The Quiet American

A Biography of George R. Wackenhut

Also by John Minahan

A Sudden Silence
The Passing Strange
The Dream Collector
Jeremy
Sorcerer
Nine/Thirty/Fifty-five
Almost Summer
Nunzio
Complete American Graffiti
Eyewitness
The Great Hotel Robbery
The Great Diamond Robbery
Mask
The Face Behind the Mask
The Great Pyramid Robbery
The Great Harvard Robbery
The Great Grave Robbery

TRANSLATION
The Fabulous Onassis

The Quiet American

A Biography of George R. Wackenhut

John Minahan

International Publishing Group

A Division of Management International Inc.

Copyright © 1994 by The Wackenhut Corporation.
All rights reserved under International and Pan-American Copyright Conventions.
Published in the United States by International Publishing Group,
a Division of Management International Inc.,
21 Stony Brook Road, Westport, CT 06880.

The text of this book is composed in 11/14.5 Times Roman.
Manufacturing by The Haddon Craftsmen, Inc.
Book design by Margaret M. Wagner.

Library of Congress Cataloging-in-Publication Data
Minahan, John.
The Quiet American: A Biography of George R. Wackenhut
p. cm.
Includes biographical references and appendix.
ISBN 0-9639395-0-5
Library of Congress Catalog Card Number 93-80474
1. Wackenhut, George Russell, 1919–

Printed in the United States of America.
First Edition

1 2 3 4 5 6 7 8 9 0

Acknowledgments

I WANT to express my appreciation for the extensive genealogy research conducted by Ernst Wackenhut of Nagold, Germany, whose investigations of evangelical parish records in Egenhousen and in the Wuttemberger main public record office in Stuttgart resulted in positive identification of the oldest known origins of all the Wackenhut tribes.

A special note of gratitude goes to the following individuals who submitted to tape-recorded interviews for use in this book (alphabetically): John Ammarell, Palm City, FL; Bud and Doris Bailey, North Port, FL; Alan Bernstein, Miami, FL; Dr. John Bonica, Mercer Island, WA; Sally Bretl, Munwonago, WI; Larry Brown, Richmond, IN; Fernando Carrizosa, Miami, FL; Eugene Charters, Philadelphia, PA; Robert Chasen, Palm City, FL; Tim Cole, Miami, FL; Edward L. DuBois III, Miami, FL; Winifred DuBois, Miami, FL; Ray Farley, Hollywood, FL; Ruth Wackenhut Feight, Feasterville, PA; Bob Frye, Melbourne, FL; Joyce Wackenhut Hilbert, New York, NY; Bud Hunter, Miami, FL; Willis Hawkins, Woodland Hill, CA; Herb Jenkins, West Chester, PA; Pam Keller, Elgin, IL; Ralph Kiel, Miami, FL; Bob Kirk, Homosassa, FL; Budd Kneip, Miami, FL; Mirtha Latour, Miami, FL; Buzz Leith, West Chester, PA; Murray Levine, Boca Raton, FL; Ted Marks, Brookhaven, PA; Jim Matson, Oak Ridge, IL; Joe McDonald, Centerville, IN; Norman Paul, Springfield, PA; Nancy Clark Reynolds, Sante Fe, NM; Gary Sanders, Miami, FL; Bill Scherle, Miami, FL; Harold and

Norman Scheule, Woodstown, NJ; George Shannon, Miami, FL; Tony Sharpe, Fort Lauderdale, FL; Jay Smith, Phoenixville, PA; Bud Thompson, Coral Gables, FL; Tanya Thorsen, Richardson, TX; Tresha Thorsen, Miami, FL; June and Tom Triol, Morganton, NC; Larry Umstead, Media, PA; Jan Wackenhut Ward, Miami, FL; Earl Warford, Miami, FL; George and Ruth Wackenhut, Coral Gables, FL; Molly and Rick Wackenhut, Miami, FL; Russ Wackenhut, Lisle, IL; Earle Waters, Boynton Beach, FL; Ken Webb, Kennett Square, PA; Dick Wilson, Merritt Island, FL; George Zeiss, Miami, FL.

For
Ruth Wackenhut,
whose love changed his life
and
whose guts changed his luck.

Trust in the Lord with all thine heart;
and lean not unto thine own understanding.

In all thy ways acknowledge him, and
he shall direct thy paths.

Proverbs 3: 5, 6

Introduction

THE NEWS STORY that would quickly be featured in virtually every major newspaper in the United States, reported by all television and radio news networks, and occupy a fourteen-minute segment on *60 Minutes* with an audience of 28.876 million households, broke exclusively on local television in Miami, Florida, late Thursday evening, August 15, 1991, on the NBC affiliate WTVJ-TV. Following is a verbatim transcription:

Tom Randles, co-anchor: A Channel 4 News exclusive that has implications from South Florida to around the globe: It involves one of the world's largest security companies, based right here in South Florida, the Wackenhut Corporation, and the focus of a massive investigation linked to the oil industry. Channel 4's David Bloom has been working on this investigation for some time and tonight has details from our Miami newsroom. Dave.

David Bloom reporting: Well, Tom, this case involves a secret congressional investigation, uncovered by Channel 4 News, into a covert operation run last year by the Wackenhut Corporation. It reaches from Miami to Washington to Alaska and beyond, and, depending upon who you believe, it is either a case of a security company just doing its job or a rogue operation out of control.

The Coral Gables-based Wackenhut Corporation employs more than 40,000 people around the world. Wackenhut security guards patrol neighborhoods and nuclear plants, embassies and the Alaskan pipeline. Two years ago, the oil tanker *Exxon Valdez* spilled almost eleven million gallons of oil into Alaska's Prince William Sound, and now Wackenhut is caught in the mess.

This letter from California Democrat George Miller informs Wackenhut Chairman George Wackenhut that the company he founded is now the subject of a congressional investigation, accused of conducting an undercover investigation of this man, Charles Hamel, who was suspected of leaking confidential oil company documents to the congressional committee investigating the *Exxon Valdez* spill.

Unidentified Person: The purpose of the investigation was very clear and it was very well focused. It was to determine where high-level internal leaks were occurring in Alaska.

George Wackenhut (Wackenhut chairman): I worked for thirty-eight years to build the reputation of this company and you can be absolutely, positively sure that we're not doing anything that's illicit, illegal, or even irregular. That I guarantee.

Bloom: But the letter from Congressman Miller reads, in part: "The Committee on Interior and Insular Affairs is investigating allegations that the Wackenhut Corporation and/or its contractors conducted undercover surveillance and investigation of Mr. Charles Hamel on behalf of the Alyeska Pipeline Service Company and any of its subsidiaries or related entities for the purpose of obtaining information and/or interfering with Mr. Hamel's communications with the committee."

Wackenhut was already providing security for Alyeska, the company that runs the Alaskan pipeline, when it began a covert investigation in March of 1990 to try to put a stop to the leaks that proved devastating to the oil industry. Here's an example of how the leaks hurt the oil industry: Miller's committee recently used internal Alyeska documents in an attempt to prove that one year before the *Exxon Valdez* spill, oil companies knew their spill-fighting capabilities were inadequate, but did nothing.

In a Houston court case, and in this statement released tonight by Charles Hamel, Alyeska and Wackenhut are accused of engaging in, quote, "covert electronic surveillance, wire tapping, burglary, and outright deception for the sole purpose of identifying the people who risked all they had to bring environmental concerns to Congress and the public through me." But both Wackenhut and Alyeska insist what they did was both legal and right.

James Hermiller (Alyeska president): All I would say is Wackenhut conducted the investigation in a completely professional and legal way.

Bloom: Now, after being informed by Channel 4 News that we were aware of this congressional investigation, Alyeska late today decided to issue a news release basically detailing both their and Wackenhut's involvement in this covert operation. Now we have some videotape that we can show you, that Channel 4 News obtained, that shows videotape shot by Wackenhut's undercover people at a company that Wackenhut set up in the Washington, D.C., area to try and convince Charles Hamel, the activist who was campaigning against Exxon and the oil companies, that they wanted to help them.

Now, according to Wackenhut, the sole purpose of this investigation was to try and find out, in a legal and above-board manner, how Hamel got the documents that they—allegedly—illegally obtained from inside Alyeska. Now, again, according to sources that Channel 4 has talked to, illegal means were used to obtain that evidence, and that is at the heart of this dispute. That's why Congress is investigating, and that is why there is a federal court case—a civil court case—in Houston going on right now. We'll have much more on this story tomorrow on Channel 4 News.

Early next morning, August 16, 1991, the story was featured on the *Today* show on NBC, with an audience of 5.067 million households, and the mass-media snowball started rolling. The same day, the Associated Press released the first detailed print account of the investigation, and the following morning the story ran in newspapers from Anchorage to Boston, Chicago to Miami. By Saturday evening, August 17, it was an item on television and radio news programs nationwide.

But it wasn't until Monday, August 19, that the first substantive article appeared, in *The Wall Street Journal,* under the by-line of Allanna Sullivan, a staff reporter who brought to light significant facts, figures, and individuals connected with the investigation that were not previously reported:

House Panel Demands All Data, Files Of Firms' Surveillance of Witness

A congressional panel investigating oil industry activity in Alaska has demanded the results of a complex surveillance operation that a consortium of oil companies ordered done on a government witness.

Rep. George Miller (D., Calif.), who heads the House committee on Interior and Insular Affairs, sent a letter to Wackenhut Corp. of Coral Gables, Fla., the security agency hired by the oil companies. Wackenhut has until September 6 to turn over all documents and files, including videotapes and audiotapes, from its surveillance of former oil broker Charles B. Hamel, a harsh critic of the oil industry who was providing information on Alaskan pipeline corrosion to Mr. Miller's group last year when the oil companies had him shadowed.

The House committee is following up on allegations that the surveillance was aimed at "obtaining information on and/or interfering with Mr. Hamel's communications with the committee." Even if the consortium—Alyeska Pipeline Service Co.—is found not to have interfered with Congress's business, the episode compounds the image problems Big Oil has where Alaska is concerned. Mr. Miller's committee investigated the huge Exxon Corp. Alaskan oil spill and will soon resume hearings on whether the oil industry should be allowed in the Alaskan Arctic National Wildlife Refuge, a prospect worth billions to the industry.

In an interview, Alyeska President James Hermiller said, "No way were we interested in trying to inhibit Hamel's relationship with Miller's committee." Alyeska said that it will cooperate with Miller, and the information Wackenhut gathered will be released to committee members. Mr. Hermiller said that he personally initiated the seven-month investigation last year "to plug some significant security leaks. Privileged documents had been stolen, and we knew Mr. Hamel had them. We were trying to trace those internal leaks."

Oil company executives have long considered Mr. Hamel "a thorn in our side." He says Alyeska ruined his business as an oil broker by selling his clients watered-down oil. In addition, he has become entangled in litigation with several oil companies over the price he and his partners received when they sold their share of some North Slope oil leases to the oil companies.

An affidavit from a former Wackenhut employee who participated in the surveillance says that Wayne Black, the Wackenhut official heading the Hamel case, told her part of the investigation was "to target Congressman Miller and other unnamed congressmen to whom Hamel was providing information for use with their hearings about environmental wrongdoing by Exxon, Alyeska and other oil companies in Alaska." Several requests to talk to Mr. Black went unanswered.

Mr. Hamel and others familiar with the surveillance say Wackenhut used questionable tactics, including wiretapping and burglary, but Mr. Hermiller of Alyeska and Wackenhut officials deny this. "We reviewed everything we did, and we did nothing illegal," said Patrick Cannan, an official with Wackenhut. "But some things legal in one state aren't legal in others. We were always legal in the state in which we were operating."

Many people familiar with the case suggest that Wackenhut was working for Exxon separately, as well as for Alyeska. But the oil giant issued a statement saying, "Exxon has never conducted or authorized any undercover surveillance or investigation involving Mr. Hamel. The security investigation was conducted by Alyeska without any prior knowledge of Exxon." Mr. Hermiller said that none of Alyeska's owners—Exxon, Atlantic Richfield Co., British Petroleum Co., Mobil Corp., Amerada Hess Corp., Unocal Corp. and Phillips Petroleum Co.—knew of the surveillance while it was under way. But the Alyeska executive knew what measures Wackenhut was using.

Affidavits and statements taken from former Wackenhut employees who participated in or had knowledge of the investigation say that those measures included monitoring Mr. Hamel's home, business and hotel accommodations electronically; videotaping him in hotel rooms; going through his garbage; obtaining consumer credit reports; and obtaining months of telephone logs. (The affidavits were filed Friday in the Southern District federal court in Houston, as part of the litigation over the price of the North Slope oil lease share. That litigation is unrelated to the surveillance question.)

At one point about a year ago, Mr. Hamel says he saw a man in a ski mask race across his lawn in the middle of the night, grab his garbage and throw it into the open trunk of a small red car that slowly cruised by.

In addition, Wackenhut's Mr. Black, head of the firm's Special Investigations, set up an elaborate sting operation called Ecolit to lure Mr. Hamel into divulging what information he had on the oil companies and who his sources were. Mr. Hamel said his first contact with the so-called Ecolit Group happened when a woman claiming to work there introduced herself to him on a flight from Anchorage.

Ecolit was described to Mr. Hamel as an environmental litigation support group. The woman contacted him again and he agreed to work with Ecolit, actually turning over one document. He visited an Ecolit office in Crystal City, Va., replete with props such as environmental literature on Alaska, and received correspondence from Ecolit's Coconut Grove, Fla., headquarters. Ecolit was a Wackenhut creation.

Alyeska says that the Wackenhut investigation of Mr. Hamel came to an end last September when it informed owner companies of the activities.

David Bloom's WTVJ-TV exclusive in Miami and Allanna Sullivan's article in *The Wall Street Journal* are quoted verbatim and in their entirety, because, at the beginning, they reflected the range and mood of the hundreds of broadcast and print stories that appeared nationwide. However, as the weeks turned into months, headlines would become more irresponsible, stories would become more titillating, and innuendoes would proliferate. The months leading up to the congressional investigation, which took place November 4–6, 1991, would prove to be a nightmare for George Wackenhut because, under state law, he was not allowed to respond to any media allegations, however inaccurate or misleading, to protect his client. Florida Statute 493.6119 is quite specific:

Divulging investigative information; false reports prohibited.—

(1) Except as otherwise provided by this chapter or other law, no licensee, or any employee of a licensee or licensed agency shall divulge or release to anyone other than his client or employer the contents of an investigative file acquired in the course of licensed investigative activity. However, the prohibition of this section shall not apply when the client for whom the information was acquired, or his lawful representative, has alleged a violation of this chapter by the licensee, licensed agency, or any employee, or when the prior written consent of the client to divulge or release such information has been obtained.

The Wackenhut Corporation never received prior written consent of the client, Alyeska, to divulge or release such information, but received permission from Alyeska to testify before the congressional committee. Therefore, with no legal way to defend itself against media allegations, Wackenhut became the prime target for investigative reporters who wanted to create the classic David and Goliath scenario: Charles Hamel versus Big Oil, with Wackenhut in the role of the heavy.

The news media questioned George Wackenhut's integrity in public. And he couldn't legally defend himself. It's not a unique situation, of course, it's happened to countless people in this country, particularly since 1974, when Bob Woodward and Carl Bernstein of *The Washington Post* elevated investigative reporting to its present popularity among the young, during the Watergate scandal. In 1974, Woodward was thirty-one and Bernstein was thirty, and they were already famous. By the time *All the President's Men* became a blockbuster movie in 1976, they were celebrities. Heady stuff at that age. By 1978, journalism schools across the country were experiencing an unprecedented increase in enrollments. Newspapers were deluged with applications. Investigative reporting became one of the glamour jobs of the decade.

And there were plenty of people to investigate in the early 1990s: Ivan Boesky, Michael Milken, Charles Keating, the list goes on and on. But George Wackenhut?

Pat Cannan, Wackenhut's director of Corporate Relations, has accumulated a huge stack of news clippings about the investigation, provided by a clipping service, hundreds of newspaper articles and verbatim television and radio clips. When you read them all several times, patterns and common denominators emerge. Clearly, the overwhelming majority of these stories were written by young journalists working against tight deadlines. That's the polite way of putting it. Journalists would put it another way: This copy was written fast and dirty. By kids. Kids who were either too lazy or too rushed or too oblivious to write news that reflects balance and perspective. One excerpt will suffice because it's typical of the one-dimensional approach. It appeared as the lead story on the front page of *The Anchorage Daily News,* September 1, 1991, together with a photograph of Charles Hamel, and it was written by reporter Richard Mauer.

The details of deception
Dirty tricks used against Alyeska critic Hamel leave him bruised.

The blonde was alone at the bar. Two men caught her eye. The woman knew just what she wanted. The men had no idea.

She stood up and breezed by their stools. She punched out a number on the bartender's phone. Her gaze bore into the men.

She hung up the phone and struck up a conversation. Her name was Ricki Edelson. She was tanned, 40ish, attractive and alone at Fletcher's, the bar at the Captain Cook, a long way from home.

One of the men was short and balding and 60 years old. The other was 37, with a beard and the features of a Norseman.

The men were talking about the Exxon Valdez and saving trees in Prince William Sound. They were, in fact, two of the principal critics of the oil industry in Alaska.

She was an environmentalist from Florida, here for a conference at the hotel. She walked back to her stool.

"She must be after you, Steiner, not the old guy here," said Charles Hamel, the balding man, pointing to himself.

"Naw, she wants you, Chuck—you're the distinguished one," answered Rick Steiner.

They went back to talking about trees and the Exxon Valdez. The woman used the phone again. And again. The two men were curious, but there were important things to do. They paid for their beers and walked to another hotel across the street.

The woman went back to her boss and laid new plans.

That seemingly chance encounter, on the evening of March 22, 1990, opened the undercover phase of a dirty tricks and spy campaign directed against Charles Hamel on behalf of Alyeska Pipeline Service Co. and perhaps Exxon.

According to investigators who took part in it or were told about it by those who did, the campaign was designed to embarrass Hamel, one of the industry's most effective critics, and reveal his sources inside the oil companies.

Hamel's bulldog persistence, coupled with documents and information he passed on to federal and state agencies, Congress and the media, has cost the industry millions of dollars and years of aggravation. He has exposed air and water pollution at Alyeska's terminal in Valdez, in tanker traffic at sea and at a Fairbanks refinery. He was one of the first people to draw public attention to corrosion of the trans-Alaska pipeline, years before Alyeska acknowledged the problem.

The investigators say Hamel's conversations were recorded in his home and at the office of the Ecolit Group, a phony environmental organization set up for the sting. They wooed him with cash for his expenses, stole his garbage, took documents from his house and tricked him out of others. They listened in on his telephone conversations, they said, and surreptitiously got records of his long-distance calls.

> From interviews over the past two weeks with sources in Miami, Coral Gables, Tampa, Washington, Virginia and Alaska, and from documents and tape recordings obtained in Florida and Texas, the Daily News has pieced together part of what happened in the massive investigation.
>
> Much still is not known. Several of the investigators who worked the case for Wackenhut Corp. of Coral Gables, Fla., said they won't talk out of fear of retaliation from Wackenhut or its personnel. . . .

Incredibly, the story goes on for more than 5,000 words, weaving its web of almost laughable intrigue. That same Sunday morning, over 4,000 miles away, the lead story on the front page of *The Miami Herald* carried the banner headline "Spy web ensnared whistleblower," and included a large four-color photograph of George Wackenhut.

In Sydney Pollack's controversial 1981 movie *Absence of Malice*, a legitimate businessman, played by Paul Newman, picks up his morning newspaper, sees his picture, and reads a front-page article stating that he is the subject of a federal investigation. Without warning, his integrity is questioned in public, and everything he's worked for is placed in potential jeopardy. He confronts the investigative reporter, played by Sally Field, and eventually they discover that the story was intentionally leaked to her by the government's chief investigator, who is grasping at straws, with no solid evidence of any wrongdoing whatsoever. The investigation is dropped, but the consequences of the adverse publicity are devastating and, in fact, lead to the suicide of a peripheral character.

Panned by most critics, *Absence of Malice* ignited such widespread journalistic indignation that it took a second beating on editorial pages across the country for daring to imply that investigative reporting was an imperfect discipline at best, capable of inflicting permanent damage at worst, and that First Amendment guarantees should be tempered by reasonable and responsible parameters at least. Clearly, the film struck a raw nerve throughout the news media.

Yet more than a decade later, it's not surprising to find that investigative reporting techniques have not changed in the slightest, and that one of the key legal equations used to defend such journalism is still an "absence of malice" on the part of the reporter. In other words, as long as the reporter exhibits an attitude of benign indifference to the subject(s) of an investigative report, and the consequences thereof, the reporter theoretically qualifies for full protection under the First Amendment.

When reporter David Bloom broke his exclusive story about the congressional investigation of the Wackenhut Corporation on WTVJ-TV, Miami, August 15, 1991, he held in his hand a copy of a letter that had been written by Congressman George Miller and sent via Federal Express to George Wackenhut on August 7, 1991. A similar letter was mailed to James Hermiller, president of the Alyeska Pipeline Service Company, plus a few senior officers of both firms.

How did Bloom obtain a copy of that letter? Who leaked it to him?

Obviously, Wackenhut and Alyeska did not want it leaked to the press and took measures to make sure that it would not be. They had nothing to gain by the publicity.

On the other hand, Congressman Miller, a consummate politician who initiated the investigation for the purpose of bringing the issue before Congress and the public, had everything to gain by such publicity.

So did Charles Hamel, who, by his own admission, had been soliciting and receiving confidential documents from employees of oil companies in the Alyeska consortium and turning them over to Congressman Miller for action by his committee. Hamel thrived on such publicity for more than a decade. The fact that he was allegedly breaking the law by conspiring to commit industrial espionage always seemed to be buried in the David and Goliath hype of investigative reporters. Hamel was their darling. He gave them juicy stories about the bad boys in Big Oil. He beguiled them with details about exotic undercover *femmes fatales* in faraway hotel bars, trying to play dirty tricks on their hero, wooing him with cash, tapping his phone, even stealing his garbage. But when Wackenhut finally caught their boy Hamel in the act, up to his elbows in the cookie jar, that was somehow immoral, if not illegal, and the news media responded, fast and dirty.

Even *60 Minutes,* the undisputed champion of investigative reporting, couldn't resist this one. It was made to order for their format: Here's this white-haired, prune-faced old guy, George Wackenhut, who has the temerity to make statements like: "I worked for thirty-eight years to build the reputation of this company and you can be absolutely, positively sure that we're not doing anything that's illicit, illegal, or even irregular. That I guarantee." Now, come on. *Nobody* could be that good. Send a team down to Coral Gables. Dig up some dirt on this sanctimonious old coot.

And if you don't believe that's the way people like Mike Wallace and Morley Safer and Ed Bradley and Steve Kroft operate, stay tuned. It's axiomatic that *60 Minutes* didn't make it to the top by presenting investigative reports with balance and perspective. That kind of approach doesn't rivet the attention of 28.876 million households. To draw that kind of audience on a consistent basis, you've got to get down and dirty. It doesn't matter who the subject is, you've got to hit him where he lives, you've got to make him bleed. That's why they went for George Wackenhut's jugular—his integrity—and that's why they went for it with the gloves off.

All of the sensationalism is over now. The seemingly endless newspaper stories, the television and radio reports, the congressional hearings, even the postmortems. Through it all, George Wackenhut's integrity remained intact. It remained intact because it was built on extremely solid foundations.

We will examine those foundations in this book. They would not be interesting to an investigative reporter, or a member of the television generation, or anyone who wants uncomplicated answers. In today's society, the quintessential metaphor to describe a man like this would be to say that he is a dinosaur who somehow survived. His value systems are anachronistic by present standards, almost the antithesis of those held by the majority of modern corporate CEOs in the United States. You will not find a computer in his office or a fax machine or even a window. You will not find a cellular telephone in his car. You will not find him in a restaurant at lunchtime. He is a dinosaur.

He is also a man who started with nothing and built an empire.

Of course, nobody ever accused George Wackenhut of being a saint, and you will find no such fiction in these pages. You do not build an empire without a tough, tenacious, competitive business personality, especially in the security industry. In this connection, we have the advantage of listening to some of his oldest friends and business associates, as well as his detractors, men and women who candidly discuss subjects ranging from his childhood to the present, and they are all asked the hard questions, the questions that often they alone can answer.

In researching this book over a period of four years, a conscious effort was made to achieve balance, perspective, and proportion, to reveal the man and his work as honestly as possible, warts and all, no punches pulled, no stone left unturned. Every interview was tape recorded and transcribed verbatim to ensure accuracy; every historical fact and figure was documented by a variety of sources; every historical, financial, and classified record of the Wackenhut Corporation was open for inspection.

What emerges from all this is an unusual life story as well as an extraordinary love story. When you enter the world of George Wackenhut for the first time, you should be warned that there are few conventional road signs to indicate that you are in the presence of a dinosaur. But you are.

Take a good look at him.

And remember what you saw.

The Quiet American

A Biography of George R. Wackenhut

1

THE YOUNG SOLDIER in the faded sepia photograph looks out at us from a distance of more than a century, a formal head-and-shoulders portrait, three-quarter face, and he is wearing a Prussian Army uniform with a high collar, epaulets, and polished brass buttons. His short hair is blond, as are his eyebrows, and his left eyelid appears to be squinting, as if injured. Despite the serious set of the mouth and chin, he looks almost childlike, although he was probably eighteen and the year was 1875. The cardboard backing on the print tells us that it was taken by A. Hummler in Stuttgart, and there is no date, but it is unlikely that the soldier, Johannes Wackenhut, saw any combat. Born February 14, 1857, in Zwerenberg, he was too young for Chancellor Otto von Bismark's three wars, with Denmark (1864), Austria (1866), and France (1870–71). When William I was proclaimed emperor of Germany in 1871, Prussia assumed great power in the new German Empire, and there were no more major conflicts until 1914, with the outbreak of World War I. By that time, Johannes had long since immigrated to the United States, the first of his family to do so, in 1881, at the age of twenty-four. He traveled by steamship to Philadelphia, got a job as a machinist in the Philadelphia Navy Yard, sent for his German fiancée, Christina Doraday Sweitzer, married her in 1884, and had six children. He died August 31, 1911, at the age of fifty-three, and was buried in an unmarked grave at Hillside Cemetery in Roslyn, Pennsylvania, north of Philadelphia, in an area designated as the

German Veterans Section. Johannes was the grandfather of George Wackenhut.

Although Johannes was the first to imigrate to America, Wackenhut genealogy has been accurately traced to fifteenth-century Germany. The oldest tribe father to be positively identified, through evangelical parish records and the Wuttemberger main public record office in Stuttgart, is Aberlin Wackenhut, who was born in 1475 in Egenhousen, deep in the Nagold region of the Black Forest in southwest Germany, where all the Wackenhut tribes originated. Today, the Black Forest is a popular tourist area, famous for cuckoo clocks and music boxes, and its current major industries are lumbering and cattle raising, but it remains a heavily wooded mountain region, ninety miles long, between the Rhine and Neckar rivers to the Swiss border. With its many lakes and mineral springs, the area was ideal for farming, and Aberlin Wackenhut's occupation was listed as farmer and judge. His wife's name is unknown, but the records confirm that one son was born in 1510; his name was Jakob and he was also a farmer and judge. Aberlin Wackenhut died in 1531 at the age of fifty-six.

Nine generations later, when Johannes Wackenhut imigrated to Philadelphia, in 1881, there was no requirement to pass through Ellis Island in New York. The U.S. Immigration and Naturalization Service was not established until 1891, charged with the responsibility for administering the laws relating to the admission, exclusion, deportation, and naturalization of aliens in the U.S., and Ellis Island was not designated as the chief U.S. immigration station until 1892.

Before 1890, immigrants were primarily Anglo-Saxon Protestants from the British Isles, Germany, and Scandinavia. Germans immigrated to Pennsylvania in response to the guarantee of religious freedom by its founder, William Penn. The Homestead Act of 1862 encouraged potential immigrants; steamship lines vied for their patronage, and young American industries advertised in European newspapers for workers. Many steamship and railroad companies actually preferred to carry immigrants, because they loaded and unloaded themselves, rather than cargo that did not. The steerage fare from Liverpool to New York in the 1880s was only three pounds. More than 46 million people imigrated between 1831 and

1915. The rate of immigration corresponded to economic cycles in the U.S., increasing when prosperity was high.

In congested urban centers such as Philadelphia, housing was frequently inadequate, wages were low, poverty was widespread, and these conditions gave rise to the U.S. trade union movement. In 1878, the Knights of Labor, a secret group formed in 1869, became a national order. Open to both the skilled and unskilled, it was the first successful U.S. union, and was superseded by the American Federation of Labor (AFL), established in 1886. As a machinist in the Philadelphia Navy Yard, we can safely assume that Johannes Wackenhut was a union member, although we have no written record that he was.

We don't know the name of the steamship he took in 1881, or the exact date he arrived at Pier 53, the traditional immigration pier, but it was probably during the summer months. We have no record of where he lived before his marriage to Christina on September 13, 1884, but his death certificate lists his address as 2311 Adams Street, which is in northeastern Philadelphia, near Tacony Creek. In nineteenth-century Philadelphia, Market Street separated the social strata. The northern district, now called Olde City, was considered the wrong side of the cart tracks. In the late nineteenth century, it was largely inhabited by immigrants.

Looking at the year 1881 from an historical perspective, the population of the U.S. was officially 50,155,783, an increase of more than 12 million over the previous decade. On July 2, 1881, President James Garfield was shot by Charles Guiteau, described as a disgruntled office-seeker, in a Washington, DC, railroad station; Garfield died September 19, 1881, and was succeeded the following day by Vice President Chester A. Arthur. That summer, Sitting Bull and the Sioux Indians returned to the U.S. from Canada after the Canadian Government refused to provide them with a reservation; although the U.S. Army had promised to pardon Sitting Bull if he returned, he was held in a military prison for the next two years.

The second oldest photograph we have of Johannes Wackenhut is also a sepia print, larger, in sharp focus, and it is a formal family portrait, the only one of the entire family known to exist. It was taken at the studio of R.R. Haug, 2447 Kensington Avenue, Philadelphia, which is about five miles northeast of City Hall and Market Street, well into the northern district of Olde City, near Frankford Creek, relatively close to the Delaware River. Although the photograph shows no date, the eldest son, William Henry, was born in 1888 and appears to be about fourteen here, which would place the date circa 1902.

The dominant impression of the family group is that the six children are extremely attractive, despite their stiff postures and uniformly serious faces. Molly, the first-born, looks to be about sixteen. She stands behind her seated father, tall, slim, long dark hair piled neatly atop her head, thick dark brows, eyes with a somber, almost sad expression, no earrings, no lipstick, and she wears a dark pleated dress with high lace collar, surrounded by a white scarf tied in a graceful bow. She would go on to marry a man named Paul Gentsch, live in the Philadelphia area, and have no children. Standing to her left, behind his mother, is the second-born, William Henry, who would become George Wackenhut's father. His hair is short and dark, parted just to the left of center, high forehead, oval face, with eyes and mouth not quite as serious as Molly's, but certainly not happy. He wears a white shirt with a light-colored bow tie, and his dark three-piece suit has very high lapels, which was the fashion. He would marry Frances Mabel Hogan, go into the printing business, and father two extraordinary sons.

After Molly and William, there is a sharp drop in the children's ages. Third-born Fred, standing to the right of his father, appears to be no older than twelve, hair thicker and lighter than his big brother's, framing a more rounded face. His right forearm rests on the back of a couch, obviously at the direction of the photographer, but he looks anything but relaxed. He, too, wears a white shirt and bow tie, but his double-breasted sport jacket is wrinkled, and his dark trousers are baggy at the knees because they're too narrow to fit over his high-button shoes. He would go on to marry Frances Fleish, have two children, and operate a successful plumbing and heating business in Philadelphia.

The two youngest boys stand between their parents, dressed identically in dark jackets with what appear to be dark silk scarves around their necks, tied in large bows. Frank, the fourth-born, is probably six, but short for his age. Like all his brothers, he obviously had a haircut for this occasion, making his ears seem to jut out. He would marry Laura Shaw, go into the plumbing business with his brother Fred, have two children, and commit suicide in his early fifties. John, the youngest, is at least a foot shorter than Frank, and looks to be about four. At the age of eighteen, he would see combat in World War I, return changed, never marry, and live alone until he died in 1969 at the age of seventy-three. Standing to the left of her mother, Caroline (Carrie), the fifth-born, is a hauntingly beautiful child of about ten, long blond hair parted in the middle and pulled back in braids, just visible, tied with a white bow. Her lovely eyes seem transparent, probably blue, her lips are tight, and she rests her left hand against the arm of a wicker chair. Her dark, high-necked dress has long sleeves like her sister's, the hem is well below her knees, revealing dark stockings and high-button shoes. She would marry Joseph Scheule, have two successful sons, and live to be seventy-three.

Christina, born in 1854, was about forty-eight when this photograph was taken, but looks considerably older. She is the only one in the group who is smiling, although a tight-lipped smile, and there is a bright quality in her wide transparent eyes, almost a twinkle, that has been passed on to future generations, known today as "Wackenhut eyes." Her thick gray-blond hair is parted in the middle and pulled back in a braided bun, her face shows no pronounced wrinkles, and the apparent discrepancy in age is probably related to her physique and clothes. Of obviously robust German stock, her full figure is accentuated by a dark, high-necked and long-sleeved silk blouse, and a heavy black silk skirt that extends to the floor. When Christina died, April 7, 1940, she was eighty-six, and had outlived her husband by nearly twenty-nine years.

Johannes, sitting ramrod straight in the small wicker chair opposite her, is the most stilted of all, and one glance at his eyes tells us why his children have such serious expressions. He was only forty-five that year, but his short hair is gray-white, receding at the temples, and his eyes appear cold to the point of glaring. He has a full mustache now, extending over the upper lip and down the corners of his mouth. His chin is lifted above a high wing-tipped white collar, and we can only see the four-in-hand knot of his tie because his dark suit coat is buttoned at the top; the other buttons are open. The three-piece suit looks new, a watch chain extends across the vest pockets, and the crease in his trousers is sharp. But his high-button shoes are quite worn, and turned up at the toes.

In fairness to the man, for all his apparent stiffness, Johannes comes across as a proud father, a strict disciplinarian because he wanted his children to have strong moral and religious values, and this is obviously a rare and important moment in his life, which would turn out to be relatively short. We have few other photographs of Johannes Wackenhut. We don't need others. This one tells us what we need to know, understand, and place in perspective, before we begin the story of George Wackenhut.

ON SEPTEMBER 3, 1919, exactly eight years to the day that Johannes was buried in the German Veterans Section of Hillside Cemetery in Roslyn, Pennsylvania, north of Philadelphia, George Russell Wackenhut was born at home, in a row house on Mervine Street in north Philadelphia. He was delivered by a midwife, which was a routine medical practice in those days. His mother, Frances (Hogan), was thirty-two at the time of his birth, his father, William, was thirty-one, and his brother Harry, born December 11, 1908, was almost eleven.

There had been another son born to the Wackenhuts, named John, who lived only two hours after his premature birth on September 29, 1913. According to the baby's birth and death certificates, the family residence was then 3741 North 15th Street, Philadelphia, and the child was buried at Greenmount Cemetery, Front and Luzerne streets, in a crypt set aside for premature births. The cemetery had the child's name spelled "John Wagenbutt."

When George was born, ten months had passed since the end of World War I (the Armistice was signed November 11, 1918), the U.S. population had jumped to 105 million, and President Woodrow Wilson was serving his second term. On September 22, 1919, more than 350,000 steelworkers went on strike, followed forty days later by 400,000 miners, increasing the number of striking U.S. workers to more than 4 million that year; the unions were demanding a reduction in the average work week of 68.7 hours, and an increase in the "inhuman" pay scale.

William Wackenhut was finding it difficult to make ends meet in 1919. A printer by trade, he worked for a number of firms in the Philadelphia area until he opened his own printing company with a partner in 1928. George remembers his father as about five-foot-nine and roughly 160 pounds, maybe less as a younger man. His eyes were blue and he wore steel-framed bifocal glasses at all times. Although his hair was originally dark brown, he grayed prematurely and was totally white during his last twenty years or so. George is not sure he ever remembers seeing his father without gray hair.

"He was very fastidious," George recalls. "Neat to the point of pain. He dressed reasonably well, not expensively, and he was a good-looking man. On the other hand, my mother was not a very pretty woman. She had blue eyes and her hair was dark brown in her early years and gray later on. As she got older, she wore glasses, but not all the time like my dad did. She was a lovely person and I attribute to her a reasonably strict upbringing, although I don't recall being curtailed in my activities to any extent. She was a very important influence in my life. She had very sound moral values. The feature I remember about my mother more than anything else was her ability to stretch a dollar. Beyond any reasonable means. She'd walk blocks to save a penny on an item of food, for example. She was able, sometimes with no money at all, to keep the family in food and clothes. She was very, very frugal."

Shortly after George was born, the family moved from Mervine Street to another row house on Blavis Street, also in north Philadelphia. Blavis is a relatively short street that extends east and west and is intersected by Broad Street, the city's main north-south thoroughfare (Route 611). The house is still there, on the west side of Blavis, facing south, in a very poor section. Although George remembers that the house was directly across from St. Luke's Hospital, the hospital is long gone. His grandmother and grandfather, on his mother's side, lived with the family from the time George was born, and he remembers them vividly: "From a physical standpoint, my grandmother was a beautiful woman, compared to my mother. On the other hand, my grandfather was not handsome at all. He had exceptionally large ears and a large nose. And my mother, I think, took after him as far as facial features are concerned. That's where I got my nose!"

His grandmother used to tell a story about something George did when he was about five years old, just before they moved from the Blavis Street house. Apparently, his mother and grandmother had gone out while he was taking a nap. He awakened, looked around the house, couldn't find them, and went out in the street to continue the search, in the dead of winter, with only his Dr. Denton pajamas on. A neighbor spotted him, took him in until his mother and grandmother returned. His grandmother scolded him, of course, and he turned and told her: "The next time you leave me alone, I'm going to go all the way to heaven. As a matter of fact, I'm going even farther than that—I'm going to go all the way downtown!"

In December 1924, when the family moved to Upper Darby, a suburb in the Bywood section, west of Philadelphia, they purchased a semi-detached house at 7438 Miller Avenue, and George lived there for the next seventeen years, until July 1941.

Herb Jenkins, born June 5, 1916, in Selbyville, Delaware, now retired from his own personnel business, and president of the Upper Darby Senior High School Alumni Association, remembers George at a very early age: "The first time I met George, he was just a tot, back about 1924. He lived at 7438 Miller Avenue, I lived four doors away, at 7430. I'm probably his oldest living friend. When his family moved in there, he was about five and I was eight. When we were a little older, I remember we used to play marbles all the time. And I was a good marbles shooter. My knuckles were always rough and bloody and with scabs on them. And I used to win most of the time, because I was older. So it got to a point where I guess he lost all his marbles, and my mother found out somehow, and she made me give him back all the marbles I won.

"The one thing George always did, if he got his hands dirty, he'd always hold his fingers up to his nose to smell them. I remember one time, we were playing football, no helmets, no uniforms or anything, and he tackled me, and his hands came down in what he called dog poop. That's what he called it. That's as bad a word as he used, dog poop! And I never, ever, forgot it. *Dog poop!* Of course, he washed his hands constantly. That was his father's influence. Just the other day, George asked me whatever happened to Edgar Powell. That was the kid who lived next door to him. I told him that Edgar's been dead for a long time. But, anyhow, Edgar always used to tease George, because we'd be playing some kind of ball out front and George's mother would call him in for supper. Well, when one of us had to quit, the game would have to break up, because you wouldn't have enough players. His mother would come to the door—and it wasn't dinner in those days, it was supper—she'd open the door and she'd call: *'Geooo-ridge, come in and get your supper!'* And as soon as she'd close the door, Edgar Powell would yell as loud as he could: *'Geooo-ridge, come in and get your supper!'* That's something all the kids remember. That's about as much as anybody ever teased George about anything."

George has vivid memories about moving to Upper Darby and being awed by his new surroundings. "When I go back and look at the house—it seemed so big to me at the time—it looks quite small," he explains. "It was semi-detached. By that I mean it was one house cut longitudinally through the middle. We were on the right side. The front porch was enclosed and had windows between us and our neighbor on the left. People get very close, unless there's a reason not to, and they were very lovely people. They were from Delaware, and the people on our other side, with a driveway between, were from Delaware, and the people next to them, going up the hill, were also from Delaware. From the enclosed porch, you went back through into the living room, then the dining room, and back further was a breakfast room, and off that was the kitchen. Then there was an outside unheated little refrigerator room, I guess you'd call it, where we kept the refrigerator. And a back door going to the back porch, which was not very large, and steps down to the driveway, then more steps down to the back yard, and then a single-car garage at the end of the driveway. And the house had a full basement and an original coal stove. I remember helping my brother put the ashes out every Wednesday night, I think it was, for collection in the morning. There was a coal bin, where the cat would do her number, and it smelled like hell all the time. The laundry facilities were down there, a couple of wash tubs, and the washer with a wringer on it. Upstairs, there were three bedrooms and one bath. Mother and Dad were in the front bedroom, my brother and I were in the middle bedroom, Grandmother and Grandfather in the back bedroom. And only one bath! Then there was a full attic, unfinished. And as my brother got older, he slept there all the time, he liked it. He had a bed up there and an old Victrola, a wind-up Victrola."

His brother Harry, eleven years his senior, whom he remembers as six-foot-two, slender, good-looking, and the light of his life, transferred from Northeast High School in Philadelphia to Upper Darby High School in the middle of his junior year, December 15, 1924; he had just turned sixteen. The following September, at the age of six, George was enrolled in the Keystone Public School, within easy walking distance of his house.

The original building that was once Keystone Public School, constructed in 1909, is still standing, on West Chester Pike, west of Sixty-ninth Street, but it's now a police station, namely, the Emil T. D'Alesio Public Safety Building. The exterior is unchanged, from its graceful white pillars at the entrance, to its three stories of gray stone with high windows, to its four tall chimneys. When he was a little older, George recalls playing with a friend near the entrance of the school and throwing snowballs at the front door. One of the snowballs hit the stone archway over the door at an angle that actually chipped off a sliver of stone. "I didn't know my own strength!" he says, smiling. He spent six years there, 1925–30, and every time he passed the entrance he would recall having thrown the snowball. Today, the chip remains, unrepaired. One of the most vivid memories George retains from his years at Keystone is the gathering of all the students on the stairs to sing Christmas carols every year, on the day Christmas vacation began.

Ted Marks, who was George's classmate for twelve years, all the way from first grade at Keystone in 1925 through graduation from Upper Darby Senior High School in 1937, and who lived on Elm Avenue, just a block from George's house on Miller, has unusually clear memories of those times, places, and people.

"I can remember we played in the school yard behind the Keystone School," Marks says. "We used to play soccer, and those are probably my earliest memories of George. We had sliding boards back there, we had a maypole with ropes, kids used to swing on that, we had a high-jumping pit there, I used to fool around with high-jumping. In Keystone School, we went home for lunch, we had recess, and our janitor was Mr. Banks, he used to sell penny candy down in the basement, in the boiler room. Mr. Banks was a thin man with gray hair, the kindest man, always treated you nicely, and you loved the guy. He was just like a parent to us. I never remember him raising his voice to anybody. And he kept that boiler room down there just as neat and clean as possible. He and his wife lived in the little stone house next to the school, just off to the left of the front entrance, and the house is still there.

"Our principal was Mr. Anderson, who was a very nice young gentleman. I remember one teacher, Mr. Herzog, and there was a lady who would come in occasionally, and we would do gym exercises. No gym suits or anything like that. We had a fire escape in the back, and when we had a fire drill, if you were upstairs, you'd come down the fire escape."

Born July 25, 1918, in Philadelphia, Marks went on to become an extraordinarily successful salesman, and believes his high school teachers and coaches played dominant roles in his life. "Upper Darby Senior High School had marvelous, dedicated teachers, who cared about you," he recalls. "They didn't punch a time clock, they were always there to help you, if you wanted help. You respected them, you honored them, and they honored you. I particularly remember the help given to me by our principal, Mr. Tyson, and our coaches, Mr. Wolfgang, Mr. Gous, and Mr. Strange. Although we had a beautiful gym in junior high, and a lovely athletic field, we had a horrible gym in the high school, low ceiling, and when we came out of the locker room to go out to the athletic field, we had a rotten approach, we had to run up a concrete-like ramp. But we had a good football field, a pretty good track, very good soccer field. We didn't have permanent bleachers like they have today."

Norman Paul, another of George's oldest friends, was a classmate at Keystone School in the fifth grade. "As I remember it," Paul says, "we all stayed in one room, and George sat directly across the aisle from me. So we became close friends at an early age. There were just two seasons, football season and baseball season. And we played every day in the school yard. If somebody got there ahead of us, there were many empty lots where we could play, but the school yard was the best."

Born in Philadelphia, December 5, 1917, and now a retired engineer, who lives in Springfield, Pennsylvania, Paul is an energetic five-foot-ten, 170 pounds, white hair, and his hazel eyes have life in them and humor. "We used to get together at George's house on Miller Avenue," he says with a smile. "I remember we were interested in boxing, and one time we got up a boxing club, and it was in this kid's basement. We didn't own any gloves, so there was a kid down the street who had some gloves, so we invited him into the club. He wasn't very good at boxing, we knocked him all over the place, but we made sure he was in good enough shape that he was going to stay in the club!

"I remember George's mother and father used to sit in the living room in the early evenings and listen to all of these programs on the radio, but we were usually out and doing things all the time. Of course, in those days, you went to the movies and things of that sort, Saturday afternoon matinees. Upper Darby, at that time, the Sixty-ninth Street section, was sort of the social center. There wre several theaters there, the Sixty-ninth Street Theater, the Tower Theater, and later on there was a small one called the Terminal Theater.

"George, of course, went to a Christian Science church. I'm not exactly sure of the location. I usually went to a Methodist church that was nearby. As I understand it, the reason they went to the Christian Science church, I think George's grandmother had been sick, and had been given up. I might have the story wrong, but I think that's what the story was, and this was his mother's mother, Mrs. Hogan. She evidently got well on the basis of her faith, and I think that's what convinced the family that this was the church for them. His father and mother and his mother's parents all lived together, so I think he was influenced by all four of them. And I think his grandmother and his father were the softening influence, and the hardening influence was his mother and maybe his grandfather."

On June 10, 1926, when George was seven years old and completing the second grade, his brother Harry graduated from Upper

Darby High School. In his senior year, Harry was the starting shortstop on the varsity baseball team; he did some pitching, but shortstop was his main position. His academic record was outstanding, to say the least. George feels strongly that if ever anyone in the family deserved to go to college, it was Harry, and his academic transcript, maintained by the high school registrar's office on microfiche, leaves no doubt about it, particularly in the final semester of his senior year, when he carried a difficult course load:

SUBJECT	TEACHER	GRADE
English IV	Woolley & Brubacher	A
Trigonometry	Wentworth & Smith	A
Latin IV: Vergil	Bennett	A
English III	Claxton & McGiniss	A
Algebra III	Wells & Hart	A
Physical Training	Spec. Supervisor	A

Unfortunately, at just about the time Harry graduated, in 1926, his father lost his job. According to George, Harry had such a strong sense of responsibility that he went to work to help support the family. Had he spent all of his years at Upper Darby High School, he would almost certainly have won a scholarship, but having attended for only one and one-half years, he was ruled ineligible. In those days, scholarships were not as plentiful as they were later. Consequently, Harry never went to college.

Instead, at the age of seventeen, he took a job as an errand boy with Penn Mutual Life Insurance Company in Philadelphia. Later, he was promoted to the real estate section of the company and, by the time he was twenty-two, in 1930, he had shown enough promise to be sent to the firm's Chicago office to conduct a special study. When he returned, his report was so well received that he was promoted and eventually transferred to the Chicago office in September 1932. That was a disappointment to George, of course, because he didn't see much of Harry from that point on. When he was transferred, Harry's title was assistant loan supervisor, and he traveled the Midwest. Then, when the loan supervisor passed away, Harry was promoted to his job. George remembers that Harry always called himself a job-hopper: He was with Penn Mutual for forty-seven years.

"He moved to Chicago on my thirteenth birthday," George recalls. "That was the last day he was home on a permanent basis. We were down in Ocean City, New Jersey, and he took me for a walk on the boardwalk, as sort of a farewell gesture, and then left. That was September 3, 1932, and I didn't see him again until December, when he came home for Christmas. That left a big void in my life. As far back as I can remember, he was basically more of a father to me than my dad was, because my dad was always working. Anyway, I wrote to Harry every week, and he wrote to me, and he helped Mother and Dad financially for more than fourteen years, until he was married in 1940."

The financial help was badly needed. In 1928, his father had formed a partnership with a man named Bill Miller and started his own printing business. They rented a storefront shop on Lancaster Avenue in Philadelphia, and it was a job printing shop, stationery, envelopes, business cards, primarily small printing orders. William was the "inside" man, running the shop, and his partner was the "outside" man, attempting to generate business. But the outside man didn't deliver. In 1929, William finally bought him out. Then, after owning the business outright for only a few months, the Great Depression took over, and he had a difficult time remaining solvent, as any small business did in those days.

George recalls working for his father in the summers, part-time, from the age of twelve. "I can picture the building in my mind," he says. "I remember the streetcar ran past, I think his store was the second from the corner. I could come and go by streetcar. I learned Philadelphia that way, as a kid, I learned how to get around by public transportation. That's how my father got around, he didn't have a car until much later. The shop was like a little store, he had the counter, the storefront with a window, and the back room had the typesetting and binding equipment. The presses were down in the basement. They had Linotype machines in those days, but my father didn't have one, it was all hand-setting. I would collate pages, deliver packages, run errands, and proofread with him, mostly at home, during the evenings. I remember he used to try to trip me up. He'd read something wrong to be sure I was awake!"

When the Great Depression started in earnest with the stock market crash of October 1929, William Wackenhut, called Bill by his brothers and sisters, was forty-one; Molly Wackenhut Gentsch was forty-three, with no children; Fred was thirty-nine, with two children, Fred and Ruth; Frank was thirty-four, with two children, Frank and Myrtle; Caroline Wackenhut Scheule was thirty-seven, with two sons, Norman and Harold; and John, the youngest at thirty-one, was unmarried. All lived in the Philadelphia area, and kept in touch with each other, primarily through visits to their mother, Christina, who was then seventy-five, and living with the Scheule family in Brookline, Pennsylvania.

Norman Scheule, Caroline's eldest son, born February 19, 1918, retired after thirty-one years as a mechanical engineer at DuPont, and lives in Woodstown, New Jersey. He was eleven in 1929 (his brother Harold was eight) and remembers the year very clearly. When his mother, Caroline (Carrie), married his father, Joseph, she was living with her mother, Christina, and she was the last of the family to leave the home.

"So she was more or less stuck with her mother," Scheule explains, "because when she left, there was no more home. So she took her mother with her to our place and Dad agreed to take care of her, with us. Hal and I were born into her presence. The way it was, with Grandma being there at our house, it meant that we were going to be visited by the other families. Fred was going to come there with his family, Frank with his family, and Bill with his family. It meant a lot of extra work for Mom. Almost every weekend, one of these families would be there for dinner. In fact, she got a little bit miffed by it all, she felt that she was kind of being taken advantage of, because whenever she wanted to do anything, it was hard for her to go anywhere, because she had the responsibility for her mom. Her mom couldn't travel, she got carsick. So she felt kind of put on by the family as a whole. But I guess it's typical. Somebody's got to carry the bag. And Mom was the one. But it was through that circumstance that we got to know our cousins and our aunts and uncles.

"I remember there was friction between three of the Wackenhut brothers—Fred, Frank, and John. From what I can put together, Fred was perhaps the most ambitious, the most aggressive, because he got out and got himself established in a business. Frank was sort of a follower, maybe, he followed his brother in his occupation, the plumbing and heating business, and then, when he learned the trade, I think he was more or less absorbed by Fred, or he went to work for Fred. Now, this is probably not the healthiest arrangement in a family. And John, he was the only one who had never learned a trade. He never got married. When he got back from overseas, he didn't have anything. He must've had some money, but I don't know where he got what he had. Couldn't have been military pay at that time. But he had some money, and it seems like Fred borrowed it from him to use in his business. And John never got it back. This made for trouble between the three of them. I don't know the details. But something was bad in there all the time. How much this had to do with what Frank did, I don't know.

"Ruth [Feight, Fred's daughter] tells me that Frank was a manic depressive. But he finally stuck a gun in his mouth and did it. That's what I'm told. I don't want to talk to the kids about it, you know, to talk to Frank or Myrtle about it. They'd just as soon forget about it; they never will, but I don't want to ask them about it. Frank was relatively young when it happened, probably in his early fifties, I don't know."

Ruth Wackenhut Feight, born May 10, 1925, has fond memories of her uncle Frank, but confirms that he suffered from manic depressive psychosis, which was probably related to his suicide. "My brother Fred was also a manic depressive," she says. "It is hereditary. Frank had a violent temper. So did my father, but he mellowed through the years. But Uncle Frank was very nice to me. That's all I can say, he was really a nice uncle. I knew about his temper—with his son, mostly. Uncle Frank had one eye, one kidney, and he was a diabetic. He had a glass eye when he was working for my dad. Uncle Frank started his own business, but that didn't work out, so he went to work for my dad. I know my father went bankrupt around 1932.

"My father was working in Atlantic City when my grandfather died, and he came home to stay with my grandmother and take care of her. That I know. I attended the funeral of my grandmother Christina. I was about fifteen. She had been in a nursing home prior to that, and I remember going out practically every week to see her. There was quite an argument about the fact that she was there. And then my uncle Frank's mother-in-law took care of her. I don't remember the name of the nursing home, it was out in west Philadelphia. I remember the nurse who took care of her, her name was Kelly. Toward the end, my grandmother only spoke German. Once in a while she would speak a little bit of English, but most of it was German. The funeral home was Oliver H. Bair, a huge funeral parlor in downtown Philadelphia. In fact, my brother said he thought he was walking into an embassy. It was quite elaborate. I know my uncle Frank stayed all night at the funeral parlor. We went from there to Hillside Cemetery. I can remember my dad and I going up there quite often, every Memorial Day, and other holidays. Today, I work right near there."

Ruth has only vague memories of her uncle John Wackenhut; she recalls that he very rarely came to see her father.

But Norman Scheule and his family saw John frequently: "Mom always felt responsible for John," Scheule says. "Mom often had him come out to the house for supper or something, he used to come out every Wednesday or Thursday for supper. She tried to take care of him because he was the youngest of the group and she figured he had gotten a bad deal in life. He just lived in a boarding house, a rooming house, it wasn't much, he didn't have much of a life. He did whatever he could pick up. Mostly, that was following the sports groups. Like, he worked at The Arena, where they had boxing and that kind of stuff. That was in the winter. Then, in the summer, he worked at Shibe Park, he sold tickets there. Later on, I think he was in charge of the vendors or something. I think he did some vending for a while, and when he was there so many years, I think he was in charge of the vendors, seeing that they had their material, and hiring vendors so that there were always so many vendors in the stadium. And then he'd go to Florida for some of the winter months; gave him a place to hang his hat. John Wacky, they gave him the nickname of Wacky. That's what the ballpark people called him."

As the decade of the 1920s was drawing to a close, it became apparent that the Upper Darby High School would no longer suffice as the sole educational facility to accommodate the district's entire eighth-grade population. Rapid growth in the community (8,920 in 1920 to more than 46,000 in 1930) dictated that expansion was necessary. In November 1927, the Upper Darby taxpayers authorized a $1 million loan to the school board for the construction of a junior high school. The new building was to house grades seven through nine. The site chosen for the new structure was Garrett Road and Sherbrook Boulevard, on land that belonged to the McGrath Estate and was previously called Brookside Farm. Originally, only six acres were allocated for this project; however, it soon became clear that this would not provide adequate athletic, recreational, or parking space. Several adjacent tracts were then added, and an agreement was reached with the township commissioners that provided use of the nearby Marshall Road field.

Georgian Colonial architecture was selected and the building was constructed in the form of a rectangle around an enclosed courtyard. In keeping with authentic Colonial design, the entire structure was built of red brick, with tall white columns adorning the portico at the entrance, to create an appearance reminiscent of Thomas Jefferson's Monticello. The interior consisted of fifty-six classrooms, many of which were specifically equipped for science, industrial arts, or music instruction. The original structure also had one gymnasium, an auditorium, and a large library that housed more than 13,000 volumes.

On September 7, 1930, George was one of the 1,630 students who entered the brand-new Upper Darby Junior High School, where he would spend the next three years in grades seven through nine. The first principal was Wallace C. Savage. According to Norman Paul, who entered with George's class, the exterior is completely unchanged today, except for the name—it's now called the Beverly Hills Middle School—but the interior was gradually modernized.

In 1970, an additional gymnasium was added. In 1982, the library, originally built with bay windows, a fireplace, and white columned walls, was remodeled and expanded to become a modern media center and research facility. About the same time, a fully equipped five-room apartment was added as a teaching aid for the home economics curriculum. Finally, a large and modern student cafeteria was constructed, as well as a private faculty dining room.

The name of the school was changed twice. In 1958, when Drexel Hill Junior High School was opened because of increasing enrollments, Upper Darby Junior High School became Beverly Hills Junior High School. In 1981, new educational philosophies brought about a district-wide structural reorganization, and Beverly Hills Junior High became Beverly Hills Middle School. Under the new system, grade nine was moved to the high school, and grade six, previously an elementary grade, joined grades seven and eight as part of the middle school.

But when the school opened in 1930, it took all the seventh, eighth, and ninth graders from all the schools in the Upper Darby township—Keystone, Highland Park, Stonehurst, Primas-Secane, and Drexel Hill.

Norman Paul recalls that he and George became better students in junior high, and always compared their report-card grades, but then they started to get separated, because they were with students from other sections of Upper Darby, and, for the first time, they were no longer confined to one classroom, but moved to a different room for each course they took.

George remembers those years as being extremely hard financial times for his father, who was struggling to keep his business going. "My mother handled all the money," he says, "and there was a good reason for that. She was so tight-fisted, she should've handled it. I can vividly remember my father coming home on Fridays, which was payday, and telling my mother that he didn't have any money to give her. And seeing her go into quite a depressed state, not knowing how she was going to handle it the following week, with food and whatever. Most times he had enough money to pay his employees, there were two or three, but sometimes he didn't even have enough to do that. That's when I decided that I'd never go into business for myself. It scared me to death."

HILLSIDE CEMETERY is situated at the intersection of Susquehanna and Easton roads in the peaceful little settlement of Roslyn, Pennsylvania, about twelve miles north of downtown Philadelphia. Opened in 1890, it encompasses over 300 acres filled with stately trees, carefully trimmed shrubbery, and colorful flowers. There are forty-seven sections, including four that are dedicated to veterans who have served their country during times of war and peace.

Dominating the German Veterans Section is a tall, multi-tiered granite pedestal holding the weathered bronze statue of a German soldier, wearing a uniform of pre-World War I, rifle in his left hand, right hand held high, as if in victory. The inscription, written in German, states: "Dedicated to the War Veterans of the German Army, State of Pennsylvania, 30 May 1903."

The statue was there, and the cemetery was only twenty-one years old, when Johannes Wackenhut bought Deed No. 5246 to Lot No. 115 in section *Central Verband der Veteranen und Krieger der Deutschen Arme,* on February 1, 1911, almost seven months prior to the day that he would die. Lot No. 115, which cost Johannes $30, contains four graves, and is located in the third row of graves directly behind the statue. Almost all of the graves surrounding the statue have gravestones, situated in neat rows. Most are granite, some upright, some flat, but at Lot No. 115, graves one and two are unmarked, and graves three and four have one gravestone between them. It is an attractive rectangular granite stone, flat, with flowers chiseled into the upper corners, and the inscription reads:

SCHEULE

CAROLINE W.   JOSEPH E.

1892–1965   1891–1978

According to the records in the Hillside Cemetery Office, all four graves are occupied, and number two contains Johannes and Christina. Details are typewritten on a standard cemetery form:

DATE OF BURIAL	NAME OF DECEASED	AGE	GRAVE
September 3, 1911	John Wackenhut	53	2
April 9, 1940	Christina Wackenhut	86	2
October 7, 1965	Caroline W. Scheule	73	3
November 24, 1969	John Wackenhut	73	1
March 9, 1978	Joseph E. Scheule	87	4

Johannes had obviously changed his name to John, probably soon after beginning work at the Philadelphia Navy Yard. He purchased the cemetery lot just seven months before he died, and wanted to establish a family burial place that was relatively close to his home. The four graves in Lot No. 115 may have been all that he could afford at the time.

The typewritten cemetery form tells us that his undertaker was Gus A. Kirchner, that he was buried in a "wooden case" at a depth of *nine* feet. It lists Christia's undertaker as O.H. Bair, states that she was buried in a "Sartin case" at a depth of seven feet, in the same grave, and identifies the cause of her death as myocarditis. Johannes's death certificate tells us that he died of "heart disease" on August 31, 1911, and that his physician's name was John W. Ford.

Some questions are immediate and obvious: With a family of six grown children, why is there no gravestone for Johannes and Christina? What possible reason could there be? One might understand an unmarked grave for John, their son, the loner, buried nearly three decades after them, who had no family of his own. But the parents? Was the family so poor in 1911 that they had to bury Johannes, their father, in a wooden case in an unmarked grave? Twenty-nine years later, in 1940, when Christina was buried, was the family still so poor that they couldn't afford a joint gravestone for their parents, however simple, however inexpensive?

Until research on this biography was started, George Wackenhut did not know what year his grandfather died, did not know where he was buried, and had never seen a single photograph of him. Given the fact that his father William was a perfectionist, as George has always been, it seems incongruous that such information was not passed on from father to son. William was twenty-three at the time of his father's death in 1911, and working in Philadelphia; surely he must have attended the funeral, along with the rest of the family. The fact that the date and place were never revealed to George gives one pause.

Logic would indicate that there must have been a good reason. What was it? All six children of Johannes and Christina Wackenhut are long gone now, of course, and all have taken that reason to their graves.

2

THE OLD OAK TREE is gone now, and so is the classic high school building that it graced for more than fifty years. There are pictures and drawings of the old Upper Darby Senior High School in George's 1937 yearbook, *The Oak,* named after the tree, and it was a distinguished two-story gray stone structure with tall gray pillars, high white-framed windows, and architecture similar to the Keystone School. The present high school building, opened in the autumn of 1970, is sprawling, ultramodern, and almost indistinguishable from many other modern high schools constructed in that decade. It is actually the fourth building in the 200-year-plus history of the school, and its origins can be traced to the late seventeenth century, when a land grant was made to William Garrett in 1684 by William Penn. In 1779, settlers on this land assembled to purchase ground on which to erect a school, and seven years later the first little gray stone schoolhouse was built on a portion of the ground now known as Upper Darby Township. A free school system was adopted in Pennsylvania in 1835 and the first free public school in Upper Darby was placed under the direction of Isaac Garrett. The first alumni reunion was held in 1891 in a new brick building that replaced the smaller stone one. Upper Darby High School was established in 1894, the principal was Elizabeth D. Turner, and the commencement of the first graduating class (of five students) was held in 1896. The magnificent gray stone building that

George attended, 1934–37, was completed in 1919, the year he was born. The following year, the ground in back was graded and named Memorial Athletic Field in honor of those who lost their lives in World War I. Between 1926 and 1928, a total of thirty-nine classrooms were added to accommodate the tremendous growth in enrollment. Overcrowded conditions were temporarily alleviated in 1930 with the opening of the new Upper Darby Junior High School, but George's senior high school class of 1937 still had 502 graduates.

In the "Seniors" section of the 1937 yearbook, which comprises 114 of the 192 total pages, we find that George was not one of the four Class Officers; he was not among the thirty-two members of the Senior Executive Committee; he was not among the twelve couples selected in the "Who's Who" section (ranging from "Hardest Workers" to "Biggest Flirts"); he was not one of the six students whose names were inscribed on The Scholarship Plaque for having the highest three-year scholastic averages; and he was not one of the six classmates whose names were inscribed on The Service Plaque for outstanding activities in sports, publications, music, dramatics, student government, or other school activities. His name is not even mentioned in the long and humorous "Washington Wanderings," a narrative record of the class's trip to the nation's capital, April 8, 1937. And he did not belong to a single club of the dozens available in the school.

In fact, there are only three pictures of the seventeen-year-old George Wackenhut in the entire yearbook. One is in the "Seniors" section, under the alphabetical listings, a head-and-shoulders photograph of an average-looking young man, dark hair neatly trimmed but unparted, slight widow's peak above a high forehead, deep-set eyes, long nose, thin lips in a tight smile above the strong chin. He is wearing a light-colored tweed jacket, his shirt collar is held fashionably snug by a pin, and his striped tie appears to be of a knitted material. Compared to the somber-looking suits and ties of the other two boys on the page, John W. Van Inwegen, Jr., and William H. Viney (who have somber expressions to match), George looks positively sporty. The inscription to the left of the picture reads:

GEORGE RUSSELL WACKENHUT
7438 Miller Avenue, Upper Darby

*General * Purple*

SCHOOL: Athletic Association, 2, 3, 4; Honor Roll; Volley-ball, 3, Captain 4.

SPORTS: Soccer Numerals 4; Varsity Soccer 3, 4.

The second picture of George is with the nine-man volleyball team. As the captain, he's sitting front and center, wearing his tweed suit and a striped silk tie. In his junior year, the team surprised everyone by winning the regional championship.

The last, and best, picture of George appears on the page devoted to varsity soccer. In the team picture, he is front-row center, with the ball between his feet, and of all twenty-seven players, he looks the most mature and has the biggest smile. Clearly, he's in his element. He wasn't the captain, but he was the star goalkeeper, as he would be in professional soccer.

Herb Jenkins recalls what he believes to be the genesis of George's career in soccer: "We played sandlot baseball together, the old Upper Darby Barons. He played shortstop. Instead of picking up a grounder and throwing it, he would always *dive* after it. Had to fall on the ground and get up and throw it. I think that's really how he came to become such a good goaltender in soccer. Our soccer coach's name was Thomas J. Milne. And the assistant coach was Fenn Minacci; he's the man who's the father of our present high school principal. Fenn was a hell of a man. Very similar personality to George. Meticulous, quiet, conservative. I remember Fenn said something to me, like, 'Hey, Jenkins, where're we going to find a goaltender?' George had come out for soccer. And I said, 'There's the one, Wackenhut.' I said, 'Hell, he plays baseball, you'd think he's playing soccer, because he *dives* for everything that comes at him!' He made the soccer team and he went on to star in college and in pro soccer."

Norman Paul has a slightly different version: "I remember in intramural sports—I guess you could call it gym—we used to go out and play different sports, and that's when George really found himself in the game of soccer and in the position of goalie. And from then on, he was very good in soccer. He made the varsity team very rapidly. Upper Darby was very good in soccer, because they got a lot of their players from these families who were from the mill district of Cardington-Stonehurst, where the mills used to be, and these people were used to playing soccer. So George not only made the team, but he made it on a very good team."

George recalls the beginning of his soccer career vividly: "In my sophomore year, I went out for cross-country, and I was a total failure at that. On tryout day, I always finished next to last. My brother kept asking how much I was paying the guy to come in behind me! Then I tried wrestling; I don't know if I stayed at that too long or not. Sometime toward the end of my sophomore year, which was my first year in high school, we were out during gym class, playing soccer. Not good soccer, just soccer. And somehow or other, I ended up in the goal, and found out I was a pretty good goalkeeper. So the following year, I went out for soccer as goalkeeper and made the team. Played every game. There was another guy who could tend goal, so the coach had me playing fullback from time to time. And that followed me into college. There was another guy there, he was just a goalkeeper, couldn't play anything else. So, in college, a couple of times I played center forward and fullback. Then in semipro and professional, I ended up playing goalkeeper.

"In high school, I think I started out at like 150 pounds or so, then probably 175, maybe 180 by the time I finished. I remember when I was a junior in college, I was up to 206. But my best weight was around 190. Senior year in high school, I was about five-nine, I guess. Didn't reach my full height until much later. I know that because, when I went back to the thirty-fifth high school reunion, I saw guys that I recall being taller than I was, and now I'm taller than they are."

In 1937, Upper Darby's varsity soccer team finished in a three-way tie for the prestigious Suburban League championship, with Abington and Berwin, despite an ostensibly mediocre won-lost record of 9–7.

Prior to entering junior year, students at the senior high school were required to decide between four courses of study that they would pursue for their final two years: Scientific, Academic, General, or Commercial. Both the Scientific and Academic would qualify a student for college; General and Commercial would not.

"The General Course was for people who didn't know what they wanted to do, and that's where I was," George says. "At that point, I didn't know if I could get to college because of my parents' financial condition. But those high school years were fun years, I'll tell you. That high school prepared me for just about anything I confronted at college or in later life. Why? The teachers, the curriculum, the no-nonsense approach, that's the way high schools were back then. We had a dress code: I was required to wear a coat and tie to every class, just as I was required to do in junior high. Going to school was a very serious business. You passed or you failed. You had to put in a sufficient amount of work to get through. I don't recall working very hard. One time, I had a math exam the following day—a final, I think—and there was a guy who lived next door to me, across the driveway, Edgar Powell. He was at least three or four years older than I, and he had the same middle bedroom that I had. The houses were the same. And he'd throw things across to me and I'd throw things back. So he shouted over this one night, he said, 'How about some Ping-Pong?' I had a Ping-Pong table in the basement. I said, 'I can't, Ed, I have a final exam tomorrow.' He said, 'Aw, come on, let's play some Ping-Pong.' So I played Ping-Pong all night and never opened a book, and still got either a perfect score or next to it on the final exam. But I paid attention in class, that was the secret."

Norman Paul recalls his first—and only—"business venture" with George in high school. They became the school "bookies," taking bets on college football games. At ten cents a bet, the venture was so popular that word spread through the school like wildfire, members of the faculty heard about it, tracked down the culprits, and reported them to the principal. It was quite profitable—while it lasted.

"We made up our own football pool card," Paul says. "As I remember, we listed ten prominent college games. To win, one would have to pick eight winners out of ten games. We studied the teams and tried to pick all games that looked as if they would have close scores. We hoped we'd get some ties, which would count as a loss for both teams. Our business lasted for three weeks, at which time we were told by the school authorities to quit the business. In the course of our dressing-down by the school principal, he made the remark, 'Wouldn't you be ashamed to wear a new pair of shoes that you bought with money made on these football pools?' At that moment, George's lowered eyes were staring at the new shoes he'd bought with his earnings!"

In 1935, after struggling for seven years, George's father finally went out of business. He was forty-seven years old then, but had twenty-nine years of experience in virtually all aspects of the printing trade. Consequently, he found a steady job as a supervisor with a large printing firm on Market Street in Philadelphia. For the first time in many years, he was able to save some money, and George believes that's when his parents started to enjoy life again.

"While I was still in my junior year in the spring of 1936," George remembers, "a high school buddy and I decided to go down to Ocean City, New Jersey. We decided we'd go down and look for a summer job. And we got a job. Got a job working in a hot dog and hamburger joint called Bob's. Came home, told my mother that I was going to spend the summer in Ocean City, I had a job. She said, 'By God, *I'm* going to spend the summer in Ocean City!' Of course, in those days, you could rent an apartment for about $125 for the season. So, at least she had enough money to do that. She came down, rented a nice place. So I lived there, I had a job for the summer, I really had a ball."

In the summer of 1936, Ocean City was a vastly different resort than it is today. First settled as a fishing village in 1790, it is situated in southeast New Jersey on the chain of barrier islands known as the "Jersey Shore," extending from Sandy Hook to Cape May. Ocean City's closest neighbor is Atlantic City, and both resorts began to develop after a railroad link was completed in 1854. During more than a century, both resorts prospered as conservative, fashionable summer retreats for primarily upper- and middle-class vacationers from neighboring states. However, in 1976, casino gambling was legalized in New Jersey, and Atlantic City experienced a tremendous increase in tourism after the first big hotel-casinos opened in 1978. As a result of the job opportunities generated by increased tourism, the population of Atlantic City today is well over 40,000 and growing rapidly, while Ocean City, still without hotel-casinos, has stabilized at about 14,000.

Ocean City was about half that size in the summer of 1936, when George met William C. (Bud) Bailey, and started a friendship that would remain strong for the rest of their lives. Born in Philadelphia, April 4, 1916, Bud grew up in Frankford, Pennsylvania, and remembers going to an elementary school that still had gaslights. "We used to get these Philadelphia pretzels and we'd heat them over the gaslights in the halls," he recalls. "Then I went to Frankford High School. I went out for football and they threw me off because I was 130 pounds. Coach wouldn't let me play. I hid in the line for two weeks one time, and he caught me when he went to play opposite me to show somebody something. He said: 'What're *you* doing here?' And I also ran the 100-yard dash in track, twice.

"My family had a house in Ocean City, and we'd been going there for years. I can't recall the first time I met George. I think it was down at the shore, and somebody I knew from Upper Darby knew him, and we got together that way. I believe that was in the summer of 1936. He was still at Upper Darby Senior High School. George was one of our group in Ocean City. Most of us were from Frankford. We usually spent all day at the beach, throwing the football around, wrestling; I used to wrestle with George a lot. Then, in the evenings, we'd all go home to get dressed, then we'd meet somewhere. And then we'd wait, and we'd wait, and we'd wait for George to show up. It took him the longest while to get dressed. Because he learned from his father; his father was meticulous. Absolutely a meticulous dresser. And very neat all the time. Any time you saw him. I guess George inherited that meticulousness. So we had to wait for him.

"Then we would go out on the boardwalk, and we'd walk up and down, as a group. And sometimes we'd go up to the bowling alley and bowl. We were all pretty good bowlers. But I thought George was going to throw the ball right out through the back of the building! *Ka-boom!* He'd throw that thing down and pins would fly over into the other alleys. I remember the pin boys would move away from their positions and go to another lane so they wouldn't get hit with the flying pins. He really used to crush it.

"When we walked on the boardwalk, we would go from shop to shop and continually eat and drink all night. Some of our favorites were hot dogs at the Hole in the Wall; ham sandwiches on a bun with lettuce and mayonnaise at Ryan's; birch beer and ham sandwiches at Taylor's; candy and Coke at Shriver's Salt Water Taffy Shoppe; and popcorn at Jimmie's. Almost every Saturday night we'd go over to the Steel Pier in Atlantic City and listen to the big bands. I think we listened more than we danced.

"Prior to 1940, I remember a couple of spots that we used to go to over at Sommer's Point, there were a lot of them, and they'd have bands, too. Talk about famous big bands! Benny Goodman was my favorite. Tommy Dorsey, Harry James, Guy Lombardo, Artie Shaw, Red Nickels and his Five Pennies, Cab Callaway, Duke Ellington, Count Basie. We'd go from one band to the other. Vocalists like Frank Sinatra, Liltin' Martha Tilton, Peggie Lee. And then, after the band had finished, we'd go out on the Atlantic City boardwalk, down to Child's Restaurant. We'd have breakfast there and sit right next to some of the band members. Because that's where they ate. We stayed out all night, we usually got in about two to four o'clock in the morning. And the last two people were George and I.

"In Ocean City, we used to stop in the Chatterbox, where young people used to congregate, and get a sandwich or something. Then, every night, after we left the Chatterbox, we were walking home, it was about six or seven blocks, we stopped at this sundry store across the street, right on the corner of Asbury Avenue and Eleventh Street, and we'd each get a half-pint of Breyer's ice cream. And we'd eat that on the way home. One night, a bunch of us, I think there were four or five of us, we ended up finishing our ice cream on our front steps. And we started singing. Four o'clock in the morning, we're singing and harmonizing, five of us! The next day, we got a lot of compliments! People enjoyed our singing! Nobody complained that we woke them up!"

Summers in Ocean City would become routine for George throughout high school and three years at West Chester State Teacher's College, until he was inducted into the U.S. Army in the summer of 1941, and he has warm memories of those days, of his friends, and of the big bands. Musicologists have labeled the years 1935–45 as the "swing era," when big bands dominated popular music in the U.S. Such bandleaders as Glen Miller, Benny Goodman, and the Dorsey Brothers achieved fame and popularity equal to that of legendary black big-band leaders such as Duke Ellington and Count Basie. During the same decade, radio, movies, and records created a huge audience for popular music, the center of which was New York, nicknamed Tin Pan Alley.

George considers himself fortunate to have actually seen and heard the most famous big bands during the heyday of the swing era. Those years also represent an age of innocence in this country, compared to the stark realities that would evolve during World War II and afterward, an age of innocence that future generations would find difficult to believe, much less understand.

Forces were already set in motion that would lead to the devastation of World War II and forever alter George Wackenhut's life, because he would be actively involved in it. In 1936, Hitler remilitarized the Rhineland, and Mussolini, having already invaded Ethiopia, proclaimed the Rome-Berlin Axis. Japan began its attack on China in 1937.

On June 16, 1937, when George graduated from Upper Darby Senior High School, he didn't have the slightest desire to go to college, but he'd hedged his bets anyway. "I looked at the requirements for most colleges," he says, "and most of them required at least two years of a foreign language. So I worked that into the General Course. But I also took bookkeeping, I took commercial geography, and typing, so I had a mix. Which didn't hurt me any. At least I had the requisite subjects when I did apply for college. Then, by the time I graduated from high school—you know how teenagers hit the doldrums and get disgusted with everything?—I was so fed up with everything at that point in time, I didn't even want to *think* about going to college. And my grades were such—I made the Honor Roll—that I probably could've gotten a scholarship. It never even occurred to me. My brother probably would've been guiding me if he were home, but he wasn't there. I was on my own. In fact, I don't think I even told my parents when the graduation was."

For a young man who admittedly didn't work very hard, and didn't really want to go to college, the academic transcript of his senior year is deceptive:

Subject	Grade
English III	B
World History	B
U.S. History	B
Bookkeeping I	B
Physical Training	A
English IV	B
Commercial Geography	C
Plane Geometry	C
Typing B	B
Bookkeeping II	B
Physical Training	B
Citizenship	B

Seen in historical perspective, 1937 was a year of intense domestic unrest and international political upheaval. The U.S. population was nearing 130 million, President Franklin D. Roosevelt was starting his second term, having defeated Republican Alf Landon by a landslide, carrying every state except Maine and Vermont, and auto workers in Flint, Michigan, began the year with an organized sit-down strike that spread quickly through General Motors' factories nationwide; the most decisive labor struggle of the decade had begun. After a forty-four-day occupation of GM factories, including violent clashes between strikers and police, all of Chrysler's plants in Detroit were closed by sit-downs; when police threatened to expel the strikers by force, more than 150,000 auto workers rallied in downtown Detroit. On May 30, striking workers at Republic Steel were parading with their families toward the Republic factory when, without apparent provocation, they were attacked by the police; ten were killed and hundreds wounded in an incident that would become known as the Memorial Day Massacre.

Shortly before George Wackenhut graduated from high school, the first student strike against a war took place at colleges throughout the country and students vowed against participation in any war. About the same time, New York City Mayor Fiorello LaGuardia was telling the American Jewish Congress that he wished he had a "chamber of horrors" at the upcoming World's Fair where he could exhibit a figure of Adolph Hitler, who was "menacing world peace."

The summer of 1937 was the second summer that George worked full-time for a printer in Ocean City. It was a small printing shop called Mywood Press, located on the corner of Ninth Street and Wesley Avenue, and the owner was Fred R. Woodruff, a man he liked very much. George's duties included setting type, redistributing type, running the press, proofreading, plus wrapping packages and making deliveries, the same basic jobs he did for his father when he was younger. And, as usual, he lived in the apartment that his parents rented for the summer.

"My hours at the printer were eight until five," he says, "with an hour for lunch, and I'd walk home for lunch and walk back. For a time, I'd go to the beach after work, but that got pretty tiring to me. The main thing was the boardwalk area at night with Bud Bailey and his group from Frankford, wandering around. Sometimes I'd go to the beach, but most of the time I'd just go home, get a shower, get dressed, have dinner, and go off to the boardwalk. I don't think I did a great deal of sleeping during those summers. I had to work five and a half days a week; Saturday from eight till twelve. And, of course, Saturday afternoon and all day Sunday, I was on the beach with Bud and his group. Unless I was still in bed from being out at Steel Pier all the night before!"

Then, after Labor Day, when his parents gave up the apartment and moved back to Upper Darby, he started looking for a full-time job in the Philadelphia area. The General Electric Company had a large plant in southwest Philadelphia, and when George learned that they were hiring, he applied for a job.

"I remember you had to fill out an application and you had to take a test," he says. "The test had some mathematical questions and some English questions, as I recall. And I was interviewed and ended up getting a job in the mailroom. I was in the mailroom for only a few weeks, at twelve dollars a week, and then they had an opening in the cafeteria, and I was chosen for that. And that paid fifteen dollars a week. I had to keep a cart stacked with all sorts of candies and chewing gum and peanuts and all kinds of snacks. Also, I helped with lunch. I don't recall if I did any serving. We had about two dozen workers in the cafeteria.

"When I was hired, one of the requirements was that I had to go to night school. That's when I enrolled in the Wharton Evening School, University of Pennsylvania. I don't know if GE dictated the courses I was to take or not, but I almost think they must have, because I don't know why I'd have taken courses in business law and accounting. I don't think they were my favorite subjects at that point in time. Toward the end of 1937 and the early part of 1938, the economy started to pick up. Then we were hit by a recession in the spring of 1938, and GE started laying people off. I was laid off in March, 1938, and I was unemployed for about six weeks, but I continued to attend the Wharton Evening School. I went to the unemployment office, but I never collected an unemployment check, because I got a call from the registrar of Upper Darby Senior High School, who said that he had just learned of a job.

"It was with a commodity broker in Philadelphia, a firm named C.L. Wood, and it was another mailroom job. I'd pick up the mail at the post office in the morning, which was quite a chore, these big bags full of mail, and I'd have to lug them several blocks. I was there for about six weeks, getting along fine, although it was a dead-end sort of thing for sure, and I was continuing to take my two courses at the Wharton Evening School. But I'd made up my mind by that time that I was going to go to college, if I could find a way to work my way through on the little amount of money that my parents could afford. While at GE, I got friendly with a guy who had graduated from Penn State, and he was always extolling the virtues of Penn State, so I sort of had it in my mind that's where I wanted to go.

"During the first part of June, I knew I could have my job back at the printing shop in Ocean City, and it would certainly be a better place to spend the summer than Philadelphia, so I gave notice and said I was going to take the job in Ocean City and then I was going to go to college in the fall. They were nice about it, and that was that. Six weeks' duration, it kept the wolf away from the door. I finished the year at the Wharton Evening School and received credit for the two courses."

During the time he was working for GE, George had been playing semipro soccer every weekend with the Cardington Soccer Club, down in the section of Upper Darby where mill workers lived. At GE, he met a man named John Hagen, who was a fullback on the Cakebakers Soccer Club, a German semipro team in the Kensington area of Philadelphia; the Cakebakers were considered one of the best clubs in the Pennsylvania League. Hagen saw George play goalkeeper, was favorably impressed, and approached him to play for the Cakebakers. George switched teams, starred as goalkeeper for the Cakebakers in 1937 and 1938, and has pleasant memories of those seasons. The reputation he established as a semipro would turn out to be a critical factor in his quest for a college education.

In the late summer of 1938, while working in Ocean City, George received a letter that would alter his life. It was from Earle "Muddy" Waters, the varsity soccer coach at West Chester State Teachers College, in southeast Pennsylvania. Waters had seen George play for the Cakebakers, believed he showed promise of developing into a fine college player, and asked if he would be interested in applying to West Chester for the fall term. Although West Chester did not offer soccer scholarships, Waters felt certain that he could arrange for a job at the college, waiting on tables in the dining room three times a day, that would defray at least part of George's expenses.

"One thing I remember very clearly," George says, "I still had in mind that I wanted to go to Penn State, but it was getting kind of late to make application. And then I got this letter from Muddy Waters, which my parents read, of course. And all I remember of that whole period was my mother scolding the hell out of me: 'Forget Penn State, we can't afford to send you there! You can go to West Chester for much less money!' So that was really what prompted me to go. I answered the letter and I submitted my application, but I don't think I met Waters until I got up there. I know I had to have a complete physical exam, and I had to go up to Philadelphia from Ocean City to do that. A complete physical exam was five dollars, I remember that!"

ON SEPTEMBER 12, 1938, when George entered West Chester State Teachers College, in West Chester, Pennsylvania, twenty-five miles west of Philadelphia, there were only four academic buildings, although the institution itself was founded in 1871. It began as West Chester Academy in 1812, and the first school building was constructed on a one-acre lot purchased from a local butcher for $600. In 1871, it became a State Normal School, which was defined as a school offering a two-year course, and certification to high school graduates preparing to be teachers, especially elementary school teachers. A new building was constructed at a cost of $75,000, built primarily of serpentine, and the cornerstone was laid on September 14, 1870. The building survives today as Old Main. To promote the new institution, an eight-page circular was published, in which the location, building, and course of study are described:

Location

The situation of West Chester is unsurpassed for the beauty and fertility of its surroundings, and for the healthfulness of its climate. Elevated nearly 500 feet above tide, it is free from all malaria. Access is had several times daily by railroad from Philadelphia, or by a branch connecting with the Pennsylvania Central, as also by stage from the Wilmington & Birdsboro Road.

The Building

Is situated on the south side of the Borough, half a mile from the Court House, is entirely new, of stone, 150 by 112 feet, four stories high, with a basement. It is furnished throughout in the best manner, with new furniture of the most approved patterns. It is heated by steam throughout, and lighted with gas. Water closets, wash rooms and bath rooms are all complete, and under one roof. Pupils boarding in the Institution will be furnished with single beds with bedding complete, wardrobe, toilet tables and glass for each, and are expected to furnish only their own towels and table napkins. Boys must also furnish themselves with slippers for use in the building.

The Course of Study

Is intended to be at once thorough and comprehensive. "Cramming" will be discouraged; but it is designed that students faithfully availing themselves of their privileges, shall be thoroughly fitted as teachers in the Common or Classical Schools, or to enter the first Colleges and Scientific Schools in the land.

When the West Chester State Normal School opened on September 25, 1871, the official register listed the names of 102 boys and 52 girls. The principal was Ezekiel Hanson Cook. A faculty member by the name of Caleb S. Cope wrote his impressions about the first day: "This morning at 10 o'clock, the brazen occupant of the cupola, of clamorous iron tongue, was lifted into position and put down upon its bearings. We have heard its first sonorous peals sent forth on the breeze of the morning, over the fertile fields of the Goshens, and the Bradfords, to awaken our valleys, and be re-echoed back by the rolling hills of the Brandywine."

West Chester was accredited as a State Teachers College in 1927, and became West Chester University in 1969. Today, more than 11,000 undergraduate and graduate students and over 1,000 faculty and staff study and work at the 388-acre campus. Among the many modern facilities supporting the university's nearly 200 academic programs are the Francis Harvey Green Library with more than 465,000 volumes, 2,800 periodical subscriptions, and a micromedia collection of 350,000 titles; extensive computing services provided through a network of hundreds of microcomputers linked with the IBM 4381 mainframe; and state-of-the-art scientific instrumentation.

"A few days after I matriculated at West Chester, I was called to the office of a man named Clarence McKelvie," George recalls. "I don't know what his title was, but he had something to do with college personnel. He's still alive and I still communicate with him. He proceeded to tell me that through the intercession of Earle Waters, the soccer coach, he was going to be able to get me a job through the NYRA, the National Youth Recovery Act. It would be a job waiting on tables, and for that I'd get all my meals free, which would be a big financial help.

"I guess I asked him if I could have weekends off, because I was playing soccer for the Cakebakers on weekends. At that particular time in my life, soccer was the only thing that really mattered to me. I even had visions of playing in the First Division over in England. In those days, those guys made ten pounds a week, and that was fifty dollars a week at the existing exchange rate. And fifty dollars a week sounded like an awful lot of money to me, right in the middle of the Depression.

"Anyway, Clareance McKelvie said I couldn't have weekends off. There were a lot of students who didn't go home on weekends and they had to be served. So I got up and started to walk out of his office! He said, 'Where are you going?' I said, 'Well, if I can't have weekends off, I can't take this job, because of the soccer situation.' I was very serious. And also very foolhardy! He said, 'Well, let me talk to Earle Waters some more.' So he did, and Waters arranged that I could have weekends off! I didn't want the weekends off to socialize, I wanted to play soccer. Anyway, I think that's interesting. If I had walked out of his office that day, it could have changed my whole life!"

Today, any type of physical or mental hazing is strictly prohibited at West Chester, under terms of the comprehensive anti-hazing policy, but it was a standard practiced when George was a freshman in 1938, and the entire college numbered about 1,200 undergraduates.

"During the freshmen hazing process," he remembers, "if you did something you weren't supposed to—and you had a whole book of freshmen regulations—you were punished for it. Well, some upperclassman caught me doing something, I don't recall what it was. And then I had to go to what they called lower court. Usually, they'd stand you up on a pile of mats in the gym, blindfold you, make you bend over, then they'd take a big paddle with holes in it and whack your ass. Well, the first time, I got whacked pretty good. And I was home that weekend and I told my mother and father about it. Dad got furious: 'I'll go up there, and I'll do this and I'll do that!' I said, 'Hey, wait. This is part of the game, you can't get involved in any way!'

"I was such a jackass, I was just too young to know differently, I guess. I got gigged again, I don't know what for. This time, I'm up on the mats, and there's this great big football player, a monstrous guy—I mean he could really wield that paddle! *WHACK!* I saw stars of red, white, and blue! I took about three of those and then I just got infuriated, I couldn't stand any more. I pulled off my blindfold and I came up swinging! And here's this guy, this monster, trying to fend me off, he says, 'Take it easy! Take it easy!' I was just beside myself and I made some stupid remark to the effect that my father was opposed to this sort of thing. So, after you go to lower court, in addition to getting your ass whacked, they have you do something, you wear a sign or something. And this, I guess, is one of the best things that could've happened to me. They had me wear two cardboard boxes! One was a big one with my arms going through it and my head going through it. The other was a small box that sat on top of that with holes for my eyes! And the sign on the back read: *They're Going to Ship Me Home to Daddy!* So everybody's coming up: 'Who's in the box?' So everybody got to know me! I had to wear those boxes every day for a week!"

Not everyone in the freshman class took hazing as well. One of his classmates, Jay Smith, who later become a special agent in the Federal Bureau of Investigation, and would be instrumental in recommending George to the FBI, remembers the hazing vividly. "I received a lot of rather severe treatment by the upperclassmen," Smith says. "There were two or three *day* students, a couple of them from Philadelphia—*men!*—who appeared one evening in the gymnasium to discipline me for having dated a girl, or whatever, some violation, and I committed all of them. And they had me bend over and lower my trousers, and they beat me with a heavy paddle. They beat me to the point that the next day I was actually bleeding.

"Subsequently, I learned the identity of one of the individuals who beat me, I recognized his voice. And, after the freshmen regs were over, I waited for him at his car. I told him what he'd done to me, and then I proceeded to thoroughly beat *him.* Left him totally bloody, cut, to the point that onlookers ran to get help. Yes, I did that. Carefully and methodically beat him. That's the kind of person I was. But he deserved it. He was a bully and a coward. And I never in my life participated in any hazing."

Born Jay F. Smith, Jr., August 25, 1920, in Philadelphia, he was a straight-A student at West Philadelphia High School, played varsity basketball and baseball for three years, and received the Best Athlete award of the Class of 1938. Needing an athletic scholarship to go to college, Smith received offers from virtually all of the local colleges, including Temple, the University of Pennsylvania, LaSalle, St. Joseph's, and Villanova, primarily because of his ability in basketball.

"But none of those offers appealed to me," he says, "because I would have had to attend college as a day student. It was very important for me to leave home and become a resident student, at almost any college. West Chester came to my attention and they offered me an athletic scholarship in basketball and baseball, which paid for all of my tuition, and I served as a waiter in the dining room, which paid for my room and board. I had very little, if any, spending money. Essentially, I left home at the age of eighteen and really never returned, other than short visits."

Smith and most of the other physical education majors lived in Wayne Hall, the men's dormitory, but George rented a room in a private house at 806 Church Street, owned by a Mr. and Mrs. Gibson, and paid $2 a week rent. He lived there throughout his three years at West Chester; there was only one room in the house to rent, and George shared it with a roommate named Don Kunz. The two-story white frame house with bay windows was just across the street from the small campus. In those days, the college was bordered to the south by West Rosedale Avenue, to the north by University

Avenue, to the east by South High Street, and to the west by South Church Street. Ironically, 806 Church Street is now the Veterans Memorial Alumni House. Today, more than half a century after George lived there as a student, the refurbished house is used as many as twenty-five times a month by a myriad of university alumni, faculty, and students. For the fiftieth reunion of the Class of 1942, George was co-chairman of the reunion gift drive that increased the endowment of the house from $150,000 to $250,000. The other co-chairmen were Jay Smith and John Gardner.

The soccer season started in September, of course, and freshman were not eligible to play varsity soccer. From the beginning, it was obvious that the freshman soccer team was loaded with talent, indirectly recruited by Earle "Muddy" Waters, who considered that freshman team, directed by Coach Benner, to be potentially one of the best varsity squads he would ever coach, his so-called dream team. They had quite a tradition to uphold. According to West Chester's 1939 yearbook, *The Serpentine,* the varsity soccer teams coached by Waters since 1920 had amassed an almost unbelievable record: "Winning soccer games at West Chester is rapidly becoming second-nature to the men who are so ably coached in the use of their feet by one Earle C. Waters. Nine of the ten opponents encountered felt the stigma of defeat administered in the Purple and Gold manner. An examination of the records of the Rams to date brings to light the sparkling string of 74 out of 78 battles won by the Waters-coached elevens."

The freshman soccer team lived up to its potential. Directly under the picture of the freshman squad on page 195 in the 1939 issue of *The Serpentine* is the history of their season:

> The frosh booters recorded one of the greatest seasons in freshman soccer history. Blanked only by a scoreless stalemate with Avon-Grove High School in the opening encounter, the Ramlets went on to win their seven remaining games with little trouble.
>
> Beacom College, Harrington High, Whitpaine High, and Hill School all fell by the wayside, as did Episcopal, Avon-Grove, and Goldey. Only once was the Ramlet net dented, and this lone enemy tally deprived the boys of another remarkable record.

Captain Ken Webb led the team ably from the goalie post and was supported by such promising players as "Wacky" Wackenhut, Paul Buono, Pollock, Hoch, Leith, Challen, Cavanaugh, Robinson, Whitman, Klank, and Kramaroff. These men blended their talents under the direction of Coach Benner into a winning machine, and it looks as though the varsity squad of next season will have little trouble in adding to that impressive string of victories when its ranks are swelled by these capable yearlings.

Ken Webb, captain of the freshman team, looks back at that season with genuine pride. Born in Philadelphia, September 17, 1915, he graduated from Abington High School in 1933, then worked for five years before entering West Chester in 1938, just days before his twenty-third birthday. "I was a secondary student, not a physical education major," he says, "so I didn't take any classes with George, but I played soccer with him from the beginning. I was goaltender, although George played that position some of the time. I'll tell you, I hope I'm not bragging when I say this, but, at that *time,* I was probably a better goaltender than Wacky. He was good, but I had the advantage. I had played in Philadelphia on the lots. The team that I played with had just won the Allied Amateur Cup in Philadelphia. In August, before I came to school, I was playing Gaelic football with the Philadelphia Gaelic Club, and I had an opportunity to play against the Irish champions who were on tour. So, that, plus the fact that I was five years older than Wacky, gave me sort of an edge. Now, George, while he was a good goaltender, I got more playing time at West Chester than he did. I'm not sure how much he played in the goal, but he was able to do things which I wasn't able to do. He could play in the field. And if he wasn't playing in the goal, he was playing in the field. I wasn't able to do that. He was all over—he was fullback, he was up on the line, he was all over. He was that sort of guy, any place you'd put him, he was going to give it his best shot.

"There was never any friction between us, I never felt that. The only thing I ever heard him say—and it goes back to long after college—he went into Philadelphia to play, he played for the Philadelphia Nationals in the American League. And he said to me at one time, 'Well, I could never play goal at West Chester, but I was good enough to play for the Philadelphia Nationals!' That griped him, although there was no friction between us as to who should be in the goal. As freshmen, I believe that Muddy Waters was setting us up to become one of his best teams. We beat the varsity several times as freshman. We had a good reputation as a soccer school. I remember, during my freshman year, when we just started, we played a team from Philadelphia, the Lighthouse Boys Club, I think, and after the game a kid came in to Waters's office—I was in the office—and he said to Waters: 'What're you offering?' Waters looked at him, smiled, and said, 'Nothing but a damn good education, son!' That was that.

"I remember George was always probing, he was always trying to get better. Wacky had an expression: 'Naturally aggressive.' And that described him, I think: 'Naturally aggressive.' He'd walk around campus with a sponge ball in his hand, squeezing that ball, building up the muscles in his arms. At a class reunion, I told him, I said, 'Hey, Wacky, we're going to chance off a sponge ball and say: *This is the ball that George Wackenhut used to develop the muscles in his arms!*' "

Horace "Buzz" Leith was also a starter on the freshman team and later on the varsity. Born February 18, 1920, in Tacony, Pennsylvania, he graduated from Frankford High School in 1937, where he played soccer and baseball. "The first time I ever heard of Wackenhut was in my senior soccer year," he recalls. "There was a fellow by the name of Fred Wackenhut, who was George's cousin, and Fred and I played baseball at Frankford. We were scheduled to play Upper Darby that year, so Fred came to me, and everybody else on the soccer team, and said, 'Boy, wait till you play Upper Darby, you're going to get beat! My cousin is the *goaltender* for Upper Darby!' I think we beat them, we beat pretty near everybody we played in those days, but it wasn't George's fault. Because I remember looking for him especially, after being warned by Freddie. And he was good. That was the first time I ever saw him.

"It was very disappointing at the start of our freshman year, because the first week that we were in school, it rained for a solid week. And I know anybody who played soccer was looking forward to practice and getting started in college soccer. I think the first day of class was September 12, and it rained for like a solid week, and the only way we could practice was indoors. We practiced in the gymnasium. And I remember I was homesick, my clothes were all wet, you know, running back and forth to class, it was horrible! I went home the first weekend, my cousin was going to get married, and I had to go to the wedding. And I almost didn't come back! But things kind of cleared up.

"We had a very, very strong freshman team. In fact, Mr. Waters said he considered that was going to be his dream team. By the time we got to be seniors, he felt that we would be the best team he'd ever had up to that point. But, unfortunately, most of us never got to play in our senior year; I was one of the few who got to play that year. As freshmen, we didn't lose a game. We had only one goal scored against us, and that was scored by our own fullback, who pushed the ball back to the goalie, only the goalie wasn't there! That was the only goal scored against us all year!"

Another classmate who was a physical education major, and in all of George's classes during freshman year, is Larry "Monk" Umstead. Born April 11, 1918, in Pottstown, Pennsylvania, he attended Pottstown High School, where he played football and baseball, graduated in 1936, and entered West Chester in September 1938. "Gym and athletics were the two physical education classes," he remembers, "and then we had everything from history to sociology to English to chemistry to anatomy. I don't recall Wacky being particularly outstanding in any given academic class, but his determination was obvious. In gym class, he would be the last one off the mats, and also the last one out of the locker room. However, he was never late for classes. Another thing I recall, when we were waiting on tables in the dining room, Wacky was usually the last one out. As waiters, we would eat after we served, three times a day, and I guess most of us would rush out for different activities, but I don't recall George ever rushing out of the dining room!

"When we went to West Chester, there were only four basic academic buildings: Recitation Hall, Anderson Hall, Philips Memorial, and the Demonstration School. It took them three years to get the furniture for Anderson Hall, so we didn't get in it until senior year.

There were two permanent dormitories. One was Wayne Hall, for the men, and the other was Old Main, for the girls. Years and years ago, I think Old Main was probably the only building there. The Old Gym had a swimming pool in the basement, only the second college pool in the country; Yale had the first. All the old buildings were constructed with serpentine stone, that's why the yearbook was named *The Serpentine*."

Tom Triol was a sophomore that year, playing first-string varsity soccer, and he felt a kinship toward George, because he had also come up the hard way, and worked several years before entering West Chester. "I guess I met George on the soccer field first," he recalls. "I was glad to see him come along, because that year I had to play goalie and I wasn't a goalie. George came, and he was a great goalie, and Ken Webb came, so we had two outstanding goalies. When I say 'outstanding,' West Chester at that time was one of the four top teams in the country. The others were Syracuse, Princeton, and Penn State. That attracted some of the best players around."

Born December 1, 1917, in the town of Abington, Pennsylvania, several miles northeast of Philadelphia, Triol was one of five children. His father died when he was six. His mother had no money to take care of the family, so he and a brother went to a Presbyterian orphanage in Philadelphia, didn't like it, and transferred to Girard College, a heavily endowed school for fatherless boys in Philadelphia, when he was seven. He stayed there until he was eighteen and built a reputation as one of the finest soccer players in the history of the school.

"There were 1,730 boys, the largest and wealthiest school in the nation, and it didn't cost a cent to get in," he says. "I was really a very fortunate person. Mr. Girard put in his will that the boys would not only take academic subjects, but learn a trade. So, when I graduated in 1935, I went out as an apprentice tool and dye maker and worked at Standard Press Steel Company in Jenkintown, Pennsylvania. After several years of this, I realized I was not a real artisan, I was a people-oriented person, so I went to my mother and asked if she'd mind if I went to college. She approved. So I pooled all of my resources, which amounted to $300 after several years of work, and left for West Chester in September 1937."

Triol met his wife-to-be, Jane, whose maiden name was Harris, during her first day at West Chester, September 12, 1938. Born in Mt. Carmel, Pennsylvania, October 29, 1920, she was in George's class and a physical education major. "The way we met," Jane says, "my 'big sister' was taking me around campus, the first hour I was on the campus. Along comes Tom. She introduces me to him, and Tom decides he's going to walk the rest of the way with us around the campus. They had some stupid rules there at the beginning, where the freshman girls were not supposed to have any dates, or even *talk* to boys for the first six weeks, after the first couple of days of orientation, the hazing. And it was the *stupidest* thing! If you were caught talking to boys, even saying hello to a boy, you had to wear white cotton stockings and a dumb hat of some sort. Well, Tom got me into difficulty with the dorm council right off the bat! He *insisted* on coming up and talking to me! I said, 'I can't talk to you, I can't talk to you, go away, go away!' I had to go down to lower court again and again. In fact, I was in lower court so often in my freshman year, they made me the head of it in my sophomore year. They didn't paddle the girls, but they just humiliated them in any way they could. And the boys! They wouldn't permit the freshman boys to have any dates with any girls on the campus for six months!"

Although Jane didn't have many classes with George, she had one that remains frozen in her mind: "I remember, I guess it was my sophomore year, that I had a couple of classes with him. He was always determined to know; if something bothered him, he would pick at it until he got the right answer that he wanted. Well, one of the classes was an anatomy class. Of course, this was 1939–40, and we weren't quite as outspoken in those days about sexual things. Well, we came to the anatomy of the sexual parts of the body, and George came out with a question that made *all* of us girls want to just *slide* right under our *seats!* And afterwards, I was so shocked by the question that I didn't hear the answer, and I was furious! His question was: 'What, exactly, is it like for a woman to have an orgasm?' Well, after a stunned silence, he got an answer. I don't recall the answer at all, as I said, I was so shocked. The instructor was Dr. Tresize, who was also the wrestling coach. He was an excellent teacher; he wasn't embarrassed by the question. So George got his answer!"

JAY SMITH remembers his freshman year with mixed emotions, largely because of a serious personality conflict with the Dean of Men, Dr. Glen Killinger, who was the varsity coach in football, basketball, and baseball, and had been an All-American football player at Penn State in 1929. Killinger had become head football coach in 1934. According to the *Centennial History of West Chester State College,* by Dr. Russell L. Sturzebecker (Tinicum Press, 1971), Killinger had come on strong from the beginning:

> The big event in May was heralded by posters proclaiming the First Annual (it was the only one ever held) Men's Steak Night. At Darlington Seminary, a defunct private school, at that time used as a recreation center by the college under the eyes of A.W. Thompson, Athletic Director, Dr. Cameron [president of the college] introduced to the assembled males the new football coach, All-American Glen Killinger. A compactly built man of average height stepped forward and dropped a bombshell. In a few clipped and well-chosen words, he announced in no uncertain terms what he intended to do and how he would accomplish this with what appeared to be a dynamic, forceful change from his predecessor. From within the group addressed came such remarks as "Who does he think he is?" "Look at the size of him." Telisport Putsavage [football player] led out in an audible guffaw. By the end of the first week of the coming fall season the cynics and scoffers found football had changed and they had to also. Putsavage in particular had more extra laps on the track assigned to him than any athlete in the history of the college. A new era in athletics had arrived with the new coach.

"In baseball, I played third base and second base, and I played on the varsity as a freshman," Smith says. "Killinger and I entered into a deep conflict situation in my freshman year, which was not unusual for him. When I was a freshman, Killinger didn't know about me, I was recruited by the freshman basketball coach at that time, Mr. Lloyd Lux, a fine, wonderful individual who understood youngsters and was kind and considerate. Killinger informed me that I had to play football if I wanted to stay at the school. And I told Killinger

I'd never played football, didn't know how to play football, didn't want to play football. Didn't want to get hurt. He immediately dragged me down to the locker room, and I put the uniform on, and I played football. And I didn't know how; I wasn't very good. He put me at halfback and we played the Temple freshmen, who were huge fellows, and I had four ribs broken. So I was excused, with great profanity, by Killinger, as being a sissy, that I should be on the women's team, and I was excused for the balance of the football season.

"Subsequently, I played freshman basketball, under Mr. Lux, and we had an outstanding team, and I broke all scoring records for the freshman team. Recently, I was selected for the West Chester University Basketball Hall of Fame. But *Killinger* didn't think I was any good! You notice that I'm laughing about the whole thing, because this honor—and I say that with tongue-in-cheek—was bestowed upon me in 1990, I believe because I may be one of the few basketball players still alive who played during the 1940s decade! I suspect that's the truth, and that's exactly what my dear friend Killinger would've said!

"West Chester, for me, was an unbelievably lovely, gentle place in a sweet, small town, and totally opposite anything I'd ever experienced, having been raised in the semi-slum city streets of Philadelphia. The student body, I might add, was about two-thirds female and one-third male, and I just found that to be a joy to behold! I lived in Wayne Hall at that time; it was subsequently demolished and a new building was constructed that I think may be called—God forbid!—Killinger Hall! I hate to even imagine that, to perpetuate that person's name.

"Killinger did his very best to have me thrown out of college in my senior year. He had a special committee meeting with all the heads of the departments and tried to have me removed. He said I was morally and ethically unworthy of being at West Chester. That's a pretty low level, because there weren't many saints there. He hated me because I had consistently thwarted him and would not do as he said, and I had good grades, so he couldn't throw me out because of my grades, and I never opened a textbook in college. Never did. Didn't have to. Not at West Chester.

"Otherwise, I had a beautiful time at West Chester. I met my wonderful wife there, as a freshman. Her maiden name was Elinor Barkley—George knew her very well—and we've been married more than fifty years. That was the greatest thing that happened to me at West Chester, and the second best thing was receiving a BS degree.

"The reason that I didn't get to know a great deal about George was because, in my view, at that time, George was the personification of an absolutely decent, honest, straightforward individual—which was a *mystery* to me! I could not relate to anyone that good. I was just a bad guy. I violated all the rules, they didn't mean anything to me. I ran around after the girls, I didn't care. George was the exact, diametric opposite. He was a good person. I mean, as far as I knew, a *very* good person. Solid, straight, decent, honest. That's the way I perceived him. That's how I perceive him now. I have the highest regard for him, I always did, and so did his classmates."

Bud Bailey, George's longtime friend during the summers at Ocean City, had a similar personality conflict with Killinger at West Chester, but not nearly as serious. "Glen Killinger was considered the outstanding coach for the T-formation, at its very beginning," Bailey says. "He got offers from large colleges and universities, but never left West Chester; he liked the small college. He was Dean of Men. I was on *his* list! I played that freshman year with three teams, I had more fun. I thought a football game lasted fifteen minutes, that's how much I loved it. So, the next year, in spring, I was playing lacrosse. And Killinger came across the lacrosse field, and he got on me for not coming out for spring football practice. He said, 'I understand you're a football player.' He knew me. And I said, 'Well, I try.' He said, 'Well, we're having spring practice.' I said, 'I don't believe in spring practice.' He asked me why. I said, 'Well, it's hot weather, you get two weeks, people are not really in condition, you rush it, you're scrimmaging, people get hurt, and then, in the fall, you've got all new people coming out, and you start all over again. I don't believe it has a place in my life. Besides, I have to play six different sports and I have to make two teams a year. I want to play lacrosse.' He looked at me, he said, 'Well, if you're gonna play football, you better be at spring practice this afternoon.' And I said, 'Mr. Killinger, you can take your football team and go to hell!' That's why I didn't play baseball—he was also the baseball coach! Baseball was one of my better sports. After college, I played three years in the minor leagues."

In fairness to Dr. Killinger, he spent thirty-six years at West Chester (1934–1970) as a physical education teacher and head coach, and actually did have a men's dormitory named after him. According to the *Centennial History*, on October 25, 1968:

> Governor Shafter came to West Chester to dedicate the men's dormitory as Killinger Hall. Glen would be honored with the gift of a portrait by Ted Hallman and a metal plaque by the Men's Resident Government. His dedicated service in many capacities since that day in May 1934 well warranted the honor. (Within a week the metal plaque will be stolen and later mysteriously be found.) This dedication was part of the Rampage Weekend program.

In 1970, Dr. Killinger was named to the Coaches' Hall of Fame by the American Association of College Baseball Coaches. He retired that year, and Dr. Sturzebecker noted in the *Centennial History*:

> The end of the year found Dr. Killinger retiring. After thirty-six years he had seen a lot of changes. Finally he would escape all the responsibility thrust upon him. The present college world was utterly foreign to him. Remember when he moved into Wayne Hall in 1936 to straighten out things? There were no "task forces" or committees to go through. The game was simpler and direct. Killy looked happy as he walked away from it all.

If there were doubts about the popularity of Glen Killinger, at least for the Class of 1942, there seems to be no question about the genuine affection felt for Earle "Muddy" Waters. Born in New Haven, Connecticut, in November 1897, Waters was working in the employment office of the Winchester Repeating Arms Company in New Haven when World War I started on July 28, 1914. He enlisted in the U.S. Army in November 1915, at the age of eighteen, was sent to the Officer Candidate School at Clark University in Worcester, Massachusetts, and was stationed there when the war ended, November 11, 1918.

"I got my fifty-dollar bonus and was honorably discharged," Waters says. "I went home to New Haven and a buddy of mine said, 'I'm studying at Arnold College to be a physical education teacher; why don't you come with me?' So I went with him and met with Dr. Arnold. He admitted me and gave me credit for one semester at Clark University. I only spent a year and a half at Arnold, but I could see at the time that you needed a degree to get anywhere.

"I took a job at Waverly High School, in Waverly, New York. P.C. Meserve was superintendent of schools, and I was the seventh physical education instructor that the school had had in four years. They just couldn't stand P.C. He made life miserable. He didn't believe in physical education. I stayed there a year, then I went to the Columbia University Summer School in New York and took three courses: Conversational French, Literature, and English. The following year, I went to Syracuse University and transferred my credits up there. I carried an overload at Syracuse, so I earned a BS degree in less than three years.

"My first job after graduation was in Westhampton Beach on Long Island. And it was there that my wife-to-be chased me in her automobile and caught me. That's *my* story! Then we got married and proceeded to have a child. The first year I was there, the principal and I got together and decided that we needed sports activities for the girls. So we tried field hockey and they didn't like it worth a hoot. The second year, we tried soccer. Well, it caught on like nobody's business. We had a four-team league. My girls won the soccer championship three straight years that I was there. And I got a raise every year, until the last year.

"Then a friend of mine told me to go down to West Chester State Teachers College in Pennsylvania, that there was a job open there. I drove down there in September and had an interview and the athletic director asked me when I could start. I said, 'Well, in about a week.' I went back, we packed, we didn't own much in those days except clothes. This was in 1920, I was twenty-three at the time.

"At West Chester, we had an apartment on the main street, High Street. I found out at that time that the previous year they had two other physical education instructors and they couldn't control this freshman class of thirty-one boys from the coal regions. Jim McGovern, the football coach, had recruited them; he was going to have a winning team. I had to battle them, they were smart and tough. That's why the other phys-ed men had left.

"I remember very well. In the gym, they had a big box with the basketballs in it, and there was a lock on it. All my predecessors had always left the lock open. My first day of class, these thirty-one kids were all shooting baskets. And you'd say, 'Fall in,' and it didn't mean a thing to them, they'd keep right on. Well, that happened once. The second day they came in for class, the box was locked. They came to me, and one of them said, 'Unlock the box.' I said, 'No.' He said, 'Why not?' I said, 'Because you don't get any balls until you do what I *tell* you. When I say line up, I want you to *line up*, tallest on the left, shortest on the right.' Well, they sort of milled around and milled around. About five minutes later, they lined up! I started talking to them and I took the rings down. I was pretty muscular in those days. So, I was talking to them about what we were going to do, and I took hold of the rings and did a full pull-push-up, talking all the time. And I got down, and they were looking at each other: Geez, this guy's got some muscles! And I had no trouble from then on. But the next day, when they came in, the basketballs were there, but they had the rings down and they were all trying to do a full pull-push-up! The trick to that is, you use a false grip on the rings. But they didn't notice that I had a false grip and they were trying to do it with just their hands! That's one of the ways I won the respect of the class. And at the end of four years, they gave me a banquet at the hotel there. They all graduated and they all got a job.

"Wait a minute, there was one who didn't get a job. And he called me up the next September and he said, 'I'm the only one who didn't get a job.' And I said, 'Well, what're you going to do about it?' He said, 'I don't know; that's why I called you.' I said, 'Well, you have a college education, haven't you? You learned to think, didn't you?' He said, 'Yeah.' I said, 'Well, *think!*' And I hung up! About six years later, he came around in a Cadillac, parked it out in front of the gym, sent one of the boys in to ask me to come out and see him. I walk out, here's this big Cadillac with the top down, his wife next to him, his two kids in the back. He looks at me, he says, 'I learned to *think!*' I said, 'What're you doing now?' He says, 'I own a string of six gasoline stations out in California. I don't have to work any more!'

"As far as George Wackenhut is concerned, I never went out to recruit anybody. They came to West Chester because they wanted to; they knew we had an excellent soccer program. And the same was true of George. He was a goaltender and he'd played semipro soccer—I think it was with the Kensington Bluebells, which was a good semipro team. He waited on tables in the dining hall. He was a good student as well as a good soccer player.

"This was about 1939, George's first varsity season, and we had another good goaltender by the name of Ken Webb, but Ken couldn't play any other position. So, half the time I played George as the goaltender and half the time Kenny Webb. When George wasn't the goaltender, he played fullback. When we were playing a tough team, like Temple, I'd use both players, and George played fullback. Well, George didn't like it, and I didn't blame him, but what was I going to do? I had to put my best team on the field. George understood. I told him at the time what I had to do. He played fullback and he was a good fullback too.

"We had very good seasons when George was there. We had one string of fifty-nine wins in a row, and it was getting to be too much pressure, so I scheduled a three-day trip in which we played three teams. I could only carry twelve men, plus the manager and myself. We won the first game against Ithaca College. The next day, we lost to Syracuse University. Boy, they had a tricky field. At one goal there was a tree that extended over the goal, and they would kick the ball up into the tree. It would trickle down and they'd all be waiting for it. They beat us, four to three! I had to hand it to my alma mater, they played a smart game. Then to Bard College on the Hudson River, and we won that game with only ten active players!

"On the trips, George would always sit in the front seat with me. The rest of the players would all be in the back, talking about girls. George was a darn good student, and we would talk about things that George would be wondering about. That was a natural thing about George. I don't remember if he went with any girls in the college. He didn't have much spare time. He was more interested in studying and learning. That's the main thing that I remember about him. He would ask me questions that I didn't know the answers to."

Earle Waters coached varsity soccer at West Chester for thirty-eight years (1920-1958). During that time, at an average of fourteen regular-season games per year, he coached more than 500 games. In all that time, he never had a scholarship to offer, he was never paid anything at all for coaching, and he always carried a full teaching schedule. Waters was president of the National Soccer Coaches of America, 1942-44, and is the author of a book titled *Soccer,* written while he was head soccer coach, U.S. Navy, at the University of North Carolina Pre-Flight School, published by the U.S. Naval Institute in 1943; it had eight editions. When he retired in June 1958, West Chester had the soccer field named Waters Field in his honor. On May 26, 1963, the Board of Trustees of West Chester State College awarded Waters the distinguished academic rank of Professor *Emeritus.* On January 12, 1965, Waters was elected to the NSCAA Soccer Hall of Fame by the National Soccer Coaches Association of America.

Following is an excerpt from an introductory speech by Ken Perrin, then-president of West Chester University, delivered September 30, 1987:

> It is significant that on the eve of the 200th anniversary of the signing of the United States' Constitution that tonight's speaker is the thirty-eighth President of our country.
>
> As you probably know, President Ford, who holds a bachelor of arts degree from the University of Michigan, and a law degree from Yale, served in the United States Congress for twenty-five years. He was Vice President and then President of the United States from 1973 through 1977.
>
> What you probably didn't know is that in 1942, when he was enrolled in the Navy's Pre-Flight Training program, President Ford received ten soccer lessons from West Chester University's Professor *Emeritus* Earle "Muddy" Waters.
>
> In a recent letter, Professor Waters asked me to tell you that President Ford was an outstanding soccer player in that he always did exactly what Muddy told him to do!
>
> Would you now please join me in welcoming Professor Waters's most successful soccer player, President Gerald R. Ford!

Probably the most frequently told anecdote about George's collegiate soccer career involved a game at Salisbury State Teachers

College, in 1940, when he lost his cool, and Buzz Leith tells it best:

"George Wackenhut and Ken Webb, in my opinion, were the best two collegiate goalies in the country. They both played in Philadelphia, in the Pennsylvania League, on two different teams. At West Chester, Waters had a tough time choosing between the two guys to play goalie. And it led to an incident in our junior year. George didn't lose his cool very often. But in this particular game, we were playing down in Maryland, down at Salisbury State Teachers College. I had injured my ankle in practice and aggravated it in the previous game. So, when we went down to play Salisbury, Waters told me, he said, 'You stay home.' I said, 'Ah, can't I make the trip?' He said, 'Well, okay.' So I made the trip and I got dressed and I practiced with them before the game, but he didn't start me. And that was the only game in my three years on the varsity that I didn't start.

"Well, in that game, Waters started George at fullback. Wacky was a big, rugged guy, good fullback, he could hit the ball pretty hard. And in the particular defense that he was using in those days, the fullback was strictly a defensive guy, he stayed back. Waters was a very innovative coach, and he was using his halfbacks in what they now call 'overlaps' with forwards. So the halfbacks sometimes scored goals. After the first quarter, we had no attack against Salisbury. It was zero-zero, we should be beating these guys, and so Waters looked at me and he said, 'Can you play?' I said, 'Yeah.' So he says, 'All right, you go in for Wackenhut.' But he didn't want me as a defender. The fullback Wacky had replaced had moved up to halfback, so what he wanted me to do, I was going in for Wackenhut, but Waters was going to send this other guy back to fullback, and I was going to play my regular halfback spot.

"The teams switched at the quarters, so I went in, and as I did, I said to the official, 'I'm in for Wackenhut.' There was a movie called *Gulliver's Travels*, I think it was a Disney thing, and at one point in this movie, one of these Lilliputians goes down to the beach and he sees Gulliver. And this little guy hollers: *'There's a giant on the beach!'* And the veins in his neck are standing out, if you remember the movie. Well, that reminded me of George. Because when George saw me coming, he yells: *'FOR ME?! FOR ME?!'* It was incredible to him! And it wasn't that he hadn't done a fine job. It was just that

Waters wanted to get on the offense, he wanted to get something on the board. But I'll never forget Wacky's expression as long as I live!"

THE OUTSIDE FORCES that would have such a devastating impact on George and most of the men in his class were building slowly during his freshman and sophomore years. On September 30, 1938, the Munich Pact, which effectively turned over Czechoslovakia to Nazi Germany, was signed by Great Britain, France, Italy, and Germany. Later, a Gallup Poll showed that most Americans approved of this act of appeasement. In the U.S., the top grossing film of 1938 was Walt Disney's *Snow White and the Seven Dwarfs.*

In August, 1939, Henry Ford was decorated with the Grand Cross of the German Eagle by the Nazi regime. On September 1, German troops invaded Poland. Two days later, France and Great Britain declared war on Germany. Using revolutionary *blitzkrieg* tactics, Germany defeated Poland in eighteen days, and the country was partitioned between Germany and the Soviet Union, with whom Germany had just signed a nonaggression pact. That September, the American Psychological Association, meeting in convention, placed the question of Hitler's sanity on the agenda. In October, Charles E. Lindbergh received a medal from Hitler; Lindbergh blamed the potential war with the U.S. on "the British, the Jews, and the Roosevelt Administration." In the U.S., more than 10 million people were unemployed despite the efforts of the New Deal.

In April 1940, Germany overran Norway and Denmark; on May 10, it invaded Holland, Belgium, and Luxembourg, which had been neutral. German tanks burst through the Ardennes and reached the English Channel. The Allied army was forced back into the Dunkirk region. On May 15, British Prime Minister Winston Churchill wrote to President Roosevelt, asking for U.S. aid; in negotiations ending on September 3, the U.S. delivered fifty overage destroyers, in exchange for ninety-nine-year leases on eight military bases in Newfoundland and the West Indies. Between May 29 and June 3, a total of 338,226 British and French troops escaped to England by sea. The Germans occupied France. Hitler expected Britain to make peace, but, under the leadership of Churchill, it fought on defiantly. The

Luftwaffe, under Hermann Goering, then attempted to destroy the Royal Air Force, so that an invasion of England could be launched, but the Germans were unsuccessful in the Battle of Britain, August–October 1940.

Two months before the Battle of Britain began, the twenty-year-old George Wackenhut was back in Ocean City, working days at Mywood Press, playing nights and weekends with Bud Bailey and his group, enjoying what would prove to be the last full summer vacation of his life, and, unlike most Americans, conscious of the fact that the war in Europe had the potential to expand into the largest conflict in human history.

BUD BAILEY remembers how it was that summer of 1940 in Ocean City, New Jersey, and laughs out loud at the vivid images, along with his wife Doris, who was his girl friend then. Crazy days on the wide Twelfth Street beach (*the* beach for high school and college people), evening strolls on the two-mile boardwalk, with amusements, shops, stores, and restaurants, the unforgettable swing-era music of the famous big bands, the all-night parties, even the names of the kids in their "crowd," and what became of them: Ben Rylah, a paratrooper who would be killed in Germany; Jack Bremme, who would be a design draftsman; Claude Merzbacher, who become a professor at the University of San Diego; Harold Emminger, his roommate in college, who would own a pineapple plantation in Florida; Billy Bertolet, who would be an industrial soap manufacturer; Bob Derby, who would be an oil company engineer, later a consultant; and, of course, George. He particularly recalls that George met Janet Blair (real name Lafferty), who sang for Hal Kemp's orchestra, and later was an actress in the movies; she and her sister became part of that Ocean City crowd.

That was the summer when George taught Bud how to play lacrosse. It wasn't an officially sanctioned sport at West Chester, because it lacked a faculty coach, but it became a club; George played lacrosse for the first time as a freshman, then became the player-coach as a sophomore.

"If George had gone to a larger school, he'd have been an All-

American lacrosse player," Bailey says. "He's the one who taught me, one-on-one. We used to knock heads on the beach, and he'd teach me the techniques and everything, and when I transferred to West Chester that autumn, I played on the team.

"Well, he'd just started this, he brought the sticks down to the beach, and I think we had fooled around with them for maybe half an hour for two days, and he said: 'We have a game!' I said, 'What do you mean, *we* have a game?' He said, 'Well, every year in Ocean City, the South Jersey All Stars—college lacrosse players—play the North Jersey All Stars.' So we went up to the field at Sixth Street, the public area where they had parks and ball fields and tennis courts and everything. Well, I have a *pin* head—six and seven-eighths or something like that—so I couldn't find a helmet to fit me. He taught me how to play, but I'd never played in a game, I'd only seen the sticks for two days! So I said, 'I'll sit on the bench and watch.' He was in charge of the South team, so finally he got me in the game. Every time I'd get the ball and run down the field with it, I'd feel great, and then this big helmet would go flop over my face and I couldn't *see!* I got the ball once and stopped to fix my helmet and somebody hit me. I couldn't *see!* And he taught me to do this—when you scoop the ball up, it's called 'goosing' it. But I was pushing it along, I wasn't scooping it up, and somebody came along from behind and flattened me! Every time I got the ball, George would shout for me to pass 'Over here!' But with my helmet flopped down over my eyes, I couldn't see where '*here*' was! That's all I remember of *that* game!"

Doris Bailey, who was born in Drexel Hill, Pennsylvania, and graduated from Upper Darby Senior High School in the Class of 1940, was a friend and classmate of Ruth Bell, who would marry George Wackenhut in 1944. "Years before George met Ruth, we would be on the boardwalk, and we'd walk behind young girls," Doris recalls. "And Bud and George would rate the girls according to whether they were 'side-to-siders' or 'up-and-downers!' It was so funny, I used to die at that. We'd be walking along and I'd say, 'Hey, there's a good side-to-sider over there,' and they'd look and they'd say, 'Yeah, she's good, but not as good as the up-and-downer over here!' Then, after George met Ruth, the four of us would do the same thing."

Bud laughs at the memory. "I don't specifically recall, but I think George liked side-to-side and I liked up-and-down," he says. "When we were at the shore before we were married, there was a group of girls George and I used to go with. Not steady. I'd date one girl, then the next time I'd date another. We didn't date much, but we went with different girls. But we used to do something special maybe two or three times a summer: We'd separate in couples, and go on the boardwalk, and see a couple our age and go up and ask them if they wanted to go to a party. We'd tell them where it was, that food and drinks would be served, and when it began. And everybody would show up! We'd go out and get cases of soft drinks and get some sandwich meat and bread and potato chips. And we'd have a great time. Then the party would break up and we'd never see them again!

"Another thing we used to do: George ran cross-country, and I was more of a sprinter type in school, and I also ran the mile. But I wasn't a distance runner. And every day, our whole crowd would take a run from Twelfth Street down to the gardens at the end of the island and back again. That was maybe six, eight miles, I don't know. We did this every day. And, of course, we were always competitive, we had to be better than our buddy—in everything. That's the way we were. So, I could never beat George. And I'd think: I'll save it until the end, because I can sprint faster than he can. But he knew just how to do it. He'd start stretching out, coming up from Eighth Street, and then he'd open up and do what I'd call a fast cruise. I would try to open up faster than he did, I tried to stay with him until the end and then fast sprint, but he always beat me, every time. I guess we ran six to eight miles every day, all summer.

"We all have fond memories of Ocean City. Actually, we had an idyllic life there every summer. George's father rented a place at the shore at 1141 Asbury Avenue. It was a typical shore house, a full apartment-like setting on the first two floors, a third floor with some bedrooms and baths. And he had a front porch and a balcony porch on the second floor. I think they rented it every summer. It's probably still there. The house my father bought in 1917 is still there and it's still in beautiful condition.

"I'll say this about George: We had the same ideas about people and family and relationships with others. We thought the same way. As I look back, three things in George's younger years indicated assurance of success. Perseverance: He was aggressive in pursuing knowledge and understanding of any challenge he was faced with, whether it was work, academic schoolwork, sports, or social functions. I think he inherited that from his father. Organization: He was always well organized in whatever he was doing. He knew what he was there for, what he had to do there, when to do it, and then he would do it successfully. Spirituality: He was always religious in the Christian sense of high values and beliefs. He knew and practiced living according to what is commonly referred to as the old basic Christian values. He has always had a strong feeling of loyalty to his friends, his family, and his country."

THE SELECTIVE Training and Service Act of 1940, the first to mandate compulsory military training during peacetime, called for registration of men between twenty-one and thirty-five years of age, and ordered training of 900,000 men in 1941. If George had not worked for a year before entering West Chester, he would have graduated with the Class of 1941, at the age of twenty. But on September 3, 1940, just prior to beginning his junior year, he turned twenty-one, and was required to register for the draft.

George had hoped for a deferment until he graduated. "The head of our local draft board lived just across the street from our home in Upper Darby, and I had known him practically all my life," he says. "This made me reasonably hopeful that I might get a deferment to finish college and then have an opportunity to go into service as an officer. But all they would give me was a deferment until I finished my junior year. I was very disappointed, primarily because of the sacrifices my family had made in an attempt to give me a college education."

That autumn, the atmosphere at West Chester reflected the national sense of alarm. In *Centennial History,* Dr. Sturzebecker writes:

> On October 16, the first peacetime Selective Service and Training Act was put in operation. West Chester alumni and students would be placed in the crucible being heated.
>
> President Swope, in the October 18 issue [of *The Quad,* the student

newspaper], on the front page, presented a sober message much applicable in current times. "The air is filled with recriminations, the middle aged have been accused of negligence, gross cupidity, and stupidity; the young are charged with bad manners, cynicism, lack of idealism, and lack of courage . . . let no belligerent belief in individual freedom weaken us—let no foolish pride on our part blind us to the danger of the present." This was written in 1940!

Perhaps as a result of this changed atmosphere, the varsity soccer team got off to a slow start and fell far short of the dream-team potential that Muddy Waters had anticipated, although they finished with an impressive record of nine wins, two losses, and two ties. Highlights of the season were victories over Towson, the champion of the Delaware, Maryland, and West Virginia League; and Wheaton, the titleholder of the Midwest.

Bud Bailey, who transferred from Drexel University in Philadelphia to West Chester that September, remembers his first impressions of Muddy Waters: "I always liked the first day when you went out to practice. Muddy Waters would say, 'All right, let's get a line here and one over there.' And he'd throw some balls between the lines and tell us to go ahead and kick the balls at one another. He'd go along and have us doing this for, I don't know, maybe half an hour. Then he'd say, 'Okay, that ought to be enough to give you shin splints for tomorrow!' Then he'd say, 'All right, now I want to talk to you. If you think I'm going to be responsible for you adult, mature men on your physical condition, you're wrong. I'm going to leave that up to you. I'm not going to have you come out here and run laps; I'm not going to have you go through exercises. That's up to you. If you drink a case of beer a week, you might want to cut it down to half a case. If you smoke a pack of cigarettes a day, you might want to cut it down to half a pack. That's up to you. But when you come out here, if you can't run *full speed* for ninety minutes, you're going to be sitting on the bench. And if you *are* sitting on the bench and wonder why—*that's* why! When you go out there, you run *full speed* all the time you're out there! You must be in condition to do that. If you're not, you're going to be picking up splinters.' And he got results with that philosophy."

That spring, the lacrosse club didn't win many games, despite George at center, Bud Bailey at one wing, and his roommate Harold Emminger at the other. According to the 1941 issue of *The Serpentine:*

> Lacrosse, starting its fourth year on our campus, finds itself with a major schedule for the first time. During the Easter vacation, starting April the fourth, the team traveled southward to compete against such teams as Navy, Washington Lacrosse Club, North Carolina University, and Duke University, respectively.
>
> The team, lacking a faculty coach, is under the guidance of player coaches William Van Buskirk and George Wackenhut.
>
> As this book goes to press, the lacrosse team has played only one game, losing 13–0 to the professional champions of New York State, the Brooklyn Lacrosse Club. As this was the first game, and one played against an experienced team, there is no certainty as to the outcome of the season.
>
> Lacrosse is seriously handicapped here at West Chester because of the lack of a faculty coach, of players who have had previous experience before entering West Chester, and of financial support.

That trip during Easter vacation is branded into Bud Bailey's memory. "We came up with a foolproof play," he says. "George would get down at center, and he'd beat the center, it didn't matter who it was. As soon as the ball was dropped by the referee, I'd take off, and he'd beat the center and flip it to me, and I'd get it and go down the field. One game, we got four goals in a row like that. Then they got on to me and they were putting two men on me, so he flipped it off to my roommate on the other side, same play. And there were times when George would take the ball and he'd go right down the field with three guys beating on him.

"We played Duke on that road trip. I remember Doc Prothro, who became the coach of the University of California's football team, he played lacrosse defense at Duke, and he was six-four and weighed about 230 pounds. Like all little guys, I thought: I gotta knock him down! So, I got a real good shot at him one time, and I lit into him with everything I had. And I *bounced* off the guy! He looked down at me and he said, 'Did you *learn* anything?' I said, 'I sure *did!*'

"I don't believe we won any of the games on that trip, but we had some close ones. George handled the entire trip, although a faculty representative was with us. George was involved in all aspects of that trip—hotel reservations, meals, arrangements with our mighty foes, and the travel schedule. We traveled in private cars and a college station wagon to hold our gear. George kept stressing that we were representatives of our college and to think of that in all of our actions. We didn't let him down. He also stressed that we were operating on a small budget, and to stay within reasonable limits on our meals, which we did. As a matter of fact, when we returned to college, we stopped at the Four Corners, south of the college on Route 100 and the Baltimore Pike, and he distributed the meal money that was left over. As I recall, we each received $2.36 as our portion."

Buzz Leith remembers that junior year with particular clarity. "During the soccer season, we would practice every day until five-thirty, when it was almost dark, and everybody would go in, except Wacky. And then Wacky would grab me, sometimes, or somebody else, and he'd say, 'Shoot some at me!' He'd get in that goal and he wanted you to take shots at him. And he'd pick the guys who were going to be a challenge to him. He was one of the most determined guys I ever met in my life. In fact, it carried over, and Wacky was like the father of lacrosse at West Chester. They started the team as a club; a guy by the name of Bill Hickman actually started it. Then, when Wacky was a sophomore, I guess, he sort of took it over, he became the coach. I remember in junior year, I'd be coming in from baseball practice, and there would be Wacky with his goalie's mask and all that crap, and he'd say, 'Throw some at me! Throw some at me!' So he'd get in the goal. I was an outfielder on the baseball team and I prided myself on being able to throw pretty good, and I'd get a few feet away from Wacky and try to throw a ball past him. He was absolutely fearless! You know, goalies in those days, one of their main objectives in life was to intimidate the opposing forwards so they wouldn't take many liberties. If they jolted a guy a couple of times, he wouldn't be too anxious to get that close to the goal.

George was very good at that and so was Ken Webb. They got that from playing in Philadelphia. Those guys played pretty rough ball.

"I remember I double-dated a couple of times with Wacky that year, he was going with Marie Carroll at that time. They had two theaters in town, the Warner, and I think the other was called the Rialto. And they used to give free tickets to the coaches. So, almost every week, the coaches would give us tickets to the movies. And it was funny, you take a date, and sometimes you had to tell her to pay her own way! They had a balcony and a downstairs. I'm not exactly sure of the prices, but I'm going to say that the downstairs was forty cents and the balcony was twenty-five cents, something like that. And our tickets were for downstairs. So, you'd take a date, and you'd say, 'I'm going to sit downstairs.' She'd have to pay forty cents to sit next to you! I mean, we didn't have any *money!*"

GEORGE dated Marie Carroll for about eighteen months and admits that it was relatively serious. "I met her at college and I started going with her on January 11, 1940, and went with her through the whole year of 1940, until July of 1941, when I was drafted. Before Marie, I was going with a girl named Eleanor Follett, and she had been in Upper Darby Senior High School, I guess she was two years behind me. She had a regular boyfriend who was still in Upper Darby and that always kind of hampered my style. Eleanor was on the petite side, very attractive, nice figure, but she thought a lot of herself. She was good-looking and she knew it. Marie had a fairly decent figure, she was Irish, and she looked as Irish as Paddy's Pig—blue eyes and black hair. Not very tall, but a bigger girl than Eleanor. Marie was a year younger than I.

"As far as dates were concerned, the girls living in the dorm had to be in by eight o'clock. And I think dinner was at six. So, by the time you'd finished serving in the dining room, and had dinner yourself, there wasn't much time left. The girls would normally wait outside in the sitting area, the lounge outside the dining room, until you came out. There were dances almost every night in the Old Gym—there were two gyms, one was an old one, built way back— and we danced to records. West Chester was noted for its health and physical education, but also for its music. We called music supervisors 'music sups,' and they had some very good musicians. They had a band called the College Criterions, and their music was outstanding; this was big band music."

Jay Smith recalls one humorous incident during a class in dancing that was a required course for physical education majors. George was required to take the course (Dancing I and II) during both semesters of his junior year.

"We would meet in the little old gymnasium," Smith says, laughing at the memory, "the girls on one side of the gym, the boys on the other. They had a nice little old lady playing the piano. We would walk up the sides toward the center, then go down the center in pairs, male and female. Off we'd go, and then we'd all pair off and dance with our partner. Well, there was one colored girl in the class, and the guys didn't want to dance with this colored girl. So, George, being very straightforward, would just get in line, while all the rest of us were counting, moving around, maneuvering, to make sure George would wind up with the colored girl. He didn't object to that. He wasn't that way, he didn't feel that way. He was *straightforward!* I never really understood George in that area. He was *decent, honest,* I can't emphasize that enough! So every week, twice a week, he'd get the colored girl—every time! I mean, what the hell, there were twenty or thirty girls, and he always got the colored girl!

"So, finally, after about seven or eight times, George just said: 'Stop the music!' The lady stopped the piano. Dead silence. George says: 'I've danced with this girl eight straight times. I just don't think I should have to dance with the same girl every time. I would like to dance with other girls.'

"That was that. He made a statement. From that point on, we didn't do that any more. But the point is, George was tolerant; he had no racial prejudice at all, none! He was the only one there who didn't! Because our activities, if you look at it, were just the reverse. But we were doing it more for fun than anything else. I remember we all laughed about it, but I've never forgotten that particular incident."

OUTSIDE the college, on January 7, 1941, the Office of Production Management was created in Washington, D.C., to oversee U.S. defense programs. On January 13, President Roosevelt addressed a joint session of Congress and appealed for its support to defend the Four Essential Freedoms: Freedom of Speech, Freedom of Religion, Freedom from Want, and Freedom from Fear. On March 11, Lend Lease Bill No. 1776 was signed into law, providing $50 billion in arms, services, and supplies for the Allied Forces. Britain, nearly bankrupt after draining its Treasury of cash for war supplies, advised the U.S. of its dire financial situation through a letter from Churchill. Roosevelt learned of an 1892 statute that gave the Secretary of War the right to lease, for a five-year period, any Army property that was not needed for public use; he applied the statue to aid Britain. On March 27, the U.S. Joint Chiefs of Staff, meeting with their British counterparts, agreed that if the U.S. became militarily involved with both Germany and Japan, the best strategy would be to make a concentrated effort to beat the European Axis powers first.

At West Chester, the recently formed Red Cross organization became extremely active in January, and the following month the Civil Aeronautics Authority granted approval for the college to engage in a Civilian Pilot Training Program. Dr. Sturzebecker notes in his *Centennial History*:

> The war touched the campus in actuality on April 17 when President Swope paid tribute to the first West Chester man, Ensign George Nelson Blackburn, killed in the service. Ten days earlier, his PBY-1 patrol plane was caught in a storm off Virginia. George was the first of a group of thirty-three West Chester alumni and students whose names are memorialized in this book for their total and final contribution to their country. George Blackburn is particularly memorialized by the Friars Club through their award of the annual Blackburn trophy to the men's champion intramural basketball team.
>
> Graduation day found the seniors sobered by the immediate future indicating a deferment from the planned practice of their profession. The immediacy of the world situation crowded out the unreal college milieu.

According to the official academic transcript issued by the Registrar at West Chester University, George Russell Wackenhut took forty-eight courses during his three years there, for a total of 146 semester hours, earning 101 credits, plus a total of eight transfer credits for two courses from the Wharton Evening School, University of Pennsylvania. In those days, before the Grade Point Average (GPA) was calculated, his three-year cumulative average was defined as B − . An examination of his required courses, and particularly his electives, gives a more dimensional perspective:

First Semester	Grade
English I, including Library	C
Biological Science I	B
Chemistry	C
Personal Hygiene	B
Appreciation of Music	C
Gymnasium I	B
Athletics I	A
Aquatic Activities I	C
Second Semester	
English II	B
Biological Science II	B
Chemistry of Nutrition	B
Appreciation of Art	B
Education	B
Intro. to Physical Education	B
Gymnasium II	B
Athletics II	C
Aquatic Activities II	B
Third Semester	
Literature I	B
Physiology I	B
History of Civilization	C
General Psychology	A
Gymnasium III	C
Athletics III	A
Fourth Semester	
Hygiene (Community)	B
Physiology II	B
Descriptive Anatomy	C
Gymnasium IV	C
Athletics IV	C
Fifth Semester	
Speech	C
Economic Geography	C
Mech. Analysis of Activities	B

Gymnasium V	A
Athletics V	C
Dancing I	C
SIXTH SEMESTER	
Physical Education Tests	A
Mechanical-Anatomical Analysis of Activities	B
Principles of Sociology	B
Gymnasium VI	C
Athletics VI	B
Dancing II	C
ELECTIVES	
Trigonometry	D
Algebra I	C
English III	D
Algebra II	C
History of Math	B
Analytic Geometry	B
Nature & Function of Play	B
Literature II	C
TRANSFER CREDITS	
(University of Pennsylvania)	
Commercial Law	4 credits
Accounting	4 credits
	8 hours

Although a three-year cumulative average of B − (percentage equivalent of 80–82) was certainly respectable, it gives us little indication that George Wackenhut was a particularly good student. Granted, any academic transcript is a clinical document that was never intended to address the more important questions about an individual's potential. In academic circles today, studies clearly indicate that entirely too much emphasis is placed on grades as opposed to the acquisition of knowledge and genuine learning skills that will be retained for life. But, having listened to the various voices of classmates and teammates who shared these years with George, who lived with the young man on a day-to-day basis, who saw him in the classrooms, on the playing fields, in social situations, year after year, several personality factors emerge that give valuable insights into the man's potential.

Listen to Buzz Leith: "I can remember so many times when Wacky would not take a simple explanation from anybody. You couldn't say, 'Well, that's the way it is,' to Wacky. He'd say, '*Why? Tell me why?*' In class, I mean he was being polite, he wasn't being obnoxious or anything, but he had that kind of inquiring mind that wasn't going to be satisfied with a yes or a no. You had to tell him. He wanted to know exactly why it was."

Listen to Jay Smith: "George is an extraordinary person; I knew that when I was a silly, dumb college boy. I always thought of George as being tenacious and determined. Those are the words. And straight and honest and reliable. Those are the words I've associated with George since I knew him in college. I was not like that at all, so I looked up to him. I respected and admired him."

Listen to Ken Webb: "Back at West Chester, I don't think I ever thought about the idea of Wacky having special qualities that would be important to him in later life, but I've thought about it since. And it certainly was his persistence, his always striving to get a little better, you know, and it sure has paid off for him."

It would pay off for him in the long run, but it would not happen soon, and it would be an uphill struggle all the way. There would be fortuitous factors involved, of course, starting with the only "lottery" he ever won, in June of that year. Words like inquiring and tenacious and determined and persistent would account for part of his success; Bud Bailey's observations about his perseverance, organization, and spirituality would account for even more. All of these qualities were present and starting to mature in the twenty-one-year-old George Wackenhut in 1941, but none of them would be charismatic enough or powerful enough or ambitious enough to eventually propel him from relative obscurity into the man who built an empire.

The catalyst was missing. The trigger mechanism.

And that summer, George didn't even know her name.

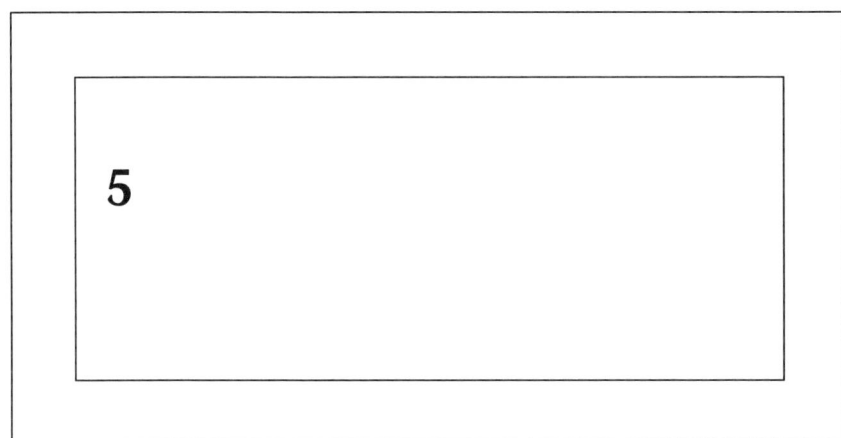

5

IN THE EARLY SUMMER of 1941, the Selective Service System ordered all local draft boards throughout the country to conduct a random selection of the names of men between the ages of twenty-one and thirty-five who had been required to register under terms of the Selective Training and Service Act of 1940. This drawing of names, popularly known as the draft "lottery," determined the numerical order in which all of the young men would be inducted into the service for mandatory peacetime training.

"It was the only lottery I ever won," George says. "When my draft board picked the names out of the fish bowl, I was number four. Then, the last week in June, I got a letter from the President: 'Greetings.' It told me where and when to report for induction: New Cumberland, Pennsylvania, July 11, 1941."

There, after five days of physical and mental examinations, he was classified as a mimeograph operator. Being fresh from three years of college, he had no qualms about speaking his mind. "A *moron* can run a mimeograph!" he told the sergeant in charge. "You must have some better classification than *that!*"

"We'll see what we can do," the sergeant told him.

So, even though George couldn't drive a nail straight, in typical Army fashion he was reclassified as a construction foreman.

After induction, Private George R. Wackenhut, Army Serial No. 33079314, was shipped off to Fort Belvoir, Virginia, eighteen miles south of Washington, DC, the home of the U.S. Army Engineers, for basic training. "Training there in the summertime was murder," he says. "I remember taking these hikes and training missions, and you were just absolutely drenched with perspiration. You had a canteen of water, and the more you drank, the more you perspired."

That summer, President Roosevelt placed a "freeze" on all German and Italian assets, all assets belonging to European countries already invaded or occupied, and all assets owned by the Japanese. He also prohibited all shipments of gasoline or scrap iron to Japan. Meanwhile, the Italians had begun the North African campaign, and by that summer Germany had overrun Denmark, Norway, Greece, Crete, and Yugoslavia, and gained Romania, Hungary, Finland, and Bulgaria as allies in the invasion of the Soviet Union. On August 3, Roosevelt left Washington for an announced "fishing trip" off Martha's Vineyard, Massachusetts, but continued on to Placentia Bay, Newfoundland, for the Atlantic Conference with Winston Churchill. The Atlantic Charter, drawn up there, laid out the common war aims of the two countries. Technically still a neutral, the U.S. agreed to join in "the final destruction of the Nazi tyranny." Well aware of Japan's menacing southward movement in the Pacific to establish the so-called Greater East Asia Co-Prosperity Sphere, FDR told Churchill: "Leave that to me. I think I can baby them along for three months."

Basic training at Fort Belvoir was supposed to last thirteen weeks, but it was shortened to eleven weeks. "They wanted to move the entire regiment," George says, "and some companies were ahead of us in the training cycle. As I recall, they took the whole regiment, so they had a whole train load. The train down from Washington, DC, stopped right at Fort Belvoir, and we all boarded it one evening in early October, 1941. My mother and dad were there to see me off, and so was my girl friend, Marie Carroll. It was a memorable evening, but we didn't know where the train was going."

In fact, as it turned out, apparently *nobody* knew where that train was going. First, it headed north to Washington, DC, then turned around and went south through Virginia and the Carolinas, passed through Augusta, Georgia, then changed direction again and headed west through Alabama, Mississippi, Louisiana, and Texas, then northwest into Colorado, then due west through Utah, Nevada, and into northern California.

"It was sheer monotony, broken only by speculation as to where we might be heading next," George remembers. "The train crews were changed frequently and could only tell us where they were going before turning us over to another crew. The troops slept, ate, swapped lies, and played cards or craps. The gambling didn't interest me; I had too healthy a respect for money to throw it away. Our last train crew finally gave us some useful information: 'We're taking you guys to Mason Docks,' the Pullman porter told us. 'Where the hell's *that?*' somebody asked. 'San Francisco,' he said. 'What the hell *is* it?' somebody else asked. 'It's a debarkation point,' the porter explained. At that point, everybody started yelling gripes like: 'They can't ship us *overseas!* We're *inductees!* It's the *law*—they can't ship us abroad!' We had been on that train for more than a week, and it was the first time anyone in our regiment had heard any specific destination."

When the train finally pulled into Mason Docks, the regiment boarded a troop ship, but they still didn't know their final destination until the next morning, when they began an eight-day voyage to Honolulu. Upon arrival, the troops boarded a convoy of Army trucks that took them to Schofield Barracks, situated near the center of the island of Oahu. Most of the troops at Schofield were regular Army, a hard-bitten lot, and George recalls that "they ran us through the wringer to complete our basic training." The group was designated the 34th Engineer Regiment, the last such combat regiment formed, because after December 7, they were all combat battalions.

It was then early November and, having been in the Army five months, George was promoted to corporal just as the Second Battalion, to which he was assigned, was sent to Kaneohe, a small town on the windward side of Oahu, hard by Mokapu Point, to build a complete camp for a coast artillery battalion. They started from scratch in an old cow pasture, putting up tents and digging slit trenches for latrines. Only then could they start erecting barracks, which were wooden buildings without glassed windows, but with a large overhang to keep out the rain. Eventually, the windows would be screened. But without screens, the mosquitoes were a serious problem.

"At night, I'd roll the mosquito netting up at the foot of my cot," George recalls, "then jump under the blanket with a flashlight. Sitting up, you'd wave your arms like a wild man while getting the net in place, and then it would take another ten or fifteen minutes to swat all the mosquitoes that had been able to get under the net with you. One night, I was on guard duty and had to awaken my replacement. He'd gone to sleep with his shoulder against the netting, and his shoulder and arm were a mass of welts. Mosquitoes were bad even in the daytime; so much so that the officers never required us to stand at attention. We'd just line up with one hand in a pocket and the other waving a handkerchief to keep them off our faces and necks.

"One Saturday afternoon shortly after we arrived, I walked the half mile or so to the Kaneohe Naval Air Station, where the sailors were housed in a brand-new building, and I happened to meet a sailor I had known in high school, David M. Mann. Well, when you're that far from home, a familiar face is a welcome sight. We were instant buddies. I went to the air station after duty hours every evening, got some good hot Navy chow, instead of eating out of my mess gear, saw a movie, and returned to the Army camp to sleep. On Saturday nights, I would sleep comfortably at the air station barracks.

"I made a habit of doing that. On Saturday afternoon, December 6, 1941, I took another GI over to the naval base with me, thinking that he, too, would enjoy some good Navy food and a mosquito-free night. But when we arrived, we found that a new group of naval replacements had arrived that day and there was only one bunk left. 'You've been coming over here,' the GI said, 'so you stay and I'll go back to camp.' I disagreed. 'We came over together and we'll go back together.' So we walked back that night and battled the mosquitoes all over again."

IN THE DECEMBER 2, 1991, issue of *Time* magazine, the cover story, "Day of Infamy," by senior writer Otto Friedrich, attempts to retrieve truths about the Pearl Harbor attack from the perspective of fifty years. "All of the elements in the way the world is organized today derive from World War II," says Friedrich. "It's part of our lives, and we need to go back and examine and explain it." Here is a brief excerpt:

In American mythology, Pearl Harbor still represents, even after a half-century, a classic moment of treachery and betrayal. Certainly it was a moment of historic surprise, a moment when the impossible happened, when warfare suddenly spread, for the first and only time in history, to virtually the whole world. This was the moment that changed Americans from a nation of provincial innocents, not only ignorant of the great world but proud of their ignorance, into a nation that would often have to bear the burdens of rescuing that world. The same cataclysm also changed the Japanese from a people trying to find their place on the rim of the great world into a nation that would eventually redefine that world and place itself at the very center.

The surprise, when it first exploded over Pearl Harbor, was shattering, and everyone who experienced it can still remember what was going on when the news interrupted that quiet Sunday: the Washington Redskins playing the Philadelphia Eagles, Arthur Rubinstein as soloist in the New York Philharmonic broadcast, or just a visit with friends. Trying to explain the national sense of bewilderment, the TIME of that time reflected the kind of racism that implicitly underlay the basic American attitude. "Over the U.S. and its history," declared the weekly newsmagazine, "there was a great unanswered question: What would the people . . . say in the face of the mightiest event of their time? What they said—tens of thousands of them—was: 'Why, the yellow bastards!' "

As often happens in surprise attacks, however, the surprise of Pearl Harbor was largely a matter of national illusions. The leaders on both sides fully expected a war, indeed considered it inevitable, even to some extent desirable, but neither side really wanted to fight unless it had to. Up to the last minute, each antagonist thought the other was bluffing.

Japan's navy had already begun planning and training for the attack on Pearl Harbor when Emperor Hirohito startled his assembled advisers on Sept. 6 by asking an imperial question. In the midst of a fervent debate over when and how to go to war, the Emperor, who traditionally never spoke during such gatherings, suddenly pulled out and read in his high-pitched voice a poem by his revered grandfather Emperor Meiji:

> *All the seas, in every quarter,*
> *are as brothers to one another.*
> *Why, then, do the winds and waves of strife*
> *rage so turbulently throughout the world?*

Roosevelt, re-elected to a third term in 1940 after pledging that "your boys are not going to be sent to any foreign wars," knew that Hirohito was just a figurehead ruler over a militarist government dominated by the flinty General Hideki Tojo. Still, Roosevelt staked his hopes for peace on a last-minute message to the Emperor. "Both of us," Roosevelt said, "have a sacred duty to restore traditional amity and prevent further death and destruction in the world."

Japanese military censors delayed that message for 10 hours, so it was almost midnight on Dec. 7 in Tokyo when U.S. Ambassador Joseph Grew sped with it to the Foreign Ministry. It was past 3 A.M.—and Fuchida's bombers were within sight of Pearl Harbor—when Foreign Minister Shigenori Togo, in full diplomatic regalia, reached the Imperial Palace. He found the Emperor listening to his shortwave radio. Togo read him the message and then the response that the government had already written for him. It said that peace was the Emperor's "cherished desire." This would "do well," Hirohito told Togo. The Foreign Minister bowed low. . . .

December 7, 1941, dawned bright and clear in Hawaii and George awakened in the unfinished barracks building at Kaneohe, wishing he was almost anywhere else but lying on a hard cot with the world's largest mosquitoes buzzing impatiently outside his netting. He thought how nice it must be down at Waikiki, about twelve miles away, where the officers had their quarters. Then he thought about last night. If he hadn't been so stubborn, he could at least have spent the night at the Kaneohe Naval Air Station in the new barracks.

"I was asleep, Sunday morning, December 7, and I was half-awakened by the loud rat-ta-tat-tat of machine guns," he remembers. "I was dreaming of dogfights I had seen in movies of World War I. Finally, the noise was so persistent that I was fully awake. I got out of bed, looked out the window, saw a number of planes circling overhead, and big billows of smoke coming up from Kaneohe Naval Air Station, about half a mile away. I saw members of our battalion on the roofs of the barracks, taking photographs of these planes that were swooping overhead, then going toward the air station.

"I dressed, got my toothbrush and other gear, and went down to the latrine. When I got down there, the first sergeant of our company was sitting on the throne, cursing about the fact that the Navy would pick Sunday morning to have maneuvers. I told him that smoke was billowing right out of what looked like the middle of the air station. He passed that off.

I returned to the barracks, put my gear back in my footlocker, and gathered my mess gear to go over to the mess for breakfast. I remember we had French toast that morning with some kind of syrup on it. There were about three or four others there at the same time, and we sat down at a table and started to eat. I remember remarking, 'This would be funny if this attack were for real,' and they kind of laughed that off. Of course, in the meantime, we kept hearing explosions and the sounds of the planes.

"After washing my mess gear, I went back to the barracks, put that away, and a radio owned by one of the GIs started blaring: 'All Army, Navy, Marine personnel, return to your bases immediately; the island is under *attack!* I repeat, the island is under *attack!* This is *not* a maneuver, the island is under *attack!*' But even with that, it was difficult to visualize that we were really being attacked, and he didn't say by *whom.*

"Planes kept circling and bombing and strafing the Kaneohe Naval Air Station, and, shortly thereafter, the officers for the battalion were beginning to arrive from Waikiki Beach, where they were all living. We were on the opposite side of the island from Pearl Harbor and Waikiki. The officers, having *seen* the destruction of Pearl Harbor, didn't realize that we were still in the dark about what was going on.

"Our company commander, who was a second lieutenant, fresh out of West Point, called for an assembly of the company. He then began to expound on the military theory that attacks usually take place at dawn and at dusk, so that another attack might occur when it begins to get dark. And, this being December, it got dark reasonably early. He said that when he blew his whistle once, he wanted us to assemble again, and when he blew it twice, we could disperse. He continued to talk, and none of us really knew what he was talking about.

"With that, a whole squadron of twin-engine bombers were flying more or less right in front of us, up high. Prior to that, they had flown over Kaneohe Naval Air Station and seemed to simultaneously drop their bomb loads. We could see all of these eggs dropping at the same time, and there was just a tremendous roar and a shaking of the ground. As they passed in front of us, heading in a southerly direction, I saw antiaircraft fire just missing their tails, sort of goosing them along. Although we were either standing at attention or parade rest, I nonetheless said to the GI next to me, 'Look at those gunners, how great they're firing, purposely just missing them!' Not yet realizing that they were firing at the enemy.

"You have to remember, it was still very difficult to distinguish between the insignia and markings on the Japanese planes, which was a big red circle, the rising sun, and the insignia *we* had, which was a red circle with a white star in the middle. From a distance, you just really couldn't tell the difference. Right after that, we came out with the bars—we had the circle, the star, and the bars.

"We were dismissed from that formation, then called together a short time later by another whistle blow, and now we were all lined up in the company street. Now, here's an entire company of over 200 men standing in formation between two rows of barracks, with a mess hall in the middle at the end. No one yet had told us officially that the island was under attack by the Japanese or anyone else. Everyone still thought it was a great big game, we were having these maneuvers, because we knew the island was on alert.

"All of a sudden, during this monologue that the company commander was giving, we hear *rat-ta-tat-tat,* and we look up to the left, over our shoulders, and here we see a plane with fire spitting out from underneath its lower wing! Instantly, we all hit the ground! Fortunately, the plane had dipped down too late, overshot all of us, and the bullets ended up in the mess hall at the end of the company street. As he passed by, he was practically on the rooftops of these single-story barracks. I looked up from the ground, saw this big rising sun, and it looked like an old World War I biplane; it had fixed landing gear, an open cockpit, and synchronized machine guns that went under his lower wing. As he passed us, he looked over his right shoulder to see if he had hit anyone, and his face was as clear as it could be, he was that close.

"It was a hell of a way to get indoctrinated into the fact that you're at war. But even with that, as we were getting up and brushing ourselves off, one of the GIs said to me, 'You can't tell me this thing is for real.' I said, 'Well, I'm not going to stand here and argue with you, but if he comes back again, you hide your ass or he's going to shoot it off!'

"Moments—seemed like moments—later, someone announced that the ammunition truck had finally arrived. What had happened there, the supply sergeant, who lived in Honolulu or Waikiki, first had to get up to Schofield Barracks, amid all the confusion. He was the only one who had the key to the supply room; he had to open it and load all the ammunition on the supply truck. He arrived, and he's parked right out in the middle of this wide-open field, away from the barracks. I ran out to get my ammunition. For some strange reason, they asked us to take our rifles with us when we were sent from Schofield Barracks down to Kaneohe. They never gave us ammunition, we just had the rifles.

"I ran across that open field like a character from *The Exorcist* with my head spinning around! Arrived at the supply truck and I was handed two bandoleers that you put over your shoulder, containing ammunition in Springfield clips, 1903 ammunition clips. And we had the M-1 rifles, which were eight to a clip, entirely different clip. So the only way we could use them was to take one bullet at a time and shove it into the breech. It was almost like we were back in the 1800s, when you had to load a ball of ammunition and fire it.

"Fortunately, the attack was just about over. It started just a little before eight, and now it was a quarter to twelve, or maybe closer to about twelve noon. We saw no more planes. There was a big discussion about where they came from. I remember talking to the battalion commander, who was a West Point graduate, a major. I said, 'Major, where did they come from?' He said, 'Apparently, they had carriers off the coast here.' Of course, we later found out they had two carriers to the north and one to the south, launching flights. They were far enough away to avoid detection. We had the PBY and PB-2Y patrol boats that left Kaneohe Naval Air Station every morning, and did their rounds, all around the islands, and they would arrive back in just before eight o'clock. As they came in, the Japs came right in behind them and blew them out of the water. That's when the attack on Kaneohe got started.

"And this good friend of mine from high school, David Mann,

who would fix me up with a bunk every weekend down at Kaneohe, I never did see him again. Don't know what happened to him, if anything.

"Eventually, we were told that we would be leaving Kaneohe and traveling by Army truck—in my case, I was in an ambulance—back to Schofield Barracks, but we were going to go around the north border of the island, heading east, until we turned off the road that went up into the hills toward Schofield. They immediately placed a rigid blackout on the entire island. That night, there was no moon, and it was so black you couldn't see your hand in front of your face. So our unit had more casualties en route back to Schofield than we did during the attack. As a matter of fact, one of the sergeants in our unit was in a truck that went off the road, and he ended up with a broken arm.

"We had to have one of the GIs walk ahead of the trucks with a white handkerchief hanging out of his belt in the back. And it was almost impossible to see *that*. We traveled at a very, very slow pace. To the best of my recollection, we left about six o'clock and arrived back at Schofield about midnight. That was a distance that you'd normally traverse in about a hour and a half to two hours.

"When we arrived back at Schofield, I remember it felt kind of funny sitting in an ambulance holding an M-1 rifle with a bayonet on the end of it, and wearing a World War I helmet. That was the issue. They didn't come out with the other type of helmet until much later. Which gives you an indication of how totally unprepared we were for war. It wasn't until we got in it that we really started to gear up. Matter of fact, during the month of December, they were sending troops over to Hawaii with wooden rifles. They didn't have enough rifles to go around. They were drilling with them, you know, close-order drill with wooden rifles.

"It was a madhouse at Schofield. As we started to go in, I spoke with the MPs at the gate, and they told me they threw everybody out of the Army hospital who could possibly walk, to make room for the wounded. Since I had some degree of first-aid training, having been a physical education major in college, they detached me to the infirmary that serviced our regiment.

"I slept in the infirmary that night, which was kind of scary, because they just had these very muted blue lights, so you could see where you were going. Everything else was totally blackened out, with all kinds of drapes hanging over the windows.

"The next morning, another one of the corpsmen and I took two stretchers—they were folded, so each of us had one in each hand— and it was raining, so we wore our raincoats and crazy flat helmets, and we left the infirmary and started walking toward the parade ground. During the night, the 24th Infantry Division, which was stationed at Schofield, had dug in, and they had trenches all around the perimeter of the parade ground. As we were walking down, it had just started to turn dawn. We walked past these trenches, carrying the stretchers, and we got some funny looks from the poor guys in the trenches.

"Then we heard the noise of an aircraft engine overhead. Everybody was listening intently, trying to figure out where the noise was coming from. It kept getting louder and louder. And when it got to a particular point, either some GIs started to fire, or somebody gave a command to fire, but it was the greatest display of pyrotechnics you ever saw, because it was still dark enough to see all the *flashes!* Bullets were going *everywhere!* Nobody knew what the hell they were firing at, they were firing at what they thought they heard, but we never saw the *plane!* I don't know to this day whether it was one of our planes or another Japanese plane coming back to see what damage was done. Nobody was ever able to tell me what it was.

"The noise got so loud, it was deafening. Of course, it continued to rain, and the trenches were full of water and mud by now, and as that noise got louder and louder, the guy who was carrying the stretchers with me yelled, 'The hell with *this!*' He *dove* into a trench with a big splash of water and mud. I was thinking: It's got to get worse than this before I splash into *that* mess. But, sure enough, I couldn't take it any more either, I jumped into the trench.

"Right after that, I went into one of the barracks and turned on a radio. Of course, remember, we were five and a half hours behind Washington time, and President Roosevelt was just giving his 'War Message to Congress' and asking for a declaration of war. It was interesting to hear that. That's when he said: 'Yesterday, December 7, 1941—a date which will live in infamy—the United States of

America was suddenly and deliberately attacked by naval and air forces of the Empire of Japan.' "

CASUALTIES were heavy and one-sided. The U.S. lost 2,433 killed (1,102 of them on the *Arizona*) and 1,178 wounded. The Japanese lost fifty-five airmen, nine sailors aboard five minisubs, and sixty-five crewmen in one sunken submarine. In terms of destruction, eighteen U.S. surface warships were sunk or seriously damaged; the Japanese lost none. The U.S. lost 188 planes destroyed, 159 damaged; the Japanese lost only twenty-nine.

In eight official U.S. investigations, scapegoats were sought for the humiliating defeat. Roosevelt was accused of deliberately ignoring final warnings and permitting the attack, to shock the American people into outraged support of his plans to lead the country into war. His critics called attention to his statement that if war was to come, it had to result from a first strike by Japan.

Exactly what did FDR know, and when did he know it? Spencer Warren, a member of the State Department's Policy Planning Staff in the Reagan Administration, addresses that question in his cover story, "Why America Slept," in the December 16, 1991, issue of *National Review*. Here are his opening paragraphs:

> "We interrupt this program to bring you a special news bulletin. The Japanese have attacked Pearl Harbor, Hawaii, by air, President Roosevelt has just announced." John Daly's hurried radio announcement on that quiet Sunday afternoon can still send a chill through the heart. Ever since, the nation has asked, How could we have been caught so naked? Who was responsible? In particular, what did FDR know?
>
> Several books published after the war, by Charles A. Beard, William Henry Chamberlin, and others, argued that Roosevelt, finding himself checked by isolationists at home, deliberately misled the country about his intentions, baited the Japanese into war, and perhaps even knew of the impending attack and failed to warn the commanders.
>
> This view has been contested on almost every count. To begin with, Roosevelt saw Nazi Germany as the chief threat and did not wish to become embroiled in a two-ocean war in the midst of our defense build-

up. Nor would war with Japan necessarily have meant war with Germany. FDR's freeze on Japanese assets and partial trade embargo were intended to deter, not provoke, the Japanese into war. But no settlement could be reached in the negotiations up to December 7, as the militarists running Japan demanded that the U.S. acquiesce in their conquest of China. No appeaser, Roosevelt refused.

The strength of the revisionist case lies in the wealth of stunning intelligence we held on the enemy, based mainly on our breaking of their diplomatic code, "Purple." Among our coups was intercepting the "bomb plot" message, in which Tokyo, in September 1941, asked its Honolulu consulate to map Pearl Harbor into five sections, identifying the warships in each; and the late November "Winds" messages advising that if certain "execute" signals were subsequently received, they would mean danger of a diplomatic break with the U.S., Britain, or Russia. We also knew on December 3 that Japanese posts in Washington, London, and Southeast Asia had been ordered urgently to destroy their codes, and that Honolulu was doing likewise. Revisionists note that much intelligence was being withheld from the Hawaii commanders, Admiral Kimmel and General Short, to safeguard our precious "Purple" secret.

To be sure, the danger was not entirely ignored. U.S. naval commanders in the Pacific received a "war warning" on November 27, and the next day army commanders were warned: "Hostile action possible at any moment." Had they taken appropriate precautions, December 7 might have told a different tale. But General Short, more concerned by local sabotage than an air attack, ordered aircraft at Hickam Field parked wing to wing, making them perfect targets. And Army Chief of Staff General Marshall failed to make clear to Short that he had other measures in mind.

What now stands out as obvious evidence of an impending attack, however, was at the time buried among a multitude of signs which, taken as a whole, certainly did not single out Hawaii as a target. Further, the system of evaluation was relatively amateurish, and was hindered by inter-service rivalry and bureaucratic attitudes born of long years of peace. Washington and Hawaii knew late in November of growing enemy troop convoys and naval movements south of Formosa and in Indochina. We were expecting war any day, most probably against Thailand, Malaya, and the Dutch East Indies, and maybe the Philippines, or perhaps Siberia—*not* Pearl Harbor. Indeed, the attack by carrier aircraft far from base, coupled with the offensive against Malaya, the Philippines, and the Dutch East Indies, was so audacious and unprecedented that even many in the Japanese high command had opposed it as impracticable. . . .

"Two things are certain," George points out. "The sacrificial lambs in Hawaii didn't know what was going on. And our regiment was among the last to find out."

Not long afterward, the Second Battalion, which included George's old company, was sent down to Fort de Russy, adjacent to Waikiki Beach, and he remained behind with the medical detachment. But in early January 1942, he developed a bad cold. The major in charge of the medical detachment, a fatherly type, asked George if he would like to join the Second Battalion as a medical specialist and soak up some sun on the beach to cure his cold. "I must have been the world's luckiest GI," George says, "because they never did recall me to Schofield."

ACCORDING to *The People's Almanac*, by David Wallechinsky and Irving Wallace (Doubleday & Company, Inc., Garden City, New York, 1975), on February 19, 1942, "President Roosevelt signed into law Executive Order No. 9066 which allowed the military to move 112,000 Japanese-Americans from their homes on the West Coast to concentration camps inland. Apparently, the U.S. Government hoped to use them as bargaining items to regain American POWs after the war, because the Government arranged to have 2,000 Japanese living in Peru rounded up and incarcerated in the camps as well."

On March 17, General Douglas MacArthur, obeying a direct order from FDR, abandoned the hopeless fight on Bataan, traveled by submarine from the Philippines to Australia, and took command of the Southwest Pacific forces. The Bataan Death March began on April 10, when Japanese soldiers forced 10,000 U.S. prisoners of war and 45,000 Filipino Scouts to march 120 miles to San Fernando, in Pampanga Province. At the end of each day, all sick and wounded prisoners who were unable to continue were shot, stabbed, or buried alive. Restricted to one meal of rice per day and no fresh water, more than 5,200 Americans and uncounted thousands of Filipinos died in the six-day atrocity.

In the first U.S. offensive strike against the Japanese, April 18, Colonel James Doolittle's carrier-based flyers bombed Tokyo on a one-way trip; they continued past Japan, bailing out over mainland China. During the Battle of Midway, June 3–6, the U.S. halted Admiral Yamamoto's thrust into the Central Pacific; he lost major units of his fleet, including four carriers, two cruisers, and eleven other vessels. On July 25, Roosevelt and Churchill executed "Operation Torch," calling for an invasion of French North Africa, and then using it as a stepping stone into Sicily and Italy. The Battle of Guadalcanal began August 7, followed by six months of savage jungle fighting on the 2,500-square-mile island; General Vandegrift's 16,000 Marines, supported by Army elements, forced Japanese ground troops to retreat.

CONSTANTLY trying to find a way to get a commission, George had applied for navigator in the Army Air Corps, but the papers were returned with the statement that, without a degree, he was basically unqualified. Next, he applied to be a bombardier. Same old story. Unqualified. Finally, he learned that a person could become a meteorologist in the Air Corps with three years of college if his studies had included calculus and thermodynamics, both of which he lacked.

"Then fate stepped in again," he says. "I was shooting the breeze with another fellow when he let it drop that he was taking a course at the nearby University of Hawaii. I asked myself: Why not take the courses I needed to become a meteorologist?"

At that time, Army personnel in Hawaii didn't have much to do and, because of the jittery morale of the troops, they were being given a great deal of time off. There was a three-day pass every other week, a twenty-four-hour pass every week, and a two-week pass every other month. So George asked his company commander if, instead of all that time off, he could get off two days a week to attend the university. The commander readily agreed.

George entered the University of Hawaii at the start of the spring term, 1942, on what was called a conference course method. A professor gave him assignments in a calculus course and as soon as he completed one assignment satisfactorily, he was eligible to go on to the next. As a medical specialist, he had virtually nothing to do, so he was able to study every afternoon, then go to the recreation hall and study every night. As a result, he sailed through his calculus course in a matter of a few weeks. At that point, the registrar, a lady named Helen MacNeill, called him into her office and encouraged him to enroll as a degree candidate.

"The result was that we arranged for courses that would lead to my BS degree," George says. "The registrar simply waived such things as residency requirements and ROTC, since I was in the Army, and accepted virtually all of my transfer credits from West Chester."

That May, more than 5,000 miles away, the Class of 1942 was about to graduate from West Chester. Sixteen members of the senior class, as well as hundreds of alumni, were already serving in the armed forces, and the yearbook was touchingly dedicated to all of them:

> Dedication of the 1942 *Serpentine* to all the men from West Chester answering their country's call to serve in the armed forces is natural, logical, and heartfelt in this anxious year.
>
> During the school year 1941–42, we have experienced great changes in feeling and thinking. First we thrilled at "playing war" for the sake of national defense; some of our friends and classmates were drafted, it is true, but we were still here, and we could laugh over everyday happenings and over a cigarette advertisement that made a joke of being "On the Land, In the Air, and On the Sea." After December 7, 1941, however, when Japan attacked Hawaii, the cigarette slogan gained stark significance, became a true pen picture of "modern design."
>
> In the rush of world events there has not been much time for reflection, but even a little thought has made us realize that we have a great deal to fight for and protect, and that our men from West Chester are doing that fighting and protecting for us. The cannon on Wayne Field campus is a useless symbol of an older war, but perhaps the picture of it will bring to the minds of our men the memory of happy days that will surely come again and the thought that we are working for and with them.

To our friends in any and all branches of the service of their and our country, and especially to those who would have graduated in the normal course of things with the class of 1942, we dedicate this book with greetings and best wishes "from all of us to all of you."

A two-page spread in the yearbook is devoted to the sixteen members of the senior class who were in the service, including a photograph of each man in uniform, and updated information about each. George is included with six of his classmates: "GEORGE WACKENHUT entered the service July 11, 1941, being sent to Fort Belvoir, Virginia, with the 34th Engineers. Later sent to Hawaii, he underwent the first attack upon United States soldiers. He was active in soccer, lacrosse, and Varsity Club."

Pictured among the graduates of the secondary education program is George's girl friend, Marie Carroll, who must be described as beautiful rather than pretty, oval face with bright eyes and perfect teeth, medium-length dark hair slightly curled, wearing the same dark V-necked blouse as all the other girls. Her caption reads: "MARIE REGINA CARROLL, 21 West Avon Road, Chester, Pa. Prepared at St. Robert's H.S. and Immaculata College. Activities: French Club 2, Newman Club 3, 4."

George recalls two of the last letters he received from Marie in Hawaii. "I remember getting one letter from her after the attack on Pearl Harbor: 'Can't live without you,' and all that kind of stuff. Didn't hear from her for several weeks, and the next letter I got, she was going with somebody else; she didn't love me any more! It was a 'Dear George' letter!"

In September 1942, while George continued to study for his BS degree at the University of Hawaii, he applied for Officer Candidate School in the Ordnance Department. He was interviewed, accepted, and received his orders to return home for OCS. However, he still needed one course (three credits) to graduate. At this point, Mrs. MacNeill, the registrar, arranged for him to take the course, Physics 261, via correspondence with the professor, while he was attending OCS in the states, and, if successful, he would receive his degree by mail the following June. He left Hawaii in October. It turned out to be a voyage he would never forget.

"There were five thousand men aboard when we sailed out in a convoy," he says, "and destroyers zigzagged in front of us while we went as slow as the slowest ship. We were about three days out of Honolulu and I was napping in my hammock below decks when a soldier came running into our area. 'We're going like *hell* now,' he yelled, 'but we're going the *wrong way!*' We asked him what he meant by the wrong way. 'The convoy is going *one* way,' he said, 'but we're going the *other* way!'

"All of us ran up to the stern. Sure enough, the convoy was slogging slowly off into the distance, while we were headed back toward Hawaii.

"We steamed back much faster than we had come out and arrived off Honolulu about midnight, unable to go into the harbor until they raised the submarine nets at daybreak. It was a long night. There was a full moon, the sea was calm, and we were clay pigeons for any Japanese submarines that might have been in the area. Everywhere you looked, you thought you could see a periscope!

"Dawn came at long last. While we were despondent at having been returned without explanation, we all had to laugh when we were greeted by a coast artillery band in the port playing 'California, Here I Come!'

"Once again, we were loaded into trucks and taken to Schofield Barracks. There we were put into a 'casual' outfit, which meant we didn't have a single thing to do, and we sat there for eleven days wondering what it was all about. What it was about, we learned later, was that the 25th Infantry Division had been shipped off Oahu to New Guinea. The 27th Division was on the big island of Hawaii, which wasn't nearly as strategically important as Oahu because of Pearl Harbor, and it was decided that the 27th would be moved in as a replacement for the 25th. That was why they needed our ship.

"So we were loaded on trucks again, placed back aboard ship, and, without being slowed by being in convoy, we steamed into San Francisco only five days later."

At almost exactly the same time, October 20, 1942, Captain Eddie Rickenbacker boarded a Pan American Sikorsky Clipper in San Francisco, bound for Hawaii, to begin a mission in the South Pacific Theater as a special consultant to the Secretary of War, Henry L.

Stimson. Rickenbacker was entrusted with a message from Secretary Stimson to General Douglas MacArthur at Port Moresby, New Guinea, a message of such sensitivity that it could not be put on paper.

Edward Vernon Rickenbacker (1890–1973) was truly a legend in his own time. During World War I, he was sent to France with General Pershing's American Expeditionary Forces, and finally worked his way into what was then called the U.S. Air Service. As a member of the famous "Hat-in-the-Ring" air squadron, he battled in the skies with Baron Manfred von Richthofen's Flying Circus, shot down twenty-six German planes, became America's Ace of Aces, earned nineteen decorations for bravery in action, including the Congressional Medal of Honor, and was universally known as "Captain Eddie."

Rickenbacker, fifty-two in 1942, was already a hero to the twenty-three-year-old George Wackenhut, and, by the odd ways of fate, they were to become close friends in Miami, when George was starting the Wackenhut Corporation, and Captain Eddie was president of Miami-headquartered Eastern Air Lines, a position he held from 1934 until he retired in 1965 at the age of seventy-five; he was a member of Wackenhut's board of directors, 1968–1972.

When Rickenbacker's Pan Am Clipper landed in Honolulu on October 20, 1942, after a fifteen-hour flight from San Francisco, he was driven to Hickam Field, where he boarded a B-17-D bound for Canton Island, 1,800 miles southwest of Hawaii, the first leg of a circuitous route that would take him to Port Moresby and his meeting with General MacArthur. The plan was to refuel on Canton, then continue southward to Suva in the Fiji Islands, New Caledonia in the Loyalty group, and Brisbane on the east coast of Australia. From there, they would fly north to Port Moresby. The reason for the roundabout route was that the Japanese controlled the straight-line area between Hawaii and New Guinea.

The flight to Canton, departing 1:30 A.M., October 21, and estimated to require about eight hours, turned out to be a nightmare. In his autobiography, *Rickenbacker* (Prentice-Hall, Inc., 1967), which became *The New York Times'* number-one best seller in January, 1968, Captain Eddie relates:

I'd been lost in the air before, but never over such a vast expanse. The ocean seemed endless. Our charts showed other small islands and island groups, but we saw none of them. To the northwest of Canton was Howland Island, the destination of the famous aviatrix Amelia Earhart's round-the-world flight in 1937. She and her navigator Fred Noonan had been trying to find that tiny atoll when they disappeared, never to be seen again. There has always been a persistent rumor that they fell into the hands of the Japanese, but I have always doubted it.

Some five hundred miles west of Canton were the Gilbert Islands, of which Tarawa is one. We hoped that we weren't that far off course; the Gilberts were in the hands of the Japanese.

By then it was obvious to all of us that we were in grave danger. De Angelis, the young navigator, was naturally on the defensive. He shot the sun with his octant and gave Cherry another course. Thirty minutes later he made another reading and changed the course he had given only a half-hour before. He simply couldn't figure out what was wrong. Then it occurred to him that the instrument, which was assigned to him personally, had been damaged when the first B-17 ground-looped back at Hickam Field. If that were true, every reading he had made had been erroneous. We could be hundreds of miles off course in either direction.

The radio station on Palmyra broke in with the suggestion that we climb to five thousand feet and circle for thirty minutes, sending out a radio signal, while they took a bearing. We did. They supplied us with a compass course, which meant nothing; we could be on it, yet a thousand miles below or above the island. Nevertheless, we let down through the cloud layer and lined up on the new course, which took us west. We flew on, at better than three miles a minute, but all we could see was water and more water.

"Get on that radio and tell Canton to start firing antiaircraft shells into the air," I told Sergeant Reynolds. "Tell them to time their shells so that they burst at seven thousand feet, above the cloud level. We'll keep a look out. Ask them if they have planes they can send up."

Reynolds got busy with his key. "They answer affirmative," he cried.

In the meantime I had suggested to Captain Cherry that he box the compass, an old maritime-navigation operation. We would go west for one hour, then turn north for an hour, then east, then south. But I knew that the gas would not hold out for all four legs.

Canton reported that the shells were being fired and the planes were taking off. We saw nothing. We were running on the leanest possible gasoline mixture. Cherry cut the two outboard engines in order to save more gas. The clouds began to thin out, and he climbed higher in order to be able to see a greater area. But there was no land, no ship, as far as all our eyes could see.

"One hour's fuel remaining," Cherry said.

I wrote a message to that effect and passed it over to Sergeant Reynolds. That was the last word anyone heard from us.

"Send out an SOS," Cherry told Reynolds. The sergeant began banging the key. Again, again and again. But there was no answer, no acknowledgment. Wherever we were, no American could hear us.

That meant that, even if we made a successful crash landing on the water, nobody would know which way to look for us. . . .

Two full days later, on Friday, October 23, 1942, the news finally hit the wire services, resulting in headlines across the country the next morning. The banner headline in the October 24 edition of *The Los Angeles Times* was typical, and carried a huge photo of Captain Eddie:

RICKENBACKER'S PLANE MISSING
Pacific Hunt Started for Noted Air Ace
Hope Not Abandoned for Stimson Adviser Flying Among Islands

WASHINGTON, October 23 (UP)—Capt. E.V. Rickenbacker, the United States' greatest air ace in World War I and confidential adviser to Secretary of War Stimson in this one, is overdue on a flight between Oahu, Hawaii, and another Pacific island, the Army announced tonight.

Rickenbacker, president of Eastern Airlines and one of the most colorful figures in aviation history, last was heard from in the early evening of Oct. 21, when he was winging his way over the Pacific southwest of Honolulu with only a little more than an hour's supply of gasoline remaining. . . .

6

IN SHARP CONTRAST to Hawaii, the late autumn was freezing cold at the U.S. Army's Aberdeen Proving Ground in Maryland when Corporal George Wackenhut arrived to begin Officer Candidate School in early November 1942. Maintained by the Ordnance Department, the very situation and terrain of the Proving Ground complemented the work there by highly trained scientists and engineers, skilled mechanics and machinists, whose duty it was to know exactly what could be expected of every type of ordnance material and ammunition used in the various branches of the Army. Nature endowed the 67,700 acres with everything needed but a hill, and the department soon took care of that by building its own. The Proving Ground is located along the western shore of the upper arm of the Chesapeake Bay, a wisely chosen site, because it provides a water surface for approximately 50 percent of the vast acreage. The establishment came into being in 1917, when the limited scope of the old proving ground at Sandy Hook, New York, handicapped the testing of material and ammunition during World War I. Congress approved the purchase of land in October 1917, and within a few days the necessary survey was started. In all, $3.5 million was spent in acquiring the post (an absolutely gigantic sum in those days), which included a three-mile right-of-way for a government railroad and highway to connect with the Pennsylvania Railroad at Aberdeen, the town from which the proving ground took its name.

In 1942, The Ordnance Training Command consisted of the Ordnance School and Ordnance Replacement Training Center. The Ordnance School was further subdivided into Enlisted School, Shop School, and Officer Candidate School.

George had picked up another bad cold during a week's layover in San Francisco before receiving his orders, and the train trip back had been a miserable experience. The day before his group was processed at OCS, he remembers spending most of the time crouched beside a potbelly stove in a utility room, wearing all the warm clothing he had, in a fruitless attempt to stay relatively warm. He recalls a conversation with another GI in the room who was telling him about the setup at Aberdeen.

"They're bringing in a lot of retreads," the soldier explained. "There's a standing joke in the automotive section that if you were a Ford dealer, they make you a second lieutenant. If you were a Chevrolet dealer, you get first lieutenant. But if you were a Cadillac dealer, you make lieutenant colonel."

There may have been some truth to that. Because some time later, George was in the quadrangle when a newly processed lieutenant colonel appeared in his brand-new uniform. Just about that time, the post commander came along, a full colonel out of West Point who had been in the Army all his adult life. The new lieutenant colonel walked up to him and his voice was full of indignation.

"Hey, Colonel," he said, not even giving the post commander a salute, "I'd like to ask you something. How come you got to be a *bird* colonel and all I get is *lieutenant* colonel?"

George laughs at the memory. "Well, sir, I've heard some dressings down in my time, but the post commander cut that guy to *ribbons!*"

ON NOVEMBER 14, 1942, the wire services released the news that Captain Eddie Rickenbacker had been found alive in a rubber lifeboat 600 miles north of Samoa, three weeks after his plane went down in the Pacific. It made headlines in newspapers from coast to coast, and *The Boston Evening Globe* (which sold for three cents in those days) was typical:

RICKENBACKER FOUND ALIVE
Condition Good; Raft Off Samoa;
5 Others Rescued, 1 Dead

WASHINGTON, Nov. 14 (AP)—Dauntless Eddie Rickenbacker has been rescued, in good condition, the Navy announced today, three weeks after his airplane radioed that it was about out of gasoline, and then vanished in the Pacific.

Rickenbacker, America's ace of aces in the first World War and the country's embodied proof that you can't keep a good man down, was picked up from a raft bobbing in the sea by a Navy Catalina flying boat along with two of his crew. They were 600 miles north of Samoa.

Three other Army fliers who were with him on a survey of Pacific war zone Air Force operations have been located on an island. The rescue of one was announced yesterday and the seventh man of Rickenbacker's crew died in the long wait for rescue.

Col. Hans C. Adamson and private John F. Bartek were Rickenbacker's two companions at the time of rescue. . . .

In his book, *Seven Came Through* (Doubleday, Doran & Company, Inc., 1943), which appeared initially in three issues of *Life* magazine (*Life*'s first serial), Captain Eddie spoke directly and persuasively to American factory workers, urging them to increase production for the war effort:

> Perhaps it is presumptuous of me to lecture, but I know what I saw—I was there. A terrible responsibility faces us people back home, a responsibility to which we are not yet fully awakened. Everywhere I went the cry from the troops was for more of everything—more planes, more guns, more tanks, more ammunition, more medical stores. It is hard for them to understand why this rich country cannot send them more.
>
> I have said, and I repeat, that if we were to bring back the troops from the hellholes of the world and place them in the factories, and if we were to take the factory workers and place them in the fox holes, in the filth, vermin, diarrhea, malaria, and Japanese, I will guarantee that production would be increased and in many instances doubled within thirty days. Some have called me a "labor-hater" for saying that. No, I am not a labor-hater. I believe in honest labor unions who are doing their darnedest to turn out the weapons we need. I have been laboring for

forty-odd years—since I was twelve years of age—in many lines of endeavor. I come from humble parents. I know the value of honest labor. I have served labor as well as employer. And to those millions of honest men and women war workers go my heartfelt thanks—to those whom the shoe fits, I say wear it.

My answer is that after you have seen the stink and corruption of New Guinea and Guadalcanal, after you have come to understand the nature of the enemy, all the talk of social security, old-age pensions, wages and hours, means nothing. We either win the war or we lose it. And we'll lose it if we don't produce. . . .

During the autumn and early winter months of 1942, the U.S. nearly lost its carrier capability in the Pacific. In October, the *Wasp* was sunk, the *Hornet* was lost, and extensive damage was inflicted upon the *Enterprise* and the *Saratoga*. Admiral William Halsey appealed to Washington for help, because he had no other carriers under his command. Prime Minister Churchill finally came to his aid in December by temporarily reassigning the British carrier *Victorious* for Halsey's use.

Throughout this period, the Japanese made a concentrated effort to send troops and supplies to their land forces on Guadalcanal. Moving at night with such speed and predictability that U.S. troops there dubbed them the "Tokyo Express," the Japanese troop transports slipped into the so-called Slot (a channel through the Solomons), slowed to discharge the troops at the closest approach to Guadalcanal, then hurried away to be beyond range of an air attack before daylight.

Also that year, the Declaration of the United Nations was signed in Washington; women's military service was established; Italian physicist Enrico Fermi achieved the first nuclear chain reaction; and the Manhattan Project, the code name given to U.S. atomic bomb research, suggested by Albert Einstein, J. Robert Oppenheimer, and other scientists, was carried on with great secrecy at several locations in the United States under the direction of General Leslie Groves.

RETURNING to Aberdeen after a ten-day leave over Thanksgiving, George began Officer Candidate School on a very significant date:

December 7, 1942. According to his Report of Physical Examination, dated January 11, 1943, and signed by Adam J. Rapalski, Major, Medical Corps, the twenty-three-year-old George was five-foot-ten and one-half, and weighed 171 pounds. When he graduated from OCS on March 6, 1943, he was commissioned a second lieutenant in Ordnance and, having finished tenth in his class, he was assigned to remain at Aberdeen as a tactical instructor. This was a fortunate assignment, because he was only sixty miles from Upper Darby and could visit his family more often.

In November 1943, a book was published by the OCS, titled *The Commandos: Company H, Class 57* (Army and Navy Publishing Company, Inc., Baton Rouge, LA), in which Second Lieutenant George R. Wackenhut is prominently featured in his role as a tactical instructor. Apparently written by one of his students, although there's no by-line, it begins with a brief biography, below a half-page photo of the twenty-four-year-old George in uniform, then goes into humorous details of the physical education program of that particular class of sixty-two candidates:

> Born in Philadelphia, September 3, 1919, the lusty offspring of William Henry and Frances Mabel Wackenhut, George Russell lost no time in growing up. Discovering that flexing one's biceps at strategic times could scare off would-be opponents, he early became an exponent of the body beautiful and animated anatomy.
>
> At Upper Darby High School, he participated in all sports, and upon graduation enrolled in the University of Pennsylvania. One year later, he was wheedled away to State Teachers College, West Chester, Pennsylvania. The bait? A scholarship in a school famed for its Physical Education Courses and a three to one Coed ratio. At State Teachers, he played varsity lacrosse and soccer and coached the varsity lacrosse team.
>
> Summoned to the Colors in July, 1941, he spent eleven grinding weeks at Fort Belvoir before entraining on a transcontinental trip to a P.O.E. Transported to Hawaii, he dodged bombs at Pearl Harbor, and helped speed up the defenses of the Island. Ambitious, and hankering for a degree, Corporal Wackenhut induced his CO to permit him to pyramid his free time so that he could attend classes at the University of Hawaii and earn his B.S. degree.
>
> He returned to the States to enter Ordnance O.C.S. December 7, 1942. Three months later he emerged a Second Lieutenant and was assigned to

the 8th O.T.C. A short time later, he transferred to the Military Section and thence to Company H, O.C.S. to become Tactical Officer of Class H-57.

Inspiring mutual devotion among his men—Wackenhut's Commandoes will always cherish his byword—"Always alert, never hurt!"

Permanent address: 307 Long Lane, Upper Darby, Pennsylvania.

The Physical Education of H-57

It was that first Saturday afternoon so long ago. Captain Craig had outlined to the new and eager class his expectations of an officer candidate. Lt. Cady added remarks.

All during their talks we saw a lean, athletic-looking young man sitting at the side of the room, wearing the gold bars of a second lieutenant.

"Lt. Wackenhut, your tactical officer, will now have a few words to say," announced the captain. "During the next four months he will be your instructor in all military subjects, and will be with you at all times."

Lt. Wackenhut gripped the instructor's stand a moment, looking over the new class . . . and, in turn, being scrutinized by 62 pairs of eyes.

"You men are going to be tough," he said. "The day of the Ordnance Officer who couldn't fight is past. I'm not going to teach you how to die for your country; I'm going to teach you how to live . . . and kill! Today's warfare needs officers who can lead their men into battle. The good officer can do anything his men can do, and do it better!"

That was our introduction to Lt. Wackenhut and his program. Entirely new to OCS were his principles, and the other OCS classes snickered when, on Monday evening, as they relaxed after evening chow, they saw us straining awkwardly at general physical fitness tests, which included a coordination test that reminded the onlooker of a burlesque of a Russian dance. Long-rusty muscles creaked and often-used vocal cords sounded groans as we attempted to follow the energetic lieutenant, who easily went through the movements, at the same time discoursing about the benefits it would do triceps, biceps, pectorals and femorals. We took his word for it and struggled.

By Saturday he decided we might be ready for the obstacle course. Obediently, and a little fearfully, we marched to the torture course in the woods, and started off rapidly in squads. The painful details will be glossed over here—overhanging ropes, walls, on and on—it seemed endless—until at last, very sore but satisfied, we tenderly settled our aching bodies on the ground for a break; but not nearly so tenderly as we eased them out of bed the next day.

But we were now convinced we needed the exercises, and as the days passed we could actually feel ourselves improving and going through each routine more easily. We were getting good.

Our joy was short-lived, when one night, the order was, "Draw bayonets and line up in two lines facing each other." While we held the unfamiliarly unbalanced bayonetted rifles, our instructor thrust, jabbed, slashed, whirled, and slammed the butt of his rifle at purely imaginary foes in such a manner as to leave no doubt as to the fate of the unlucky Jap.

But we had to start from scratch. "On guard!" "Lo-o-ong THRUST." "Growl at him and lunge as though you meant to kill him! Don't push the bayonet out there as if you were presenting it for inspection. GET TOUGH." And we improved. And we exercised. And we hiked. And we double-timed. Belt-lines narrowed. Groaning subsided and was replaced by normal good-natured complaining, tinged with cockiness.

Came bivouac. The other platoons still snickered—a little. We merely tore the bayonet course apart, breezed through forced marches, and jabbed and thrust bayonets when aching bodies wanted the comparative comfort of lolling in our tents in the evening. And Lt. Wackenhut, still thinking of combat soldiers, devised a new combat course—dummies that popped out from behind trees, fell from the branches and crawled across the path of the unsuspecting soldier; and machine guns spit at the surprised competitor. Perhaps we hesitated at the first couple of obstacles; from then on the reaction was to immediately attempt to destroy the enemy by the most effective means.

So we came back to the post. And ran the obstacle course each morning for a week. Now it was a breeze. Hah. What next.

Once a paperhanger had a dream—and built an army. Once a plumber had a nightmare—and built the trainasium! And in due course, it became our lot to mount the steps of what looked strangely like a scaffold. We hung from bars, crawled in and out of pipes, jumped, balanced on ladders and catwalks seemingly high above the ground, and quickly it became easy.

Bivouac again. Now we were teaching the bayonet to our juniors. And learning to take them away from armed opponents.

Then one day we heard there was to be a party of visiting officers, and a general. A review must be held. And an exhibition would be given. Lt. Wackenhut summoned his ablest Commandos, and for two days they practiced until their bodies ached from bruises as well as exhaustion.

Came the exhibition. Swiftly and smoothly the Commandos exhibited to the startled visitors the technique of the bayonet. And stabbed and banged at each other until it seemed certain this was not entirely play. And battered Ed Gales warily stalked Jerry Smolinsky with a knife again and again, but Smoky, who comes from Brooklyn, where a knife is used only for eating peas, disarmed him again and again. A final sham battle left "dead and dying" soldiers all over the field, and a limp but excited audience. There was no longer doubt in any onlooker's mind that Lt. Wackenhut had succeeded.

But we weren't through. . . . Unarmed defense . . . boxing . . . wrestling . . . more athletics.

Wackenhut's Commandos have graduated. They're officers now. And on battlefields in distant theatres, surprised enemies will discover that Ordnancemen CAN fight, trained by these new officers, carrying on.

"I'm not going to teach you how to die for your country. I'm going to teach you how to live . . . and kill!"

Oh yes, we can shoot, too.

James B. Matson was one of George's "commandos" in Company H, Class 57, and remembers those four grueling months very clearly. He was twenty-four that year, married, and had one semester to complete at the University of Cincinnati, Class of 1942, when he was drafted (he received his degree in 1946). "At Aberdeen, when you first met George," he says, smiling, "he was just another lieutenant—that we had to find out about. And we quickly found out. He had sixty-two guys in the physical education class, as I recollect. The thing that had happened not too long before we went into this class was Kasserine Pass, in Africa, where our troops were rolled back to where the actual supply outfits were fighting, doing infantry stuff. It was one of the first engagements we had over there where we got our nose bloodied. So the orders had come down, I guess, and, not too long before that, OCS had been increased from three months to four months. Some of that was to provide infantry training through Ordnance officers, in case we ever got into another Kasserine Pass situation. It was a wake-up call!

"So George explained that some of our training was going to be infantry. And I've got to say that at the end of those four months, I was in the best condition I've ever *been* in, or ever *will be* in! Because he was—he was very physical. I still remember playing what George liked to call 'Wackenhut's Christmas Present.' I think it was a soccer ball we were using, and it was played on kind of a soccer or football field, and there were two balls in play at all times. We would divide the platoon up in half. Opposing teams. There was only one rule, and that was, you had to get the ball in-between the goalposts over the goal line! Any way at *all!* There were only two officials, and they were there to count the score and return the ball to the infield to put it in play again. The reason George called it this, we were playing this maybe in September, and he said, 'You'll still have the marks by Christmas!'

"The only thing that kept it from being *murderous* was at the end of each month we had a rating, which was secret, where you rated every one of your other platoon members on a scale of one to sixty-one. The only question was: 'Would you serve under this person?' So that was what kept the game within bounds. I mean, we had no protection! And there were some injuries. The length of the game was whenever George decided we'd had *enough!* But the purpose was bodily contact.

"When you got done with the four months with George, you really weren't afraid of much of anything. Bayonets were used with lacrosse equipment, we did use the helmet and the gauntlet gloves. But the bayonets were not sheathed. We had one guy, we always called him 'The Knife Fighter'—Eddie Gale, Johnstown, Pennsylvania. He was just *tough!* Knew how to use a *knife!*

"Strange combination of ages. Ordnance had decided that automobile dealers would make Ordnance officers! And they picked some of these automobile dealers, and some of them didn't make it. When they got to the physical part, they just couldn't hack it. Particularly after these 'rating' things were turned in. You'd come back to the barracks, and everything was gone, the bunk, clothes, everything, you never saw the guy again. I'm just guessing, but I'd say over 10 percent were washed out. I'm sure George had to make some of these decisions.

"My wife Georgia had come down and had a trailer in a cow pasture just outside the post. And I always accused George of going out to my trailer while we were on bivouac or something, and getting home-cooked food from my wife! We had him over for dinner once in a while, and he never forgot it, because we didn't get off the post too much, so you couldn't get that kind of food. We'd take these night hikes, and the road out of camp went right past this cow pasture where the trailer was. So Georgia would be standing out there with cookies for me, and, in the fatigues and helmets and everything, it was hard to tell who was who. So she'd have to keep asking, 'Where's Jim? Where's Jim?' They'd keep pointing back, and finally I'd come along!

"At Aberdeen, George's phrase, 'Always alert, never hurt,' was somewhat famous. He kept saying it over and over. And, I mean, he'd be explaining a rifle or bayonet tactic to somebody and, all of a sudden, he'd *toss* it at somebody! So, you stayed awake!"

IN THE MEANTIME, George was completing the one three-credit course he needed for his BS degree from the University of Hawaii, Physics 261, via correspondence with the physics professor. He graduated on June 15, 1943, and was mailed his diploma. According to his official academic transcript, he took eleven courses for a total of thirty credits. He was allowed 103 transfer credits from West Chester State Teachers College, and four credits from the Wharton Evening School, University of Pennsylvania, for a total of 107 transfer credits.

1941–42

Subject	Grade
Math 153	B
Math 154	B
Physics 200	W
Geology 150	B
Geology 151	B
Math 155	C
Physics 151	C

Summer School 1942

Math 200	C
Math 275	B
Physics 255	B
Physics 261	B

Second Lieutenant Wackenhut, Officer Serial No. O-1554297, was finally appointed post athletic officer, a position he held until September 1944.

George had been at Aberdeen about a year when Jimmie Mills, head coach and manager of the Philadelphia Nationals first-division American Soccer League team (now a member of the National Soccer Hall of Fame), learned that he might be available for weekend play and wrote to him. The offer was accepted with enthusiasm and that autumn of 1943, George traveled to Philadelphia every weekend to play goaltender for the powerful Nationals, his first major league team. That autumn, the following article appeared in the sports section of the *Philadelphia Inquirer:*

Hispano Loses to Nationals in Cup Soccer

The Philadelphia Nationals, playing a vigorous brand of soccer, took the Brooklyn Hispanos into camp, 4–1, in the second round of the American League's Lewis Cup playoff series yesterday at Cambria Stadium.

Charles (Chili) Altemose and Walter Bahr, former Northeast High star, each booted two goals for the winners.

The Hispanos, who will shortly play at the Polo Grounds for the National Open Challenge Cup, were blanked in the first half, which ended 3–0.

It was the first victory in two games for the Philadelphians in the cup play.

The large crowd was enthusiastic over George Wackenhut, Philadelphia goalie, who played bang-up ball to deprive the visitors of points. In the first half alone, Wackenhut made nine brilliant saves from difficult positions. . . .

Wackenhut provided one of the greatest displays of goal custodianship ever seen in this league, barring nobody. The Hispano might have scored ten goals only for this tender.

Even when caught out of position by the rapid movements of the forwards, the Nationals' rapidly developing goalie simply bobbed up from nowhere, getting his fingers, sometimes, and hands, at others, on the ball to divert it from its true course.

When a fellow can dive from nowhere and get one of those low drives by Bill Gonsalves at the opposite side of the goal, he must have something. That is just what Wackenhut did. And he was not yelling foul, he was just getting them. . . .

(Almost fifty years later, on May 20, 1993, it was announced that George Wackenhut had been appointed to the National Board of the National Soccer Hall of Fame.)

IN DECEMBER 1943, George went home on Christmas leave, looking forward to seeing his mother and dad and his brother Harry, not realizing that within a matter of days an event would occur that would change his life forever. On Christmas Eve, he was idly reading the dozens of Christmas cards his parents had received. One was from the family of a man named Harry Merz, who had been friends of his mother and dad for many years.

"Harry Merz," he said to his mother. "Didn't I meet his stepdaughter about five years ago when we were at Ocean City?"

She nodded. "Yes, Ruth Bell, a lovely young lady."

He remembered her vividly, although she had been only about sixteen at the time. That was the summer of 1939, when George had just finished his freshman year at West Chester. It was a weekend afternoon, he was on the beach, and he tried to show her how to manipulate the ball with a lacrosse stick. She had left a towel on the beach, stopped by the apartment to pick it up that evening, and he recalled how pretty she was.

"Mother," he said, "why don't we go over and see them tomorrow? There isn't much to do and it might be fun for me to see them again."

Ruth Bell lived in a stately three-story white Tudor house at 937 Cornell Avenue, on the corner of Bond Avenue, in a relatively affluent section of Drexel Hill. The graceful old Scotch pine on the corner of the lawn is still there, and the white stucco and brown wooden panels look freshly painted today. Most of the homes along the quiet, tree-lined street appear to be old and solid, constructed in an era when architects and contractors and carpenters took genuine pride in their work, when houses were called for generations by the family name.

George can visualize that house on Christmas Day, 1943, with snow glistening on the lawn, the sidewalk and driveway shoveled, a cold brace in the air, and a big wreath on the front door. Although 7438 Miller Avenue in Upper Darby is only about two miles to the northeast, the difference between the two houses and the neighborhoods is as striking today as it must have been then, to say nothing of the lifestyles of the residents.

Born Ruth Johann, in Philadelphia, September 17, 1922, Ruth was the youngest of two other sisters, Evelyn and Blanche. Her father, Andrew Johann, a real estate broker, and her mother, Bessie Johann (nee Bell), divorced when she was a child. Her mother went on to marry Harry Merz, a successful entrepreneur, the owner of Merz White Way Tours in Philadelphia, a large fleet of tour buses. All three girls then assumed their mother's maiden name, Bell.

Ruth graduated from Upper Darby Senior High School, June 12, 1940, three years after George. She was twenty-one on that memorable Christmas morning in 1943.

"First of all, I was in bed," Ruth remembers, smiling. "I had been away for a weekend party on the Main Line. So I came home in the morning sometime, and I went to bed. It may have been four or five in the morning, something like that. So, my mother came up the steps, she came into my bedroom, I was sound asleep, I didn't know she was in the room. 'Ruth? Ruth? *Ruth!*' I pulled the sheet over my head. She said, 'The Wackenhuts are downstairs, and they have their son with them, George, and I want you to get up, I want you to get dressed, and I want you to come down immediately. I would like you to meet George.'

"I said, 'No, mother, another time. I don't want to meet anybody, I want to *sleep!*' She said, 'I'm going to say it one more time: I want you out of bed.' And I said, '*I'm* going to say it one more time: I'm not getting up! I'll see them another time!'

"With that, she grabbed me bodily, and I landed on the *floor!*

Bang! 'Get dressed!' All right, what can I do? So, I got washed, I put on a shell-pink cashmere sweater, a tailored skirt, and pumps. And my hair was long, I had dark hair, but I had a natural gray streak that started at the widow's peak and just went right down.

"Anyway, I went down the steps half-asleep. I walked in, and he was sitting there in uniform, dress-uniform, and I did a double-take. Now, I had been dating Marines, and Air Force, and Navy officers, and he was a second lieutenant. Anyway, I walked in, and I thought: Um, he's attractive. So, I said, 'Hello, Mr. and Mrs. Wackenhut.' His father did the printing for my father's company, that's how they knew each other.

"Now, I hadn't seen George since I was sixteen, on the beach in Ocean City. And, of course, at that time I was going with Walt Satterthwaite, who was from a well-to-do family, and was a student at Cornell University.

"Well, there was an antique iron bench in front of the fireplace, so I went over, sat on it, and crossed my legs. I didn't know that George was *zooming* in on me, but, according to *his* story, that was it. I started getting very uncomfortable, because his eyes were just penetrating right *through* me! And he's a very quiet person. He had really an introverted personality, compared to my extroverted personality, and I think that intrigued me, too, because he wasn't really *trying* anything, he was just looking, and he was very quiet. I always had so many men trying so hard. So this was something new."

"She was even prettier than I remembered," George says, "and when we hit it off famously that day, I asked her for a date on New Year's Eve. She told me she was sorry, but she already had a date. It didn't surprise me."

By that time, George was getting home just about every weekend, playing for the Philadelphia Nationals, so he kept calling Ruth, and they had their first date in the middle of January 1944. Actually, it was a double-date, they went out with a married couple, George's old friend Norman Paul and his wife Dotti. Norman did the driving.

"We were going to go to their house for dinner," Ruth recalls. "I got in the car, and we were sitting in the back, and he started *staring* again! Now, I was about to be engaged, but I think I was on the rebound at that point, because I'd been engaged twice before, and I kept giving rings back! Because I really didn't want to get married. Everybody was getting married between eighteen and twenty-one, that was the thing to do. And I used to tell everyone, 'I'm not getting married until I'm *thirty.*' And, of course, that's what people are doing *today.*

"Anyway, he was sitting in the car, and instead of sitting like *this,* straight ahead, and talking to the people, he was sitting like *this,* facing me, and staring at me. So I said to Norman: 'Turn the car around.' George said, 'Why?' I said, 'I want to go home.' He said, 'Why? What'd I do?' I said, 'I can't put up with this. You keep staring, and I don't know what you're looking at.' He said, 'Well, you have entirely too much eye-shadow on.' I said, 'I do not. I have *daylight* eye-shadow on, and I have *daylight* mascara. This is *not* what I wear in the evening.' Now it was early evening; it was daylight when we started out. He said, 'What's that between your teeth?' I had a space between my two front teeth, a little space. I said, 'I'm glad you asked. That's my *personality!*' He said, 'Don't ever cut your hair.' I said, 'What *is* this? I don't like this at *all!*'

"I said, 'Now, let me study *you.* Your *nose* is almost touching your *chin!* And where's your *mouth?* And why don't you hold your shoulders back more?' Then we both burst out laughing. Well, of course, the car never turned around.

"Then we went to the apartment, and I helped Dotti Paul put dinner out, and she went into the dining room. George came out, and, all of a sudden, he grabbed me and he gave me a *kiss!* And I said, 'Wait a minute, this is running too fast here!' He said, 'Did you like it?' I said, 'I don't know if I *liked* it or *not,* but you should've asked first!' That was our first date.

"Next, he came around the night that I had a date with my fiancé, Chuck Vogel. And he wasn't supposed to be there. Chuck had come in, and he was about six-foot-four, blond, and a civilian at the time. I opened the door, and George was standing there, and I said, 'I don't have a date with you tonight!' He said, 'I know you don't, I just came over to say hello. Can I come in?' Well, he came in, and I introduced him to Chuck. George looked at him like a *bulldog.* Now, George was tall, but not as tall as Chuck, so Chuck was looking down at him—in more ways than one. It wasn't a good meeting, to say the least. In fact, I said, 'This is *ridiculous!* Can't either of you smile and be pleasant?' Anyway, George left, and he told me later, 'I feel sorry for you, dating a guy like that. You ever shake *hands* with him?' I said, 'Why would I shake hands with him?' He said, 'Try it sometime—it's like a *wet fish!*' "

When did the relationship become serious? Almost immediately, according to Ruth, but she was in no hurry, and she wanted to see how he reacted to a variety of situations. She recalls one humorous anecdote vividly:

"One night, he said, 'We're going to dinner; where would you like to go?' I said, 'The Bellevue Stratford.' A *very* expensive hotel restaurant. He sort of cleared his voice, and he said, 'All right.' So, we went to the restaurant, and we had cocktails, and looked at the menu. And, of course, the menu prices were very high. Naturally, I *knew* he couldn't afford to pay for these dinners. And I did this purposely. I wanted to see how he would handle *this* one. I mean, we were always playing games. He was always testing me in his subtle way, and I was always testing him.

"So, he was straightening his tie as he studied the menu and the prices. I said, 'What're you going to have, George?' Which was normal, in those days, when you were having a date, to get a feel for what the man wanted to spend, since the women weren't paying. He told me that he wasn't particularly hungry. He said, 'I think I'll just have a shrimp cocktail—but you have whatever you wish.' I glanced down the menu, I selected the most expensive things I could find. I could see him sweating. So I picked out an appetizer, the salad, the entrée, and I said, 'Oh, the *desserts,* look at the *desserts!*' When the waiter came for our order, George said, 'The lady will have—' I interrupted him, I said, 'You know what? I don't think I'm hungry. I think I'll just have a shrimp cocktail.' I never saw anybody look so *relieved* in all my life!"

7

THE MILITARY WEDDING was scheduled for Saturday, April 8, 1944, at three o'clock, in the nondenominational post chapel at Aberdeen Proving Ground. By 2:45, all the guests had arrived, about 100, including dozens of relatives from both families, scores of old friends, and even a good showing of officers from the post in full-dress uniforms. All had been greeted at the door of the small frame chapel by Chaplain Ira A. Kirk, who was to perform the ceremony in the East Chapel. By 2:55, everyone had taken their seats, the organist was warming up, and all was in readiness. George waited nervously in the small front room with his best man, Major Doughty. The bride was to arrive with her stepfather, Harry Merz, whom she had always considered to be her real father, because she was only four when her mother married him. At 3:05, the chaplain asked one of the officers in the last row to step outside and see if they had arrived.

They had not. By 3:15, George was visibly upset. By 3:30, whispering in the chapel had gradually changed to open conversation, squirming had changed to standing. Officers in the back rows were routinely stepping outside to see if any cars were approaching. By that time, George was becoming concerned, for the first time, that she was not going to show up.

What was happening? "Her stepfather had picked her up from a guest house on the post," George recalls. "They were en route, and she said, 'Daddy, I've got to go back and change my panties!' She said they showed through—you could see the lines on them through her wedding dress. So he took her back. After what must have been a lot of frantic changing, she finally decided not to wear *any* panties. She didn't have a damn thing on underneath her wedding gown. She wore a long white wedding gown with a train."

Ruth finally arrived with her father about 3:45. Everyone returned to their seats, and the organist started playing the traditional wedding march. George, standing near the altar with the chaplain, remembers looking at Ruth, framed in the chapel doors that faced west. "The sun was shining right through her wedding gown," he recalls, "and I got a preview of things to come! When she started down the aisle, all her old boyfriends were treading on her train!"

Ruth remembers those moments clearly: "I think that I was in shock when I started walking down the aisle. I couldn't believe that I was getting married. It was like he had utter control of me. I'd never experienced anything like this. There were so many fellows that I had been dating, and they were there in the chapel, and I had not invited them! I'll never forget standing, just before I was to go down the aisle, and they all had their *feet* on my *train!* And they were saying under their breaths: 'You said you weren't getting married until you were thirty!' And: 'Why are you getting married—you don't *know* this guy!' George was standing there next to the chaplain with an expression on his face as if to say: *When* is she going to start walking down the aisle? Well, I was *trying!* And I'm not talking about two former boyfriends, I'm talking about *several* who were holding that train! Then I started thinking: Maybe I shouldn't! Maybe I shouldn't! I was so *scared!*"

Immediately following the ceremony, with the organ playing, the newly married couple walked under the traditional military swords in the bright April sunlight just outside the chapel, then headed directly for the Officers' Club, where Mr. and Mrs. Merz had arranged a reception and buffet dinner.

"That was very pleasant," George says. "There was a band, and dancing, and we had a wedding cake, and a wonderful dinner. Afterward, as we were about to leave, we stood on the steps of the club, and Ruth threw her bouquet. Her niece Dusty caught it, as I remember. 'Dusty' is Barbara Knoblauck the daughter of Ruth's sister, Evelyn Ricker, and her husband, Renard."

George had rented an apartment not far from the post, and Ruth had furnished it, at a complex called Mars Estates, named after the Martin plant nearby that was building the Mars Seaplane. The idea was to spend their wedding night there, then drive to Atlantic City the next day for a brief honeymoon. However, the twenty-minute drive to the apartment turned into a mini-nightmare.

"We had an old Ford, a coupe," George recalls. "We had to drive twenty miles, I'd say, south, toward Baltimore. That was on US-40, I think. We got about halfway there, and the damn car conked out! Fortunately, there was a garage right across the street, so I got it over there. It took an hour and a half to get the damn thing fixed. I don't know what was wrong with the car, I think the water pump or something; this was an old klunker. And Ruth had to sit in the garage in her wedding gown!"

Understandably, Ruth remembers sitting there longer than an hour and a half. "I sat *five hours* in a garage while the car was being repaired!" she recalls, laughing. "And I was thinking: *Oh, what a horrible way to be married, sitting in this dirty, greasy garage!*"

In any event, they spent their wedding night in the rented and furnished apartment in Mars Estates, then drove to Atlantic City the following evening. "You know how you remember some things vividly?" George asks. "We were on the way up to Atlantic City, and it was dark, and we were going down this lonely two-lane road. And, all of a sudden, a deer runs out in front of the car, and I came awfully close to hitting it. If that wasn't bad enough—that was the doe—the *buck* came right after it! So I was just *inches* from hitting the buck! I didn't want to hit either of them—for a lot of reasons!"

After only one night in Atlantic City, they drove to Ocean City, and spent the last few days there. "We had a good time," Ruth remembers. "We had fun on the boardwalk. It was April, and there weren't a lot of people there, because it was still cool. Of course, there are many people who live there all year 'round. We had a room in one of the boarding houses. We walked on the boardwalk, and we were eating french-fried potatoes in cups in the rain! We had fun! That was our honeymoon. I think it was maybe three or four days; it was very short. He had to report back to duty. I got pregnant on my wedding night. He got me anchored right away!

"When we returned home to the apartment, I saw him play with the Philadelphia Nationals on weekends. He was fantastic. He was always my Knight in Shining Armor. Truly. I admired him tremendously. He was a great athlete. I also used to watch him when he performed hand-to-hand fighting, jujitsu, and wrestling. He was great. Very fast on his feet, very quick, loved every minute of it. When he was teaching, he had a lot of respect from the students. I guess part of my appeal for him was that I felt he could be stronger than I was. I needed a strong man. I'm not talking about physical strength, I'm talking about the individual. Because I can be a very strong woman, and I needed that strength to overpower me—at the right time. I needed that.

"When his mother and dad could visit us, they would come for a weekend. It was a little bit difficult getting close to a mother-in-law. Here she was with two sons, and a husband, who she ran pretty strongly, and now here comes daughter-in-law. So it was a little difficult. I admired my mother-in-law, although I didn't always agree with her as woman-to-woman. But she had a lot of intelligence that she did not get from education. She was a good woman, and I think she raised two fine sons. I understand why it was difficult, because now I'm a mother-in-law. I remember one day she said to me, 'You know, I never really approved of the marriage, Ruth.' I said, 'I know, but I never knew why.' She said, 'Well, it wasn't so much you, but I just felt you were accustomed to more, and would demand so much more from George. And, you know, George doesn't have the ability that Harry has.'

"I took a deep breath. I think, from that time on, from what I had heard from her, it was obvious she favored Harry over George. Now, don't misunderstand me. They adored their children, and it was a good family, but I felt she believed that Harry was the one. And George—well, there's George, and he'll make out all right, but he won't go very far. And I made up my mind that I was going to do nothing but *build his confidence.* I had confidence in him. And I wasn't afraid of anything. Because I *truly* had that much confidence in him. It wasn't what *I* wanted, it was what I felt *he* could accomplish. I knew he had it inside, but he couldn't let it out."

ON D-DAY, June 6, 1944, Allied forces under Eisenhower landed in Normandy, crossed France and the low countries, to reach the Rhine by November. In Italy, Rome had been captured on June 4, while a Soviet offensive that had started in June drove the Germans out of the Soviet Union and swept into Poland and the Baltic states.

In the Pacific, U.S. forces destroyed the remnants of the Japanese fleet at the battles of the Philippine Sea and Leyte Gulf, and invaded the Philippines in October 1944. The Allies crossed the Rhine in March 1944, and drove deep into Germany.

General Mark W. Clark, who took control of the U.S. ground forces in Europe in 1942, and commanded the Fifth Army during the Italian campaign in 1943–44, became a good friend of George Wackenhut after joining the corporation's board of directors in 1967, when he retired as president of The Citadel (1954–66); he served on the board until 1975, then became director emeritus.

In his book, *Calculated Risk* (Harper & Brothers, New York, 1950), General Clark gives particularly interesting insights into the war in the Mediterranean, during the time frame June-October 1944:

> The meeting with my four corps commanders on Capitoline Hill in Rome that morning of June 5 will always stand out in my mind as a kind of turning point in the Allied attack on the soft underbelly of the Axis.
>
> The meeting itself, of course, resulted in no momentous decisions. After a caretaker had appeared in response to our pounding on the door, General Roberto Bencivento, the Italian military commander in Rome and a splendid patriot, came to make us welcome. When General Truscott, General Keyes, General Crittenberger, and General Juin arrived, we quickly got down to the immediate problem of following up the badly battered Germans and giving them no chance for rest.
>
> But to me the meeting was significant because of the men present and because of decisions, made in higher echelons, that were soon to affect all of us. On that morning I felt that the corps commanders of the Fifth Army made a great team; that we had finally developed a winning combination of leaders with the desire and the ability to conquer almost any circumstances. It was interesting that my three American corps commanders—Truscott, Keyes, and Crittenberger—were originally all cavalrymen and that, in a time when the cavalry was disappearing, they had what it took to meet the stern tests of the war in the mountains of

Italy. I have already told of my admiration for Juin—there was never a finer soldier.

There was no question in my mind that day that we could soon destroy the enemy in Italy and drive him beyond the Alps and go on to whatever objective was set for us. The Fifth Army, it seemed to me, had at last become a tremendous fighting machine and its horizons were unlimited.

That, however, was not the way it worked out. For various reasons, which will appear later, our team soon was broken up and the Fifth Army was sapped of a great part of its strength. A campaign that might have changed the whole history of relations between the Western world and Soviet Russia was permitted to fade away, not into nothing, but into much less than it could have been. These were decisions made at a high level and for reasons beyond my field and my knowledge; but I do not think that it is outside my bailiwick to discuss, from a military viewpoint, what might have been achieved had the Fifth Army been kept together and strengthened in the coming months instead of being torn apart.

Such speculation, I already have indicated, comes under the heading of Monday-morning quarterbacking. It's a lot easier to see mistakes when you look back on them; but in Italy there was plenty of opportunity to see what might be done, and the possibilities were exhaustively discussed before it was decided to ignore the opportunity they offered. Not alone in my opinion, but in the opinion of a number of experts who were close to the problem, the weakening of the campaign in Italy in order to invade southern France instead of pushing on into the Balkans was one of the outstanding political mistakes of the war. . . .

"It is incomprehensible why divisions were withdrawn from the front," according to one German general, whom we interviewed after the war. "Whatever were the reasons, it is sure they all accrued to the benefit of the German high command." It was some time before the Germans understood what had happened to the American troops in Italy; for weeks the Counterintelligence Corps under the able direction of Lieutenant Colonel Stephen J. Spingarn were catching enemy agents who had orders to find out "where in hell" were various Allied divisions that were being sent to France. . . .

On September 5, 1944, when George was assigned to take a four-week course in physical reconditioning at Washington and Lee University in Lexington, Virginia, Ruth accompanied him. When he graduated on October 4, he was immediately ordered to Atlanta,

Georgia, to await reassignment in the physical reconditioning program. Ruth, being pregnant, returned to her mother's home in Drexel Hill. She joined him in Atlanta after he found a place to live.

"The day after she arrived," he says, "I received orders to report to the School for Physical Reconditioning at Fort Lewis, in the state of Washington. There was nothing to do but drive back to Philadelphia, but Ruth refused to stay there and we took the train to Seattle. It was almost a fatal mistake. The train tracks were in disrepair and the ride was a jolting one, so much so that, passing through the Dakotas, Ruth began to have labor pains. Luckily, I found a doctor on the train. He gave her some medication, told her to lie perfectly still, and that if she didn't lose the baby that night, she probably wouldn't. Fortunately, she didn't."

In the November, 1944, elections, Roosevelt ran for an unprecedented fourth term, although clearly in poor health, with Harry S. Truman as his running mate. During the war, Senator Truman (D.-Missouri) had headed a committee to stop waste in government spending. His success at that task—and his acceptability to all factions of the party—made him Roosevelt's choice. The ticket won easily, but Truman was to be vice president for less than three months.

When the Wackenhuts arrived in Seattle, George found a hotel room, then set out frantically trying to find a place to live. However, because of the huge influx of military personnel at that particular time, there simply wasn't anything to be found.

"I was desperate," George recalls, "so I pulled a sneaky deal I wouldn't have thought of under other circumstances."

In the lobby of the hotel, there was a desk where women volunteers were on duty to help servicemen, giving them any assistance possible, as well as trying to find lodgings for those with families. As George walked through the lobby and passed the desk, he overheard one of the women answer the telephone.

"Yes, Mrs. Lee," the woman said happily. "An apartment at 121 Foot Street. Well, thank you very much. We have a long waiting list and we'll send someone over to see you immediately."

George ran out of the hotel and, having no idea where he was going, spotted a small metal workshop nearby. He went in, saw an elderly man working, and asked him how to get to 121 Foot Street, where he hoped to rent an apartment. The man grinned and gave him explicit directions.

"By the way," the man told George dryly as he started to leave, "I'm Mr. Lee."

The Lee home was located in a pleasant middle-class neighborhood and George was greeted by an attractive, motherly looking woman. He was shown the basement apartment and accepted it at once.

"There's just one thing," Mrs. Lee said. "We don't allow children or animals. You don't have any children, do you?"

"No, we don't," he said, and handed her the rent.

As he was leaving, a young blond woman arrived and asked to see the apartment.

"I've just rented it to the lieutenant," Mrs. Lee told her.

The blond gave George a hard look. "Weren't you in the hotel lobby when this call came in?"

"Yes, I was."

"Well," she snapped, "that sure was a dirty trick you pulled!"

"I'm sorry, ma'am," he said. "I was desperate."

That night, back at the hotel, Ruth was able to get out of bed and go down to the dining room. This was late October and the baby wasn't due until the middle of February, but George recalls that she already looked like she was about to have triplets. As luck would have it, they bumped into the blond woman and her sergeant husband going into the dining room.

The blond stared at Ruth, then smiled at George. "Lieutenant, now I don't feel so bad about your getting that apartment."

But when they moved into 121 Foot Street the next morning, Mrs. Lee was wide-eyed when she saw Ruth, and her voice was cold. "Lieutenant, I told you we don't allow children. The last couple who were here had a child who did nothing but cry all day and half the night."

"Mrs. Lee," George said quietly, "the baby isn't due for about four months. If you want us to leave after it arrives, we will. But at least it will give me time to look around."

She agreed to those terms and they moved into the basement

apartment, which was an interesting experience in itself. "We didn't have a refrigerator," George recalls, "but merely a receptacle cut into the cold earth with two doors on it. We also cooked and heated the apartment with wood stoves, Mr. Lee cutting the wood and stacking it by the back door. Being a city boy in the country, I had a hard time adjusting. Once I put a damper on the stove and the whole apartment filled with smoke. But Mrs. Lee taught Ruth how to bake bread and make other delicacies. Then, when our daughter Janis Lynn was born on February 16, 1945, she was such a good baby that Mrs. Lee fell in love with her and didn't want us to leave."

Shortly after assuming his assignment at the school, George was transferred to Madigan Army Hospital, also at Fort Lewis, twenty-six miles south of Seattle. In 1945–46, Madigan was a 7,700-bed facility, one of the largest American military hospitals, and George was assigned to the physical reconditioning section. He had enlisted men under him and they gave exercise programs designed for three classes of patients: Those ready to return to duty, the ambulatory, and the bedridden.

There he became friendly with Lieutenant John Bonica, who was chief of the section of anesthesia, and "Man Mountain" Dean, who was a master sergeant on his staff; both men were former professional wrestlers.

Dr. Bonica, who went on to become one of the foremost anesthesiologists in the world, and eventually professor and chairman of the Department of Anesthesiology at the University of Washington's School of Medicine, was born February 16, 1917, on the small island of Filicudi, one of the seven islands that make up the Eolian archipelago, situated about thirty miles northeast of the island of Sicily. In 1925, his father Antonino decided to imigrate to the U.S. in order to give his children better educational opportunities and a more stable and democratic future. In 1928, after fulfilling the requisites for imigration, Angela Zagame Bonica, together with her son John and daughters Maria and Elisabetta, left Filicudi for Brooklyn, New York, to join her husband. Because of the severe currency restrictions of the time, the family was unable to transmit its funds, then considered a fairly large family fortune, to the U.S. Despite this, and despite the severe economic crisis of 1929, Antonino Bonica was able to keep his family comfortable through his work, first as a common laborer, and, two years later, after he had mastered the English language, as a supervisor of the American Telephone Company.

During these early years, John and his two sisters continued their studies in Brooklyn, and John continued to pursue his goal to become a physician. Tragically, his father died unexpectedly in 1932 at the age of fifty-five, leaving the family with only the meager savings they had accumulated in the four years since their arrival. John, at the age of fifteen, assumed responsibility for the family, and almost lost hope of continuing his education. However, through the sacrifices of his mother, who immediately went to work in a factory, and through his own tenacity and hard work, the family survived, and John was able to continue his studies.

During the period 1932–36, while attending high school and the first two years at Long Island University, Bonica sold newspapers in the evenings and worked as a grocery clerk on weekends, activities that earned him $20–$22 per week, which at the time was sufficient to help sustain the family. Despite the workload, he continued to be an honor student. At the same time, he became interested and active in amateur wrestling. In 1934, he won the New York City middleweight intercollegiate championship, and two years later, won the middleweight regional intercollegiate championship.

In the summer of 1936, John began his professional wrestling career to finance his last two years of college and four years at the Marquette University School of Medicine. It was no easy job to fight and remain an honor student. John would get excused from his Thursday and Friday classes, fight in different cities Thursday through Saturday nights, then hurry back to campus for his Monday morning classes. "If I didn't have three fights in a row, it was a waste of time and money," he recalls. In 1939, wrestling under the name of Bull Walker, Bonica won the light heavyweight championship of Canada, and, in 1941, held the light heavyweight championship of the world for seven months.

"John also worked his way through college and medical school by wrestling in carnivals in the summer," George says, "where he and the barker worked out a clever dodge to handle all the collegiate wrestlers who accepted a challenge to wrestle him. Most of the collegians were out of shape in the off-season, so the barker—who, along with Bonica, only got the purse if they won—would ask the crowd if it wanted three-minute or six-minute rounds. The crowd wanted longer action, of course, and yelled for the six-minute rounds. During the first three minutes, the college wrestlers would be all over Bonica, but then they would tire and he'd pin them."

Today, Dr. Bonica and his wife Emma remain good friends with George and Ruth, and John has pleasant memories of their association at Madigan Army Hospital: "We worked out in the gym where George was athletic director, and we became very good friends rapidly. Soon thereafter, we started to go to their house for German food, and they would come to our house for Italian food. Both wives were—and are—excellent cooks. The fact that we worked out regularly meant also that we were able to bring into the gym such wrestlers as Jim Londos, one of the greatest wrestlers of all time. I used to organize exhibition bouts for the soldiers, which was very much appreciated during the war. Other than that, we just had a lot of fun together.

"I should mention that, at that time, professional wrestling was a serious sport. The fact that I had eighteen orthopedic operations as the result of injuries during my professional career attests to the fact. When I was working for the circus, I used to take on twenty to thirty men in one day, in six-minute rounds, from ten o'clock in the morning to eleven o'clock at night. But I was in terrific shape, forty-six chest, thirty-five waist. I used to run around Prospect Park in Brooklyn with fifty pounds of sand in my pockets.

"When I was an intern in New York, 1942–43, I used to catch trains at four o'clock in the afternoon, wrestle in various cities in Pennsylvania, Connecticut, Massachusetts, come back at three o'clock in the morning, and be up at six-thirty for surgery with a black eye and other injuries. One morning, a director of the hospital saw me come in all banged up and he said, 'Doctor, please go to the nurses quarters and get treated, because you're going to scare the *patients!*' "

Dr. Bonica has written and edited forty-one books, has been a collaborator and contributor to sixty other books, and has written

274 scientific articles, two-thirds of which have been devoted to pain research and therapy, including acupuncture. His work has been the subject of feature articles in *Time, Newsweek, U.S. News & World Report,* and *Realites,* the prestigious French magazine. In a cover story on pain, *Time* magazine called Bonica the "founding father of pain research and treatment."

Man Mountain Dean, long a noted professional wrestler, weighed 450 pounds on the circuit, but was down to a svelte 385 when he was on George's staff, although he was known to pack away about as much Army chow as any soldier in World War II.

George smiles at one memory: "We had an early noon mealtime at 11:30 and then the regular chow at 12:30. One day I needed Dean about 11:30. I asked one of the enlisted men if he'd seen Sergeant Dean. 'Yes, sir,' the soldier said. 'He went to early chow.' So, at 12:30, I went looking for him again, and asked another man if he'd seen Dean. 'Yes, sir,' he said. 'He went to regular chow.' Every day he had to have both meals, he said, 'to keep up my strength.' He sure had it, too. Because John Bonica and I worked out with him just about every day, and he was something to behold, particularly if he fell on you."

DURING THE MONTHS that George was assigned to Madigan Army Hospital, the war in Europe was inexorably drawing to a close. On April 12, 1945, Roosevelt died suddenly, and Truman became president. Although many believed him to be unprepared, Truman took quick control of the reins of power. Seen from an historical perspective, he was in the right place at the right time. In mid-April, Mussolini and his mistress were captured at Lake Como by Italian partisans, while trying to flee the country; they were shot, and their bodies exposed to the execration of the mob in Milan. Hitler committed suicide on April 30, 1945, and the Third Reich survived the death of its founder by seven days. The signing of the unconditional surrender and the final days are perhaps most powerfully expressed by William L. Shirer in his monumental history of Nazi Germany, *The Rise and Fall of the Third Reich* (Simon and Schuster, 1960):

> In a little red schoolhouse at Reims, where Eisenhower had made his headquarters, Germany surrendered unconditionally at 2:41 on the

morning of May 7, 1945. The capitulation was signed for the Allies by General Walter Bedell Smith, with General Ivan Susloparov affixing his signature as witness for Russia and General Francois Sevez for France. Admiral Friedeburg and General Jodl signed for Germany. . . .

The guns in Europe ceased firing and the bombs ceased dropping at midnight on May 8–9, 1945, and a strange but welcome silence settled over the Continent for the first time since September 1, 1939. In the intervening five years, eight months and seven days millions of men and women had been slaughtered on a hundred battlefields and in a thousand bombed towns, and millions more done to death in the Nazi gas chambers or on the edge of the S.S. Einsatzgruppen pits in Russia and Poland—as the result of Adolf Hitler's lust for German conquest. A greater part of most of Europe's ancient cities lay in ruins, and from their rubble, as the weather warmed, there was the stench of the countless unburied dead.

No more would the streets of Germany echo to the jack boot of the goose-stepping storm troopers or the lusty yells of the brown-shirted masses or the shouts of the Fuehrer blaring from the loudspeakers.

After twelve years, four months and eight days, an Age of Darkness to all but a multitude of Germans and now ending in a bleak night for them too, the Thousand-Year Reich had come to an end. It had raised, as we have seen, this great nation and this resourceful but so easily misled people to heights of power and conquest they had never before experienced and now it had dissolved with a suddenness and a completeness that had few, if any, parallels in history.

In 1918, after the last defeat, the Kaiser had fled, the monarchy had tumbled, but the other traditional institutions supporting the State had remained, a government chosen by the people had continued to function, as did the nucleus of a German Army and a General Staff. But in the spring of 1945 the Third Reich simply ceased to exist. There was no longer any German authority on any level. The millions of soldiers, airmen and sailors were prisoners of war in their own land. The millions of civilians were governed, down to the villages, by the conquering enemy troops, on whom they depended not only for law and order but throughout that summer and bitter winter of 1945 for food and fuel to keep them alive. Such was the state to which the follies of Adolf Hitler— and their own folly in following him so blindly and with so much enthusiasm—had brought them, though I found little bitterness toward him when I returned to Germany that fall.

The people were there, and the land—the first dazed and bleeding and hungry, and, when winter came, shivering in their rags in the hovels which the bombings had made of their homes; the second a vast wasteland of rubble. The German people had not been destroyed, as Hitler, who had tried to destroy so many other peoples and, in the end, when the war was lost, themselves, had wished.

But the Third Reich had passed into history. . . .

On July 11, 1945, George was reassigned again, this time to the Convalescent Hospital in Camp Pickett, Virginia, and began another cross-country odyssey. George and Ruth had bought an old Plymouth coupe and when they loaded it with all of their belongings, the springs were down to rock-bottom, and the roads, which hadn't been maintained during the war, were full of potholes. Jan was still an infant and Ruth felt that the jolting and jouncing would be bad for the baby, so she insisted on holding her on a pillow all day long until it seemed her arms would break. When they stopped at night, Ruth would wash the diapers and George would prepare Jan's formula. The following day, they would continue the journey with diapers hanging out of the car windows to dry.

In addition to his travel time, George also had ten days leave, so they stopped in Chicago to see his brother, Harry, and his family. Then they headed for Ocean City, New Jersey, where George's parents were vacationing, and really surprised them while they were playing cards with some friends.

Doris and Bud Bailey, George's old friends from college vacations at Ocean City, had just been married, were spending their honeymoon at the shore, and bumped into George and Ruth at the beach.

"The next time we saw George and Ruth was on our honeymoon," Doris recalls. "They were also newlyweds, they'd been married for about a year. We were married at the end of July, and we spent the month of August, 1945, at Ocean City. Bud and George were still in the military. Germany had surrendered, Japan was still fighting, and we were down there when Japan finally surrendered after the atomic bomb. Because Bud's orders were that he had a thirty-day leave, then he was going to the West Coast, then he was going over to a base in the Philippines. But then everything changed and they got out of the service after that.

"I don't remember how we met at that time, whether we were on the beach and, all of a sudden, we saw them there. We certainly didn't know they were there. But then we just spent the rest of the time together. We would meet in the morning, spend all day on the beach, then go home and dress, and go out to dinner together. We were staying at Bud's father's place and they were staying at George's father's place. And those houses were quite close.

"In the service, George had taught special physical education. So, when we were down at the shore that summer, he taught Ruth how to walk along and to throw someone. Well, Ruth is small and George is big, and we would be walking along the beach and, all of a sudden, she'd just take hold of his arm and—zoom!—he'd be down on the ground, and she'd just continue to walk along calmly. He'd get up and he'd say, 'I *never* should've taught her how to do that!' It was a judo thing and it looked so easy the way she did it. We'd just be walking along and she never even changed stride. Down he'd go, wham!"

And, as both couples remember so clearly, it was while they were in Ocean City, Sunday, August 6, 1945, that the first atomic bomb was dropped on Hiroshima, killing approximately 130,000 people, and destroying 90 percent of the city. Three days later, the second one fell on Nagasaki, killing 36,000 and destroying the inner city. The following day, Japan offered to surrender, and did so, unconditionally, August 14, 1945, under the supervision of General Douglas MacArthur, aboard the battleship *Missouri*.

"By the time I reported to Camp Picket in early September," George says, "they were already beginning to discharge men on the basis of points, and on October 22, 1945, I was out, my terminal leave carrying me through until late November."

Although reliable statistics about World War II were not available for years, it was by far the largest conflict in human history, and eventually engulfed every occupied continent in the world. The toll in human life was staggering, with roughly 40 million to 60 million dead, of which at least 20 million were Russians and at least 6 million were Jews executed in Nazi concentration camps.

According to the U.S. Department of Defense, more than 16 million Americans saw combat, and U.S. casualties amounted to 1.076 million, including 405,399 dead.

8

HISTORIANS have labeled World War II as "The People's War," because no previous conflict had so directly involved the civilian populations of the combatant countries or caused them so much suffering. But if the war years brought unprecedented hardship to civilians, they also brought many tangible benefits. In both Germany and Britain, because of the fairer apportioning of food supplies, and full employment, poor families achieved a higher standard of living than they ever had before. Everywhere, including the United States, rigid price controls kept the cost of living within reasonable limits. In the U.S., for factory worker and farmer alike, these were boom years, but the new prosperity masked deeper, long-term changes. The migration from country to city was accelerated; there was increased pressure for amenities to be extended to the countryside; it was clearly demonstrated that full employment in the U.S. was not impossible; and everywhere the shared sacrifices and wider opportunities led to demand for a fairer social order after the war.

Yet, like millions of returning servicemen, finding a post-war niche proved difficult for the twenty-six-year-old George Wackenhut that autumn of 1945.

"Arriving back at my parents' home, I was almost immediately bedridden with a virulent attack of influenza," he remembers. "Lying there helplessly, I was gripped by despair because I had a wife and baby to support, I didn't have a teaching certificate in the

Pennsylvania school system, and I had already failed in a bid to get into the FBI.

"My futile attempt to land with the FBI had been made when we left Camp Pickett for the last time and started driving home to Philadelphia. While I was stationed at Madigan General Hospital, I had met an FBI agent and he told me that they started at $4,500 a year, a sum that sounded like a fortune to a first lieutenant who had barely been able to make ends meet. As we drove north, I told Ruth, 'I've thought a great deal about trying to get into the FBI. Maybe it would be wise to go home by way of Washington, so I could stop at the Justice Department and see if they'll accept my application."

Ruth agreed, they drove to Washington, DC, and George changed into his best first lieutenant's uniform before entering the Justice Department, where he was ushered into the personnel department of the FBI. It was a brief interview.

"You must be either an accountant or an attorney," he was told. "You have your bachelor's degree, so why don't you go back to school under the G.I. Bill and become an attorney?"

"Thank you, but no thanks," George said. "I've spent a great deal of time in school, I'm qualified to teach physical education, and I have no desire to become an attorney just to get into the FBI—as much as I'd like to."

That had been that, and then came his stringent bout with the flu. But as soon as he was beginning to recover, he began to write letters and send resumes to a variety of private schools and colleges throughout the state. Surprisingly, he had interviews with two schools almost immediately, both within driving distance of Upper Darby, the first with the Valley Forge Military Academy, the other with the Haverford School. Both schools made offers to begin teaching in the fall term, which started in late September.

He decided on Haverford, long regarded as one of the finest preparatory schools for boys in the country. Today, the school looks much the same as it did in 1945, except for several modern buildings, including a new gymnasium, and the surrounding athletic fields are spacious. A handsome hardcover book, *The Haverford School: A Century of Service, 1884–1984,* by Edward Lawson, gives an intriguing history of its founding:

There seems to be a difference in basic history—and why The Haverford School was founded. Some say The School was organized to teach the sons of the Haverford College professors. According to others there was a need for another boys' school in the neighborhood. Whatever the reasons, a dedicated group of Haverford residents did yeoman work in establishing a new boys' school.

Thus, in 1884, practically coinciding with the Pennsylvania Railroad's expansion and the development of the 15-mile-long Main Line as a residential and resort area, was born The Haverford College Grammar School, which metamorphosed into The Haverford Grammar School until its final change into The Haverford School.

One of the prime movers behind the development of The School was Alexander Cassatt. During the 1880s he was a resident of Haverford, a transplanted Pittsburgher who had been passed over for the presidency of the Pennsylvania Railroad in 1877 (he later headed up the Pennsy in 1899). Cassatt's wife, an equally determined person, the former Lois Buchanan, was the niece of the 15th President of the United States, James Buchanan.

They were the force. They had sons of school age, as did a number of their friends, as did a number of the professors and instructors at the college.

Then an announcement was made during the summer of 1884:

Haverford College Grammar School

There will be opened, on ninth month 23rd, 1884, a Day School for Boys, embracing Primary and College Preparatory Departments, at Haverford College Station.

It is intended to erect, for the use of the school, a commodious and convenient building, on the grounds of Haverford College. Until its completion, the School will occupy a rented building.

The School will be under the care of the Board of Managers of Haverford College, and in addition to the teachers regularly employed, PLINY EARLE CHASE, ISAAC SHARPLESS, and THOMAS NEWLIN, professors in the College, will give instruction in the School.

Arrangements now being made will secure for the School the regular service of teachers of experience and culture. Appliances will be added to make it first-class in every respect. Boys will be fitted for College or the Technical Schools.

The healthful country location, ample grounds, careful training and responsible management, will give advantages not usually possessed by schools.

The prices of tuition will be $100 a year in the Primary, and $150 a year in the College Preparatory Department. A warm dinner will be served at The School about midday; the charge for this will be extra. A few boarders will be taken into the building; the charge for board and care of these, exclusive of tuition, will be $350 a year.

Until the appointment of the permanent Head Master, the Dean of Haverford College will act as Principal, and receive entries of students.

WALTER F. PRICE, A.M. (Harvard), one of the teachers, will call upon any one thinking of entering, if notice is sent to the Dean's office.

Address,

ISAAC SHARPLESS, Dean
Haverford College, P.O., Pa.

When author Lawson reaches the section devoted to the Class of 1946, he gives us telling insights into the general atmosphere at the school immediately following the war, as in this brief excerpt:

During the late spring and summer of 1945 the war ended and peace treaties were signed. The most awful statistic of the war from The School's standpoint was that 46 alumni gave their lives in the conflict. It was to their memory that the graduating class dedicated *The Haligoluk*.

Normalcy began to return as many of the younger faculty members were demobilized and came back to the school. On campus now there seemed to be a stronger awareness of what were important issues of the day. The Polemics Society debated on such topics as "Resolved: That the United States give the atom bomb to the rest of the world." "Resolved: That Negroes should be admitted to the Major Leagues." In a formal debate at Episcopal the subject was "Resolved: That Socialism is a better form of economy than Capitalism." . . .

"I started there that fall of 1945," George says, "teaching arithmetic, geometry, and physical education. I also was soccer coach and assistant tennis coach and started a varsity wrestling team. But working in the intermediate school wasn't teaching. The main job there was being a disciplinarian. So I continued filling out applications and sending resumes to various colleges."

In the school's yearbook, *The Haligoluk,* published in the spring of 1946, there is a picture of George in the faculty section, looking every inch the academician in a dark three-piece suit, holding a book, and with the obligatory bookcase in the background. The inscription reads:

GEORGE R. WACKENHUT, B.S.   Mathematics; Athletics

> Mr. Wackenhut is the most recent addition to the Haverford faculty, having taken up his duties here upon his discharge from the Army. In fact, he taught in uniform for a week in September because he was unable to find any civilian clothes. In the fall he was assistant coach of the varsity soccer team, and in the winter he organized a wrestling team which attracted many students. He is a graduate of the University of Hawaii, and, among his other accomplishments, plays professional soccer.

George laughs about having to wear his first lieutenant's uniform during that week in September "because he was unable to find any civilian clothes." The truth, of course, is that he couldn't even begin to afford any decent civilian clothes, not even a tweed jacket, until his first paycheck. At the time, he, Ruth, and Jan were living in Ruth's parents' house at 937 Cornell Avenue, Drexel Hill, because they were almost flat broke, and they would continue to live there until the following September.

In the athletics section of the yearbook is another picture of him, looking much bigger in a white sweatshirt, even a bit mean, posing with nineteen uniformed members of the school's wrestling team. A whole page was devoted to this team with a summary of the season:

> This year, wrestling was introduced into Haverford School for the first time in several years. Mr. Wackenhut, a new master at school, is mainly responsible for the renewal of the sport. . . . Wrestling was greeted enthusiastically and a great many boys turned out. Mr. Wackenhut arranged four matches for the team. These were with Penn Charter, Episcopal, Hill School and Lower Merion. In view of the fact that this was the first year that any of the boys on the team had wrestled, the team showed up very well and deserves a lot of credit. Horatio Wood, who was

one of the bulwarks of the team, unfortunately was forced out by an illness for most of the season. Dick Lau was the heavyweight of the team at 220 pounds and did very well in the heavyweight class. Fenny Johnson wrestled in the 175 pound class and, although a little light for this class, showed up excellently. Bob Kimbrough in the 165 pound class, Charley BreMiller in the 155 pound class and Bud Wooley in the 145 pound class—all did very well, and anybody who had been on the mats with them felt as if he had been through a ringer. There were many boys who wrestled in the lighter classes and did very well. Among these were Scotty Kimmich, John Africa, Fred Fuchs and Bucky Scott. Mr. Wackenhut and the team are to be congratulated for their good season and for bringing wrestling back to school.

During the summer of 1946, George enrolled in the summer session of the Teachers College of Temple University, in downtown Philadelphia, and took three graduate courses in physical education with a view toward eventually obtaining his master's degree in education.

His official transcript from Temple:

COURSE	CREDITS	GRADE
P. Ed. Care of Injuries to Muscles, 143	2	A
P. Ed. Modern Trends in Orthopedics, 229	2	A
P. Ed. Modern Trends in Orthopedics, 205	2	A

Among the colleges that George had applied to for a teaching position was the famed Johns Hopkins University in Baltimore. Late that summer, he received a call from Dr. G. Wilson Shaffer, the director of the Department of Health and Physical Education at Johns Hopkins, and was invited to have an interview. As a result, he was offered a position as an instructor, at a salary considerably higher than he was earning at Haverford, and he was delighted to accept it.

In early September 1946, George, Ruth, and Jan (who was then sixteen months old) moved from the spacious house in Drexel Hill into a modest apartment, 6909 Dunmanway, in Baltimore, Maryland, within commuting distance to the university.

Today, Johns Hopkins University is substantially larger and more diverse than when George was an instructor and master's degree candidate, 1946–1950, but the basic educational philosophy of the university remains essentially unchanged. The unique educational philosophy of Johns Hopkins was first articulated more than a century ago by Daniel Coit Gilman, the university's first president. Gilman believed that the highest quality education must be carried out in a research environment and that the best training, whether undergraduate or graduate, takes place under the supervision of an active researcher. This belief in the inseparability of education and research has become the distinguishing feature of the university's academic programs. In both the School of Arts and Sciences and the G.W.C. Whiting School of Engineering, undergraduate education, graduate education, and the conduct of primary research are interrelated in an organic way.

The School of Arts and Sciences and the G.W.C. Whiting School of Engineering are the heart of a small but unusually diverse coeducational university. Privately endowed, Johns Hopkins was founded in 1876 as the first true American university on the European model: A graduate institution offering collegiate preparation where knowledge would be assembled and created as well as taught. The men and women engaged in scholarship and research here achieve a balance between that work and their commitment to teaching. Their active involvement as leaders in their professional fields cannot help but benefit their students.

The university now comprises six other academic divisions in addition to Arts and Sciences and Engineering. The School of Medicine, the School of Public Health, and the School of Nursing are in East Baltimore, contiguous to the renowned Johns Hopkins Hospital. The School of Advanced International Studies is located in Washington, DC, and includes centers for foreign studies in Bologna, Italy, and Nanjing, China. The Peabody Institute, recognized as one of the leading professional schools of music in the United States, became formally affiliated with Johns Hopkins in 1977. It is located in the historic Mt. Vernon section of Baltimore, approximately one mile from the Homewood campus. The School of Continuing Studies provides courses at night and during the summer on the Homewood campus and at its three off-campus centers in Columbia, Maryland, downtown Baltimore, and Montgomery County.

Johns Hopkins also operates the Applied Physics Laboratory,

midway between Baltimore and Washington, noted for its contributions to the applied sciences in a variety of fields. In addition, the Homewood campus is the site of the Space Telescope Science Institute, the ground base for NASA's Space Telescope project. The Institute is managed for NASA by AURA, Inc., a seventeen-university consortium.

The School of Arts and Sciences and Engineering (the Homewood schools) are located on a 140-acre wooded campus of great beauty in a residential area of north Baltimore. The campus was originally the Homewood estate, built for Charles Carroll, Jr., son of the signer of the Declaration of Independence. The university was given the estate in 1902 and the Faculty of Philosophy began instruction on the campus in 1915.

Despite the growth of the university academically since that time, Arts and Sciences and Engineering have maintained a relatively small student body and a low student/faculty ratio. In 1992, there were 3,042 undergraduates, 1,293 graduate students, and 94 postdoctoral fellows, with the faculty numbering 334 for both schools.

In the fall of 1946 at Johns Hopkins, George initiated a program for students who wanted to major in health and physical education. He was also head coach of the university's varsity soccer, wrestling, and track teams. In addition, on October 9, 1946, he enrolled in the university's McCoy College (the graduate school of education), taking six courses that first year, attending classes two nights a week and on weekends, determined to continue work for his master's degree in education.

The 1947 issue of the university's yearbook, *The Hullabaloo,* gives insights into George's first year as a college coach:

Soccer

In the first year of competition for the formerly mythical crowns, the '46–'47 Blue Jay soccer squad hit a new sports high in winning the Mason-Dixon Championship and the Championship of the Southern Division of the Middle Atlantic States. Possessing a precision machine from the forward wall to the goal, the Hopkins booters out-scored their opponents 24–19, winning five of their nine scheduled games, tying two, and losing only to the top-ranking powerhouses of Muhlenberg and the Navy J.V.

With an auspicious nucleus of five former varsity players, Coach Wackenhut, in his first year at Hopkins, built up a team that was undefeated in the last five games of its schedule. The Jay booters rolled over Delaware 4-0 to win their most crushing victory of the season. In the last and decisive game in the race for the Mason-Dixon Championship, the Jays eked out a thrilling 3-2 win over the booters from Washington College.

As a fitting climax to their superb performances, the great one-two punch of the Hopkins forward wall, Charlie Huang, center forward and top scorer in the conference, and Roderigo Nunez, the colorful Costa Rican inside, were given first place births on the All-Middle Atlantic States team, along with the great defensive halfback, Bill Kinling. Honorable Mention was given Armin Brunning, sparkling fullback. Officially unsung but deserving of mention were the yeoman exploits of Jerry Cooper at goal. Coach Wackenhut sees a bright soccer future ahead when a powerful varsity squad returns next year to defend their Mason-Dixon Championship. . . .

Wrestling

Coach George Wackenhut carried his winning ways from the soccer field to the mat as he led the Jay wrestling squad to one of its most successful seasons.

After dropping the opener to Franklin & Marshall early in December, the Hopkins grapplers went on to post eight consecutive victories, capped by a runaway in the Mason-Dixon tournament. In the stronger Middle States Conference, the Blue team placed second to Franklin & Marshall.

In the Mason-Dixon tournament, the Hopkins matmen captured five titles and two second places. Harry Tighe won the 121-pound crown; John Leopold, the 145; Fred Smith, the 155; Captain Francis Brown, undefeated during the season, the 175; and Jim Hunt, the unlimited. The two second-placers were Bob Latane in the 128-pound class, and Mort Disney in the 165.

In the only December match, F&M set back the Jays 20-8. January found Wackenhut's wrestlers taking the measure of Gallaudet, 31 to 5; Loyola, 26 to 6; and Swarthmore, 16 to 12. During February the Jays defeated Western Maryland, 23 to 9; Washington College, 22 to 6; Haverford, 35 to 3; and Gettysburg, 14 to 12. . . .

"Our first wrestling match that year was against Franklin and Marshall, always a powerhouse in intercollegiate wrestling," George says, "and what happened comes under the heading of 'small-world department.' The Franklin and Marshall coach, Dr. W. Austin Bishop, who at this time held a reserve commission in the Army, had been the officer in charge of special services at Washington and Lee University when I attended the special four-week course in physical reconditioning before going west to Madigan General Hospital. The Franklin and Marshall wrestling team was really good, which wasn't surprising, since Dr. Bishop had been a member of the U.S. Olympic wrestling team in the 1924 games at Amsterdam. His team defeated us, 20-8, but it wasn't indicative of the closeness of each individual match, and he was highly complimentary about what I had been able to do with my kids.

"However, despite that loss, we had a good year. Johns Hopkins was a member of the Mason-Dixon Intercollegiate Conference, and my wrestling and soccer teams both won the conference championships that year. We would also have taken the track championship, but finished second by a scant couple of points when our high hurdler, who easily was the class of the field, tripped over a hurdle and failed to finish."

One of the stars of George's 1947 track team was Leon Schwartz. At the Penn Relays, the mile relay team of Sterns, Glenner, Hurka, and Schwartz won the conference title in 3:27.8, coming within .6 seconds of the school record. At the Mason-Dixon Conference Championship, Schwartz set a new conference record when he won the quarter-mile run.

More than forty-seven years later, George was surprised when he received a letter, straight out of the blue, from Leon Schwartz, who was then vice chancellor, emeritus, University of California, Irvine. Schwartz was retired, living in Newport Beach, California, and the letter was dated May 27, 1994:

> I was in Florida last month and seeing the Wackenhut Protective Services all along the highway rest stops was a good reminder for me to

write to you. For some time I have thought that I wanted to let you know how farsighted your ideas of training were.

I was on the Hopkins track teams in the late 'forties and remember your leadership and friendship with a great deal of fondness and admiration. I also remember how I was somewhat dubious about your ideas for a weight program for runners. Of course, this is taken for granted now.

I have watched your company grow over the years and, remembering your values around discipline and control, I am not surprised at the success that you have achieved.

"My second year at Johns Hopkins is memorable to me for a number of reasons," George says, "the first of which was that our son, Richard Russell, was born on November 11, 1947, at Johns Hopkins University Hospital."

Jan Wackenhut Ward, who was two years and nine months old at the time, has vivid recollections of that particular event. "Rick's birth is my earliest memory," she says. "I think I remember my mother pregnant, but I'm not sure; that might be from pictures. We lived in an apartment on the third floor in Baltimore—in Dundalk, as I remember. It was a brick apartment and there were a lot of trees. I remember being bundled up and cold, and that probably would've been about right, because he was born in November. And I remember the day I went with Dad to pick up Mother and the baby. We were in a taxicab. I was in the back seat, and they let me hold him on the way home. That was a big treat, and I think Mother and Dad both did a very good job at incorporating me into the event. I wasn't slighted in the least, that I can remember.

"What ended up happening was that he got very ill. He contracted pneumonia. And, in those days, they had him in isolation. He was at the hospital, I don't know what hospital, but Mother would sneak me up with her to see him, because nobody under a certain age was allowed to go there. I remember seeing him. Either it was from the elevator, or peering in the window. It was like a nursery, just like when the newborns come out. He was close to a year old when he got sick. I remember how distraught they were because he wasn't eating. He was like wasting away, they would say. And, what it was, he was terribly lonely, and he missed his house and his mom and dad. I remember they were talking that he was going to die if they didn't get him home.

"And so, one day—I thought it was an illicit, sneaking-up type thing, but that might've been that *I* wasn't supposed to be there—but Mother ripped out cords and took him home. And she kept *feeding* him and *feeding* him, and *holding* him, and I helped. He was in a little high chair and he was *so* happy to be home, and he bounced right back. A whole different way of caretaking. That was a big part of my life, when he was a baby, because I was like the little mother, I would play with him and care for him."

To supplement his instructor's salary, George had retained his reserve medical unit status in the Army. During the summer of 1948, he went back in for six weeks and was assigned to the Pentagon, Washington, DC, under Colonel Cecil Morgan. Together, they worked on a revision of the physical reconditioning manual, and, in the end, Morgan voiced his extreme satisfaction at the result.

Then, during the summer of 1949, George was assigned to the Valley Forge General Hospital for thirteen weeks to work on physical reconditioning for those in the psychiatric ward. He describes that experience as an interesting "touch-and-go" assignment, because many of the patients were dangerous and he had to be extremely cautious of those with maniacal tendencies.

He was back at Johns Hopkins in the fall of 1949 when he received a call from Dr. Bishop, his friend from Franklin and Marshall. Only it was *Colonel* Bishop now. There had been a buildup of tensions, and the Korean War was in the offing. Bishop had gone back into the service and was now in charge of the Special Services Department, Adjutant General's Office.

"George," he said, "I have a spot tailor-made for you as a civilian consultant in sports and recreation for the Department of the Army."

"We discussed his offer at length," George recalls, "and the salary offered was quite a jump over what I was making at Johns Hopkins. Having a wife and two children to look out for, I finally decided to take the job. I left Johns Hopkins at mid-term in February of 1950 and reported to Fort McNair in the District of Columbia."

Meanwhile, after three years of classes at nights and on weekends, George was awarded his master of education degree at Johns Hopkins on June 14, 1949. One glance at his official transcript tells us how much he had matured academically:

COURSES	WEEKS	EXAM
1946–47 ($160)		
Phys. Ed. 9T (Administration of Physical Education)	16	A
Phys. Ed. 3T (Methods of Teaching Physical Education)	16	A
Ed. 3T (The History of Education)	32	A
Ed. 2T (Philosophy of Education)	32	P
Ed. 8T (History of Physical Education)	16	A
Ed. 1P (Introduction to Seminary)	32	P
1947 Summer		
Independent Study	13	
1947–48 ($240)		
Ed. 11P (Philosophical Backgrounds for Education)	16	S
Ed 33P (Problems in Psychological Study of Education)	32	S
Ed. 42 MEd (Statistics)	16	B
Psychology 4C (Abnormal)	16	C
1948 Summer		
Independent Research	16	
1948–49 ($120)		
5.613 (Educational Psychology: Recent Developments)	16	A+
5.614 (Modern Psychological Theories in Education)	16	A+

In those days, in the graduate schools of Johns Hopkins, professors were not required to give conventional grades (A-F), or even to give examinations. Thus, the two "P" grades that George received during his first year represent "Passed," and the two "S" grades during his second year represent "Satisfactory," as no examinations were given.

A total of thirty points were required for the master of education degree, and each course passed carried two points of credit. Counting the three graduate courses he took at Temple in the summer of 1946 that were accepted as transfer credits, George took a total of fifteen courses. He received an "A" or "A+" in nine of the fifteen. It's also interesting to note that as a member of the faculty he paid a total of only $520 in tuition for the twelve courses taken at Johns Hopkins.

John B. Whitelaw, chairman of the Department of Education, wrote George a letter dated June 4, 1949, and addressed to him at Valley Forge General Hospital, in which he said: "I am happy to advise you that you have passed the comprehensive examination satisfactorily." In a handwritten postscript at the bottom of the letter, Whitelaw added: *"You ranked #10 out of 45. Good stuff!"*

Dr. G. Wilson Shaffer, who was then director of the Department of Health and Physical Education, and who would serve nearly four decades as a faculty member, psychological counselor, and administrator, with a classroom building in his name at the Homewood campus, wrote a book titled *Recreation and Athletics at Johns Hopkins: A One-Hundred-Year History* (Johns Hopkins University Press, 1977), in which he mentioned George's accomplishments in his chapter on "The Post-War Period":

The period following the Second World War was in one way disappointing since the tremendous sports boom all over the country made it unlikely that a large number of colleges would follow Johns Hopkins' noncommercialized program. . . .

Because Gardner Mallonee was the only full-time athletic staff member remaining, it was necessary to engage a new staff. Howard Myers, who had had a very successful coaching career at St. Paul's School, was engaged to coach football, basketball, and lacrosse, sports which had been handled formerly by Mallonee, who would now be engaged in managing the full program. Marshall Turner, Myers' assistant at St. Paul's, would work again with Myers in coaching and also assist Mallonee in the required physical education program. The Hopkins Y.M.-C.A. director, Frank Wright, agreed to take over the cross-country program, and George Wackenhut, formerly of West Chester, joined the staff to coach soccer, wrestling, and track, and to play an important part in the required physical education program. . . .

During this period, George Wackenhut's soccer teams performed remarkably well. In the fall of 1946 the team won the Mason-Dixon championship and were also champions of the Southern division of the Middle Atlantic States, losing only to Navy and Muhlenberg. Charlie Huang, center forward, was the top scorer in the Conference. Huang, inside right forward Roderico Nunez, and the great defensive halfback, Bill Kinling, won places on the all-star Middle States team. Fullback Brunning and goal keeper Jerry Cooper received honorable mention.

Wackenhut's second soccer team in the fall of 1947, with most of his players remaining, won second place in the Middle Atlantic conference. His 1948 team won spirited victories over Washington College, Western Maryland, Delaware, Gettysburg, and Towson Teachers, but were defeated 3-2 by Loyola in the Mason-Dixon championship game. Bill Kinling, Bob Lang, Rudy Behonneck, Harry Tighe, and Malmut Tulezogler carried the burden of the team by consistently producing when the chips were down and the tension was highest. . . . Captain Bill Kinling starred for his fourth year and was chosen as an All American, and Harry Tighe was selected as a member of the All Maryland team. During this year it was decided to have a freshman team and to refuse to allow freshmen to play on the varsity team.

Wackenhut also coached three wrestling teams and was even more successful with wrestling than with soccer. In the 1946–47 season, after losing the first match to Franklin and Marshall, the team won eight straight matches to score a runaway victory of the Mason-Dixon conference, but because of the early loss to Franklin and Marshall, had to be satisfied with second place in the Middle Atlantic conference. Harry Tighe won the 121-pound championship; Captain Francis Brown, at 175 pounds, was undefeated; and John Leopold at 145, Fred Smith at 155, and Jim Hunt, unlimited, scored impressive victories throughout the year. The 1947–48 team had an almost identical record, losing the first match and winning all others and another championship. Harry Tighe, at 121 pounds, and Francis Brown won Mason-Dixon championships; and Bob Lang and Bill Schaefer were outstanding. In the following year, featuring five Mason-Dixon wrestling champions, Tighe, Phillips, Smith, Leopold, and Brown, the wrestling team won still another championship, losing only one match to the University of Maryland. Individual honors went to Brunsman at 121 pounds, Harry Tighe at 136, Ernie Leopold, who was undefeated, and Howard Goodrich and Fred Smith were co-holders of the "Wrestler of the Meet" at Gettysburg.

In the 1949–50 year, Wackenhut left the University early in mid-term to accept a physical education post in the Army, and Ed Czekaj finished the year as coach. The team went on to another championship with Harry Tighe, now at 145 pounds and again undefeated. Brunsman was again a winner in his four bouts at 121 pounds, and Cromwell had an excellent record at 128 pounds. . . .

When George left the faculty at mid-term in February, 1950, and reported to Fort McNair in the District of Columbia, it necessitated moving the family from Baltimore to another apartment in Alexandria, Virginia (1023 Wakefield Drive), but long-suffering Ruth was well accustomed to packing by this time.

Jan, who had just turned five and entered nursery school, recalls several events clearly: "I remember 1023 Wakefield Drive in Alexandria. It was exciting, because it was across the Potomac, and we'd go to the Capitol building and visit, and I went to a little nursery school called Evergreen. We used to sing songs, Dad would always try to kid and sing the songs with me: 'Evergreen, Evergreen, boys and girls at play,' that sort of thing. I remember the apartment and playing in the back with Rick. Two big memories there. One year, Mother got very ill; I don't know what happened, it might've been the flu or something. But she couldn't cook, shop, anything, and they hired a woman to take care of us. She was a German *army sergeant,* is how I would explain her. She had an accent and didn't speak English as I knew it. She was very gruff, a real mean lady. She made us eat turnip greens! So that didn't last very long.

"The other thing, on one of our tours to the Capitol building, we had purchased these little bells. It was just a little bell that you would ring, but on the top of the bell was the Capitol building, as the handle. So it was very tall and thin and pointed. It was a Saturday afternoon; Dad used to stay at home on Saturdays. And he and Rick would wrestle. Dad taught wrestling and was trying to teach Rick real early on. We were all in this little living room and the television was on. Dad was squatting in front of the television, and Rick made this beeline run over to him and climbed up on his back. And Dad must have been off-balance, and fell back, and landed on the sharp handle of this bell. Toys were all around. All I saw was his face in complete agony. He couldn't talk. When he stood up, we could see that the handle had gone all the way into his back. He was pointing to it, to Mother, for her to pull it out. And she couldn't. Just couldn't pull it out. And I wanted so much to help. We went into the bathroom, and he pulled it out himself, and I remember just crying, just wanting to help. So he handed me the bottle of Mercurochrome—remember that red stuff that stunk?—to clean the area. The next thing I knew, I woke up in the bathtub with ice cubes all around—I had *fainted!* My little way of helping. And I remember being in the bed, and they were all very nurturing, and I had Popsicles. To this day, if I see needles and blood, I get real light-headed."

Working as a civilian consultant in sports and recreation for the Department of the Army under Dr. Bishop at Fort McNair was an enjoyable experience for George, and the increased income helped considerably. But then the Korean War erupted four months later, on June 25, 1950, and he began to get constant calls from Colonel Cecil Morgan in Washington, DC, the man he had worked for at the Pentagon in the summer of 1948. He remembers one call vividly.

"Where do you want to be sent?" Morgan asked him.

"What do you mean, where do I want to be sent?"

"Well," Morgan told him, "you're the only reservist in the entire District of Columbia Military District who has the qualifications we're going to be looking for in reconditioning officers."

"You've got to be *kidding!*"

"It's no joke," Morgan said. "Count on it. You're going to be called back into service the first time they come to DC for a quota. You're it, George."

Colonel Morgan kept trying to pressure him from time to time, as the war gradually escalated, and the last thing in the world George wanted was to go back into the Army as a first lieutenant, even though they might have jumped him a grade. He found himself thinking about the subject constantly. Then a thought occurred to him. His reserve medical unit met periodically and the adjutant of the unit was an attorney in the Department of Justice. So he approached the attorney at the conclusion of one of their meetings.

"You know," George explained, "I once tried to get into the Federal Bureau of Investigation, but at that time an applicant had to be either an accountant or an attorney. Have they made any changes in those requirements?"

"Funny you should ask," the man said. "I understand that the Bureau hasn't been able to get enough lawyers and accountants to apply, and they're in some sort of a bind because of a speeded-up program due to the Korean War. I'll check it out, but I think that now an applicant only has to be a graduate of an accredited university, and has to pass some oral, written, and physical tests."

George's hopes soared. "Who do I call to find out?"

"Call me tomorrow and I'll have all the information for you."

The attorney kept his word and his initial understanding had been accurate. The requirements had changed, due largely to the Korean War, and the FBI was now accepting applications from college graduates who were not accountants or attorneys.

George went to the Justice Department and applied immediately. He passed his oral, written, and physical examinations just prior to Christmas, 1950, and received orders to report for FBI training on January 11, 1951.

In the interim, Colonel Morgan was still breathing down his neck and George knew he'd have to sweat out the days until January 11, because until then he could be recalled by the Army. So he decided to turn to his friend Colonel Austin Bishop.

"Austin, I have a problem," he said. "As you know, I'm in the medical service reserves, and I'm in this district where I might be one of the first men called back in. As you also know, I have a wife and two children, and now I have an appointment to the FBI, which will let me take better care of them than I could if I were a first lieutenant in the Army. So, naturally, I don't want to be called back into service now. It's no place to be unless you want to make a career out of it, which I don't. What do you suggest?"

Colonel Bishop smiled. "Leave it to me, George. I'll just have you transferred to the Adjutant General's Department."

Bishop did exactly that, within a matter of a few days, and George walked the papers through himself.

When it was *a fait accompli,* the transfer papers naturally wound up on Colonel Morgan's desk, as an advisory to his department. He called George one last time, made just one statement, and hung up.

"George," he snapped, *"that was a real dirty trick!"*

One of the standard requirements for all FBI candidates in those days was that you had to have the recommendation of an individual who was presently serving in the FBI. The only person George knew to be in the FBI was Jay Smith, his former classmate at West Chester State Teachers College, who was at that time a special agent assigned to the Philadelphia office. So George called him and asked for a recommendation.

Jay Smith remembers it well, and recalls how he went through the same process of recommendation and background investigation. "After the war," he says, "I was out of the service, I was fumbling around, as most returning servicemen were, and this is where George comes into my life again. I got out in 1945 and had four or five jobs, then I taught school for about three months. I was making $200 a month. Married. As a lieutenant in the Navy, I was making significantly more than that. By chance, I was walking down Chestnut Street in Philadelphia and ran into a person who knew me from high school; I didn't know this individual.

"He stopped me and told me who he was, and we chatted. He asked me what I'd done, and I said, 'Well, I'm just out of the Navy.' He said, 'Did you ever go to college?' And I said, 'Yes.' He said, 'Would you have any interest in becoming an FBI agent?' 'Well,' I said, 'I'd love to be an FBI agent, but I'm not a lawyer and I'm not an accountant; I'm not qualified.' He said, 'Well, you really are—now.' What I didn't know, and subsequently learned, is that immediately after the war, the FBI lost about 35 to 40 percent of its agents, because they'd jumped into the FBI to avoid going into the service. Everybody jumped wherever they could. The FBI's usual complement was somewhere around 5,000, so they lost about 2,000 agents. There weren't any lawyers or accountants. Anybody who was a lawyer was working—quickly. So they had a special designation, which was special agent/employee. Which no one knew about. This was Hoover's way of moving the qualifications around to suit himself.

"In any event, I applied. This individual said, 'I'll recommend you.' Then he told me, 'The FBI is engaged in rather aggressive, selective recruiting. We've all been asked to go back through our college yearbooks and to contact those people that we thought might be suitable.' Well, I didn't think I was suitable, but I didn't tell him that. Then the investigation started. But Hoover, who was an administrative genius, was also very savage. He really was. His standard was perfection. He wasn't kidding. It was a tough deal. If you were less than perfect, you had no credit in the bank to draw upon. You were just flat-out, you had no credit.

"The way the investigation works, wherever you've been—you may have worked in eight cities—an agent in each of those cities does that part of your investigation. It's not one agent running all over the place. But I'd spent almost all of my life in Philadelphia, so one agent did most of my investigation.

"He went out to West Chester and he ran into *Deean* Killinger! Dean of Men. This is ironic and amusing. Dean Killinger, the great, gentle educator. He couldn't speak ten words without swearing. He was almost illiterate. Chewed tobacco. Spit it all over me in the shower. Oh, yeah, real nice fella. So, this agent went to various faculty people who were still there, almost all of them were, and all of them were very pleasant. Then he got to Killinger. Killinger said that I was probably the worst person who ever attended the college. Worst individual who ever graduated. He said, 'Over my objections, mind you!' And he was so vociferous and so stupid in these remarks—and the only reason I know this, I was able to see my file, subsequently, when I came back to Philadelphia as an agent. I was transferred a number of times. I wasn't supposed to see my file, but I had a friend who got my file.

"Well, the agent was so shocked by this testimony from Killinger that he sent a report to the Bureau that said, in effect, that this testimony was so severe that he felt it could not have been objective. Therefore, unless he was advised to the contrary, he would proceed with the investigation and widen his scope at the university to make certain that the Bureau had a fair appraisal of the applicant. Which he did. And he received good appraisals. Therefore, they rejected Killinger's comments as prejudiced.

"So, I got in the FBI, in spite of Killinger, and I went through training, as George did. I went to Washington, then to Richmond, then to Louisville, and finally I got to Philadelphia. I was the first person from West Chester who was ever appointed to the FBI. After Hoover recruited enough agents, he went back to the old rules. I guess I'd been in the Bureau about a year and a half, and it was still 'special agent/employee.' After a year, Hoover would drop the 'employee' designation, and you'd be a special agent. He could always say that he never hired anyone as a special agent who had not been a lawyer or an accountant.

"Well, George called me, and he said, 'Jay, I understand that you're in the FBI.' I said, 'Yes, I am, George, I sure am.' He said, 'I would like to become an agent; I don't want to be involved in education any longer.' I told him, 'George, it's tough.' He said, 'Well, I've been told it's tough, but I also know that I have to have someone recommend me who's in the FBI.' I said, 'George, you are one of the *only* people that I can *imagine* who I would recommend for the FBI!' I had a number of people who asked me to recommend them; one was Doug Connelly, my dear friend, and he was rejected.

"I recommended George, and I couldn't have been more right, obviously. I had nothing to do with his investigation, I just wrote a memorandum saying that he would like to become a candidate, and that I would recommend him without qualification. I don't know how many people I can say that about, except George, and I was very happy to do it. Subsequently, with no surprise to me, he was investigated, passed, no problem, went to the training school, graduated, and was appointed an agent.

"The Bureau taught me to speak; they should've taught me to speak *softer*. I became a speechmaker for the FBI, among other things. I became the supervisor for all communist activities in the eastern half of Pennsylvania. I had fifty agents working for me. I had a nice, solid ulcer. If you didn't have an ulcer in the FBI, you weren't loyal! But they wanted to transfer me to Washington to take over the espionage desk, which meant that my partner would be John Edgar Hoover. At that desk, you would last there maybe ten or twelve weeks, and then you were finished, because Hoover was always second-guessing everybody. At this point, I resigned from the FBI, rather than transfer to Washington, DC.

"I had a number of changes, and then, at the age of about fifty-four—and this is the thing that I will never, ever, forget about George—I resigned from Kiwi. At that point, I was executive vice president, acting president, of Kiwi Polish Corporation. It was an Australian corporation with an American division. I'd been with the company for twelve, thirteen years, it was the longest I'd been with a company. I'd taken the company from a million dollars in sales to twenty million dollars in sales. Esquire, our primary competitor, had been twenty million, and they wound up with three million. So we took it all from them. All my life, I seemed to get into conflict situations. I wanted to do it one way and they wanted to do it another. So I told them to shove it. Just like that, at the age of fifty-four.

"So then I wondered what I was going to do. I called George. I owned stock in George's company at that time, I was very proud of him, I read about him in the annual reports. I called and I said,

'George, I don't know if you'll even remember me, Jay Smith.' He said, 'Sure, of course I remember you.' And I said, 'Well, I'm in a situation now where I left a company rather suddenly, and I'm looking for employment. I wonder if you would have any spot for a former FBI agent who also has a number of years of marketing and administrative knowledge.' He said, 'Jay, I'd love to have you come down, fly down at my expense, and we'll meet.' I did. I went down to Coral Gables and I met with George and he couldn't have been more warm, friendly, gracious, kind, understanding, all those things. He said, 'Jay, I've never forgotten that you played a role in my entering the FBI. I'll never be able to repay you for that, but now I may have an opportunity to do something for you.'

"We went through a series of jobs that he thought might be of interest to me, all of which were quite attractive, and I was overwhelmed by his kindness and his response to me, when I was obviously in a rather difficult position at age fifty-four. One job he asked me to consider was traveling around the world developing his international operations. I remember saying, 'George, I travel so much, I don't know if I want to do that much traveling.' And he said, 'Well, you pick any of my offices, and I'll transfer the manager and put you in charge.' I was again overwhelmed. He said, 'Well, if you need me, I'm always here.' I was touched deeply then, and I'm touched now.

"As it developed, I found other things that I thought were more suitable for me, but the thought of his generosity and his kindness will remain with me always."

9

THE BUREAU OF INVESTIGATION, a branch of the Department of Justice, was founded in 1908, during the administration of Theodore Roosevelt, as an investigative agency working against the trusts and monopolies of that time. In 1924, a young attorney named John Edgar Hoover was appointed to take control of the Bureau and reorganize the agency that had been unable to deal in a satisfactory manner with espionage during World War I, or with the anarchists in the years afterward. Hoover established high standards, strict training, and uniform operating procedures for his agents, and the success of the new regime became apparent when the newly named Federal Bureau of Investigation began its campaign against gangsters like John Dillinger, "Baby Face" Nelson, and "Pretty Boy" Floyd in the 1930s. The Bureau's jurisdiction was extended at that time to cover kidnaping, bank robbery, and extortion.

During World War II, the FBI also became an intelligence agency, working with the Army and Navy to combat espionage, sabotage, and subversion, a responsibility it maintains even in peacetime. After the war, FBI investigation uncovered communist activities such as Dr. Klaus Fuchs's plot to steal the secrets of the atomic bomb. More recently, the Bureau has become involved in the struggle for civil rights, the war against organized crime, and investigations into political corruption.

Dozens upon dozens of books have been written about the FBI

since its inception more than eight decades ago, but one of the most recent, titled simply *The FBI*, by Robert Lovegrove and Tim Orwig (Exeter Books, 1989), offers particularly interesting and incisive research into the Bureau's earliest days:

> The trail started in 1871, when the United States Congress for the first time earmarked federal dollars for the "detection and prosecution of crimes against the United States." That first $50,000 allotment went to the new Justice Department, an agency created only the year before and placed under the administration of the United States attorney general. With the allocation, Attorney General Amos T. Akerman organized his department for prosecutory work and appointed one detective, or "special agent," to conduct limited investigations for the prosecutors. All other detective work required by the department was either handled by United States attorneys and federal marshals in the field offices around the country, farmed out to investigators of other government agencies (particularly the Secret Service agents of the United States Treasury Department) or assigned to private detectives hired on a case-by-case basis.
>
> Throughout the 1880s, United States attorneys general continued the practice of borrowing or hiring detectives from outside the Justice Department to meet the growing caseload. Attorney General Benjamin Brewster introduced the practice of routinely using men from the private Pinkerton detective agency. This practice alarmed some lawmakers, and in 1892 Congress passed a law prohibiting the use of private investigators for government work. The Justice Department was forced to take its investigative assignments to an assortment of bank examiners, customs inspectors, and, in most cases, the Secret Service men in the Treasury Department.
>
> As the investigative workload of the Justice Department grew, it became painfully apparent that relying on a makeshift setup of borrowed detectives was not getting the job done. By 1906, Congress approved the use of up to 32 Treasury Department Secret Service agents for temporary Justice Department assignment, subject to the year-to-year funding of the House Appropriations Committee. The Secret Service, which had been established to investigate counterfeiting "and similar related outrages" (and, after 1907, was tasked with providing physical security for the President of the United States), was haphazardly becoming an interagency detective pool.

Not only were Washington-based government prosecutors stymied by the lack of in-house investigators, but United States attorneys and federal marshals in the field were severely hampered by the detective-hiring restrictions. Indeed, the sluggish bureaucratic process of manning investigations weighed heaviest on the Justice Department men in the outposts farthest from the nation's capital. Cumbersome procedures required that all investigators be assigned from Washington, making it next to impossible for prosecutors in the hinterlands to move quickly in gathering evidence. But whenever a United States attorney or a federal marshal asked to be allowed to hire his own detectives, they were denied on the grounds that there was no precedent for authorizing them to pick their own investigators.

The twentieth century brought the country a vigorous, reform-minded president intolerant of corruption and impatient with bureaucratic sludge. But when President Theodore Roosevelt began advancing his trust-busting agenda in Washington, he immediately butted heads with a suspicious Congress, many of whose members took a dim view of "that damned cowboy" and his energetic efforts at reform. They were particularly alarmed when Roosevelt's beacon of reform was shined on government officials. . . .

Roosevelt's attorney general, Charles Joseph Bonaparte, capitalized on the sleazy reputation of the detective profession as part of his argument in favor of a professional class of government investigators to be hired and trained by the Justice Department. For whatever combination of reasons, the fear of a secret police ran deep in the Congress, and the votes were there to block, at least temporarily, Bonaparte's efforts to establish in the Justice Department an agency for professional government investigators.

In 1908, Congress took the additional step of blocking the appropriation of funds to the Justice Department "for any person detailed or transferred from the Secret Service," thus plugging the department's last source of investigative manpower. The bill was to take effect at the beginning of the 1909 fiscal year. In a 6 May 1908 editorial, *The New York Times* castigated Congress for "having become the tools of thieves." President Roosevelt, too, was outraged. "Only criminals need fear our detectives," he wrote to a congressman.

But Bonaparte did not retreat. Using funds already in his department budget, the attorney general hired nine Secret Service officers who had worked primarily on Justice Department cases. The men were transferred to the Justice Department payroll just days before the appropriations bill took effect. Bonaparte had met the letter of the law, but had also gotten the trained detectives he needed.

The new men joined the Justice Department's 14 special agents and examiners to form a permanent subdivision under the direction of Chief Examiner Stanley W. Finch. A year later, Bonaparte's successor, Attorney General William W. Wickersham, christened the new unit the Bureau of Investigation. In 1935, under the leadership of J. Edgar Hoover, it would formally become the Federal Bureau of Investigation. . . .

In 1935, Hoover also started the National Police Academy in Quantico, Virginia, which has been called the FBI Academy since 1940. Today, the Academy is a huge ultramodern complex, but it was relatively small when George reported there for training on January 11, 1951.

In 1926, Ruth's stepfather, Harry Merz, bought a winter home in the old and fashionable Shenandoah section of southwest Miami, and the family spent winter seasons there from the time Ruth was four years old. Shortly after Harry died in the autumn of 1946, Bessie Merz moved into the home in Miami as a full-time resident. Before George reported to Quantico, he took the family to the Miami home for a short vacation, and Ruth and the children stayed with her mother when he reported for three weeks of training in firearms and defensive tactics.

"Our instructor was George Zeiss," George says, "a huge man, who was something of a legend in the FBI even then. But back there at Quantico in 1951, to me, he was just another large man who didn't appear too fearsome to a fellow who had wrestled almost daily with Man Mountain Dean."

When George A. Zeiss retired from the FBI on December 31, 1977, after more than thirty-five years in the Bureau, he was indeed considered a "living legend." Born in Philadelphia, July 31, 1921, Zeiss graduated from Yeadon High School in Yeadon, Pennsylvania, in 1940, and was working for J.T. Ryerson Steel Company in Philadelphia when he was accepted by the FBI to work at its headquarters in Washington, DC, on April 13, 1942.

His first FBI assignment was in the identification division, fingerprint section. Within a year, he was transferred to the training division at headquarters, where he was a physical education instructor, and also taught the art of self-defense to new agents, National Academy students, and conducted a training program for FBI agents to train local, county, and state law enforcement officers. This training consisted of techniques used in the carrying out of an arrest, such as personal search, handcuffing, and transporting prisoners. While assigned to Washington, he completed his law studies at Southeastern University. He was later transferred to the FBI Academy in Quantico, VA, where, at the time, he was the only physical education instructor on the staff. He continued to teach the same subjects that he taught at headquarters, but added firearms training to the list.

"In those days, the Academy was just a red brick building," Zeiss recalls. "First floor was all classrooms, plus a kitchen and a dining room. Second and third floors were bedrooms, and could accommodate about 300 men. The basement of the building, what we called a gymnasium, was a long, narrow room. And there was a gun-cleaning room and a gun vault down there. The range was about a mile from the building, and each instructor drove his class out there in our little Ford bus."

While instructing new agents in the gym on the art of self defense, he first met special agent trainee George Wackenhut.

"I recall that his class was unusually large, eighty men, so we had to break it up into two classes of forty each," Zeiss says. "The way it worked, the people in the class would report to Washington on a Monday morning, go through indoctrination and so forth up there, then they would come down by bus to Quantico, usually that Monday night. Which meant that I would meet them in the gym for the first time on Tuesday. Working alone, as I always did, I always had to call on a class member to assist me. I would request that the biggest, strongest man in the class step forward. The class practically *pushed* trainee Wackenhut forward, because they looked on him as their leader, and if I could disarm George Wackenhut, they would believe disarming was certainly a possibility. He told me years later that he wanted to kill me that day, because I embarrassed him in front of the group. But, as I used to tell all of the classes after the demonstration, 'But for the will of the Lord, any one of you would've been up here, because we do this every Tuesday afternoon.'

"We had some revolvers that were beyond economical repair, and we had the gunsmith rig them up. He'd take the firing pin out and he'd replace the grips with bright-red grips, so these weapons would stand out from the regular service revolver. After showing the class that this weapon could not possibly fire ammunition, I then placed it in the student's hand—in this case Wackenhut's hand—and had him pull the trigger a few times as he held the weapon close to my body, to show that he had no fear, no hesitation.

"Now you have him give a sharp command: *'FBI—put your hands up!'* And, of course, I put my hands up. I tell him that if I should try to grab the gun, he should pull the trigger—*instantly*. Then, after that, I'm looking at the class, I'm talking to the class, I have my hands moving around, and every time I'm making a point to the class, I'm pointing with one hand and pushing the gun away with the other. Well, of course, he doesn't expect me to do that. So I look at him and I say, 'What's the *matter,* son? Don't you understand? You're supposed to pull the *trigger!*'

"Now I go back to the same type of demonstration, talking, moving my hands, grabbing the piece from time to time, and shoving it aside—each time glancing at Wackenhut and saying, 'What's the *problem,* son? Do you understand your instructions?' At this point, he's getting very upset with me. All he wants to do is fire that thing at me and win the favor of the class. Well, the only problem is, the class is rolling on the floor with laughter. After a while, then, I'd say, 'Well, I'll tell you what, maybe it was unfair: I kept my hands moving, I kept talking, maybe I was distracting you. So, from now on, I'm going to put my hands down close to my sides. I'm not going to move a muscle until you tell me.'

"So he'd shout: *'FBI—put your hands up!'* And, of course, as I bring my hands up, I make a little *motion* toward the gun, then put my hands up—but it's too late, he's pulled the trigger! They *always* pull the trigger! With this, the class will laugh, because he can't believe he's done it. Now you explain to him, you say: 'Son, that badge they gave you yesterday is not a *hunting license!*' Of course, the class roars at that. So then, the next time, he's not going to pull that trigger if *hell* freezes over. So, the next time he gives the order, I go straight for the gun and disarm him easily. I did it routinely every week!"

In November 1951, Zeiss was transferred from the Academy to Birmingham, AL, then to New Haven, CT, where he continued to train agents of the FBI, along with local law enforcement officers, and handled all fugitive matters in those two states. One of the finest marksmen the FBI ever produced, he returned to Quantico in 1954, where he eventually became the special agent supervisor in charge of the firearms range. From 1942 through 1977, he trained all special agents of the FBI, literally thousands of men. Aside from J. Edgar Hoover, "Big George" Zeiss, as he was called, was probably the most widely known FBI agent in the world. He has been honored by law enforcement agencies throughout the world, including the French *Sureté,* and Scotland Yard's elite group known as the "Murder Squad."

During his assignment at the FBI Academy, he was often called upon to put on firearms demonstrations. Some of the techniques included firing a .38-caliber revolver at the edge of a playing card, splitting the card in half with one bullet. Another shot that he was well-known for was to use the reflection in a diamond ring to hit targets hanging behind him. Still another accomplishment was to fire a .38-caliber revolver at the edge of an ax, splitting the bullet into two segments that would break two targets; high-speed photographs of this sharpshooting technique appeared in national magazines, including *National Geographic.*

He also served as technical consultant (and actor) for the major motion picture *The FBI Story* (1959), with Jimmy Stewart and Vera Miles, and was technical consultant for the filming of *The FBI* television series (1965–74), with Efrem Zimbalist, Jr. In June 1968, Zeiss was specially selected by J. Edgar Hoover to return James Earl Ray from London, after Ray was arrested in England as a suspect in the murder of Dr. Martin Luther King, Jr.

Following his retirement from the FBI at the end of 1977, Zeiss joined The Wackenhut Corporation, September 25, 1978, as director of special service sales, and later became vice president of client relations. He celebrated his fifteenth anniversary with the company in 1993.

During his training at the Academy, George Wackenhut clearly recalls meeting J. Edgar Hoover for the first time. He smiles and shakes his head at the memory: "One of our counselors kept telling us, 'You're going to meet Mr. Hoover one of these days real soon, and there are two things he can't abide. One is to see an agent wearing a sports jacket. The other is to see an agent wearing a bow tie.' He paused and then suggested, in what was a thinly veiled order: 'Over the next few days, until you meet him, be sure you wear regular neckties and ordinary business suits.'

"The problem for me was that I didn't have that many civilian clothes. Several days passed, and I wore my suits until they looked shabby and unpressed. So there was nothing else to do, this one particular day, except to wear a sports jacket and bow tie. And, of course, that was the day when our counselor told us, 'Gentlemen, today we meet Mr. Hoover.'

"I was in a panic as we lined up in preparation for walking up to him, introducing ourselves, and shaking his hand. I thought: If he sees me dressed like this, I'm *doomed!* So I decided that when it came my turn, I'd grab his hand and squeeze it so hard he wouldn't see anything but *stars!* Or, at least, he wouldn't pay too much attention to what I was wearing.

"The line moved along in front of him and, just before it came my turn, I saw a slender man standing beside him giving me a narrow-eyed stare. This was Clyde Tolson, the associate director, who was Mr. Hoover's right-hand man and constant companion. But then I was standing in front of Hoover, the man who had fashioned the FBI into one of the world's greatest law enforcement agencies, and I gripped his hand with all the power I could muster. He smiled broadly, so I think I made some kind of an impression on him—or at least on his hand. Then I was moving on down the line, and my ruse must have worked, because I never heard anything about having appeared in a sports jacket and a bow tie."

Following three weeks of training in Quantico, George's class was sent to FBI headquarters in Washington to continue training during

February and March. This was convenient for George, because he was able to stay in his rented apartment in Alexandria. However, when he graduated on April 7, 1951, he was assigned to the Atlanta office, and this, of course, necessitated moving the family again. Ruth was uncomplaining, as usual, but this was the ninth move in their first seven years of marriage.

Shortly before graduation, George received a letter from Special Agent in Charge (SAC) John C. Bills of the Atlanta office, dated March 27, 1951, welcoming him to his first assignment, telling him the names and addresses of the hotels in town that offered special rates to Bureau agents (average of $4.50 for a double bed, $5.50 for twin beds, and $1.50 for a child requiring a cot), and even offering assistance to help move his furniture to Atlanta.

When Special Agent George Wackenhut, employee number 937640, arrived at the Atlanta office in mid-April, 1951, it was situated in a brand-new six-story building at 805 Peachtree Street that was highlighted in the August, 1951, issue of *The Investigator,* a black-and-white magazine published monthly by the FBI Recreation Association, and that included seven pages of photos of the new office and staff. George looks happy sitting at his desk in the open and brightly lighted "Agents' Room."

The first commendation contained in his official FBI file is dated April 19, 1951, in the form of a short memo from SAC John C. Bills:

> I want to take this opportunity to thank you for the splendid cooperation in voluntarily assuming additional overtime in reference to the AIKEN M. STANTON et al, CASE.
>
> As you well know, it is the esprit de corps and willingness to pitch in when a job is at hand which makes our organization the organization it is today.

But George's first important assignment revealed to him what was, at that time, a basic flaw in FBI training. "The manual they used then was a thing that, like Topsy, just grew," he remembers. "As new methods were devised, they simply were added to the back of the manual, and thus it lacked cohesion." It was a fault that he took great pains to avoid when he helped put together the first manual for The Wackenhut Corporation.

"On the first actual FBI report that I wrote, I committed an administrative sin," he remembers. "I left out the term 'armed and dangerous' from the synopsis of the report. It was important from the standpoint that the next agent involved in the case should be forewarned that the suspect might be armed and dangerous. Being new to something that later became second nature, I inadvertently omitted the phrase. And my supervisor didn't notice it. But the inspectors caught it, and so did we, both of us receiving a letter of censor. Bureau policy at that time was that if you received a letter of censor, your pay raises were held up. Which is what happened to us, although the raises in those days weren't of the size to pay for a weekend at the Waldorf."

The censor was in the form of a letter addressed to George, signed by J. Edgar Hoover, and dated August 25, 1951:

Dear Sir:

During the recent inspection of the Birmingham Division it was observed that you submitted a report under date of May 29, 1951, in the case entitled "Lawrence P. O'Donovan, WAS.–Fugitive–Interstate Transportation of Stolen Property," in which you set out leads for an auxiliary office which had no previous information regarding this case, and that you failed to reflect in your report the fact that the subject was reportedly armed and should be considered dangerous.

The possible consequences which could result from an omission of this nature should be apparent to you and it is accordingly essential that you make sure there will be no recurrences of an error of this type on your part in the future. If you should fail to do this and again be responsible for a mistake such as this, it may be necessary to take more severe administrative action.

"Then came the first arrest that I was in on," George says, "and I was determined that if I got my hands on him there was no way he was going to escape. This determination stemmed from an incident that happened with another agent in Atlanta shortly after I arrived. He had gone on what was called a 'road trip' to pick up a U.S. Army deserter, and the agent found the soldier at the man's mother's house. The AWOL pleaded with him, 'Please let me go to my room and change from civilian clothes to my uniform. It won't go so hard on me if I go back in uniform.' The agent agreed. The soldier went into his room, changed, and went out the window. Then he turned himself in at the base, wearing his uniform. The base commander called the agent in charge of the Atlanta FBI office and told him about the escape. However, the agent had already falsified his daily report, not wanting it known that a prisoner had escaped from his custody. The agent was discharged with prejudice, making it difficult for him to get a job anywhere else. So I decided right then that anyone I apprehended was going to stay apprehended.

"Actually, the first arrest in which I participated came off rather tamely. An informant told us that a certain man on our fugitive list was in the city and could be found at a designated place. We nailed him on a downtown street, two of us taking him from behind and two from the front. It was all done so quietly and quickly that none of the passersby knew anything had happened."

Jan was six years old that year and in the first grade. "Atlanta was very traumatic for me," she recalls. "We lived in Decatur and I went to Druid Hills Elementary School. It seemed very big to me. There was still a North-South problem in Atlanta in the 1950s. I didn't know anything about the Civil War in the first grade. I remember getting an upset stomach whenever I went to school. I loved school, always loved studying and all of that, and this was very unusual. What was happening was that I was the brunt of the jokes of the teacher and the kids, because I had come from the North. I didn't *speak* like they did. And I remember one day the teacher yelled at me, because she said I wasn't printing my *e* correctly. She sat me on a stool in the corner with a dunce cap on. Kids were there and everybody was laughing. I guess that does something to you. It sure didn't help self-esteem. I don't think I said anything to Mother or Dad. Finally, I guess Mother found out about that story, and she can be very undiplomatic when she's angry, and she went marching down—and I remember I was so embarrassed—she went to the *principal's* office, and he was like God! I went in with her. Whatever she did worked, because from then on, the teacher was nice to me, and we didn't have any more incidents.

"But after that, for my birthday, Mother had this little luncheon, and one girl came, out of the eight who were invited. There was no indication that they wouldn't be there. All I felt was devastation for Mother. Because she had all the little sandwiches fixed, all the chairs, favors at each place in the dining room, and I kept thinking: Oh, gosh, she's gone to all this trouble, and they're not here. And we had pin-the-tail-on-the-donkey, Mother had all these party games, but it was kind of hard to play with only two. I remember her excusing herself and going into the kitchen—she said she had to make a telephone call—and I heard her saying: 'What do you mean, you made a *dentist* appointment, you *knew* this party was today!' She must have been calling each of them to find out where they were. The bottom line was, the moms wouldn't let them come to a *Yankee's* house!"

According to George's official FBI file, he received his first raise in grade, effective January 2, 1952, and defined as "Retroactive pay adjustment from 7-8-51 through 10-27-51," elevating him from $5,000 to $5,625. His gross biweekly pay was $216.35, minus a retirement deduction of $12.98 and a tax deduction of $20.50, for a net biweekly "take-home" pay of $180.87.

In those days, agents received "monthly accomplishment" reports, and those received by George from J.J. Casper, who was the new SAC of the Atlanta office, were outstanding. During January, all Atlanta office agents closed an average of nineteen cases, but George was credited with closing twenty-nine cases. In February, all agents closed an average of sixteen cases, and George closed twenty-eight cases.

"However, after only eleven months in Atlanta, I was transferred to the Indianapolis office in March of 1952," George says. "At that time, Indianapolis had an outstanding reputation for criminal cases. It seemed that almost everyone who had any criminal stature passed through there at one time or another. This meant moving again. Ten moves in almost eight years of marriage."

When he drove his family from Atlanta to Indianapolis, he submitted an expense voucher of $70.15. Included in that amount was his actual driving expense, which he calculated at 590 miles and the normal 7 cents a mile. He received the following document:

Federal Bureau of Investigation
Voucher Unit
STATEMENT OF DIFFERENCES

Name: *George R. Wackenhut* Division: *Indianapolis*
Period: *March 1 to 31, 1952*
Approved amount of Voucher: *$66.23*   Claimed: *$70.15*
Account reduced in amount for the following reasons:
   1. Error in addition
 *2. Error in mileage
   3. Error in Per Diem computation
   4. Long-distance phone for compliance with P.69 G.T.R.

Claimed:
  Mileage from Atlanta, Ga.,
  to Indianapolis. Ind.
    590 @ .07 $41.30
Allowed:
  By Rand McNally Highway Mileage
  Guide from Atlanta, Ga., to
  Indianapolis, Ind.
    534 @ .07 $37.38
        Suspended $3.92

"When we moved to Indiana, in the car, I'd never heard of Indiana," Jan remembers. "Seems kind of strange, I was going to be in second grade. I was a year ahead in school because of the way my birthday fell. It really culminated in Indianapolis, because we moved midyear and I had to take some kind of a test to make sure I could be in second grade. But I remember in the car, driving up there, I said, 'Where *is* Indiana?' We got out the map and Mother showed me where we were going. I wasn't traumatized to leave Atlanta. I mean, it wasn't like I was leaving a lot of friends or anything like that. We lived on a street of apartments again, and all the apartments on one side of the street were more expensive than the ones on the other side. And all the FBI agents were on the side that was least expensive! They looked the same to me, but, of course, I didn't see inside them. The address was 2132 Winfield Avenue. We were at the dead end of a street. There was a fence, just a chain-link fence next to us, and fields. We were at the end and it was a two-story apartment—well, they were two-story duplexes. Our entrance was to the front, and the entrance next door was to the side. I had a little kid over there I used to play with; Rick had some friends there, Greg and Terry, that were brothers.

"I went to Ernie Pyle Number Ninety. The first day of school, they had me stand up in front of everybody and introduced me, and everybody laughed at the name. They thought Wackenhut was the funniest name they ever heard! That was *devastating* that they were laughing at me. I would always get knots in my stomach the first time I would go to any school. I had my first boyfriend there, but that was third grade, this is second grade. But I met him in second grade, his name was Don Motionross. He had blond hair and he had this wave. I don't know if he put anything on it in those days, but it was hysterical. He just seemed to really take care of himself, and the other little boys were just little boys."

Larry Brown was George's supervisor in Indianapolis, and remembers him vividly. Born Lawrence E. Brown in Indianapolis, August 23, 1911, "Brownie," as he was called by the agents, graduated from the University of Indiana in 1933 and received his law degree there in 1935. After practicing law in Indianapolis for about two and a half years, and "almost starving to death," he joined the FBI as a special agent on January 10, 1938, was married to Berniece Jeannette, April 19, 1938, and began his travels in the Bureau. His offices included three cities in Massachusetts and three in Kentucky before he was transferred to New York City in 1939. In the latter part of 1948, he was transferred to Washington, DC, as supervisor on the communist desk. Then, in 1951, his wife was diagnosed as having polio of the spine.

"We had three young children by then, and I almost went crazy," Brown recalls. "So I contacted Mr. Hoover. Very nice to me. He knew about the situation, because I had kept the Bureau advised of Berniece's condition. I said I needed help with the children, they'd have to be cared for by close relatives back in Indianapolis. He understood perfectly, transferred me to Indianapolis. I was made a supervisor there, but instead of being on the communist desk, I was made supervisor of criminal cases. Our office was on the third floor of the old Custom House and Post Office Building on Ohio Street. I had thirty-two agents assigned to me on that particular desk.

"George was assigned to my squad in 1952. We had what we called the '87' cases, the bad-check cases. Now, I can't remember all the agents that were on that squad, but I've never forgotten George Wackenhut. I'll never forget George because he was one of the best agents I had on the squad. He handled his cases well, he wrote excellent reports, he was an excellent agent. Very tenacious. And very dedicated to his work. I remember that because, as a supervisor on the desk, my big problem, of course, was *assigning* cases. Which agents to assign. And then approving their reports, written reports, because I had to sign them. If the report wasn't proper when it went to Washington, *I* was in trouble! Never had any problems with George's reports. I had no qualms about giving George *any* case that came on the desk. Bad-check cases were not what you'd call high-profile cases, but they were among the most difficult to solve. Why did I pick out George? Because he was tenacious. And meticulous. At that time, we had several 'master' check writers going throughout the country. That was sort of a big thing at the time.

"I never worked with George on the street, of course, I was at the desk all the time. I don't know whose case it was, but one of the agents came in one day and said, 'Hey, did you hear about George?' I said, 'No.' He said, 'Well, he and another agent tried to arrest a guy in a store, and the guy resisted arrest, and had a pair of scissors, and started to attack George.' And George, of course, being the physical, defensive expert that he was, he overpowered the guy, put him down on the floor, and took the scissors away from him. Physically, he was a well-built, very *physical* type of agent. He was considered that in the office, a defensive expert."

The bad-check cases that Brown assigned involved interstate theft with a value of $5,000 or more. It was something George thoroughly enjoyed, because it entailed matching wits with con-artists, and they were extremely clever. "One guy who led me a merry chase was a con-man who posed as a Bible salesman," George recalls. "He was slick. His dodge was to pick out three small towns within a ten-mile radius. On Monday he would go to one bank and deposit a large check, fraudulent, of course, drawn on a bank in some small town in

New York State. In those days, it would take at least a week before word finally came back that the check was invalid. On Tuesday, new checkbook in hand, he'd go to the next town and open another account, transferring a large amount from bank number one to bank number two, and getting another checkbook there. Wednesday, he'd go to the third town, open a fat account with checks drawn on banks number one and two. On Friday, he'd go around to all three banks and draw out all the money. Then he'd move on to another area and work the same racket all over again.

"But his luck ran out in Washington, Indiana. A cashier was astonished when she looked at the address he'd written on the new-account card—it just happened to be the house next to *her* house and she knew those neighbors well! She notified her supervisor, who called the police, and they detained him while checking with the FBI in Indianapolis. It was a Saturday afternoon, and Ruth and I were getting ready to go to a party at another agent's home when Larry Brown, my supervisor, called me: 'George, they've picked up a man in Washington on suspicion, and it may be one of the men you're looking for. You'd better call them.' From what the police there told me, I figured this was the pseudo Bible salesman I'd been looking for over quite a period of time. His operation fitted the pattern that had been established elsewhere, a pattern almost as identifying as fingerprints. I jumped in my car and started the three-hour drive to Washington.

"As soon as I started talking to him, I knew I had my man. He was a devious character, but he confessed early on, and, as I continued to question him far into the night, he also confessed to a pile of other cases. In the end, I asked him how he ever got started doing this. 'Well,' he said, 'I just found out how easy it was to cash a check in these small-town banks if you have any kind of identification at all.' He grinned at me, shrugged, and said, 'Maybe I just have an honest face.' The judge didn't think so. He drew a stiff sentence."

After only five months in the Indianapolis office, George received his first official commendation in a letter signed by J. Edgar Hoover, dated August 11, 1952:

Dear Mr. Wackenhut:
 I was most pleased to learn of your splendid participation relative to

the investigation and apprehension of Fugitives Frazier D. and Floyd H. Taylor, subjects of Deserter cases.

I want to take this means of expressing to you my sincere appreciation and commendation for taking such prompt and affirmative action when faced with the difficult situation which arose during the apprehension of these subjects. You may well be proud of your splendid contribution to the successful results which were accomplished.

The agent who worked that particular case with George (and who also received a letter of commendation), was Joe McDonald, who recalls that it was the most violent arrest in his twenty-eight-year career in the Bureau. Born Joseph Carl McDonald, November 9, 1924, in Carmel, Indiana, he enlisted in the Navy in 1942 before his high school class graduated; his mother received his diploma about the time that he was in the Marianas invasion. He was a torpedoman and missed only two of the major Pacific invasions: Guadalcanal and Tarawa. Following his honorable discharge in 1946, he entered Ball State University in Muncie, Indiana, where he received his bachelor's degree in 1949 and earned his master's degree in education in 1951. He entered the FBI under the modified program in 1951 and stayed until he reached the mandatory retirement age of fifty-five in 1979. Counting his five years in the Navy, his government service totalled thirty-three years.

"In the Indianapolis office, I was just a special agent, like George, and we worked together," McDonald says. "George saved my life during the Taylor case, two deserters who were fugitives. Basically, we rewrote some federal law on that one. What happened, we believed they were in the Indianapolis area, and primarily in Whitestown, Indiana, which is north of Indianapolis. We went to that area and found out that the father had picked them up, and they were back in Indianapolis. So we located the apartment in Indianapolis.

"The next thing was to determine if, in fact, they were in the apartment, and we were able to do that. There was a young man painting on the side of the building, and he could see in the apartment, so he informed us, yes, in fact, they were in the apartment. We attempted to interview them and they turned us down. They became a little bit heated. We were not given permission to come in. So, as the case unfolded, we eventually kicked the door in, and went in.

They had a dog, and they sicked the dog on us, and we put the dog in the restroom, and continued with the apprehension.

"During the apprehension, the one fugitive was handcuffed in front. George bent over to say something to the mother, who was seated in the chair, and at that time this fellow swung his handcuffs around just like a ball bat, and would've hit George in the head. I hit him about the same time. I broke my right fist in six places. Then the sister, who was involved in it, started kicking me, and I went back over a davenport and broke it in two, and the old man came out of the kitchen with a knife, a butcher knife, and came after me. George ended up throwing him across the room, and he landed with his feet on the window ledge. If he'd thrown him a little bit harder, he'd have thrown him out the second-story window of that apartment. Of course, I was amazed. Here's the father, who weighed pretty close to 200 pounds, and—I'm not kidding—George threw him at least fifteen feet, completely in the air.

"Anyway, he saved my life by doing that. That was on West Washington Street in Indianapolis. Of course, he received a commendation on that one, and so did I. I kept that one because of my first [Hoover's letter specifically mentioned the injury]. I damaged it pretty good and I thought, you know, I might want to refer back to that in time. It's hampered me at times. I turned his lights out, but I'm not sure where the blow landed. He was unconscious for a little bit. He was swinging, and I knew I had to deflect that blow, because he would've slammed George in the back of the head. When the fight was all over, Larry Brown, I think, went back to the apartment to arrest the father and the mother. And the door fell off and fell over a lampstand and a lamp, and broke them, and those were the only two pieces of furniture left that we hadn't torn up. That was the most violent case we were involved in.

"As I mentioned, we rewrote some federal law. Judge Stecker was the judge. The daughter was charged with assault on me, and I'm sure that the father was charged with assault. The women went to Alderson, West Virginia, the mother and the sister, and I'm not sure where the father went. Of course, the two boys were returned back to the military. But the thing that the judge ruled in that particular case, we had federal warrants already outstanding for the two deserters, and that was our primary reason for being there. The judge ruled that because there was ample time for us to have obtained a search warrant, we should have obtained one. At that point in time, that was unheard of in the type of case we were working. Because we were interested in two individuals, and there were already warrants out for them. The law was rewritten to say that if you have *time* to obtain a search warrant before entering a home, you must obtain the warrant. Realistically, we couldn't do that, unless one of us would have stayed there, and the other one gone after a warrant, which was not really practical."

GEORGE was the only agent in the Indianapolis office who was invited to attend a General In-Service Training Course in Washington, D.C., in a memo from Hoover to SAC Leonard Blaylock, dated August 15, 1952. It was a twelve-day training course scheduled from Monday, September 8, through Friday, September 19, and involved advanced training in firearms, including seven days at the FBI Academy in Quantico, Virginia. In addition to marksmanship training with a variety of weapons, agents were required to take extensive notes, have their notebooks graded, and take a written final examination. The results would be made part of their permanent files.

George's grades in the course were sent from Hoover's office to SAC Blaylock in a memo dated October 3, 1952:

SAC, Indianapolis
Re: GEORGE R. WACKENHUT
    SPECIAL AGENT
General In-Service Course, 9/8 to 9/19/52

Dear Sir:
    The above-named Special Agent attended the above General In-Service Training Course at the Seat of Government and attained the following grades:

Notebook	Satisfactory
Examination	94
Double Action Course	98

Practical Pistol Course	96
Shotgun (Skeet)	13
.30 Rifle	87
Machine Gun	90

The firearms grades, with the exception of the Shotgun Skeet Course, should be entered on the individual's field firearms training record.

Minus the embarrassing Shotgun Skeet Course grade of 13, George's cumulative average turned out to be 93. When Blaylock sent a carbon copy of the memo to George, he humorously penciled in the word *Bad* after the 13 grade.

There was one case in Indianapolis that turned out to be particularly satisfying for George, because it was what they called an "old dog" that had been laying around for nearly five years. It concerned a man and woman who had been papering the whole country with bad checks. There was an indictment on them, because they were longtime fugitives who had bilked a long string of companies out of a staggering amount of money. But they were hit-and-run artists who never stayed in one place long enough to be caught.

"Then came the break we needed," George says. "I received a call one cold day in March, 1953, from the sergeant who was in charge of the rubber-check detail at the Indianapolis Police Department. 'A man just filed a complaint with us,' he told me. 'It doesn't mean much to me, but maybe it will to you. This guy tells me he rented his furnished house to a couple with two children and a dog. They had a station wagon with Florida plates on it. Anyhow, a couple of days after they rented the house, they backed a moving van up to the place and took off with all his furniture, leaving a bunch of bad checks behind. The thing that got me wondering if they might be wanted in another state was—what would people from *Florida* be doing up *here* this time of year?'"

When he went through the complaint filed by the landlord, George was more certain than ever that these were the people he was after. And he thought it was possible that they had moved to some other area of the city to work the same racket. But a comprehensive check of real estate agents failed to provide him with any new renters who fitted the descriptions. Then he reasoned that they might have moved out of greater Indianapolis and into the suburbs. At that point, he mapped out all the smaller towns in the vicinity of Indianapolis and began to hit them one by one, visiting local police departments and leaving Identification Order (IO) posters with photographs of the mother and father, information about the family, plus his phone number. He also checked the local banks for anything suspicious with newly opened checking accounts, and left his phone number.

"Finally, about six o'clock one evening," he says, "after I'd been at it for about three weeks, I decided to hit one last town about ten miles from Indianapolis. The chief of police was not in his office, but I gave the officer on duty the IO poster and told him we were looking for this couple with two kids, a dog, and a station wagon with Florida plates. 'If the chief finds out anything, I'd appreciate a call,' I said, and left my phone number.

"I drove the ten miles back to the office, went upstairs to sign out, and received a call from one of our agents who lived in that particular town. 'I just arrested those people with the Florida tag that you were after,' he told me. I did a slow burn, because I'd wanted so badly to nail them myself, after working so long and hard to track them down. But I managed to thank him civilly and asked him what happened. 'The police chief here is a friend of mine,' he explained. 'When he returned, not long after you left, he knew them immediately because they were new in the area and had rented a farmhouse just outside of town. He figured it was easier to get hold of me, rather than call you, so we went out there and made the arrest.'"

George took over from there and spent a week interviewing the man, who was in his late twenties, and his wife, who was a couple of years younger. They hoped that if they told everything they might get a lighter sentence, so they spilled the whole story, laughing from time to time over the gullibility of the public.

And it was quite a story.

"I'd get a job as a bookkeeper in a plant, a factory, or some kind of big company," the wife said. "I'd find out, of course, where the checkbooks and the checkwriter were kept, and learn the authorized signature. I'd only work there one week."

"Then," the husband continued, "I'd burglarize the place on Friday night and grab the checks and the checkwriter. It wasn't any problem to forge the authorized signature. We'd make up fifty or more checks, like payroll checks, and we'd cash them all day Saturday at different stores. The company would be well-known, so it was easy. Then we'd blow town."

The first thing the company would discover on Monday morning was that the new bookkeeper hadn't reported to work. Then it would receive a call from the bank that it was overdrawn. And there were some major companies involved, so the couple was making quite a haul each time they executed the operation.

"After a while, we got to thinking that we were taking too many chances," the husband said, "and that I might get nailed burglarizing some of those places. So we started printing our own checks. We got a little press, a checkwriter, and a whole bunch of our own checks. Then we'd just pick out a big company, print its name on the check, and do our 'shopping' all day Saturday before blowing town again."

He burst out laughing when he told one story: "I just printed this batch of checks, I go to a grocery store, buy a few things, and ask the guy to cash my payroll check. When I hand it to him, his thumb smears the ink, and he says, 'Holy mackerel, this thing must've just been printed.' I take it out of his hand, study it, I says, 'Well, I'll be a son of a bitch. I just picked it up this morning. Listen, I'm going to take it back to payroll and have them issue a new one. Hold the groceries. Be back as soon as I can." He laughed again at the memory. "So I go back to where we were staying and dry all my checks out in the oven. They all have the same company name on them, made payable to me. Then I go back to the same guy at the grocery store and hand him a new check. Well, this time the paper is kind of brittle, and it *cracks!* The guy looks at it, he says, 'What the hell's wrong with *this* one?' I say, 'Damned if *I* know!' He shrugs his shoulders, he shakes his head, he goes ahead and cashes it anyway!"

His wife was laughing, too, and followed up by relating how she took one of their "company checks" to a bank teller. He handed it back to her because she forgot to endorse it. "I forgot what name was on the front," she said, "so I wrote the first name that came to my mind. He looked at my signature, then at the name on the front, and he said, 'This isn't the same name.' So I said, 'Oh, what the hell is wrong with me? Here, let me fix it.' I crossed out the name I'd just written, wrote the name that was on the front, and handed it back. Damned if he didn't cash it!"

But the judge didn't think the confession was funny. She was sentenced to three years, and he drew seven years.

George's second pay raise became effective January 9, 1953, and increased his annual income from $5,625 to $5,750. After the standard deductions, his net biweekly "take-home" pay increased from $180.87 to $183.38.

Less than two months later, he received his second official letter of censor, signed by J. Edgar Hoover, and dated February 25, 1953:

Dear Mr. Wackenhut:

During the recent inspection of the Indianapolis Office it was noted that copies of five drafts which had been stolen at Grand Rapids, Michigan, on or about July 15, 1952, in connection with the Interstate Transportation of Stolen Property case involving an unknown subject with alias Lawrence N. Stetler and other aliases, were made available to you on August 4, 1952. The copies of these drafts had not been submitted to the FBI Laboratory at the time of the inspection of the Indianapolis Office in January, 1953, and you failed to submit an investigative report in this matter until January 29, 1953.

Your delay in submitting a report in this case and your failure to promptly transmit to the FBI Laboratory copies of the stolen drafts are not in keeping with the high standards of performance expected of Bureau Agents. Prompt submission of this material to the FBI Laboratory might have effected the identification of the subject with a resultant savings of investigative time and funds. In the future you will be expected to handle your assignments with greater efficiency and dispatch in order to prevent a recurrence of such deficiencies as occurred in this instance.

However, just four months later, he received his second letter of commendation from Hoover, dated July 3, 1953, which evened the score:

Dear Mr. Wackenhut:

Your admirable work in the Interstate Transportation of Stolen Property investigation involving James Edward Mescall and also in several other cases in this category has been directed to my personal attention as deserving of particular commendation.

The enthusiastic and tenacious manner in which you have devoted yourself to these assignments conforms to the highest ideal of Bureau service, and I want you to know of my sincere, personal appreciation.

George genuinely enjoyed his work with the FBI, especially in Indianapolis, and looked forward to the challenges every day. Ruth loved the FBI atmosphere, the active social life, and made many friends. But when George's next raise in grade became effective, March 1, 1953, he was still earning only $5,875 a year, and, with two children, they were finding it difficult to make ends meet.

"We talked at great length about our future," George recalls, "and Ruth always came around to voicing a desire to live in Miami, her memories bright with thoughts of early days she had spent there with her family. And then one evening at a dinner party with other agents and their wives, I was jolted when one of the older agents told me in confidence that he worried constantly about how he could exist on his retirement pay. He said, somewhat bitterly, that after twenty-odd years in the Bureau, the only thing he could call his own was his Ford automobile, and that wasn't paid for."

In retrospect, that particular conversation had a profound effect on George. The following week, he went to a Dun and Bradstreet office, obtained their rating book, and began to send his resume to major corporations in the Miami area.

In October of 1953, he got his first nibble. The vice president of industrial relations at Eastern Air Lines responded to his letter and resume, said the company was contemplating the idea of starting its own security department, and invited George down for an interview. George accepted, received a round-trip ticket, and the interview with the vice president went quite well. But about a week after his return to Indianapolis, the man called back to say that the plan for a security department had been cancelled.

"I decided then that if I were going to get a job in Miami," George recalls, "I would have to go there and concentrate my efforts. So, in

April of 1954, I took three weeks' leave from the Bureau and headed for Miami. I split the gasoline costs with a friend who was driving as far as Atlanta, then took a night flight to Miami, and spent three weeks pounding the pavements."

10

THE SOCIETY OF FORMER SPECIAL AGENTS OF THE FBI is very much like a fraternity today, as it was in 1954, when George arrived in Miami in early April and began looking for work. He didn't go down cold by any means. Long before he left Indianapolis for his three-week leave of absence from the Bureau, he had studied the confidential *Membership Directory* of the Society, published annually, that lists the names, addresses, home and business telephone numbers of every ex-agent who is a member of the Society, sections of which are broken down by geographical location, cities within each location, and specific companies with which the ex-agents are associated. At that time, there were dozens of ex-agents working at a variety of professions in the city of Miami, and those were the people he called first. Throughout those three weeks, he was staying at the home of Ruth's mother, Bessie Merz, in the Shenandoah section of southwest Miami.

One of the first ex-agents George contacted was C.W. "Bud" Thompson, who had been in the Bureau 1951-1953, before he became a special investigator in the Dade County Sheriff's Department, and he was chief of the administrative division when George called and met with him for the first time that April.

"When George first came to town, he was still in the FBI," Thompson recalls, "and he went around looking for the various ex-agents, because he wanted to move here and live in Miami. His wife had lived here during the winters since she was a child, and they both liked it and wanted to move here. He had this idea of building an investigative company. He talked with me about going with him. At that point, he didn't know who the partners were or how many he was going to have, but he was going to get some people to be partners."

Born Cyrus W. Thompson, in Miami, January 14, 1927, he graduated from Miami Senior High School in June 1945, and went into the U.S. Army immediately; he received his diploma and his notice to report for induction the same day. When he was being trained for the invasion of Japan, the war ended, and he was sent to Europe for the occupation. He was in the medical corps, and the task of his company was to care for 40,000 German prisoners of war. When he was discharged in November 1946, he returned home, and entered the University of Miami in January 1947. Helped by the GI Bill, he worked his way through college, graduated in three and a half years, and went to work in commercial credit; repossessing autos was his first job. In 1951, the FBI was still engaged in aggressive, selective recruiting of men who were not necessarily accountants or attorneys, but simply graduates of accredited colleges.

"One of the men that I worked with went in and applied, and was accepted by the FBI," Thompson says. "He came back, told me what to expect, and encouraged me to apply. I was making $185 a month, the Bureau paid $5,000 a year, which sounded like a million dollars. So I went down and applied, was accepted in September 1951, attended the FBI Academy, where one of my instructors was George Zeiss, and I was assigned to the Detroit bureau. Shortly afterward, my wife and I had our second child, but she almost died in the childbirth, and the baby almost died, so she had to go back to Miami to have somebody take care of her. In the meantime, I was being transferred to Hammond, Indiana, in the Bureau, and I decided that I didn't want to work there, that I'd try to get back to Miami.

"One of my fraternity brothers, who had been in the FBI, was working in the sheriff's office, and my wife ran into him, and she said, 'Do you know of any other jobs?' He said, 'Yeah, the sheriff is looking for another man; he needs four.' So they made an offer to me for a job with a salary matching what I was making in the Bureau.

So I resigned in September 1953, and came back here and went to work for the sheriff.

"The main reason I decided not to become a partner with George at that time is that I had my first position as a manager of people. Up to that point, I'd always been a worker type. Although I started off as a special investigator for the sheriff, he promoted me and made me administrative assistant to him, and then quickly promoted me again to chief of the administrative division. So that was the first time I had ever supervised people. And, as a young man, I had divided my life up into three areas: Up to thirty, try to *learn* the most; thirty to fifty, try to *earn* the most; and fifty and over, do as I please. At that particular point, I considered myself to be in the learning part of it; I was in my twenties. I was like twenty-seven, something like that, and all of the other division chiefs were in their fifties. So this was really quite a good thing for me, to have that exposure.

"I knew I could do investigations, I had done that before, so I told George, I said, no, I didn't want to go into a partnership with him at that time. However, one of the ex-agents I suggested he should see was Ed DuBois, an excellent investigator who had left the Miami Bureau less than a year before, but seemed to be doing very well on his own. I had done work for DuBois on the side, because he was always a guy who wanted to do top-caliber work, and he paid good money to investigators. He was one of the best surveillance men I ever knew. He was outstanding with that and loved it."

Edward L. DuBois, Jr. (pronounced Du*Boys*), who would become George's first partner, was born in New York City, July 27, 1911, where he attended public grade school, until his father retired from the New York City Police Department, moved the family to Kissimmee, Florida, and then to Miami Beach. He completed grade school, then graduated from Miami Beach High School in 1930, where he was president of the student body, captain of the football team, and editor of the yearbook. Without taking an undergraduate degree, DuBois then attended the University of Florida School of Law, and received his LL.B. in 1937. At law school, he was a member of Phi Alpha Delta legal scholastic fraternity, served as a captain in the ROTC, and was president of four groups: Chi Phi Fraternity, the University Glee Club, the YMCA, and the Florida Players. He also served as a student minister for Congregational churches in Florida and Georgia, 1931–1934.

From 1937 to 1939, he was an associate attorney with Shutts & Bowen in Miami; he was also a municipal judge in Surfside, Florida, 1938–1939.

DuBois joined the FBI on February 6, 1939, and began a fifteen-year career in cities all over the country. In Indianapolis, he served under Harold Reinecki and Ed Sackett; in Kansas City under Dwight Brantley; in San Antonio under Gus Jones; in San Francisco under Nat Pieper; in Seattle under Art Cornelius, Howard Fletcher, and Lee Boardman; in New Orleans under Paul Kitchin; on specials in Alaska under Clint Stein, Al Schlenker, and Henry McConnell; in Tampa and Miami under Dick Danner, Roswell Smith, Joe Thornton, Crawford Carson, Ed Mason, Bob Wall, and Ed Powers.

He was a counselor for the forty-ninth session of the FBI National Academy, attended FBI Police Instructors School, Traffic School, and Inspectors School. Finally, he conducted police and traffic schools throughout Florida for two years, until February 6, 1954, when he resigned from the FBI.

DuBois then practiced law with George Bolles, former FBI agent and partner, and Edward F. Boardman, a law school roommate. But when he met with George Wackenhut for the first time in mid-April 1954, he was attempting to establish a law practice of his own.

A handsome man, six feet tall, 185 pounds, with trim and curly brown hair, dark brown eyes, and a meticulous, analytical approach to investigative work, DuBois was forty-three that year, married to the former Winifred Hagan, and the couple had five children.

"Clients are slow in coming," he told George, "so I've been doing investigative work on the side. I have one case that's been taking me all over the country, and at fifty dollars a day, plus expenses, that's not too bad."

George remembers being astounded at the idea of $50 a day, plus expenses, for private investigative work. His last raise in grade, effective February 28, 1954, had increased his annual salary from $5,875 to $6,000, which gave him a biweekly net of only $193.12. Naturally, he was extremely receptive to the possibility of working with this man.

"What we should do is form a partnership," DuBois suggested.

George readily agreed. "But first of all, before I move my family down here, I'll have to find a steady job to keep food on the table."

That steady job wasn't long in coming. Actually, he received two offers, and decided on Giffen Industries, a roofing and building supply company, where he accepted a job as director of personnel, security, and safety. The salary was only $5,000 a year, plus an average package of benefits, but with the promise of investigative work on the side, in a partnership with Ed DuBois, he reasoned that he could support the family quite well. And his future looked much brighter than it had with the FBI.

At the end of April, he returned to Indianapolis. Naturally, Ruth was elated at the news, even though it meant their eleventh move in just ten years of marriage. Maybe, at long last, they could finally settle down and live a relatively normal life.

That first morning back at work, as soon as George arrived at the office, he went directly into the office of SAC Leonard Blaylock to formally submit his resignation, but he didn't have a chance to open his mouth.

"I understand you're leaving us," Blaylock told him.

George looked at him wide-eyed. "I just got in last *night!* How the hell did you find out about *that?*"

Blaylock smiled. "The pipeline. It's a shame, too, because you were scheduled for a promotion to Bureau Supervisor in July. You would've been transferred to headquarters."

"It wouldn't have made any difference," George told him. "Money would always be a problem in the Bureau. Besides, I've already accepted a position in Miami."

George gave the Bureau twenty-five days' notice, in a formal letter to J. Edgar Hoover, dated April 27, 1954:

Dear Mr. Hoover:

I herewith tender my resignation as a Special Agent of the FBI, to become effective at the close of business on May 21, 1954.

The aforementioned resignation is offered with the greatest reluctance, as my experience with the Bureau has been most enjoyable, gratifying, and educational. However, a position of exceptional possibilities in private industry has been offered to me, an opportunity too valuable to overlook, and I feel that I owe my family the benefits that are certain to accrue from such an opportunity.

I shall ever cherish with pride my associations with the agents and officials of the Bureau, an organization worthy of the public respect and esteem it enjoys.

I shall always be at the Bureau's disposal to serve this organization to the best of my ability in any capacity to which I am suited, both as a citizen and former employee, and will so serve at any time with enthusiasm.

The date of George's letter, April 27, 1954, was a Tuesday. Mailed from Indianapolis, it probably reached Hoover's office in Washington on Thursday, April 29—or, at the very latest, Friday, April 30. In any event, the fact of the matter is that J. Edgar Hoover wrote a letter to George that was dated April 30, and arrived at the Indianapolis office on Monday, May 3, with no mention of having received the letter of resignation:

Dear Mr. Wackenhut:

I am indeed pleased to advise you that you are being promoted from the position of Special Agent Employee, $6000 per annum in Grade GS 10, to the position of Special Agent Employee, $6140 per annum in Grade GS 11, effective May 9, 1954.

On Monday, May 3, 1954, the same day George received Hoover's letter, an official "Notification of Personnel Action" was written and approved at FBI headquarters, promoting SA George R. Wackenhut to Grade GS 11, $6,140 per annum, with a biweekly net salary of $198.18, effective May 9. A carbon copy was mailed to George.

On May 6, 1954, Hoover wrote to acknowledge the resignation:

Dear Mr. Wackenhut:

Receipt is acknowledged of your letter of April 27, 1954, submitting your resignation as a Special Agent Employee in the Federal Bureau of Investigation, and you are advised that same is being accepted effective at the close of business May 21, 1954, active duty to cease at the same time. The computation of accrued annual leave payable to you will be furnished at a later date on the personnel action form reflecting your resignation and the amount of such payment due.

There is enclosed an Application for Refund of Retirement Deductions which should be executed by you, in duplicate, and returned to this Bureau for appropriate action in the event you desire to withdraw your retirement deductions at this time. It should be noted your application cannot be processed until your final payment is scheduled by this Bureau, which is approximately three weeks after your resignation becomes effective. It has been our experience that it takes an additional four weeks for an account to clear both the United States Civil Service Commission and the Department of the Treasury. For your information, deductions will not be taken from your salary for retirement purposes subsequent to the effective date of your resignation.

It is requested that you keep this Bureau promptly advised of your forwarding address and any changes therein until such time as all salary matters have been settled. This will eliminate considerable delay in transmitting checks to you.

I am indeed pleased to know you have enjoyed your association with this Bureau and I wish to thank you for your kind offer to be of further service should the occasion arise.

Joe McDonald remembers when George left, and hated to see him go. "He was motivated to do a lot of good things for the Bureau," McDonald says. "It's too bad that they lost him, because I think he could've been an outstanding SAC. I knew that George was very torn. I considered us to be pretty close friends through the time at Indianapolis. Neither one of us had too much time to spend socially, or any money to be sociable. We both had our families and, basically, that was your life—your family and your work. We would put in hours and hours and hours of overtime. I know an eighty-hour week wasn't anything unusual. We'd give up holidays, because that's when you usually caught your people—Thanksgiving, Christmas—they didn't think anybody would be working. I've caught a lot of bank robbers that way.

"I remember Rick and Jan when they were small children. I remember Ruth, she was a model, a model for car sales and things like that, to bring in some extra income. I truly believe that George is a solid American citizen. His loyalty to his country is beyond reproach. Maybe his methods were a little unorthodox in ways, but he got the job done. By 'unorthodox' I mean that George was the kind of fellow that might take files from the office, and go home and do them, and baby-sit at the same time that Ruth was working. Again, it was a matter of economics. It wasn't because he wanted to do something different.

"I had to loan George ten dollars one time, he was broke. As a matter of fact, Ruth got arrested that day, she didn't have enough money to pay the laundry bill. And she got into it with the laundry delivery man, and he ended up calling the police, and she got arrested. I don't know how far it went, but I know that she got arrested. So I assume that they probably booked her, but I really don't know that. There wasn't much George could do other than pay the laundry bill. But that was the same day I loaned him the ten dollars, so he could catch a bus in Indianapolis and go to Detroit to buy a new Buick, so they could drive to Miami. It was that bad. He paid me back the ten bucks." (Through a contact, George was able to buy the car at cost, directly from the factory, with no down payment, and a low-interest installment payment plan.)

Ruth laughs out loud whenever she hears the story of her "arrest," which spread like wildfire, of course, but was not true. Joe McDonald merely repeated the story, in good faith, as it was told to him. What actually happened is even more bizarre, and gives a clear indication of how "broke" they really were. "His shirts had been sent to the laundry," Ruth recalls, "and I was very anxious to get them back, as he was leaving town the next day. I was so happy to see the laundry truck arrive. The driver made weekly stops at the various houses on our street. Around the neighborhood, our street was known as 'FBI Street,' because the majority of houses were occupied by agents and their families.

"When he got out of the truck, he had to come up a walkway, up five steps, and onto the front porch. He never went around to the back of the house. I was anxiously awaiting him, and had opened the screen door and reached for the package. He pulled back from me and said, 'Oh, no, money first!' Now, he was asking for *seventy-five cents,* and I didn't happen to *have* seventy-five cents! I said, 'Please give me the shirts; I'll make sure you get the money tomorrow. I must have the shirts, because my husband will need them on his trip.' Well, he became very nasty. But he was distracted by some noise down the street, looked away, I grabbed the package out of his hand, slammed the screen door, and locked it!

"He turned back to me and said, 'I'll call the police,' and started down the steps. I tossed the package on a chair, dashed out the door, ran past him to the truck, and took the *keys* out of the ignition! Then I sprinted back to the house, dodging him all the way, ran up the steps, slammed the screen door, then locked the inside door! I saw him from the window, walking down the street. He was so *mad!* I then sat down and started to cry! I was so upset, angry, irritated, because I didn't have *one cent* in my purse!

"Then I composed myself and thought: What have I *done!* My temper sometimes gets out of control. I thought: My husband is in the FBI, and this *weasel* of a man is calling the police. I could picture the newspaper story: *FBI Wife Arrested After Fight with Delivery Man!* I also thought: J. Edgar Hoover will fire him! Next, I saw not one, but *two* police cars pulling up in front of the house! Two police officers rang the bell, and behind them was the laundry man. I opened the door and let the policemen in, but put my arm across the door and said, 'Not this idiot!' He stayed outside.

"I was teary-eyed as we walked inside. Suddenly, our boxer 'Krugie' ran into the room and started *attacking* the policemen, growling, baring his teeth, and biting the legs of their pants! I took Krugie in another room. One of the policemen asked for the keys to the truck. I gave them to him. I said, 'I'm so sorry to have caused this problem, but the driver was so unreasonable. My husband is an FBI agent and he'll be very upset about all this.'

"Within minutes, a very good friend of ours, who lived across the street, came up on the porch and rang the bell. When I opened the door, I could see that all the wives and children of the FBI agents were out on their porches watching. I let our friend in and he said, 'What are they doing to you?' I then told the whole story to him and to the policemen. He asked the officers if they would step out on the porch with him, which they did. He called the driver to come up on the porch; the driver had returned to his truck. He then threw the seventy-five cents down on the floor of the porch and told the driver:

'Pick it up, consider this account closed, and no one wants to see you on this street again!' The driver picked up the money, was handed his keys, walked back to the truck, and drove away fast. To my astonishment, all the wives and children out on their porches gave me a big round of *applause!*

"My friend and the two police officers wished me well and left. What a *relief!* I had the shirts, the damn driver had his seventy-five cents, I had neighbors who cared, two understanding policemen, and a happy husband who left the next day with clean shirts! Of course, I didn't *dare* tell George about it until he returned from the trip!"

IN LATE MAY, when the Wackenhut family started the long drive to Miami, their furniture to follow by van, Jan was nine years old and would enter the fourth grade in September; Rick was seven and about to enter the second grade.

"I always wanted to live in Miami," Ruth recalls, "because I had such pleasant memories from our winter visits. In those days, it was so lovely, like an island paradise. I *asked* George to consider going into business for himself. He was very hesitant. I told him that he had a good record with the FBI, and, if his new venture did not work out, he could always apply to return to the Bureau. We certainly needed more income. He had the intelligence, a business mind, and a strong determination to succeed at everything he did. I was so happy when he finally said, 'Okay, let's try it!'"

ON SUNDAY, JUNE 6, 1954, Casey Stengel's New York Yankees were in first place in the American League, as usual, and had won five straight World Series championships; the sitcom *I Love Lucy,* starring Lucille Ball and Desi Arnaz, was the most popular television show in the nation; Henry David Thoreau's *Walden* was banned from U.S. Information Service libraries, and categorized as "downright socialistic"; the Supreme Court (May 24, 1954) upheld the constitutionality of the Internal Security Act, making membership in the Communist Party sufficient grounds for the deportation of aliens; the U.S. population had increased to 150.697 million, and the Wackenhuts arrived in Miami after the long drive from Indianapolis, eager to settle down at last. George was just thirty-four years old, Ruth was thirty-one.

That evening, they had dinner with Ed and Winnie DuBois in the dining room of the old Everglades Hotel, 244 Biscayne Boulevard, in downtown Miami (it's still there), and both Ruth and George remember the couple as particularly attractive. Winnie, a diminutive, bright, and charming blond, elegantly dressed for the occasion, was the daughter of Louis Hagan, who became one of Miami's first real estate brokers when he moved there in 1909. Born in 1912, she graduated from Miami Beach High School in 1929, where she was its first queen, vice president of the student body, and where she met Ed, who graduated the following year. She went on to attend Florida College for Women, now Florida State University, where she was a Sigma Kappa.

"But the beginning in Miami wasn't all too promising for a variety of reasons," George recalls. "There was an initial shock when Ruth and I met Ed and Winnie for dinner that Sunday evening. That was when I learned, to my disappointment and dismay, that while I had been up in Indianapolis serving out my notice with the Bureau, Ed had brought two more former FBI agents into the partnership."

In addition, George learned that DuBois had a concept of partnership that didn't coincide with his original understanding.

"When I mentioned a partnership," DuBois told him, "I didn't mean we would pool all the income and share it. What I meant was that we would share office space and secretarial expenses, but each partner would keep what he made individually. When we've had a chance to build up our case load, there'll be plenty to go around."

The two other partners, whom George met the following week, were Ken Altschul and Bill Stanton, both natives of Miami, and both thirty years old. Altschul held a BBA degree from the University of Miami, had served three years in the U.S. Navy, and recently completed seven years as a special agent in the FBI. Stanton held a BS in chemistry from the University of Miami, spent nine months as a chemist with E.I. DuPont before entering the FBI, and resigned after three and one-half years as a special agent.

The oldest documents in the history of what would become The Wackenhut Corporation, dating from June 1954, were obtained from Edward L. DuBois III, the son of Ed DuBois, Jr., who is now president of Investigators, Inc., in Miami, a firm started by his father in 1955. A total of eighty-five original documents were maintained in a manila file folder that DuBois allowed us to examine and copy in April 1992.

The oldest document, handwritten in pencil by Ed DuBois, Jr., on a yellow, lined, 8½"-x-14" legal pad, is not dated, but its contents indicate that it was written in June of 1954, when the four partners-to-be were temporarily operating from the small office of Ed DuBois in Suite 1403 of the Ainsley Building. Although this first "memo" was probably written at least a month prior to the signing of the official Partnership Agreement (July 21, 1954), it is clear that DuBois had already changed the financial philosophy that he enunciated to George at their meeting of June 6, in which he indicated that the partners would not pool all the income and share it, but each partner would keep what he made individually, while sharing the expenses equally.

1. Selling
    Between now and July 12:
    Employer contacts
    Attorney investigations
    Others

2.A. *Then, if we have $2000 collected, we open own office & operate as 4 man partnership.*
  B. *If we don't have that amount, we make up difference by each paying an equal amount up to $500 each to open our own office & operate as a 4 man partnership & $500 monthly expenses.*
  C. *Or we continue to operate out of my office with all four of us paying equally on expenses of steno—$240 month.*
  D. *Get out announcements & cards.*

3. *On the first of every month after we have commenced operation, the net profit, if any, up to a maximum of $2000, will be paid as follows: 1st*

$500 to Stanton, 2nd $500 to Altschul, 3rd $500 to DuBois, 4th $500 to Wackenhut.

4. Any money of net profit over the $2000 shall go into the partnership fund to be divided on July 1, 1955, as follows:
   10% each to Stanton and Altschul.
   15% each to DuBois & Wackenhut.
   50% to remain in the partnership fund and divided only in event partnership is dissolved or upon unanimous vote of 4 partners.

5. The above arrangement will permit all partners to pursue other lines of endeavor except Stanton who will devote his full time to the partnership & except if the business is too much for him to handle, then Altschul will be expected to give more of his time to the partnership & then if too much for both, then DuBois & then Wackenhut.

"When we first moved down, we lived with my grandmother," Jan recalls. "I remember Mother knew where she wanted to live, south, so she enrolled us in Pinecrest Elementary, which, in those days, were portables. I thought I'd died and gone to heaven, because there were parrots from the Parrot Jungle that would fly free, and at 104th and the Dixie Highway we had something called the Rare Bird Farm; it's now a Howard Johnson's motel. And we would have a lot of classes out in the yard, under the pine trees! Wow! This was great. We'd have to leave fairly early to get from Eighth Street to 104th and Red Road, where Pinecrest was. Mother would stop on the corner of Schoolhouse Road and Kendall Drive, and comb my hair! I had real long hair, and she'd either braid it or put it in a ponytail or fix it, and that was our little morning ritual. Why in the world, don't ask me! Mother isn't a morning person, so maybe it took her that long to get awake before she got down there."

Rick Wackenhut, then seven years old and in the second grade at Pinecrest Elementary, has happy memories of those days, particularly when they moved from his grandmother's house into an apartment building at 1515 San Remo Avenue near Riviera Park in Coral Gables, directly across the street from 1500 San Remo Avenue, where the headquarters building of The Wackenhut Corporation stands today. "When I was in the second grade, we lived in the apartments across the street from where this building would be constructed thirty years later," he says. "That's where I learned to ride a bicycle. I remember riding a bicycle, and it was too big for me, I think it was somebody else's bike, or else it was a new one that I had to grow into. I recall one time, I had on a pair of shorts and a shirt, and there were two little old ladies sitting on the steps of the apartment, and I was trying to ride this bicycle, and I lost my balance. And when I fell, I ripped my pants, and I was so embarrassed that they were going to *see* something, so I went running inside and didn't come out till they left the steps!

"Where our headquarters building stands, there was nothing; I believe there were woods there. Pinecrest started becoming overcrowded at that point in time, and they brought in a number of portables, some of which are still there today. They were in the process of building Palmetto Elementary."

During this time, of course, George was working full-time at Giffen Industries, as director of personnel, security, and safety. So, to uphold his end of the partnership, he did a great deal of work at the temporary office in the evenings, helping prepare reports, and later proofreading and addressing the new-partnership announcements.

There are no existing documents to indicate how much business was generated during June and July of that year, but the four men must have met their goal of collecting $2,000 by July 12, because they leased an office in Suite 1402 of the prestigious Ainsley Building in the center of downtown Miami, agreed on the name of the company, and the legal Partnership Agreement was written by DuBois, who was the only attorney in the group, and signed by the four partners on July 21, 1954, the official start of Special Agent Investigators, which was the first predecessor company of what would eventually become The Wackenhut Corporation.

The original five-page document, typed with a manual typewriter on 8½"-x-14" legal paper and double-spaced, was the only copy known to exist (apparently no carbon copies were made) until loaned to us for copying by Edward L. DuBois III. When George examined the original document on April 20, 1992, it was the first time he had seen it in over thirty-seven years.

PARTNERSHIP AGREEMENT

THIS AGREEMENT, made this 21 day of July, 1954, by and between A. KENNETH ALTSCHUL, EDWARD L. DuBOIS, JR., WILLIAM STANTON and GEORGE RUSSELL WACKENHUT, all of Miami, Dade County, Florida.

WITNESSETH:
That, WHEREAS, the parties hereto are desirous of forming a partnership to operate a private investigative agency,
NOW, THEREFORE, IT IS AGREED AS FOLLOWS:

I.

The name of the partnership shall be the Special Agent Investigators.

II.

The business of the partnership shall be carried out at 1402 Ainsley Building, Miami, Dade County, Florida, or at such place or places as the partnership shall hereafter determine.

III.

The parties hereto will become and remain partners in said business for an indefinite term of years commencing July 21, 1954.

IV.

All partners hereto will at all times diligently employ themselves in the business of the partnership and do all in their power to carry on said business for the greatest advantage of all.

V.

The expenses of the partnership shall be borne equally by all partners, and the term "expenses" shall include all expenses connected with the operation of said partnership.

VI.

The parties further agree to contribute equally to said business, and thereafter each will share equally in the profits and in the real and personal assets as well as the good will of the Special Agent Investigators, which assets are listed per the attached inventory signed by the parties and incorporated herein by reference.

VII.

It is understood and agreed that the parties hereto shall have reasonable equal drawing accounts, as shall be later agreed upon as the business progresses.

VIII.

No partner shall, without the previous consent in writing of the others, enter into any bond or become bail or security for any person, or do, or willfully suffer to be done, anything whereby the capital or property of the partnership may be attached or taken in execution.

IX.

Books of account shall be kept by the partners and proper entries made therein of all the sales, purchases, receipts, payments, engagements, transactions and property of the partnership, and the same books of account and all securities, papers and writings of the partnership shall be kept upon the premises aforesaid or any such other place where the partners shall designate, and each partner shall have free access at all times to examine and copy out the same.

X.

On the 1st day of June, 1955, and on the 1st day of June, in each and every succeeding year, or oftener if necessary, a general account shall be made and taken by the partners of all the sales, purchases, receipts, payments, engagements and transactions of the partnership during the then preceding year, and all of the capital, property, engagements and liabilities for the same time being of the partnership and the said general account shall immediately, after the same shall be made and taken, be written in a book of account and be signed by each partner, and after such signature each partner shall be bound by every such account, except that if any manifest error be found by any partner and signified to the other partner within three (3) months after the same shall have been so signed by each of them such error shall be rectified.

XI.

In the event that the partners hereto deem it necessary to establish a checking account, said account shall be established with the checks to be endorsed by any two partners, and shall be established in any reputable banking establishment in Dade County upon which the partners shall agree.

XII.

Any partner leaving the partnership whether voluntarily or involuntarily shall give or shall be given thirty (30) days notice. The leaving partner shall not have any monetary interest in the assets, either real, personal or inventory property, nor in the good will of the partnership except to receive his proportionate share of the net partnership fund, hereinafter defined, as of June 1st last past.

The leaving partner for one year thereafter binds himself not to operate a competing investigative agency in Dade County, Florida.

XIII.
The partnership can be dissolved only by unanimous vote. When the partnership is dissolved, a general account within three (3) months shall be taken by the partners of all the capital, property, engagements and liabilities of the partnership, and immediately after such last mentioned account shall have been so taken and settled, the partners shall forthwith make due provision for the payments of the debts and meeting of all other liabilities of the partnership, and subject thereto, all of the property of the partnership shall be divided between the partners in equal shares, and such instruments in writing shall be executed by the partners respectively for facilitating the getting in of the debts due to the partnership and for vesting the whole right in the said respective shares of the property in the partner to whom the same respectively shall upon such division belong, and for releasing to each other all claims on account of the partnership and otherwise as are usual in cases of a like nature.

XIV.
In the event of the death of one of the partners, then the surviving partners shall have made by a qualified disinterested third person, within three (3) months after the death of the deceased partner, an appraisal of the value of the net assets, including real, personal and inventory property and the partnership fund, but not the good will of Special Agent Investigators. When this value is determined, then the heirs of the deceased partner shall be paid the proportionate share that would have been due the deceased partner had the partnership been dissolved under paragraph XIII.

XV.
A partnership fund shall be established and maintained in a banking institution and shall be separate and apart from any other funds of monies maintained.

The partnership fund shall be established June 1, 1955, by placing in the fund at least twenty per cent (20%) of all money remaining after all expenses, salaries and liabilities have been provided for the past year. Thereafter on the 1st of each succeeding June the fund must be enhanced by at least twenty per cent (20%) of the net money remaining for that current year.

This partnership fund can be dispensed only by unanimous vote of all partners except a leaving partner or deceased partner's heirs automatically become entitled to the proportionate share of this fund which share shall be calculated by dividing the number of partners into the total amount of the partnership fund.

The remaining net money as of June 1st each year may be dispensed by majority vote of the partners.

XVI.

A partner may be dropped from the partnership thirty (30) days after he receives notice in writing signed by all the remaining partners.

XVII.

Except where otherwise specifically provided in this written agreement, the policies and decisions of the partnership shall be governed by majority vote of the partners. In the event of a tie vote, if DuBois and Wackenhut in accord then their vote shall carry.

IN WITNESS WHEREOF, the parties hereto have hereunto set their hands and seals the day and year first above written.

Signed, Sealed and Delivered
in the presence of:

Each Other   /s/   (L.S.)
                                A. Kenneth Altschul
                                /s/   (L.S.)
                                Edward L. DuBois, Jr.
                                /s/   (L.S.)
                                William Stanton
                                /s/   (L.S.)
                                George Russell Wackenhut

As required by law under the State of Florida, County of Dade, Fictitious Name Statute (Chapter 20953, Laws of 1941), on Friday, July 28, 1954, a notice was published in *Miami Review,* printers of law briefs and transcripts of record, to wit:

NOTICE UNDER FICTITIOUS NAME LAW

NOTICE IS HEREBY GIVEN that the undersigned, desiring to engage in business under the fictitious name of
SPECIAL AGENT INVESTIGATORS, 1402 Ainsley Building, 14 N. E. First Avenue, Miami, Florida, intend to register said name with the Clerk of the Circuit Court of Dade County, Florida.

DATED at Miami, Florida, this 23rd
day of July, 1954.
A. KENNETH ALTSCHUL
EDWARD L. DuBOIS JR.
WILLIAM STANTON
GEORGE R. WACKENHUT

Simultaneous to the publication of intention to register, several hundred announcement cards were mailed to present and prospective clients. The cards, 4½"-x-5½" and of heavy stock, were handsomely engraved, like the business cards and stationery, and the logo, behind the name Special Agent Investigators, was a fine-line border profile of the United States, giving the clear impression that the firm was national in scope. This was George's idea, and it became the logo of The Wackenhut Corporation for many years.

SPECIAL AGENT INVESTIGATORS

1402 Ainsley Building—14 N.E. First Avenue
MIAMI, FLORIDA
Telephone 9-3093

IS A PARTNERSHIP FORMED BY
A. KENNETH ALTSCHUL, B.B.A.
EDWARD L. DuBOIS, Jr., LL.B.
WILLIAM STANTON, B.S. CHEM.
GEORGE R. WACKENHUT, B.S., M.ED.
All former F.B.I. agents with 29 years aggregate
F.B.I. investigative experience,
specializing in civil and criminal investigations
for attorneys, individuals, corporations, partnerships
in–accounting, negligence, science, documents,
insurance, industrial surveys, plant protection,
personnel security, uniformed & plain clothes guards

On Saturday afternoon, July 24, 1954, the partners held an announcement party at the home of Ed DuBois, Jr. His son, Ed DuBois

III, recalls it clearly: "I can remember a big party my dad threw in the backyard of our house, kind of an announcement party that this was going to happen, Special Agent Investigators. There was a big barbecue in the backyard; our house used to have a double lot from one street to the next. Address was 530 Northeast 59th Street, same house my mother has right now. They invited, I'm sure, law firms, potential clients. This house, for its time, I think, was a big, fancy house. It was an old Spanish style, built in the 'twenties type of home, two story, with an elevator and a big, giant yard. I think it was an impressive house for its time. I was about twelve years old at the time of that party. I knew it was a big deal. We were probably tapped-out financially, stretched pretty thin. But we were always stretched, because, with the FBI, you didn't make a lot of money. The first bicycle I got, it was won at the Boulevard Theater. I used to take that around sometimes and pick up Coke bottles just to get a few more nickels to buy some milk and bread and stuff, you know? I mean, it was pretty hard times during the late 'forties, early 'fifties."

George recalls those first days of the new partnership with great pleasure: "We set up an office on the fourteenth floor of the Ainsley Building in downtown Miami. It was a good address, but the quarters were not exactly plush, having space for only three desks against three of the walls, each with a chair beside it, and a desk for a secretary in one corner. But since only DuBois and Stanton were in the office eight hours a day, the space was adequate, and the rent was reasonable, $260 a month, for an office in the most prestigious building in the business district."

In fact, the Ainsley Building, constructed in 1952, was one of the most luxurious office buildings in South Florida, located at 14 N.E. First Avenue, which was then the diametric center of downtown Miami, at the corner of Flagler Street and N.E. First Avenue. At fifteen stories, it was also one of the tallest buildings in the city. The wide windows of Suite 1402 faced due east, offering a magnificent panoramic view of Biscayne Bay and, in the distance, the long expanse of Miami Beach. Today, the exterior of the building remains unchanged, the lobby is still impressive with its tall green marble walls, but since 1980 it has had a new name: The Israel Discount Bank Building. Suite 1402 is occupied by Carlos Velazquez & Ruben S. Barge. There is a small reception area inside the front door, leading to a relatively small office beyond, which is the way it was originally designed.

Today, the Israel Discount Bank Building is dwarfed by the dozens of modern skyscrapers that dramatically altered the skyline of Miami during the building boom of the 1980s, office towers such as the nearby forty-seven story International Place (formerly CenTrust Bank Building) and the fifty-five story Southeast Financial Center. It is also surrounded by the elevated tracks of the 1.9-mile Metromover, a "peoplemover" that winds its way through the downtown canyons to link with the twenty-one mile elevated north-south Metrorail.

One aspect of the building's location has not changed. It is still within easy walking distance of clusters of office buildings occupied by the majority of law firms in the city (the Dade County Court House is nearby), which was one of the prime reasons the partners of Special Agent Investigators selected this particular address.

"Domestic cases were a big thing at that time," George says, "but we decided that we wouldn't handle this type of action, not realizing at the time that we were not only turning away cases, but also clients who might have more reputable cases for us later on. Despite our selectivity, however, business improved steadily."

In September, 1954, Special Agent Investigators hired Orville W. Dixon, a certified public accountant, to design its first accounting system. His first invoice:

ORVILLE W. DIXON
CERTIFIED PUBLIC ACCOUNTANT

September 30, 1954

Special Agent Investigators
1402 Ainsley Building
14 N. E. First Avenue
Miami, Florida

Services rendered setting up partnership books of accounts and records and posting for July, August, and September, 1954. Reconciling bank and establishing accounts receivable control. $20.00

Supplies Purchased:
20 Column Ledger Sheets	$2.60
Debit & Credit Balance Pages	2.10
Index	1.50
Binder	4.25
	$10.45
Sales Tax	.31
	$10.76

                                                            10.76

                                                           $30.76

In mid-November, with business increasing steadily, DuBois, Altschul, and Stanton were working full-time for Special Agent Investigators, and George would start full-time on November 27. It was obvious that Suite 1402 in the Ainsley Building would not accommodate all four men, plus the stenographer, Jackie Powell, so the decision was made to rent the small office next door, Suite 1403, that had been DuBois's original office. For convenience, a carpenter was hired to construct a doorway, with a door, between the two offices, and Ed DuBois moved back into his old office.

"By late November," George recalls, "business continued to expand, and it was obvious that I would have to leave Giffen Industries and join our partnership full time. So, on Friday, November 26, 1954, the day after Thanksgiving, I tendered my resignation, and told them I would give them as much notice as they desired. They told me that as long as I was resigning I could make it effective immediately."

The very next day he received a call from Bill Stanton, asking him to replace him as a bodyguard at the Fisher Island residence of Gar Wood, one of the world's foremost speedboat drivers. According to Stanton, Wood had received some threats and wanted someone watching out for him over the following three days until he left town. This was George's first taste of $50 per day plus expenses, and compared to the $96 a week he had been paid at Giffin, he felt like a millionaire.

"The first case I ever handled for SAI, I had to spend a night in jail," George remembers with a smile. "We got a case from a law firm, J.B. Spence, that has become very successful in negligence work. Only in this case, they were working for the defense for an insurance company. Spence asked me to see what I could come up with. I interviewed an elderly man who gave me information to the effect that absolutely ruled out any possibility that the main plaintiff's witness, who testified that she had seen the accident, could've seen the accident because she wasn't even there, she was somewhere else on that day. J.B. Spence, the lead attorney in the law firm, and another attorney, who were representing the insurance company, were all excited about this, because the case was ready to go to trial.

"So, of course, I was to be there and testify, and the elderly gentleman was there as well. He was seated on the bench just outside the courtroom, and I think the attorneys told me he was going to change his story, the one he told me. So I went up to him and started selling him on the idea that he shouldn't do that, because he'd be perjuring himself. Not realizing, being a neophyte in this sort of thing, that when you do this in and around the courtroom, you can be charged with contempt of court. The two attorneys and a man, I can't recall his name, who was the chief investigator for the State Attorney's Office, and I were all involved.

"When the case was being heard, and they called the elderly fellow to the stand, and J.B. Spence started asking him questions, the plaintiff's attorneys objected on the basis that he'd been harassed by me outside the courtroom. So the judge dismissed the jury. The judge was Pat Cannon, who was famous down here in those days. He was immense. For descriptive purposes, he was bigger than George Zeiss. They called him 'Fat Pat.' No attorneys enjoyed arguing a case before him because—especially if it was right after lunch—he'd fall asleep while they were arguing their case!

"So, when the judge heard this, he dismissed the jury, called me up, and put me under oath. He said, 'Mr. Wackenhut, did you talk to this gentleman outside the court?' And I said, 'Yes, sir.' He said, 'Did you tell him this, that, and the other?' And I said, 'Yes, sir.' He said, 'I'm surprised at you, sir.' I said, 'Well, I didn't think he should perjure himself, and I knew what he told *me,* and I had every reason to believe he should tell the court the same thing.'

"Anyway, the judge held me, the two attorneys, and the chief investigator for the State Attorney—I've forgotten now exactly what his involvement was—in contempt of court. A $100 fine each, or thirty days in jail. So we left the courtroom, we went out in the hall, and I said, 'Well, let's get up our hundred bucks and be done with this thing.' The two attorneys said, 'Hell, no, we're not guilty of anything, we're going to *fight* this!' I said, 'Wait a minute, I just got out of the FBI, I don't want to go to *jail!*'

"But the following day, I think it was about one o'clock in the afternoon, we turned ourselves in. We were fingerprinted, photographed, the whole routine. This was at the old courthouse, the top floor. We were put in the holding tank there. And as we came in, of course, we all had coats and ties on, and the bums who were in there said: 'Look, here come a whole bunch of *bankers!*'

"It was an interesting experience. So I had to spend the night there. Talk about food? What they served was uneatable! We were in a cell with bunk beds, and the mattresses on the beds were *black!* It was *not* a good experience. I think I threw my clothes away after I got out of there. The only appeal in those days was to the State Supreme Court, so we appealed to them on the basis of habeas corpus, and the following day we were let out. In the meantime, my wife got in touch with Ed DuBois and says: 'You're an *attorney,* why are you letting my husband *rot in jail!*' I think eventually we paid our fine and that ended that.

"But then, at a later date, we were fighting the union down in Puerto Rico, trying to keep them from organizing us. I think it was the United Plant Guard Workers of America. And they *publicized* the fact that I had been arrested and sent to jail! Well, that was hitting pretty close to home, so I got hold of my own attorney, Dick Maloy, and he in turn got another attorney who was friendly with the judge and knew how to go about this. So we went in and met with Cannon in his chambers, and the attorney asked that my sentence be expunged, because I had proven to be a good citizen and the whole thing had been a comedy of errors. Anyway, the judge did that. He sealed the records, and they're salted away somewhere, if they're still in existence. But that night in jail was a real experience."

Seen in perspective, the four partners must have shared a certain

Johannes Wackenhut, age 18, Prussian Army, 1875, George's grandfather, first of his family to immigrate to the U.S., in 1881, at age 24. (A. Hummler, Stuttgart)

First Wackenhut family photo known to exist (circa 1902), left to right: Fred, Johannes, Molly, Frank, John, William, Christina, Caroline. (R.R. Haug, Philadelphia)

First-born Molly, as a young lady.

Second-born William on the Boardwalk in Atlantic City.

Third-born Fred as a young man in Philadelphia.

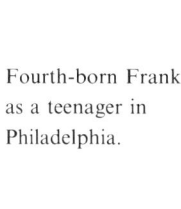

Fourth-born Frank as a teenager in Philadelphia.

Youngest son John, age 19, U.S. Army, stationed in France during World War I.

Johannes with son William (George's father), and Harry (George's brother) at age three, in 1911.

George at eight months, with his mother Frances, May 1920.

Frances with George on her lap, and Harry (circa 1922).

Christmas 1930: George, age 11, and Harry age 22.

The 50th wedding anniversary of George's grandparents (mother's side), left to right: Richard Pancoast (cousin), George (age 12), William Harry Hogan, Rebecca Hogan, Harry Wackenhut, Howell Pancoast (cousin), circa 1931.

William Henry Wackenhut, George's father, in 1931.

Wackenhut family occupied the right side of this house, 7438 Miller Avenue, Upper Darby, west of Philadelphia, where George lived from 1924 to 1941.

Original building that was once Keystone Public School, Upper Darby, founded in 1909, where George spent six years, 1925–30. It is now a public safety building.

On September 7, 1930, George entered the brand-new Upper Darby Junior High School, studied in grades seven through nine.

George's graduation photo from yearbook, *The Oak,* of Upper Darby Senior High School, Class of 1937. School was torn down in 1969, replaced by modern structure.

One of the older buildings at West Chester State Teachers College, 25 miles west of Philadelphia, which George entered in 1938; he was drafted before his class graduated in 1941.

House at 806 Church Street, on the college campus, where George rented a room for $2 a week. Refurbished, it is now the Veterans Memorial Alumni House.

Earle "Muddy" Waters, George's coach, coached varsity soccer at West Chester for 38 years. Photo was taken when he was 94.

The 1943 Philadelphia Nationals of the American Soccer League: George's photo was inserted at top, second from left, because he was on duty at the Aberdeen Proving Ground when the picture was taken.

Lieutenant Wackenhut as he appeared in a 1943 book published by the OCS at Aberdeen, titled *The Commandos: Company H, Class 57,* in which his role as a tactical instructor was featured.

Second Lieutenant Wackenhut, soon after he was appointed post athletic officer, a position he held until September 1944.

A painting of Ruth's mother, Bessie Bell, circa 1916, who was born in Philadelphia in 1893, and died in Coral Gables in 1988.

House at 937 Cornell Avenue, Drexel Hill, PA, where Ruth lived from the age of four until she was married at age 21 in 1944.

Herb Jenkins, who has known George since 1924, stands near the historic (1808) Lamb Tavern in Springfield, PA, where George often took Ruth for dinner on weekends when they were dating.

George and Ruth had a military wedding in the post chapel at Aberdeen Proving Ground on Saturday, April 8, 1944.

As FBI agent in Indianapolis, George interviews notorious forgery felon he arrested in 1952.

George and other FBI agents have breakfast at sheriff's home outside Indianapolis after apprehending a forgery team in 1953.

The Ainsley Building in downtown Miami, where George and partners had their first office, July 21, 1954, Suite 1402.

George's first partner, Ed DuBois, Jr., and his wife Winnie on vacation in Ocho Rios, Jamaica, circa 1954.

sense of euphoria during the Christmas holidays that year. Despite the substantial odds, particularly in a recession year, they had established a new firm that had the ostensible shape and feel of solidity. When we examine the most tangible evidence about the company that has survived from that year, the documentation, simple logic indicates that these relatively young men, with only one true common denominator—FBI training—had created at the very least an illusion of *permanence*. It is a quality seen in the tasteful, authoritative, engraved letterhead and imaginative custom logo of the obviously expensive stationery, in the new case forms and case reports that are almost exact replicas of those used by the FBI at the time (George collected all the standard FBI forms), in the engraved invoices, even in the daily time sheets. It is a quality seen in the selection of the new building that would house their first office, a building so well known in the community that most of the mail they received was simply addressed to "1402 Ainsley Building," with no street name or number.

Permanence. It was an important illusion in a time of nationwide insecurity, often bordering on paranoia. But the illusion would not last. The four-man partnership would be irrevocably destroyed before even one year had elapsed, not because of the tangibles of permanence, but because of precisely the opposite. Two of the men would discover that their strong-willed opinions about the future of the company were emotionally and philosophically incompatible, resulting in a heated confrontation, a fistfight in which only one punch was thrown, and the intangible, delicate balance of the partnership, based on mutual respect, understanding, and trust, was finished in an instant.

Unfortunately, there were deep wounds.

11

BUD THOMPSON, who was then chief of administration in the Dade County Sheriff's Department, was the only outsider who knew all four of the partners, had lunch with them regularly, and understood what the major problems were. In effect, he became a sounding-board for the frustrations that were building, and he talks about it candidly.

"Ed DuBois was an absolutely fantastic investigator," Thompson says. "Very, very intelligent investigator. Very high-caliber guy. But he had a totally different feeling about what the company should be from what George wanted it to be. Ed wanted it to be an outstanding investigating company that would cover South Florida and be pros in it. Good men doing a good job. And George has always been one of the guys that, he gets this thing going and then he wants to go to something else. And George's thinking, when he would talk with me, was: I want to make a nationwide security company. First he talked about a nationwide investigative company, but then he got talking security. And I kept thinking, hey, this guy here, he's way out here, he's talking about nationwide, they're hardly getting started here.

"Ken Altschul was a nice guy, no great ambition, not what I would call much leadership at all, he was just a 'doer' type. A nice guy, I liked him, we were good friends. Went to lunch a lot, talked. But no leader type guy.

"Bill Stanton, I knew him very well. Kind of a strange guy, a loner, Lone Ranger type of guy. Not a very good man to be part of the team. He was not a team player at all. I wouldn't say a real good investigator, but he wasn't a bad investigator. You couldn't say, 'Well, Bill, you take seven men and go work this thing out.' That was not his style. Give him something to do, he would do it.

"George was very determined in what he was going to do and where he was going to go with the company, and that kind of flew in the face of some of the thinking of the others. So if you sided with one, then you usually were against the other. And when they started in business, Special Agent Investigators, the intention was to be this big, or at least very good, local investigative company. And it wasn't too long till George wanted to spend his time developing in the guard business and the polygraph and these other things, particularly the guards. It caused a commotion between them, because Ed was saying he busted his butt to build in the investigative business, and George is out here playing with these guards all the time and trying to get this going.

"To me, let's say, each one had their own intentions and ideas. Ed was a very strong individual in his opinions and his ideas. So the two of them were clashing with this, and the other two guys were like sitting there watching the Ping-Pong ball go back and forth; they had no real input into it at that point. Because the two people were truly the strong people of the company. I always felt it was a shame that they could not have stayed together, and Ed run the investigative facet of the business, and George go ahead and do all these other things. But George is a very strong-willed individual and he wanted to do his thing his way."

The first full-time investigator hired by the partners was Earl F. Warford, a former FBI agent, who had been in the same fraternity as Ed DuBois at the University of Florida (Chi Phi, although their graduating classes were twelve years apart, 1937 and 1949). Born in Miami, August 10, 1925, Warford graduated from Savannah High School, Savannah, Georgia, in 1943, where his father was building Army camps during the war. He turned eighteen that August, enlisted in the Army Air Corps in September, and served until March 1946. After graduating from the University of Florida in 1949, he accepted a job with Maas Brothers in Tampa, and applied to the FBI on his twenty-fifth birthday. DuBois, then in the Miami office of the

FBI, recruited him for the Bureau and provided his primary recommendation. Warford's first FBI assignment was in the Baltimore, Maryland, office for about nine months, in 1950, then he was transferred to Newark, New Jersey, where he remained for the next four years.

"The reason I left was not necessarily the money," Warford remembers. "My wife and I had twins, and we didn't particularly like the Newark area, so we just decided that we would try and come back to the Miami area. My wife's parents lived there, my parents lived there, my sister lived there, so we just wanted to return to where we had family. I applied for a transfer, but they weren't accepting transfers at that time, except for hardships.

"When I came down to Miami on vacation in October 1954, I went to see Eddie DuBois, and he told me they had formed a company, Special Agent Investigators. He had me talk to all the people involved. I talked with Eddie first, then I talked to Bill and Ken. George was still working at Giffen Industries then, and I went to Giffen Industries on Ponce de Leon in Coral Gables and talked to him there. So, they hired me then. I went back and gave a month's notice to the Bureau, then came back and started to work for them in early December 1954. I was the first full-time investigator to work for them—and the only one, too, at the time.

"Basically, what I remember about our office, 1402 Ainsley Building, as you came in the door, you had the secretary's desk, and Sonja Kirk was the secretary, then there was a relatively small office with desks for the partners, and a little library there. I only came in the office and got assignments in the morning if I had completed the case that I was working on before. And, for a long portion of the time I worked there, we were the investigators for the grand jury. I spent an awful lot of time doing that. The grand jury was investigating the Dade County Aviation Department. The most important result of the investigation was that the man who was the airport director was replaced, and Dick Judy became the airport director. Judy worked for the state accounting office, and he was the one who was doing the investigation of the accounting practices of the airport. And he got the airport directorship out of it. [Judy retained that position until 1987.]

"Other than that, I would come in and they would give me an assignment. One that stuck out, other than the grand jury, was an investigation for White Shoulders Perfume. There was a small company in the southwest section of Miami that was counterfeiting their perfume, and sold it under the name of White Showers Perfume. I went in their garbage and got a lot of information from their garbage, and turned it in, and it was a successful case for the company, and for the perfume manufacturer. And I think it led to other work.

"I seem to remember I was paid a regular salary, rather than by the hour. On the surveillance nights, we worked long hours. I don't remember ever feeling that I was ever treated unfairly, so if we were working overtime, I'm sure I must have been compensated on an overtime basis. Basically, my recollection is that I was paid $100 a week. And, of course, I got mileage on top of that.

"Eddie DuBois was the type of guy that always seemed to have a serious look on his face. Actually, he was a lot like George. George, at that point, was a very serious person, because they were trying to establish the business. Eddie was the same type of personality, but he had a dry sense of humor. He was very athletic, he and another friend of mine, when we went to the University of Florida, were the handball champions at Florida. Eddie was in the neighborhood of six foot, and he had dark wavy hair and brown eyes.

"Ken Altschul, to me, he had a salesman's personality. He was very outgoing, he had a good vocabulary, he was very articulate. He was the only one of the partners who had any weight on him. He wasn't obese, he was just stocky in build. He was about five-foot-ten, probably weighed a couple of hundred pounds. His hair was brownish; I don't remember his eyes.

"Bill Stanton was probably six-foot-one, very thin, dark hair. He wasn't trained as a lawyer or investigator. He actually was a chemist. To me, he was sort of a misfit. I don't think he ever really belonged in the company, because he was so different from the others. They were all investigators. The general impression I had was that he wasn't contributing that much to the firm, that he was a drain on it.

"My feeling was that George was the one who provided direction to the company, and I know he was supported very strongly by Ruth. He was the one that predominatly was responsible for building the company and taking on new types of work. I mean, originally we were just investigators, and there wasn't money in that, unless you had an awful lot of employees to support the firm. So George was the one who tried to go out and sell. You know, he was very articulate and made a good impression on these companies."

In one of the first lengthy memos George wrote to his partners, he demonstrates exactly how much time and effort he was spending on research into patrol, guard, and undercover services, with very specific recommendations. Although he was researching and writing this document in the office, in December 1954, and had the verbal agreement of the other partners to explore these areas, according to Bud Thompson the consensus opinion of the others seemed to be that he was not pulling his weight, that he was "playing" with the idea of guards, instead of making a substantive contribution by generating revenue to the investigative side of the business. An excerpt from George's memo that includes crucial facts and figures:

January 4, 1955
TO: AKA, ELD, WS and FILE
FROM: GRW
SUBJECT: PATROL, GUARD and UNDERCOVER SERVICES

Pursuant to verbal agreement of all partners, the writer's time during the latter half of December 1954 was devoted to the development of information concerning the listed services. For the edification of all concerned, the following data is set forth:

I-PATROL SERVICE

A. General Information

1. Personnel—Available thru use of Sheriff's Office deputies, National Association of Retired Police and Firemen, Inc., or others.

2. Salaries—Will range from 80 cents per hour for the least qualified up to $2.00 per hour for Sheriff's Office deputies.

3. Uniforms—Sheriff's Office deputies will wear their "on duty" uniforms, National Association of Retired Police and Firemen reputedly have their own and others are available from Donald S. Levine, Miami, Florida, priced below:

Trousers $16.00

Shirts:
- Short sleeve 3.95
- Long sleeve 5.00

Cap 5.00
Shoulder Patch .... .60
Leather goods including Sam Brown
belt, holster and cartridge line 11.00
Jacket 35.00
Black Leather Jacket 29.75

Minimum uniform would include trousers, long-sleeve shirt, cap, shoulder patch and leather goods for a total of $37.60.

4. Revolvers—To be furnished by personnel employed.

5. Automobiles—Privately-owned cars to be furnished by personnel employed at either 7 cents per mile or amount per hour to be designated.

6. Radios—Use of own radios operating on our frequency out of the question. Alternate plans follow:

(a) Two-way rentals available thru Rolfe Armored Truck Service at $40.13 per month, per unit, plus $25.00 rear installation and $15.00 front installation cost. If units are owned, Rolfe will monitor, maintain and service for $17.50 per month, per unit.

(b) Paging systems are available at $11.00 per month, per unit.

(c) Telephones are available at $22.00, plus tax, per month, per unit for 20 calls each at a minimum of three minutes. Over 20 calls are billed at rate of 30 cents for first three minutes and 10 cents for each additional minute.

7. Special police commissions are available to employees at the Miami Police Department for $15.50 per man, per annum. This commission provides powers of arrest within confines of the city, authority to carry a gun and the right to wear a badge. Ten dollars of this fee purchases a $1,000.00 city firearms bond, $5.00 is the city's fee and 50 cents is for notary fees. The necessity of the city firearms bond is waved if the employer is covered by a minimum liability policy in the amount of $200,000.00.

Special deputy commissions are available from the Dade County Sheriff's Office to employees for $22.00 per man, per annum. This fee entitles the employee to membership in the Sheriff's Association, provides powers of arrest within Dade County, authority to carry a gun and the right to wear a badge. Here again $10 of the fee purchases a $1,000.00 firearms bond, $11.00 purchases false arrest insurance and $1.00 is charged by the county for administrative fees.

8. Insurance—Compensation insurance will cost approximately $2.00 per $100.00 of salary annually. Liability insurance for coverage of $100,000–$300,000 plus $10,000 property damage will cost $2.17 per $100.00 worth of receipts. A blanket bond on employees runs about $10.00 per year, per man. Liability insurance and the blanket bond can be purchased thru an insurance agent, whereas the compensation insurance will most probably be obtained only thru Assigned Risk, F.I.C. Cash in advance of roughly $400.00 for compensation insurance necessary.

9. Cost of Service to Clients—Rates will range from $5.00 to $50.00 per month depending on the size and type of installation and depending on the client's ability to pay.

10. Hours of Service—During statistically pertinent periods only, which in most cases and in most areas will range from 11:00 p.m. until 4:00 a.m., a total of five hours nightly.

11. Licenses—No additional licenses necessary in order for SAI or any of its principals to operate a patrol service; however, county and state license fees to be charged SAI for each employee so engaged. This additional license charge averages to approximately $4.00 per employee, per annum. No such additional license fees are assessed by the city.

B. Cost of Operation Per Month–

It is estimated that a patrol car will average 15 m.p.h. which totals 75 miles for a 5-hour night. At 7 cents per mile this amounts to $5.25 per night. In compliance with the above figures, each car can cover 1 square mile every 15 minutes.

1. If Sheriff's Office deputies are employed:
    Salary $300.00
    ($2.00/hour, 5 hours/night,
    30 nights/month)
    Mileage 157.50
    ($5.25/night, 30 nights/month)
    Compensation Insurance 6.08
    Liability Insurance 8.34
        Total per person.. $471.92

Alternate Plan–
    Salary and Mileage Combined $375.00
    (Salary at $1.50/hour,
    automobile expenses at $1.00/hour)
    Insurance 14.42
        Total per person.. $389.42

2. If NARP and F are employed:
>Salary $187.50
>($1.25/hour, 5 hours/night,
>30 nights/month)
>Mileage 157.50
>County and State Licensing .... .34
>Compensation Insurance 6.08
>Liability Insurance 8.34
>Blanket Bond .... .83
>Special Deputy Commission 1.83
>>Total per person $362.42

Alternate Plan
>Salary and Mileage Combined $262.50
>(Salary at $1/hour and auto-
>mobile expenses at 75 cents/hour)
>Licensing, Insurance, Commission 17.42
>>Total per person $279.92

From the figures listed above, it is to be noted that 32 clients must be obtained at an average rate of $15.00 per month in order to meet expenses if Sheriff's Office deputies services are utilized, and 24 clients under the same set of circumstances if men of the NARP and F are hired.

It is further to be noted that 30 to 35 separate establishments are to be found in an average block of a commercial section. Let it also be pointed out that between 10–15 city blocks are found in a linear mile. . . .

Selling these services without a track record was predictably difficult, and almost all of SAI's income during the winter and spring of 1955 came from investigations, while George continued to plug away, in his spare time, on generating new business, primarily in the area of guard services.

In anticipation of the June 1, 1955, general accounting deadline of all the sales, income, assets, liabilities, and capital of the partnership during the preceding year, as required by Article X of the Partnership Agreement, Orville W. Dixon, the certified public accountant used by SAI, prepared and submitted the fledgling company's very first financial report on Monday, May 23, 1955.

ASSETS

CURRENT ASSETS
Cash on Hand and in Banks $156.41

FIXED ASSETS
Office Equipment $1,650.11
Less: Reserve for Depreciation 79.67 1,570.44
TOTAL ASSETS $1,726.85

LIABILITIES AND CAPITAL

CURRENT LIABILITIES
Notes Payable $163.19
Payroll Taxes Payable 67.20 $230.39

CAPITAL

	Balance 1-1-55	Profit Distrib.	Less Drawings	Net Capital
Altschul	$221.87	$3,581.05	$3,428.80	$374.12
DuBois	221.87	3,499.34	3,347.09	374.12
Stanton	221.87	3,389.82	3,237.58	374.11
Wackenhut	221.86	3,736.24	3,583.99	374.11
	$887.47	$14,206.45	$13,597.46	1,496.46

TOTAL LIABILITIES AND CAPITAL $1,726.85

STATEMENT OF PROFIT AND LOSS
Period Ended May 23, 1955

INCOME
Services $25,551.54

EXPENSES
Expenses Advances $1,059.76
Salaries and Wages 1,280.00
Rent 1,300.00
Taxes and Licenses 110.34
Depreciation 68.75
Credit Report 34.99
Repairs and Maintenance 254.60
Gifts 21.00
Office Supplies 586.45
Steno Service 95.00
Outside Labor 5,648.83
Telephone 771.79
Legal and Auditing 100.00
Bank Charges 13.58
TOTAL EXPENSES 11,345.09
NET PROFIT for Period Ended May 23, 1955 $14,206.45

THE DATE is Monday, May 23, 1955, the place is Suite 1402 of the Ainsley Building, the time is dusk. The wide windows of the suite face due east, revealing hundreds of lighted windows in the low buildings bordering Biscayne Bay. With the oncoming darkness, the bay is changing color, and the portholes of anchored boats throw ribbons of yellow across the calm water. Miami Beach is flat and wide and gold in the shimmering distance. George Wackenhut, thirty-five, sits alone at one of the three desks, in shirtsleeves, tie pulled down, studying background investigations. The silence is broken by Ed DuBois, forty-three, also in shirtsleeves, who walks into the suite through the new doorway to his office in 1403, hesitates when he sees George. Apparently, Ed has been experiencing severe mood swings lately, and this scene has been repeated three or four times over the past few weeks. The tensions between the two men are revealed in their bodies and voices, and the conversation is essentially the same.

"What're *you* doing here?" DuBois asks.

"Background investigations."

"Bullshit. You're playing around with your *guards!*"

"No, I'm not."

DuBois walks over to him. "I ought to kick the shit out of you."

"I'm tired of hearing that, Ed. Knock it off."

"You're wasting *time!* I ought to kick the shit out of you!"

George stands up. "Knock it off, Ed! I *mean* it!"

"You son of a *bitch!* I ought to kick the *shit* out of you!"

The two men move closer, glaring, adrenaline pumping, short of breath now, beads of sweat on their foreheads, both ready to fight. George feints with a right to the body, throws a hard left to the head, splits Ed's chin with his wedding ring, knocks the man back, but not down. It's over. It's finished. The four-man partnership is dead.

In fairness, both sides of this story should be heard, but Ed DuBois, Jr., died of a brain aneurysm in 1968 at the age of fifty-seven. Ed DuBois III vividly remembers his father coming home the night of the fight; he was twelve years old at the time: "It's my understanding that George threw the first punch. Who won the fight, I don't have any idea. I knew my dad came home really upset that day with a big cut on his chin. And he was a big guy, he was six-one. I don't know how many punches were thrown, I don't have any idea. I know it was a fight. George hit him. Whether my dad hit back—I can't imagine my dad not swinging back. Probably did. I never heard the story in any more detail than that. I know when he came home, his chin was cut open . . .

"Anyway, after that confrontation, after that night, it was all over. He knew it was over. He resigned probably the next day. He told the partnership that he was going to form his own company and specialize in investigations, and see you later. I think the time frame is in this folder. I may be off a day, I'm not sure, but it was instantaneous, that was the end of it. My dad went and it was a three-man partnership after that. They kept the name and the logo, and that logo evolved into the Wackenhut logo.

"Unfortunately, there were deep wounds. I think George passes through life, and passes by people, without really knowing what people are about, and who they are, and what they care about, what their feelings are, what they want to do with their lives."

Earl Warford, who had been an investigator with SAI about six months by that time, and was a personal friend of DuBois long before he joined the company, has several insights about the confrontation. "I know Eddie had a hot temper," he recalls, "and I think that you could describe George that way, too, if you really got him mad. I mean, he was one of these people who were very self-controlled, but, after a certain point, he can have a temper, too. All I know is that it ended in fisticuffs, no further than that. After that, I don't know whether you'd call the mood in the office depressed or not, but I think the others thought that Eddie was a capable person, and a very excellent investigator.

"But my recollection is that Eddie had left the Bureau for almost the same reason, that he had gotten into some kind of contest with either the ASAC or the SAC, and was sort of insubordinate to him. He was like an eighteen-year agent, if I remember correctly, and thought that he knew more than the people he was working for, and he was probably insubordinate. I don't know if there was an altercation, just insubordination. He was in the Miami office at that time. I don't remember who the SAC was at that time."

Bud Thompson heard first-hand accounts of both sides of the story: "There was a real battle that took place in the company, it exploded. I guess it depends upon who you talk with as to what was behind what happened. And I heard both sides of it, one from George, and one from Ed. Because both were friends, and I was not in the company at the time. But it basically had to do, in my opinion, with a difference of opinion about what the company should be and where it was going and how to get there. So they knocked heads on that. I don't know how many blows, I know there was one blow struck, I guess George hit him because Ed called him a son of a bitch or something like that, and George was short-tempered and flew at him, and that caused total disruption in the company at that point."

DuBois resigned the next day, May 24, 1955, but gave the partners ten days' notice, to make the resignation effective June 2. Following is an excerpt from a memo he dictated the morning he resigned:

May 24, 1955

TO: AKA, WS, GRW
FROM: E.L.D., Jr.

The following is my itemization of monies due me as of May 23, 1955, as compiled from the Accounts Receivable file:

[He lists the file number of twenty-one cases, the amount due SAI on each case, and the fees and expenses due to him on each case. He was owed a total of $1,207.90 in fees, and $21.65 in expenses.]

The above amounts, you will note by checking the file, are not in all cases the "net fee due SAI" because, in some cases, the expenses and amounts paid to others were already paid, and therefore, where those amounts have already been paid, it has been added as the total amount due SAI, which latter amount I have divided by four to arrive at the amount due to me.

I have not asked for any share of fees owing SAI for the year 1954.

Pending cases worked, or being worked, during the month of May, 1955, and not yet billed, should be calculated by SAI to show the proportionate share due ELD:

13-6 Schwab Case
11-4 Christopher Case
14-3 Ware Laboratories
 2-5 Bornstein
 3-20 Stamates
 4-5 Black
 4-8 Pope
 1-45 Miami Beach Hotel Association as to work conducted subsequent to May 17, 1955.
5-20 thru 5-53, with the exception of 5-29 (Martin), which was billed on May 23, and 5-20, (Parsons), which was also billed on May 23, 1955.

In addition to the above, the balance in the checking account as of May 23, 1955, through Check No. 651, is $53.72, and one-fourth of that is $13.43 due ELD.

Exactly seventy-nine days passed before his memo was answered on August 11, and then very formally, on the engraved stationery of Special Agent Investigators, which still listed his name as one of the partners, of course, because they couldn't afford to change such expensive stationery until the supply was exhausted. The inside address gave his title as Attorney-at-Law, and his office as 1403 Ainsley Building.

Dear Mr. DuBois:
Reference is made to your memorandum dated May 24, 1955, in which you itemize all monies allegedly due you as of May 23, 1955, compiled from the accounts receivable file for the calendar year 1955. Also listed were pending cases, worked or being worked, during the month of May 1955, but not yet billed, which you asked SPECIAL AGENT INVESTIGATORS to determine the proportionate share due you. It is also noted that you arrived at the figure $13.43 due you as your share of the bank balance as of May 23, 1955.
Attachments to this letter, listed below, are itemizations prepared by the undersigned individuals of your financial status with SPECIAL AGENT INVESTIGATORS as of the close of business May 23, 1955:

A–One-fourth share on cases where payment has been received.
B–One-fourth prorated share of those pending cases worked or being

worked during the month of May 1955, but not yet billed as of May 24, 1955.

C–One-fourth prorated share of cases 5-21 thru 5-53.

D–$53.72 in checking account as of May 23, 1955, one-fourth of which is $13.43.

E–One-fourth proportionate share of accounts not collected as of August 11, 1955.

F–Explanation concerning those cases listed in the referenced memorandum, but not listed on Attachments A, B, C and E.

G–One-fourth proportionate share of monies owed SPECIAL AGENT INVESTIGATORS by you.

H–Itemization of your share of the potential bad debts for the period January 1 thru May 23, 1955.

I–Recapitulation sheet.

J–Letter from Orville W. Dixon, C.P.A.

K–"Financial Report, SPECIAL AGENT INVESTIGATORS (A Partnership), Miami, Florida, May 23, 1955," prepared by Orville W. Dixon, C.P.A., Miami, Florida.

The document was signed by all three partners. A meeting of the four men was held that day to discuss the attachments A–K, and another meeting was held on August 19, also for the purpose of trying to settle financial arrangements with DuBois in his partnership dissolution.

The next correspondence we have is a pencil-written memo/invoice from DuBois to the partners, not dated, but obviously subsequent to the meeting of August 19. Curiously, DuBois refers to himself throughout in both the first and third person:

To: Special Agent Investigators
For Services rendered up to June 2, 1955, the effective date of DuBois' resignation:

Total due DuBois.....$_____.00

Amount approximated in my memo filed under "Partnership Dissolution–File #1." They are to confirm by letter & if disputed DuBois & a C.P.A. will examine their records. They may claim not to owe DuBois anything, per the Partnership Agreement, but DuBois will claim that argument was amended several times–see above file which contains memos–last one by Altschul–which disregarded the Partnership Fund.

> Since DuBois' resignation, he received from SAI as part-payment on above total due:
>
> | | |
> |---|---|
> | June 6, 1955 (SAT file 1-45) | $200.00 |
> | June 10 by SAI check #697 (file 11-4) | 75.00 |
> | June 14 by SAI check #705 (file 1-45) | 200.00 |
> | June 28: credited DuBois on rug & drapes, which amount is full payment by DuBois to SAI for rug, drapes in Room 1402. | |
> | Door from 1402 to 1403 | 100.00 |
>
> August 19, 1955, Wackenhut said SAI will not prevent me from operating Investigators, Inc., if I will cancel balance they owe me, allow them to use my name on their stationery until present supply exhausted, and if I will forget Wackenhut's assault.

That last sentence contains the essence of the deal that was eventually struck. The one-year non-compete clause in Article XII of the Partnership Agreement was waived by the partners in return for his agreement to cancel the balance owed to him, and he further agreed not to file any charges of assault against George. In September 1955, DuBois opened his own firm, Investigators, Inc., operated out of Suite 1403, and the company has been in business ever since, carried on by his son.

"Ed went off and started his own company and did a very fine job," Bud Thompson recalls. "He was known as being an outstanding investigative company. He was a fine leader and was well liked by the investigators. His technique was not to hire a whole flock of people, but have like seventy-five people in his rotary, and he could call up whoever he needed, whatever he needed, and he could put twenty men out on the street or fifty to a hundred. I worked for Ed while I was in the Sheriff's Department in those times, because he'd call up and say, 'Bud, I got something that needs to be done, you could do it, you want to make some extra money?' And he paid the highest of anybody in Dade County. But he wanted good people. He used a lot of ex-agents, he used a lot of people in law enforcement that had special talents, guys that would be very good in certain areas, and he would use them. He only had a secretary and, later on, one man who really was reviewing the cases and putting them all together, and all that, but they turned out wonderful work.

"There was a very bad feeling among the ex-agents about George. Because the stories that went around, and, you know, I'm not going to say I knew all about what all the stories were, but there was bad feelings, and everybody knew DuBois to be a very fine investigator and do very nice work. He was stationed in the Miami office here before he left, and he was very well respected. And George, being the new kid on the block, they didn't have the same feeling about him. It was very difficult for George.

"And then, afterwards, it was a lot of jealousy, because George became very successful and very wealthy. And, you know, there's always some guy mumbling in the background. I don't pay any attention to that crap, because there's no way you can play games with all those people. It's never ending. My mother used to say that all your life you're going to meet a lot of small people, and if you stop and fight with all of them along the way, you're never going to get anywhere, so just get out and do the best you can every day, and the hell with all those people, you'll pass them by. And it's true, there were a lot of little people in there that didn't understand, didn't know, and it was very bad. I felt sorry for George in those times, because I think he always wanted to be a part of the group, but he was not as well accepted as maybe he would like to have been."

Ed DuBois III was twenty-five when his father died in October 1968. He had graduated from Florida State University in 1966, joined the Air Force before he was drafted, and graduated from OTS in 1967. Then he decided that as long as he was going to be an officer signed up for three years, he would sign up for another year and be a jet pilot. He was accepted in the pilot program and started training in October 1967.

"Then, in October of 1968, the week of completion of the program, my dad died," DuBois says. "He had an aneurysm in the connecting artery of the right frontal lobe, and had probably had it for a long time. The aneurysm, at the time it popped, was about the size of a golf ball. For the last couple of years, he had been experiencing a lot of problems associated with that. At that time, they didn't know what it was. He had pressure in his head, he rubbed his head in the mornings, he had a lot of personality swings and personality problems. Looking back on it, we should've seen it, but, you know, in the mid- to late-'sixties, they really didn't know a lot about that stuff. We thought he was having a late middle-age crisis, or something, we didn't know what it was. But he was on the way to the airport, and it popped, it actually exploded, burst, and wiped out his right frontal lobe, and that was it.

"This was hanging on the wall in my dad's office [referring to a typewritten, framed motto; see below], and, really, that's who he was. He was not a joiner, he hated to join anything, he wasn't a member of this and that, he wasn't a self-promoter, he was just an anonymous, excellent investigator. That was their way of life. I mean, there's a new breed now, but back then, those guys were like that. That's the way they were, that's how they operated."

The following was written by Ed DuBois, Jr., and hung in a frame over his desk from the time he started Investigators, Inc., in 1955.

A PRIVATE INVESTIGATOR

A Private Investigator is a public servant for clients of the last resort;
A Private Investigator must use a fool-proof pretext as his credential;
A Private Investigator keeps his eye on the beam, not on the bounce;
  A Private Investigator must have a burning desire to succeed;
  A Private Investigator is a fact-finder, not an advocate;
  A Private Investigator makes luck the refuge of design;
  A Private Investigator must use pinpoint concentration;
    A Private Investigator keeps private affairs private;
    A Private Investigator reports facts, not opinions;
      A Private Investigator must lack inhibitions;
      A Private Investigator must be dependable;
        A Private Investigator is anonymous;
          A Private Investigator–
          REPORTS RESULTS–
            NOT ALIBIS!

12

THE ONLY PHOTOGRAPH known to exist of the four partners together was taken in December 1954 at the Biscayne Terrace Hotel in Miami by Bert Henry, the hotel's photographer, whose name appears on the back. It is a formal shot taken at a dinner party of the Society of Former Special Agents of the FBI, and the four partners appear in a group of ten men arranged in two rows. Earl Warford is in the front row, sitting at the table with a large shrimp cocktail before him, and his face looks much younger than his twenty-nine years. Bud Thompson, sitting one chair away, could easily pass for a college boy, although he was twenty-seven. Ed DuBois, standing behind the table with his partners, is the oldest of the group at forty-three, and looks it. Bill Stanton, at thirty, appears to be extremely thin compared to George on his left, who is at least 175 pounds at thirty-five, crew-cutted, square-jawed with a pronounced cleft in his chin, and the only man wearing a bow tie. Next to him, Ken Altschul, at thirty, has a bald pate and seems a bit chunky, but has a naturally heavy build.

Although George always insisted that no photographs had ever been taken of the four partners together, Earl Warford found this slightly faded 8"- × -10" black-and-white print more than thirty-nine years after it was taken, and in a very unusual way.

The time is Wednesday morning, February 5, 1993, and Warford is sitting with his wife Aileen in the small living room of a rented thirty-five-foot trailer, a Fleetwood Limited, parked on the front lawn of his extensively damaged house at 9635 Dominican Drive, in the Cutler Ridge section of South Miami. It is an area hit particularly hard by the devastating Hurricane Andrew on August 24, 1992, labeled by the media as the worst natural disaster in U.S. history, far surpassing the damage inflicted by the legendary San Francisco earthquake and fire of 1912. More than five months after the hurricane, virtually every house on Dominican Drive is still badly damaged, has a trailer parked on its front lawn, and the same is true for many miles around. According to statistics compiled by *The Miami Herald,* more than 103,200 homes were damaged, 50,000 homes were destroyed, 107,348 buildings were damaged, 625,000 insurance claims were filed, and $15 billion was paid by insurance companies.

As we tape record Warford, carpenters are working inside his house and the sound of hammers and power tools is constant. White-haired, tanned, wearing glasses, Earl glances at the house, shakes his head. "I bought this house while I was working for Wackenhut. We moved in February 4, 1955. Hurricane Andrew did pretty extensive damage, our insurance settlement was like $72,000. We got this trailer November 1; the trailer actually belongs to my niece, but the insurance company allowed me to rent it from her. They were very happy, because most of the people were having to buy trailers. We're scheduled to move back in the house February 16. The outside won't be completed, but the inside will be. Our van over there had $6,000 worth of damage to it, but it was fairly new, so we went ahead and had that repaired. We had a ten-year-old second car that had $1,200 worth of damage to it, so we decided it wasn't worth fixing. We haven't been able to replace it yet, because we have no place to park. I don't want to get a new car and put it out in the street."

When the Warfords put all of their furniture in storage after the hurricane, they also packed and stored ninety-five boxes of belongings. One of the boxes contained old photographs, and Earl said he seemed to remember a few from his days with Special Agent Investigators. As it turned out, he found only one. Naturally, he recognized the four partners, plus Bud Thompson and himself, but he couldn't identify the four other men, although their faces were extremely familiar.

George was delighted when he saw the photo, and recognized one other man, Don Lohmeyer (FBI 1951–54), but he had never seen a copy of the photo before, and didn't even recall posing for it. Bud Thompson had seen it before, consulted the roster of ex-agents in the Miami area during 1954, and remembered the names of the three others: Paul Williams, Jim Hayes, and Bill Robinson.

MAY 1955 was a pivotal month for SAI in a variety of respects. Several weeks before the May 23 altercation with Ed DuBois, George had met Gene Brawner, a former FBI agent, who was an official at National Airlines in Miami. During their conversation, George mentioned that he knew National had a large guard force.

"Yes," Brawner said, "and we aren't too pleased with the present setup."

"You know, of course, that we're in the guard business," George told him with tongue in cheek, because, at the time, SAI had no guard contracts.

"I didn't know that," Brawner said. "As a matter of fact, we're going to ask for bids. Would you like to bid on it?"

"By all means."

At this point, George's extensive research into the financial aspects of initiating a guard service, outlined in his lengthy memo to his partners, January 4, 1955, became the basic operating rationale behind his formal proposal to National. He made a few inquiries to ensure that his facts and figures were still up to date, and finally submitted a bid of $1.25 an hour. The minimum wage at that time was still 75 cents an hour, and he planned to pay $1 an hour to the guards. He felt that a 25-cent spread would be sufficient. Fortunately, he had taken into consideration such items as the cost of social security, unemployment taxes, and insurance. However, he hadn't considered the cost of office overhead and a few other items.

"Yet, that probably saved me the contract," he says, "because, after all, we had no track record as a guard service."

Since the price was right for National Airlines, SAI was awarded the contract, which was subsequently held for twenty years. This was the start of the Wackenhut security guard service.

Although George had no practical experience in the security guard business at the time, and the contract was scheduled to commence July 1, 1955, he immediately met with an officer of the National Association of Retired Police and Firemen, Inc., who told him that he could secure all the ex-policemen he would need at $1 an hour. George needed about twenty men to get started at National, and this solved his major problem.

"Now I needed uniforms in a hurry," George recalls. "Close by the office was a uniform company operated by Donald S. Levine, who had quoted prices to me when I was doing research on patrol and guard service in December 1954. So I went back to see Levine. I told him that I needed twenty uniforms. The minimum uniform would include trousers, long-sleeved shirt, cap, shoulder patch, and leather goods, for a total of $37.60 per man. For twenty uniforms, that worked out to a total of $752. So I told him I needed a little credit until we got started."

"Nothing doing," Levine told him. "There are about forty guard agencies that spring up here every year and go out of business about as quick as they get started. With me, it's cash on the barrelhead."

"Well, this is *one* outfit that *won't* go out of business!" George bristled. "And I'll promise you this: As I get bigger, you'll get *all* my business!"

George smiles warmly at the memory. "He must have liked the cut of my jib, my vehemence, or something. Because, before I walked out, I had the credit I needed."

(Although this was the beginning of the Wackenhut security guard service, the first twenty guards had uniforms with sleeve patches that read "Special Agent Investigators." Eventually, the problem was solved when, on July 25, 1957, a Certificate of Incorporation was filed in the office of the Florida Secretary of State for the name "Special Agent Security Guards, Inc.")

In early June, 1955, less than one month after George's altercation with Ed DuBois, the company moved from Suite 1402 in the Ainsley Building to larger quarters in Suite 811 of the same building, with a luxurious reception area, and three rooms. That became the first office that Ruth designed for the firm. "I remember the day Special Agent Investigators moved into Suite 811 in the Ainsley Building," Ruth says, smiling. "I was handed $100, and George asked me to 'furnish' the office. This, you might say, was the beginning of my ambition to be a designer/architect. Surprisingly, it turned out well—with additional money. My favorite room was my husband's office. On the wall behind his desk chair, I hung a large framed painting, *Silver Knight in Shining Armor*. In my heart, he *was* my Knight, and would eventually win his 'battle' to be the tremendous success he has become. But I had no idea—nor did he, at the time—that he would eventually expand worldwide."

An interesting observation is the fact that, just prior to starting the National Airlines contract, on July 1, 1955, the balance sheet of Special Agent Investigators showed current liabilities of $4,140.32, and current assets of $195. The Statement of Income for the months ending October 31, 1956, showed an income of $72,082.48, total expenses of $48,314.89, and a net profit of $23,767.59.

By December of 1955, the three remaining partners had decided to form a corporation, and filed a Certificate of Incorporation on December 28, 1955, under the name of Special Agent Investigators, Inc. George Wackenhut was designated as president, Bill Stanton as vice president, and Ken Altschul as secretary-treasurer.

A special meeting of the stockholders and board of directors of Special Agent Investigators, Inc., was held on January 25, 1956, at which time it was noted that the assets of the partnership of Special Agent Investigators had been transferred to the new corporation. It was mutually agreed that there should be an adjustment of capital stock, so that the interest of each stockholder would be shown as follows: George R. Wackenhut, 3,700 shares; A. Kenneth Altschul, 3,700 shares; William Stanton, 200 shares. It was also decided that the salaries of each officer, as of January 1, 1956, should be $1 per year, and that each should share $33\frac{1}{3}$ percent of the operating costs and capital investment, and that their salaries should be determined by the gross income produced by each of them, less the $33\frac{1}{3}$ percent of cost of operation of the company and capital investment.

As a result of obtaining the National Airlines contract, the company now began to establish a track record in guard service and was able to win other security guard jobs. Contracts came from International Minerals and Chemicals Corporation at Bartow, Florida, for which the company had been conducting investigations; from Riddle

Airlines, Detroit Diesel of General Motors Corporation, Ware Laboratories, and Dade Drydock, all in the Miami area. In addition, Crown Cork and Seal Company contracts were obtained, both in Bartow and Orlando, Florida Tile Industries, and Kraft Foods, along with Food Machinery and Chemical Corporation in Lakeland, and the Grandway Discount Centers in the greater Miami area.

However, the investigative end of the business was holding its own, and Earl Warford has pleasant memories of those days: "I think it was the policy of the company not to do divorce work, unless the attorney that asked them to do it gave us a lot of other work. But the few divorce cases that we worked on were ones that stick in my mind. I believe we had a lawyer whose client was the wife of a National Airlines' pilot. And she suspected him of cheating on her, so we surveilled him. They thought, of course, that it would be better to have a couple doing the surveillance, rather than a single man, so my wife accompanied me on several of the divorce cases that we did. Plus, George and Ruth also were in on the early surveillances."

Earl's wife, Aileen, a graduate of the Florida State College for Women (now Florida State University), recalls those cases clearly. "The first time I met Ruth was when the four of us went on surveillance," she says, smiling. "We went bar-hopping on Miami Beach and along the causeway. That was kind of fun. And we sat outside a hotel all night that the subject went into with this woman, in order to establish the fact that he was in there all night with her."

Earl has particularly strong feelings about the significance of the role Ruth played during the early days. "Personally, I feel that Ruth had a lot to do with the growth of the firm. I think that she was the type of wife that provided the drive, part of the drive, that George had. I think she was very astute and had a lot of business sense herself. I think she was behind George. Not being the type of wife that wanted him home and with the kids, and all that kind of stuff. She understood that to develop a business, you had to put in the time and effort to do it. I think she had a lot to do with the success of the business."

Warford left SAI in mid-February, 1956, to accept a position with Jordan Marsh on March 1, where he would remain for thirty-one years and become a vice president. "I had been through their executive training program before I entered the FBI," he says, "and they wanted somebody to administer that program for them. It was a better job, and had all of the benefits that you get for working for a large company. It seemed to me at the time that it had more stability than Special Agent Investigators. I really enjoyed what I was doing, and I liked the people that I worked with, but I was agonizing between taking a chance on how that company would develop and going into something that I knew world provide the income and benefits and security that I thought I needed for my family."

Then, although the business was prospering, in April of 1956, Ken Altschul accepted a business offer from Kelly Garges, an ex-agent who ran an armored car service in Atlanta, and the company bought out his stock. Just five months later, Bill Stanton, who held a degree in chemistry, accepted an offer from Nat Klein, an ex-agent who owned Key Pharmaceuticals in Miami. As a result, in September 1956, George Wackenhut became the sole owner of Special Agent Investigators, Inc.

During 1955, George was one of the founders (along with Charles B. Allen), of Fidelifax, an organization of former FBI agents formed to do background investigations throughout the country. The idea was prompted by John Fisher, head of the American Security Council, who at that time was head of security at Sears, Roebuck & Company, in Chicago. It was at the second ex-FBI convention, in 1955 in Detroit, that George met Eugene J. Charters, who eventually replaced Bill Stanton in 1956.

Born in Philadelphia in 1906, Gene Charters graduated from the University of Pennsylvania's Wharton School in 1927, and from its law school in 1930. In 1931, he joined the law office of John J. McDevitt, Jr., in Philadelphia, before becoming a special agent of the FBI in 1934. He remained with the FBI for twelve years, assigned to various offices, including Washington and New York, where he was a supervisor. After resigning in 1946, Charters started his own investigative agency in Philadelphia, E.J. Charters Associates, Inc., which he has continued to maintain to the present.

"I met George at the ex-FBI convention in 1955 in Detroit," Charters recalls. "That was the second convention; the first was in Chicago. I think he told me about his company at that time. I don't remember how it came about, but I know that we met again in New York, sometime in 1956, before I started in Miami in September 1956. I was in the throes of some personal problems, and it kind of fitted in, and we got to talking. I know that finally he said that he needed somebody to run his investigative branch, and we came to an agreement. Bill Stanton had just about left in 1956, and that's why I came in. I never met him there. Ed DuBois was long gone by that time. The other partner, Ken Altschul, I can picture him, he went to Atlanta. When I came on board, there was only George left of the original four partners. We were in the Ainsley Building. He had a fellow by the name of Lew Whitworth. We had a secretary by the name of Sonja; I don't know her last name. She was a whiz. The nature of the business then was still investigative, but I think he was more interested in the security end of it.

"Now, it's a funny story, when I first came down there, I was looking for a place to stay, so Ruth said she'd drive me around. So I met her, she picked me up, we went around to different places. And a couple of places, they'd look at her, they'd look at me, they didn't want to rent to a single guy, and that sort of stuff! Well, we had lunch. So then, I don't know if it was the next day or a couple of days later, and I don't remember the exact language George used, but it so happened he was telling me that Ruth mentioned my name in her *sleep!* And he was kind of concerned whether anything went on, I think. At that time, I was in a certain situation with another gal, and I pointed out to him: How the hell could that happen? But I liked George coming to me with that, that was smart, I mean the guy would talk about those things. We socialized with them—out—but I don't recall dinner parties or anything at their place. They may have had them. But I went out with them to various other parties.

"But I have to say this about George, he treated me beautifully, very fair. I admire him. He was very serious about making good, because of his background. Because his family had suffered during poverty, and he vowed it would never happen to him. In fact, he was very straight-talking about that. I don't know whether he still does or not. But he had a sense of humor, he had a good sense of humor, and he had a wonderful mind. A curious mind. If he'd hear something new, he'd want to know about it. And he'd store it away. He was the kind of guy who it was good to be around. I liked to be with him. He was very responsive to you, he'd listen to you. And you always felt as though he was listening to you to find out what he didn't know. In other words, he wasn't picking your brains—he'd do that sometimes, every executive does that—but there wasn't a question that he was doing that to your detriment. He was persistent, he was a hell of a good investigator, too. I went out with him one time, and I could see what kind of an intense, persistent investigator he was. He covered all bases, making sure he had the stuff right, the details and everything like that, so he was a very good man in that way, too. I think that's the way he was with all problems that he had, very detailed about solving them. Very intense type of guy and a very hard worker.

"You know, hard work is always rewarding. And especially when it's day in, day out—and *night* in and night out. Because this guy worked. In fact, you know, it's the same old story, I guess, where Ruth was wondering what was going on. He'd say that to me, I'm not making that up. So he put in a lot of hours, and he worked at it, but not only that, you see, he was goal-oriented, he knew what he wanted. And that's another thing that a man has to know in order to be successful. You have to know where you want to go. You can't just go slopping around and waiting for something to happen to you. George didn't do that. George made it happen. He was very bulldoggish on that sort of thing, when there was something that he wanted. And I noticed another thing about George: With all the problems on his desk, he'd never plop around from one to the other; he'd pick the most important one and work on it. Everything else could just sit there. And he had a knack of picking the ones that were important to him, that needed to be solved.

"One of the things that we did when I was there, a case that we got, was from the Miami Beach Council. I can't remember the councilman that was the instigator of it [Mel Richard]. They had a city manager there, and they were having problems with reports of the chief of police, corruption and that sort of thing, and they wanted an investigation. And they got George, and I was in charge of the investigation. It was quite a voluminous thing. We ended up writing a very thick report, but all the important witnesses were termed 'confidential informants'—Number 1, Number 2, Number 3—and nobody was supposed to know who these men were. That's the only way they would talk to us. I don't think it ever did come out. Maybe it did later, but I didn't know about it. The thing I wanted to mention here, there are a couple of points: When it came time to present this report, it was a meeting of the council, and George got up in front of the microphone and he says, 'We have the report here, but we're not turning it in unless we're guaranteed indemnification." And they were really squirming in their seats on that one. But it didn't take them long, they decided, okay, we'll give you indemnification. And George had never told me anything about that, that he was going to do that."

George still considers this particular investigation one of the most fascinating, because of the incredible corruption involved. "Now, on the Miami Beach Police investigation, this was in 1957," he says with a smile. "The whole thing was political. There were seven members on the Miami Beach Council. One of them was an attorney named Mel Richard. He was disenchanted with the chief of police, and he started raising a lot of hell, and it got into the press, and then it became a cause célèbre type of thing. Mel actually wanted a fellow named Bernie Weider as chief of police. So he kept beating the drums until there was public pressure and it became necessary for the council to get somebody to investigate to see if there was any fire, because there was sure a lot of smoke.

"They knew perfectly well there was a lot of fire. And Mel Richard said, 'Now, I want it to be a group of former FBI agents; I'm not going to settle for anybody else.' So this all impressed them, and he had them by the shorts then, they had to do pretty much what he asked them. So the city manager called us. Gene Charters was now part of the company. So Charters and I went over and met with the city manager, and we told him what our price was, I think it was $50 a day, plus expenses. So he told us what the limit on the total cost would be, and when we reached that point to come back and he'd see what he could do. He didn't think—nor did the other councilmen—that we were going to come up with anything. But we came up with *so much,* we could've filled *volumes!*

"During the course of the interviews, it seemed like everyone had something to say. It was either because they were trying to down this one or they were trying to down that one. So one of the things I thought was fascinating was that Bernie Weider was a sergeant, plainclothes, and he had a partner with the rank of patrolman, but plainclothes, who was *constantly* with Weider. And Weider grabbed him and used him in the capacity he did because the patrolman was alleged to have been a 'runner' for the S&G syndicate, which was renowned in those days down here as the top gambling organization. And, by being a runner, you know, you'd run information and money form one to another. So he knew all the top gamblers—by sight as well as by name.

"Weider was in charge of the hotel detail at that time, So he'd take this plainclothes guy into a hotel and they'd nose around, and if the guy saw any of his gambling figures, Weider would collar them and take them to the police station.

"This one day at the Fontainebleau, his partner pointed out a man who was a top gambling figure in those days, and apparently was a convicted felon, and should have reported in to the police department when he came to town; when you were a felon, you had to do that. He was pointed out by Weider's partner, and Weider went up to him and asked if he'd reported in. He hadn't, so Weider arrested him and took him down to the police department, which was down toward South Beach. He didn't have him there more than ten or fifteen minutes, and the police chief ran in wearing his robe and bedroom slippers, and said: '*Bernie,* what're you trying to *do to me!*' Well, it was pretty obvious what was going on.

"Now, this went on for many weeks. After we ran out of money, we went back over to the city manager, and said, 'We have so much—about 345 pages—we don't want to stop now, but we don't have any more funds approved.' He said, 'Well, I can't get any more money!' He changed his tone completely. Because he didn't think we were going to get anything. Now he sees we've got so much, he's not going to pay us to get any more. So, after we left there, I said to Gene, 'We have no choice, we'll just have to keep on going, out of our own pocket, and bring this thing to some sort of a logical conclusion.'

"So we continued on and centered the report on the chief. When the report was almost complete, we invited the councilmen to come to our office and read the report, separately and privately. They were all dying to know who was in the report, of course. One or more of them, after reading it, when they were talking to the news media, said, 'It reads like a *best-seller!*' I remember that clearly. Then, after the councilmen had read it, they had to decide how to get rid of the chief. There had to be a sacrificial lamb somewhere.

"During the course of the investigation, we also learned that—and we got this from the wives of police officers, some of the wives who were about to divorce their husbands, or otherwise were upset with them. They told us that every morning there would be a series of phone calls among the wives: 'What did you get last night?' 'Well, I got a fur coat, what did you get?' 'Well, I got a diamond ring.' What the police were doing, whenever there was an alarm, or a report that a burglary had taken place at such-and-such a store, the police would converge on the store, *clean it out,* and give the stuff to their wives that night! It was a marvelous police department.

"But, you know, investigating something like that was just absolutely fascinating. The things that you learned, you could hardly believe they were happening. The bottom line is, the chief got fired, and when we went over to the council meeting to turn in our final report, I remember saying, 'I don't want to turn in this report unless we can get indemnity from the council.' Because it was chock-full of corruption. And they hesitated to do that, but they finally agreed.

"Then, afterward, something extremely interesting happened. I had a good friend, who's since deceased, who was a sergeant with the Sheriff's Office, before it became Metro. His name was Charley Zmuda. He was originally from Chicago, he was on the police force up there. Zmuda had a legal wiretap on the home of the reputed leader of organized crime down here. He was the boss. What they used to do in those days, I think it was before the Sunshine Law became active, the Miami Beach Council would meet in private, down on a lower level, decide how they were going to vote on something, then they'd come up and have a public meeting. Of course, everything was foreordained at that point.

"The night before the council meeting—and this is on tape—every single one of those council members, with the exception of Mel

Richard, called the boss and said, 'How do we vote tomorrow?' So the boss told them. To three of them, he said, 'You're going to vote for a certain sergeant.' The three others were told to vote for another man. They all asked, 'Who's *he?*' The boss said, 'Well, he's the city's hot-plate inspector.' They had an ordinance in Miami Beach that people staying in hotel rooms were not allowed to use hot-plates. So, if there were any complaints, the inspector would check to see if they were violating the hot-plate law.

"Then, the next question from the councilmen was, did the inspector know where a certain room was? That's where they all got their payoffs! That's where they met every week to get their share. And the boss said, 'Yes, he knows.'

"Now, the boss also said that the first ballot would be three for the inspector, three for the sergeant, and one for Weider. So, it's a tie, which made it look good, and they had to have another vote. And when they voted the second time, the three who voted for the sergeant would switch over to the inspector. Then it would be six to one, and the inspector would be the new chief.

"The evening they voted, I turned the radio on, and they were broadcasting the council meeting. Sure enough, that's *exactly* what happened. I remember thinking: This is really fascinating."

SEEN in historical perspective, the years 1954–1957 included a number of significant events. The infamous Army-McCarthy hearings began April 22, 1954, and the daily inquiry became one of the most popular television shows of the year; after thirty-six days of testimony, Senator McCarthy was discredited, and later "condemned" by the U.S. Senate. May 7 of that year, the Supreme Court handed down its unanimous decision (in *Brown v. Board of Education of Topeka*) that racial segregation in public schools was illegal. On February 8, 1955, Nikolai A. Bulganin became Soviet Premier, replacing Malenkov; April 6, Winston Churchill resigned as British Prime Minister and was succeeded by Anthony Eden; May 5, the Federal Republic of West Germany became a sovereign state; December 5, the American Federation of Labor merged with the Congress of Industrial Organizations, to form the powerful AFL-CIO, with George Meany as president. May 21, 1956, the first aerial H-bomb was tested over Namu islet, Bikini Atoll, equivalent to 10 million tons of TNT; August 1, the polio vaccine developed by Dr. Jonas Salk was made available on a mass basis; November 6, Dwight D. Eisenhower defeated Adlai E. Stevenson in the presidential election. In 1957, Senator John F. Kennedy won a Pulitzer Prize for his book *Profiles in Courage*; Dr. Martin Luther King, Jr., started the Southern Christian Leadership Conference; the Soviet Union launched *Sputnik I,* the first earth-orbiting satellite, marking the start of the Space Age.

IN MARCH 1957, John Ammarell visited Miami as director of security for Air Products and Chemicals Corporation (APCC) of Allentown, Pennsylvania, which was in the process of constructing a classified liquid hydrogen manufacturing facility about a mile or so adjacent to the Pratt and Whitney Research and Development Laboratories, west of Palm Beach in the Everglades. Ammarell had to meet with officials of the Florida Power and Light Company (FP&L), which had a large electrical contract wtih APCC for the manufacture of liquid hydrogen. During a discussion with Bob Wall, vice president of personnel for FP&L, who had formerly served in the FBI, Ammarell learned of Wackenhut's success with Special Agent Security Guards. He visited with George and told him that he planned to secure proposals from three firms in order to arrange for a contract security program at the APCC plant near Pratt and Whitney. Pinkerton, Burns, and Special Agent Security Guards were requested to submit proposals.

Eventually, the contract was awarded to Special Agent Security Guards, and approved by the Philadelphia Air Procurement District, since this was an Air Force classified contract. Service began in August 1957. Because this was a classified contract, it required that the firm be granted a secret security clearance and that all personnel assigned to the APCC facility have interim or final secret clearances. On January 8, 1958, Special Agent Security Guards was granted a secret security clearance, authorizing the receipt and use of classified information required in connection with the pre-contract negotiations for contract performance by the secretaries of the Army, Navy, and Air Force, by authority vested in the secretary of the Air Force.

The liquid hydrogen being manufactured by APCC was for the purpose of testing an engine utilizing liquid hydrogen as its fuel, and eventually resulted in the Saturn engine program, which was the engine used to propel our satellites into space. Wackenhut has been continuously involved in the satellite and missile program since August 1957.

Bud Thompson was still working in the Dade County Sheriff's Department that year, but occasionally he did work on the side for George, and he remembers one humorous anecdote about the Air Products contract: "John Ammarell used to work for Air Products, and they were able to pick up a facility which was a liquid hydrogen plant out in the Everglades. I mean, it sits right out in the middle of nowhere. I had been up there to inspect the thing a couple of times. Well, the plant went on strike. And the plant decided to keep going with supervisors. I had to go up there and set up the guard operation for a strike.

"The guards had a pet *alligator* out there. The guards had taken an alligator, and they would bring food to it. If they found an animal hit in the road, they'd pick it up, put it in the car, take it out there, and feed it to the gator. That gator, they called him 'Peg'—pegleg—he had one leg gone, another gator had taken his leg off. They would go up to the side of the canal there, and they'd go: 'Peg! Peg-Peg-Peg!' Down the canal come this damn alligator. And they'd feed the gator. And when I was up there, first time I saw it, the supervisor—I liked to died when I saw him—little short dumpy guy, he had sandals on, and I said, 'Jesus Christ, George would crap if he saw this guy.' But, anyway, he has a hambone or something there and he wants to show me how they feed Peg, and he went down the edge there, and he goes, 'Peg-Peg-Peg!' Peg comes around, he comes up the side of the bank. He's holding this meat out, and that gator makes a lurch—he dropped the thing and fell backwards! He's laying there on the ground, I'm thinking I'm going to stand there and see my supervisor eaten by a gator, right there on the job! How do you claim Workers' Comp when a guy has his leg eaten off by an alligator?

"But, anyway, that was the guard post out there, and those guards fed all kinds of animals, they had bobcats, they had raccoons, everything you can think of; this is a wildlife area. They would come out there, and the guards made pets out of them, they were feeding them all this stuff. They used to say, 'Ain't nobody going to row around the fence and go through the Everglades to get there with Peg out there.' They're just not going to do it, because there's gators all over, but particularly Peg stayed there all the time.

"Anyway, I went up there for the strike, and we had a mess. God damn it, I was sleeping on the desk for a while, and they ran out of food, pretty soon they didn't have any food. So the people in the plant said they had lined up a whole station wagon full of food, and I was to be the one, because they let me come and go through the picket lines, because I was not one of the employees, and they knew I was with the security company, so they let me go through the thing. So they said, 'You got to take the station wagon and go into Palm Beach and get us some food.' They let me out, all right, and I went into town, and I came back in, and they saw me and waved at me, and I went on through and went in there. And I had that son of a bitch—everything in that wagon except where I was sitting was solid with food. Well, they found out about it after I got back in the plant. The next time I came out, they jerked me out of the car, and they said, 'We're going to tell you a little something, friend.' And these were not old bummy workers, these were people working, making liquid hydrogen, they're not peasants. They said, 'We're going to take and stick you in the swamp out here if you try this one again.' So I said, 'Well, I was only doing what they told me to do, I'm sorry, but that's what I did.' Well, we got through that one, and made it, and it wasn't too bad of a deal. But that was one of our first experiences with labor disputes."

The growth of the security guard business required the company to secure supervisors in the Miami, Lakeland, Orlando, and West Palm Beach areas, in order to provide the clients with the necessary supervision. In Miami, the area supervisor was Raymond Giesler, who, with other supervisors reporting to him, handled the training and operational responsibilities for more than 100 guards in that area. Dale Wilson in Lakeland and Marvin Barnes in Orlando were area supervisors, working out of their homes. They handled the hiring, uniforming, payroll, and other administrative duties from their residences, and often were required to stand guard duty when insufficient personnel were available due to illness or other reasons.

Expansion outside South Florida occurred when Special Agent Investigators, Inc., filed a Certificate of Incorporation in San Juan, Puerto Rico, on April 26, 1957. Russell Carver was the first president. M. Fred Rayne took over as president of Special Agent Investigators, Inc., of Puerto Rico in July 1958 and began an accelerated expansion program. But, of course, all of this did not happen easily.

"As our guard service flourished, there was one fiasco after another," George explains, "because in many instances we had to resort to untrained guards, a situation which finally was solved by hiring guards at the right salary who remained with us on a permanent basis. But in the early days, it could get hairy, and often did.

"There was the time when there was a strike at the Florida Power and Light plant in Miami Beach, and at two o'clock in the morning the guard called his supervisor in near hysterics, reporting that he had shot a pink elephant. What happened was that a carnival elephant, powdered white for a show, had escaped. When he loomed up out of the darkness, the startled guard fired a round which went through the elephant's ear. The guard promised never to take a drink again.

"It wasn't always easy to get the caliber of men we desired. A case in point was that on another occasion one of our guards was locked inside a picketed store for the night. He got a six pack of beer out of a store refrigerator and drank it. Then he got another six pack and drank it. Then he fell asleep on a pile of bags, but his cigarette set fire to the bags. Dashing for a pay phone inside the store, he discovered he had no change. So he fired six rounds through the front door, which aroused the neighbors, and firemen were called. They had to chop down the door to free him. Yes, he left money for the two six packs.

"One of our early guards, believe it or not, was standing post when a snake crawled up his pantleg. He did a war dance, twisting and turning, and, in attempting to hit the snake, he shot himself through both feet.

"In another incident, a guard was inside a building with a metal roof when pickets began throwing rocks that clanged off the roof in a thunderous crescendo. Whipping out his pistol, he began firing at the pickets. They hid in some trees while other pickets called the police, who in turn summoned our supervisor. Both the police and the supervisor did an Alphonse-Gaston until the guard, fortunately, ran out of bullets.

"In labor disputes, it always has been our policy that we are there only to protect private property. We are not police and we are not strikebreakers. But, as I said, until we had built up a force of properly trained and indoctrinated guards, almost anything could happen, and usually did, in one way or another.

"At another strike site, where we had two guards on duty at the time, the pickets began demonstrating, and one of them walked toward a guard in a menacing manner with a bottle filled with a clear liquid that the guard thought might be nitroglycerine. 'Hey, buddy, what's that?' the guard demanded. 'Water,' the picket sneered. The guard pulled his pistol and shoved it under the picket's nose. 'Then drink the son of a bitch,' he ordered. The picket drank it, but filed a suit that was eventually dropped.

"On another occasion, during a sudden strike situation, I received a call from the sheriff that one of our guards had built a big bonfire, had his shirt off, and was dancing around the fire while shooting at every window in sight. When we arrived at the scene, the sheriff took one look at the guard and shouted: 'Jesus Christ! This guy's the village *idiot!* He's as nutty as a *fruitcake!*' After that, we cleared all quickly-hired guards with the local sheriff to make sure we hadn't hired either an idiot or a criminal."

As GENE CHARTERS observed, hard work is rewarding, especially when it's day in, day out—and *night* in and night out. But if we look at the personal side of the equation, it's axiomatic that when an entrepreneur like George puts in those kinds of hours, six to seven days a week, year after year, the emotional and psychological price paid by the family can be progressively very high, and the Wackenhut family was no exception. In 1958, Jan was thirteen years old, in the eighth grade, and Rick was eleven, in the sixth grade, obviously important formative years for both, and Jan was—and still is—especially sensitive to what was happening.

"In Miami, there were a lot of bad memories," she relates. "Most of it was due to—all of it—was due to the work schedule. And Mother's lack of having something—you know, she's so talented, and I think if things had been different, or if she'd been born a little bit later, she would've been working and had her own interests. I went through the whole thing, repeated it in my first marriage. Unfortunately, the years when you have to do all this are also years when children need nurturing most.

"I related very, very closely to my father. He wouldn't get in until real late at night, and Mother just couldn't adapt to that at all. You can't have it both ways. I mean, if you want it, you've got to sacrifice.

"I used to suggest to her, even when I was little, of all kinds of things maybe she could get involved in. I seemed to have—she would always say I didn't understand. And yet it seemed very, very clear to me. I could see both sides. It's the same old adage: You keep doing what you've always done, and you always have what you've always had. You've got to change, somewhere; somebody's got to do something differently.

"I remember that he was not there. But *she* wasn't either. She was in the house, but she wasn't there. And those are the things that I've learned in later life. Because I couldn't understand *why*. I mean, a lot of my problems with, 'Well, your father was never there,' and I later found out that *she* wasn't either. Because the times that she could have taken to fill in what Rick and I weren't getting, she was too absorbed, and rightfully so, with her own loneliness. Because he wasn't there for *her* either.

"She spent a lot of time on the house, she loves gardening. In fact, she really could've been many things. She could've been a landscape architect; she definitely could've been an interior designer, and was; she could've been an architect. She loved clothes and design. Knew how to put things together. Had very exquisite taste. When they didn't have any money, she could really put things together well, in that line. While my talents and loves were more into studying and reading and research, and stuff that wasn't artistic. So we couldn't really—we had no basis of anything to *talk* about. There didn't seem to be that—knowing how to go from *your* interests to learn about the other. I always felt like I was very *un*talented, because I couldn't draw, instead of being able to pick up on what I *could* do. Consequently, she probably felt very inadequate when I'd have a trigonometry problem and she couldn't help me with it. I would always wait up for Dad. Even midnight, he'd come in and sit down and help me with math.

"They built the house, 7795 Southwest 122nd Street, and she was very consumed with that. I thought she was a *sub*contractor; I remember her telling me in those years she subcontracted it. Today, she tells me she contracted it; they didn't have a general contractor. So, I don't know. I remember seeing all the cement blocks going up. They paid $3,250 for one acre. Incredible. And I remember her lamenting, because she wanted to be in an area called Town and Ranch, which is closer to Red Road, between 67th Avenue and Red Road, where Gulliver Prep is. A lot of the families in those days, the kids I went to school with, their dads were pilots for National Airlines, most everybody was in some way involved with Pan Am, National, or Eastern Airlines. That was very heavy in that school.

"When we first moved into the house, Palmetto had not been built, and I had originally started at Southwest. That was in junior high; it was called Southwest. It was west, and far away, and there seemed to be a rougher crowd than Mother wanted us to be in. Now, I guess that was the zoning or something, I don't know, Southwest. And she got around that, somehow, and we ended up at South Miami Junior High, on 67th, between Sunset and Miller. Dad used to take me in the morning with a friend of mine, Patti McCulley, who lived three doors down, and I'm still friendly with her. Her dad was a pilot at Eastern. And she had a brother, Rick's age, Jimmy. Mother and her mother were good friends. And then Mother would pick me up in the afternoon.

"I did seventh and eighth there, and then they built Palmetto, and I spent ninth through twelfth at Palmetto. Patti and I had our first dates together. Jean and my mother made sure we were together. There was a boy next door, Teddy Kundtz, and his mother taught Spanish at Palmetto, and I had Spanish with her, and I used to *love* to go over and talk with her, because she was a real crazy lady, she was nutty! Dressed funny, and a more Bohemian type, but she had an academic background, you know, she was a teacher, and I would love to go over and just sit and talk with her. And she had twin girls that were Rick's age, and then she had this older son, Ted, Teddy, and he had a little crush on me, and I thought he was just—yuck, a greaseball, I couldn't stand him. He asked me out, and then the boy across the street—there were two guys across the street, one was Rick's age, that he used to play with, and his brother, I think his name was Don Pope, he asked Patti out. So that was our first time to go out in a *car!*

"I remember Mother telling me a funny story, that Jean called and asked what she was letting me *wear.* My mother said, 'Well, I don't know, I think she's wearing a dress.' On this first car date. Because I had had dates before, when they couldn't drive, and I remember fathers picking us up. So Mother said I was wearing a dress, and Jean said, 'Oh, there's no way I'm allowing Patti to wear a dress. She's wearing *slacks!*' I mean, we were just so—naive. She just didn't want anything to happen, and it was much easier with a dress!"

Ruth recalls the incident vividly: "I said to the mother, 'Why should you be so upset? Didn't you prepare Patti on how to conduct herself on a date? You know, Jean, you can *drop* a pair of slacks just as quickly as you can *lift* a dress! I *trust* my daughter!' We've had many laughs over that incident. How times have changed! Mothers today prepare their daughters for automatic *protection!* They're not interested in how they dress. Jan was naive in her manner, but well schooled in what a young lady should know about boys!"

Ruth remembers how difficult it was to raise the children when George was working an average of twelve hours a day, often seven days a week. "It was difficult for Jan and Rick to adjust to my taking the part of Mother *and* Father," she recalls. "I've always loved a 'home,' and although I was very enthusiastic about the progress of the company, and I was willing to cooperate with my husband in every way, I was quite social and joined clubs, did charity work, and deliberately made circumstances happen to express good will, and to circulate the name Wackenhut.

"Fortunately, I have a husband who was content to know I enjoyed taking care of a home, but I found he was always totally consumed in his work—seven days a week—arriving home most of the time after nine o'clock. I always had his dinner ready for him; most of the time the children had been put to bed. Every evening, I would prepare the table with candles, and truly enjoyed cooking—quite an experience for me, as I never cooked or knew anything about it until after I married. I would always sit with the children at dinner and tried to have talks about their days. Jan was not cooperative most of the time; she was always disappointed that her dad was not there to join us. Even on weekends, he sat at a desk and very seldom partook in what I felt should be 'normal' family togetherness.

"I was quite aware of my talents, and, although I had several things in mind for my own business, to express my interests, I found the demands of being the wife of a man with a growing company had to be my first consideration. I also knew my husband did not want me to have my own business, as he knew that whatever I do, I try to do my best, and put my 'blood' into it. In the meantime, I was designing uniforms, decorating offices, meeting prospective employees with my husband, and planning various types of social-business meetings. I was giving of myself in whatever manner my husband needed me.

"I could adapt to his schedule, but my biggest problem was that he was not *there*, as I felt he should have been as a father, and I knew my children were missing a great deal, not having him around to do things with them.

"But I gave many parties at the house for Jan's and Rick's friends. I took them on short excursions and long weekends. Sometimes they each had a friend to go along with us. I often drove my convertible with the top down to various football, baseball, basketball games with Rick's crowd in the car. I encouraged Jan and Rick to take part in tennis lessons, dancing lessons, swimming lessons, and so on. I was a Room Mother many times for both of them in the lower grades. I attended Scout meetings and outings with Rick, and encouraged Jan to join the Blue Birds, then the Campfire Girls, and she seemed to enjoy the outings and activities.

"Jan has always adored her father, and, unfortunately, did not have sufficient experience of doing things with him. I truly believe he felt 'lost' concerning how to be a father to a girl. The little time he spent with Rick, it was easy for him—wrestling, weight-lifting, soccer, and so forth, but he never attended any activities that the children participated in at the schools. No father could love his children as much as he did, but it was difficult for him to show it.

"Yes, it was lonely for me, many times, but I was married to a special man, and I had to decide at a very early time to 'go with it' or to take off. But how can you just 'take off' when you love someone, and he has so much faith and trust in you?

"Raising children in those early years was much more difficult than today. Both parents usually work now, and many husbands have taken over the role of 'Mom,' doing the shopping, cooking, cleaning, and care of the children. Many women today truly just want to be on the run, and do not feel like a 'nester' as I did. They don't want to be bothered learning homemaking. It was fun and a challenge for me.

"Russ [as Ruth has called George since his FBI days; short for his middle name, Russell] was so excited when he came home one time and said: 'We're off to Hawaii! I have so much to show you, and it's been many years since I was there!' I wanted to go with him so badly, but Jan was graduating from high school, and I suggested that he take her alone. I wanted them to be together. He insisted that I go, too, but I said, 'I think Jan will be happier just with you.' They had a wonderful time for two weeks, and she arrived home a very happy girl. The next time, when I went along, we took Rick with us.

"I love children and would have enjoyed more, but Russ felt that two were enough. We've always been proud of them, and I don't believe they were neglected in any way. In fact, they were spoiled quite a bit by my 'doing for them.' I'm so pleased about how Jan has raised her two daughters. They were taught early to stand on their own two feet, and it prepared them in a realistic way to handle things as they grew older."

IN SEPTEMBER 1958, George received a telephone call from Walter Levine, son of the uniform dealer he had convinced to advance him credit on his first guard job with National Airlines. Levine said that he had just finished a conversation with Charlie Taylor, director of security at the Martin Company plant in Orlando, who advised him that they were dissatisfied with their guard force and had plans to make a change. At that time, they had a contract guard service provided by General Plant Protection of Los Angeles, a firm that Wackenhut eventually acquired in the summer of 1962. Levine also said that the general manager at the Martin plant was unhappy with the current guard force and wanted military-looking guards, snappily dressed, and with proper bearing. The word was out that the Martin plant had about $2 billion in back orders of government work, basically in missiles.

George had visited Eglin Air Force Base some time before that and had noticed that the Air Police, although in khaki, acquired a super-sharp military appearance by wearing paratrooper boots. He then visualized that the addition of paratrooper boots, with the company's regular powder-blue uniform and white helmets, should give his guards a distinctive appearance. George asked Levine to order a small quantity of black paratrooper boots and white helmets. It should be noted that in previous dealings with Levine's father, and over the elder Levine's objections, George had settled on a visored cap for his guards that was extremely military looking but somehow resembled Nazi storm troopers' caps. These caps were very upsetting to many Jewish people and, in subsequent years, when the company expanded into the New York area, he was requested to change the caps because some people felt that they were a grim reminder.

In aiming at the Martin contract, George wanted white helmets, white gloves, white Navy gunbelts, and white holsters with a flap that would completely conceal a revolver with a five-inch barrel. Levine obtained all of the equipment and George selected three of the most handsome men in the company, dressed them in the outfits, had them professionally photographed, and prepared a presentation that he hoped he would be able to make to the Martin executives. He then called the company's director of industrial relations and arranged to meet with him.

It was clear from the outset of the meeting that this man wanted guards with a military appearance, and that he wanted young men, who would have to be paid a higher rate. When George showed him the striking photographs of his three men with their white helmets, gloves, gunbelts, and neckties, against powder-blue uniforms with navy-blue stripes on the trousers, tucked into black paratrooper boots, it was obvious that their appearance satisfied him completely. He asked George to submit a proposal with the understanding that they didn't want minimum-wage guards and wanted the very best men they could get.

Immediately after the meeting at Martin, George made a survey of the wages paid by most of the regular law-enforcement agencies in Florida and came up with an hourly rate of $1.70, a figure that was exceeded only by the Miami Beach Police Department. With the minimum wage at that time being $1.00 an hour, he felt that if he could obtain the Martin contract he could offer a forty-hour week, with additional fringe benefits, that would attract high-caliber men. As it turned out, that rate of pay did secure high-quality men, many of them former Marines, and accustomed to guard duty.

"With the financial figures and my proposal in hand, I went back to the Martin plant," George says, "and when I had made my proposal in detail, the director of industrial relations called in the general manager. The GM took a long look at the figures, and when he came to the photographs of my carefully selected guards in their military-like uniforms, I knew I was in. He turned to the director, told him to run the figures through accounting, and that was that. The contract that we eventually signed was worth $700,000 that first year, with a renewal option, putting my company over the million-dollar mark for the first time."

The contract was to start January 1, 1959, and required seventy-seven top-grade men, including a staff of supervisors, and responsibilities for security, fire protection, and ambulance service. It provided the opportunity of demonstrating a concept of combining fire and security services with cross-training of fire and security personnel, and with fire and security being under one top commander.

Prior to the time the contract was awarded, George realized only too well that he needed someone to step in and run the operation. The man he had in mind was John Ammarell, who had made an extraordinary impression on him when he was negotiating the contract for Air Products and Chemicals in 1957. The two men had kept in touch since the awarding of that contract. In the interim, Ammarell had become manager of personnel for Air Products and, at the same time, had a director of security reporting to him. He had been considering leaving Air Products, arranged to visit George in the latter part of October 1958, and spent three days at George's home to review the company's operations and decide if he wanted to leave Air Products and move back to Miami where he had once served in the FBI.

Born near Reading, Pennsylvania, March 21, 1920, John Ammarell received his BA degree from Muhlenberg College, Allentown, Pennsylvania, in 1941, attended George Washington University Law School, 1942–43, and served with the FBI from 1943–1955, in Savannah, Miami, Richmond, Pittsburgh, and Washington, DC. He was a resident agent in Gainesville, Florida, and Augusta, Georgia, and his last seven years with the Bureau were spent in Washington at FBI headquarters. During his last four years there, he was assistant chief of the liaison section of the Domestic Intelligence Division. This post included responsibilities for six units within the section.

Studying the company in Miami, in late October 1958, John expressed his concern to George about the use of the term "Special Agent" in the names of Special Agent Investigators, Inc., and Special Agent Security Guards, Inc. He noted that J. Edgar Hoover frowned upon the utilization of the term "Special Agent" by former FBI agents in their commercial activities after leaving the Bureau. As a result, much discussion ensued concerning the selection of an appropriate name to replace Special Agent Security Guards, Inc. The name Security Services Corporation was finally selected, primarily because it described the type of work in which the corporation was engaged.

Once this was resolved, John agreed to commence employment with the firm, effective December 15, 1958, to assume the duties of executive vice president of Security Services Corporation at its inception on January 1, 1959. He was to receive a weekly draw against future percentage of $150, and the percentage agreement on which he was to be recompensed was as follows: (1) the State of Florida—$33\frac{1}{3}$ percent of the net profits of all guard business; (2) Eastern Pennsylvania, South New Jersey, and Delaware, or that area described by Eugene Charters as "his area"—1 percent of all the gross billings of all guard business; (3) All other areas within the continental United States—20 percent of the net profits of all guard business. For annual computation purposes, John was to receive $150 per week for fifty-two weeks, or a total based on the percentages set forth above, whichever sum was greater. It was also understood that he would be eligible for stock ownership in the various corporations, details to be decided upon in future discussions.

After this decision, John submitted his resignation to Air Products, where he was earning more than $11,000 annually (equivalent to about $50,000 by 1990s standards), and moved to Miami at his own expense. While the proposal for the Martin Company was being prepared, he had provided George with considerable material concerning a training program, selection of personnel, and other administrative matters, and the administration and responsibilities of the security guards. He left Allentown, Pennsylvania, the afternoon of December 12, 1958, and drove to Rocky Mount, North Carolina. When he arose the next morning, he learned that a severe snowstorm had struck North Carolina during the night, and it took him an entire day to drive from Rocky Mount to Lumberton, North Carolina. On Sunday, December 14, John drove from that point to Winter Park, Florida, near Orlando, where he met George and a man named Jackson "Jack" Flowers, who had been retained as a safety consultant, and who later became the company's director of safety and fire prevention. On the morning of December 15, the three men met with Charles Taylor, director of security of the Martin Company, to plan the takeover of the security and fire forces at Martin, scheduled to begin at midnight, January 1, 1959.

One of the requirements of the Martin job was that all new personnel had to be hired from outside the Orlando area, and none of the current guards or supervisors of General Plant Protection could be utilized. Another requirement was that all new personnel be given a forty-hour training program before assignment. John drew up the training program and arranged to use the facilities of the Florida Police Academy in Miami Springs, near the airport, where he conducted the forty-hour program from December 26 through December 30, 1958. John taught many of the courses and also secured the assistance of other experts in fire fighting, firearms, first aid, safety, and other training subjects. George taught defensive tactics and hand-to-hand fighting.

Bud Thompson also played an important role in the training, taking a brief vacation from the sheriff's office. "At that time, I was the head of training in the sheriff's office," Thompson remembers. "George calls me, he says, 'Bud, will you come help me design this training program, because I've got to train these people, and we're not allowed to tell them where they're going to be stationed until the last minute.' And I would say, any sane human being would've said, 'What you're asking for, I can't do.' Because they wanted seventy-seven men, or whatever it was, I think it was seventy-seven men, I can't remember. Memory is the second thing that goes; I can't remember what was first. George said, 'I can furnish seventy-seven men in Orlando.' They said, 'Fine. *But,* you can't have anybody from the Orlando area, and nobody can be told where they're going! Because the guard force at the Martin plant in Orlando, which was then a very prized plant, was from a company in California, called General Plant Protection. They were a very independent group. And they had the facility, and they had a lot of turmoil, they had a man who ran the thing who was a pain in the ass and he caused a lot of turmoil with the group. And the Martin Company were worried that they were going to strike the place. Because the employees were unhappy, and they weren't getting paid on time, they had a lot of things they weren't doing that caused problems.

"And the guards there did get wind of a change. They didn't know what, but they knew it was a change, and they gave us one hell of a welcome. They took all of the keys from the key control boxes—and in a plant like that, you'll have thousands upon thousands of keys, all in these boxes with hooks on them. Pulled the tags off of all the keys and threw the keys in a barrel. And they had a barrel like a fifty-five gallon drum of keys, with nobody knowing where the hell any of them went. They had to re-key the whole plant. They left such a bad taste that, ultimately, I think it helped kick them down the drain in the other places. It wasn't a gentle shake-your-hand and go out the door. They hated the Martin Company with a passion; they blamed a lot of their problems on them. And then here they threw them out and this new group came in, and they left a mess. We had one hell of a mess on that one in the beginning. They took all the guard orders and destroyed them. We went in with nothing. Most difficult situation. We didn't get any blame for it, of course, because it wasn't our fault that it happened. All it did was make us look even better. And we got such high raves out of that, many, many contractors started calling and wanting to talk to—at that time—Security Services Corporation, that was the name of the company."

As of December 31, 1958, Special Agent Security Guards, Inc., conveyed all of its equipment and uniforms to Security Services Corporation. On the same date, Special Agent Investigators, Inc., also transferred to Security Services such guard equipment, furniture, and equipment as it owned. Total payment to Special Agent Investigators was $7,372.20, and to Special Agent Security Guards, $8,585.45.

With the contract for the Martin Company secured, George was now the owner of a million-dollar corporation at the age of thirty-nine, he had surrounded himself with the best and brightest people he could find, his horizons seemed virtually unlimited, and it was an extraordinarily exciting time in his life.

A special joint meeting of the stockholders and directors of Security Services Corporation was held on January 29, 1959, in Suite 811 of the Ainsley Building. At that meeting, the office of executive vice president was created, and John Ammarell was elected to that position. In addition, George Wackenhut, John Ammarell, Eugene Charters, and William MacReynolds were elected to the board of directors.

Just six weeks into the new contract, George received the following letter from E.G. Uhl, vice president of the Martin Company, dated February 10, 1959:

Dear Mr. Wackenhut:
   Since the time your company took on the plant security responsibility on 1 January, 1959, I have been carefully observing your conduct. I want you to know I am pleased by what I have observed.
   It is our aim to make Martin-Orlando the outstanding missile and electronics plant in the entire United States. We want it to be outstanding in every respect, beginning with the reliability of our products, the intelli-

gence of our employees, going down through the appearance, orderliness and cleanliness of our plant.

To go with this ambition, we must have an outstanding security force. Frequently, our customers and visitors make their first contact with us through you—the people charged with our plant security. It is important that your uniform be flawless, your carriage military, you handle difficult situations intelligently—but firmly, and that you be courteous under all conditions. You have made a good beginning toward the achievement of this goal.

From time to time, we will observe deficiencies in the way you are doing your job and we intend to bring these to your attention through your supervisors. I know you will also observe deficiencies in our operation, and I would appreciate it if you would bring these to our attention through Mr. Taylor and the people in his organization.

I hope the good beginning is an indication of a long and mutually profitable association.

Bud Thompson has particularly intriguing insights about the early days of the Martin contract. "One of the things that I think made the company very successful in the beginning was that we had a very handsome group of uniformed guards," Thompson says. "They looked good. George is a man who really likes physical appearance. He will make a determination on the physical appearance of a guy before he even opens his mouth. He's always been that way. In fact, sometimes it's been to his detriment, because he'll think somebody's really great when they ain't got enough brains to go to the men's room, but they look great.

"But, anyway, he wanted a military look. Not necessarily copying our military, but to have something that made a very striking appearance. The guards at Orlando, at the Martin Company, wore a white ascot, they wore a white rope that hooked to their pistol like the British army has, they wore white helmets, they wore combat boots—very, very striking. I got a lot of pictures that were made of those guys, and they were a very handsome group. One of the things that we taught the guys, and it was George's idea, and a good one, we got pictures of all the Martin brass, and every guard post on the outer perimeter had pictures of the brass. So when that man came around there, he was called by name. You didn't just say, 'Excuse me, sir,' it was 'Mr. Smith,' or whoever it was.

"Another thing, he employed an ex-Marine to work in the parking lot where the visitors' parking was, and this guy was like a ramrod. He was one of the men that wouldn't come out of the rain, he was so dumb, but he looked sharp. He walked like he was guarding the Tomb of the Unknown Soldier, and wore white gloves on top of it, and when a car pulled into the visitors' lot, he was there and: *'Sir, can I help you?'* I mean, he snapped it out like he was in the Marine Corps. And those people who came there from the Cape, and from major companies all around the country, I mean, they said, 'Where in the hell *am* I? I've never seen *anything* like this in a guard force.' He would escort them up to the visitors' entrance, and he would see that they were properly passed, and on to this, and back out. He was very, very good at that, he did a super job. He was probably very influential in making us stand out in the eyes of every major contractor that came to the Cape. Very good thinking, because the people at Martin thought this was the greatest thing; they had a slovenly bunch that was there before. Here we had these real sharp cookies—I mean, saluting, and when they directed traffic, we taught them the military ways of directing traffic, whistles in the mouth, white lanyards, and the whole works on the thing, and people ate that up. They thought we were the greatest thing since root beer.

"If I were to say what major thing in The Wackenhut Corporation, other than George's being the man who did it, because he's brilliant, other than that, I can't think of anything that made that company catch hold better than the Martin Company job we had. Very selective group, nice-looking, clean-cut. They were paid above the average. They were like military guys, looked like military police.

"But, anyway, the Martin Company was really the kickoff. One of the trips up there, up to Orlando, George used to drive a convertible, and he's always been one hellaciously fast driver. He'd always take the back roads, so he could drive as fast as he wanted. Well, he comes back one day, his windshield is all cracked, his back seat is splashed red, and we said to him, 'George, what the hell happened to you?' He says, 'Well, I hit a buzzard, and it cracked my windshield and made a real mess.' He's got buzzard guts all over him, the inside of his car is covered with buzzard feathers and guts and blood. And somebody asks him, 'Where the hell did you hit the buzzard?' George thinks about it, he frowns, he narrows his eyes, then he remembers, and he smiles and says, 'Right in the *ass!*' "

13

GENE CHARTERS sits across the polished mahogany conference table in the private room he's reserved on the twelfth floor of the Jenkins Law Library at 841 Chestnut Street in downtown Philadelphia. It is Wednesday morning, January 22, 1992, and he has agreed to a tape-recorded interview for this biography, but it had required a formal letter from George Wackenhut himself to convince him that the interview was legitimate. "How do I know you're not a *con*-artist?" he had asked on the telephone. "How can you prove you *are* who you *say* you are?" He demanded positive identification before he agreed to an interview, and even then he questioned motive. Charters has been a private investigator for forty-six years (1946–1992), preceded by twelve years as a special agent with the FBI. He's intuitively suspicious of everyone now, but good-humored about it. White-haired, grizzled, soft-spoken but blunt at age eighty-seven, he adjusts his glasses and smiles thinly as he opens his mint-condition copy of the first brochure ever published by The Wackenhut Corporation, in October 1959, one month after the name of the firm was legally changed. The conservative four-page, two-color brochure measures $8\frac{1}{2}"$-×-$11"$, has a 100-pound glossy cover with a blue, highly stylized *WC* logo in a black circle against a white background, and, below that, bold black typography reading:

THE WACKENHUT CORPORATION
*Protection and Safety
for Business and Industry*

"I remember I eventually got into a different phase of the business," Charters says. "I did certain things for the security end, and I got into—not PR so much—advertising, images, that sort of stuff. I even have a brochure here that I made up. And when it came time to pick a name, I said, 'Why not The Wackenhut Corporation?' I said, 'What's wrong with your name?' I thought it was a very strong name. So I have to take credit for naming that corporation. [Actually, Ruth had suggested it months earlier.] I thought it was a heck of a strong name. I based the idea of this inside cover [of the brochure] on Modigliani, the artist, it was my own idea. I pictured the page and just worked this stuff up. And then one time we were in an art gallery, George and I—there was a museum near the Dallas stadium there, we were going to a football game—and we came across a Modigliani, and I said, 'That's the guy I was talking about.' And he knew it, of course. After I had written the whole thing, he got it all together, he went over it and changed some parts of it. It didn't bother me, because it's his brochure, and it can always look better. It's just another instance of his thoroughgoing methods."

On the left-hand page of the center-spread are individual black-and-white photographs of nine young-looking executives of the newly named corporation: George R. Wackenhut, president; John S. Ammarell, Jr., executive vice president; Eugene J. Charters, vice president, Research, Information, and Promotion; George W. Ryan, director, Sales; C.W. Thompson, director, Training and Inspection; Jackson G. Flowers, director, Safety and Fire Prevention; Robert C. Haas, director, Retail Store Protection; John E. Kyle, director, Internal Security Methods; and M.F. Rayne, director, Puerto Rico Operations.

Charters studies the young faces, shakes his head, points out each man: "There's John Ammarell; there I am; this was a great guy here, Haas, died in an automobile crash with his wife, he was a terrific worker, fantastic guy. This guy was Puerto Rico—Rayne, I guess you never got to talk with that guy. Ammarell was a real stolid guy, a guy you could depend on, a man who took hold of an assignment and it was done, it was on its way; a very, very efficient guy, and serious minded. Now, Ryan was a very colorful guy, a great big fella, this George Ryan, he came from the FBI in Indianapolis. He traveled around the country, he did some sales work for George, somewhat successfully, I think, and he later went out for himself in Indianapolis and he started a business like that, and I did some work with him. Thompson, he was former administrative assistant to the sheriff in Dade County. He was our director of Training and Inspection. I remember him as being in charge of the uniforms, taking care of them, making sure everything was okay. I didn't like him. I think he was bigoted. Matter of fact, the year I left, I came down to Miami, I don't know whether we had a convention in Miami or not, ex-FBI, but I met George, of course, and I got into the pool, and this guy was there with his son, and he wouldn't even talk to me. I mean, I didn't want to force him to talk to me, but he acted like—cool, you know, cool it off. For what, I don't know. Anyway.

"I don't remember Flowers too well, he'd been safety director of Dade County. Kyle was just—he wasn't anything special, as far as I remember. He was a nice fellow, I don't know what he did. This Rayne was supposed to be a very, very top-notch guy. I think he was German. It says, 'Formerly, Intelligence Division, British Army,' but I think he came from Germany and he did work back there on the Continent for them. But he was a terrific guy. The last thing I remember about him, he came to me when he went in business for himself, and had me do something up in Philadelphia. He never paid the bill. Charters, this is a rotten picture of him, but he—vice president, huh? You know, my wife said to me, she said, 'Now, George wanted to make you vice president.' I said, 'Uh-huh.' I mean, that didn't really mean anything to me, being a vice president."

According to John Ammarell, 1959 proved to be an extremely busy year for the expansion of operations. After starting the Martin Company contract on January 1, Security Services Corporation, as it was still called, was successful in obtaining guard service for the five missile-tracking stations on the Eglin Gulf Test Range. This contract was with the Vitro Corporation and began in February 1959. Security Services had to secure personnel who could be cleared to a secret level of clearance, and initially staffed the station at Fort Walton Beach, Florida. The next step was the station at Port St. Joe,

Anclote near Tarpon Springs, Marco Island near Naples, and finally Pine Island near Key West. In addition to being cleared, these employees had to be trained in guard duties and firearms.

Grandway Discount Centers continued to expand to Hollywood, Fort Lauderdale, and St. Petersburg. After completing the Eglin Gulf Test Range staffing in May, Security Services secured an Air Products job at Glassmere, north of Pittsburgh, and a contract with Federal Electric Corporation at the Dew Line Training Site in Streator, Illinois. Ammarell recruited, trained, and assigned the men for both locations during late June and early July of 1959.

In the meantime, Bud Thompson joined the firm on July 1 as director of Training and Inspection. In fairness to Thompson, despite the private opinion of Gene Charters, George had his own opinion of the man, which he still holds:

"Always, as the years passed," George says, "I remained alert for the type of men I would like to have at the top of my organization, and one such was Bud Thompson, a man I had known virtually since I arrived in Florida. Bud had served in the Army in Europe during World War II, returned to graduate from the University of Miami, and then entered the FBI. After serving as an agent in Detroit, he resigned to take a post as a special investigator for the Dade County sheriff's office. He had risen to chief administrator, became disenchanted with the job, then worked six months for the Florida attorney general's office. I had heard that he was bored with the inaction of his position, so I went to see him and he accepted my offer to join us in July of 1959. Bud, who would remain with us for more than twenty years, and eventually become an executive vice president, moved in quickly to take charge of Training and Inspections. As it turned out, he joined the company at a particularly propitious time, because that summer and autumn things began to break wide open."

Bud Thompson remembers: "Then George picked up another contract, which was the Eglin Gulf Test Range. That was where they were firing missiles from under airplanes at Eglin Air Force Base, and they were then tracked down the west coast of Florida, over Cuba, and then were picked up going downrange. The Cape fired out across the ocean, across Africa, and down through that area, and these two ranges more or less crossed as they went farther down. This was basically the British thinking for missile launching—not to put silos in the ground and shoot them up, but to put them on the bottom of airplanes and drop them, and then fire them from the air. Two different systems. That was being tested. George picked up the job, he called me, he says, 'I now got enough money, I want you to come to work for us now.'

"I was hired at the beginning and ran the training programs and the selection of people for the Eglin Gulf Coast Range. Which was Panama City, Anclote, Marco Island, were the missile-tracking places, they were starting to build them, and I had to go and hire thirteen people or so in each one of these locations, and train them to meet the government standards that they wanted for it. Then we would furnish the guards. A bitchy situation, trying to find people in these areas that could get clearances and all. It was very difficult. But we did it, and got it going, and started it. That was the beginning, for me, of a number of years of running my ass off."

That August, the firm was asked to handle two strike situations at the same time. Ammarell handled one at the International Minerals and Chemicals Corporation mines near Bartow, Florida, and the other was supervised by George at Peoples Gas Company in Tampa. Both strikes lasted several weeks and provided early experience in handling labor dispute security situations.

In late September 1959, Ammarell traveled to Los Angeles with Charles Taylor, the Martin Company's director of security, to attend the convention of the American Society for Industrial Security. While there, Ammarell became acquainted with Robert Hodgkins, director of security for the Martin Company's Activation Division, which was preparing to set up bases under the Titan Missile Program. Security Services was requested by Martin to submit a proposal. While George, John, Gene, and their wives were attending the annual convention of the Society of Former Special Agents of the FBI, in Dallas, word was received that Security Services was awarded the contract to provide security for the Titan Missile Program at its new headquarters in Denver. Ammarell and his wife left the convention and flew to Denver, where he spent two weeks getting that program started.

"John subsequently took on another important job," George recalls, "that of putting together a manual on guard procedures. Obviously, the time was coming when we would have to move fast into certain situations, the urgency precluding the type of training we wanted our people to undergo, and being able to give such guards a clear, concise manual spelling out their duties and code of ethics, as well as certain prohibitions, was an utter necessity.

"Meanwhile, as our operations spread farther and farther afield, I began to ponder just where detection stopped and protection started, and vice versa. We had Security Services Corporation as a protective agency, and Special Agent Investigators, Inc., functioning as a detective agency. It was perfectly obvious that if you had a guard in uniform, he was protective, and if you had a man doing an investigation, he was a detective. But if you had a man detailed to a store as an undercover observer, the question, for me, was whether he was there for prevention or detection. And there were other of our services that were also borderline situations.

"This question plagued me so much in the summer of 1959 that I retained the law firm of Smathers, Thompson, Maxwell and Dyer. One of the partners, Jack Thompson, suggested that we look into the law, but it was such a vague, confusing area that we could come to no definite decision. I corresponded with the General Services Administration in Atlanta and was told that a wholly owned subsidiary of a detective agency could contract with the government, but this was merely a supposition and not actually a fact."

In an attempt to clarify the situation, Gene Charters communicated with the secretary of state or attorney general in each of the fifty states, and eventually learned that there were twenty-two states in which the name Security Services Corporation could not be used, because similar names had already been registered by other companies.

Jack Thompson discussed the idea of establishing a new corporation, and also setting up a subsidiary for the purpose of contracting solely protective work with the government. This was suggested because of the so-called Anti-Pinkerton Law of 1893, which had precluded the federal government from contracting with private firms for security services if that same firm also conducted investigations. Globe Security had established a subsidiary called Plant Security Inc., while Burns Detective Agency had set up Federal Services Inc., for the purpose of contracting with the government to provide protective services.

After Ruth first suggested the name The Wackenhut Corporation, George discussed the idea at length with John Ammarell and Jack Thompson. John agreed that the name should be changed to The Wackenhut Corporation, because it didn't conflict with anything, and because Burns and Pinkerton had been successful by utilizing their family names. George still liked the idea of having a name that described the nature of services that they provided, but Jack Thompson concurred with John's idea, that this seemed to be a good way to go. Following a week of discussion and thinking about the matter, George finally agreed that the name should be changed from Security Services Corporation to The Wackenhut Corporation. At the same time, the decision was made to bring the assets of Special Agent Investigators, Inc., into The Wackenhut Corporation, and to form Wackenhut Services, Inc., which by its charter would be forbidden to do any detective work, and therefore would be a company that could do work for the government.

On September 10, 1959, amendments to the Articles of Incorporation of Security Services Corporation were enacted so that the name of the new corporation would legally become The Wackenhut Corporation (TWC). This was approved by George and Ruth Wackenhut, sole stockholders of Security Services Corporation, and, on the same date, by George Wackenhut, John Ammarell, and Gene Charters, sole members of the board of directors of Security Services Corporation.

Around the middle of November, the company won the contract to provide security at the Atlas Missile Site in Salina, Kansas. After Thanksgiving, Ammarell left for Salina to help in starting the security and fire-force at that location, then proceeded to Denver for a review of the security and fire-force at Buckley Field, near Denver, where the first missile squadron under the Titan Program was to be initiated. During that year, the firm also set up a small guard force for North American Aviation at Eglin Air Force Base and McDonnell Aircraft Corporation at Eglin.

Obviously, 1959 was a breakthrough year, the year in which the company first reached the $1 million level in business volume. And, significantly, the expansion in the guard business exploded in comparison to that of the investigative volume.

As 1959 came to a close, TWC was providing security services in five states—Florida, Pennsylvania, Illinois, Kansas, and Colorado—plus the island of Puerto Rico. The firm had 356 employees and gross sales had more than tripled in a single year, from $386,900 in 1958 to $1.346 million in 1959.

"Success obviously breeds success," George says, "because, all in all, it had been a year which had given us fantastic nationwide exposure to giant corporations that was to pay off handsomely in the years ahead."

IT HAD BEEN a memorable year in many historical respects. Cuban President Batista resigned and fled, as Fidel Castro and his guerrilla army marched triumphantly into Havana on January 1; the Cuban revolution had apparently succeeded, and Castro was hailed as a hero. On January 3, Alaska became the forty-ninth state. March 31, Tibet's Dalai Lama escaped to India. April 9, NASA selected the first seven astronauts. April 25, the St. Lawrence Seaway opened, allowing ocean ships to reach the Midwest. June 8, the Supreme Court upheld the right for Congress and individual states to investigate communism. June 11, D.H. Lawrence's novel *Lady Chatterley's Lover* was banned from the mails by the U.S. Postmaster General. June 15, the United Steelworkers began a nationwide strike that ended only when President Eisenhower invoked the Taft-Hartley Act, forcing them back to work. August 3, Vice President Richard Nixon debated Soviet Premier Nikita Khrushchev in the model kitchen of a U.S. exhibition in Moscow. August 21, Hawaii became the fiftieth state. And, in the autumn, Clark Kerr, chancellor of the University of California, made his famed prediction about college students in the 1960s: "The employers will love this generation. They aren't going to press many grievances. They are going to be easy to handle. There aren't going to be any riots."

IN MARCH 1960, TWC was awarded the Titan Missile Site at Ellsworth Air Force Base, Rapid City, South Dakota. Just prior to that, Ammarell had performed security surveys at all the plant and operation sites of Maule Industries, a large concrete and rock manufacturing and distribution firm on the east coast of Florida. In April, TWC was successful in winning the contract to provide security services for the administrative offices and the twelve plant locations.

"One of the secrets of George's success," Bud Thompson says, "is that he's always been a thinker of the future. He doesn't get satisfied with today; he's off in the future. I use the Jimmy Dean 'bear story' to describe George, and I've done this in front of audiences. A bunch of guys are talking about going bear hunting. And this one guy says, 'Hell, I catch 'em with my bare hands.' And they say, 'Baloney! We're not talking about little baby bears, we're talking about big, mean, nasty bears!' The guy says, 'That's nothing, I still catch 'em with my hands.' So they say, 'Come along, you go with us.' They go off to the cabin in the forest where they're going to be doing the bear hunting, and that night they're sitting around and talking, telling bear stories, and this guy says, 'I'm telling you, I'm going to catch 'em with my bare hands.' They say, 'Okay, you're first out tomorrow morning.' So, next morning, the sun comes up, he says, 'Okay, I'm off.' He says, 'You guys wait here now and I'll bring you back one.' Pretty soon, they hear this *thump!-thump!-thump!-thump!* coming down the mountain path, and they look up, and here's this guy running like a son of a bitch—and right behind him, running flat-out, roaring mad, is a big black *bear!* The guy scrambles up on the cabin porch, throws open the door, steps aside fast—*boom!—crash!*—the bear leaps inside! The guy slams the door, he shouts: 'Skin that one and I'll be back with another!'

"Well, that's George to me, because he was always bringing us a bear to skin! And, my God, I used to think: I'm going to go out of my nut trying to keep up with this crap, because just about the time when we think we've got something under control, he's throwing another bear in the door."

TWC WOULDN'T BE in the Ainsley Building much longer. Since landing the Martin contract, George had realized that the company would soon be outgrowing its quarters, and, in anticipation of rapidly expanding operations and increasing management personnel to keep pace, he had arranged to lease (with an option to buy, which he later did), a new two-story office building at 3280 Ponce de Leon Boulevard in Coral Gables that would more than quadruple the space available in Suite 811 of the Ainsley Building.

The move took place over the Memorial Day weekend, May 28–30, 1960, and the brand-new headquarters building, on the northwest corner of tree-lined Ponce de Leon Boulevard and Sarto Avenue was ready for occupancy Wednesday, June 1. The recessed and palm-filled front entrance faced east, flanked by a red-brick facade, and the rest of the modern structure was white stone with wide windows sweeping across both floors. Steel paneling above and below the windows was the traditional Wackenhut blue. All the front windows were equipped, inside, with classic white louvered shutters, double-doored, to screen the strong morning sun. George occupied the second-floor corner office to the left, overlooking Ponce, with John Ammarell's office next door. Across the wide white stone frieze above the second floor were huge steel letters, raised, and backlighted at night: THE WACKENHUT CORPORATION. The firm would remain in that building for the next twenty-four years.

Today, the four lanes of Ponce de Leon in that area are still divided by a center island of grass and trees, the white stone exterior of the building is basically the same, minus the red-brick facade at the entrance, and the modern sign just above the first floor reads: HEALTHSOUTH Sports Medicine & Rehabilitative Center. When HealthSouth bought the building in 1984, they had both floors gutted to construct therapy rooms and facilities, and added a large hospital-like elevator to the small existing one, but the winding wooden staircase near the front entrance is unchanged.

In June 1960, TWC opened its second area office outside Miami (San Juan, Puerto Rico, was the first, in 1957), in Tampa, Florida, with Robert Hopler serving as the first manager. Hopler was a former special agent of the FBI and had been employed by the company for a brief period as an investigator in Miami. In July, TWC was awarded the Titan III Site at Larson Air Force Base, Moses Lake, Washington, with responsibility for security and fire protection services. In September, the company acquired an investigative firm owned by Harry Manicas in Buffalo, New York, and opened its third area office in Buffalo. During the same month, TWC opened a Boston area office with Frank Horbert as the area manager.

In the meantime, Gene Charters had maintained his own investigative agency in Philadelphia, E.J. Charters Associates, Inc., which he founded in 1946. His routine, sanctioned by George, was to spend an average of two months in Miami, then a month in Philadelphia to look after his own business. Eventually, some of the executives at TWC resented this special status.

"I decided to leave because I think my position there was becoming more on the fringes," Charters says. "It wasn't in the substantial end of it, it was in this image thing, with advertising and that sort of stuff. When they started to list the value of the different guys, Ammarell was given that job, and I was at the bottom of the list, see, because George showed me the list. And I had a business in Philadelphia, my home was there, and I think that's why I left, I just eased out, that's all. I don't think Mary, my wife, particularly wanted to live in Florida. We had an apartment in Miami, and when I'd come down, she'd come down with me. I thoroughly enjoyed my stay there. But I was the boss in Philadelphia, and in Miami, when I saw myself at the bottom of the list there, I didn't see any point in hanging around. I didn't feel unwanted, just unnecessary.

"I remember when I was working for Wackenhut, traveling back and forth between Philadelphia and Miami, George and Ruth came up to Philadelphia. I think we had drinks at the Barclay here, a very nice, cozy little bar in the hotel, and then we had dinner, and I think we saw a show, and I was putting out some of the money. I don't know if I paid for everything, but I may have. Now, I have a business up here, so it looks like I was the host. When I got back to Florida, whatever the amount was, I put it on my expense account for The Wackenhut Corporation. And I got it back, crossed off, he didn't want to pay that. I don't know if we had any conversation about it or not, but I'm thinking about it now. George was right about that. Because he enjoyed himself tremendously. And here he enjoyed himself, and he finds out he's *paying* for it! It's a different feeling altogether than to think: Well, Gene, that's his place of business up there, he was entertaining us, and that's the way it should be. And I want George to know that I agree with him."

In November 1960, G. Ralph Kiel joined the company as director of Public Relations, and this was to result in the start of a well-coordinated and expanded public relations program. Kiel was an experienced newspaper man and, through his media contacts, helped to further establish the credibility and reputation of the corporation. Sam McKee, a highly regarded former special agent-in-charge with the FBI, joined the company in December 1960.

By year's end, TWC had 855 employees, gross sales of $2.139 million, and had expanded to nine states and the island of Puerto Rico. That was also the year when the *Forms Manual* was initiated to provide identification of forms, as well as procedures for their use. During the course of the rapid growth in 1959 and 1960, there was a great amount of concentrated work done in training new hires at all locations. This necessitated developing the *Training Manual,* as well as lesson plans and materials for the various subjects that were taught in the training programs. In many cases, certain portions of the training programs had to be customized for the conditions involved with each particular client's needs and desires.

"My worst year was 216 days on the road," Bud Thompson recalls. "Because we just started exploding out all over the place, we started picking up stuff. My job, when I was hired, was to be the head of Training and Inspection. I was to set up and work out training programs so we could train people, and the inspection was to go to all the facilities, see that they were running right, help them get started, do whatever had to be done. And it was a bitch.

"I found George to be a very interesting man to work with, because he always was looking at the future, and things that I was so busy with today, he didn't worry about them any more, that was my problem, he was out getting me another bear to skin. So we would solve one problem and then take on another one, and get that underway, and do it. But he had good thinking, because I remember him saying in the beginning, one of my jobs was to write down and prepare all of the manuals we would use in the company. And we devised an operations manual, an administrative manual, and a forms manual. He said to me, 'When we sit down and have a conference, and we come up with a conclusion, what we're going to do, I want this written up as a procedure, so that as we keep growing, we don't waste time to stop and do that. We can't keep doing it over and over and over again. We do it one time, write it down, and then that becomes our bible. So that, we open up in Tampa, then we've got a manual, we give them the manual, we got the forms, here's how the forms are filled out. We will have this as a procedure.'

"I remember very vividly when he said this to me, in the early days of the company, I think we were down in the Ainsley Building at the time, I know we were, and I used to think: This guy is nuts, because he wants me to sit down and spend all this time writing this crap up, when I can pick up the phone and talk to every one of the guys we have that's running anything. Why do I need all this? But as we grew, I could see that this was the answer, because we could open an office and that office would run like the next office, or another office, because they had some guidelines to go by. Thank God, because I think it was the first five years, or something like that, we doubled our size every year."

Maria Hester, who celebrated her thirtieth anniversary at TWC on November 18, 1993, was Bud's secretary during those hectic early years and Bud has pleasant memories about her: "This is during the time when all hell was going on around the place, and I was running around all over the place. I've been around secretaries a lot of my life, I've never found any better than Maria Hester. Absolutely fantastic person. Sharp, intelligent, super-nice. I used to be gone for two weeks. When I came back, she had all my mail answered, she had all the things set up that had to be done. I mean, I never read things. She would come in with a pile of material and tell me, 'This letter says this,' and I'd say, 'Answer him back: Yes, I will, or no, I won't, or whatever.' And it was done. I would say to Maria, 'Tomorrow, I've got to talk to Charley Brown. I don't want to, but it's important.' She'd walk in next morning, she'd say, 'Now, what time do you want to call Charley Brown? Do you want me to call him now?' I'd say, 'No, not now, please.' And I'd put it off and put it off, and then, about eleven o'clock, she'd say, 'Do you want to call Charley Brown now?' I'd say, 'No. Not yet. Maybe after lunch.' Always some excuse. Two o'clock: 'Do you want me to call Charley Brown now?' I'd say, 'Oh, Maria, God damn it, no, I really don't, I mean I got something I just got to do right now.' At four o'clock, she'd buzz me: 'Charley Brown is on the phone.' She'd called him at four o'clock—I *had* to do it then!

"You could not escape. There was no way of escaping. She would do it. And every night, I had a card on my desk that said, 'Tomorrow at eight o'clock, you have this meeting; at ten-thirty, you have to be here; at noon, you're having lunch with this man; two o'clock; four o'clock.' And if I was in a meeting, and was not there at the time, she brought it to me. Or, when I came out of the meeting—and I don't wear a coat if I can help it—the coat, hanging behind the door, had a card clipped to the lapel, telling me what I had to do tomorrow. Never let me forget. Never. I could not escape. Whatever I said I wanted to do, she'd make sure I did it. She's really a fabulous person!"

During this period, the firm's Retail Store Protection service continued to increase through a program that combined the utilization of security guards—store detectives—to combat shoplifting, and to develop the technique of "shopping" to determine the integrity of cashiers in the stores. These shopping teams also determined such conditions as stock supply, general store appearance, parking facilities, courtesy, knowledge, and the efficiency of sales clerks. At the same time, TWC's Internal Intelligence service, which obtained information through undercover investigation, was utilized to expose and control inside thefts that could range from employee pilferage to embezzlement and poor working conditions. The Investigative Division was continuing to provide various investigative services for business and industry, insurance companies, attorneys, banks, and retail establishments. The company began publishing *The Wackenhut Case Report,* a monthly journal containing synopses of actual cases compiled from TWC files. Each case was disguised to protect those concerned, but identified the investigative and security requirements of business, industry, and the professions, and illustrated the manner in which these needs were being met.

In January 1961, Jack Bevan joined the company as director of the Polygraph Division. In February, another former agent, Phillipe Moore, became director of Sales Promotion.

Early in 1961, TWC introduced the use of guardetts at retail stores with security responsibilities. Experience had shown that the public would react positively to a woman in uniform, and guardetts were trained in the same manner as the Wackenhut guards.

As the company continued to grow, the need for strong leadership in the Accounting Department was apparent, and Marshall Bell, a former FBI agent, who had joined the firm in September 1960, was appointed controller in March 1961. At the special joint meeting of the shareholders and board on March 6, 1961, George Wackenhut, John Ammarell, and Robert F. O'Mallay were selected directors. In June 1961, William Bitter, the former head of personnel and safety at Maule Industries, was employed by TWC as director of Personnel Relations. Also in June, Hugh A. Page, another former FBI agent, became the company's director of the Scientific Services Division, and Robert E. Clift was named director of the Guard Forces Division.

During the summer of 1961, George vacationed in the mountains of North Carolina, and while there read the *Washington Report*, published by the American Security Council. The report listed a board of directors composed primarily of generals and admirals. He reasoned that if an organization such as the American Security Council could obtain individuals of that caliber for its board, perhaps he could do the same for his company.

"My idea, of course, was not only to enhance my company's image," he recalls, "but also to give direction to management in a variety of areas, and, since we were engaged in a wide variety of military-related and government-related work, I thought it would be a good idea if we had some people with military backgrounds on the board.

"I discussed this with Phillip C. Crowen, president of the Peoples Gas Company of North Miami, who had been one of my early advisors as well as a good friend and client. There were valid reasons to respect his business ability. On one occasion he told me that his wealthy father had a stipulation in his will that Phil had to be worth a million dollars in his own right by the time he was thirty years old to collect any of his father's estate. Phil made the deadline. I asked him one time if he was a graduate engineer. 'No,' he said, 'I can hire engineers. I'm a businessman.' So when he heartily approved my idea, I set the wheels in motion.

"At that time, I had an executive in our organization who had been a colonel in the Air Force and personally knew former Major General Joseph V. Dillon. Prior to his retirement, Dillon had been air provost marshal, U.S. Air Force, and was one of the judges in the Nuremburg trials of Nazi war criminals following World War II. I invited him to join and, to my delight, he accepted.

"Dillon, in turn, interceded for me with his friend, former Major General Kenneth P. McNaughton, U.S. Air Force, to see if he would join our board. McNaughton had been deputy commander of the Far East Air Forces prior to his retirement. While he would never discuss it, there had been talk that he would have been made Air Force chief of staff except for some altercation with Lyndon Johnson when the former president was chairman of the Senate Armed Services Committee. It was two feathers in our directorial cap when McNaughton also acceded to our request.

"Next came Richard Glavin, who had retired as assistant director in charge of the administrative division of the FBI; Samuel K. McKee, retired agent in charge of the FBI's office in Newark, New Jersey; Will M. Preston, a partner in the law firm of Scott, McCarthy, Preston and Steel, and chairman of the board of Dade National Bank; Robert Weadock, Washington manager of Beloit Iron Works, who knew all the ropes in the capital, and was the youngest member of the board, but died not too long afterward of a heart attack; James Darbaker, president and CEO of the Copperweld Steel Company; Raymond A. Quadt, president and general manager of Reactive Metals, Inc.; Eric Barr, then director of security, electric boat division, General Dynamics Corporation; plus John Ammarell and myself.

"I asked my advisor, Phil Crowen, what I should pay my directors and he suggested that $100 per man for each of our four annual meetings would be suitable. This proved to be satisfactory, because they liked the philosophy of our company, all being political conservatives, and they enjoyed gathering at our meetings."

In November 1961, the first issue of *The Wackenhut Security Review* was published. Ralph Kiel, TWC's director of Public Relations, authored this publication and it was the company's contribution to the nation's growing fight against the communist conspiracy. Before publishing the first issue, an inquiry was made to Florida's secretary of state to obtain a ruling on a Florida law prohibiting corporations from contributing to political campaigns, the wording of which was all-inclusive. When the secretary of state learned of the company's purpose in publishing the series on communism, he raised no objection; thereafter, the publication was distributed to all employees, clients, and other interested individuals.

"George and I are both conservatives," Kiel explains. "Always have been. We were both tremendously concerned about the communist setup. And the way the Russians had been devoting all of their resources to the military buildup, they were way ahead of us in many areas. All the liberals over here were always ha-ha about it. They don't realize how close we came to war."

Born in Hackensack, New Jersey, September 24, 1911, Kiel graduated from Hasbrouck Heights High School in 1929, then received his BS degree from the University of Virginia in 1933. "Then I went back up to New Jersey and worked as a newspaper reporter. I had worked as a reporter in high school, believe it or not, and I went back to that same newspaper, which was *The Bergen Evening Record*, and then I did some work for *The New York Times*. That was when I decided that the money in the future was not in that field, and I had to get into public relations.

"So I went over to New York, got a job in public relations, worked there several years, handled a lot of interesting accounts, and then joined a new firm, Hal Leyshon and Associates, which had offices in Miami and New York. And they needed somebody down here, desperately needed help, so I came down to Miami in 1941. Then I had my own firm for a while, went over to Nassau for four years, starting in 1950, and then came back to Miami in 1954. And I was still in public relations when I joined The Wackenhut Corporation in November of 1960.

"We started publishing *The Wackenhut Security Review* about a year after I joined the company, and I wrote it, at George's suggestion. It was an excellent suggestion, because we were able to publish it along the lines that we wanted. We developed a large mailing list to concerned citizens, as well as to our prospective clients. The *Review* was monthly, and it had only two pages at the most, and we wanted to keep it that way. Because the businessman is reading so much that's coming across his desk every day, he wouldn't have the time to read a longer publication.

"Sometimes, we'd get challenged by the liberals. I researched everything that went into the *Review*. I selected news clippings from a variety of newspapers and magazines, respected publications like *The New York Times* and *Newsweek* magazine. Our editorial format went along the lines: 'Here's a report from Moscow by the Associated Press.' We used those things to call attention to the buildup that was going on in the Soviet Union. Many people didn't realize the magnitude of that buildup."

In 1963, *The Wackenhut Security Review* won the prestigious George Washington Honor Medal awarded by the Freedom's Foundation at Valley Forge, Pennsylvania, and in 1964 it won the Vigilant Patriot Award from the All-American Conference to Combat Communism.

"I think George just has this intuitive instinct for management and leadership," Kiel says. "Right there in the very beginning, maybe in the first few weeks I was there in 1960, we were just starting in our sales work and starting to get business. He said, 'I want every one of our department heads to go out and make at least one sales call a week!' I remember going out and calling on the *nunnery* of the Catholic Church down on Biscayne Boulevard! She was very receptive. I almost sold her a con-job! Anyway, that only lasted temporarily, because everything was growing fast anyhow. But he wasn't wasting any talent. He was saying: 'Don't let it go to your head, get out on the road and produce some business around here!'"

November of 1961 saw TWC open an area office in Jacksonville, Florida, with Sheldon Cooper, another former agent, as manager, and an office in Denver, Colorado, with former agent John L. Myers as manager.

The month of December found the year ending on an emotional note with the retirement of Captain Raymond A. Giesler, the company's oldest supervisor in terms of service. Captain Giesler was a former sergeant with the Chicago Police Department, who had retired from that city in 1956, moved to Miami, and served with Wackenhut's predecessor companies and TWC, from April 1957 until December 31, 1961. He had established an outstanding record for Wackenhut security guards in the Miami area, where he supervised more than 100 guards and supervisors, and did so with the lowest overtime ratio in the company.

It was another record-breaking year, as TWC continued to operate in nine states and Puerto Rico. Gross sales more than doubled, from $2.139 million in 1960, to $5.415 million in 1961, and the number of employees also doubled over the same period, from 855 to 1,741.

14

JOHN AMMARELL smiles as he looks at the first issue of TWC's employee newsletter, dated January 1, 1962, and as yet unnamed. He was only forty-one years old when it was published and had just completed his third year as executive vice president. During that three-year period, he had seen the company grow from a small agency in Miami, with an income of under $300,000, to a relatively large organization in nine states and Puerto Rico, with an income of more than $5 million. His full head of white hair is neatly combed, as usual, he wears glasses now, and his tanned features show the mileage of seventy-two years, but he's obviously in good shape, lean, vigorous, and his blue eyes have sparkle and humor. When he took charge of the breakthrough Martin Company contract on January 1, 1959, he was thirty-eight, married for sixteen years, with two teenage sons, and had given up a lucrative executive position with Air Products and Chemicals, Inc., in Trexlertown, Pennsylvania. It was a risk. There were no guarantees. It was also a wrenching experience for his family, particularly his sons, to pull up roots and move to Miami, which wasn't much of a city back then. Twenty-five years later, he would retire as one of the most valuable executives George Wackenhut had ever had, the strong right arm who had helped build TWC into one of the world's largest security and investigative organizations, with revenues that year (1983) of $238.936 million. And he would retire a wealthy man. After two years as president of Newberry College, Newberry, South Carolina

(1984–1986), where he had been a trustee since 1970, he returned to TWC as chairman of the executive committee of the board of directors, and senior consultant to the president. In January 1994, he retired from the board.

Looking through the first newsletter brings back a flood of pleasant memories. "Ralph Kiel wrote this back in December 1961," he recalls, "and we didn't know what to name it, so we asked the employees to submit names, and offered a $25 Defense Bond for the winning name. In the February issue, it was announced that Sergeant Stephen Pastiva, Sr., a security supervisor on our force at the Atlas Missile Base in Salina, Kansas, had submitted the winning name, *The Pipeline*."

Sergeant Pastiva had submitted a total of twenty-three entries, and the entire guard force at Salina had submitted 174 entries. There were 227 suggested names submitted during the contest.

In that first issue, there was a "Message from our President," together with a photo of George at the age of 42, when he still sported a crew cut:

> Dear Fellow Employees:
>
> It gives me great personal pleasure to present to our more than 2000 employees this, the first edition of our company "house organ."
>
> It often comes as a surprise to our employees when, in my personal discussions with them as I visit our far-flung installations, I mention that we have over 2000 people in our employ. This surprise is undoubtedly due to the fact that our employees are so widely scattered throughout the many areas in which we serve our clients.
>
> It is this same geographic dispersion which makes it difficult at times for our employees to associate themselves with other employees whom they have never seen, or of whose existence they were not even aware, at least until the medium of this company publication came into being.
>
> We do not have the advantage of working together under one roof, nor that of working under exactly similar circumstances. Our working conditions are not identical, due to the differences in our contracts with various clients (although we are making every effort to standardize these wherever possible).
>
> But, regardless of these variances in location and operation, I am pleased to say that I feel, in making my visits and meeting many of you

personally, a sense of pride and of belonging, a feeling of being a part of a growing organization which is making a substantial contribution to the security, not only of the American industry which has made our country great, but to our American way of life itself.

I am very pleased that from time to time, I will have a chance to visit with you and your family through the medium of this new publication, so that we may get to know each other better.

Pipeline became a valuable means of communication with the company's employees, because TWC's forces were becoming so widespread throughout the U.S. and Puerto Rico. A great deal of emphasis had been placed on the hiring of former FBI agents, and, at the time the newsletter was published, there were sixteen ex-agents in various executive and investigative positions. One of the interesting features of the newsletter during 1962 was the publication of background profiles on various executives. These profiles included John Ammarell; M. Fred Rayne, who was vice president of District Offices at the time and had been manager of the San Juan office in Puerto Rico; Marshall J. Bell, Treasurer; Richard H.W. Maloy, who joined the company in February, 1962, as its first in-house general counsel. G. Ralph Kiel, director of Public Relations, was in the June issue, and Bill Bitter, director of Personnel, in the July issue. Bud Thompson appeared in August, and Victor P. Keay, director of Operations, was highlighted in September.

Keay had retired as an inspector from the FBI in 1956 to accept a five-year appointment as deputy head of the Security Bureau of the North Atlantic Treaty Organization (NATO), based in Paris. Ammarell had been Keay's assistant for five years at FBI headquarters, and was successful in convincing Keay to join TWC, February 1, 1962, after his five years with NATO.

In the October, November, and December issues of *Pipeline,* profiles included Sam McKee, director of Investigations; Robert C. Haas, director of Southeastern Regional Development, and Robert M. Kirk, executive director of Development. TWC had become acquainted with Kirk when he was with the Martin Company as supervisor of security at the Titan I Base in Denver. He resigned from Martin to go into business in Florida, but soon determined that he preferred to be in security work and joined Wackenhut in January, 1962, as contracts manager.

Early in June, 1962, TWC made its first major acquisition when it purchased General Plant Protection Company of California and its affiliates. This move combined the country's fourth and fifth largest security firms and included Protection Engineering Corporation, which provided a central burglar and fire alarm protection system for the Los Angeles area and General Plant Protection Corporation, which had branches in San Jose, California, and Honolulu.

General Plant Protection was headquarters in Los Angeles and had many clients in Southern California and at Edwards Air Force Base. It had been headed since 1940 by Ralph E. Davis, a Los Angeles businessman; this was the guard organization that TWC replaced at the Martin plant in Orlando in 1959. Ray J. Abbaticchio, Jr., a former FBI special agent in charge, and more recently chairman of the Nevada State Gaming Control Board, was appointed to supervise the new acquisition's operations. This was an excellent acquisition at the time and, through the cooperation and efforts of the management personnel of General Plant Protection, it was possible to retain almost all of that company's clients by the time the takeover was concluded in August. At the same time, TWC recognized the United Plant Guard Workers of America for the officers who worked at various chemical plants for General Plant Protection in the Martinez, California, area; these were the first unionized employees to become part of the company.

TWC's board of directors was expanded by the addition of two new members by vote, May 31, 1962, when Ralph E. Davis, the chief executive officer and one of the founders of General Plant Protection, and Loyd Wright of California were added. Wright was the senior partner of the law firm of Wright, Wright, Wright, Goldwater and Mack of Los Angeles, and was a past president of the American Bar Association.

Both men attended the board meeting in Miami on September 10, 1962. That month, TWC began phasing out the Atlas Missile Site Program at Salina, Kansas, and reducing the size of the security force in Denver. At the September board meeting, George Wackenhut announced that the company had recently received notice from

Martin-Marietta Corporation (formerly the Martin Company) that it intended to cancel its contract at Orlando, Florida, and install every member of The Wackenhut Corporation guard force at the Orlando plant as a Martin employee. The reason given by Martin was the desire to have its own guard force, but senior management expressed the highest praise for TWC, both orally and in writing. General McNaughton said that he had made inquiries of the Martin headquarters in Baltimore and learned that the decision was purely a local one, emanating from a request by the Martin/Orlando security director to have his own guard force. George Wackenhut received a letter from J.M. Holliday, director of industrial relations at the Martin/Orlando plant, dated September 6, 1962:

> Dear Mr. Wackenhut:
> In the past four years, the efficiency of the Wackenhut guards in carrying out their assigned duties in their courteous demeanor has brought many favorable comments to my office. I would like to assure you that severance of the contract with your organization was taken only after consideration of all aspects of a subcontracted guard force. It was in no way related to your performance, but rather we thought it was to our advantage to have this group of employees as a part of the Martin team, because the nature of their duties makes it necessary that they work closely with all of our employees as well as with management.
> I would like to take this opportunity to express my appreciation to you and the members of your organization for the outstanding services rendered the Martin Company.

That year, Jan was seventeen and a senior, and Rick was fifteen and a sophomore, both at Palmetto Senior High School. Rick has particularly pleasant memories: "My favorite subjects? My father would tell you that it was girls, girls, and girls, which is probably close to accurate. I enjoyed history a fair amount, I enjoyed civics and geography. Did not enjoy math that much. I think that was because, when I was in sixth grade, I was scared to death by students and teachers who said, 'Boy, when you get to junior high school, it's going to be really, really tough.' So, when I hit seventh grade, I think I was scared into making good grades. And I made straight-A grades almost every report card. By the time I hit eighth grade, I discovered girls, and it was A and B grades, and maybe a sprinkling of C. By the time I hit ninth grade, it was B and C, and I said, 'Hey, I better wake up, or I'm not going to get into any colleges.'

"But going into seventh grade, and doing so well, they put me in an advanced math class for eighth grade, and it was right about that time that I started having trouble with my vision and needed glasses. So I went into an advanced math class with some eye problems, and really did not do well in math. I was nearsighted. And, being a 'W,' they always sat us alphabetically, and, inevitably, I was always in the back right or left side of the room.

"I did not grow to any appreciable size, as far as bulk is concerned, until I was a senior. So, as much as I wanted to play football, I never played. I think I went out for junior varsity in eighth grade and did not do well. But I wrestled all during high school, and went to a couple of state meets, and did fairly well. In high school, I was in the 154-pound class, and I continued wrestling in college. I wasn't tall enough for basketball, and never really had the desire for baseball.

"I was probably in the ninth or tenth grade when I started working in the Wackenhut mailroom during summer vacation. I continue to threaten my father with taking him to court, because he only gave me twenty dollars a week, out of his own pocket, and I tell him that he violated child labor laws! Twenty dollars a week for a forty-hour week! Another summer, I was on the 'scissors brigade,' it was extremely boring work. It was simply cutting out of newspapers anything that had to do with arrests or violations or anything criminal—or even civil—matters related to crime, to begin building files on anyone that we may come across at a later time during an investigation. We had newspapers from all over the country. Basically, we had our own clipping service. Summer work as a guard came a bit later. I was probably a senior in high school at that time. I was a guard at the Winn-Dixie warehouse. That was just a miserable place to work. Diesel fumes from the trucks coming in all the time. Later, I drove a patrol car in Gables Estates when the house was being built. That shift was from eight at night to eight in the morning. Those were basically the two guard assignments."

Jan worked as a receptionist and switchboard operator at Wackenhut during several summer vacations in high school and enjoyed it. "Downstairs, they had the switchboard, little tiny switchboard, it was more fun," she recalls. "I imagine I would have done it the summer of my junior year; maybe it was both years, junior and senior. That was exciting, to be around Dad. The bottom level in those days was the garage. Half of it was a garage. Getting to meet all those people was enjoyable, but it was not mentally challenging. It was fun to be there, but I wasn't busy enough, and I couldn't get my teeth in it. Maybe I did it during the time the normal operator was on vacation. It was a real close-knit situation and I didn't feel any animosity. I felt everybody was eager that I was there. We had an old—I think it was a 1954 Buick that they had given me in high school. It was a stick-shift. When they were ready to get a new car, they got an Oldsmobile. And then I gave the Buick to Rick when I was finished with it, at the end of high school. I really didn't even use it to take to school; I walked.

"I loved all my subjects in high school. Had a hard time with math in junior high, but, you know, geometry and trig and algebra, I just ate up, I didn't have a problem with any of them. I had a straight-A average. I remember one time I brought a B home, and that was a big thing: 'Why the B?' I studied all the time, that's all I did. I enjoyed it, but also I think it was an escape. I stayed after school for all the activities that I would be involved in—Spanish Club, Math Club, National Honor Society. Volleyball team, basketball team, I loved sports, but I wasn't real good at them. I danced, I took dancing. I'd come home fairly late, then study till one or two in the morning. I don't know, it was like an escape for me.

"I used to date a guy fairly steadily, named Mike Wedge, his dad was a captain for National. And they also had this egg farm. His house and property were turned into a nursery school, it's on South Dixie Highway and 160th. Colonial Drive, but it's east of the Highway, and there's a big auto dealer there now. Next to the auto dealer was his house, and there was a park, a pretty park with ducks. We spent a lot of time in the park! Across the street, where the car dealership is, was a blank field. And they had their own Piper Cub. He used to fly with his dad, and he always wanted to fly. Many times he wanted to take me up in the plane; Mother and Dad would never let me go. He ended up being a pilot with TWA. But that was my first 'true love.' We dated from tenth through twelfth grade. Off and on. He was into music, he had a music group with a couple of other people, real good boys, and he used to play the guitar.

"He graduated the year before me, and his grades weren't real good. He was kind of—he kind of swept me up, because he had all the right things to say, and he was much more mature, and he just knew what to do with dating, this whole thing. He'd serenade you and write songs and made you feel like a queen. But his grades were abominable, and we had no classes together, because I was in college prep type things, all honors courses, and really carrying heavy loads. I ran for every office there was, every club, I was into all of that, and he was not involved in school.

"Senior prom? Mike Wedge was never around for proms. He would be dating other people on the sly that I didn't know about, a lot of 'broken heart' type stuff. I remember when it was *his* senior prom, I was a junior, he had been chosen a 'superlative'—I think he got 'most talented' or something. We were supposed to go to the dance together, and then he decided he wanted to take someone else, but he didn't tell me that, he just said he couldn't go. Just couldn't make it. I said, 'You can't go to your senior prom?' Well, he just made up this big story. I remember sitting down, telling my dad. And he said, 'Jan, isn't he a superlative?' I said, 'Yeah.' He said, 'Don't they *have* to go?' Because there's this big presentation and everything. So I thought: *Bong!* I remembered this foreign student, who was a Spanish student, and we didn't have many of them. He was in my Spanish class, which was the only like 'rip-off' class I took, we just kind of joked and everything, because my neighbor was teaching it. He invited me, he was a senior. And, oh, I didn't want to go with him at all, but I went, because I wanted to see if Mike showed. He was there. That was the end of *him!*

"The night of the senior prom, I met my husband-to-be, John Thorsen. He had come to Palmetto from Southwest, of all funny things. His parents decided that the element over there wasn't good for him, either, and they bought in the Palmetto area. He came into school and he was on crutches. I don't know what had happened, playing football or something, he was injured. He was very nice-looking and all the girls went *'Ahhh!'* So I didn't get involved in any of that. But I knew about him. The night of our senior prom, Mother and Dad had met his parents through King's Bay—that was a country club in those days—and they had invited them over for cocktails, I think with some other people, and then they were going to go out to dinner. I was dressed to go to the prom with this other person, and my mother-in-law-to-be, Arline, said, 'Oh, you look so gorgeous!' I remember she was in my bedroom, watching me get ready; Mother was in there. I was real nervous, trying to get ready. And she said, 'I've got to call my son, you've *got* to wait, he just *has* to come by and *see* you!' Okay? He drives up in this *Triumph!* TR-4, I think it was, which was a real snazzy car, and he was on his way to *his* prom at Southwest. Even though he'd transferred over to Palmetto, it was so late in the year, he was going to his prom. And we met. And that was it! I graduated in June of 1962 and we started dating that summer."

MIRTHA LATOUR joined TWC as a typist in the Accounting Department on October 19, 1962. Now director of Payroll and Billing, she celebrated her thirtieth anniversary with the company in 1992, but has vivid recollections of that first year. "In 1962, when I started, we had maybe twenty-five headquarters employees," she says. "In Accounting, there were only seven of us. From that time, only a few of us are left. Maria Hester was here when I started, but then she left for a short time, because she got married and went to live in California. The office manager was Anne Pelton, a former chief clerk of the FBI field office in Buffalo, New York. She was very strict. We had a dress code. It made people dress professionally, which made a big difference."

Born in Havana, Cuba, one of four children of Luis and Maria Merino, Latour graduated from Sagrado Corazon de Maria grammar school in Havana, and the Havana Business Academy, then studied for two years at the Havana Business University. She was married in 1948 to Edward Latour, an American citizen born in New York City, who was an acting vice consul in the U.S. Foreign Service, stationed in Havana. Three of their four children, Mirtha, Lianne, and Eddie, were born in Cuba as American citizens.

In 1950, her husband was transferred to Santiago, Cuba, as acting vice consul. Then, in 1952, he was asked to transfer to Juarez, Mexico, but declined to accept the position. The family moved from Havana to Miami on May 21, 1955.

"Because of the children, I didn't work until 1958," recalls the slim, attractive Latour. "Then I accepted a job with Pan American World Airways in the Accounting Department. But they transferred that department to New York in 1959. After that, I worked for Florida Gas." Her fourth child, Charlie, was born in Miami, July 6, 1962. Today, she has six grandchildren, five boys and a girl.

She began work with TWC at the "new" (1960) headquarters building, 3280 Ponce de Leon Boulevard, in Coral Gables. "I was hired by Bill Bitter, who was personnel manager at that time," she says, "and I worked for Stanley Kokan, who was the supervisor of the Accounting Department. I stayed in billing from day one for the next thirty years."

But the year 1962 was particularly memorable to Latour for a variety of reasons. In December, TWC was granted the Mack Truck security guard contract at Mack's headquarters in Allentown, Pennsylvania. A forty-five man force started in January, 1963, headed by James H. Dunn, who had served as a captain in TWC's force at the Martin Company in Orlando, and was subsequently placed in charge of the Atlas Missile Site force at Salina, Kansas.

Latour's first impressions of George Wackenhut in 1962, when he had just turned forty-three: "He was a very powerful man, the way he carried himself," she recalls. "He had a crew cut, but he always had white hair. He was a handsome man. The impression you got, you knew when Mr. Wackenhut was there, his presence. Once, he bought himself a red Corvette, and I told Mr. [Bud] Thompson one day, 'You know, Mr. Thompson, tell Mr. Wackenhut that car doesn't go with his job or his personality.' He laughed a lot about that, Mr. Thompson told me. But I understand Mr. Wackenhut liked to go very fast, to press the pedal a lot—so the car *did* go with him!"

The year 1962 closed with TWC reporting revenues of $7.772 million and a total of 1,816 employees in fifteen offices located in twelve states and Puerto Rico.

ELSEWHERE in the U.S. during 1962: On January 26, Orsen Welles's classic *Citizen Kane* (originally released in 1941) was voted the best film ever made by a poll of seventy film critics from eleven countries. On February 20, Lieutenant Colonel John Glenn orbited the earth three times in the space capsule Friendship 7, to become the first American in orbit; more than 135 million Americans watched his flight on television. On April 25, the U.S. resumed nuclear tests in the atmosphere above the South Pacific in response to the U.S.S.R.'s breach of a four-year unofficial test moratorium the previous autumn; the U.S. exploded thirty-six nuclear devices through November 4.

On May 12, *The New York Times* reported: "U.S. aid to South Vietnam reached a peak and will start to level off, Robert S. McNamara, Defense Secretary disclosed today. Before departing for Washington, Mr. McNamara said he doubted whether U.S. personnel assigned to South Vietnam would be increased above the present strength. After 48 hours in South Vietnam, Mr. McNamara was tremendously encouraged by developments.... 'I found nothing but progress and hope for the future,' he said."

On June 25, the U.S. Supreme Court barred the use of a "nondenominational" prayer in New York State schools on the basis of the First Amendment, separating church and state; Justice Douglas condemned the conduct of school prayers as "a public official on the public payroll performing a religious exercise in a governmental institution before a captive audience." On July 18, the first privately owned satellite, Telstar (AT&T), relayed television programs across the Atlantic. On August 5, Marilyn Monroe was found dead of a barbiturate overdose in her Los Angeles home; her death was officially ruled a suicide. On October 23, President Kennedy ordered a Cuban blockade, announcing that he had photographs of Cuban-Russian missile bases capable of launching nuclear weapons 1,000 miles into the U.S. Kennedy threatened to invade Cuba if the bases were not dismantled, and Russia threatened nuclear war. On November 8, the Pentagon announced that the bases had been dismantled, and on November 20, the blockade was lifted. On December 8, typographers struck all nine major New York City newspapers, leaving 5.7 million subscribers without daily papers until April 1,

1963; Cleveland and St. Louis newspaper workers also struck. That was also the year when Rachel Carson's best-selling book *Silent Spring* exposed the widespread damage to all life caused by pesticides, and heralded an increasing concern with ecology and the risks of destruction inherent in man's technological progress.

IN SEPTEMBER 1962, Jan entered Florida State University in Tallahassee, while her husband-to-be, John Thorsen, entered Dade Junior College in Miami, with the idea that he would prove himself academically and qualify for a scholarship to Florida State. In view of Jan's outstanding achievements in high school, the fact that she selected Florida State over the academically superior private colleges in the northeast "was a real bummer for Mother and Dad, they were horrified," she remembers. "I had grades to get into any school I wanted to get into. See, I didn't know the northeast at all, I was very sheltered as far as my high school years went. I didn't really like Miami, because I knew that there was more culture elsewhere. For that reason, I wanted to go away to school, but I think I was emotionally very immature. Very afraid. Because I knew no one. Dad was so engrossed in the business that, you know, he figured it would take care of itself. So I sent away for every college catalogue you can imagine. And I'd get all excited about Colorado, then I'd get excited about Texas. I didn't know where I was going. I didn't know what I wanted to do.

"I was accepted at both Vassar and Smith. And when it came down to it, I got scared to death. Mother always pushed status on me and I rebelled like crazy. I never went up to visit those schools. See, all these things I did with *my* girls [Tanya and Tresha], because it was important to me that they really get out of here and see what it is, and not just read about these schools in catalogues. I had nobody I knew there, nobody to talk about it. So I went out on my own and really didn't have the resources available to me to make the best decisions. It was more of a rebellion type thing. The way I had pictured Vassar and Smith, they were a bunch of snooty women, no football games, no sororities, no interaction with men, an 'old money' type thing that, you know, you get these reputations in some of these northeastern cities from the time you're a kid. I just didn't want it. Didn't want it.

"I don't think I decided to go to Florida State until the very last minute. Now, Mother says it's because my friend Jane went. Jane Franzino. Mother thought I was very—always said I was so influenced by friends. It wasn't so much that as a need of—I just didn't have enough inner strength to go off and do something by myself. I wanted to go to Principia, the Christian Science college that Tresha ended up going to. But nobody knew anything about it, we didn't know anybody that was there. That scared me.

"When I got up there, I mean, it was huge, and I was missing John terribly. So happy to get away from home, but missing him terribly. And I became anorexic. Nobody knew what it was. I didn't want to go in the cafeteria and eat by myself, this huge thing. I hadn't joined a sorority yet; I tried, but didn't get the bids. Then I just didn't eat. And then it was fun. Because at home, I could not go out on a date until I finished my dinner, you know, and it was always everything was centered around food. I was always feeling uncomfortable. I weighed about 135 when I entered. I went down to 105, and I'm five-seven and a half. There were bones everywhere. It didn't dawn on me until—none of my clothes were fitting, and I remember being involved in several fraternity parties, not having anything to wear, and I had a few girl friends from high school who were very slim, and I had gone to their dorms to see if I could borrow some slacks, and they were too big for me. Then I realized what was going on. Because you still see yourself as this cow, and you're not.

"Mother and Dad didn't know anything that was going on, but my period stopped. Now, John wasn't there, and we didn't have intimacy until we were married, so there was nothing like that, but I didn't know what was going on. I knew I must be sick, something's happening. I went to the infirmary. No empathic reaction. The first thing she said was, 'Well, are you pregnant?' And I was aghast. She just treated me like I had no head on my shoulders and dismissed me. Didn't know what was wrong. Then, reading about it, when your body fat goes below a certain percentage—female athletes have the same problem—all that stops, your hormone system is all changed. It's very interesting. So I got caught up in that.

"I remember coming home that first Thanksgiving. If you could've seen me going to school, it was like really comical. I was afraid to leave anything at home, it was like: Well, I'm *leaving!* So I took *everything!* I must've had forty trunks. I remember my residence counselor telling me at the end of the year her view of this entourage: My mother, me—Dad didn't come—I don't know who else was there, and all these *clothes!* Well, of course, Mother was aghast at where I was living, she thought it was just awful.

"It gets worse. I don't know when it happened, it must've been after the holidays, into the next semester, I'm doing my thing, going to class, whatever, and, all of a sudden, I get paged out of a class. And I thought: Oh, my God, who's *dying,* what's *wrong?* I was sent to the president's office. My parents had called. What had happened is, John had decided he had to come to Florida State to see if he really loved me! Because if he did, he was going to come up there, and we were going to have this future, and he was going to go to school there. He was just mixed up, where he was going. Mother and Dad assumed we were getting *married!* It was the farthest thing from my mind! Marriage? I wasn't ready for marriage!

"So they had the dorms barricaded, that I couldn't get in without the president of the dorm knowing, and I was going to be sequestered in an office until they could talk to me, and they were going to make sure that I didn't leave campus, and that nothing happened. Really weird. I remember the campus police got John, and he didn't know what was happening. His mother must have been hysterical, thinking: *He's run away!* I don't know. Crazy."

HARRY WACKENHUT, George's brother, was divorced in 1962, after nearly twenty-two years of marriage to the former Mary Frances (Fran) Boyd. The couple had four children, Pam, Russell, Joyce, and Sally, ranging in age from twenty-one to eight at the time of the divorce. Harry was fifty-four that year and Fran was forty-two. At that time, he had been working for Penn Mutual Life Insurance Company for thirty-six years. According to the children, it had been a tumultuous marriage for as long as they could remember.

Pam Keller, the eldest, was born in Chicago, November 9, 1941, graduated from Downers Grove Community High School in June

1959, and was married shortly afterward. She has two children, Terri and Rick, four stepchildren, and lives in Elgin, Illinois.

"My earliest memories of my father are him coming in the door at night and being so thrilled to see him home," she remembers. "He played. Dad played with us. One of my favorite memories was when *The Lone Ranger* was on, and that part would come at the end with 'Hi-yo, Silver . . .' Dad would repeat 'Hi-yo, Silver . . .' and he'd hang on to it, and he'd pretend he was lost somewhere in the room, and what we were waiting for was the *'Ha-waaay'*—because that was the key, we could all jump on him and wrestle!

"Mostly, he was home at a reasonable hour every day. I remember incidents where he had to go out of town sometimes, and my mom was drinking very heavily, and we hated and feared how she would get when he was away. There was one time in particular that was very frightening, when we waited in the bushes till one in the morning for him to come back from out of town. Because we were so frightened. I think I was about twelve or thirteen when it hit me the hardest.

"I learned about her promiscuity by picking up the phone and hearing. That was her big affair, I think. He would come over a lot, and I heard a lot going on. This was when my father was at work. And I'm talking summertime, when I was off school, or when I'd come home from school. Yes, he'd be away, absolutely, he'd be away. But she had what I called her 'drunk voice.' I've got her down perfect; one time she said to me: 'You *know,* don't you, I've *never liked you!*' And one time, talking about the promiscuity, she said to me, in the same tone of voice, that now that she had quit selling her body to my father, she was going to *'live!'* Tell me that isn't frightening.

"I remember her going into Hinsdale Sanitarium, of her own volition, and the psychiatrist telling my dad he can't help her, she has to want to help herself, she knew as much as he did. Mother was *extremely* intelligent. Extremely. I think she was around thirty-six about this time; I could be wrong. I remember greeting her with my dad when she came out of the hospital, and saying, 'Does this mean you're not going to drink any more, Mom?' And she said, 'Yes.' And then the first time I saw her drinking, I confronted her, and she called me a Pollyanna and all sorts of things.

"My brother reacted to all this by hiding in his room. Played sports games. I did that too, we both did that, hid in our respective rooms. I read. A lot. In essence, I'm a speed-reader today. I average six books a week now, and that's working ten-hour days. That was from hiding up in my room all summer, reading.

"I was in court to testify against my mother when my mother and father finally divorced. Sally was eight years old, and Mom agreed to give him custody if he would pay her $10,000, and $100 a month for ten years. Dad raised Sally alone after that, the happiest years of his adult life. I *hated* being in court. I didn't have to testify, but I was frightened of my mother and the hurt I was inflicting on her by being there."

Sally Bretl, the youngest, was born July 12, 1954, graduated from high school in 1972, received her bachelor's degree from Northern Illinois University in 1976, and her master's degree in 1981. She was married to Jim Bretl in 1981, and they have three children, Mat, Ben, and Nick. They live in Mukwonago, Wisconsin, near Milwaukee.

"One thing my mom did was bring me to places a lot," she recalls. "It was routine for her, we lived in the Chicago suburbs, and it was routine for her to bring me in to visit my special wax museum in Chinatown, or other museums, and the zoo was a regular place to visit. That was the part I remember about my mom, that was among the happy parts about my mom. I'm much younger than the others, my next oldest is about ten years older, that's Joyce, way up to Pam, who's thirteen years older. I'm a *great aunt* for the fourth time! I think I began to be a great aunt ten years ago. I mean, it was weird!

"At home, I was removed from knowing what was happening maritally, but I had my own adjustments to make. I don't think the divorce was a surprise to me. One knew that they didn't get along, just from the way my mother would talk. She would be more likely to say something derogatory than Dad would.

"I went to live with my dad after the divorce, and I missed not having Mom around. For me, it was tough, because I think being so much younger, I was the pet, you know, for everybody. I went from living with my mom and dad and the four of us kids, to just Dad and me in the apartment. It was lonely, that was the most difficult part for me. The other part was that we moved into an apartment, and I lost my school, and my normal neighborhood, and my family as I knew it. Then we moved again, within a year. So I had to start in another school in a farther off town that I didn't know, and try to pick up other friends there.

"When you're eight years old, and you only have one person, and you wait for him to get home, and often it's not until after dark, it's lonely. I worried a lot about my father not being home. It frightened me, but I don't think I let myself know it at the time. When our school would go on vacation, I had nothing all day.

"I have completely opposite feelings about both my mom and dad. I have real positive and negative feelings about each one. The positive about my mom: I believed she loved me in her way, and tried in her way to parent me the best she knew how, which was by exposing me to things, teaching me things, showing me things I should know about life. She made a point of taking me to the Bowery in New York. Negative about my mom, of course, was her drinking. I wasn't really aware of her drinking at the time. I was used to there being a glass there, but I was too young to know its full meaning. One didn't walk up and hug her, she would often have caustic remarks, she would be unpredictably morose or cruel in her remarks. My older siblings had fights with her when she had been drinking. Only once was her abuse directed toward me, but you sense this woman may be one way or the other at any time, so you kind of keep at arm's length, even though you love her. She didn't really direct a lot of it toward me, but I knew what it was like, what the others had experienced.

"There were a lot of positive things about my dad. He was very consistent, he made me feel very secure, I always felt that he loved me. I lived alone with him from when I was eight until I left for college. The negative things: I always felt real responsible for him. He never made an effort to have a social life of his own. Whenever I would try to socialize with my friends in high school, he would give this big audible sigh as I left. That made me feel very bad for leaving him alone at home. But I felt I had to get out and get with people, because it was just him and I at home, and I really needed more people in my life. When I moved out, Pam more or less took that spot."

Joyce Wackenhut Hilbert was born in Chatham Park, a suburb of

Chicago, on May 31, 1945, before the family moved to Downers Grove, and graduated from Downers Grove Community High School in 1963. After attending the University of Illinois for five semesters, she moved to New York, attended the New School for Social Research, then dropped out of school and worked several years as a legal secretary in entertainment law. In 1970, she entered the Hunter College night school program, worked at several large advertising agencies, received her bachelor's degree in 1976, and decided to remain in New York. She entered Hunter's graduate program in 1977 and received her Ph.D. in philosophy in May of 1987. She married Charles (Chuck) Hilbert on October 13, 1984. They have an adopted son, Tommy, and live in Manhattan.

"One of my memories of my mother is when we lived at Hillcrest, and a vague memory of a neighbor coming over. I don't have it straight, I just have a memory of everyone was up in arms, and that my mother then went away for a few days, and it was referred to later as a nervous breakdown. I remember that. And I remember my mother sequestering the children, one at a time, when my dad would travel, and talk to us. She would drink and then she would tell us how horrible our father was. It was a very devastating experience for a young child to go through, having your mother tell you that your father is bad.

"I remember one time she was doing this to me when my father drove in the driveway. This is really a funny thing, but I think it does make sense from a child's perspective. I said, 'Mom, Dad's *home!*' And she said, 'So?' Or something like that. But, anyway, I couldn't deal with it, and I just ran out of the house. And I just ran, probably close to a mile, just ran and ran, and hid in the bushes somewhere. Finally, someone came to look for me and found me. My dad or someone did.

"Then I was in Florida once, visiting at 'The Wacken Hut,' you know, where they had the sign 'The Wacken Hut,' it was the Miami home before the Castle. There's a story about my uncle there which I'll never forget, which is, I was out riding Rick's bike or something, and I happened to get shot in my arm with a BB gun by two boys in the bushes. This is so different from the way my father would've handled it, which is another thing that struck me. I went home crying, it *hurt,* it stung like the bejeepers. I went home crying, Uncle Russ was there, he found out what happened, and he said, 'Show me where it was!' He takes me, we storm out, go to exactly where it took place, he rushes through, *finds* the two kids, and says to them, 'Do you realize that you could've put her *eye* out!' He says, 'Don't you *ever, ever* do that again!' He took very concrete action. Whereas my dad would probably not have done that. He would've just soothed me or whatever. The two brothers are a study in contrasts, my uncle and my dad. My dad's the more soft, maternal, more passive. My uncle's the archetypical, stereotypical, male, masculine, authoritarian *man!*

"So, my dad was my mother. I could go to my dad and cry on his shoulder, to a fault, because I feel I grew up as a crybaby. I'm glad Dad gave me so much nurturing and love, but I wish my dad had given me more of a backbone. I wouldn't have wanted to have been Uncle Russ's child instead of my dad's child. But I would've liked a *flavor* of my uncle Russ's perspective inside my dad. That would've been better, I think, for me.

"But my dad was always *there.* I always felt, and to this day I feel, if there was anyone in the whole world I could go to, it was my father. I knew my father loved me. Unconditional love."

Russ Wackenhut, whose full name is George Russell Wackenhut II, was born in Chicago, October 10, 1942, graduated from Downers Grove Community High School in 1960, attended Drake University in Des Moines, Iowa, but did not graduate. After spending six months at the Harris Trust in Chicago as a messenger, he accepted a position as a file clerk at the Downers Grove National Bank in 1963. He celebrated his thirtieth year there in 1993, and has been president since 1989. He married the former Carolyn Rimnac on December 23, 1966. They live in Lisle, Illinois, and have two sons, David and Robert.

"I was named for my uncle," he says, laughing softly. "How that came about, I'll tell you the version I got. My dad fully expected Rick to be William Henry Wackenhut, to be named after his uncle Harry. He thought he had a bargain with Uncle Russ, but, obviously, Ruth had something to say about that. She didn't want a little boy named Harry. I wouldn't either, to be honest. I don't think that was anything that my dad lost sleep over, but that was the story that was related to me.

"We don't have a lot of relatives in my family, there are very precious few Wackenhuts, I guess, in the world. On my mother's side, we were never close to any relatives, and she had a number of brothers and sisters. My dad's family was much more a part of my life than my mom's. My dad was the one who took us to church. He did a lot of things that mothers do in traditional families, I think. I remember both my grandmother and grandfather vividly, George's mother and father. Everybody called him Bill and her Fran, although I don't know what her name was, really, it might have been Mary Frances, but everybody called her Fran. On my side of the family, my dad was William Henry, they called him Harry; my mother was Mary Frances, they called her Fran; I grew up George Russell II, but I was always Rusty as a kid. Uncle Russ, even though he's George Russell, he was always Uncle Russ. Everybody seemed to use their middle names for some reason.

"I remember Uncle Russ in Indianapolis, I remember when we were visiting them in Indianapolis. He was still with the Bureau at that time. There was a moment there that I've cherished all my life. The two moms, my mom and Ruth, and the kids—and it seems to me there were maybe all five of us—we all went to the movies one day. I don't know what my dad did, maybe he went to work with Russ or whatever. We went to the movies, and we parked the car in the downtown parking garage. I remember this vividly. One of the parking attendants was a black man who had enormous shoulders and chest, and a very narrow waist, and he had particular features that, in my mind, I could not help but have flash through my mind that the guy looked like an ape! And I no sooner formulated that thought when my cousin Rick said, 'Hey, mister, you look like an *ape!*' Well, I wanted to crawl into a hole and die, but Ruth, of course, apologized profusely, and the guy said to her: 'Don't worry about it, I *do* look like an ape!' That one is real distinct in my memory. I think I was ten or eleven and Rick was five or six. He was irrepressible at that age.

"My dad and my uncle used to trade five-dollar bills with birthday cards. My dad, when he was in Philadelphia, he was a major support to the family. When he moved to Chicago, he continued to support the family in Philadelphia. He was single, and he just took what he needed and sent the rest back to his mom, because, I gather, that she pretty much handled the finances. He was the support for George and the family for many, many years. He didn't get married until December of '40, so he was thirty-two years old when he got married. And he was in Chicago for quite a long time, living at the YMCA, before he was married, living minimally. He didn't save anything, he sent it all back. One of the things he would invariably do would be to send my uncle Russ a five-dollar bill with his birthday card every year. Well, of course, it got to a point where my uncle started sending my *dad* a five-dollar bill with *his* birthday card. And I guess they carried that tradition on, maybe forever, I don't know.

"Pam and Joyce and I lived in the same room, shared the same room, until 1951, the first eight and a half years of my life. We had a two-bedroom apartment in Chatham Park, Illinois, just outside Chicago, 619 East 84th Street. We moved to Downers Grove on Valentine's Day, 1951, and I remember we built that house, my parents built that house. I remember coming out to see it any number of times, and walking on the boards that were going to be *my* room, and *only* my room, that kind of thing. I think we did okay from that point on. You know, I couldn't get a new baseball mitt or anything like that, but we did okay.

"My dad was a very special man, very loving. More than anything else, he was the straightest, most ethical human being I've ever known. I got a lot from him. It's lasted a lifetime. Dad worked for Penn Mutual through the Depression, he was very fortunate, he felt, to have a job. He was with Penn Mutual for forty-seven years."

15

July 1, 1963, Wackenhut Services, Inc., took over the security responsibilities for the National Aeronautics and Space Administration (NASA) at its Lewis Research Center, Cleveland, Ohio. This was the first cost-plus security contract in the history of the industry. Captain James Dunn was placed in charge of this new operation, transferred from his responsibilities at the Mack Truck headquarters in Allentown, Pennsylvania. His thirty security officers included supervisors who had transferred from TWC's Titan Site in Wichita, Kansas, as well as two Miami district representatives.

In the autumn, George Wackenhut was named to the Florida Committee on Agency Licensing by the Florida Secretary of State. George was selected as chairman of a special advisory committee on private detectives, investigators, watchmen, guards, and patrolmen set up to advise the Secretary regarding revisions to Florida's laws relating to private investigative and guard organizations. TWC security forces were also started in North Carolina, Maryland, and New Hampshire.

It was announced in November that TWC had been selected to serve Westinghouse at its plant in Large, Pennsylvania, just outside Pittsburgh. Robert L. Yadon was transferred from his position as branch manager in San Jose, California, to head this force. Yadon was originally employed in 1959 to serve as a supervisor at the Titan Missile Site in Denver, and when TWC was awarded the Titan Missile Site at Moses Lake, Washington, he was named the captain in charge of that force.

The single most important historical event of the year 1963 was, of course, the assassination of President John F. Kennedy on November 22, during a midday motorcade in Dallas, Texas, a tragedy that shook the nation and the world.

At TWC, the year closed with a volume of $9.553 million, seventeen offices, operations in twenty states, and the number of employees had increased to 2,642.

The year 1964 started with a great deal of enthusiasm and optimism, much of which was demonstrated by the attitude of the various managers from the thirteen districts and areas who attended a special staff training conference at headquarters in January. All looked forward to increasing TWC's impact on the industry and to achieve an even firmer and higher position in the security field.

This contrasted sharply with consensus attitudes the previous July, when it became necessary to streamline the executive staff and operations of the company. At that time, among other things, the Miami district office was abolished and its functions were passed on to the executive staff. In addition, Samuel K. McKee, a director and head of the Investigative Division, was placed on leave of absence status for an indefinite period, and Arthur T. Potter was appointed director of that division. Potter had previously served in the FBI as an agent and administrator. The position of director, Administration, was abolished, and Victor P. Keay was placed on a leave of absence for an indefinite period. In addition, Fred Rayne, vice president, Development, was given notification of discharge for cause on June 25, and Robert Kirk was promoted to the position of director, Development.

George always considered Bob Kirk a marvelous addition to his staff. Born in Alpha, Illinois, August 14, 1918, he graduated from Oxford Township High School in 1936 (with only twenty-one students in his class), then stayed on the farm about a year and a half; he was born and raised a farmer. In 1938, he became a salesman for Roundy-Peckham-Dexter, a wholesale grocery firm in Milwaukee, Wisconsin. His draft number was eleven in August of 1940, so he joined the Army Air Force.

Kirk had a spectacular record with the 14th Air Force in China during World War II. He was a tail-gunner, flying B-24s, when he made sixty-eight round trips over The Hump, and finally was shot down over Hong Kong while bombing the Kowloon docks. Taken prisoner, he escaped four days later and made good his bid for freedom by walking 850 miles to return to the Allied lines. Home from the war, Kirk operated a dude ranch in Arizona where Eleanor Roosevelt was a guest for three months in 1946. Restless, he gave that up to reenlist in the Air Force and to engage in counterintelligence in Germany, then went to SHAPE headquarters in Paris with General Eisenhower in 1951. Subsequently, he worked security for Pan American at Cape Canaveral, and after that he was placed in charge of security at the Martin Company's Titan Missile Site in Denver. Later, he was NASA's chief of security in directing recovery of the rocket nose cones launched from the Cape, wherever and whenever they happened to splash down. He joined TWC in September of 1961, and, with his knowledge of the Cape and its needs, he played a major role in TWC's winning that contract.

"In the spring of 1963, the contract for NASA's Kennedy Space Center went out for bid," Kirk says. "In other words, the Space Center was just being built, and they were going to let a contract for the operation. They requested bids from twenty-seven companies, and twenty-one responded. Now, in that bid package for prime contractors was the security item, but the companies involved did not know whether they were going to subcontract the security portion or do it themselves. I wrote the proposal on the security aspect. I didn't know a God damn thing about fire protection, and George wrote that, he called some people in, he did a hell of a job with it. He wrote all that himself. I did all the costing on the security portion, and what have you, because, having been chief up there, I had a pretty good idea of what we could actually do and how it could be accomplished. It wasn't any intelligence on my part, it was just things that I'd experienced.

"Now we had our proposal written, so we had to go out and sell the idea that the prime contractors should subcontract to us. George and I got on planes and visited with every one of the twenty-one companies that had submitted bids. We were then selected by seventeen of the twenty-one companies. So our only hope was that one of those seventeen would get the prime contract. I felt confident that

Westinghouse was going to get it, but George said, 'No, I think some other company will get it.' There's the first place I had a little bit of trouble with George. Because in discussing our proposal with all these companies, they kept trying to get us down in price. George, a couple of times, wanted to come down in price. I said, 'No way, George, because if we do that, we're done.' I wanted to be locked in at the same price with each one of the prime contractors. Because all we'd have to do is let one of them know we're giving someone else a lower price, and you're dead. So that's where we had our first argument, really. But George agreed, and he did a tremendous selling job at each one of the meetings we had with these companies. As a result, we were tied in with all but three of them. When the results came out, first it came out with nine companies, I believe it was, then five, and then it was down to three. And when it got down to three, we were locked in with two of them. Pan American would not consider subcontracting to anybody. The other two companies were Westinghouse and TWA."

In February, it was announced that TWA had been awarded the prime contract by NASA. On April 1, TWC implemented a complete security, fire, and safety program that included a 450-man force for NASA's Kennedy Space Center. This contract totaled more than $44 million during a seven-year period that climaxed with the Apollo program that landed men on the moon.

The April issue of *Pipeline* reported that Edward V. "Captain Eddie" Rickenbacker would join TWC's board of directors. America's "Ace of Aces" during World War I had been Eastern Air Line's chairman of the board, director, and general manager prior to his retirement in December 1963.

In May, 1964, TWC took over the space vacated by the last tenant other than Wackenhut in the headquarters building at 3280 Ponce de Leon Boulevard in Coral Gables. Since moving in, June 1, 1960, TWC occupied the second floor of the building, and two other tenants rented the first floor. In 1963, one of the tenants moved out, and his place was assumed by TWC to be utilized for the newly installed IBM tabulating machine, along with the billing and payroll departments. The expansion of the company since the previous year led to TWC taking over the space vacated by the last tenant. From that time on, the building was occupied entirely by Wackenhut.

The May issue of *Pipeline* profiled the First National Bank of Miami, at that time the largest in Florida, and one of TWC's principal clients in the Miami area. Special recognition was also given to security officer Fred Porod, who was regarded as the "most decorated" officer in the Miami district—and probably in all of TWC. Porod had gained an outstanding reputation in pleasing clients and the general public because of his courtesy and kindness in handling people.

The month of May was saddened by the tragic death of Robert C. "Bob" Haas, TWC's director of Retail Store Protection, and his wife Estelle, who were killed as a result of an automobile accident in which a car fleeing from the police crashed head-on into their vehicle. Bob was a former FBI agent and, at that time, the oldest Wackenhut staffer in terms of company service. The accident occurred on the evening of May 27, 1964, as they were en route to visit his parents.

THE SUMMER of 1963 was particularly hectic for Jan. Delta Zeta, her sorority at Florida State, had elected her rush chairman, a critically important assignment that was traditionally given to seniors, and as soon as she returned home in late May, she began work on the bidding process for freshmen, scheduling and organizing the rush parties for the fall, and soliciting letters of recommendation for potential candidates. She was continuing to date John Thorsen, who had achieved a straight-A average during his first year at Dade Junior College in Miami. That spring, John submitted his application and academic transcript to Florida State, and was accepted. Because of his parents' proven inability to finance his expenses, he was also granted a full scholarship.

"He was set to enter in September," Jan says. "And in July of that summer, Mother and Dad told me I couldn't go back to Florida State. Because of John. They still thought we were going to get married. It was devastating. They didn't think he was right for me. And, in retrospect, they were probably right. They wanted someone who was—especially my mother—wanted someone who was established and wealthy. And he wasn't good enough, and his parents didn't have any money. See, there was always that dichotomy, because my mother was on that end, and my dad is very spiritual, and was very spiritual. He was the solid part of my—he was like the rock. Whenever I was fearful about anything, we would sit down and talk about it in a spiritual vein. And it was so comforting.

"But then there were all these different messages that you're being fed. I resented that they didn't feel that I had enough intelligence to make that decision. I resented the control, terribly. A lot of different things. And I think it forced me into decisions that I maybe wouldn't have made, had they not been so controlling. It was a very frightening thing for me, because I wasn't twenty-one, and, in those days, you could not live off-campus at a state institution unless you were twenty-one.

"I wrote to different colleges in *July*, trying to get in. No problems with grades, but they were full! Dorms were full, everybody's full. I was at the grocery store one day and I ran into a high school friend of mine who had been a cheerleader, Dee Black. We weren't close friends, but we were good friends, and she had spent her first two years at a college in North Carolina or Virginia, and she was transferring to the University of Florida in Gainesville. And I said, 'God, are you staying in a dorm?' She said, 'No, I got an apartment with another girl friend; it's actually a house, and we're renting a couple of rooms.' And she said, 'There's a back porch, and you're welcome to stay with me until you can find a place to stay.' So that's what I did.

"Now, Gainesville did not have my sorority, which was a big part of my life. It did not have my major. I was majoring in child development, and a food and nutrition minor, it was under what then was home economics. I don't know what you end up doing with the degree, child development, I guess some people go into social work, other people teach. I really didn't think about what I was going to do. I was going to get married after college. Everybody was going to get married after college in those days.

"I was never encouraged to go the business route, which was really too bad, because I've got a good head for it, and I would have enjoyed it. And with the company—I mean, it never dawned on Dad that a woman could get involved in business. Most of the girls majored in elementary ed or nursing. That was it. Some art, some English majors, I almost did that. I didn't like reading all the poetry,

I loved reading English grammar and stuff like that, and I loved writing, I used to write a lot. I had some things published locally.

"Anyway, when I switched to Gainesville, and they didn't have any of that, I even looked up design, because I thought that would please Mother. And I was in these drafting classes, and I hated it. Hated it. The only way I could continue, to graduate, was if I lumped all my credits into elementary ed. And I didn't have any desire to ever teach. Although I'm a good teacher. The classes were *easy* for me, I *loved* college, but I wasn't in anything really meaty that you could do a life's work on. I hadn't gotten into that thing, and it bothered me terribly, because I had so many interests. And then, when you have all of these personal, emotional things happening, it was very hard.

"Now, you have to visualize this: I'm on a screened-in porch, on a cot, with no closet. And no transportation. And the threat of being booted out. I cried myself to sleep every night. I had a few dates with people. I mean, that was the deal, to get me away from John, but I hated it. And so, on weekends, I would take the bus up to Tallahassee. He never came to Gainesville; all of my friends were up there.

"That pushed us closer, because I was just miserable where I was. He had gone out and dated too, because that was the thing we were supposed to be doing. He used to drink beer a lot and I thought it was an immature college thing that he'd outgrow. He really didn't ever do that. Of course, I was going to change all that. What ended up happening, he got an apartment, because he couldn't afford the fraternity payments. He got an apartment with a couple of other guys, so I started coming up and staying at the apartment on weekends. And that never would've happened if I'd stayed there. I don't think it ever would've happened. It just was a lot more convenient.

"So that fall of my junior year, we decided to get married. I mean, that's when he asked me to get married. He gave me a ring that Christmas. Then we were engaged a year, and I finished school, I graduated in 1965, and started working. I had an internship in Miami for teaching. John hadn't finished. He hadn't decided he wanted to go into accounting until the year before. He had a teacher that he really liked in the business school that geared him that way. I remember he was trying to decide whether he wanted to be an attorney or an accountant, and he took out the Miami telephone directory, and when he saw the difference in how many attorneys there were versus how many CPAs, he decided to go into accounting. That was it!"

A MAJOR turning point in the fortunes of TWC was the five-year struggle to find a way to comply with the Anti-Pinkerton Act of 1893, which resulted in the award of the Atomic Energy Commission's Nevada Test Site contract to Wackenhut Services, Inc. (WSI), in 1965, a major government contract for protective services that WSI has held to the present day. The security force at this facility, where explosive nuclear devices undergo live testing, is equipped with helicopters and armored vehicles capable of crossing vast areas of rough terrain at the 1,350-square-mile site, now controlled by the U.S. Department of Energy.

The genesis of the Anti-Pinkerton Act is a fascinating, often humorous, history in itself. In the latter part of the nineteenth century, there was a serious outbreak of industrial labor difficulties in the U.S., including the railroad strikes of 1887–88 and the steel riots at Homestead, Pennsylvania, in 1892. These and other disputes between labor and management, together with the organizational activities in the hard coal area of Pennsylvania by a union known as the Mollie Maguires, resulted in numerous riots, and a considerable loss of life and property.

During this period, the Pinkerton Detective Agency was engaged by management to protect property from damage, and to protect non-striking employees from physical violence. The detective agency employed in these operations recruited and armed large forces of men and placed them at the disposal of management. The presence of these "outside forces," as they were sometimes called, frequently served to inflame the tempers of the workers, causing much bloodshed and strife. In addition, private detectives were employed, from time to time, as labor spies. Pinkerton, the detective agency employed in these operations, seemed to have had at that time the only trained and armed force in the country, outside of the U.S. Army and the militia.

Leon Wolff, the author of *In Flanders Fields* (1958), and *Little*

Brown Brother (1961), gives insights into reasons behind passage of the Anti-Pinkerton Act of 1893 in his book, *Lockout* (Harper & Row, 1965), that includes a study of the "Homestead Massacre," one of the bloodiest labor-management struggles in U.S. history:

> By 1892, Andrew Carnegie, so-called "angel of the workingman," once a penniless lad from Scotland, had established himself as steel master of the world and majority shareholder in the all-powerful Carnegie Steel Company, focused in western Pennsylvania. Of all the iron, steel, and coke works contained within his peerless semimonopolistic empire, none compared in magnitude and output with the unit at Homestead.
>
> That grim borough lay near Pittsburgh on the south bank of the Monongahela River. Together, Homestead and the adjacent town of Munhall had a population of 12,000, and practically every able-bodied man and boy was employed by the mill. The unalleviated peril and harshness of their working conditions are hard to believe by modern standards. In and near Pittsburgh during 1891 alone, about 300 men were killed and over 2,000 injured while "working aside of hell ahead of time," as one employee put it. Except for a few isolated acts of feeble generosity, the Carnegie company offered no financial compensation to the mutilated men or their survivors. On the other hand, wages were adequate and the men and their families by and large satisfied with their way of life. The great majority worked twelve hours daily, seven days a week. Only Christmas and the Fourth of July were holidays.
>
> Semiretired, Carnegie spent half of each year in Europe and left affairs to his lieutenant, Henry Clay Frick. A multimillionaire in his own right, general manager of the company and its second largest shareholder, this withdrawn, gelid individual detested the concept of labor organization and was determined to break the union's grip on Homestead. Of necessity this narrative must deal with superlatives; thus it should be noted that the American Federation of Labor, though only six years old, was already the world's largest and wealthiest union, and that its most powerful component—the world's mightiest single craft union, in fact—was the conservative Amalgamated Association of Iron and Steel Workers, almost 25,000 strong. Its president was a huge, amiable former steelworker named William Weihe.
>
> Although Amalgamated members at Homestead numbered only 325 out of the work force of 3,800, they ran the local show. This small, elite

group of highly paid specialists, a bone in the throats of Carnegie and Frick, negotiated wage scales for all employees (except the thousand-odd illiterate Slavic day laborers, who earned fourteen cents per hour), fought incessantly over work rules, enforced the adjustment of complaints, and in general badgered the company into acceding to most of its demands. By the mere threat of a strike, the Amalgamated had won a moderate victory in 1889. A contract rather humiliating to management had been signed, to expire June 30, 1892. As the deadline neared, a battle of giants loomed. That spring Mr. Carnegie had left for Scotland. Now, in essence, it was Frick vs. the Amalgamated.

Suddenly, it dawned upon the Homestead local that a showdown was imminent and that the union's very existence in all Carnegie plants was at stake. Hurried recruitments brought in 400 new members. An advisory (strike) committee was formed, headed by an intense, quick-thinking young man named Hugh O'Donnell. Measures were taken to block ingress to the mill, should negotiations fail. A launch (the *Edna*) was chartered, arrangements were made for dozens of skiffs to patrol the river, especially near the mill's waterfront entrance, and an elaborate picketing system was drawn up.

Meanwhile, Mr. Frick had not been idle. He had a twelve-foot board fence, topped by barbed wire, erected around the plant. It curved from the waterfront east and west and contained loopholes, shoulder high, every twenty-five feet. Sardonically the workers termed the arrangement "Fort Frick." He began preliminary correspondence with the Pinkerton Detective Agency to furnish guards for the purpose of taking over the mill.

Three conferences between union and company officials took place between March and late June; but despite compromises on both sides the talks collapsed. Frick then announced that he would no longer deal with the Amalgamated and that work would commence as usual on July 6, on management's terms and without recognition of the union.

In a mass meeting, all 3,800 workers voted to strike—a shock to Frick, who had expected to confront only the small minority of union members. He then contracted definitely with William and Robert Pinkerton for an armed force of 300 men (at $5 per day per man) to be towed up the river in two barges early on July 6 and placed inside the works. The stage was set for one of the most murderous and dramatic tragedies in U.S. labor-management annals. . . .

The opening phase of Mr. Frick's maneuver had proceeded like clockwork. The Pinkertons had collected a total of 316 men in New York and

Chicago. Mostly unemployed or drifters, with a few college lads trying to earn a little money between semesters, a hard core of Pinkerton regulars, some hoodlums and out-and-out criminals on the run, they comprised a typical group of agency guards. The superintendent of the Chicago office had tried to be reassuring. "You men are hired to watch the property of a certain corporation, to protect it from harm," he told them. "The element of danger which is usually found in such expeditions will be here entirely lacking. . . . A few brickbats may be thrown at you, you may be called names, or sworn at, but that is no reason for you to shoot." He refused to answer the question, "Where are we going?"

John W. Holway, a twenty-three-year-old medical student, was one of many who began to feel qualms. Shoot whom? With what? No weapons were visible. But the papers were full of stories about the great Homestead lockout, and Holway had a feeling he was going there, and that there would be gun play. After dark he and the rest of the Chicago contingent were placed (smuggled, one might say) aboard a train standing at the Lake Shore depot. As it rolled east, Pinkerton detectives stood guard to prevent anyone from departing, particularly during stops at Toledo and Cleveland. The thought struck Holway, annoyingly, that he was a sort of prisoner. An identical procedure was meanwhile taking place on a train speeding westward from New York. Both journeys, no doubt, were sufficiently gloomy. . . .

Wolff's book goes on for more than a dozen pages to describe the battles that ensued while the Pinkerton men were still on the river. Highlights: The Carnegie Steel Company did not want to bring in the guards during daylight for fear that the strikers would believe they were strikebreakers. Therefore, Frick arranged to have them floated down the Monongahela River on barges under cover of darkness. Rumors spread that the Pinkertons were, in fact, strikebreakers, and that they were arriving on barges that night. Thousands of strikers ambushed them from the riverbank, firing rifles and revolvers, throwing sticks of dynamite, and floating lighted oil across the water toward the barges. Trapped, outnumbered, and outgunned, the Pinkertons waved white handkerchiefs of surrender and were finally allowed to come ashore. The narrative continues:

> After dousing the barges with barrels of Mr. Carnegie's oil, the workers put the torch to them. Hot, dry as dust, they blazed beautifully, the

process being accelerated by light northerly breezes. The crowd cheered the great flames and billows of black smoke, and cheered again when the nearby company pump house also caught fire. With surprising speed the *Iron Mountain* and the *Monongahela* burned down to their waterlines, the pump house to the ground.

Temporarily these diversions had distracted the onlookers, but now they turned their hard, collective attention upon the prisoners forlornly awaiting escort to the Homestead railroad depot. They were marched around the western edge of the plant toward deliverance, about half a mile away, fortunate that O'Donnell was an honorable man and that the crowd, at long last, was under control. They were sneered at, laughed at, sworn at, even threatened; but as they started up the long slope not a man had been touched.

Bedlam did not break loose until the first captives were halfway up the hill, when a few were slapped across the face. Next, clubs were used, and children pelted the prisoners with rocks. Then the women started in. One shoved an umbrella into a Pinkerton's eye and poked it out. When a guard dropped to his knees and begged for mercy he was kicked sprawling; while trying to flee he was clubbed into unconsciousness. Blocked right and left by the mob, the Pinkertons were unable to break through and escape. One striker carefully slugged one captive after another behind the ear with a large stone wrapped in leather, tied to the end of a short rope. An elderly gray-haired Pinkerton man, already streaming blood, was shown no more mercy than the others; and while in general those suffering from bullet wounds were spared, a few received additional whacks for good measure.

Reluctantly, young John Holway started up the embankment, appalled at what was taking place ahead of him. Three strikers knocked him down. "You have killed two men this morning," said one; "I saw you!" As they shoved Holway up the hill, he was hit in the head by a stone. He decided to make a break for it. He bulled his way through the crowd and began to run, pursued by perhaps a hundred people. In his words: "I ran down a side street and ran through a yard. I ran about half a mile, I suppose, but was rather weak and had had nothing to eat or drink, and my legs gave out, could not run any further, and some man got hold of me by the back of my coat, and about 20 or 30 men came up and kicked me and pounded me with stones. I had no control of myself then. I thought I was about going and commenced to scream, and there were two or three strikers with rifles rushed up then and kept off the crowd. . . ." Ironically, Holway does not appear to have fired a shot all day.

Sand was thrown into the eyes of some of the Pinkertons, temporarily blinding them. Most of the Slavs disdained weapons; they simply grabbed men around the neck and punched their faces with bare fists. Over forty victims, severely pounded and unable to move, were dragged toward the skating rink and its adjacent theatre, while the rest staggered on. A few were divested of their money and watches. One striker pumped a bullet into a guard named Conners and then clubbed him; another bashed in the head of a wounded man with the butt end of a musket. Both victims died that evening. One Pinkerton may have lost his mind as a result of his beating, for he killed himself with a pocketknife.

In tiny print two days later the New York *Tribune* meticulously listed the dead and wounded: "Peter S. Prash, kicked in the back and badly cut back of right ear . . . J. Emmet, New York, shot in the body in three places with buckshot, and struck on right ear with a club . . . Edward Milstead, Chicago, mouth terribly bruised and lacerated . . ."—the list went on for 118 lines. Hardly a man among the Pinkertons avoided injury. Hugh O'Donnell and other Amalgamated members were struck and bruised in attempting to protect the Pinkertons, but they were able to save many of them from further mistreatment. . . .

These events caused considerable concern throughout the nation, which was reflected by numerous speeches on the floor of the House and the Senate. Resolutions providing for full and complete investigations of the Pinkerton Detective Agency were introduced in the House of Representatives in May and July, 1892, and in the Senate in July and August of that year. Some of these resolutions called for an investigation of the circumstances of the Homestead riots, involving the workers and the Pinkerton detectives; another directed the Attorney General to cause the arrest, indictment, and trial of all persons armed and in the service of the Pinkerton Agency and engaged in the Homestead riots, and of all persons who employed them or directed their actions. Some of the resolutions requiring an investigation were ultimately adopted, after considerable debate.

An act was finally passed on March 3, 1893, set forth in Title 5, U.S. Code, Section 53 (27 Stat. 591), which, in effect, prohibited the federal government or the District of Columbia from employing, for any purposes, employees of organizations that engage in investigative work.

The pertinent portion of the act of March 3, 1893, reads as follows:

> That hereafter no employee of the Pinkerton Detective Agency, or similar agency, shall be employed in any Government service or by any officer of the District of Columbia. . . .

As early as 1959, George Wackenhut understood the enormous potential consequences this act could have on the future of TWC, and he started work in earnest to attempt to find a way to comply with the act. In the legal department of TWC today, there is a thick file titled simply ANTI-PINKERTON LAW, and numbered 99-15, containing literally hundreds of documents pertaining to the act, dating from February 25, 1959, including numerous letters between George and then-Florida Senator George Smathers, then-Florida Congressman Dante Fascell, and then-Comptroller General of the United States Joseph Campbell.

On August 20, 1963, the objectionable portion of the act was finally repealed by the U.S. Senate (it would subsequently be submitted to the House of Representatives). Senator McClellan, from the Senate Committee on Government Operations, submitted the following report, quoted in part:

> The Committee on Government Operations, to whom was referred the bill (S. 1543), to repeal that portion of the act of March 3, 1893, which prohibits the employment, in any Government service or by any officer of the District of Columbia, of any employee of the Pinkerton Detective Agency or any similar agency, having considered the same, report favorably thereon, without amendment, and recommend that the bill do pass. . . .
>
> Over a period of many years, the Comptroller General has uniformly held that this statute is a prohibition against the employment in Government service of employees of detective agencies of firms or corporations as well as the contracts with, or appointments of, individual employees of such agencies. Thus, whereas firms or organizations which furnish

only protective services may be employed by the Government, organizations which do both protective and investigative work may not be employed even to supply protective services. The statute, therefore, results in discrimination against organizations which provide both types of services, and is detrimental to the interest of the Government since it serves to eliminate from competitive bidding numerous major detective organizations which would otherwise respond to Government invitations to bid on contracts for the furnishing of supplementary guard service. According to the Administrator of General Services, it may be causing an increase in the cost to the Government of contract guard service.

It is the purpose of S. 1543 to repeal this restrictive legislation, which was enacted 70 years ago as an expression of disapproval by the Congress of the practice, once prevalent in private industry, of employing certain detective agencies to recruit and furnish armed guards who were allegedly used as strikebreakers and labor spies, giving rise to acts of violence. . . .

However, the struggle was far from over. Senate Bill S.1543, reported from the Senate Committee on Government Operations on August 20, 1963, was passed by the Senate October 17, 1963, and immediately sent to the Government Activities Subcommittee of the House Committee on Government Operations.

Within days, Congressman Jack Brooks of Texas, Chairman of the House Committee on Government Operations, received a letter from officials of the United Plant Guard Workers of America (8,500 members) to protest the repeal of the Anti-Pinkerton Act. The union's letter alleged that Senate Bill S.1543 was designed to "fire" Civil Service guards. The union's members were Civil Service employees, not connected with the AFL-CIO. As a result of the protest letter, Congressman Brooks considered holding hearings on the bill, because 1964 was fast approaching (an election year), and he wanted to avoid antagonizing labor by expediting passage of such a bill. However, open hearings were never held. The bill languished in the subcommittee, was never passed by the House, never became law, and the so-called Anti-Pinkerton Act remains in effect to this day, with only slightly different wording from the act of March 3, 1893, and a different section number under Title 5, U.S. Code:

3108. Employment of detective agencies; restrictions

An individual employed by the Pinkerton Detective Agency, or any similar organization, may not be employed by the Government of the United States or the government of the District of Columbia.

In 1964, the security contract for the Atomic Energy Commission's Nevada Test site was held by Federal Services, Inc., an affiliate of the Burns Agency, and it had held the lucrative contract since the early 1950s. Conscious of the Anti-Pinkerton Act, Burns had formed Federal Services, Inc., as a distinctly separate corporation. Thus, when Wackenhut Services, Inc., made its formal bid for the Nevada Test Site contract, George anticipated that Burns would contest the proposal on the grounds that Wackenhut Services, Inc., was still, in fact, a wholly owned subsidiary of a detective agency, and therefore was in violation of the act.

Early in 1964, an Atomic Energy Commission Evaluating Team visited TWC's headquarters. Wackenhut Services, Inc., was one of three firms being considered by the AEC. The Evaluating Team had been particularly interested in the question of whether or not the affairs of Wackenhut Services was sufficiently separated from the affairs of TWC, so that it could sign a contract with the government without being in violation of the act.

Following the report of the Evaluating Team, the Acting Assistant General Manager of the Atomic Energy Commission requested a ruling on this question from the Comptroller General of the United States.

Wackenhut's bid for the contract was upheld when George received a seven-page copy of a letter from then-Comptroller General Joseph Campbell, dated June 22, 1964, and addressed to Glenn T. Seaborg, then-Chairman of the Atomic Energy Commission.

Comptroller General Campbell stated, in part:

> Assuming that the above is a correct statement of the facts, we fail to see how the provisions of 5 U.S.C. 53 would preclude a determination that the subsidiary is a responsible bidder. In other words, even though the parent corporation is ineligible to receive a contract award, we see no reason why its record of performance might not be taken into considera-

tion in evaluating the dependability and responsibility of its officers who are also officers of the subsidiary company. Furthermore, we understand Wackenhut Services, Incorporated, is presently performing and also has satisfactorily concluded contracts covering guard services with several other agencies of the Government, so that its responsibility as a bidder apparently could be determined to some extent, at least, on the basis of its record with those agencies.

Accordingly, it is our view that the provisions of 5 U.S.C. 53 are not applicable to Wackenhut Services, Incorporated. . . .

July and August, 1964, were particularly busy months for Wackenhut. During that time, the company was studying the desirability of purchasing Dawn Patrol, a security guard organization in the greater Los Angeles area. A special meeting of the executive committee of the board of directors was held on Wednesday, July 29, 1964, in order to consider an agreement involving the purchase of the assets of Dawn Patrol, and approval was given. The purchase was effected to supplement the activities in the Los Angeles area of General Plant Protection, acquired in 1962. At the time of acquisition, Dawn Patrol employed approximately 375 people and was operated by TWC as the Dawn Patrol Division.

On July 31, 1964, Wackenhut Services, Inc., was notified of its selection to provide security services at the Nevada Test Site, and was invited to enter into negotiations preliminary to the signing of a contract.

Following the announcement, Federal Services, Inc., filed suit in Federal Court in Carson City, Nevada, requesting an injunction against four officials of the Atomic Energy Commission in Las Vegas, prohibiting them from entering into a contract with Wackenhut Services, Inc. However, upon hearing the request, the federal judge denied this injunction. Federal Services, Inc., through their attorney, also filed a complaint with the Atomic Energy Commission in Washington, D.C., based essentially on the same points that had already been considered by the Evaluating Team.

The Atomic Energy Commission designated an inspector to make a complete investigation of these allegations and write a report to the Commission. The inspector spent several days in Miami, not only interviewing officers and current employees of Wackenhut Services, Inc., and examining books and records, but also interviewed former employees, most of whom had been dismissed for cause and were extremely antagonistic to the company.

But once again, the ruling was in TWC's favor, and Wackenhut Services, Inc., started providing security services to the Atomic Energy Commission at the Nevada Operations Office and the Nevada Test Site, outside Las Vegas, at 6:00 A.M. on Sunday, January 31, 1965. It is a contract the company has held ever since, and was recently renewed again by the U.S. Department of Energy (successor to the Atomic Energy Commission) with a five-year, $140 million contract, extending from October 1, 1992, through September 30, 1997. TWC's functions under the contract involve providing a security guard force, pass and badge services, sensitive services, and test-related activities, with a personnel force of 383.

On December 7, 1964, the regular quarterly meeting of the board of directors was held at King's Bay Yacht and Country Club. It was learned that the lease to the building that headquarters occupied at 3280 Ponce de Leon Boulevard would expire on May 31, 1965, and that contained in the lease was a favorable option to purchase, which had to be exercised within 120 days before expiration of the lease. The board unanimously adapted a resolution that authorized management to purchase.

At year's end, TWC was continuing to expand dramatically, with operations in twenty-two states, plus Puerto Rico, seventeen offices, 3,274 employees, and an annual volume of $10.821 million.

Ten years and five months had passed since George signed the original Partnership Agreement on July 21, 1954. Volume for the first year had been $25,551.54, and current assets (cash on hand and in banks) had been $156.41.

AT MIDNIGHT, June 30, 1965, the sixty-eight-man guard force at the Goddard Space Center in Greenbelt, Maryland, went on strike, represented by the United Plant Guard Workers of America, and just hours later, the entire guard force at the Nevada Test Site went on strike, represented by the International Guard Association of Nevada. John Ammarell spent the entire month of July in Silver Spring, Maryland, working with the Goddard security staff, replacing the striking guards, and George Wackenhut devoted his full attention to the strike at the Nevada Test Site.

During the Goddard strike, which lasted four weeks, there was great pressure from the government at the last minute, including a federal judge, before whom a request for an injunction against the union had been filed by the National Labor Relations Board. This was apparently based on the fact that the operation at Greenbelt was an extremely important one to the projected Gemini launch from Cape Kennedy, since Goddard controlled the communications system around the world. In view of the virtual ultimatum from the government, agreement was reached on July 28. The union settled for exactly what Wackenhut Services, Inc., was prepared to give before the strike began. It was estimated that the employees would have to work about three years at the higher rates in order to make up what they lost in wages and benefits during the strike.

In the strike at the Nevada Test Site, the head of the union made contact with two Nevada senators in Washington and they, in turn, made demands to the Atomic Energy Commission that the strike be ended. After eighteen days, an agreement was negotiated providing that the strikers would return to work for ninety days with a no-strike pledge, and Wackenhut Services agreed that it would negotiate further with the union for a contract. Atomic Energy Commission officials praised the stand taken by the company.

George recalls an intriguing anecdote that happened during the start of the strike in Nevada. "I was at headquarters in Miami when this happened, and I spent the next few days glued to the telephone," he says. "There were constant long-distance conferences with the head administrator of the Test Site, and calls had to be made to our top personnel at various other sites to get guards rushed to Nevada. Once there, of course, they had to have security checks and health clearances. Trying to pull all the strings together seemed to take endless hours.

"Bob Kirk and I worked around the clock. He had been a major influence in securing the AEC contract, and we didn't want it to get off to a bad start. So neither of us paid too much attention when the receptionist called one afternoon from the lobby and told us that three gentlemen were waiting to see me. But then the telephone started ringing again—'Nevada calling'—and we forgot all about the three men, who hadn't had an appointment to begin with.

"Quite a while afterwards, when the wires cooled down, I remembered the three men and I called downstairs. The receptionist told me they were tired of waiting, so they gave her their business cards, and left the office. It was simply another unsettling factor in a bad day. I told Kirk that I felt terrible about those people. I didn't know who they were or what their business was, but I didn't mean to offend them. He said he'd try to locate them and make our apologies."

That afternoon, Kirk telephoned the three office visitors at a hotel on Miami Beach where they were registered.

"I apologized and explained what had been happening around here today," he told George. "I invited them to come back tomorrow and told them we'd give them all the time they needed. So everything's all right and they'll be here."

"What's it all about?" George asked.

Kirk shrugged. "I'm not too certain about any of the details, but a Señor Jose Olavarria said something about being from Venezuela and wanting to talk to us about forming a security company down there."

Next morning, two of the Venezuelans who had departed in exasperation were ushered into George's office. The elder of the pair, a courtly man who spoke excellent English, introduced himself: "I am José Antonio Olavarria, and this is my son, Dr. Carlos Domingo Olavarria Jimenez."

George exchanged greetings, apologized for the fiasco of the previous day, and, as soon as they were seated, the senior Olavarria launched into the purpose of their visit.

"Señor Wackenhut," he said softly, "I represent a group of my country's most important industrialists and executives. We are extremely concerned about communist activities in Venezuela. Our idea is to set up a security operation which we can use in various trouble spots, more or less a uniformed guard service to start with. Your name was suggested to us as being an expert in these kinds of affairs. Can you help us?"

George nodded. "I'm certain we could work something out, Señor Olavarria. We could probably form a corporation to handle that kind of work for you."

Olavarria handed him a typewritten list. "Here are the names of some of my associates and the names of their companies. You might call it a Who's Who of important people in my country."

George studied the list. "The best thing to do would be for us to come down and visit you to discuss just exactly what should be done and how to go about it."

They agreed that George and Bob Kirk would make a visit to Caracas as soon as possible to set the wheels in motion and, following a bit of friendly conversation, the two men prepared to depart.

Turning at the door, the elder Olavarria smiled. "Señor Wackenhut, I assure you that if you will supply the know-how, we will supply the know-*whom!*"

When they had gone, George called in Bob Kirk and gave him the list of names. "There's just one thing," he said. "Anybody can drop a lot of names. We'd better check them out. And we'd better check out some of the names on this list."

Kirk initiated a thorough background investigation on Olavarria and his son, plus a random sample of some of the other names. They proved to be among the most respected people in Venezuela. Once this was established, they made plans to visit the Olavarrias the following month. However, that August, George had to be hospitalized to have his gall bladder removed, and they postponed the trip until September.

Then, following another necessary delay, they finally set up the trip for November, advising Don José of the date and time they would arrive on a Pan American flight. He replied that he would meet them at the gate and also make their hotel reservations.

The day before they were scheduled to leave, one of George's employees who had worked in Venezuela asked him how they were going. George told him via Pan Am with an intermediate stop in San Juan.

"Don't take the Pan Am flight," the man said. "The Viasa flight goes nonstop from Miami to Caracas. You leave later and get there earlier, and the service aboard is superb."

George took the advice, asked his secretary to change the reservations, then to send a telegram to Don José advising him of the new flight plans.

"However, upon our arrival in Caracas," George says, "we were surprised to find there was no one at the airport to meet us. So much for international telegrams. Neither Bob nor I spoke Spanish, but we bumbled our way through customs and finally stood on the sidewalk with our luggage, not knowing what in the world to do, because Don José hadn't given us the name of our hotel. 'I'll bet they never received our telegram and are expecting us on the Pan Am flight,' I told Bob. He agreed: "You stay here with the luggage and I'll go down to the gate where that Pan Am flight is due and see if they're waiting there.'

"After what seemed like hours, Bob came back alone: 'They weren't there. I looked all over, but didn't see them.' As it developed later, Don José had been there, but somehow, in the confusion caused by the crush of passengers and waiting friends and relatives, they had missed each other. 'Well,' I said, 'I know at least one word of Spanish—*publico!* That means taxi. And the fellow who told us to take the Viasa flight also told me that the Tamanaco Hotel was one of the better hotels in town. Maybe that's where Don José made our reservations.'"

When they arrived at the Tamanaco, Kirk waited in the taxi while George went inside. Fortunately, the desk clerk spoke English.

George smiles at the memory. "I asked him if he had a reservation for Wackenhut. He checked. 'No, señor.' How about Robert Kirk? He checked. 'No, señor.' How about Olavarria? He checked. 'No, señor.' Well, how about a double room? 'I am very sorry, señor, but we are completely booked. We have absolutely no rooms available.'

"By now, it was getting quite late and I was tired and frustrated. 'Listen, friend, this is our first time in your country. I don't speak Spanish, we've missed connections with the people who were supposed to meet us, and we don't know the names of any other hotels. Could you suggest one?' He said he was sure we could get a room at the Hotel Luna, wrote the name and address on a slip of paper and told me to give it to the cab driver.

"We drove and drove, gradually entering poorer sections of the city, and finally the driver turned from a main street into a grimy alley. 'Dear God,' I said to Bob, 'I hope the hotel isn't up this alley.' It was. The Hotel Luna was never going to become a tourist attraction. The shabby character who assigned us a room was the entire staff on duty. He carried our luggage to a creaky elevator and took us to a drab little room with one rickety bed and a couch. Kirk grinned: 'Rank has its privilege; I'll take the couch.' I looked at the bed and laughed: 'I'm not sure I got the best of the deal.'

"Downstairs, we found a dilapidated bar with a few patrons. The combination porter-room clerk-bellboy was also the bartender!

"We rose early in the morning after tossing and turning through an uncomfortable night. When we went down to what passed for a lobby, there was a woman on duty who spoke a smattering of English, and I asked her to try to contact Señor Olavarria at his office, which was the only telephone number we had. As I expected, no one was at the office that early, so I asked the woman to keep trying, and told her we'd be in the hotel cafe for breakfast. It was one of those places where the flies fight you for the food. The menu was stained worse than the apron of the waitress. And, of course, the menu was in Spanish. Using gestures and pidgin English, we hopefully ordered bacon and eggs, and, to our surprise, that's what we were served. We'd just started to eat when the public address system started sputtering a stream of rapid Spanish. We couldn't understand a word, but I went to the desk anyway.

"Sure enough, the woman at the desk nodded and handed me the telephone. 'Don José?' I asked. 'Señor Wackenhut! Where in the hell *are* you?' It was a genuine relief to hear his voice. 'We're at the Hotel Luna.' There was a pause. 'Hotel *Luna!* Where in the hell is *that?*' I couldn't help laughing at the tone of his voice. When I told him I didn't know, he laughed too, asked me to put the desk clerk back on, that he'd get directions, and not to move until he arrived.

"I went back and told Bob and we finished breakfast and packed before he arrived about forty-five minutes later and whisked us out of there. He drove us to the Avila, a plush hotel that the Rockefellers had built, and our reservations were in order.

"We finally did get around to working out a 50-50 partnership arrangement with Olavarria and when we drew up the contract, it was Don José who corrected our attorney's English. He was of Basque descent, not Spanish, educated in England, and also spoke fluent French and German. Subsequently, we sold our interest down to 20 percent in compliance with the Andean Pact, an extremely satisfactory move as events developed. Sadly, Don José passed away in 1977, and, in another family tragedy, his son Carlos was killed the same year, when he crashed in his own aircraft. However, at that point, Carlos's older brother José took over, and made the operation even more successful, doing uniformed guard work and building a complete security operation, including electronics, which happily returned more for our 20 percent than our former 50 percent."

This represented TWC's first expansion into South America. When the original contract was signed in October 1965, the name of the company became Venezolana de Seguridad y Vigilancia, C.A., and TWC sent Henry J. Brentari to Caracas as vice president and general manager.

WHEN RICK graduated from Palmetto Senior High School in June 1965, he had been accepted for admission to The Citadel, the famed military college in Charleston, South Carolina, where retired four-star General Mark W. Clark had been president since 1954. During his summer vacation, Rick worked at TWC as an apprentice investigator under Murray Levine, who had joined the company the previous year, and is presently vice president of the South Florida Region and CPO Services.

"That was a lot of fun," Rick remembers. "Murray was the most lovable character at that time, he was a prince of a guy to his employees. He was tough when he needed to be, but he was always very amiable. I looked up to him and admired him very much, and had a lot of fun with him. Played tennis with him, joked around a fair amount, when it was appropriate, and really learned a good bit of the business from him. The first time I worked for Murray, I was his number-two person in Supply, out of the Miami office. At that time, there was a Captain Ketchum, who was my immediate boss. Captain Ketchum worked in the uniform room, basically, and when applicants would come in, he would screen them, or a personnel person would screen them, and, once they were hired, uniforms had to be issued. So I would take their uniform record, see what their sizes were, pick out their uniforms, and pass the uniforms out to them.

"In September 1965, when I entered The Citadel, my major was political science. I ended up enjoying The Citadel very much, and, to this day, have some very strong ties, both to the school and to Charleston. But the first year, I can truly say, was one of the most miserable years of my entire life. It was the first appreciable time away from home, but it wasn't really *that,* I think, that bothered me, as much as the drastic change of environment from being in a public high school, male and female, to a very, very strict military and academic environment. All male, in a *plebe* system, was a little too much. That was a rude awakening, but it taught me an awful lot of good basics that I recognize that I have today.

"My worst subjects, again, were the sciences. I had a terrible time with chemistry and physics. Absolutely terrible time. I think I finally completed sophomore physics in my senior year. Favorite subjects: I was a political science major, so I enjoyed a number of the international law courses, the political science-type courses. History, again, I enjoyed. I was taking ROTC at that time, because it was a military school, and I continued my ROTC even when I realized I was behind my class academically, and probably would not get a commission. I continued it because I enjoyed it, number one, and also I didn't think it could hurt me if I applied for a direct commission upon graduating. This was Vietnam in 1965, it was really starting to heat up, and by the time '69 and '70 rolled around, it was really something. So I just felt that it would be beneficial to continue the ROTC.

"I was very active in intramural sports. In fact, one year, I think it was my junior year, I won the obstacle course race for all the battalions in the school. It was an intramural thing, we were against other cadets, but I excelled in that. Really enjoyed intramural football. Enjoyed all the intramural sports I was involved in. In my freshman year, I got involved in wrestling, because I wanted to continue that from high school, and really had a very good start. There was a junior who was in my weight class, and I think my weight class then was 167, which is a very fast, very tough weight class, and in tryouts I won against him, and he was the captain of the wrestling team and was really a star guy. He outshadowed me in wrestling, but I put on enough of a showing that the coach put me on the team. Shortly after that, I injured my ankle. It was a wrestling injury, it was on a takedown, and my ankle got turned underneath me. It put me out for that season, and I just didn't go out for it the following year.

"General Mark Clark was a living legend, of course, especially in a military school environment. He was a giant of a man, not only in physical height, but also in reputation and in general stature. We would be in formation on the parade ground—there was a parade every Friday—the public was invited, and the whole corps of cadets would march out, the cannons would go off, they would have a pass-in-review. And I remember in the warmer months, we'd be on the parade ground, having to stand at attention, and the gnats were just miserable, and you couldn't move to knock them off, because you were in formation. And we're all mumbling under our breath, 'Geez, these *gnats,* what're we gonna do, they're *killin'* us!' And he'd come by on the Jeep, you know, as he's reviewing the troops, and we knew they were bothering him just as bad as they were us. And he didn't *flinch,* he didn't *move,* he used to drive us all *nuts!*

"He was quite a guy. I got an opportunity to meet him, my freshman year, when my father had invited him to join our board. Both of my parents were in Charleston and were invited to—he had a penthouse apartment in the Francis Marion Hotel, that I believe was donated to him by the city. Really quite a nice place, with all kinds of his memorabilia from his career. I was invited to go to that dinner. And I'll never forget, when I first shook his hand—I'm a freshman, I had just been to The Citadel for a month or two—I shook his hand and I said, 'Very nice to meet you, *Mister* Clark,' rather than *General* Clark! So I was immediately corrected, and from that point forward I didn't want to say *anything* to him! But he was quite a guy."

In 1893, at the semicentennial celebration of The Citadel, founded in 1842, Colonel John P. Thomas, who was connected with the institution by the ties of graduate, professor, superintendent, member of the board of visitors, and historian, presented to the Association of Graduates his monumental study, *History of the South Carolina Military Academy*, covering the first half-century of its operation. The next historical volume was written by Colonel O.J. Bond, published in 1936, and titled *The Story of The Citadel* (Garrett & Massie, Inc., Richmond, VA); reprinted in 1989 (Southern Historical Press, Inc., Greenville, SC). Bond's work, intended to tell the story "in an informal way," includes a fascinating narrative of a little-known historical fact: On January 9, 1861, Citadel cadets actually fired the first shots of the Civil War:

> And now the scene was set for the first act of the tragic drama of the War Between the States.
>
> News had been received of the fitting out of the *Star of the West*, a steamer with provisions, munitions, and a reinforcement of two hundred and fifty men for Major Anderson at Fort Sumter, and the little battery at Cummings Point was charged with the duty of seeing that they should not pass. The guard boat was notified of the expected coming of the steamer, and sentinels kept watch along the beach of Morris Island.
>
> At daybreak on January 9, 1861, the guard boat sighted the *Star of the West*, and gave the signal. What then took place at the sand battery is

thus described by Sergeant S.E. Welch, of the Zouave Cadets, who was on duty at the time:

"Cadet W.S. Simkins, on post on the Battery, gave the alarm, the sentinels along the beach took up the call, the long roll was sounded, and the men immediately took their positions, the Citadel Cadets at the guns, the Zouave Cadets and German Riflemen just in their rear as an infantry support.

"The Ship was soon inside the channel and rapidly approaching. The guns were loaded, the lanyards stretched, the men awaiting orders. There seemed to be some hesitation among the higher officers; the commanding officer, evidently impressed with the seriousness of firing on the United States flag, appeared to be in doubt just what to do.

"Major P.F. Stevens, commanding the Cadets, turned and gave the command: 'Commence firing.' The cadet captain passed the order: 'Number One, Fire!' Cadet G.E. Haynesworth of Sumter, pulled the lanyard and fired the first gun of the War, the shot going across the *Star of the West*.

"Cadet S.B. Pickens fired the second shot, directly at her, and the firing then became general, each gun in turn. The vessel paid no attention to the first shots; then slowed down; turned, and put out to sea."

The report of the action made by Captain McGown, who commanded the *Star of the West*, is as follows:

"When we arrived about two miles from Fort Moultrie—Fort Sumter being about the same distance—a masked battery on Morris Island where there was a red palmetto flag flying, opened fire upon us—distance about five-eighths of a mile. We had the American flag flying at our flagstaff at that time, and soon after the first shot hoisted a large American ensign at the fore. We continued on under the fire of the battery for over ten minutes, several of the shots going clean over us. One passed just clear of the pilot house. Another passed between the smoke-stack and the walking-beam of the engine. Another struck the ship just abaft the fore-rigging, and stove in the planking, and another came within an ace of carrying away the rudder."

The Charleston *Mercury* of January 15 gave the following extracts from the New York *Evening Post*, which published a full account of the voyage of the *Star of the West*:

"The military men on board highly complimented the South Carolinians on their shooting in this first attempt. They say it was well done; that all that was needed was a little better range, which they probably could have obtained in a few minutes. Their line was perfect; and the opinion is expressed that some one had charge of the guns who knew his business. . . . Two guns were employed, the smaller, it is believed, a twelve-pounder, and the larger a thirty-two pounder. This however, is only conjecture. Whatever their size, they were well manned. They were fired rapidly and with will.

"One of the officers hazarded a joke soon after we left Charleston harbor; 'The people of Charleston,' he remarked, 'pride themselves upon their hospitality, but it exceeds my expectation—they gave us several *balls* before we landed!' "

The Charleston *Mercury* of January 10, 1861, in its account of the *Star of the West* incident, used the headlines:

THE WAR BEGUN.
ENGAGEMENT AT FORT MORRIS.
ATTEMPTED REINFORCEMENT OF FORT SUMTER.
THE "STAR OF THE WEST" IS FIRED INTO
AND DRIVEN BACK.
THE CITADEL CADETS FIRE THE FIRST SHOTTED GUN.
THE UNITED STATES FLAG HAULED DOWN.
THREE OF THE SHOTS TAKE EFFECT.

Similarly, *Harper's Weekly*, New York, in its issue of January 19, 1861, headlines its article on the engagement: "The First of the War" and gives its readers a picture of the *Star of the West*, and a map of Charleston harbor.

But subsequently the beginning of the war was fixed at a later date—April 12, 1861—and the events of January 9 were not charged with the burden of responsibility for the awful conflict. . . .

Back home, the quarterly meeting of the board of directors was held in Miami at the King's Bay Yacht and Country Club on December 6, 1965. General Mark Clark, who joined the board the previous day, attended his first board meeting. At that time, George noted that union negotiations had been completed between Wackenhut Services and the International Guard Association of Nevada, and that a three-year contract had been signed, effective November 3, 1965. George advised the directors that he had, on invitation, appeared six times before the four-day meeting of the Twenty-third Annual Conference of the Merchants and Manufacturers Association of California, held October 24–28, in Palm Springs, California, speaking on "Business Espionage."

On December 26, 1965, after having been engaged for a year, Jan Wackenhut married John Thorsen in the Plymouth Congregational Church in Miami. "I think by that time, my parents were resigned to it," Jan says. "They were always, always disappointed in me. That I hadn't gone to a college where I should have, that I hadn't majored in something exciting, that I hadn't met a statesman to marry or somebody from Europe. And yet I was never given the opportunity to do any of that.

"They did ask me to go on a trip to Europe with them. When I was in Gainesville, I had to stay in Gainesville, after I got engaged I was still there, but a new apartment complex was being completed. And I moved over there. It was a two-bedroom, real nice, and there were four girls. The two that I originally was with, and then they picked up this one gal, I don't know where she was from, but she was a real street-wise lady. And I could never get into my bedroom! She had parties constantly. So I was always on the sofa and I hated it. And it was in that apartment that I remember a phone call from Mother, saying they were planning a trip—I don't know where he was opening in Europe, but they were going there—and would like me to come. I guess Rick was in school now, so it would've been just the three of us.

"I just had all these romantic-type ideas of life, and I thought that kind of trip should be done with someone you love, not your parents. I mean, I was at that age where you weren't a child and you weren't really an adult, and it wasn't something I wanted to share with them. Because I knew Mother would want to do the best hotels, the best restaurants, and I would want to go in the museums, and go where the people lived. It was something that I was tabling until a time when I could share it with—a love or something. Consequently, I've never been!"

THE YEAR 1965 finished with gross sales of $17.76 million, a gain of nearly $7 million over the previous year. TWC had also expanded to

4,033 employees, had 3,182 clients, and closed the year with twenty-four offices in twenty-two states, the District of Columbia, and Puerto Rico. The new operation in Caracas, Venezuela, would not become effective until January 1966.

JANUARY 1, 1966, was the effective date for various changes at headquarters, where the Guard Forces Division was renamed the Physical Security Division, with William Lewe continuing as head of that operation. A new division, Special Services, was set up with Bud Thompson named as director. This division included Electronic Services, Retail Store Protection, and Central Records. The Training and Inspection Division that had been headed by Thompson since he joined the company, July 1, 1959, was eliminated, with the training function being performed by Elwood Trueblood as manager of Training, and the Inspection function being assumed by Victor Keay, assistant to the president. W. Jackson Jones joined the headquarters staff as manager of Labor Relations.

Bud Thompson offers insights into the direction the company was taking that year. "We mopped up the security business, an awful lot of it, in those days," he says. "I used to say—and it proved to be true—we were *good,* and that's why we could wipe out those others, but we were also *small.* And as we grew, we had the same problems they did, which is, you can't have the personal attention that you had. I could be the head of Training and Inspection, but, hell, I can't keep going for ever and ever, and I'm only one person, and we started having offices all over. But you need that type of thing, where you have a relationship with individuals. You lose that as you get bigger. And we lost that as we went along, so it made it much more difficult. We could wipe out Pinkerton or Globe or Burns, or one of those, because we were small. I could pick up the phone and call the man who ran one of the major facilities out there and talk to him like we're friends, because I went to dinner with him, you know, and I got to know him very well. Those are the good things about it. But as you went on, that got to be impossible. There's no way you can keep up with them all over the place.

"My trip up the chain was Training and Inspection, and then I became director of Special Services. What he did, he took a lot of these different services and threw them in a clump, and he says, 'You run those. Should we keep them, should we build them, should we cut them out—what should we do with them?' So I had a lot of garbage stuff that I was responsible for in that, before I became a vice president of Operations."

The regular meeting of the board of directors was held at King's Bay Yacht and Country Club on March 7, 1966. George announced the receipt of a letter of resignation as a director from Samuel K. McKee, dated February 17, 1966. Will M. Preston was designated as a member of the stock option committee in replacement of McKee. During the presentation by C.E. Moore, he noted that the financial condition of the company had improved dramatically over that of the preceding years. For example, working capital had increased from $190,000 in 1961 to $2.272 million in 1965. He stated that the current ratio had increased from about one-to-one to more than two-to-one. Moore pointed out that the improvement, in large part, was attributable to the retention of all net earnings in the business over the years and said that negotiation of a very favorable, long-term borrowing arrangement with the First National Bank of Miami was effected December 31, 1965. He also noted that the earnings per share were $1.28 in 1965 as compared to $.65 per share in 1964. It was at this meeting that Bill Bitter was elected vice president of Industrial and Personnel Relations, and Bob Kirk was elected vice president of Development.

JAN AND JOHN THORSEN were living at Florida State University in Tallahassee, in an apartment complex called Alumni Village, reserved for married students, and John was scheduled to graduate that summer of 1966. "I was presuming I was going to teach," Jan remembers, "but there wasn't anything available in the county, and the nearest teaching job was fifty miles—one way! That doesn't sound too appealing when you're newly married. So I started doing the want ads, and he was heavy into his accounting, and we found this ad for a bookkeeper in a little printing business. A one-man deal with a secretary. The woman whose job I was going to take was *very* nasty, very mean, and I didn't even know what a debit or credit was! I didn't know squat.

"But I sold myself on this job. She *knew* I didn't know what I was doing, but the boss didn't. I figured John would help me at night, I'd have all these questions, but it was coming too fast and furious. It was taking time away from his studies. He was doubling up to finish, taking tons of courses. Mortified, I had to go to the boss and explain that I had really oversold myself and didn't know what I was talking about, and he'd best get a replacement. So I was there maybe a month.

"Next I got a job with the state road department. Huge, huge state transportation building, and this guy was just a state payrollee, didn't do squat. Sit with his feet on the desk and move some little numbers around on this huge map of all the counties in the state. I didn't do a whole lot, I was a secretary."

ON MARCH 25, 1966, TWC filed a registration statement with the United States Securities and Exchange Commission, seeking registration of 247,300 shares of common stock. Of these, 135,000 were to be offered for public sale by the company, and 112,300 by George and Ruth Wackenhut. The offering was to be made through underwriters headed by Francis I. duPont, A.C. Allyn, Inc., at a maximum of $12.50 a share. Pending approval of the Securities and Exchange Commission, 7,500 shares were to be offered initially to company employees at the public offering price, less underwriting discounts.

The thirty-one-page Prospectus, published by Francis I. duPont, A.C. Allyn, Inc., on Tuesday, April 26, 1966, includes a brief but financially revealing history of the company. Following is an excerpt:

> The business was founded in 1954 by George R. Wackenhut and three associates to supply investigative services. In July 1955 the Company entered the business of providing physical security to private industrial and commercial establishments and to municipalities through the services of uniformed guards and other personnel. In July 1960 Wackenhut extended its physical security operations to United States Government installations through a wholly owned subsidiary formed to comply with

requirements of a federal statute which prohibits the Government from contracting with companies furnishing investigative or detective services.

In June of 1962 the Company extended its operations to California and Hawaii, and entered the business of providing central alarm system services for protection against fire and theft, by the acquisition of the assets of General Plant Protection Company and its subsidiaries. Wackenhut paid $352,000 in cash and assumed liabilities of $672,000 (or a total of $1,024,000) to acquire the assets of the General Plant Protection companies, which had a book value of $774,889. This acquisition brought approximately 600 employees and about the same number of new clients to Wackenhut. In August 1964, Wackenhut enlarged its California operation by the acquisition of Dawn Patrol, a company furnishing security services in the Los Angeles area. Wackenhut paid $733,000 in cash and assumed liabilities of $47,000 (a total of $780,000) to acquire the assets of Dawn Patrol, which had a book value of $467,872. The amounts in excess of book value paid by the Company for the assets of General Plant Protection and Dawn Patrol, aggregating $561,239, are not being amortized (see Note 4 to Financial Statements).

The purchase price paid by Wackenhut for these companies was based on Wackenhut's expectation that it could effect significant cost savings and increase the rate of profit in relation to sales of these companies, as well as on the Company's decision that it could most effectively expand its operations to the California area and into the central-alarm-system business by acquiring established companies with an established clientele. . . .

On January 1, 1966, Wackenhut acquired the assets of Crawford Research, Inc., a private investigative firm in Washington, D.C., for $75,000 in cash and moved its Washington office to the offices formerly occupied by Crawford. Also on January 1, 1966, Wackenhut for the first time extended its operations outside of the United States and its possessions with the opening of an office in Caracas, Venezuela, through a 50%-owned affiliate.

The Company now has 24 offices—six in Florida, four in California, three in Puerto Rico and one each in Atlanta, Boston, Caracas, Columbus, Honolulu, Houston, New Haven, New York, Philadelphia, Las Vegas and Washington, D.C. The Company also furnishes guard services to customers in 11 states in which it does not have offices.

At the end of 1961 the Company had 1,332 employees and occupied approximately 10,500 square feet of leased office space. In that year the

Company performed 2,198,565 guard hours of work. By the end of 1965 the Company had 4,033 employees and occupied approximately 42,500 square feet of owned or leased office space. In 1965 the Company performed 6,608,466 guard hours of work. . . .

The common stock offering to the public was made on April 26 and all stock had been sold by 10:00 A.M. on April 27. In fact, the issue was oversold. The following article appeared in *The Miami Herald* on Wednesday, April 27, 1966:

Wackenhut Shares Issued

More than 247,000 shares in The Wackenhut Corp. of Coral Gables went on the market Tuesday and all were grabbed up quickly at the offering price of $12.50 a share.

One Miami broker reported heavy demand for the shares but he said the price held firm at $12.50 bid throughout the day.

"Reception to the offering was excellent and the issue was oversubscribed," an official at Francis I. duPont, the principal underwriter, said.

Wackenhut provides security services to the U.S. government, industrial firms, banks, retail stores and other customers for which it furnishes guards, patrolmen, fire-fighting personnel and uniformed women receptionists.

Of the shares that went on sale Tuesday, 135,000 were offered by the company and 112,300 by George R. Wackenhut, president and board chairman, and his wife. After payment of underwriting commissions, the Wackenhuts will realize well over a million dollars from the sale of their shares.

They retain ownership of 646,700 shares, or 70 per cent of the company's outstanding stock.

Wackenhut Corp, reported net profits of $665,757 (or 86 cents a share) on revenues of $17.7 million in 1965. In 1964, the firm earned $337,573 (43 cents a share) on revenues of $10.8 million.

The stock offering was completed on May 3, 1966, when the manager of Francis I. duPont presented George with Cashier's Check No. 451107, drawn on The First National Bank of Miami in the amount of $1,302,680, made payable to "George R. Wackenhut and Ruth J. Wackenhut," and Cashier's Check No. 451108, drawn on the same bank in the amount of $1,405,920, made payable to "Wackenhut Corporation," a total of $2,708,600, after deduction of underwriting discounts and commissions.

According to the Prospectus, George's salary in 1965 was $46,800, and would be $52,000 in 1966. But on Tuesday, May 3, 1966, when George was forty-six and Ruth was forty-three, they became millionaires. The company had been in business less than twelve years.

HISTORICALLY, May 1966 began a pivotal period in the domestic and foreign affairs of the United States. Use of consciousness-altering drugs, particularly marijuana and LSD, gained national attention when, in May, LSD was the object of Senate hearings that led to a federal prohibition. Dr. Timothy Leary, an early LSD researcher, founded the League for Spiritual Discovery, in an unsuccessful attempt to legalize LSD and marijuana as religious sacraments.

That month, congressional opposition to the Vietnam war intensified as Senator Fullbright charged that the U.S. was "succumbing to the arrogance of power." President Johnson's first response was subdued—"not arrogance but agony"—but after another wave of antiwar protests, he called war critics "Nervous Nellies," and added: "If America's commitment is dishonored in Vietnam, it is dishonored in forty other alliances we have made." Titular Republican leader Goldwater asked Fullbright to resign as chairman of the Foreign Relations Committee for giving "aid and comfort to the enemy."

On May 16, Stokely Carmichael was elected chairman of SNCC, starting a shift from civil rights to "Black Power." The idea was for blacks to organize blacks into their own political groups. As Carmichael put it: "To ask Negroes to get in the Democratic party is like asking Jews to join the Nazi party." CORE also endorsed "Black Power" and "self-defense," but the NAACP and the SCLC (Martin Luther King's group) rejected "Black Power" as a separatist movement.

During June, the U.S. escalated the Vietnam War by bombing Hanoi for the first time, bombing railroad lines up to the Chinese border, and declaring that U.S. planes would pursue North Vietnamese planes into China. President Johnson stated: "We must continue to raise the price of aggression at its source." Some students refused college degrees in protest to the war, and 6,400 people, including 3,938 college faculty members, paid for a three-page antiwar ad in *The New York Times*.

On July 7, despite his conviction for taking $250,000 in union funds, and his status on bail pending appeal, Jimmy Hoffa was reelected by acclamation to a five-year term as president of the Teamsters.

August 1, Charles Whitman, a Boy Scout leader and former Marine, terrorized students, teachers, and passersby at the University of Texas in Austin. Positioned at the top of the clocktower for eighty minutes, he shot forty-four people, killing fourteen, before he was killed by police. Earlier in the day, he had killed his mother and his wife.

In September, U.S. troops in Vietnam reached 300,000 and suffered a record 145 dead and 970 casualties in a single week. The Treasury Department reported the Vietnam War was then costing the U.S. more than $1.2 billion a month.

17

EARLY IN 1966, George and Ruth began work on two outside projects, each of which would require more than seven years to complete. They had been living in a relatively modest home in Miami, 7795 Southwest 122 Street, while the children were growing up, but in 1966 Jan was twenty-one and Rick was nineteen, so George and Ruth decided it was high time to do something they had discussed frequently—and often dreamed about—to design and build a bayfront house and a motor yacht to go with it.

After looking at literally hundreds of properties fronting on Biscayne Bay, they found what they wanted at the end of Casuarina Concourse in an area of Coral Gables called Gables Estates. The home would be named "Tyecliffe," although most of their relatives and friends would refer to it simply as "The Castle." Ruth would supervise virtually every detail of the construction, landscaping, and furnishing of Tyecliffe, a multimillion-dollar project that would require her undivided attention ten to twelve hours a day, seven days a week, for more than seven years.

"I had subcontracted our first house, on 122nd Street," Ruth says, smiling at the memory. "I had no money, and I still don't know how I got the place built. I truly had no money to speak of. So, I just said, 'Well, I'll subcontract, and off we go!' I learned a lot building that first house. There were many times we could have—and should have—moved, but Russ kept saying, 'When I make a move, that's going to be *it!*' And, you know, a lot of people will go to their first house, then step up to another house. But, no, I couldn't get him to budge.

"Finally, he said, 'Okay, go out and look for some property, I'm ready, it's all yours!' So, having lived in Florida, I knew the areas pretty well, and I knew Gables Estates had not been developed yet. But I always knew this road, Casuarina Concourse. It was a little dirt road and there were two houses there. That's all that was there. All of Gables Estates was mangrove, and, of course, on the other side was Tahiti Beach, which was all mangrove and a beautiful beach. You had to pay to go to Tahiti Beach. I went there, my sisters went there, and my children went there. Then, in time, they developed it into what is now Coco Plum.

"I always liked the *feel* of the area. So I drove down the dirt road and I stopped at the larger home, which was owned by the Swensons at the time. He was on the board of Southeast Bank. It was a beautiful home, it's been sold in the meantime, and they've added to it, a family from Venezuela is in there now. The little home across the street, coincidentally, the people were from Drexel Hill, where I was originally from. They only spent one month out of the year in that little house. I stopped at the Swensons' house and knocked on the door and Mrs. Swenson happened to open the door. I asked about the street, and how long she'd been there, and so on.

"Anyway, the area that is now Gables Estates started to develop, and I looked at several lots. The one I wanted, which I feel is the prime piece of property in Gables Estates, had already been sold, but they hadn't built on it. Turned out to be the Bassett family. Now, I didn't know at the time that Casuarina Concourse was sort of ignored by the rest of Gables Estates. It had always been neglected. I drove down to the end, to the cul-de-sac. I saw *this* property, which we later purchased, and then the neighbor's lot, and another lot at the point on the bay. I wanted to purchase two large lots, which would have taken up the cul-de-sac, and then I was going to try to get the little house across the street. So I would've had that whole cul-de-sac area. Well, the neighbor was planning on building, so he wasn't going to sell. When he didn't sell to me, there was no sense in just buying the lot at the point on the bay, and the lot across the street.

"We purchased three acres. Actually, when I did the landscape design, you have the illusion of not really knowing how much acreage is here.

"After purchasing the land, I started to plan the house. I used to sit out on our patio, at our old house, and I had two card tables, and I had all kinds of tablets and books and different things. No research on architecture. I had no architectural books. I had no research books on different periods, I had nothing. There was so much in my head. And it was very frustrating for me, because I'm not a draftsman. I can lay out something, and *I* can figure it out, but don't show it to somebody else to copy, because they'd get lost.

"I remembered we had been in Caracas one time, and there was a Spanish villa that I went to see. This had a country Spanish charm that was most attractive, and I love the country feel. It was like a ranch-style old Spanish in feel. We went there for dinner one night. I had not been all through the house, just outside. I just loved the atmosphere. So I started sketching and working around this country design. Now, this was the first time I put something on paper. I started to think of the countryside of England and the thatched roofs. Don't forget, Russ had said: 'Do whatever; just do it,' giving me no suggestions of what he liked or anything. And I thought: The country English, I think I'll do that, and there is a way that I can get the *effect* of a thatched roof.

"Well, one night Russ came out and he said, 'I don't want that! I don't want that!' I said, 'Oh! Well, what *do* you want?' He said, 'I have to have a steep roof like your house had in Drexel Hill.' Well, that wasn't real steep, but it gave the illusion of the English manor house on a smaller scale.

"Now, I was leafing through a magazine, and I saw a gatehouse. That's all there was, it just showed the archway from the outside. But it had the feel I wanted to start with. From that point on, ideas began for what is now Tyecliffe. I started to cut out pictures of English manor homes. I'd show various ideas to Russ, and he would say, 'Yes, I like it.' Tyecliffe was built for him. Everything in it is my husband. He wanted stone, he wanted wood, he wanted strength, he wanted space. That's how I arrived at the style of architecture. But I knew I couldn't do the drawings. I knew I needed an architect."

George picks up the story in the spring of 1966: "We knew we had to retain an architect who, in turn, would put the plans out on bid, and a general contractor would also be retained. We both knew of a local architect whose work we had admired, by the name of James Dean. So we contacted Jimmy Dean and arranged to meet with him. We explained to him what we had in mind, and Dean said, 'Whenever I build a house for a couple, I ask each of them to list everything that they want *in* the house."

"So he gave us a few days to do that, and we each came up with our list and presented it to him. Then he came back with the floor plan that showed the house would be 300 feet in length, which, parenthetically, is the size of a football field, and just about as wide. I said, 'Well, dear God, Jimmy, we don't want a house *this* size.' He said, 'Well, if you want all these things in it that both of you said, it's *got* to be this size.' So I turned to my wife and I said, 'You don't really need *this* room.' And she said, 'Oh, yes, I *do*.' She said, '*You* don't really need *that* room.' I said, 'Oh, yes, I *do!*' So we were stuck. The moral of that story is, when an architect asks you and your wife to list everything that you want in the house, *don't do it!*

"So, each of us got everything we wanted, but in an entirely different design. Each time he would come back with plans or renderings, I would say, 'No, further back in history.' Then he'd come back with something else and I'd say, 'No, further back.' We met with Jimmy Dean every week for more than a year, from the late spring of 1966 to the late summer of 1967, but we knew his plans would not be approved by the Coral Gables Planning and Zoning Department. At which time he said that he gave up, he didn't have the infrastructure to build a house of the size we were talking about, he didn't have the engineering capability. So we were right back to square one.

"Then I started looking for another architect. Ruth and I had a personal friend by the name of Steve Little. So I visited with Steve and told him the type of house we were looking for, which was one of Medieval design. What I realized I was looking for was a house that went back to the eleventh, twelfth, thirteenth, fourteenth centuries, a combination of those centuries. When I talked to Little, I explained to him what we wanted, and he said he couldn't handle that sort of thing, but he knew an outstanding period architect in

Palm Beach by the name of John Volk. So I called John Volk and we made arrangements to go up to Palm Beach and meet with him.

"He knew immediately what we were talking about. He was born in Austria, he was familiar with castles and homes from the fifteenth century. He said, 'I think what you're really talking about is an old English manor house.' So he started on the plans. However, he thought that we should get bids from at least three builders to start construction, because he didn't want to have us wait until he completed all the plans. He gave a pretty good idea to these three building contractors of what we were after, and basically how many square feet.

"When the three bids came back, two of them were right around $710,000, if you can imagine costs back then. To build that today, you wouldn't do it for $17 million. The lowest bidder was John Avant. We called him Jack Avant, that's what he went by. So we proceeded with him and finally arranged for a cost-plus-fixed-fee arrangement, because we began to realize that this was the type of a house that it would be hard to do on a contract-price basis."

AT THE TWC board meeting in June 1967, management was authorized to enter into a contract for modification of the headquarters building in order to provide for an increase of available office space. In addition, management's actions were confirmed and approved in purchasing four lots across the street from the headquarters building, which were originally going to be paved for parking. It was resolved that the regular quarterly meetings of the board of directors, beginning in 1967, would be held on the last Monday of January, April, July, and October.

A particularly important announcement was made at the next quarterly meeting of the board on December 5. George advised the directors that the newly elected governor of Florida, Claude Kirk, had requested TWC to provide certain services for the governor's office, the details of which were to be negotiated. He said that the corporation was requested to furnish service in three fields: Physical security for the governor and the Governor's Mansion and offices, including electronic security; personnel security (TWC was already conducting background investigations on all of the appointees of the governor); and investigative services in connection with the governor's war against crime and corruption. It was the governor's intention to finance this fight against crime and corruption with funds donated by private individuals and corporations.

On December 20, TWC announced further expansion in Latin America with the formation of Wackenhut de Colombia, S.A., and the opening of offices in Bogota, Colombia. Frank M. Smallwood, a former FBI agent, was elected president of Wackenhut de Colombia, owned 51 percent by TWC.

The executive committee of the board held a special meeting on December 22, attended by all members. George announced that Governor Kirk wanted to appoint him a member of the governor's staff, at a salary of $1 per year, to direct all aspects of the project that was to be called the Governor's War on Crime. Kirk was scheduled to make an announcement of the project during his inaugural address on January 3, 1967, and at the same time would announce that he had commissioned George, as director of the War on Crime, to employ investigative personnel from TWC on a cost-plus basis. Resolutions to this effect were approved by the executive committee.

The year 1966 closed with gross revenues of $22.427 million, an increase of 23 percent over the previous year. At this point, TWC had become the third largest investigative and security organization in the nation, based on sales volume. The company had thirty offices throughout the U.S., the District of Columbia, Puerto Rico, Venezuela, and Colombia. In addition to opening up in South America, TWC opened new area offices in Chicago, Detroit, Houston, Kansas City, and St. Louis.

Although 1966 had been a year of almost astonishing success for the twelve-year-old company, 1967 would become a year of particular importance because it would represent a significant step forward toward George's goal of establishing TWC offices in all the major market areas of the United States. Gross revenues would increase by nearly 30 percent, new clients would increase by 10 percent, and the company would open nineteen new offices. But the year would be among the most memorable for reasons not directly related to financial success. As director of Governor Kirk's War on Crime, George would see TWC receive an avalanche of national publicity on a day-to-day basis, mass-media attention he never dreamed would be possible for such a young company, publicity that even a giant corporation could not afford to buy.

Not all of it was favorable. And, in the end, TWC would lose $180,000 on the project, and have to write it off.

But it was one of the most exciting times in George Wackenhut's life.

LISTENING to a tape recording of Governor Claude Kirk's inaugural address, delivered in Tallahassee on Tuesday, January 3, 1967, hearing the rhythms and nuances and pauses, gives you insights into the man's intensity, motivation, and visionary convictions, especially when he discusses the subject that would prove to be the most controversial and widely publicized issue of his term in office, the Governor's War on Crime:

> Florida has suffered too long the crime of an antiquated constitution, the crime of too expensive government, the crime of high taxes, the crime of an inadequate educational facility, and, finally, the crime of crime itself, the insidious, brutal crimes committed upon the citizens of Florida by storm troopers of the underworld, by the thugs, murderers, and gamblers. Today, I totally and irrevocably commit myself to ridding Florida of all these crimes. I pledge to you again that in our fight against the sources of organized crime that I mean business.
>
> The momentous battle is now joined. Today I am proud to announce to you that I have commissioned Mr. George Wackenhut of Miami as director of the Governor's War on Crime. Mr. Wackenhut heads the third largest private investigative firm in the United States. I am happy to say he is providing his services to the state for one dollar a year. It will be his responsibility to marshal the forces for this great fight: The investigators, the computers, the prosecutors, the attorneys, the accountants, the people. Although Director Wackenhut is donating his services, I have authorized him to secure from his firm whatever manpower is needed in this campaign. Now, the costs involved in all phases of this endeavor will be paid from funds volunteered by interested private citizens. This means that this important and crucial fight will be led by me without additional taxes.
>
> I hereby put our underworld adversaries on notice that this is not just

another temporary campaign with a flair for publicity. Ours will be an effective, professional, and responsible campaign, a campaign in which we push the criminal element not only from Florida, but beyond national boundaries. I have and will continue to confer with officials of New York, Illinois, and California, as well as others who share our desire to rid America of this cancerous growth. I intend to make sure that Florida leads them in this battle against our joint enemy.

Professional crime fighters have been employed for this war; they are our "reserves." Responsible law enforcement officers from all levels of state and local government will be mobilized to carry forward this campaign; they are the "regulars." But no war is ever won by the regulars alone; it is always the reserves who provide the margin of victory, and into this fight we will throw every reserve we can muster. And when the cancer of crime is removed, the professionals can carry on without our having created another governmental division or empire. And yet these reserves can always be recommitted when and if needed. . . .

Claude Roy Kirk, Jr., who was Florida's first Republican governor in ninety-four years, since the days of Reconstruction, was born in San Bernardino, California, in 1926, where his parents both worked as railroad clerks. When he was a child, the family moved to Chicago, where his father tried unsuccessfully to sell mobile homes. Next, the family moved to Montgomery, Alabama, where the elder Kirk tried his hand at manufacturing vending machines, trailers, axles—as Kirk himself put it: "He was kind of spotted around."

Following stateside service in the Marine Corps during World War II, Kirk entered the University of Alabama to study law, helping to pay his way by giving jujitsu lessons (one of his specialties) to officers of the Alabama Highway Patrol. While in law school, he married the daughter of Montgomery's only Ford dealer, an unusually attractive girl who was the product of an exclusive Episcopal academy for young ladies in Virginia.

Soon after receiving his law degree, Kirk was snatched out of civilian life again by the Korean War. When he returned, he informed his father-in-law: "You know, Pops, the Lord's been mighty good to me. I buried many a buddy over there with my bare hands, but I did find the Lord. And He has given me an idea—an idea to form an insurance company that nobody else has ever formed." The idea was to create an insurance company exclusively devoted to policies on the lives of upper-income executives.

After experimenting with several insurance firms in Alabama, including one that sold policies through airport vending machines, Kirk and an accountant from Atlanta named Ashley Verlander went to Jacksonville, Florida, in 1956, and started the American Heritage Life Insurance Company. While Verlander worked behind the scenes as administrator, Kirk tirelessly approached top executives with the message he had received while under fire in Korea. Within three years, American Heritage was turning a profit, and by 1963 was one of the more robust insurance companies in the country.

But seven years with American Heritage was enough for Kirk, who abruptly quit and sold his stock for a reported $3 million. "I'm only happy when I'm building something," he explained. "I like to feel the wind in my face." Later, he formed his own firm, Kirk Investments, conducting business enterprises primarily in Latin America.

George recalls his first meeting with Kirk in 1964: "He was a Republican candidate for the Senate, running against Spessard Holland, and he struck me as just what the doctor ordered. He was a big man, rather handsome, tastefully dressed, well spoken, and urbane. He came to see me, he said, because I was noted to be conservative in my political views and he considered himself to be an ultraconservative. He asked me if I'd be interested in introducing him at a fund-raising breakfast in Miami. I told him that I'd like to help him, but I was really too busy to get involved in politics, that I simply didn't have the time.

"But he persisted: 'I know you'd like to see a conservative in office and I can beat Holland.' I told him, 'Frankly, I don't think you have a chance in the world. Holland's a Democrat, but he's also a noted conservative.'

"Finally, however, I did agree to introduce him at his fund raiser. As we became friends, Ruth and I had him to our home for cocktails and later that evening to dinner at the King's Bay Yacht Club. That night, I stressed again that I didn't believe he had a chance of winning the election. And, as it turned out, he was defeated.

"It was two years before I saw him again, and this time he was running for governor. We met at a fund-raising cocktail party and I asked him how the race was going. 'The latest poll shows that I'm ahead and gaining,' he said. I told him that I was surprised, because I didn't think a Republican had a chance in traditionally Democratic Florida.

"He maneuvered me into a corner where we could talk privately and began to speak with quiet intensity: 'George, I'm campaigning hard on the promise of cleaning up crime in the state, and I think your organization could be a major help to me in keeping that campaign promise.' We discussed it at some length. I told him that I didn't believe his thrust should be in the area of street crime, because that's a police matter, and that I didn't believe we could do much in the way of organized crime either, because the government had been fighting it for years with only marginal success. A group of people moved in on us, and he said, in parting, 'George, I'll get back to you after I win the election.'

"Well, to the astonishment of virtually all the so-called political experts in the state, he did win. Two days after the election, I received a call from him, asking me to meet him right away at an office he was then maintaining in Coral Gables. 'I'm going to lay it right in your lap,' he told me. 'I want you to put together a crime-fighting apparatus coordinated with public law enforcement officials. It will be up to you to devise a means of handling complaints from any and all sources. I want this to be completely non-political.'

"In mid-December, the governor telephoned me and asked me to meet him in Jacksonville. It was at this meeting he informed me that he was going to pay for his anti-crime campaign with donations from private sources. Naturally, this gave me a great deal of concern, not only from the standpoint of paying for the investigations we would be doing, but also for the possibility that all-Republican donations might subsequently lead to reports that this was a witch hunt aimed at Democrats. 'Don't worry about it,' he assured me. 'I'll get the funds and the apparatus will be yours with absolutely no dictates from me. I give you my word, George, there will be nothing political about this.'

"After the meeting, I called our in-house attorney from my hotel room, told him what the governor was requesting, and told him that I wanted to be absolutely certain that we went about it legally. That night, I tossed quite a bit in my sleep. It was going to be a gigantic undertaking, I knew, and there were certain to be political overtones, no matter how carefully we proceeded. But we did start putting it together."

Bud Thompson remembers the whole project vividly and looks back on it with a sense of humor. "Claude Kirk, in his War on Crime, was a big subject of discussion in the company as to whether it should be done or not, because, again, political implications. And we came to the conclusion that it was probably going to take and blow up, but, most probably, would not be bad. It would make politicians unhappy, but the general public would be for it, because they think there's corruption in every facet of the government. That's what we were working on, and it was a fantastic thing. When that came about, one of the things George insisted—and we sat down and had a meeting, a bunch of us with him, and kicked around: If we're going to do this, we should have some rules of the road. One is that, first of all, we have our own private attorney to work with us on the thing to keep us legal, and not get out of bounds that way. Not have to depend upon the state attorney, county solicitor, the governor's attorney general, or anything else. We have our own. Which, by the way, the way these things were set up, we thought that Kirk would say no.

"The second one was that the public would have access to the company, to Wackenhut, *directly*, not through anybody. You wouldn't have a phone number in Tallahassee, and everybody call Tallahassee, and then they would give you the information, because then somebody can screen it, and say, 'Well, we'll give them all the ones against the Democrats, but nothing on the Republicans.' So, we said, 'No, it's got to come directly to us.' And, again, we thought Kirk would say no.

"I can't remember all of them, but those were two of the principal ones on it, and he said yes, which surprised us. We never made any money on the thing, but it was very good exposure. See, when the governor, one of the things he did in his inauguration speech was announce that he was employing George to direct the Governor's War on Crime. And, boy, that jerked a lot of people right out of their jocks when that happened. It was a very, very big item. It was a good one for the company, but a very difficult one, because it drove us nuts, we had a whole flock of investigators, they were on the road. Trying to keep up with them all over the place was chaos."

JOHN THORSEN was scheduled to graduate from Florida State University in the summer of 1967, and Jan had quit her job as a secretary in the state road department early that year, because she was expecting to give birth to their first child in mid-March. "We were living off of money that we had saved from the wedding," Jan explains. "The baby was due March 15, and, of course, you read that they can come two weeks before or two weeks after. So I asked my mother to come to Tallahassee to be with me. She moved up in, I guess it must have been the end of February, thinking two weeks before March 15. She called the university and asked if they had housing available. Dad had just been appointed director of the Governor's War on Crime. All these apartments, they were just single-row little things, all attached, were all for married students. And the couple next door to us had just finished school, and she had gotten a job with the Post Office. Anyway, they moved out and the thing was empty, and the next thing I know, my mother is next door! She was going to be there to help."

THE first national magazine to run a feature story about the Governor's War on Crime was *U.S. News & World Report*, in its issue of May 22, 1967, complete with photographs of the governor, George, and various Wackenhut investigators at work.

> WHEN A STATE OPENS ITS OWN WAR ON CRIME . . .
> *There is more to Florida's anticrime crusade than just a furor over a Governor's "private police." Investigators hired by the Governor are beginning to get results. Indictments have been made, and they may be only a starter. Now the legislature is working toward modernizing State laws. A whole new system for crime prevention is taking shape.*
>
> TALLAHASSEE
> The new Republican Governor of Florida has hit his crime-ridden State with shock treatment by hiring private investigators to clean it up.

Reaction against the "outsiders" has been sharp.

There have been charges of "Gestapo" and "private police"—and claims that Florida is being turned into a "police state." But now Claude R. Kirk, Jr., first Republican Governor in 94 years, seems to be getting what he wants from the shock treatment.

The Governor is making it popular to fight crime, by creating the issue of how to do it.

As a result, for the first time the State senate has set up its own anticrime committee. County sheriffs have made the first move toward giving up some of their broad powers to the State.

And Democratic legislators are introducing the Republican Governor's bills to create a State police force, which Florida never has had.

In addition, during the first four months of the "Governor's war on crime," 23 public officials and others have been indicted.

Among those indicted so far are: a county school superintendent, a sheriff, a police detective, and suspected dope peddlers, abortionists, gamblers, embezzlers and armed robbers.

The director of the "war on crime," George R. Wackenhut, says these cases are only the beginning—"the visible top of the iceberg."

The director is a former FBI man who heads the nation's third-largest private detective and security agency.

On May 10, Mr. Wackenhut told two legislative committees that far more serious cases are now being prepared for prosecution.

In four months, he testified, the "Governor's investigators," hired and directed by Mr. Wackenhut, have uncovered evidence that shows that "corrupt officials are operating from one end of this State to the other."

Many of these officials, he said, are in league with organized crime.

Mr. Wackenhut's testimony was reminiscent of the Kefauver crime hearings of the 1950s. He said at least 70 leaders of organized crime are operating in Florida full or part time—and named them.

These leaders, he said, were members of crime syndicates of Detroit, Buffalo, Chicago, Philadelphia, Boston, Minneapolis and Pittsburgh, or top men in the Cosa Nostra "families" of Vito Genovese, Carlo Gambino, Gaetano Lucchese and Frank La Bruzzo.

Mr. Wackenhut linked the Florida operations of organized crime to official corruption: "There is no doubt that organized crime can exist and grow only where it has the umbrella of protection of corrupted local authorities."

Cases for the courts. To illustrate this point, Mr. Wackenhut listed the following examples, which he described as cases that are about ready for legal action:

* "An official who is falsifying court records and pocketing bond forfeitures."

*"County employees who are profiteering from prison labor."

*"A county official who is busily saving his friends tens of thousands of dollars in taxes by shaving the assessments of their properties."

*"Two public officials who are in deadly competition with each other—competition to determine who is going to be king of the local *bolita* [numbers] operations."

*"Officials converting, to their own use, materials and supplies purchased with public funds."

*"A judge who juggled the facts to clear a hoodlum goon."

*"The policemen who nightly sit in parked cars outside a prostitute-ridden bar, go inside for a drink—and never make an arrest."

*"The official who solicited bribes from suspended licensees on the promise to get them reinstated."

*"A group of officials who attempted to destroy judicial process by bribery."

*"Agents of a State body accepting bribes to overlook violations of regulatory laws."

*"An official who solicits bribes and kicks back a large portion to higher officials."

*"A lawman who is Mr. Big in a county-wide *bolita* ring which is part of a national syndicate."

*"A group of lawmen involved in *bolita* and illegal whisky production."

*"Lawmen who actually protect the local *bolita* monopoly from outside competition."

However, Mr. Wackenhut continued, "even more disgusting" cases have been uncovered. He cited these examples:

*"Youths who were forced to commit vile and unnatural sex acts while in custody."

*"A group of nearly a dozen officials and their associates who engaged in a sex orgy with a woman threatened with criminal prosecution."

*"Officials who used persons in custody to pose for pornographic photographs."

*"Lawmen who regularly seduced high school girls."

Both Mr. Wackenhut and Governor Kirk insist that official corruption, organized crime and "crime on the streets" are part of the same problem.

To illustrate, the Governor draws a circle on a blank sheet on the chartboard in his office and says:

"Corruption makes it possible for organized crime to operate.

"Organized crime feeds on 'crime on the streets'—the dope peddlers, prostitutes, *bolita* operators, even armed robbers. To complete the circle, organized crime provides much of the money that keeps corruption going."

The "war" begins. Governor Kirk plunged into his "war on crime" on the day he took office, January 3.

In his inaugural address, he announced that Mr. Wackenhut was to direct the "war," and called for private contributions to pay for it.

The controversy began immediately. The Governor's opponents expressed fears—as they still do—that the Republican who moved into the Governor's chair would use his investigations against the Democrats who hold most State and local offices.

There were complaints that, since the Governor was not using State funds to pay his investigators, the State government would have no control over them.

But gradually, after the Governor presented a bill to set up a State police authority that would employ his "private investigators," the fears and the controversy began to die down.

"No alternative." For example, State Senator Robert Shevin, from Miami, a Democrat who introduced the Governor's crime bills, says this:

"I disapproved of the Governor's approach, appointing Wackenhut and private investigators.

"But I realize the Governor had no alternative. He had no appropriated funds to hire investigators.

"The very positive thing he did was to call attention to the size of the problem and the need for action.

"I doubt that this legislature could have gotten off the ground on this anticrime program if the Governor had not focused attention on the problem in this way."

Senator Shevin was working on the crime problem even before the Governor was elected last year. In the summer of 1966, Mr. Shevin spent three weeks in New York, studying the crime commission there.

State law enforcement in Florida is outmoded, Mr. Shevin insists. Policing authority is split among a number of agencies.

The State highway patrol is limited, for example, to enforcing traffic laws. The Sheriffs' Bureau in Tallahassee, financed by State funds, has investigators—but they can enter a county only at the invitation of that county's sheriff.

The bureau maintains the State's criminal files—but has no computers and not enough people to keep the office open nights and week-ends.

Senator Shevin says: "The State never has been in the law-enforcement business—and the local law enforcement has proven inadequate for the task."

The Governor's bills to turn the Sheriffs' Bureau into the Florida Intelligence Bureau, with computers, more investigators, more powers to investigate, have been introduced by Mr. Shevin.

"Healthy" changes. A senior Democratic State senator, John E. Matthews, Jr., of Jacksonville, sums up the situation by saying:

"You make a political issue and you get action. And that's good. The *status quo* is going to be changed—and that's healthy."

"Florida law enforcement will be improved."

To most observers, the shock treatment that is being given Democratic Florida by its Republican Governor seems to work.

George agrees with the article's conclusion that the shock treatment did work: "Those cases that were mentioned in the magazine's story were completely documented by our investigators before being turned over to the proper authorities with never any question on our part as to whether the perpetrators were Democrats or Republicans. And Claude Kirk never once interfered or suggested any course of action.

"One result of our investigation and surveillance was the arrest by North Miami police of Anthony Di Pascua, a heroin trafficker who supplied all five New York Mafia families with narcotics. He had been sought for eight years before we located him, kept him in sight, and informed the police so they could make the arrest. It appeared subsequently that three mobsters were 'hit' on suspicion that they had been informants in the case. We actually had penetrated the Mafia in three different places with undercover personnel and were obtaining outstanding information."

The regular quarterly meeting of the board was held at King's Bay on July 31. George advised the directors concerning the reorganization of the executive staff at headquarters which had recently been put into effect and he furnished a chart that reflected the present organization staff. He pointed out that due to the growth of the company, it was impossible for John Ammarell, as executive vice president, to directly supervise all of the operations of the company, and, at the same time, give his attention to other necessary matters such as the establishment and development of new offices and dealing with acquisitions, including new companies in Latin America. For this reason, Bob Kirk, who was vice president of Development, was appointed vice president of Operations, and would exercise direct supervision of the operational divisions reporting to Ammarell.

During the meeting, Ralph Kiel, director of Public Relations, provided copies of numerous newspaper articles concerning TWC. He referred specifically to a four-page "Progress Report" published by the Francis I. duPont firm. In addition, he referred to the fact that George's report on the War on Crime before the joint meeting of the Judiciary B and Senate Anti-Crime Commission of the Florida Legislature on May 10 resulted in large headlines and stories in all newspapers throughout the state, as well as radio and television coverage. Also, George's testimony before Senator Long's U.S. Senate Committee on Administrative Practice and Procedure, regarding Senate Bill 928, "Right of Privacy Act of 1967," produced wire service stories in newspapers from coast to coast.

A six-month progress report on the War on Crime reflected that 1,695 complaints were received; thirty-three arrests were made, fifteen public officials were indicted, and three sheriffs removed from office as a result of the investigations.

There were also humorous aspects to the War on Crime. For example, the local front page of *The Miami News,* Monday, June 5, 1967, carried the banner headline "Kirk Moves Into Dade Crime War," followed by a lengthy article, including a large photograph of Kirk during a news conference, surrounded by reporters, plus three television crews. Directly above the feature headline was a smaller headline and article, including a photograph of George, back turned to the camera, hands behind his back, head down, facing Metro Judge Thomas G. O'Connell, with the caption reading: "Wackenhut Hears Sentence From Judge." The article was written by Jack Oswald.

Speeding Charge
Wackenhut Pays $27 Fine

George Wackenhut, Gov. Kirk's general in the war on crime, paid a $27 fine in Metro traffic court today for driving his sports car 55 miles an hour through a 30-mile-per-hour zone.

"I think it was a very fair sentence," Wackenhut remarked after paying the fine. He had pleaded guilty.

Metro Judge Thomas G. O'Connell assessed the crew-cut detective agency operator an additional $3 in court costs, ordered three points to be entered on his license, and gave him the option of spending three days in jail in lieu of the fine.

"I hope I don't see you back here any more," Judge O'Connell added.

Wackenhut, accompanied by Attorney Richard Maloy, arrived for the 9 a.m. session in the Metro Justice Bldg. at 8:50 a.m. He spent 40 minutes listening to Judge O'Connell dispose of other traffic cases in a thorough but rapid-fire order.

Wackenhut, driving his red Corvette, had been stopped by Sheriff's Deputy John Stack on SW 120th Street near 77th Avenue on April 12. The arrest occurred just four hours after Gov. Kirk, at a news conference in Tallahassee, had recommended that drivers exceeding the speed limit by 25 miles an hour automatically lose their licenses for a month.

Wackenhut had three previous traffic citations, two of them for speeding. Judge O'Connell could have ordered the 46-year-old former FBI agent to traffic school, but made no mention of this possibility at today's trial.

Directly below that is the lengthy feature article by reporter William Tucker, with a very serious tone, including the photograph of Governor Kirk speaking at a major press conference. Following is one excerpt:

BAY CORPSE STILL MYSTERY
Kirk Moves Into Dade Crime War

Gov. Claude Kirk said today he is sending 24 special agents into Dade County to beef up his war against organized crime, which he holds responsible for a wave of gang killings here.

The governor held a brief press conference at the State Office Building here to announce he is sending in 12 men from the Beverage Department and 12 of his own investigators.

"Their main objective will be surveillance," Kirk said. "They will work with the state attorney and with Sheriff Wilson Purdy, and hopefully, we can make some important breakthroughs in the organized crime setup."

As the governor spoke, police sought to identify the hacked-up body of the fourth gang war victim in South Florida in three months.

Underworld circles were wild with rumors about the possible identity of the man. Two names were mentioned—but both men were determined by The Miami News to be in good health.

It was speculated that the butchered body, reclaimed in five pieces with the hands and feet still missing, was that of a bookie.

A bookie, Nat Ehrenberg, was one of the previous victims. And a car belonging to the wife of handbook figure Mickey Zion was blown up in a North Bay Village parking lot Saturday.

Rumors have been strong that a big split up among the bookies and lottery writers came recently while their kingpin was in jail. Some allegedly started "cutting up the action"—and getting in deep with the syndicate "shylocks" when a lucky seven fell in bolita and they did not have their usual insurance.

Gov. Kirk said the gang killings point up the need for a statewide crime agency and "I am confident the Legislature is moving in that direction."

He called the slayings a "major movement" in law enforcement when various agencies must cooperate to get to the facts and crack down on crime "totally."

He said his crime war has had many results—not all of which he is pleased with. He cited the gang killings as a product of his "shaking the tree" with the war on crime.

The 12 investigators from the governor's office will be under the direction of his "General" fighting crime—George Wackenhut. Kirk said he has told Wackenhut to put some 600 investigations he originated in a "hold" position so they can be studied. . . .

Among the longest and most critical articles about the War on Crime appeared in the July 29, 1967, issue of *The Saturday Evening Post,* under the by-line of Marshall Frady. Here is one excerpt concerning George's role:

In his campaign for governor, Kirk vowed to clean up the state once and for all, preaching a return to righteousness with all the refreshing gusto and simplicity of Carrie Nation bearing down on a block of saloons with hatchet in hand. "I don't know what we're going to stir up," declared Kirk, "but we're going to stir up something. I want to let them know"—one large finger tapping his chest—"that this guy is for real."

Kirk's promises of Armageddon were not so easy to fulfill. There were no provisions in the state budget for such a crusade, and Kirk knew that the Democratic legislature was unlikely to vote him the money soon. So he launched his war with a hopeful call for private donations from the state's citizenry and recruited what was to all appearances his personal police force. For a token fee of one dollar a year, Kirk appointed an old friend to head his campaign, an evangelistic arch-conservative named George Wackenhut. Simultaneously, Kirk hired Wackenhut's prosperous security agency to prosecute the war at a fee of cost plus 10 percent.

A onetime FBI agent, Wackenhut presides over an empire of 33 offices in the United States and Latin America—a $23-million-a-year operation, dealing mostly in plant security and "business counterespionage," in powder-blue uniforms, booted like paratroopers. From his headquarters in Coral Gables, Wackenhut directs his forces and issues, at irregular intervals, a two-page newsletter entitled "The Wackenhut Security Review," which grimly warns against "coexistence with Russia" and points out the Communist menace implicit in student unrest on the American campus.

Once a professional soccer player and wrestling coach, Wackenhut has a blunt and battered face with pale, flat eyes, close-cropped white hair, and an expression of blank, metallic imperturbability. At 47, he is still as stocky and sturdy as a brick, and his suits fit as flat and smooth as tin. "Carelessness makes me angry," he snaps. In the evenings after supper he trots the dark, deserted streets of his neighborhood in track shorts and tennis shoes, a stop watch clenched in his fist.

Wackenhut sent out 38 of his investigators to fight Kirk's war against crime, and the distinction between political and criminal investigations soon became muddled. The first casualty of the campaign was not a Mafia chieftain but a Democratic county school superintendent whom former Gov. Haydon Burns had appointed to the state Board of Regents shortly before leaving office. Kirk, who had brought his own list of appointees with him to Tallahassee, demanded that he retire. When the fellow refused, he suddenly found Wackenhut men swooping over his county. About the same time, a local newspaper came out with a report that the man had been guilty of certain indiscretions, and he was soon indicted by a county grand jury for theft involving such pedestrian booty as a washer-dryer and light fixtures. Though the school superintendent admitted his impropriety, the general feeling was that his was hardly an imposing head for Kirk's initial stroke.

Subsequently, the chairman of the state racing commission resigned after one of Kirk's aides phoned him Christmas Eve with the ultimatum, "Either you quit, or we're going to put you in jail. Our investigators have been investigating, and we know enough on you to do it if we have to."

After a few incidents such as these, Florida Democrats began charging that Kirk was less interested in a war against the syndicate than a complete appropriation of the state government. Some even muttered darkly that what Kirk really wanted, either consciously or unconsciously, was to reign over a kind of police state. "What I call him," snapped one official, "is *führer*-a-go-go."

For a while the capital of Tallahassee was living through what one official described as "a season of rumors—people seeing Wackenhuts under every bed." The outcry against his methods left Wackenhut aggrieved. "What everybody is implying, really, is that we are unprincipled men," he complained at lunch one day. "But look now. If the governor says to me, go get so-and-so, and if that man's gettable, he should be gotten, right? But the civil libertarians and all have said I'll be breaking down everybody's doors. Well, look at me. Can you picture me breaking down a door?"

Quickly, as if sensing this was not his most compelling argument, he ordered another bullshot—a manly mixture, like the dark old wood and olive leather around him, of beef bouillon and vodka—and continued, "I mean, if a man has nothing to hide, nobody should worry about his being investigated—right? So the implication is, since there's all this fuss anyway, that we're going to conjure something up."

Not long ago Wackenhut appeared before a special state legislative subcommittee and recited an exhaustive list of gamy characters and situations in Florida—he seemed, after four months, to have succeeded in thoroughly identifying the racketeers in the state, but virtually all the names and items he mentioned, it was discovered afterward, had been in newspaper files for years. Later Kirk announced that Wackenhut's investigators had finally cornered a prostitute of some repute. A few dope and abortion rings have been shattered and a covey of local officials are under suspension or indictment for assorted improprieties.

For such triumphs, according to most estimates, the cost of Kirk's crusade was running about $1,500 a day, but the governor's appeal for funds was drawing only a daily trickle of $30. This spring, still declaring that he was on the verge of making important disclosures, Kirk finally asked the legislature to convert his private offensive into an official, government-funded Department of Criminal Justice. But Kirk demanded that the war remain under his control, and he indicated that he intended to retain Wackenhut as "my General Grant." When the legislature balked, it appeared that Kirk would have to settle for a commission with severely restricted powers to run the war. . . .

Ralph Kiel recalls the predictable pressures generated by daily mass media exposure. "The War on Crime is a very dramatic story, and this is a great compliment to George R. Wackenhut," Kiel says. "Because of the tremendous national, state, and local media coverage. Listen, we were interviewed by newspapers and magazines from all over the country, and we had television crews in the office constantly. And they, like all great liberal reporters, were out to get us! I would prepare lists of questions they would probably ask George, and go over the list with him. And I knew there would always be a *zinger!* George was on the air, live, fielding these questions, and he was talking to the nation! This takes poise and thinking on your feet, particularly when they slip that zinger question in there and try to take you off-guard. He handled himself beautifully.

"It was a very touchy thing, it was a controversial subject. And the liberals immediately seized on it, rightly or wrongly, saying that we were invading privacy. The objective, as Kirk put it, was that the War on Crime would provide a voice for anybody who knew that something illegal was going on. They could turn to our investigators, anonymously, and reveal a whole range of illegal activities that had been going on for years. And, of course, the liberals wanted to kill the whole thing. It was a real daily battle with the press.

"One of the outstanding examples: Jack Nelson of *The Los Angeles Times,* he came and gave us a real cut-up job. Beautiful cut-up job. It was so bad that we had Dick Maloy, our attorney, write to the president of *The Los Angeles Times,* and they were so worried that they gave us a rebuttal that was as long as the original story. Nelson is still with them, stationed in Washington.

"Another experience was *Newsweek*. Very bad. They called me, this was on the telephone. We were investigating something, I gave them the facts. They always start out: 'You know, we want to give your side of the story,' or 'We want to do a story on you and it's going to be a positive story.' The *Newsweek* reporter called me, I gave him the facts, the story turned out to be the exact opposite. Of course, the way those weekly magazines operate, the leg-man calls the reporter, the reporter calls me, the editor rewrites it, then it goes to a final edit, there's probably three or four versions of it. Then the managing editor makes the last-minute decision to cut it down or enlarge it, and nobody has any real responsibility for it in the end.

"But that's not my point. My point is that here's George in a daily situation where these questions, these tough questions, are thrown at him, and he never hesitated, always handled himself so calmly, and gave intelligent, explanatory answers that were right to the point. He showed magnificent growth. It was important, too, because our corporate reputation was on the line."

WHEN John Thorsen graduated from Florida State University that summer, he finished first in his class and was subsequently wined and dined by recruiters from many of the major accounting firms in the state. "They were taking us everywhere," Jan recalls. "They would pay for his flights for interviews in Tampa and Orlando and all over. He had taken out a college loan with an accounting firm in Tampa, that he needed to pay back, and if he had gone with them, they would've forgiven the note. He wanted to come back to Miami, too, but I think he would've gone to Tampa, and I said, 'No, let's go back to Miami.' So I flew back with the baby, Tanya, and he drove back. We lived with his parents.

"I just knew the business was doing real well. One interesting thing, I don't know how old I was, I was still in high school, and we had a little den off the garage of the old house, and a gym, where Dad kept all his exercise equipment. But tiny rooms. In the den, it was all wood-paneled, and he had his desk. I guess Mother had built it hoping he'd come home at night and work there, but that never was the case. He had a map of the world, and he teasingly said one Saturday afternoon: 'Today, Miami; tomorrow, the world.' And it was so exciting, because every time a new office would open, he'd put a little flag on this map."

18

THAT SUMMER OF 1967, Rick attended the summer session at The Citadel, where he was visited by Ruth and George, and that was the summer when the nineteen-year-old cadet, about to enter his junior year, met his wife-to-be, Mariane (Molly) Hutson Ball, an extremely attractive sixteen-year-old who was about to enter her senior year in high school. The circumstances were humorous; it was essentially a blind date.

"The summer after my sophomore year," Rick recalls, "my parents were en route either back to Miami or en route up north on their fifty-foot Hatteras that they had. They stopped off in Charleston and docked at the Charleston marina. I was rooming with three other guys, this is summer now, I'm taking summer classes, so we were in civilian clothes, we weren't under the military environment, it was much more relaxed. And we had a penthouse apartment at the Ashley House in Charleston, which was right across the street from the marina.

"On a given Saturday, we went to the beach, and as we were driving to the beach, we saw a whole carload of girls who were also going to the beach. So we started shouting at them, you know, on the road and everything, and talking to them. When we got to the beach, we teamed up with them, and just had a great time for the day. I think there were three or four of them and there must have been six of us. As we were leaving, we invited these girls, the following day, to go out on a ski boat that was really the dingy on my parents' boat.

I think one or two of the girls couldn't go, they had some other commitments, but two or three of them went with us. Some of the guys couldn't go also.

"So, anyway, the following day, we had a boatload of about five or six people, two or three of which were girls. We go out, and we're going all through the rivers and canals and stuff around Charleston. And this one girl, Stephanie Larkin, she went by 'Stevie' as her name, a nice-looking blond-haired girl, she said, 'Oh, I know a girl who lives on the Ashley River.' We were in Charleston Harbor, and she pointed out where Ashley River was, so we took the boat up; she said, 'Let's see if she's there.'

"We went up to the dock that was by her house. It was a real long dock, and this fellow who was in the boat with us, named Eric Petiprin, he got out—and he was not a Citadel cadet, he was actually going to the University of Miami, but his parents lived in Charleston. We met him at some function and became friends. Eric goes up to her house, knocks on her door, and says, 'Stevie's out here on a boat, a bunch of us are out here, would you like to come out?' "

Molly recalls that day in a slightly different way. Born in Charleston, March 19, 1950, she was sixteen that summer, about to enter her senior year at St. Andrews High School. "Eric Petiprin and Stevie Larkin both came to the door together," Molly says, smiling, "and it was one of those really weird days when I had an afternoon date—probably the only one in my life!—so I couldn't really leave and spend the day, go hop in the boat with them. But I remember them coming to the door, and Stevie said, 'I met some really cute guys at the beach, come down and meet them, they're in a boat down at the dock.' So I excused myself for a short time and walked down with them and looked in that boat. And I'll never forget seeing Austin Caldwell's face! *The* most handsome guy I think I'd ever seen. He was. He was totally handsome. Italian, dark hair, bright-blue eyes, just a real sharp-looking guy. I remember looking in there and thinking: Gosh, he's adorable!"

Rick's point of view: "So Molly came out of her house and walked down the dock, and she had on a West Point sweatshirt. It was low tide, and I'm looking up at this West Point sweatshirt, and I'm saying to myself: Boy, I'd like to date *her!* We're all talking to her, and she stays up on the dock, but we're looking up pretty high at her. And there was a fellow who was sitting right in front of me, named Austin Caldwell, from New Jersey, and you hated him because he was everything you always wished you were, okay? He was good-looking, Italian, dark, the guy was just a really nice-looking fellow.

"Molly's looking down, I didn't know, I thought she was giving *me* the eyes, but she was giving *him* the eyes, sitting right in front of me! So, you know, I'm beaming all over, because I think I'm getting these smiles! She couldn't come with us in the boat then, and she goes back to the house. So we're going along, and I turned to Stevie, and I said, 'Stevie, I'd really like to date her.' She said, 'All right, when we get back in, I'll call her.' So she called Molly, and said, 'Would you like a date with the guy in the back of the boat?' Molly says, 'Oh, yeah, the *good-looking* one?' And Stevie says, 'Yeah!' And she says, 'All *right!*' So Molly thought she was dating Austin Caldwell!"

Molly remembers walking back to the house and thinking: God, that would be *fun* to go out with *that* guy! "So, later that afternoon," she says, "Stevie called and said, 'Listen, this guy wants to go out with you; do you have any plans for tonight?' And I said, 'No, as a matter of fact, I don't.' She said, 'Okay, Eric and I will double with you!' I said, 'Well, which one is it?' And she goes, 'The *good-looking* one!' And I went, 'Oh, *great,* I'd *love* to!' Thinking it was Austin!

"So I get all dressed, got ready, and when the doorbell rang, I opened the door, and I just remember my mouth opening, like a look of shock, because it wasn't what I expected! Well, we doubled with Stevie and Eric. And it was one of the most fun nights, I think, that Rick and I have ever spent. Because we went to one of those pizza parlors where you can get up from the table and sing along with the band. And Eric had a fabulous voice, he used to jump up and sing all the time. Rick didn't sing, but Rick was his best agent! He was selling this guy to the band, you know, saying, 'Eric's got a great voice!' So we had some pizzas and beers, and laughed, and just sort of got to know each other a little bit.

"One of the fun things that I remember about that night, there was this huge giraffe by the front door, a stuffed animal, it had to have been about nine feet tall. And the whole night, we were joking about how we were going to get that giraffe out and take it home! Rick swore he'd *ride* it out for me! He felt creative, I liked his ideas! We still joke about riding that giraffe out. That was a fun night."

Rick laughs as he continues the story: "Of course, I met her parents the very first time I picked her up. Her parents were not of main financial means, but were extremely mainline culturally, everything from family background to manners to ethics. Never wavered at all. In all the years I knew her mother, who's now deceased, and her dad's still alive, they had always maintained their convictions, which is extremely admirable. I enjoyed her parents very much. Her dad was quite imposing. He's a tall man, but he's imposing with a silent strength, which was hard for a young kid to really handle, because he was ever present in the living room, and would always look down over his glasses at me if I said something improper and that kind of stuff. He always made his point without saying too much. And her mother was always just a perfect lady. Molly is from a family of five kids. And they call her 'Molly in the Middle,' because she has a younger brother and sister and an older brother and sister."

It was on that first boat trip to Charleston that George and Ruth met Molly for the first time. "He wanted me to come by and meet them," Molly recalls. "We had been dating almost every night for that whole first week. And that was unusual for both of us, because we had both dated a lot of people. And, by the end of the second week, he had given me his high school ring. Well, he made me take it *off* when I went to meet his parents! He said, 'I just don't think Mother will approve; I mean, we've only known each other two weeks!' So, I remember, I had it on a chain around my neck, I had to hide it when I went to meet them.

"We went onto their boat, we may have had lunch, and I think Nana [Merz] was with them, Rick's grandmother. I think that was the time that, after spending a few hours with them, when we walked off the boat, Nana came up to me and said, 'I just think you're *so* nice, I hope he marries *you* instead of one of those *other* girls he's brought home!' That was really one of the funniest things Nana ever said to me. But I'm sure it was that trip, when she was along. I remember that first meeting was very quiet. I felt that I was being scrutinized very closely. And I remember Rick's dad as being very,

very quiet, you know—uncomfortably quiet. Of course, his mother is so outgoing, she filled in all the gaps in the conversation.

"The first trip down to Florida, I don't know, maybe it was a year after we'd been dating. Seems like it was 1968, and the only reason I'm thinking that, it was probably a date at the bottom of the picture that was taken. Rick and I decided to drive down, he wanted me to come down to Miami and get to know his parents. So, of course, Mother wouldn't let me go without a letter from *his* mother *inviting* me, you know, which seemed to create a few rumbles. But, anyway, they got that worked out, and we drove down to Miami, drove into the driveway. We were both dressed wildly, we were both dressed in *train conductor* outfits, just for fun, because we did crazy things.

"Pulled in the driveway, Rick honked the horn. Of course, his mother came to the door, she opened the door, we walked up, and she said, 'Hi, *Linda*, let me show you to your room!' I always had a good sense of humor, so I said, 'Wrong weekend!' So she goes, 'Uh-uh,' and Rick says, 'Mom, it's Molly, not Linda.' So, she was embarrassed, but it was funny, and we still laugh about that. So that was sort of an interesting way to start a weekend.

"The first time I met Rick's dad, I told you my impression was that he was very quiet. The second time, when I was in Miami, I remember—it'd been such a long period of time, I didn't recall much about him. But I remember coming out of the bathroom in their house, and, as I opened the door, there was this huge hunk of a man in the hall. At that stage, he was not only big, but very heavy. That's when I named him 'Big Daddy.' I used to call him that all the time. I still do, sometimes, it's just like an old nickname I have for him. Big Daddy was always a term of endearment, but it also represented, to me, what he was in my eyes. He was one big man, in a lot of ways. He'd built a huge business, he was a real American, and, to me, that makes people taller than they are. Gentle. Strong. Religious. Loving. My God, he's got the patience of Job.

"He's very private about his religion and about his own feelings. And yet, if a problem presents itself, I've often heard him quote from *Science and Health.* Maybe he doesn't like to advertise. A lot of people are like that about their religion."

At a later date—Rick can't remember the specific year—his parents were in Charleston again, he's not sure what the occasion was, but he introduced Ruth and George to Molly's parents, and they all went out to dinner. "We went to a restaurant called Caballeros, which no longer exists," he remembers, smiling. "We're all sitting around the dinner table, and at that time, in Charleston, which is very prim and proper, a woman like my mother—gregarious as she is, and says anything that's on her mind—was a little hard to take. Of course, Molly and I are like Ping Pong balls, looking between her parents and my parents. The subject got on a dog that my sister and I had given to my mother for Christmas. The dog's name was Rija—'Ri' for Rick and 'ja' for Jan. It was a poodle. And, for some reason, we were talking about the poodle. Elizabeth Ball, Molly's mother, said, 'Well, did you want puppies, or did you have the dog spayed?' And my mother, right in the middle of dinner, said: 'I had her spayed, of course. You don't think I'd have that dog walking around the house with a *Kotex* on all the time, do you?' Well, the knives and forks dropped—but it broke the ice. It broke the ice very, very well, and they got along beautifully."

LISTING of TWC stock on the American Stock Exchange was approved on September 14, 1967, and trading in the company's common stock began on October 9. Approval was secured for the listing of 1,044,901 shares of common stock, of which 483,698 were issued shares.

The regular quarterly meeting of the board was held at King's Bay on October 30. George reported that Governor Kirk had requested that TWC remain in the War on Crime until March 31, 1968. The budget was to be based on supplying twenty investigators and the necessary supervision, and to include payment for important informants being utilized. About twenty-one major cases were being investigated and no new cases were being opened for investigation. It had been estimated that it would take about $500,000 to pay off what was then owed TWC and to continue as requested by the governor. After much discussion, it was the consensus of the directors that possible steps should be taken to collect the money owed and that the company should phase out its investigative services as rapidly as possible without, however, taking abrupt action which might impair its ability to collect the past due debt for services.

"In retrospect," George says, "I feel that in the 299 days ending in October of 1967 that we did an outstanding job from a standing start as an investigative agency without police powers. We had investigated somewhere in the neighborhood of 900 citizen complaints, effected a number of important arrests, and provided the information for twenty-six indictments. Also, the Florida Bureau of Law Enforcement was formed as a result of the War on Crime, giving state agents the power to cross county lines without having to be invited by the county sheriff. And I believe that our work paved the way for the subsequent enactment of a state-wide grand jury which could eliminate the possibility of local maneuvering.

"We wrote off the $180,000 that we lost, but, in looking back, I would have to think that it was worth that much for the national publicity which we received. Earlier we had opened our offices in Buffalo, Boston, and New York, because we had obtained contracts in those areas. Now, with Wackenhut becoming a more familiar name, we started opening offices around the country."

Bud Thompson believes TWC could have continued investigations in the War on Crime for many years just on the leads already acquired. "We could've gone for ten years on leads," he says. "We had prisoners that were allowed to sneak out of the jail at night and be with girl friends, and whiskey coming in, and everything. One thing led to another to another to another, like a rapid train going.

"Then, when we were done, we had all these files, and we said, 'What do you want us to do with this?' *Nobody* wanted them: 'Don't give them to *me*, I don't want them!' Highway Patrol didn't want them, Department of Law Enforcement didn't want them, nobody wanted them, because there was dynamite in those things, there was so much stuff. So, I don't know what—we ended up throwing away a lot of it, then others finally ended up going to somebody up there [Tallahassee], who I'm sure immediately found some place to put them in the back archives and hope they would disappear in time.

"There were some cases in there that should not have gotten out. I mean, they were murderers, it could've been very dangerous—including lives of people, if they found out who did it, who said it, who gave them the information. So that was always kept very private and it was not—*that* was not sent. They knew it was available, but nobody, *nobody* wanted to touch any of it."

DURING 1967, a concentrated effort was made to open additional offices, and TWC was successful during that twelve-month period in opening nineteen. They included offices in Charlotte, North Carolina; Norfolk, Virginia; Melville, Long Island; Louisville, Kentucky; Cincinnati, Ohio; Cleveland, Ohio; New Orleans, Louisiana; and San Francisco, California.

In 1966, the company had a total of thirty offices, and by the end of 1967 company offices totaled forty-nine, including those in Venezuela and Colombia. TWC was also active in acquisitions, and a special meeting of the executive committee of the board was held on December 14, 1967, for the purpose of approving an agreement to buy the assets and assume the liabilities of Alarm System, Inc., Rockville, Maryland. The purchase price was $90,000, and seemed very favorable to the corporation.

In December, TWC also formed Wackenhut Protective Systems, Inc., and named James H. Roberts as president. Roy Murray also joined the company as vice president of Development. The year ended with revenue from services increasing to $29.017 million, which was a 30 percent increase over the prior year. TWC had a 10 percent increase in the number of clients, and the company's employees increased to more than 6,000. TWC's second Annual Report was a positive one, although George was still not satisfied with progress in the area of net income. The company showed a gain from $670,184 in 1966 to $713,223 in 1967. The cost of expansion and the rapidly rising operational costs which had been very noticeable in 1966 continued to be experienced. In spite of the energy devoted to the War on Crime, TWC continued to grow dramatically and expand its horizons.

EARLY in 1967, the Pentagon announced that 5,008 Americans died in Vietnam the previous year; U.S. troop strength stood at 380,000.

In February, opposition to the Vietnam War broadened as civil rights leader Dr. Martin Luther King, Jr., spoke against it; the Women's Strike for Peace demonstrated at the Pentagon; 5,000 scientists petitioned for a halt in bombing; University of Wisconsin students forced Dow Chemical recruiters off campus; and Senator Robert Kennedy proposed the U.S. halt bombing and negotiate troop withdrawal.

On April 22, the 1.6-million-member United Auto Workers voted to leave the AFL-CIO, criticizing its lack of democratic leadership. April 28, heavyweight boxing champion Muhammad Ali was arrested for refusing induction into the Army, after having been denied conscientious objector status; boxing authorities immediately stripped him of his title.

That summer, tens of thousands of young people converged on San Francisco's Haight-Ashbury district for the "Summer of Love," with similar migrations to New York's East Village, and other centers of "hip culture." The "hippies" or "flower children" dropped out of straight society and turned to communal living, free love, marijuana, LSD, spiritualism, and heavily amplified rock music. July 12-17, the Newark Riot, covering ten square miles, left 26 dead (24 black), over 1,500 injured, and 1,397 arrested. July 23-30, the Detroit Riot left 43 dead (36 black), more than 2,000 injured, 5,000 arrested, 1,700 stores looted by whites as well as blacks, and 5,000 homeless from 1,442 fires. There were riots and disturbances in 127 U.S. cities that summer.

On September 30, President Johnson signed a record $70 billion defense appropriation that included $20 billion for direct support of the Vietnam War. October 21, more than 100,000 people marched to the Pentagon, and 647 were arrested in the antiwar demonstration immortalized by Norman Mailer in *Armies of the Night*. Folk singer Joan Baez was among 125 arrested at a sit-in at the Oakland Draft Induction Center. Other antiwar demonstrations were held in Philadelphia, Chicago, Los Angeles, and on many college campuses.

In December, reports by the Census on "Social and Economic Conditions of Negroes" revealed that 41 percent of nonwhite families made less than $3,300 a year (compared to 12 percent of white families), 7.3 percent of nonwhite were unemployed (3.4 percent white), and 29 percent of nonwhite families lived in substandard housing (8 percent white). Another report showed that 83 percent of black students still attended all-black schools in eleven southern states.

THE DUPLEX PENTHOUSE on the twenty-first floor of Grove Towers at 2843 South Bayshore Drive gives a panoramic view of fashionable Coconut Grove and Biscayne Bay in the near distance. It is only a temporary residence for Jan Wackenhut Ward and her husband Roger, whose home was severely damaged by Hurricane Andrew on August 24, 1992, like hundreds of thousands of other homes in south Florida. The time is Thursday morning, December 3, 1992, and shafts of sunlight flood the elegantly furnished living room. Traffic noises, not unlike those of midtown Manhattan, can be heard, although the glass doors leading to the wraparound terraces are closed.

Jan sits on a white sofa behind a glass-topped coffee table, slim, attractive, soft spoken, relaxed in the presence of the tape recorder, and her memories of dates, places, people, are vivid, laced with anecdotes. But sometimes, when she pauses and glances away, trying to visualize the past, there is an unmistakable sadness in her eyes. We are discussing the years 1967-68, when her first husband, John Thorsen, was beginning his career as a CPA in Miami.

"We bought a little house, and John went to work with what was Haskins and Sells, one of the Big Eight accounting firms," she says quietly. "And he started putting in hours just like Dad. Because he had this thing, too, of wanting to make a lot of money, mainly because he grew up with the lack of it, and saw how hard it was on his parents. And I think the other part was keeping up with, supposedly, what I had been accustomed to. But I hadn't really been. I mean, when you look back at it, they didn't really make the money when I was growing up. Everything that I bought was a major—Mother would take me out to buy me a prom dress, and we weren't to tell Dad. That kind of thing. So I didn't grow up around a lot of money.

"When John was twenty-five, he was looking at forty to be a

partner, and I think he probably would've been a partner before he was thirty. He was getting paid more than most of the men. Of course, all of our contemporaries at school weren't doing nearly as well, so everybody was assuming that Mother and Dad were helping us financially. In those days, they gave us a car as a wedding present, which was a real big deal, but that was all.

"I admire both of them, especially Dad, for making sure he didn't spoil in any way. I see so many cases today of contemporaries of mine that have no concept of what any of that means, because it's all just been given to them. Not only contemporaries of mine, but of my kids. And they've then gone the other way, because they've had it all so much. I think of all of us as being frugal, even more than my dad. In many ways. He went through the Depression, and I think he taught me that, knowing how hard he worked. And Mother, too, in her own way.

"We stayed in the same house until Tanya was about three, I guess. One thing that happened was that John's parents had a turn for the worse, financially. They had both been singers and entertainers in New York. Beautiful voices. John's mother was Miss Michigan. Of course, in later years, she got quite heavy. But she had a beautiful face, and she was quite talented. I don't know why they moved to Miami. That wasn't his real father. He was adopted when he was a year old, so it was the only father he ever knew, but his real father's name was Trimble, and I think he's since passed away. I never met him. I'm trying to figure out how they moved to Florida; I don't know why. His dad developed polyps in his throat, and it might've been the weather change that he needed, I don't remember, but when he got here he left singing and opened up a coin laundry business. In those days, you know, I can remember my grandmother used to do her wash like that. John used to work in the summers at the laundry, folding and everything. Then it branched out. His mother became an interior decorator and his father was installing carpet. He used to pray for hurricanes! That used to be funny, when you only had water damage, he'd have a lot of carpet work.

"They had a financial turn for the worse. They had been living near Palmetto, near us, 73rd Court and 136th, and Mother and Dad bought their home from them. They bought the home, and then they were to pay them mortgage. It wasn't a natural thing for Dad to do at all, he doesn't invest in real estate at all. Doesn't want to be a banker, isn't real philanthropic that way, and it caused quite a strain between all of us. It was like, John was backing his parents, and I was backing my parents. Then, the worst thing is that I guess Dad then sold that house, and John's parents bought the house next door to where we were living. Interesting story, though. The people that had been living in that house next door to us were building a bigger house across the highway, that's all I knew. And the next house we bought was exactly next door to John's parents. Funny? It's a small world.

"It didn't last long, but it put a lot of undue pressure. I think, in retrospect, where the problem was, is that his parents always lived beyond their means, and were always trying to keep up with Mother and Dad. And, by this time, *nobody* was keeping up with Mother and Dad. Mother, I've got to give her credit, she tried to retain some of her friendships from the old days. But it's hard, because you've got a lot of envy, and she was always guarded, afraid that maybe people were befriending her because of the financial thing. A little bit too much, but she probably got stung several times. And I think that Arlene and Eric, my former in-laws, just weren't able to hack that.

"Mother and Dad were so afraid—Mother used to say the only reason John married me was because of the financial gain. For his parents, and I guess they thought, you know, Arlene and Eric thought that they were going to be on easy street because they had married into the family. Of course, that never happened, and it caused—it was one of the factors in our breakup. Because it travels into all kinds of deep-seated things. It's just being too young to be able to sort it all out.

"I married someone very similar to my father in his work ethic, and what he wanted, and I thought I wanted that, too. I admired a man who worked very hard. My thing was, you do that—it was all very partitioned—you do that, and I do the house and the children. I was very absorbed in that. I was told by their nursery school teachers that they had never seen—not that they had *never* seen— they complimented me on the obvious time I had spent with them, because they were head-and-shoulders beyond where a lot of their contemporaries were. I was always sitting down with them, you know, I was reading them books when they were six months old. Tanya would have books in her crib at seven months old. I let them explore everything, I didn't keep them contained. I used a lot of my child-development background. Mother would get upset: 'Oh, they're getting dirty, do you just let her crawl all over?' Both of them, they would touch things and look at stuff. Every time I would see an interest, I would take books, and we'd read everything about that. And I'd take them to places when they were, you know, crawling.

"That's where all of my time and energies went, and I felt like I was really very well rewarded and accomplished that way. I didn't feel that I was losing out by not working. His hours were abominable. I used to eat two dinners, one with the kids and one at midnight. I don't think he came home any night before midnight. And yet, any time of the day or night I happened to drop down at the office, there he was. I remember packing picnics with the kids, because I was so worried, he never saw the children. Worried about their relationship. And I would pack dinner: 'Okay, kids, we're going to go see Daddy,' and we'd get in the car. And he'd be furious. Because he couldn't separate the time, and I was interrupting. I was wanting him to have dinner with the kids, and then we'd leave, and he could stay there for however long. But he couldn't do that. He'd sit there and wait. I didn't do that too many times.

"The only family meal we ever had was on Sunday nights. And usually Sundays—he was a great sports enthusiast, so we had Dolphin tickets, and theater tickets, and tickets to everything. Every Sunday during football season there'd be a game. And he was drinking heavily. So even when we'd come home from the games, he was no good for the kids, and it was just breaking my heart. And yet I'm the one that—I mean, he's the one that walked out. I would still have been in there, hanging on, learning how to do this. But I took it, you know, what can *I* do to make this better? How can *I* change this? Not seeing that it takes two people.

"We went to a practitioner a couple of times, a Christian Science practitioner, and John wasn't a Scientist, that was the other thing, we never could go to church, we never had anything. He felt his success was all *inner* controlled. It was from his background, he had not had any kind of training that way. I knew he believed in God, but it was a lonely part for me, I would've liked to have had that link filled in the family. The kids wouldn't have gotten to Sunday school unless I went, all the time, with them. We just grew apart, because the little bit of time that he gave us, I would force the kids on him. It left no one-on-one."

THE QUARTERLY MEETING of the board of directors was held at Cheeca Lodge, Islamorada, Florida, on January 29, 1968. It was reported that the investigative services being furnished in connection with the Governor's War on Crime were drastically reduced on October 30, 1967, and were completely discontinued on November 30, 1967. By that time, $537,000 had been billed to Governor Kirk for services through January 1968, of which $290,583 remained unpaid at the time. It was also reported that government contracts had been renewed at the Atomic Energy Commission's Nevada Test Site near Las Vegas, at NASA at the Kennedy Space Center, at Lewis Research Center in Cleveland, and with NASA at the Goddard Space Flight Center in Greenbelt, Maryland.

The annual meeting of the stockholders of TWC was held on Monday, April 29, at the David William Hotel in Coral Gables. A proposal was presented to amend Article III of the Certificate of Incorporation to provide for authorizing 500,000 shares of preferred stock at the par value of $1 per share. It was stated that among the purposes for which a series of preferred stock might be issued would be the possible acquisition of other companies.

The board of directors held their meeting the same day at King's Bay, and discussed the proposed acquisition of Reliable Reporting Service, Inc., of Rockville Center, New York. A resolution was passed authorizing the purchase of Reliable for $442,000. In connection with this, the company exchanged 22,100 shares of its preferred stock for all of the business and net assets of Reliable. The transaction was accounted for as a "Pooling of Interests," and, accordingly, the financial statements for the year ended December 31, 1967, had to be adjusted to include the accounts and operations of Reliable. That firm specialized in the business of making pre-insurance and pre-employment investigations for more than 400 clients in the insurance, financial, and industrial fields, and was headed by Coulby Gunther. At the same board meeting, it was announced that the amount due on the War on Crime was then down to $275,583.

April 16, John Ammarell represented TWC at a "Crime Seminar" in New York for large institutional investors. The seminar received a great deal of publicity, including an eight-column story on the financial page of *The Miami News*, and a feature story in the business section of *The New York Times*. That month, George addressed a management group of Trans World Airlines, and his speech, "There is No Substitute for Victory," was enthusiastically received.

At the April board meeting, Victor P. Keay was elected vice president and assistant secretary of TWC. Bob Kirk was promoted to senior vice president, responsible for Operations and Development. At the same meeting, Bud Thompson was named a vice president of Operations and Development. O.E. Wedbush was appointed assistant director of the Physical Security Division, replacing W.T. Lewe, who resigned.

On May 31, TWC purchased National Business Security, Inc., a firm that specialized in retail honesty shoplifting services, and had offices in Dallas and Kansas City in addition to its home office in Oklahoma City. Daniel Gilliam, a former co-owner, became a member of TWC, and the operations of National Business Security became a part of the company's retail protection division. George was featured as a writer in the May 18 issue of *TV Guide*. His story, "Is Mannix for Real?," compared the fictional exploits of the TV detective Mannix with actual investigators in TWC.

According to a twenty-seven page Prospectus published on July 18, 1968, by Francis I. duPont, A.C. Allyn, Inc., George and Ruth Wackenhut offered 75,000 shares of TWC common stock, listed on the American Stock Exchange, at a price to the public of $22.75 per share, for a total of $1,706,250. Following is an excerpt from "The Offering" section of the Prospectus:

> As of May 1, 1968, the issued and outstanding capital stock of the Company consisted of 900,872 shares of Common Stock and 611,130 shares of Class B Stock or an aggregate of 1,512,002 shares of both classes combined. George R. Wackenhut and his wife (the Selling Stock-

holders) own jointly 407,570 shares of Common Stock and all of the outstanding Class B Stock and Mr. Wackenhut individually owns 19,726 shares of Common Stock. Accordingly, prior to this offering, the Selling Stockholders owned 68.7% of the total issued and outstanding stock of both classes combined.

Following the sale of 75,000 shares of Common Stock by the Selling Stockholders in this offering, they will own 611,130 shares of Class B Stock and 352,296 shares of Common Stock (including the 19,726 shares of Common Stock owned by Mr. Wackenhut individually) or 63.7% of the outstanding stock of both classes combined. The Common Stock and Class B Stock vote as a single class for the election of directors and on all other matters (except proposed charter amendments which would adversely affect the rights of either class, as to which approval by a majority vote of each class voting separately is required) and accordingly, except as to matters on which each class votes separately, Mr. Wackenhut and his wife will continue to have voting control of the Company after this offering. . . .

The stock offering was completed on July 25, 1968, when the manager of Francis I. duPont presented George with Cashier's Check No. 561538, drawn on The First National Bank of Miami in the amount of $1,597,500, made payable to "George R. Wackenhut and Ruth J. Wackenhut," representing the proceeds after deduction of underwriting discounts and commissions. This amount, added to the initial public offering of 247,300 shares of common stock, completed on May 3, 1966, produced total net proceeds to George and Ruth of $2,900,180 in just over two years. That week, the company had celebrated its fourteenth anniversary.

In late July, TWC designed the security plans and provided the security forces for the Richard Nixon headquarters at the Hilton Plaza Hotel during the Republican National Convention in Miami Beach, Florida, including around-the-clock service for assisting visitors and controlling the traffic flow. Nixon's personal security was provided by the U.S. Secret Service.

The next quarterly meeting of the board was held at the Dessert Inn, Las Vegas, Nevada, on July 30, 1968. This meeting afforded the board an opportunity to be given a tour of the Nevada Test Site, where Wackenhut Services, Inc., had been providing security since

1965. S. Wesley Reynolds, a former FBI agent, was elected executive vice president of Gor-Buc Security Systems, Inc., a wholly owned subsidiary of TWC. Area offices were opened in Pittsburgh and Baltimore, and James King, an investigator during the War on Crime, was named area manager of the Hartford office.

The quarterly meeting of the board was held at King's Bay on October 28, and it was reported that the company's War on Crime debt had been reduced to $253,286; TWC had been paid $284,320 to date. Directors Tracy, Wright, and Darbaker were appointed to a committee authorized and directed to confer with Governor Kirk about collecting the full payment of the debt.

"Meanwhile, our reputation was spreading in South America as a company which ran a straight, clean operation," George says. "In the fall of 1967, I visited our operation in Bogota, Colombia, and while there met a former FBI agent who was the assistant director of security for the USAID program. At that meeting, he stated that he was being transferred to be head of security for USAID in Quito, Ecuador, very shortly, and asked why we didn't consider opening an office and forming a company there. I told him I would arrange to pay him a visit after he was duly ensconced in Quito.

"In 1968, I made a visit to Quito by way of Bogota, paid a visit to this former agent, and began to look for a partner to join with us in the new venture. My friend with the USAID suggested one Hector Santacruz to be president of our newly formed subsidiary in Ecuador. He has been with the company ever since.

"Three interesting sidelights occurred during that first visit to Quito. When we arrived by plane from Bogota, we were met by members of the Quito police force, one of whom was their public relations officer. He couldn't speak any English and I couldn't speak any Spanish, but nonetheless we got by and did the things we had to do. Leaving the airport, we were whisked away to the Hotel Quito, a very nice hotel, at least in those days, with a beautiful suite overlooking the valley and the mountains. It was then approaching noon, so I suggested that we all have lunch up on the top floor where the restaurant was located. They all agreed, and, with that, I went in to wash my hands. When I turned on the faucet, there was no water.

"One of my executives from Miami, who was an accounting wizard named David Maya, was with us, and David, having originally been from Cuba, spoke the language, of course. So I went out and I said, 'David, call the front desk; there isn't any water.' He called and reported, *'No agua.'* Some more conversation transpired, and after he hung up the phone, he said, 'This is the dry season, and they cut off the water at different hours in the day to conserve it. The water will not be on until about six o'clock this evening.'

"Although all of us felt grubby, we went up to the dining room and had lunch. I proceeded to go about my business, the purpose for which I was there, then returned to the hotel just after six, in time to get a nice shower and dress for dinner, only to find out there *still* was no water. So we reported it again to the front desk, *'No agua,'* and the room clerk said that the water would be turned on around eleven o'clock that night.

"So we went out to dinner, even more grubby than before, and couldn't wait to get back to the hotel room to take a shower. We got back a little bit after eleven, turned on the faucets, and there was *still* no water! At that point, my wife Ruth proceeded to turn on *every faucet in the suite!* There were two bathrooms, two sinks, two showers, two tubs, two lavatories. We went to bed, feeling very uncomfortable. At five o'clock in the morning, we were awakened by a tremendous *roar*, and realized that the water had come on! So we leaped out of bed, as tired as we were, jumped into the bathtubs, and took our baths and showers!

"Having come from Florida, where hurricanes are not unusual events, we thought we would use the trick that they use in Florida when they know there will be no water for a time because of the cut-off of electricity. So, before going out that day, we filled both of our bathtubs with water, as high as it would go. When we returned that afternoon to jump in the bathtubs and have a luxurious bath, we found that the maid had *emptied both bathtubs!* So we went through *that* routine again. Finally, the water did come on at a more reasonable hour and we were able to get washed.

"The following day, we had arranged to meet David Maya in the restaurant for breakfast. We went at the appointed time, and Ruth and I had a nice breakfast, and David didn't show up, and didn't show up. Ruth and I got to talking, and we wondered what happened to him. Finally, David came into the dining room and was obviously as mad as a *wet hen*. He was just so *angry*. But he wouldn't say anything. He sat down, I said, 'Do you want to order?' He grumbled, 'No.' I said, 'David, have I done anything to offend you? What's wrong with you?' He said, 'Well, I'll tell you. I got in the shower, turned on the water, got wet, turned it off, soaped myself up totally, even my hair, turned the water back on—and it had been *shut off!* So there I was, without any clothes, soaped from head to foot, and no water to get rinsed off! I finally managed to get hold of a bellman, who—*for five dollars*—brought me a bucket of water!'

"At the airport in Quito, waiting for our Miami flight to be called, the public relations officer from the police department and I were having a discussion with my interpreter. I said to him, 'On my next visit to Quito, I bet that I will know more words in Spanish than you know in English.' And, through the interpreter, he said, 'That's a fair bet. However, before we can put a bet like that into place, we have to know how much of each other's language we know now, as a starting point.' It's interesting to note that in Ecuador they don't just say, *Sí*, they always say, *Sí-sí-sí*. So I said, 'All right, I'll go first. I know the following words: *No, sí, como no, gracias, no gracias*—and *sí-sí-sí!*' "

IN THE COURSE of the approximate year between the time architect John Volk started on the plans for Tyecliffe and the time he and the Wackenhuts had to appear before the Coral Gables Planning and Zoning Board for approval, they found that they had to submit variances for a number of irregularities. "As I recall, we went before them with requests for thirteen variances," George says, "one of which was to allow us to have three stories, whereas the Coral Gables Building Code allows only two and a half stories, the half-story being defined as what would be an attic space.

"It seemed that everybody in Gables Estates turned out for that hearing. Dick Maloy, my former in-house attorney at the company, was representing us. There didn't seem to be any objection by those in attendance to any of the variances requested."

The Coral Gables Planning and Zoning Board met on Monday,

May 6, 1968. On Wednesday, May 8, the following article appeared in *The Miami Herald* under the by-line of staff writer Mike Petit.

Wackenhut's Home His Castle

As befits Florida's most famous crime sleuth, George Wackenhut will move his family into a Coral Gables mansion that could have come out of the pages of Sherlock Holmes.

Where it came from, however, was the designing board of Palm Beach architect John Volk.

Wackenhut, president of the Wackenhut Corp. detective agency and one-time state investigator for Gov. Claude Kirk, approved the plans that illustrate the saying that a man's home is his castle.

The three-story house, with a facade resembling the best in English manors, will go up along side a boathouse, swimming pool with a waterfall and full-size tennis court in the Gables Estates area east of Old Cutler Road.

In the least, it is comfortable; at best, luxurious.

Though the city's planning department expressed disapproval of the special exception to permit a tennis court, the Coral Gables Planning and Zoning Board voted 5-0 Monday night to approve all 13 architectural modifications.

Volk's design replaced the plan of architect James Dean which failed to win the city's endorsement. Dean's plans included a lavish estate complete with a tower.

When Dean's plans weren't approved, Wackenhut went elsewhere for an architect.

The approved plans will allow Wackenhut to build a residence with 20,000 square feet that includes a dining room, galley, master suite, detached garage, guest suites, recreation rooms and rooms for Wackenhut's son.

The main residence will be three stories high. The average Gables home occupies approximately 2,000 square feet of living space.

A six-foot wall will encircle the parking, pool and patio areas. Two auxiliary buildings with guest and parking facilities will be detached from the main residence.

However, Volk's imaginative plans were not approved for long, due in large measure to an event that occurred Monday, May 27, 1968, and reported in the May 29 issue of *The Miami Herald* by staff writer Susan Miller.

Wackenhut's Castle

Neighbors Whittle His Tower Power

Plans for the luxurious fortress home of Florida's best-known private eye, George Wackenhut, were sent back to the drawing board Tuesday after Wackenhut's new neighbors charged the sleuth with "invasion of privacy."

Coral Gables commissioners voted 3-1 to chop the top off the three-story Wackenhut castle after surrounding property owners in the exclusive Gables Estates area east of Old Cutler Road complained the proposed third-story "belvedere" gave too good a view into their homes.

George Patterson, attorney for Mr. and Mrs. Edward Swenson, of 21 Casuarina Concourse, told commissioners the view from the belvedere, or gabled tower, lets the Wackenhuts "stare down into the patio-pool area" of the Swensons who live 400 feet away.

"He can look right down in the bayside of my home," added J.L. Johnson of 11 Casuarina Concourse. "I don't like the idea of people looking into my home."

Swenson and Johnson said they and other property owners previously agreed to Palm Beach architect John Volk's design for the three-story English manor after Volk assured them it would not violate their privacy.

The Casuarina Concourse residents changed their minds Monday when they looked up to see Mr. and Mrs. Wackenhut towering over them in a "cherry-picker."

The head of the Wackenhut Corp. detective agency and his wife had taken a ride in the tree-top trimming machine to see what the view from their 40-foot-tall tower would look like.

George continues the story, laughing softly. "Then, not too long after that, John Volk, who as I mentioned was from Palm Beach, decided maybe he'd better get a copy of the Coral Gables Zoning Code, so he would know what he was doing. He did, and in going through it, he noticed that a 'story' was defined simply as 'the floor from one level to the floor of the next.' With that definition, he came to me and said, 'Why don't we make the entranceway a *great hall*, two stories high, and we'll put the belvedere on top of that, and that will only be the second story.' So that's what we did. In early June, I was again able to obtain a cherry-picker from the Florida Power and Light Company, raised it to the exact height where the floor of the belvedere was to be, and took motion pictures of all three of the surrounding residences. Bear in mind now, there was no landscaping, so that when the landscaping was in place, it would have been virtually impossible to see any of the places they said we could look into.

"Nevertheless, without the landscaping, the Zoning Board was able to determine that they had no cause for objecting to the height of the belvedere, because, in fact, the motion pictures proved that we could see nothing. However, after the meeting, I told Ruth privately, 'The first piece of furniture we're going to put into the belvedere is a *telescope!*' See what a rise we could get out of them with *that!*

"Since our neighbors could not prevail at the Zoning Board, they filed suit to prohibit us from constructing the belvedere to the approved height."

The lawsuit, which quickly became the *cause célèbre* of gossip columns all over the state that summer, was detailed in a banner headline story, featuring a large picture of the crew-cutted, square-jawed George, in the August 26, 1968, issue of *The Miami News*, written by reporter William Tucker.

Now, About That Tower On Wacken's Hut . . .

Private investigator George Wackenhut said today he would fight all the way a suit by his prospective neighbors to prevent him from building what they consider a "watch tower" on his new house.

"We'll go to court with them," said Florida's best-known private eye, who was Gov. Claude Kirk's "general" in the war on crime until a new state agency took over the job.

"It's a matter of wanting three stories," Wackenhut said. "The Coral Gables Commission approved the design and there's no reason why we should not go ahead with it. There's nothing wrong with it."

Wackenhut said he already changed the design of his new home to be built in the lush Gables Estates area east of Old Cutler Road and even hired a new architect, John Volk, designer of Palm Beach millionaire homes.

But three residents of Casuarina Concourse who would be his immediate neighbors have sued to prevent inclusion of the 40-foot "belvedere" tower in his fortress-like home, which is expected to cost him more than $200,000.

They are James L. Johnson, Edward F. Swenson and R. Kirk Landon. They claim that the tower, providing a view from both the second and third story levels, would let the private eye look down on their patios and pools, the prime relaxation areas of suburban Miami.

They charged in the suit that Wackenhut should have been forced to wait a year after the Gables Commission denied him a variance for the tower. Instead of waiting, Wackenhut went back before the Commission with architect Volk and persuaded it to reverse itself.

They also charged that the Commission failed to give proper notice that the variance denial would be reconsidered.

On May 28, the Commission approved 12 variances for the Wackenhut house but denied one for the three-story tower exceeding the limit of 2 ½ stories for private homes. Wackenhut obtained the reconsideration on June 25.

The neighbors' opposition was solidified in rather dramatic fashion just before the Commission acted for the first time.

A "cherry-picker" used for tree trimming showed up on the property one day and the neighbors looked up to see Mr. and Mrs. Wackenhut peering down from the machine at about the elevation of the proposed tower.

"I need a cherry picker like I need a hole in the head," was Wackenhut's comment on the incident.

He said one of the objecting neighbors, whom he did not name, came up with the idea of the cherry picker and planned to go up in it to appraise the view.

"He didn't show up, so I went up in the picker myself," Wackenhut said.

"The suit was finally settled when I agreed to reduce the level of the floor of the belvedere by one foot and nine inches," George says, smiling, shaking his head. "Which really didn't make any difference. That's how the conflict was resolved."

The Miami Herald had the last word, a short article by Bill Amlong, but carrying a big headline in the November 22, 1968, issue.

Private Eye Lowers His Tower

Private Eye George Wackenhut, whose proposed $500,000 castle on Casuarina Concourse has been under siege by his neighbors, has worked out a truce.

"I hope it is now settled," said Wackenhut, the rock-jawed, silver-haired former general of Gov. Claude Kirk's War on Crime, whose neighbors have staunchly opposed his plans for a Sherlock Holmes-ish manor—complete with belvedere tower—at 20 Casuarina Concourse.

The revised plans call for a tower—but 1 foot, 9 inches shorter and containing only two floors instead of three.

THE CHANGES in the number of floors makes moot a suit filed by three of Wackenhut's neighbors-to-be, who claimed that the Coral Gables City Commission was wrong in granting a zoning variance in August after denying him one in May. The trio charged Wackenhut would have to wait a year before reapplying for the variance to let him build his three-story tower—one story higher than Gables' zoning permits for homes.

"Rather than be tied up in litigation, I had the architect redesign that part of the house," Wackenhut said.

The revision, which trimmed 1 foot, 9 inches from the tower and eliminated the second story in that part of his house, will make the mansion's entrance a "great hall" with a 20-foot ceiling.

WACKENHUT's home will now be built under the zoning permit he got when the commission first approved a dozen variances for his house, but vetoed his plans for the third story.

His neighbors originally complained that the 40-foot belvedere provided too good a view of their patios and back yards.

During 1968, the company opened eight new offices, including Valencia, Venezuela, and Cartagena, Colombia, and added thirteen additional offices through acquisitions. This resulted in a total of seventy-three offices. Revenues reached $36.691 million, an increase of 21 percent over the previous year, and net income rose to $818,-291, an increase of 9 percent. TWC was operating in thirty-five states, the District of Columbia, Puerto Rico, Venezuela, and Colombia, with more than 7,000 employees.

THAT YEAR, the Vietnam War continued to dominate the headlines. On January 30, 1968, the National Liberation Front and North Vietnam launched the infamous "Tet Offensive" against every major city in South Vietnam, including an attack on the U.S. Embassy in Saigon. Although U.S. troops drove them out, and General Westmoreland termed it a "go-for-broke effort" that failed, the Tet Offensive shattered any realistic belief in an approaching U.S. victory in Vietnam among most politicians and the public.

May 31, President Johnson announced he would not seek reelection. This occurred after Senator Eugene McCarthy's strong showing as a peace candidate in the Democratic primaries, Senator Robert Kennedy's decision to enter the Democratic race, and Johnson's own doubts about his Vietnam policy following the Tet Offensive. Johnson ordered a halt to most bombing in Vietnam and asked for negotiations. On April 3, North Vietnam agreed to direct talks with the U.S., which started May 10 in Paris.

April 4, Dr. Martin Luther King was assassinated in Memphis, leading to riots in 125 U.S. cities, with forty-six deaths, 21,270 arrests, and 55,000 federal troops and National Guardsmen used in riot control. June 5, Senator Robert Kennedy was assassinated in Los Angeles, after having won the California primary, which made him the front-runner for the Democratic presidential nomination.

October 31, President Johnson announced a complete halt in the bombing of North Vietnam and the expansion of the Paris peace talks to include the National Liberation Front and the South Vietnamese government. December 14, the U.S. death toll in Vietnam passed 30,000, and U.S. forces there reached a peak of 550,000 men.

EXPANSION of the corporation into a third Latin American country was announced in January 1969, with the formation of Wackenhut del Ecuador, S.A. This new company, a wholly owned subsidiary of TWC, was organized to operate throughout Ecuador from its headquarters in Quito. That January, A. Robert Frye joined TWC, and was appointed director of the Physical Security Division. A former FBI agent, Frye had been a TWA security manager at the Kennedy Space Center.

The annual meeting of the board was held at King's Bay on April 28. It was reported that Verne C. Davis had submitted his resignation as assistant treasurer and that Eugene K. Auerbach, the present auditor-general of the Navy, was retiring and would be available for the position. The board elected Auerbach treasurer, effective July 7, 1969. The directors' committee appointed to confer with Governor Kirk reported that they had met with him on February 9, 1969, in Jacksonville, at which time the governor freely acknowledged that the debt was owed and assured the committee that it would be paid, while not offering any specific plans for payment. At that time, the balance on the debt was $235,300. After consideration of the report, the board directed George to write a letter to the governor asking him to take whatever steps were necessary to collect sufficient funds in order that a substantial payment could be made in the near future. It was also announced that TWC had acquired Interstate Services of Hawaii, Ltd., and Retail Protection, Inc., both located in Honolulu, for a total price of $260,000. Both operations were absorbed into the company's Honolulu office.

"The Managers' Bulletin" was first published on April 30, 1969, and was designed to contain information on personnel changes, company news releases, changes of address and phone numbers of area offices, updates on opening and closing of offices, company happenings from the executive level, new operational methods, information on acquisitions, a synopsis of operational and administrative problem areas, and other appropriate data that would come to headquarters' attention and should be passed on to the managers in an expeditious manner. This publication was an expansion of the "Organizational Changes" memorandum that had been distributed for a number of years.

Jonathan P. Goldsmith, WSI project manager in Las Vegas, was presented with the Atomic Energy Commission's Award of Merit by Robert E. Miller, manager of AEC's Nevada Operations Office. The award was made in recognition of the WSI record of 647,878 man-hours of work without a disabling injury to an employee, between December 23, 1967, and September 28, 1968. Goldsmith had joined WSI in November, 1968, as project manager of the Wackenhut force, replacing Harvey Peters, who had been appointed area manager of TWC's Los Angeles office.

"That summer," George recalls, "I received an invitation from a group of bankers in Brazil, asking me to visit them for a consultation. Their problem was that terrorists were hitting at least a bank a day in Rio and Sao Paulo, concentrating primarily on the branch banks. They hadn't been able to devise a method of preventing these robberies or apprehending the bandits, because much of the branch banking was done from storefronts in rather isolated areas. Complicating the matter was poor telephone service. Before the police could be called, the terrorists—who robbed banks to finance their revolutionary plans—would be long gone. The bankers were frantic to have a system devised whereby the police, or a guard service, could be alerted while a holdup was in progress.

"My idea was that we would install alarm buttons which, by radio frequency, would sound an alarm at guard locations in the various areas that had response capabilities. It was a thought that led us into the electronic security business and perfected our operations in Brazil, where we're still affiliated."

19

CONSTRUCTION ON TYECLIFFE actually started September 1, 1968, although the lawsuit wasn't officially settled until November 21, because pilings had to be driven into the property to support the buildings, which would be situated on landfill that was originally mangrove swampland. That started a process that would last for a period of six and a half years.

George recalls the very early stages. "Of course, as the house proceeded, both Ruth and I—but I in particular—noticed what I considered wasted space. The best example I can think of, one weekend I was down at the property and had walked up the front stairs, the entrance stairs, and looked down. There was a big excavated area down there that was just going to be nothing. So I said, 'Why couldn't we make a wine cellar out of that?' Put another lavatory down there, we could have wine-and-cheese parties, and what have you. They all thought that was a good idea, so that's what we did. So there was reason to do this on a cost-plus basis, because of various changes we made as we went along.

"As the construction was continuing, John Volk approached Ruth and me, and said it was time that we got an interior designer—and he didn't mean interior decorator, he meant interior *designer*—so we could start to give him plans for the actual construction of the interior. We were at an absolute loss at that point, and we said, 'Do you have anyone you can recommend?' He recommended a Mr. Donghia. We met with him a few times and decided that he wasn't grasping exactly what we had in mind.

"We remembered the home on East 84th Street in Manhattan that was occupied by a friend, a very wealthy widow named Lilian Roijtman, and we wondered who had been the interior designer. The late Mr. Roijtman's grandparents were collectors of fine art, and they had a tremendous collection of Old Masters, which they managed to get out of Germany into France. Then, as World War II began and continued to get worse, they managed to get these paintings out of France and into the United States. In the meantime, after graduating from college, Roijtman formed a company that manufactured farm equipment, very much like International Harvester. He was later bought out by another large equipment manufacturer, and received in the neighborhood of $13 million for the sale of the business.

"He then decided he wanted to have a home on Long Island, and purchased some fifty acres of prime real estate on the Island. He and Lilian were in the process of building their home, and, when it was within roughly three weeks of completion, it caught fire and burned to the extent that it was beyond repair. While the home was under construction, they had purchased this townhouse on East 84th, which was a five story row house in a very exclusive area of Manhattan. What they decided was to just stay in the townhouse, and he would convert what was left of the home they had built on the Island into an office and research area for his continued work.

"During that period of time, he had developed a locking device with an alarm. He had developed this because, while living in the townhouse, he would come down in the morning to get his newspaper and, without thinking, would open the front door, and the silent alarm he had would be monitored by the alarm company. Next thing he knew, there would be armed guards arriving at the door. So he decided there should be some better arrangement. With his new locking device, anybody who tried to force the door open would set off an alarm.

"It looked like a real good thing, and Morris Goldstein, our financial advisor and later a director of the board, invited us to take a look at it. So Ruth and John Ammarell and I went up to New York and, together with Morris Goldstein, visited Lilian in the townhouse. A short time before that, her husband had passed on.

"The townhouse they renovated, a five-story walkup, they converted to authentic eighteenth-century French décor. It was absolutely like a museum, it was so beautifully done. She even had the authentic desk of Marie Antoinette. Throughout the house, where painting was done in grooves, it was done by finger, because that's the way it was done in France during that period. She had an exact replica of a bank vault on her lower level, and at that time she stored in the vault Old Masters and other paintings valued collectively at $25 million. She also had paintings on every wall, every staircase, all of which had been left to her husband, whose parents and grandparents had obtained these things for a song, back in the old days.

"Anyway, that's the background on how we knew Lilian, and how we respected her and her taste. As we came in, at the street level, she had all her staff lined up in uniform. That was really quite impressive. So, knowing her, and not knowing what to do about an interior designer, Ruth finally called her."

"I called Lilian," Ruth remembers, smiling. "I said, 'You've got to help me with something. I need an interior designer who can understand what I want to do here.' She said, 'I've got just the person, Ernest Bonammy, the man who designed my townhouse.' I called his firm, Kahn and Jacobs, in New York. I spoke to the senior partner, introduced myself by way of my friend, and he said, 'Well, send up your present plans and I'll review them.' I said, 'No way. *You* send *me* Ernest Bonammy.'

"Ernest Bonammy arrived. I went to the airport and here was this very charming Frenchman who could hardly speak English. But we could communicate. Of course, as we worked longer together, he started to use more English words. When we arrived at the job site, I had four trailers parked along the street, the kind they use on location for movies. I should have *bought* them. I was *renting* them. I would have *owned* them! I paid rent on those things for eight years. Anyway, I said, 'Ernest, I'm thinking of a color, and I'm going to put it down on a piece of board. I'd like you to go over there and mix the same color that I'm thinking of.' I either said 'orange' or 'midnight blue,' I don't know what color I said, but I gave him a color. I mixed it, he mixed it, and we compared our colors. They were *identical!* I said, 'You're hired.'

"He was the most charming man I've ever met in my life. He

started as a bricklayer in Paris at the age of eight. Not a bricklayer—*making* bricks. His life was absolutely fantastic. Drawings that would look like Picasso or Monet. He was unbelievable. I absolutely adored him and he had great respect for me. I felt quite honored. This man had renovated castles in Europe. He built the Government House in Bermuda. He worked on many wonderful projects. One day, he said to me, 'Wooth, Wooth, seet, seet down, I moost talk to you.' He took my hand and he said, 'Where? Where did you learn this?' I said, 'Learn what, Ernest?' He said, 'You see my books, all my books? Every time you say something to me, I open a book. You don't open a book!' I said, 'It's up here, it's in my head.' He said, 'I am amazed how you have such ability without training.' He said, 'We should go into *beesnoos* together!' I said, 'Ernest, nobody could have given me a bigger compliment; I feel honored that you would say this to me.'

"His wife passed away. One day he came to me, he said, 'I am in *luff,* I am in *luff!*' At that time, I guess he was sixty or seventy. I said, 'Oh, Ernest, that's wonderful!' He said, 'You know, I am French, and we French gentlemen must have a lady. We have so much *luff* to give!' We were having dinner at the house on 122nd Street, and he said, 'You must *help* me!' I said, *'How?'* He said, 'There are three women. One leeves in New York, one leeves in Paris, and one leeves in Miami. You must help me wheech one I marry.' I said, 'No-no. No-no, Ernest, I'm not going to get into *that.*' I said, 'By the way, how old are they?' He gave me the age of the one in Paris, who was *very* wealthy, but the oldest. He gave me the age of the one in New York, who was wealthy, but a little younger. Then he told me the age of the one in Miami—and mentioned her *curves!* She was about thirty-two at the time. So, I was convinced that was the one he was going to pick, but I didn't say anything. And, of course, that's the one he did pick.

"She was Italian, and he wanted me to meet her before they got married. I thought she was a charming woman, she had a nice personality, she looked and acted a lot more than thirty-two. But I thought: I don't know if this is doing to work. He told me they were going to Bermuda for their honeymoon. I said, 'Now, listen. You take care. I don't want something happening to you. I *need* you! You come back to me!' He said, 'I come back, don't worry, I come back.' He came back beaming from ear to ear. He said the only problem he had on his honeymoon, he kept slipping around in the *satin sheets!*

"I would say to Ernest, 'I want beamed ceilings, I want this shape, I want brick walls, I don't want the brick to look like brick, I want them washed, I want this, I want that.' He would make his French notes, he would do some quick sketches, and his sketches would look like complete artwork. A lot of time, I insisted on certain things, and he would say, 'No-no-no, *no-no-no,* we can't do that!' I would say 'We *can* do it!' He would say, 'It hasn't been done!' I would say, 'We can do it.' He would say, 'All right, all right, let me theenk, let me theenk.' Then he'd come back: 'We can *do eet!* We can *do eet!*'

"What was so wonderful about him, when he really felt I was getting a little carried away—and I can get carried away—he'd say, '*No,* that's too much, that's too much, you don't do that!' I would say, 'Then we calm it down, but I want this *feel.*' So that's how we worked together. And then, sometimes he would look at me, and he'd say, 'Come, come.' It would be getting dusk. He'd take my hand and he'd say, 'Now, you need to clear your mind. I want you to look up at the sky. Now I want you to look around.' And he would just unravel me, just like that.

"Well, it got so, he didn't care if he ever went home to his new wife. Because I was so enthusiastic about building, it was his love, and he was so artistic, and he gave me so many compliments, and encouraged me to go even further with so many things, that it was just wonderful being with him. But his wife became *insanely* jealous. Now, I was older than the wife. And I told her, 'This is absolutely ridiculous. I have all *I* can handle with a *German* husband, who's much younger than *your* husband!' I said, 'We are *working!*' But I think she had pangs of jealousy because of our common interests. So I said, 'I want you to do something for me. Ernest loves French food, and you're giving him Italian food. Go to a French class and learn how to cook French food, and you'll see how fast he comes home.' And, you know, it *worked!*"

The cornerstone-laying ceremony was January 25, 1969. "We had a big party," George recalls, "a tent with a dance floor, a dance band, and Ruth arranged to have a pirate ship from some movie set come down behind the house and land at our dock. It was called the Pirate Party. We had lots of people there, maybe 300, and Governor Kirk was there. Joan McHale of *The Miami News* did a fairly big story on that party. I stood on what's now the first landing, as you come up either side of the front entrance, and gave a talk. I had so much fun with Ralph Kiel, writing this talk. Among other things, I had a piece of paper with some numbers on it, and I said, 'This was the original price of the house.' Then I had a computer printout that just rolled out and out and out, and I said, 'This is the *revised* cost of the house!' We had a lot of laughs. We put those papers in the cornerstone, and some odds and ends and trinkets, but anything that was worth keeping, I kept. There was no date on the cornerstone, but I've got a gold-plated spike that one of the attendees at the party gave me, it was supposed to go in the cornerstone, but I kept it, and it had the date of the party."

Jan recalls that party clearly: "Tresha was born December 14, 1968. Then, on January 25, 1969, Mother and Dad had their cornerstone party for the new house. I remember, because that was the first time I left Tresha. That was one of the most fabulous parties I'd ever been to. Where the tennis courts are now was all tented—dance floor, band. The main steps were there, where the time capsule was put in, and part of the main building. They had a pirate's ship in the bay. Mother was fabulous at parties and themes and putting it all together. It was quite an affair."

The Miami News devoted a full page to the party, including six excellent candid photos by Sal Crisanti, in its issue of Tuesday afternoon, January 28, under the by-lines of reporters Ian Glass and Joan McHale.

Roger Jolly And So Was the Crew . . . At Wacken's Hut

The safest place to be last Saturday evening was No. 20 Casuarina Concourse, an establishment that could be termed the wackiest hut in the Gables.

It was just ALIVE with security officers, with the result that all of the 400 invited guests felt terribly, well, you know, secure, and nobody was robbed . . . mostly because they left their jewelry at home.

The scene was the four-acre estate of George Wackenhut, the fellow who provides guards for all those nervous establishments and who also directed Gov. Claude Kirk's war on crime for a bit. You'd better believe the employees were on their toes. It rained all evening, but they refused to admit they were wet.

Well. The occasion was that George, or Russ as he is known to his friends—and count us in, Russ—was laying the cornerstone of his controversial $1 million house (off Old Cutler Road) which should be ready for occupancy by next Christmas. (You DO remember all that horrid business of the neighbors objecting because Russ and Ruth wanted to build a big tower on the house, and finally the Coral Gables building department ruled they couldn't? We were sure you did.)

Everybody was invited to dress as a pirate and, by Jim Hawkins, they did. It looked like a benefit for the city's costume shops, which rent these things out at $25 a throw.

Russ wore a black top, gold bottoms, an eye patch, and carried a stuffed parrot on his shoulder called Chip. Ruth looked fabulous in silver lame dress with silver boots and wore a cavalier hat with blue feathers—which absolutely DISTRESSED her hairdresser, honestly.

It really was fun. The whole thing was held in a circus tent. There were a half-dozen bartenders (one of whom looked distressingly like LBJ), two bands and a limbo dancer. The tent stood on the site of what will be the tennis courts. Honestly, the Wackenhuts haven't left out a thing.

The pad is composed of three structures—a recreation building, the main house, and the living quarters. Actually, there are only four bedrooms, but you can't have everything.

Gov. Kirk popped in early, which was nice.

There was a funny ceremony at which Russ buried a time capsule ("to be dug up in a hundred years") in the foundations. These included plans for the tower; revised plans for the tower; a list, yards long, of local objectors; an IOU from Kirk (the governor, that old Claude, owes Wackenhut something like a quarter-of-a-million dollars for his war on crime services); the bill from his lawyer ("Which reminds me," shouted Dick Maloy. "When do I get my check?") and the zoning restriction decision from the city of Coral Gables.

Architect John Volk was there, and muttered the remark of the evening (well, Saturday evening, anyway). "It isn't every day you build a million-dollar home," he said.

Appropriately, Russ had a gorgeous 60-foot pirate ship tied up to his berth. He had borrowed it from Jack McGowen, who had brought it over from Nassau. Not that he was trying one-upmanship or anything like that, but Russ announced he was trading his 50-foot boat—Security Risk—for a 90-foot one, which is called, hold your breath, Top Secret.

Russ and Ruth had sent invitations to the immediate neighbors, but none turned up. Oh, well, you can't have everybody. Two of them snubbed it grandly by taking off for South America. Another turned her sprinklers on and barricaded her driveway. It is only a rumor she hired the Andy Frain service for the evening.

One nasty Democrat there swore Saturday night's caper would set the Wackenhuts back at least $30,000, but Russ said it had better not be a penny over $12,000.

In the late summer of 1968, George contacted a well-known naval architect, Jack B. Hargrave, of West Palm Beach. "In a discussion with Hargrave," he recalls, "we explained what type of a yacht we would like designed, with the thought in mind of the depth of the water and the waterways here. We were not anxious to go ocean cruising, except over to the Bahamas and that sort of thing. About the most we could get in length, to have a draft that would be satisfactory for these waters, would be ninety feet. After the plans were prepared and approved, Hargrave took a trip to Europe and visited two Dutch and one German yacht yard. And, upon his recommendation, we selected the de Vris Lentsch yard in Amsterdam."

Hargrave had met George's specifications for a motor yacht ninety feet in length (later expanded to 104 feet), with a twenty-two-foot beam, and a draft of seven feet six inches. It would have a welded steel hull with quarter-inch plating, two and one-half inch teak decks over steel, and a welded aluminum pilothouse and bridge. The engines would be twin Caterpillar D343TA diesels, six cylinder 460 horsepower, fresh-water cooled, twin disc reduction gears, three-to-one ratio, and underwater exhaust amidships. Fuel capacity would be 6,000 U.S. gallons. Speed/consumption would range from 10.5 knots at 1,200 rpm to 14.5 knots at 2,100 rpm maximum.

Ruth and George would name the yacht *Top Secret*, and the two seventeen-foot runabout launches were named *Cloak* and *Dagger*.

The interior décor was created, designed, and supervised by Ruth, working with her favorite interior designer Ernest Bonnamy. Following is an excerpt from a Florida yacht broker's specification sheet that was written many years after the yacht was finished, when George put the craft up for sale at $3.5 million:

> GALLEYS: Main galley is located below, just forward of the engine room. The finish is primarily stainless steel. Inventory of equipment includes toaster oven, commercial refrigerator and freezer, Toastmaster commercial eight-burner, two-oven electric stove, lighted vent hood, stainless steel sink with disposal, combination washer and dryer, electric dumbwaiter to the pantry on the main deck.
>
> The pantry is located just forward of the dining salon on the main deck. Equipment inventory includes commercial stainless steel refrigerator, icemaker, General Electric dishwasher, double stainless steel sink with disposal, Thermador two-burner counter-top electric range, Toastmaster two-drawer warmer, abundance of cupboard storage.
>
> ACCOMMODATIONS: Luxurious accommodations for six to eight in the owner's party, plus five crew. The interior displays unique craftsmanship, utilizing a number of unique materials: lead, stone, pewter, granite, fine ash and teak woods. The décor invokes a feeling of strength and sets forth a Viking theme.
>
> Below decks are three staterooms, each elegantly decorated. The walls are of rich irregularly planked ash, individually studded with wooden pegs. All fixtures and hardware are handcrafted in lead, pewter, brass or ash, and from original designs. The ceilings are cowled in suede panels separated by intricately carved beams. The rich neutral hues complete the romance and harmony for the staterooms.
>
> The owner's stateroom is the full width of the ship. Located athwartship from the port bulkhead is the kingsize bed featuring an ash plaque with brass reading lamps on either side of the headboard. There are deep hand-carved drawers, abundant storage, built-in vanity with drawers and cabinets, plus walk-in closets designed for optimum storage. All hardware is pewter. The primary art form located on the forward bulkhead is an exquisite mosaic work depicting a man and woman on the beach in a Norwegian fjord, where their Viking longboat rests nearby.
>
> The private adjoining bath features hand-painted Rocky Mountain quartz panels. Inlaid intricate mosaic works and a random-pattern slate floor exists throughout the bath. Centered is the "his and her" wash

stand. The sinks, back splash and fixtures are pewter. Stained glass, brass fixtures and pewter hardware are but a few of the exciting appointments.

Aft to port is a double guest stateroom with twin lower berths, a private bath and shower featuring a Tennessee Crab Orchard stone floor to complement the suite. A cleverly hidden "Murphy style" bed hides away, allowing a greater measure of space, and can be easily pulled out when needed. Generous storage is achieved with the built-in drawers and lockers. The same fine use of ash wood, suede cloth and distinct metals accentuate this stateroom.

The second guest stateroom is located opposite, to starboard, featuring a built-in double bed, offering drawers underneath. A built-in dressing table is accentuated by a three-way mirror, cabinetry, shelves and drawers, thus creating a useful dressing area. The private connecting head is in the same tasteful decor as the port guest head. A large hideaway is accessible via a door in the starboard guest shower. There is a built-in platform with an upholstered mattress and a storage chest. The area provides accommodations for extra guests when necessary.

A spiral staircase leads up to the main salon. A large, built-in, U-shaped lounge occupies the entire port bulkhead. The color scheme is pleasant neutral tones. A driftwood coffee table, made from an oak plank from an 1880 schooner, sits in front of the lounge. Hand-carved ash beams form square ceiling panels covered with suede cloth. On the end of each beam is a carved gargoyle head. The walls are panelled in irregularly planked ash, and the floor is planked ash.

The dining salon is forward and separated from the main salon by an open arch. The walls and floor are ash, as in the main salon. An original-design chandelier, made of pewter and stained glass, highlights the room. Two built-in buffets with hammered lead tops, located port and starboard, provide storage as well as serving areas. The forward bulkhead is a magnificent hand-carved replica of a scene from an old French tapestry depicting the Battle of Hastings in 1066. All hardware on drawers and cabinets is brass. The unique dining table will seat six and is custom made of carved ash. A service pantry is located forward.

The aft deck lounge and bar invites comfortable entertaining. This area is panelled in teak. Attention is drawn to a U-shaped, carved-ash bar with the specially designed carved-ash stools. The overhead beams are hand-carved. Walls are random planked, as are the cabinet and doors of the back bar. The back bar houses a refrigerator, icemaker and liquor storage. Two large built-in teak settees are each located port and starboard. The bar top and front insets are made of hammered lead. Forward to the main salon, via double doors with inset stained-glass windows, is a scene of the Viking invasion of northeastern England in 1066. The door handles are hand-carved ivory. The aft cockpit, with its teak deck, is an ideal private sun lounge. A large lazarette is under the sun lounge and features a special luggage storage area as well as space for extra equipment. The upper sun deck is reached by a circular teak stairway from the aft lounge. A permanent enclosure and forward wind screen afford comfort and privacy.

The den is located all the way forward and is panelled in irregularly planked ash. Running the width of the room forward is a built-in buffet which houses the color television and stereo equipment. The stereo system is piped throughout the boat. To starboard is a built-in desk. An adjoining powder room is located to port. The color scheme is in pleasant neutral tones.

The raised pilothouse access is just forward of the dining salon via a curved stairway. There is an observation lounge with a table located aft. Visibility is excellent with all navigational equipment and controls well placed for easy access. Port and starboard doors lead to the wraparound bridge deck and to the boat deck area.

Lower deck entry is from the companionway which also provides access to the pantry and den. A stairway to starboard of this den leads to the main galley which occupies the full width of the ship. Engine room access is aft and crew access forward. Under the steps to the crew quarters is a wine, liquor and food storage area adequate for provisioning a long voyage. This area also houses a large built-in freezer.

Crew's quarters provide birthing for five. To port lies the Captain's cabin with a private adjoining head and shower. Crew's lounge features a semicircular seating area with a large dining table, china storage and built-in color television. Forward are berths for four with their own head and shower area.

20

THE YOUNG CADET in the black-and-white photograph looks out at us from page 125 of *The Sphinx*, the yearbook of The Citadel, a formal head-and-shoulders portrait, full-face, and he is wearing a gray uniform with a high collar and polished brass buttons. His short hair is dark, parted to the left, worn low over the high forehead, and the face is oval. Despite the serious set of the thin lips and strong chin, he looks almost childlike, although he was twenty-one and the year was 1969. The three-line inscription under the photograph reads simply: "Richard R. Wackenhut, *Political Science*, Miami, Fla." Only ninety-four years had passed since his great-grandfather Johannes posed for a similar photograph, wearing his similar Prussian Army uniform in Stuttgart at age eighteen in 1875, and only eighty-eight years had passed since he imigrated to the United States in 1881, virtually penniless, to become a machinist in the Philadelphia Navy Yard. Three generations later, the Wackenhut graduating from The Citadel was the son of a multimillionaire.

Rick remembers those undergraduate years as among the most difficult of his life, but he emerged from that strict academic and military environment with very strong disciplinary values that he would retain for the rest of his life. He also developed many strong friendships that would endure—and some that would not.

"Handfuls of students come to mind," he says. "One of my very early roommates, fellow named Joe Eubanks, who was subsequently killed in Vietnam, was probably one of my idols, academically, because he was a very good student. I was one of his idols, physically, because I taught him—he was kind of a real thin type of a guy—and I lifted a lot of weights at that time. He wanted me to teach him how to lift weights, and I did, and he started building a little bit of bulk on him, and he was really proud of that. So we admired each other and learned from each other. When I heard that he had been killed in Vietnam, it was a very sad day. I believe he was killed in 1970 or 1971, shortly after graduation.

"Another fellow, named Christopher Clearwaters, who achieved cadet rank of lieutenant colonel, and was a cadet battalion commander, was probably one of the few on battalion staff who was not an asshole. He was a regular guy, he was a good friend, he was well liked by everyone, and yet he maintained a military bearing, maintained his academics and everything, and he was killed there also.

"So, those were some of the sad parts. A very good friend of mine, with whom I'm still in contact, named Varn Pratt Hambright III, he just went by Pratt Hambright, and Pratt is now working for the state up in North Carolina, in this general field, in an investigative capacity. Prior to that, he had two or three camera stores that fell on hard times with the economy. But I remember him so much, not only because we would double-date some of the Charleston girls and stuff, but he won what was called the Star of the West award. Star of the West was a competition that was held among all the cadets. It was a weapons drill. In effect, you would have to be standing at attention, and it would start out with maybe a hundred cadets who would try out for this. They would all be in full-dress uniform with a rifle. A command would be given—and, of course, there were monitors going all through this—a command would be given, something like, 'Right shoulder arms!' So you'd go to a right shoulder arms position. Then it would be, 'Port arms!' Then it would be 'Parade rest!' You know, all the different commands that would be given with rifles. If anyone made any slight flinch or change or did it incorrectly—out. They were eliminated from the competition. So you had to be absolutely pristine in every one of your movements.

"It went down to two people, and Pratt was one of them, and after about half an hour or more of drill, of both of them doing everything in absolute precision, the other guy made a mistake, and Pratt won the Star of the West medal. He's the only cadet, before or since, who's ever won it two years in a row."

Since he did not earn a commission upon graduation, Rick received a draft notice in 1970, and immediately applied for a direct commission in the Army's Military Police Corps. He was turned down at that time, because President Nixon had ordered a cutback, which was a disappointment. "I then enlisted in the Air Force, and made an effort to get into OSI, Office of Special Investigations," he says. "After basic training in the Air Force, at Lackland Air Force Base, San Antonio, Texas, I got into OSI, and was assigned to Washington, DC, in June of 1970."

BUD THOMPSON was executive vice president of Operations when George and Ruth were working on the new house and the yacht, 1969–1974, and provides intriguing insights and anecdotes. "I was in Operations when George was building the house," he says, "and during the six or so years that he built that house, he was more involved in the house and the boat than he was in the company.

"Those were the times when I think he and I probably had more problems, at the end of that, than any other time in my twenty years in the company. Because when he came back from being involved in all that, one day he called me in, and we were talking on something, I don't know what it was, but he said to me: 'You're too powerful in this company. You're running the company.' And I said to him, 'You're gone, somebody's got to make the decisions.' I mean, I'd kept him informed every chance, but he would be in the office one day and out two, and never seen, and when he was in, he was on the phone to Holland or he was on the phone to something or other. And I would sit down with him and go over what was happening. We increased up to 100 offices during my time in there, all over the country, not counting our foreign operations, thirteen offices across Canada, offices in the Dominican Republic, offices in Puerto Rico, which we were up 1,600 employees in Puerto Rico. We were in Colombia, Ecuador, Brazil, Venezuela. And, I mean, I was executive vice president of Operations, worldwide operations. He didn't like it, because he came back and things were running, and things were doing, and I think he kind of felt maybe left out or something, I don't know. I know I had some detractors in there that would like to stick their knife in me when they could, but, you know, what do you do? I got to do what I'm supposed to do.

"Anyway, he told me that, and he proceeded then to try to get in a position where these people were not really coming to me, he wanted to have more influence. He moved the five vice presidents that we had around the country, who ran districts of the country, he moved them into headquarters, and I told him that he would lose them all, and he said, 'No, they'll come.' I said, 'No, they won't. They'll tell you they'll come, but they won't come.' And they didn't. They told him they were coming, and never did. We lost all of them. It was not a very good thing, but George is a one-on-one person, he does best when he can sit down and talk to you across the table. He doesn't like it as well—he does okay—but he doesn't like it as well when he's got ten people out there.

"There was one thing that I think made him that way. There was an effort made, in the early days of the company, when we first moved out to the Gables, where there were a number of guys that went to him and said, 'We want you to give us parts of the company.' And it was a conspiracy. Ammarell and I were not involved. We were on the other side. They called me 'the office fink,' they wouldn't put me in on the thing, because I was very loyal to George, and I would not—I didn't think that was right, what they were trying to do. One of them told George, 'I'm not here to build a memorial to you.' And that's the kiss of death in George, you just don't do those things.

"But, anyway, that conspiracy, George just told them, you know, 'I haven't worked my ass off all these years to give away my company. You'll have opportunities to buy stock in the company when we become a public company, but you're not going to be the ones to tell me what to do with my company.' And they all, within a month or two, most all of those guys were gone. But it was a conspiracy. And I think George, from that time on, never felt comfortable with a bunch of people who may become too powerful in their place. And I think he, all through the years after that, did everything he could do to keep from that type of thing ever being able to come to the surface again. He would not trust a group. I don't blame him.

George is no philanthropist, he doesn't give anything away, and I can understand his way of being, at that point, but I do think that it could've been done a lot different. But, anyway, it caused him, I think, to change, and never again put himself in that kind of a position."

IN THE SUMMER of 1969, Gor-Buc Security Systems, Inc., which had operated as a wholly owned subsidiary of TWC since its acquisition in 1967, became a division of the corporation. It was called the Loss Prevention Division and continued to be headed by S. Wesley Reynolds as vice president. Its operations continued as in the past specializing in preventive security programs designed to fit specific needs of clients.

Six new area managers were named in the autumn. Among them were three who were promoted from other positions in the company, including J. E. "Ed" LeBlanc, who was named area manager in San Francisco; Arthur C. McPhail, area manager in Jacksonville; and Darrell G. Swezey, area manager in the new office in Portland. In addition, three new men joined the company: Paul G. Zarynoff, named area manager in Washington, D.C.; Stephen Horton, area manager in Orlando; and Peter L. O'Neill, area manager in New York City. The latter two men were former FBI agents.

The quarterly meeting of the board was held at King's Bay on October 27, 1969. B.E. Gorrill was elected vice president, Development, and Ralph Kiel was elected vice president, Public Relations. George advised that the amount due on the War on Crime debt was then approximately $192,000. He said that $35,000 had been received from Governor Kirk as payment on the debt since the last board meeting.

A special meeting of the executive committee of the board was held on December 29, at which time it was decided to acquire the assets and liabilities of Bonded Audit Services, Inc., of Greely, Colorado, for $50,000. The firm was merged into TWC's National Business Security Division.

The year 1969 closed with total revenues of $48.458 million, an increase of 32 percent over the previous year. Net income rose 71 percent and totalled $1.447 million, to produce record earnings of $.95 per share. The results represented TWC's most successful year to date, and, because it came on the company's fifteenth anniversary, the figures proved conclusively that significant corporate goals could be set and achieved. It had taken the company ten years to produce revenues of $10.8 million in 1964, and only five years to jump to $48.458 million in 1969. The year was one of consolidation. Although TWC opened nineteen new offices in 1967, and acquired and opened twenty-one offices in 1968, it opened only two new offices in 1969. One of those was the new area office in Portland, which helped the company expand into the northwest. The second was a branch office on Miami Beach. TWC ended the year with a total of seventy offices, because, through consolidation and effecting greater economy and operating efficiency, it was able to combine some offices and improve operations.

During the later part of 1969, TWC also began work on the formation of a wholly owned subsidiary in Brazil, called Wackenhut do Brazil, S.A. Established in Rio de Janeiro, this subsidiary was officially incorporated on February 16, 1970. It was the outgrowth of the trip that George had made in 1969 at the request of a group of bankers who needed increased security against bank holdups and other types of thefts.

HISTORICALLY, on January 20, 1969, Richard Milhous Nixon was sworn in as the nation's thirty-seventh president. In March, the U.S. Air Force started fourteen months of secret bombings of Cambodia, a recognized neutral country; President Nixon bypassed the chain of command when requesting the bombings. May 15, Supreme Court Judge Abe Fortas resigned after an article in *Life* magazine revealed that he had received a $20,000 fee from the foundation of Louis Wolfson, a man convicted of selling unregistered securities.

On the evening of July 18, Senator Edward Kennedy drove his car off a bridge on Chappaquiddick Island, off Martha's Vineyard, Massachusetts, an accident that killed his twenty-eight-year-old companion, Mary Jo Kopechne; Kennedy did not report the accident until the following morning. July 20, Astronaut Neil Armstrong became the first human being to walk on the moon; he said: "That's one small step for a man, one giant leap for mankind."

August 16–19, more than 300,000 young people gathered on a 600-acre farm near Woodstock, New York, to hear rock music. *The New York Times* editorialized: "The dreams of marijuana and rock music that drew 300,000 fans and hippies to the Catskills had little more sanity than the impulses that drive the lemmings to march to their deaths in the sea. They ended in a nightmare of mud and stagnation that paralyzed Sullivan County for a whole weekend. What kind of culture is it that can produce so colossal a mess?"

October 15 was proclaimed Vietnam Moratorium Day, and millions of Americans demonstrated in their towns and cities against the Vietnam War. Vice President Spiro Agnew said that the demonstrations were "encouraged by an effete corps of snobs who characterized themselves as intellectuals." November 15, more than 250,000 people gathered in Washington to protest the Vietnam War. As demonstrators marched past the White House, President Nixon and close friend Charles "Bebe" Rebozo watched a televised football game.

November 16, the U.S. media published the first reports of the My Lai massacre.

December 4, Chicago Black Panther leader Fred Hampton was shot dead by police as he slept. Subsequently, it was reported that the Panthers' chief of security was actually a police officer acting under the direction of the FBI. In early 1968, the FBI initiated a program against the Panthers called "Cointelpro" (counterintelligence program) that was ordered by J. Edgar Hoover and operated out of forty-one FBI field offices nationwide.

That year, a total of sixty-five airplanes were hijacked in the United States.

GEORGE laughs when he remembers one evening and the following day in the summer of 1970, when Jan was twenty-five and Tresha was two: "It was a Friday evening in the summertime. The phone rang and it was Jan: *'My house is on fire!'* I said, 'Dear God! I'll be right there!' We lived only about five minutes away. So I said to Ruth,

'Call the fire department—Jan says her house is on fire!' I got down there on about two wheels, ran inside, and Jan said, 'It's not all that bleak. What I'd done, I'd left eggs on the stove to hard-boil, and I forgot I'd left them there, and I went out. By the time I got back, the fire ate through the aluminum pan and the house was full of smoke that had a terrible smell from the eggs and the aluminum.'

"We had a chef with us then who was an elderly Frenchman. Ruth said to him, 'Come on, we've got to go down to Jan's house!' They raced over there, and as they got to an intersection where they would turn right, the fire engines were coming in the opposite direction, and they turned the wrong way. So Ruth said to the chef, 'Turn around, they're going the wrong way, we've got to get them!' So they finally caught up to the fire engines and brought them to Jan's house. And with that, Jan looked out the window and said, 'What's going on?' I said, 'Well, Mom called the fire department because you said your house was on fire.' Jan said, 'Oh, my God, I've got to get some *makeup* on!' I said, *'Makeup?'* She said, 'Yes, that fireman running up the walk, *I went to high school with him!*' So she went and got some makeup on, and they came in, and I said, 'The emergency is over,' and told them what happened.

"That night, it was summer, it was hot, so she had the air conditioning on, and this damn acrid smoke had gone away, but the smell was still there, and Tresha inhaled this all night long. Anyway, the next day, Tresha was out playing, and she came in. Our phone rang again and it was Jan: *'Tresha is dying!'* Two days in a row now, Friday night and Saturday afternoon. I said, 'What do you mean she's *dying?*' She said, 'Well, her temperature is below normal, she's all clammy, she's got a terrible headache, she's listless, she can hardly move!' I said, 'I'll be right down there.' So I raced down, got Tresha and Jan into my car, raced to South Miami Hospital, and into the Emergency Room. Well, if you have an emergency, never go to the Emergency Room, because it takes forever to get treated.

"They laid her on a couch, it was like an Army cot. We waited for what seemed like an eternity. Finally, a doctor came in and looked at her and said, 'What's the problem?' Jan gave him the symptoms that she had. The doctor said, 'Sounds like an insect bite. Were you bitten by an insect of any kind—by a bee?' Trisha didn't say anything. So the doctor said, 'Well, let me take care of some other things, I'll be back as soon as I can.'

"An eternity passed. I was running around, saying, 'Where's the *doctor?* This is my *granddaughter* and she needs *help!*' So, finally, he came back, and he sat down at the foot of the couch. He said, 'Tresha, how do you feel?' She said, 'It hurts.' He said, 'What hurts?' She said, 'My *foot!*' He said, 'Is that where the bee stung you?' She said, 'No, you're *sitting* on it!' "

RICK AND MOLLY were married in the beautiful Summerall Chapel at The Citadel in Charleston on Saturday, March 13, 1971, while he was still serving in the Air Force's Office of Special Investigations, and stationed in Washington. Molly laughs when she recalls the rehearsal party: "At the rehearsal party the night before, that was a big splash, it was held at the Mills Hyatt House. It was an old building that had been redone into a hotel, and they did a beautiful job. Rick's mother brought in a Bahamian band, palm trees, sand, coconuts, local dancers to act like they were Bahamian dancers, which was kind of fun, and we drank rum punches out of coconuts. There probably were some tropical birds there! I mean, it was just *wild!* She's really talented for giving parties and making a big splash. It was tons of fun.

"At the wedding in the Summerall Chapel, what I can remember of the Chapel, it was massive, beautiful, handsomely carved stone, but it felt warm. Stained-glass windows, beautiful altar, as I remember, with a lot of beautiful wood, and big granite floors. It felt like a very old place, even though it wasn't that old. It's situated in the center of the quadrangle, across from Rick's barracks, so as he came out of his barracks, he would see it. It's nondenominational, of course, because it has to service the whole corps of cadets. Our ceremony was Episcopal. We had three ministers officiating: We had to have Sidney Crumpton, who was the minister for the corps of cadets, and they used to call it 'Simple Sidney's Sunday Circus.' You know, the doddering old military kind of a minister. And then John Ball, who is my cousin, an Episcopal minister, along with Fred

Sosnowski, who is another Episcopal minister who my family had been connected with through St. Phillip's.

"We had an organist, a friend of the family, we had a very traditional wedding march. Rick's best man was John Richards, who is *still* his best friend. I would guess there were about 300 people there. Jan and John were there with Tanya and Tresha, and Nana, and Bev, his Aunt Bev, she was alive at that time. John Thorsen's parents also came. It was a lovely wedding. Our reception was just off campus, in the Alumni House of The Citadel, which is an old brick building, real pretty, upstairs and downstairs."

"Everyone was trying to find out where we were going to spend our first night," Rick recalls. "For obvious reasons, to play tricks on us. So we zoomed off, outraced a number of cars, and finally got away. And we ended up going right back to the *hotel*, which was the last place they'd look, and parked on the roof, and stayed in the Alumni House, the same hotel where everybody else was staying that night! But, as it turned out, it was a mistake, because we wanted to go to the reception party downstairs, because we could *hear* it all night!"

The following day, they left for Puerto Rico, staying two weeks at the Hotel El San Juan, and enjoyed a relaxed and memorable honeymoon, filled with humorous anecdotes. "I remember one story," Molly says. "We went to the Hunka-Munka Room in the hotel, it was the local night spot, and people used to come from all over the city to go there, because they always had great music. We met two single guys, one was from New Hampshire, I don't recall where the other was from. Bob Vigneault and Dan Debians. They had saved up money to go on a vacation and thought it'd be fun to go to Puerto Rico. So, what they did, they paid the maître d' to seat all the single, good-looking girls around them! And we were sitting *next* to them! So every girl who came in, who was single and attractive, sat near Bob and Dan. Rick was *dying* the whole night! Because here he is, he's been married just a *weekend*, and all these gorgeous girls around him! We remember that night as being great fun, you know, with all the partying going on. As it ended up, I guess Bob and Dan decided to stay with two of the girls, and we all went out and went walking on the beach, and had some drinks together. And then we watched the sun come up, walking back to our hotel. That was really a fun night, a night to remember."

Following the honeymoon, Molly joined Rick in Washington, where he continued his service in OSI. During the first week in May, he was tapped to enroll in the prestigious OSI Special Agent School, an opportunity granted to only a select few. Unfortunately, as a newly married twenty-three-year-old, he wasn't motivated to study. "So I bombed out of Special Agent School, which, I think, devastated Dad," he says. "I felt fairly bad about that. Then, in late 1971, OSI went through a major change. Instead of having investigative units, OSI for the Air Force, NIS for the Navy, CID for the Army, the Department of Defense formed the DIS, which was Defense Investigative Services. They would take a normal field office that might require three clerks, five agents, and two secretaries, and they would pull an agent or two from the Army, Air Force, Navy, and they would split them. They would do the same with the clerks and secretaries.

"So, all of a sudden, a lot of openings and shufflings came about. Just about this time, and I'd been married six months, a friend of mine who was in the placement office, OSI Washington, caught me at lunch one day, and he said, 'Rick, I just saw your orders for the Philippines.' Well, the Philippines was a stop-off spot to Vietnam. And I said, 'I just got married six months ago, what can I do? Is there anything I can do?' He said, 'There's nothing that I know of that you can do.'

"Now, there was an attorney who taught in the Special Agent School. He felt really bad that I didn't do well in the school, and just took a liking to me. I approached him as a confidante and said, 'I'm going to Vietnam, I've already been told. I just got married, I didn't try to avoid the military, but how can I leave my wife after just six months?' He said, 'Come with me.' He took me right upstairs to the colonel's office, the officer who was making all the assignments. And the colonel asked me, he said, 'Where is your preference in the country?' I said, 'My gosh, if you're asking that, it would be Miami, Florida.' He turns his pages, he looks, and he says, 'We've got a spot for your rank and specialty right now.' You can imagine how flabbergasted I was, I'd just been told I was going to Vietnam, and now I'm told I'm going to Miami. I said, 'Well, what do I do?' He said, 'Just sit back, we'll red-line your orders, and just wait until you get your orders cut to go to Miami.' I said, 'How long will that be?' He said, 'About two weeks.'

"In Washington, there was an E-6 that I reported to who was extremely likable and very, very funny, always smiling, black guy, who was your typical military sergeant who just *loved* it. I mean, it was his life. He would wake up with a smile on his face, and he'd go to bed saluting the flag, and he was just wonderful. Every morning, he'd just be laughing, and come over and put a stack of 200 updated security forms on my desk, and tell me that he wanted them all typed before *lunch!* He used to drive me nuts. But what drove me nuts more than that, and it made me reflect that I should've done better in college and in OSI Special Agent School. Here I was trained to be an officer, because I continued the military classes, the ROTC, and went through the entire military environment, and there was a first lieutenant who ran this section. This gal was a first lieutenant, and her husband was a first lieutenant also, but worked in another area. I'm convinced to this day that she would do things to irritate me because she was in a higher position than I was in. I think back on it as really comical, two kids, one was an officer and one was enlisted.

"One time, I said to her, 'Can I just go off the record for a minute?' Because I rode a bus into downtown Washington, and the bus would often be late. And if I came in late, she'd *ding* me! She'd start sending me these notes: 'You're coming in late, I need to talk to you, come in here,' and finally it just got a little bit too much for me, and I said, 'Can I go off the record for a minute?' She said, 'Yes.' I said, 'I don't know why you're riding me like you are, but I have the same education you have, I was trained to be an officer myself. It's not my place to tell you this, but, since we're off the record, you come in here considerably later than I do, many more times, but you ding me for being late. And I know you haven't been to meetings, because you still have your *purse* in your hand and you still have the *satchel* you took home with you.' I just let her have everything that was on my mind. So she said, 'Are you finished?' I said, 'Yeah.' She said, 'Okay, now we're back on the *record!*' The only satisfaction I got out of that was just *saying* it, you know? But she eased up a little bit after that."

AT THE QUARTERLY MEETING of TWC's board of directors, July 26, 1971, it was announced that Major General Joseph R. Dillon (Ret.), a member of the board, had died the previous day in Washington, DC. The directors observed a minute of silent prayer.

Approval was granted for the purchase of Anning Services Ltd., Toronto, Canada, for $850,000; Trans-Canada Protection Service Ltd., a Toronto firm, for $90,000; and Argus Protection and Investigation Service Ltd., an Ontario, Canada, corporation headquartered in Windsor, for $350,000. Approval was also given for the purchase of Professional Investigations Company, Indianapolis, IN, for $26,750.

The acquisition of the three companies in Canada resulted in the formation of Wackenhut of Canada, Ltd., which was finalized when John Ammarell, James Hastings, vice president and legal counsel, and Ulrich Becker, treasurer, spent a week in Toronto at the end of August, juggling the legal ramifications and arranging for the election of officers of that firm. Ray Anning was named president, Jack Forrest, vice president, and Robert Cullen, secretary.

The decision to acquire these companies resulted from several visits and contacts between Ammarell and Bob Cullen, the owner of Trans-Canada Security, Ltd., between 1969 and 1971. Cullen knew both Anning and Forrest, and was convinced that he could get them to agree to sell their companies and join under one umbrella to become Wackenhut of Canada. The companies brought with them their officers and staffs, more than 600 employees, some 800 clients, and a total annual sales volume of approximately $3 million. In December, Wackenhut of Canada, Ltd., purchased Baker Guard Service, Ltd., which provided security guard service in Guelph, Ontario, and surrounding cities.

That year, TWC also initiated one of the most unique services to be performed in the company's investigative and security history when it was awarded the contract in Puerto Rico to provide total collection services for the superhighway system being constructed by the Highway Authority of the Commonwealth of Puerto Rico. Ammarell visited San Juan for the formal signing of the contract with the director of the Highway Authority. Effective July 1, TWC was also awarded the contract to provide protective services at the NASA's George C. Marshall Center, Huntsville, AL.

At the meeting of October 29, 1971, the board accepted the resignation of Lloyd Wright because of illness; Wright had been a director since May 31, 1962. George nominated Vice Admiral William F. Raborn, Jr. (Ret.) as a member, to fill the unexpired term of Major General Joseph Dillon (Ret.), and nominated Lieutenant General Joseph F. Carroll (Ret.) to fill the unexpired term of Lloyd Wright. Both men were unanimously elected. A report was made about the Canadian acquisitions that required a cash outlay of $1.3 million. It was also reported that in late August the officers of TWC had purchased the building at 3310 Ponce de Leon Boulevard, Coral Gables.

The year of 1971 was one of exceptional challenges for the company. The biggest challenge occurred early in the year when TWC's fire and security contract with TWA at the Kennedy Space Center in Florida terminated on March 31, when TWA, the prime contractor, lost its renewal bid to the Boeing Company. Boeing announced that it would provide the fire and security services itself, rather than subcontracting them. This was a great disappointment after the outstanding record achieved by TWC in its seven years at the Kennedy Space Center. The contract had generated revenues of $5.3 million annually. Fortunately, the company had established a sales program with goals that more than replaced the lost revenue with new commercial business. Revenue during 1971 reached $55.791 million, an increase in excess of 7 percent over the previous year. The figure includes $1.209 million in sales generated by the three Canadian companies acquired that year. Net income was $1.682 million, compared to $1.677 million in 1970.

Moreover, the number of employees and offices continued to accelerate. In 1971, TWC employees in the U.S. and abroad increased to 12,000, compared to 10,000 in 1970, and the number of clients rose to 11,000. Both domestic and foreign offices continued to grow from a total of seventy-eight in 1970 to ninety-five in 1971. Eleven offices were consolidated during the year. TWC operated in thirty-eight states, the District of Columbia, Puerto Rico, the Dominican Republic, four Latin American countries, Canada, and Italy. In addition, five new area offices opened, as well as ten new branch offices. During this period, licensing and other groundwork was completed for the opening of Wackenhut France.

At the same time, operations in Latin America were growing rapidly: Venezuela increased its guard force from 550 to 675; Wackenhut de Colombia increased from approximately 500 to 935; and Wackenhut del Ecuador expanded from 275 to 319. Wackenhut do Brazil continued its rapid growth, which began with the start of operations in June 1970. A new growth record was set by the Latin American affiliates with total sales of $3.9 million, an increase of 50 percent over revenues in 1970. Although these sales were not consolidated in the financial statements of The Wackenhut Corporation, the company's share of the earnings were included.

As the year closed, TWC acquired the business and assets of Harrison Security Corporation and its subsidiary, Harrison Security Services, Inc., of Jackson, MS, for $300,000; the firm had an annual gross of approximately $2 million, employed 360 persons, and blended well with TWC.

During 1972, a number of organizational changes were made, including the establishment of regional directorships and providing services through three operating companies, two of which were newly formed: Wackenhut Systems Corporation and Wackenhut Protective Systems, Inc., along with The Wackenhut Corporation. The reorganization plan was intended to aid in producing greater efficiency of operations, and in order to make headquarters' support functions available to all three companies. Under the plan, electronic alarm services, and operation of the central alarm stations, came under the Alarm Division of TWC, in order to more closely combine electronic and guard security operations.

An Aviation Division was also established to serve airlines and airports across the nation. The division provided TWC inspectors for pre-departure screening to prevent hijacking of airplanes. Other services included guard forces, ramp security for parked aircraft, crash/fire rescue services, and positive baggage claim service and security surveys.

Wackenhut Protective Systems would now devote its efforts to electronic research and product development, the production and marketing of the Wackenhut Bloodhound Surveillance System, and the Wackenhut Watchdog Security System.

Wackenhut Systems Corporation brought together a specialized staff and group of services, one of which was Loss Prevention Systems, which included initial surveys and recommendations, followed by the implementation of special programs. This company also offered support services to include various types of surveys, and the operations of special projects both in the U.S. and abroad.

Nuclear security programs were also being provided for utility companies, and attitudinal surveys were provided to achieve management objectives through improved employee retention and increased production.

The Educational Systems Division operated academic and professional training programs, and conducted research through the Wackenhut Security Studies Center, and arranged seminars and conferences for business and industrial groups as well as individual clients. The Center, which had been started the previous year, produced a study of drug use by potential employees, and the data from studies of 4,000 employee applicant interviews conducted for clients on a nationwide basis by TWC personnel revealed a startling use of various types of drugs. As a result, requests for copies of the study came from throughout the nation and abroad.

Colonel Wallace E. Hawkins joined the Nuclear Security Division of TWC directly from the U.S. Defense Nuclear Agency, where he served as inspector general for two years prior to his retirement from the U.S. Army on July 1, 1972. During this period, Charles F. Hemphill, senior consultant with the Wackenhut Loss Prevention Division in Los Angeles, authored a book titled *Security for Business and Industry*. The book not only received the best reviews in the history of the publisher, for a book on security, but also had three printings by its publisher, Dow Jones-Irwin Inc. Hemphill was a former FBI agent and had supervised bank robbery investigations at FBI headquarters in Washington for an extended period of time.

Throughout 1972, development of new business was excellent and sales of the company's various services continued to be strong. Revenues of TWC's services that year were $66.854 million. When $5.4 million in revenues from the Latin American affiliated and subsidiary companies are added, the overall total sales for 1972 reached $72.254 million, an increase of 21 percent over the prior year. The Latin American sales, of course, were not included in TWC's consolidated financial statements. Net income, after taxes, was $1.765 million. Earnings per share were $.84, compared with $.80 the previous year. TWC now had 15,000 employees and more than 12,000 clients. The total number of offices increased from ninety-five to 107, and three offices were consolidated with fifteen offices actually being opened during the year. The two new area offices added were in Jackson, MS, and the reopening of the one in Denver, CO. Wackenhut de Colombia, headquartered in Bogota, became a $1 million office in 1972, and was one of the top fifty companies in that nation during the year, with 1,110 security officers.

The 1972 Annual Report also shows some changes in the structure of the officers of the corporation, with Ulrich Becker now listed as vice president of finance and treasurer; Coulby Guenther named vice president, Investigations; James E. Hastings promoted to vice president, Legal and Insurance, as well as assistant secretary; Bud Thompson promoted to senior vice president; Bud Wedbush named vice president, Physical Security; and Bob Kirk named vice president, Corporate Development. Other officers were Bill Bitter, vice president, Labor Relations; Ralph Kiel, vice president, Public and Stockholder Relations; John Ammarell, executive vice president; George Wackenhut, chairman of the board and president; and Ruth Wackenhut, secretary.

When the airline passenger pre-departure screening regulations went into effect in January 1973, TWC was already positioned to become the largest single contractor in the country for this service, because the airline industry was traditionally one of its major clients. The force of the company's male and female boarding inspectors initially involved more than 1,200 employees, and by April, TWC had over 1,500 individuals inspecting airline passengers at sixty airports for thirty airlines.

RICK WACKENHUT received his honorable discharge from the Air Force on August 24, 1973, then took a one-month vacation with Molly, during which they drove from Miami to northern Maine, joined along the way by groups of friends in other vehicles, camping all the way up. He started with TWC at headquarters in mid-September as manager, Physical Security, and reported directly to Bud Wedbush. "I think I was received differently at different times of my growth," Rick recalls. "To my conscious thought, I never intentionally tried to abuse or use my name. But, in the very early days, I was very cocky. And it was more cocky in the sense of when I was with the secretaries and the girls. For example, when I was working in the mailroom years before, I was dating some of the girls in the file room. We would take our fifteen-minute breaks, and I would meet this one girl in the polygraph observation room, that was the dark side of the polygraph room. And we'd spend our fifteen minutes in there, and then we'd come out of the observation room, and one time we came out of there, and I was fixing my jacket and she was fixing her dress and all, and I go to close the door, and there's Jim Hastings, our in-house council, right behind the door, saying, 'Uh-huh, *now* I know where you go during your lunch breaks!'

"I was probably received as a brat in the early days, the poor little rich kid, the boss's son. I think as I began showing that I had some staying power, and that I was committed to staying in the company, and as I started maturing, I gradually earned the respect of the people who may have originally felt differently.

"My relationship with my father that first year after the military was good, but I think I kind of drove Wedbush a little bit nuts. Because he, in effect, was appointed to be my guardian. I don't recall a lot of contact with my father during those times. He kept his distance, and I respected that. I'm sure he intervened a lot in the decision-making process of Wedbush. Like, Wedbush would tell him where I was good, where I was bad, that type of stuff. And then he might tell Wedbush how he wanted it handled. I think a number of those situations developed. But, for the most part, it was a distant relationship at that point in time.

"Both of my parents are perfectionists. To the extreme. And it did make it very difficult. It still does. You're following Babe Ruth to bat, no matter what you do. Because I don't care how much of a perfectionist he is, he has been a tremendous success in his life. So, trying to expect that of myself, I think, is an unreasonable expectation. I can only hope that I'm able to carry on as much of that, and enhance it, as much as I possibly can. It's been tough. In the early days, I didn't know if I wanted to go into the company. I didn't know what else I wanted to do, and yet it was the only thing I was really exposed to. I knew I didn't want to go into the military as a career. I had no other real training, because all of my summer jobs were in this business. So, it was a very tough period there. Murray Levine helped me through a fair amount of that, too, in the early days.

"I seriously considered *not* being in this company, but did not know where else I would go or what else I would do. Because, at that time, I hadn't formulated in my mind specifically *what* I wanted to do. In the numbers of months or even years that I felt I didn't want to make this a *career*, I still didn't have a sense of what I *did* want to make a career. I was still at that time in our lives where we're not sure what we want to do. And I think I just kind of grew into the company. By the time that I was really comfortable with the company, I'd sit back and say: *Why* go anywhere else, because I'm enjoying what I'm doing and I feel comfortable with it. So, it was at that point that I realized I wanted to stay."

Bob Kirk has particularly vivid recollections of Rick's first few years with TWC and the general reaction toward him. "Early in 1973, when Rick Wackenhut joined the company, the attitude toward him was rather strange," he remembers. "I never saw any animosity per se, but most of them thought: There's a playboy, he just wants to play around, and he's just putting his time in, and he's just here for whatever he can get out of it. That was the impression of a lot of fellows. They really didn't know Rick at that time, how sincere he was in his thinking. It became quite evident, I think, as he progressed in the company. Because he didn't step into one job right off the bat, you know, to running the company. I thought he did remarkably well, under the *handicap* he had of being the son of the president, chairman, and owner! But, as far as animosity is concerned, there was very, very little. I guess there was some between two or three of the fellows, but I ignore that kind of stuff, because you're going to have that anyhow."

In the autumn of 1973, Wackenhut Services, Inc., was awarded three federal government contracts for security guard services totaling over $1 million. They were located at the Internal Revenue Service Center complex in Memphis, TN, the Veterans Administration and Treasury Department in Austin, TX, and the federal facilities at eight locations in metropolitan Atlanta, GA. TWC was also awarded a one-year subcontract to provide security at the NASA George C. Marshall Space Flight Center's Mississippi Test Facility at Bay Saint Louis, MS. It was also reported that Wackenhut del Ecuador was guarding the world's highest pipeline in the Ecuadorian oil fields carved from the jungle near the Colombian border. Rising through the Andes Mountains, it reaches a crest of more than 12,000 feet before descending steeply to the coast.

The November-December *Pipeline* contained a feature story announcing the recent retirement of Captain James H. Dunn, who headed the Wackenhut Services, Inc., security forces at NASA's Lewis Research Center, Cleveland, OH. Captain Dunn had joined TWC as a supervisor on the Martin-Orlando security force that began service on January 1, 1959. He was then selected to head the new security force at the Atlas Missile sites at Salina, KS, in November 1959. After construction on those missile sites was completed, he was named deputy head of the security force at the Titan Missile sites at Wichita, KS. In December 1962, he was named to head the security forces for the new contract at the world headquarters of Mack Trucks, Inc., at Allentown, PA. In addition to the world headquarters force, he was also responsible for the Mack security forces at two major manufacturing locations in the Allentown area. Subsequently, TWC was successful in obtaining the NASA Lewis Research Center contract, effective July 1, 1963, and he was named to head the security force there. Dunn was one of the company's outstanding field security leaders for fifteen years, and did much to aid in establishing the excellent image of TWC professionalism, because he was in the forefront of establishing and directing the security forces at prominent locations.

Jonathan P. Goldsmith was elected vice president of Wackenhut Services, Inc. Goldsmith was continuing his duties as general manager of the WSI-Las Vegas, NV, project, which included providing security for the Atomic Energy Commission's Nevada Test Site at Mercury, NV.

By year's end, TWC had attained an earnings goal that had been established when the company became publicly owned in 1966: That was to reach the "dollar a share" mark, while at the same time continuing a program of declaring periodic common stock dividends, in addition to paying regular cash dividends for stockholders. In 1973, TWC's earnings per share reached exactly $1.00.

In comparison, the company's first Annual Report in 1966 reported earnings per share, on an adjusted basis, of $.31. Adjusted earnings each year thereafter were: 1967, $.32; 1968, $.37; 1969, $.64; 1970, $.73; 1971, $.74; 1972, $.77. In studying this earnings-per-share record, we must take into account the fact that during the previous eight years TWC had an approximate 235 percent increase in the number of shares outstanding through stock dividends. In other words, the initial share of Wackenhut common stock issued in 1966 now was equivalent to about 2.35 shares of the presently outstanding stock.

Revenues for the year 1973 reached $90.458 million, compared with $66.854 million in 1972, an increase of 35 percent. When we add $6.9 million in revenues from the foreign affiliated and subsidiary companies, TWC's overall total for 1973 was $97.358 million, compared with $72.254 million in 1972. This was an increase of 35 percent. Total net income, after taxes, was $2.263 million, or a 28 percent increase over the previous year.

Growth in numbers of employees and offices continued unabated. At the end of 1973, TWC had a total of 117 offices worldwide, an increase of fourteen over the previous year. The total number of employees increased to an estimated 18,000, up from 15,000 in 1972. The estimated number of clients rose to 14,000, compared to 12,000. The 1973 Annual Report contained a financial summary for the years 1966 through 1973, and contains a three-page description of the TWC "systems approach" to security. It described the various functions of the five main operating companies, and listed the three directors emeritus: Mark W. Clark, Kenneth B. McNaughton, and Lloyd Wright. It also included the photographs of three director nominees: Seth J. McKee, Bernard A. Schriever, and Cecil L. Wright. In addition, it noted with deep sorrow the deaths of Edward V. Rickenbacker and Stanley J. Tracy.

G. Ralph Kiel retired as vice president, Public and Stockholder Relations, effective December 31, 1973. He had headed the company's public relations program for almost fourteen years. Don Richards was then named director of the department.

ELSEWHERE in the country and the world, the 1970 census revealed that the U.S. population had passed the 200 million mark— 203,211,926.

On April 30, 1970, American troops began what President Nixon termed an "incursion" into Cambodia. May 4, National Guardsmen killed four students at Kent State University in Ohio after a campus protest against the Cambodian invasion. President Nixon called antiwar college students "bums." May 5, a nationwide student strike, supported on the majority of college campuses in the country, protested the extension of the war and the killing of students at Kent State.

In early February 1971, tape-recording equipment was installed in the Oval Office of the White House, in the Executive Office Building across the street, in the Cabinet Room, and in the Lincoln Sitting Room. The tape-recording system was not revealed to those having conversations with President Nixon. April 30, more than 2,000 Vietnam veterans, members of the Vietnam Veterans Against the War, rallied in Washington to protest the war; many of them threw their combat medals on the steps of the Capitol. May 3, antiwar demonstrators engaged in civil disobedience in Washington; police arrested more than 12,000 at random. All of the arrests were overturned by a court ruling that they were unconstitutional.

June 13, *The New York Times* began publishing the "Pentagon Papers," a government history of the Vietnam War, which revealed that the government had lied consistently to the American people. The same day, President Nixon authorized the establishment of a "special investigations unit," later known as the Plumbers, to "stop security leaks and to investigate other sensitive matters." On June 28, Daniel Ellsberg, a former deputy secretary of defense, confessed that he had leaked the Pentagon Papers because he had become convinced that the Vietnam War was immoral. June 30, the Twenty-sixth Amendment took effect, giving eighteen-year-olds the right to vote. During September, Donald Segretti was employed by the Committee for the Reelection of the President (CREEP) to infiltrate the campaigns of Democratic candidates and disrupt them. September 3, the Plumbers burglarized the office of Daniel Ellsberg's psychiatrist; the CIA assisted the leader of the group, ex-CIA agent E. Howard Hunt, by providing him with a red wig, a special camera, and a "speech-altering device." December 29, Daniel Ellsberg and a coworker at the Rand Institute, Anthony Russo, were indicted for espionage and conspiracy.

On April 10, 1972, financier Robert Vesco, under investigation by the Securities and Exchange Commission for fraud, contributed $200,000 in cash to CREEP fund-raiser Maurice Stans. May 9, President Nixon ordered the harbor of Haiphong mined, and authorized massive bombing raids over North Vietnam. June 17, five men, on another Plumbers' operation, were arrested while burglarizing the Democratic National Committee's headquarters in the Watergate building complex. October 10, reporters Carl Bernstein and Bob Woodward of *The Washington Post* revealed a massive effort on the part of CREEP to disrupt the Democratic campaign. October 26, Henry Kissinger announced that "peace is at hand" in Vietnam, and that the war would be over within sixty days. November 7, Richard Nixon and Spiro Agnew were reelected with 61 percent of the popular vote. December 18, President Nixon ordered the bombing of Hanoi and Haiphong. President Thieu of South Vietnam had threatened to sabotage any peace agreement; in order to placate him, Kissinger and Nixon sent B-52s to bomb North Vietnam, including many heavily populated areas. In a National Security Council meeting, Kissinger called this a "brutal ending," but a necessary one to win Thieu's acquiescence.

On January 28, 1973, The U.S. and the North Vietnamese signed a treaty ending direct American military intervention in Vietnam. The U.S. continued to fund the Saigon dictatorship, which held at least 200,000 political prisoners in jail. March 19, James McCord, a defendant in the Watergate break-in case, wrote a letter to Judge John Sirica charging that perjury had been committed at the trial, and that high Administration officials were involved in pressuring defendants to maintain silence and plead guilty. March 21, President Nixon ordered the payment of $75,000 in hush money to defendant

E. Howard Hunt. The next day, Nixon told John Mitchell: "I don't give a shit what happens. I want you all to stonewall it, let them plead the Fifth Amendment, cover up, or anything else, if it'll save it—save the plan. . . ." April 12, CREEP deputy director Jeb Magruder confessed his perjury to prosecutors of the Watergate case. April 30, H.R. Haldeman and John Ehrlichman, President Nixon's two top assistants, resigned. Nixon fired John Dean. May 17, the televised Senate hearings into the Watergate case began. July 16, White House aide Alexander Butterworth inadvertently revealed to Senate Watergate investigators that Prsident Nixon maintained a secret tape-recording system. October 20, the "Saturday Night Massacre" occurred: President Nixon ordered Attorney General Richardson to fire special prosecutor Archibald Cox because Cox was seeking secret White House tapes; Richardson refused and resigned. Deputy Attorney General Ruckelshaus also refused and was fired. Robert Bork, the solicitor general, was named acting attorney general; he fired Cox and abolished the special prosecutor's office, under Nixon's direction. October 23, Nixon reversed himself because of intense public pressure, offered to release the tapes that Cox sought, and to maintain the special prosecutor's office.

BACK IN THE WORLD of commerce, TWC first accepted the challenge in what is known as "America's last frontier" when it provided security guard services for the Atomic Energy Commission's nuclear detonation at Amchitka Island in the Aleutians in 1969. Then, in 1971, the company initiated security services in Anchorage and Juneau. Early in 1974, George received a call from a friend named Bob Miller, who had been operations manager of the Nevada Test Site, and had left to become an executive of the Resource Sciences Corporation, a firm heavily involved in pipeline construction.

"George," he asked, "are you familiar with what's happening up in Alaska with the Alyeska Pipeline Service Company?"

"I've heard they're about ready to get started," George said.

"It's going to be a fantastic project," Miller told him. "That pipeline is going to run straight down north to south, all the way through Alaska. It just struck me that they'll need security and that it might be a great thing for your company."

George discussed the subject at length with Bob Kirk, who was then vice president of Corporate Development, then asked him to go to Anchorage and make a complete study of the situation and what it had to offer.

It turned out to be a dangerous trip. Kirk covered the last leg in a rented plane. With the wind-chill factor at 68 degrees below zero, an engine caught fire and they made a forced landing at Eilson Field, about twenty miles from Fairbanks. Then, because of the weather conditions, it took three hours to drive the twenty miles.

Kirk smiles at the memory: "When I finally got to Anchorage, I met with some executives from Alyeska. Now, Alyeska was made up of seven different companies that were going to build this pipeline. I believe the original cost of the pipeline was $9 million. But the only place they could get the pipe was in Japan, because that was the only place that made forty-eight-inch pipe. Now, Alyeska, here's an organization set up, nobody knew what the hell they were doing, they didn't know how they were going to get the pipeline constructed, how they were going to get all the permits from Alaska to do it in the first place, how they were going to take care of the wildlife enthusiasts. So I met with the Alyeska people, and they said, 'Look, we're going to go out for bids on this, and we're going to put the bids in the hands of our prime contractor,' which at that time was going to be Fleur and Bechtel.

"I decided it was going to take some politics to get the job done. They said, 'We're going to have a bidders conference in Los Angeles, and you go there and we'll tell you what we're going to do about letting the contract out.' So I went, and all the big companies were there, including a company that was owned by Alaskans. And I was told real quickly that the contract would probably have to be given to Alaskan people. So, I thought, that's interesting, but I'll go ahead and work it out. I went back to Aslaska, made two trips up there, and I found a fellow who was actually in the land management area up there, and a very close friend of the governor. So I hired him to go down to the capital, Juneau, gave him a copy of our reports, and said that we were a company that would be bidding on the security contract, and here's our whole background.

"Eventually, that turned out to be a big asset, because Juneau, being inaccessible except by plane or boat, a lot of people never even get to the capital. So, we got quite a bit of favorable treatment as we started to prepare our proposal. I went up there again, and made the whole tour of everything that was going on. On the map, it showed all these towns, and I thought: Christ, we could get people who live in all those towns to work on the pipeline. Little did I know, every town on the map could be just eight to ten people!

"So then we sent our proposal in. I wrote about 95 percent of the proposal, I did all of the costing on it, and all the plans and operations on it. It was submitted to Alyeska, who then gave it to Bechtel, because Bechtel had then been named management contractor—CMC, Contract Management Contractor. Well, Bechtel took the thing, and we never heard, we never heard. I kept calling them, kept going up there. We couldn't get a damn thing. So, finally, I went to a vice president of Alyeska, early in the morning, and I said, 'Look, you're going to have to do *something*.' He said, 'Well, what do you mean, Bob?' I told him, 'Here's the story, we can't get any *answers*.' He said, 'Let me see what I can do.' By ten o'clock that morning, he had his people on the plane to San Francisco to pick up all the proposals from Bechtel and bring them back. So I stayed then for three or four more days. We worked with him, we showed him what we had. He said, 'Well, look, we can't give you all of this contract; how about half of it?'

"So, an Alaskan company—can't think of the name of it—got everything north of Fairbanks, from the North Slope down through Station 5, on the other side of the Yukon, and we got everything down from there, including Valdez. We agreed to that, signed the thing, got all set to go, and I got contacted by some people from Alaska. They said, 'Look, you folks are going to have to hire people from our towns to run this thing.' I said, 'I don't think so.' He said, 'Yes, you do!' So they came out with a stipulation that everybody working up there had to be a *resident* of Alaska! We had a little bit of a problem there, but we got the supervisors in, and we found enough people that we could get started."

The security contract for the two and one-half year construction phase was in excess of $15 million. TWC established headquarters in Anchorage and purchased American Guard and Alert which, with Wackenhut of Alaska, gave the company two wholly owned subsidiaries. The next step was to bring in Jonathan Goldsmith, vice president and general manager of TWC's Las Vegas operations, as president of both companies.

In recruiting personnel during the inauguration of the pipeline, TWC made a determined effort to bring women into the work force in all classifications, and among those selected were former nurses, teachers, secretaries, and beauticians. To overcome the requirements of Alaskan residency and security experience, a special training program was instituted for women as well as minorities. TWC found that the turnover rate for women actually was less than that for men, and women proved highly satisfactory, working ninety-six hours a week in the fourteen construction camps, pumping stations, facilities, and terminals in Fairbanks and Valdez, standing fixed posts or patrolling facilities on foot or in vehicles, regardless of weather or other adverse conditions. At some crowded camps, the women were even required to share bathroom facilities with the men and did so without complaint.

All guards worked under extremely rigorous conditions during the construction phase, working seven days a week, for nine to eighteen weeks at a time. Their duties involved various aspects of security, including the responsibility for stopping unauthorized visitors, and patrolling barracks, furnace rooms, and other buildings while the construction workers slept.

During a visit by then-President Gerald Ford to the pipeline, TWC guards provided security and won commendations from both the Secret Service and the Alaska State Police for their alertness and efficiency.

"When they were constructing the pipeline, I was up there every six weeks," Kirk remembers. "We had 121 people working during that time, and our lowest-paid man got close to $100,000 a year. We had women as supervisors at three of the facilities, and we never had a single problem where we had a woman supervisor. Now, they were on duty ninety-six hours a week, and they got paid for ninety-six hours. It was actually a cost-plus contract. Fact of the matter, to start up this whole job, out of our own pocket, including my trips and everything up there, I think it cost us less than $20,000. And I think our first year's billing was $9 million. Then I got some subcontracts on top of that, as we went along, on some alarm systems and other requirements. Every time they needed something done, we would take care of it."

When the construction phase of the pipeline was completed, the project again was put out to bid, to provide security for the operational phase. This time, TWC won the security contract for the entire length of the pipeline, from Prudhoe Bay to Valdez. In the summer of 1977, under the terms of a $12 million contract, the company began providing access and egress control, and security against fire, theft, and vandalism along the entire line, its nine pumping stations, and the southern terminal. Wackenhut has held the contract continuously since the beginning.

Today, seen in realistic perspective, the trans-Alaska pipeline runs 800 torturous miles from wind-blasted Prudhoe Bay on the bleak shores of the Artic Ocean, down across the Artic Circle and through the Yukon to the Valdez Marine Terminal on the Gulf of Alaska. It is a harsh and seemingly endless wilderness. On the northern end, Prudhoe Bay's winter climate can send the temperature plummeting to thirty degrees below zero, with an almost unbelievable wind-chill factor of 115 below, and for two months of the year there is no sun. By comparison, it may be only twenty below in winter at Valdez on the southern end, but nature complicates matters with as much as twenty-five feet of snowfall.

The entire length is still protected by American Guard and Alert, Inc., a wholly owned subsidiary of TWC, and the people who handle this demanding and dangerous assignment find there is much more to contend with than instant ice, swirling snow, killing cold, and lonely monotony. For example, there are black and brown bears, predators that range in weight from 200 to 500 pounds. Most feared, however, are the grizzly bears, extremely dangerous animals because of their savage disposition. They can rear to ten feet in height, weighing as much as 1,000 pounds, and they do not hibernate, but hunt day and night in all kinds of weather.

The bears learned in a hurry to relate man to food. It didn't take them long to realize that lunch boxes frequently were left in the pickup trucks used by the workers. With uncanny intelligence, they discovered how to hook their claws under the edge of a windshield and pop the whole thing out. On one occasion, in a parking area at a construction site, the bears ripped out the windshields of thirteen automobiles and trucks to get at the lunch boxes.

Imagine the consternation of the driver of a Wackenhut pickup truck when he stopped to make a pipeline inspection and, returning to the vehicle, found a huge grizzly sitting immobile in the back of the truck. Moving slowly, he managed to get back into the cab without attracting the grizzly's attention, but he was fearful of starting the engine because he didn't know how the bear might react. All he could do was sit there in trepidation, praying that the grizzly wouldn't decide to break out the cab's rear window to get at him. Finally, after what seemed like an eternity, the bear leaped off the truck and shambled slowly away.

One of the guards at a pumping station, Myung Chill Kim, was an expert in the martial arts. When a black bear appeared at his post, Kim used his "nunchuck" karate sticks, along with yells, leaps, and aggressive gestures, and chased the bear clear out of camp.

On another occasion, two black bears discovered that the space under a dormitory at a construction camp made an acceptable den for their winter hibernation. The bears, apparently mates, were spending a peaceful winter under the building until one night something startled one of them. The bear took off, running full tilt underneath the dormitory, until its 400 pounds slammed into a support pillar in the dark. The impact shook the whole building, awakening the men. Then, from under the floor, came terrible groans, followed by a loud *smack*. The groans subsided each time, but then began again, to be followed by another *smack*. The men decided that the female bear was chastising the male for keeping her awake.

At one lonely post, a single guard stood watch over surplus goods at an abandoned construction site, and he was plagued by a massive brown bear that continually attempted to break into the building in the animal's ceaseless search for food. There is no telling what a bear will do, particularly when it is ravenously hungry, and the guard began to think that this constant confrontation was going to end in a case of kill or be killed. However, in Alaska, you cannot kill a bear without a permit. The guard's supervisor decided that this was an extreme case, with imminent danger for the guard; he went through the necessary procedures, obtained the permit, and the guard was provided with a rifle. "Okay," he was told, "when the bear appears again, get rid of it." The problem, at least from the guard's viewpoint, was that according to the law in Alaska, when you kill a bear, you have to skin it. Contemplating what a job the skinning would be, the guard decided against the whole business, turned in his badge, and quit the job.

In addition to tales of continual harassment from bears, there are endless stories among Wackenhut workers in Alaska of man's never-ending battle to survive the cold. They tell of two men who were trapped in a stalled truck on a night when the bottom dropped out of the thermometer. The driver had been hitting snow drifts on the road and the snow jammed the air intake of the carburetor and caused the engine to stall. It was a situation in which they quickly could have frozen to death, but their ingenuity saved their lives. The men had a barrel of oil in the back of the truck. Working feverishly to beat the cold, they wrestled the barrel into the cab of the truck, punched a hole in the metal, and inserted a wick made out of a piece of cloth. Setting fire to the wick, they had a homemade heater. In the confinement of the cab, it kept them from freezing. When they were located by a search party sent out because they failed to appear as scheduled, the two men were solid black from the soot. But they were alive.

21

TYECLIFFE had been under construction for more than five years, and would not be occupied until February 22, 1974, but Ruth and George gave their first party there (aside from the cornerstone-laying "Pirate Party" held January 25, 1969), a lavish wedding reception attended by more than 100 guests, on Saturday, July 28, 1973, in the first completed structure on the estate, later named "Tyde's Tavern," as reported in a full-page story with three large photos that appeared in *The Miami Herald* on Tuesday, July 31, 1973, under the by-line of Grace Wing Bohne:

'Social Security' Was the Byword
Wackenhuts Open Gates

If a trip down the Loire Valley to view the royal chateaux isn't on your summer itinerary, you can cruise down the Gables Estates waterways and view **Ruth** and **Russ Wackenhut's** 20th Century reincarnation.

Weekend boaters, ogling as usual the slate-roofed witches' hat towers and stained glass windows of the still-unfinished pleasure dome, were startled to see fair ladies in flowing gowns waving to them from the rocky parapets. The Wackenhuts were having a party, the first ever on the premises.

The 100 or so lucky friends, members of the family and Wackenhut firm who got in on the scoop were at a wedding reception being given for Ruth's former brother-in-law, retired **Col. Renard Ricker,** and his pretty, dark-haired bride **Mikki (Dillon).**

The party wasn't in the main house, which was off-limits—uniformed Wackenhut guards were courteous but firm—but the pool house, a spacious, air-conditioned version of a ducal hunting lodge with beamed ceiling, diamond-paned windows, brick parquet floors and a giant fireplace in a tile-trimmed recess that could accommodate 20 standees.

Between the pool house and the main house is the rock-lined swimming pool, spanned by a footbridge, and a series of rock-bound terraces on which frankly curious guests promenaded in the hot afternoon sunshine, sneaking peeks at the future residence which has been five years a-building.

Ruth's sprightly mother, **Mrs. Bess Merz,** a Gablesite since 1924, echoed community sentiments. "I keep telling them I hope they move while I'm still alive to see it," she said. Mrs. M. is 78, and looks as if she had plenty of mileage left.

The silver-haired host, a sprig of stephanotis in his lapel, was noncommittal about settling in or when the housewarming will be. The house is not named. "Maybe I ought to have a contest," he mused.

Most guests stayed indoors to dance to the music of a three-piece combo, sip champagne, and flex their muscles in the elaborately equipped gym at one end of the pool house. Even the fair ladies tucked up their skirts to try the rowing machine. (Ruth's invitations had specified long afternoon dresses.)

In the dressing room, a hand basin carved from a solid piece of wood was supported by a painted woodcarving of a topless woman, like a ship's figurehead. "My first wife," Russ quipped. In the toilet a painted carving of Neptune with upraised trident discouraged dawdlers.

Social security was the watchword. Uniformed guards halted guests at the big wrought metal gates on Casuarina Concourse. "Do you have the gold bangle?" one asked me, indicating the sample dangling from his clipboard. Quelle horreur! My invitation didn't include a bangle.

The guard nestled a walkie-talkie to his cheek, purred into it, and in a moment our car was whisked away and we were escorted by a genial plainclothesman to the pool house door, passing elegant plantings and a tennis court on the way.

Col. Ricker, who headed Wackenhut operations in Europe, was the husband of Ruth's late sister. Slightly built, fresh-faced and smiling, he looks more like an astronaut than a one-time military police officer. The colonel and his bride met in Hawaii. She wore a lei of fresh pink roses with her pink and white print dress. Their 2 P.M. wedding in Plymouth Congregational Church preceded the reception.

"By February 22, 1974, we were able to move into the Hunting Lodge," George says, "which was the first structure of the four main structures that was completed. That was followed by the completion of what we now call Tyde's Tavern, which is a replica of a Medieval seacoast tavern. It wasn't until September 1974 that we actually got our certificate of occupancy, which meant that a sufficient amount of the home had been completed. So, apparently, we were living there a few months before we got the certificate. The dates on the blueprints are not accurate, because there were no final revisions. John Volk was doing the blueprints as he went along. He was trying to stay ahead of the builder. I don't think he held the builder up at any time, but it was sort of nip-and-tuck. It was aggravating, but then, that's the way it was. Prior to moving into the Hunting Lodge, we continued to live at our old residence. I said to Ruth, 'If we don't move down to the new property, it'll probably take them forever to get the house finished, but if we're down there on site, we can kind of speed things along.' "

Although newspaper and magazine articles have always tended to exaggerate the size and grandeur of Tyecliffe (one national magazine described it as a "$20 million castle in Coral Gables, Florida, complete with a moat and 18 full-time servants"), the exterior of the four buildings does resemble the architecture of a fifteenth-century English castle.

The first aerial photographs, taken March 8, 1974, by Smith Aerial Surveys & Associates of Fort Lauderdale, and enlarged to 11"-×-14" in color, give the most realistic perspective. Constructed on three heavily landscaped acres, and backing on a private waterway leading to Biscayne Bay, the estate is surrounded by battlement walls concealed by graceful trees. As you drive through the wrought-iron entrance gates, monitored by closed-circuit television and opened electronically, then turn left and continue past the tennis court, you emerge through a porte-cochere into a spacious cobblestone courtyard, flanked by three of the buildings, and there is indeed an atmosphere of England in the late Middle Ages. A set of stone stairs lead to the arched main entrance, with the two-and-a-half story "belvedere" tower directly overhead, reached by a circular staircase in a flagstone turret with stained-glass windows.

The three-story living quarters are to the left, connected to the main building by a cloister. Across the courtyard, directly opposite the main entrance, is the Hunting Lodge, which is actually two connected structures with a gatehouse in-between, the lodge to the left, and a three-car garage to the right, including upstairs living quarters for the chauffeur and his family, complete with dormer windows, front and back. To the left, past the tennis court, is Tyde's Tavern (described in the *Herald's* article of July 1973), a meticulous replica of an old English pub.

"Tyecliffe should actually be on fifty acres," Ruth says. "To have the illusion of more land, I decided to have different elevations for the landscape. When Russ and I were in England, we were very impressed with the Dover Cliffs. We could visualize a 'cliff' behind our house, much smaller scale, of course. When Hurricane Andrew hit in August, 1992, we lost all our landscaping, so I've been working on the new design for the landscaping recently. The cliff is made of coquina rock, which is similar to coral, but if you feel it, coral rock has more holes in it, more openings. When the house was under construction, a landscape architect by the name of Jonathan Seymore was selected. In explaining to him the effect needed in the rear of the house, I requested the cliff and all kinds of elevations to give illusions—tunnels and grottos and rocks and stone patios, and the wooded look of a forest.

"Jonathan selected the coquina rock, because I didn't know anything about coquina rock, I just told him that I wanted rocks for a cliff. I still wanted to stay with the English feel. And yet, when you look at an English manor home, it has so much ground around it, the trees are at a distance. I didn't have that much property, so I tried to make up for it with the grottos and the walkways. And then I definitely wanted a forest at the south side of the property, and I wanted another effect at the north side, a 'brook'-style swimming pool with cascading waterfalls, plus Italian gardens, gallery areas, courtyards, and a tennis court. Jonathan worked very well with me to accomplish all of these effects.

"Unfortunately, I was not that familiar with all trees, or the names of all the plants. But I would go to every wholesale nursery, and I'd say, 'I like that tree, and I like that one.' But I made a mistake, I didn't say, 'What does that tree do, does it shed a lot, does it have fruit, what problems will it have with insects?' All of which I've learned since, and used to more advantage to accomplish easier maintenance. I found I had to move quite a few things that he originally put in. For example, near the pool, three large trees were planted, and droppings from those trees were causing constant maintenance for the pool water.

"A landscape architect really wants to do his own thing. I had a little conflict with Jonathan, on and off, but I knew that he knew his business. I also knew I couldn't just go out and find all these rocks and all, with everything I was involved in, with the house and the boat. He did make some mistakes with some of the trees, but I will say that he brought in people who were very knowledgeable with trees and shrubs, and made a study of them. We believe he did a beautiful job. I should have had more shade trees—which he told me—out around Tyde's Tavern, because he said the bricks would get very hot. And I kept saying, '*No,* I want trees here, here, and there.' I made a mistake with that. And now I can't tear up all the brick and just bring in trees for that area.

"After the cliff was completed, one day I received a call from the City of Coral Gables. They said, 'Mrs. Wackenhut, we understand you have a very high wall behind your house.' I said, '*I* don't have any wall.' They said, 'Do you mind if we come down?' I said, 'No, not at all.' So five men arrived and asked to walk around the rear of the house. I agreed, and I suggested that we start at the north end of the property, which is called the Yacht Drive. As we walked, I went up one grotto, across the bridge, down another grotto, up another grotto, down another grotto, walked through a tunnel, until we got to the end. Then I said, 'Gentlemen, what's the definition of a wall?' They looked at one another, then they looked at me. I said, 'I'm not joking. What's the definition of a wall?' One of them said, 'It's a solid structure with no penetration.' I said, 'How many places did you penetrate?' If they had made me knock the cliff down, I think I would've *jumped* off it first! That's how the 'wall' was approved.

"When we were in London, we hired a driver and a car, and we visited Canterbury, and we were driving around and around, and it was late one night, and we went into this pub. It must've been about eleven, and it was *very* cold outside. We went in and, oh, we were so hungry, and they had this beautiful buffet with the roast beef and the lamb and everything. They had what they called their *Ingelnook*, which was the big fireplace and the seating area. And that's what I did a miniature of for Tyde's Tavern.

"Let me tell you what I *didn't* know: I didn't know a thing about stained glass. One day, John Volk said, 'Ruth, can you come up, I have a couple of pieces of stained glass for you to see.' He put two out and he said, 'I think this would be good and that would be good.' I said, 'I want to see *all* stained glass, I want to know *everything* about stained glass.' That was a fascinating experience. I hand-picked every color of stained glass. The type and color depended on where it was being used. Of course, it was so much fun doing the dining room windows, with the coat of arms, you know? Every color is in there. The same thing on the boat, when I did the Viking theme in the master stateroom, I worked *with* the artist, with the mosaics that were placed on the wall to form a scene. I'm very color conscious. I can look at something, and I remember that color, and I can go out and bring back something that's an identical match.

"The living room fireplace is an exact duplicate of an eleventh-century Norman fireplace. The plans were done by Ernest Bonammy. It's an exact duplicate. Lava rock covers the facing. That was all going to be one floor. As you step down from the great hall into the drawing room, that was going to be one floor. And I had bought one piece of antique furniture in the great hall, and I kept looking at that, and I thought: Uh-uh, I'm going to have steps going down, it's going to be a sunken area in front of the large fireplace. Then I had the furniture made to pick up the feel of the one antique piece of furniture in the great hall. Bonammy gave me a little bit of an argument on that one. But I won.

"The two dining room tables are oak. The chairs were made, the tables were made. I did make a mistake on the high-back chairs, they should've been a little lower, because if you have four on either side of the table, it's a little hard for the butler to get through because of the high backs. But the room, to me, demanded the higher-back chair. Now, if you have three and three on either side, eight at the table, there's no problem. But there are times I've had ten at each table. Then I have to put the tables together, and have a huge buffet.

Or, I'd leave them singly, and there would be a buffet of one type of food, and a buffet of another type of food.

"The chandeliers were all made, I worked on those designs, and I went to Alan Frank in Sarasota. Many of his craftsmen were from Spain. They worked over huge open fireplaces, melting all the metal and creating the designs of various fixtures. I can pinpoint every fixture that's been made at Alan Frank's. He's retired now. Everybody's retired. I mean, they're either dead or retired, the people who worked on this house. Everybody used to say, 'Well, if you work on the Wackenhut house, that's where you'll die!' "

Although Ralph Kiel retired as vice president of Public Relations on December 31, 1973, he still laughs when he relates a humorous anecdote about Tyecliffe. "I have to tell you this story, because it's so vivid in my mind," he says. "I've never forgotten, we were in George's office around 1970, talking about Tyecliffe, and he said, 'Ralph, I figure it's going to cost about $700,000, and that's *all*. That's *all* I want to put into it. *Period!* That's it, not a penny more!' Four years later, you know what happened."

George is far too modest to discuss the subject, but the fact of the matter is that when all construction was completed, inside and out, including the landscaping, the total cost to build Tyecliffe was exactly $5,214,872. Add to that the total cost of the furnishings, $659,081, and the final total was $5,873,953. Today, of course, the cost would be—conservatively—five times that amount.

To the rear of Tyde's Tavern is a cement dock flanking a long slip capable of mooring several boats. Although *Top Secret* was intended to be finished about the same time that George and Ruth first occupied the estate in late February 1974, it would not be ready until 1977. Again, George will not discuss the subject, but when completed, the cost of *Top Secret* would be $1,819,645.

"Work was commenced in 1969 in Holland at the de Vries Lentsch yard in Amsterdam," George relates. "After a year and a half, they began to have financial problems, and the big question was whether they were going to go into bankruptcy. If they did, we didn't know what the bankruptcy laws were over there, so Richard Maloy, who had been our in-house counsel, checked with a famous international law firm, Baker & McKenzie, and we retained one of their attorneys in Amsterdam. We were told by that attorney that we had to mark everything that had been sent from the United States to Holland that was going to be used in the boat, so that, in the event they went bankrupt, the creditors couldn't grab all that stuff that was sitting in the yard waiting to be put into the boat.

"The hull had been finished, the engine room had been finished, and most of the mechanical work, but it did not yet have the shafts or propellers installed, so it couldn't go on its own steam. So we arranged to have it floated down the river from Amsterdam to Rotterdam. At Rotterdam, it was put on a merchant ship headed for Miami. They took it up the Miami River and it was off-loaded at the Merrill Stevens yacht yard. They proceeded to work on an hourly basis to complete the mechanical work, including the shafts and the propellers.

"At that time, we noticed that the boat was too wide for its length. It had a twenty-two-foot beam and it just didn't look right. So we arranged to add another fourteen feet to give it an overall length of 104 feet. So they had to cut it in half with a welding torch, add the fourteen feet, and put it back together. All that was done at Merrill Stevens, all of the electronics were installed. The wheelhouse was not completed, we did a lot more things there, but it was completed enough so that a captain could pilot the boat from Merrill Stevens down the river. While he did that, while he had it out in the bay, they did what they call 'sea trials.' Then they brought it up right behind the house.

"We were just finishing work on the house at that time. I used the carpenters from the house, the painters, the plumbers, the air-conditioning people, the electricians, just moved all of those workmen over to the boat. They completed the entire interior and the air conditioning and mechanical work. This is what took so long, because the whole thing was just so disjointed. It was eight years before we could finally take it away from behind the house and use it. All work was completed in January 1977.

"The reason de Vries Lentsch was having problems, and it looked like they were going into bankruptcy, was that they had entered into an agreement with Merrill Stevens whereby Merrill Stevens would get like 10 percent of the total cost of the yacht if they could refer customers to them, to de Vries Lentsch. They referred one man to them who was a very well-to-do individual. He wanted a ninety-foot, all-aluminum hull, with a tremendous, oversized engine that could move the yacht up to thirty-five or forty knots or better. So they completed the hull, and they put this souped-up engine in, which they had to get from the United States. They had gotten that far when the man's daughter was killed in an auto accident. He lost all interest and told Merrill Stevens to just keep the deposit, which was on the order of $100,000 to $300,000—it was a lot of money. He gave that up and de Vries Lentsch was stuck with a different type of boat, and something that would probably cost a lot of money because of the all-aluminum hull and the engine, certainly an out-of-the-ordinary type of yacht. I don't think they ever did go into bankruptcy, I think they managed to pull out of it somehow. They may have found somebody before the curtain was drawn on that boat. They had laid out all this money for building the hull and putting in this engine, so it was a lot more than the deposit, whatever the deposit was."

THE YEAR 1974 was particularly significant for TWC. It was the twentieth consecutive year of successful operation, and the company had passed the $100 million mark in combined total domestic and foreign revenues for the first time, domestic revenue amounting to $93.686 million, and foreign revenue totalling $9.320 million. It was reported that the company had more than 10,000 domestic clients and approximately 14,000 employees, excluding foreign operations. In analyzing the summary of operations of TWC for 1973 and 1974, the impact of two of the company's specialized security services is noteworthy. Revenue from services increased from $66.854 million in 1972 to $90.485 million in 1973, and $93.686 million in 1974. It was believed that the unusual increase in 1973 resulted from the company's pre-departure screening service, plus the continued growth in all services, coupled with a stronger than normal demand for TWC's emergency support services rendered during labor-management disputes.

AT THE QUARTERLY MEETING of the board, January 27, 1975, twelve directors were present, with directors Darbaker and General Schriever absent. A resolution was adopted reducing the number of directors from fourteen to thirteen. Darbaker was not included for reelection. Certain promotions and title changes were discussed and approved. John Ammarell was named chairman, Executive Committee, and executive vice president, Administrative Group, and Bud Thompson was named executive vice president, Operational Services Group. Wackenhut Services, Inc., celebrated the completion of its tenth year of providing protective services for the Atomic Energy Commission at the Nevada Test Site. At the same time, it was announced that a total of 149 employees had completed ten years of service in conjunction with that anniversary. During the year, Arthur C. McPhail was elected vice president, South Central Region, and Cliff Reader was promoted to director of Purchasing.

On June 6, a special meeting of the Executive Committee was held for the purpose of approving the purchase of the assets of American Guard and Alert, Inc., for $125,000. A special meeting of the Executive Committee was held by conference call between Messrs. Ammarell, Wackenhut, and Preston to approve the organization of a wholly captive insurance company, to be called Titania Insurance Company, Ltd., with offices in Bermuda.

The quarterly meeting of the board was held on October 27. Approval was granted for the formation of an electronics company in Colombia, South America, and the investment of an additional $26,000 to an original investment of $30,000. Although 1975 was another year of progress for the company, it was achieved during a difficult period of business recession. The consumer market was strongly depressed by inflation, high prices, and unemployment. Revenues rose to the record level of $102.441 million, and net income totalled $2.574 million. The board was pleased with the growth of affiliates and subsidiaries in Canada, Brazil, Ecuador, Colombia, Venezuela, and the Dominican Republic.

DURING 1974 and 1975, the ramifications of the Watergate scandal still dominated the news. On April 30, 1974, President Nixon released an edited version of the transcripts of White House conversations concerning Watergate. It became an immediate best seller. May 9, the House Judiciary Committee began formal hearings on the impeachment of Nixon. July 24, the Supreme Court ruled unanimously that President Nixon had no right to withhold evidence in a criminal case, and ordered him to release sixty-four tapes to the Watergate special prosecutor. July 27, the Judiciary Committee voted twenty-seven to eleven to recommend to the full House of Representatives that President Nixon be impeached for criminal acts committed while covering up the Watergate break-in, and for obstructing the subsequent investigation. August 8, Richard Milhous Nixon resigned as president of the U.S. September 8, President Gerald Ford granted Nixon a "full, free, and absolute pardon" for any crimes he may have committed.

On January 1, 1975, after a thirteen-week trial in Washington, DC, a jury found four major Nixon Administration officials guilty in the Watergate cover-up case. Nixon's closest aides, H.R. Haldeman and John D. Ehrlichman, as well as former Attorney General John N. Mitchell and assistant Robert C. Mardian, were the defendants found guilty. On January 16, in a landmark decision, the U.S. District Court in Washington, DC, awarded $12 million in damages for false arrest and infringement of rights to 1,200 protestors who had been jailed during the May Day antiwar demonstration of 1971. Each of the 1,200 protestors would receive an average sum of $10,-000. The successful suit had been filed by the ACLU against the District of Columbia. *The Los Angeles Times* reported that it was "probably the largest amount ever awarded in a civil suit in which no large corporations were involved. . . ."

On April 30, 1975, an emergency helicopter evacuation removed the last 1,000 Americans from South Vietnam, ending over two decades of U.S. military involvement. A few hours later, the South Vietnamese government surrendered, and soldiers representing the communist-led Provisional Revolutionary Government occupied Saigon, renaming it Ho Chi Minh City. The war cost the U.S. 56,555 lives, 303,654 wounded, and, during the last fourteen years alone, $141 billion. The total Vietnamese fatalities amounted to over 1.250 million.

AFTER spending about a year as manager, Physical Security, at headquarters, Rick Wackenhut was promoted to manager, Development, in 1974, with responsibility for the administrative and marketing support to domestic field offices for the nationwide sales expansion programs. "As manager of Development, I reported to Curt Bachmann," he says. "I had no people reporting to me at that time. The title 'manager' was somewhat of a misnomer. Basically, I assisted in proposals. I would take the bid specifications of large government proposals and highlight the key ingredients of what needed to be included in the proposal, to make sure we didn't miss anything, so that we qualified in the proposal process, those types of things. I would then go out in the field and make sales calls. We'd have sales blitzes, where three or four of us would go into an area office and just blitz the city, to try to get as many leads for the area manager as possible, as much exposure as possible, then let him follow up and try to make the sales. Those types of things. Pretty much what the sales groups do today.

"Back then, I was starting to mature. I was much more mature emotionally than I was when I was working for Murray Levine and in the earlier days. But I was also beginning to mature from the standpoint of business, and what I wanted to do. I was starting to focus a lot more. At that point, we didn't have any children yet, my wife and I were trying to have children. So I was settling down."

Then, in August 1976, the decision was made to give Rick some experience in the field, and the city selected was Columbia, SC, an area office that had been losing money on a consistent basis for several years. As area manager, he was responsible for physical security administration, operations, airport pre-departure screening operations, plus the hiring, screening, and training of new personnel.

"As area manager in Columbia, I reported to Art McPhail," he recalls. "Reporting to me were two clericals in the office, a manager of Physical Security, an area supervisor, a manager of Investigations. Five in the office and, of course, all the guards that were out there reported to me indirectly. That was a good time. We lived at 146 Cokesdale Road in Columbia.

"Prior to going up there, we had been trying to start a family. I think after about our third year of marriage, we said, 'Okay, let's have kids.' Nothing, nothing, nothing. So we went through the tests, and the problem was on my side. We continued trying, we even tried artificial insemination, with me as the donor, and it did not take. So we were not given a lot of encouragement. In fact, I believe the doctor said he'd probably give Molly a one-in-500 chance of getting pregnant. So that was it. It came right up around the time of moving to South Carolina, and Molly said, 'Look, let's just forget it for a while, let's move up there, put our roots in the ground up there, and take things as they come.' Well, when we went up there, we immediately started looking for housing, of course. You're given thirty days in a hotel until you can find a place to live. And we were fortunate to team up with a real estate guy who was a Citadel graduate, took real good care of me, he found us a home, but the home was under construction. So we had to wait until it was completed.

"We got a room at the Holiday Inn. Well, what *else* do you do in a Holiday Inn? So, my wife got pregnant in the Holiday Inn! And whether you can say it was the change of atmosphere, getting away from the tensions down here, whatever it was, whatever the chemistry was, she got pregnant in that Holiday Inn. But other strange things happened there. I mean, we knew the maids on a first-name basis, we brought potted plants into the Holiday Inn, we rearranged the room. I think we were in there for forty-five days, something like that. And, you know, you don't want to be in a Holiday Inn room for forty-five days. Molly got pregnant during the first thirty days. We moved in there in August of 1976, and she was pregnant in September. Our daughter was premature by three or four weeks, and she was born May 10, 1977. That was Jennifer."

Molly has strong emotional insights into what actually precipitated the pregnancy. "I don't think it was the change of atmosphere, or a psychological change, getting away from the tensions, that triggered the chemistry," she says quietly, reflectively. "No, I don't. I think it was God. I think God decided this was the time. No doubt in my mind, God has decided every time for us. Of course, Rick's mother said, the first thing she said when we told her was, 'I knew the minute you'd get across the state border you'd get pregnant!' She still swears that's why, she still swears, 'You moved away so you'd get pregnant!' But, no, I really believe that each one of our children has been preordained. Especially when the doctors tell you you're not going to have children. Well, I'd love to go back to that guy now and show him my kids! No, every single one of them has been decided for us. I have a very strong faith.

"This was a miracle for us. I mean, we truly believe that. I'm a good Presbyterian. I believe everything happens for a reason. Religious reasons. And I do feel that everything that's happened to us in our lives has been guided by God. You know, He gives you so many choices, and the road may fork, but at the end, ultimately, it's the same road."

After taking over the Columbia area office, Rick was fortunate enough to really cut some costs. "I did not follow a wizard of a manager, so it did not take a whole lot to turn that office around pretty quickly," he recalls. "We started making money, basically, the first month. And I think after the first four months we eliminated the year-to-date loss and started being profitable. We never were like a Fort Lauderdale or a Miami, a huge office, because the market in Columbia, South Carolina, was, you know, a two-tooth minimum for your guards. They were all farm boys, it was minimum wage—I'm being obviously facetious—but very low billing rates, lot of competition, lot of good-ole-boy outfits, Southern Security, and these types of groups that were up there. So it was a battle. We never really grew to a tremendous size. I think the best we achieved was maybe 5200–5400 hours a week, which is a decent size, but not setting the world on fire. But we maintained it profitably and we were growing on a consistent basis. They were $32,000 in the red when I got there. Eliminated that loss pretty quickly and then we stayed profitable.

"That was a real good feeling. Because I knew what I was doing, I *knew* I knew what I was doing. It was clicking, we started getting some extra business. I hired a real good guy for Investigations, he did a good job of getting Investigations into the black. Things just moved along well. My wife was pregnant, we had a house of our own, we were away from *this* environment, away from the folks. It was just nice. It was a good time in our lives."

A SPECIAL MEETING of the board was held at 20 Casuarina Concourse on December 21, 1976, for the purpose of discussing the proposed contract between TWC and Sonatrach of Algeria for the industrial security project at Arzew, Algeria. The contract had been negotiated by Bob Frye, Henry Smyler, and Les Lobaugh. The board authorized management to advise Sonatrach of the approval of the terms and conditions of the contract, and resolved that disclosures be made to Sonatrach regarding contractual relations between TWC and Calcusearch, Inc., and American Trade and Finance company. At this meeting, management was also authorized to enter into a leveraged lease agreement with a reputable and financially secure corporation providing for an investment by TWC at a reasonable rate of return, and with perfect guarantees to safeguard the assets of the corporation.

Although 1976 was a relatively successful year for the company, it was also difficult. One spectacular contract was awarded by the supervising architects for the Jeddah International Airport in Saudi Arabia, the largest project of its kind in the world. The contract called for complete conceptual design and engineering services for security on the entire project. Also that year, through a loss prevention and internal fraud investigation, TWC was able to pinpoint $1.3 million in losses suffered by a U.S. construction company working in Saudi Arabia, effectively ending the losses.

However, while revenues increased from $102.441 million in 1975 to $110.417 million in 1976, net income declined from $2.574 million in 1975 to $2.258 million in 1976. Earnings per share were $1.14 in 1975 versus $1.00 in 1976. Not included in the company's consolidated financial statement were revenues from operations in South America, Europe, and the Caribbean, which totalled $12.713 million in 1976, compared to $10.136 million the preceding year.

Rate increase resistance was apparent during the year. This was not unexpected in view of profit pressures which typified the year. Other factors also affected the company's performance and contributed to the downturn in earnings. Liability insurance increased in cost some 76 percent, which resulted in an additional expense of almost $400,000 for the year. Workmen's Compensation, Unemployment Insurance, Social Security payments, and increases in the minimum wage combined to sharply raise the company's costs of doing business during a period when customers were extremely reluctant to accept rate increases.

The January 1977 issue of *Pipeline* headlined the fact that TWC had been responsible for security at Exxon headquarters in Rockefeller Center, New York, since 1970. The company's Physical Security responsibilities had a vital role in providing security for the offices of the top management of Exxon. A special meeting of the Executive Committee of the board was held on June 2, to consider authorizing management to enter into a leveraged lease transaction with Chase Manhattan Bank for the purchase of an IBM 370/15 computer that would require a maximum equity investment of $3.6 million. A resolution was unanimously adopted, subject to approval of the Finance Committee.

The quarterly meeting of the board was held at 20 Casuarina Concourse on July 25, with all directors present. At this meeting, it was reported that the contract negotiations between Sonatrach and TWC on the Arzew industrial security program were finally terminated on June 27. Wackenhut and its associate, Calcusearch, Inc., had expended more than $500,000 in two years of extensive effort in attempting to develop a viable contract. There was also discussion concerning the new contract with Alyeska in Alaska, which was a seventeen-month contract commencing August 1. It was also reported that arrangements had been made to sell 434 shares of stock owned by TWC in Wackenhut de Colombia to Dr. Salvador Otero Espina, the president of Wackenhut de Colombia, for the sum of $175,000. The company's original investment in Colombia was $57,000. John Ammarell then reported on the sale of the Central Alarm Station in Los Angeles, saying that a sale had been negotiated with Alarmco, Inc., for approximately $1.4 million, plus inventory valued at about $57,000, on the basis of $100,000 cash and a promissory note for the balance over a period of years at an interest rate of 8 percent per annum. George then explained his new organizational concept, stating that the company had finally eliminated the regional idea and that ten districts had been formed. He noted that the company was being divided into smaller geographical districts, placing those offices within each district under closer and more constant supervisional scrutiny. He added that fifteen more districts would be formed when the company had qualified managers.

IN THE MEANTIME, *Top Secret* was finally finished and ruled seaworthy, so Ruth and George decided that it was time for their first cruise. "When our boat was finally completed in 1977," George says, "we used the chef from the house, we used the butler as a steward, and we had an engineer at the house who took care of all the mechanical things. So the only two people we had to hire from the outside were a mate and a captain. We went through mates like potato chips and the same thing with captains.

"The first cruise we took, we wanted to go up to Charleston to see Rick, who was manager of the Columbia office at that time, and Molly was pregnant with Jennifer, her first child; she was seven years in the coming. Anyway, they came and spent time with us on the boat, and we went up to see them at their place. It was a nice visit, we stayed in Charleston about three weeks."

Rick has vivid memories of that visit in the early spring of 1977. "They came a couple of days later than they anticipated, because they ran aground in Savannah, as I recall. I remember there was a considerable amount of fanfare in Charleston about the arrival of *Top Secret*, because it was such a magnificent boat."

"Fanfare" is putting it mildly. *Top Secret*'s presence in Charleston's Ashley Marina prompted a front-page story with two large photos (one of the yacht, another of Ruth in the master stateroom), in the April 1, 1977, issue of the *Charleston Evening Post*, written by special assignments editor Fred Rigsbee.

A 'Woodcarver's Paradise' Docks Here

If a Viking were to find himself aboard the yacht *Top Secret*, he'd think he was in Valhalla.

The 104-foot yacht has been docked at Ashley Marina for about three weeks while her owners, Mr. and Mrs. George R. Wackenhut, visit the area and have some repairs made to the vessel.

Wackenhut is the soft-spoken president and board chairman of the multimillion-dollar security corporation that bears his name. It took eight years to build the yacht which is now on her shakedown cruise.

Top Secret was selected as the vessel's name for two reasons. First, it ties in with the corporation's security business, and second, the exterior of the yacht conceals her unanticipated decor, although the vessel does have an impressive Viking figurehead on her bow.

Going along with *Top Secret* are *Cloak* and *Dagger*, her two 17-foot launches.

Wackenhut says the boat's construction was a joint venture between him and his wife, Ruth. He was "Mr. Outside" and she was "Mr. Inside." He looked after the yacht's design while she designed, with the assistance of an architect, the boat's interior.

Top Secret's structure was about half completed in Holland when the shipyard ran into financial difficulties. The unfinished vessel was loaded on a merchant ship and sent to a Miami shipyard for completion.

The vessel was then docked near the Wackenhuts' home at Coral Gables, Fla., where the interior was worked on for two years and nine months.

Skilled craftsmen to do the detailed, artistic carvings had to be brought in from Europe and South America.

Mrs. Wackenhut said she sketched designs of what she wanted and the architect converted them into plans for the workmen.

Research revealed that the Vikings, which terrorized the coastal areas of Europe from the 8th through the 10th centuries, used mostly ash and birch in the construction of their vessels, Wackenhut said. Since birch is a plain-looking wood, it was decided to use mostly ash for the interior work. The decks are of teak.

The vessel is a woodcarver's paradise. It has carved bucket seats at the bar, a main salon where fierce Vikings and dragons glare at the heads of passengers, scenes copied from an ancient tapestry on a wall in the dining salon, and carved enclosures that conceal the toilets. Lead, stone and pewter are used in the bathrooms where the mosaic tiles depict Viking scenes.

The toilet adjoining the master stateroom is a small art museum. Large panels of framed granite with nearly lifesize figures painted on them circle the walls.

All fixtures from handles to cabinets to lights were handcrafted from Mrs. Wackenhut's designs.

Animal skin rugs cover the main salon's floors.

Originally, *Top Secret* was designed to draw five and a half feet. With extra reinforcement put in the vessel's hull, plus all the heavy materials in the interior, the boat now sits two feet deeper than originally planned.

She's a little too deep for comfortable cruising along the Intracoastal Waterway, her owner says, and there was some difficulty coming to Charleston from Coral Gables. Wackenhut is hoping to sail back to Florida on the open sea.

"I don't know the total cost. I think if I did I might be unhappy," Wackenhut said.

But the vessel isn't for sale at any price, he adds. "There's too much love in it."

While in Charleston, the Wackenhuts have visited and entertained friends. They have a son, Richard R. Wackenhut, who graduated from The Citadel and now heads up one of the corporation's offices in Columbia.

Is *Top Secret* the end for the Wackenhuts in luxury vessels? Mrs. Wackenhut's eyes light up. No, she's already got some more plans in mind for another that's bigger.

She also designed their Coral Gables home—a medieval village which took seven years to complete.

George laughs about that first cruise. "On the way up, the first captain got as far as Boca Raton, and he pulled into the Boca Raton Yacht Club. He got off the boat and he came back and he said, 'Well, my brother-in-law is going to take you the rest of the way.' He quit. I don't know why he quit. Then the brother-in-law took us all the way to Charleston. This engineer that we had, who bragged about the fact that he was an engineer in the Finnish Navy, but wasn't worth the power to blow his nose, the captain fired him as soon as we got to Charleston. Then the captain left the boat, took a motel room, and proceeded to stay drunk for the whole time we were there. So I ended up calling Miami and finally got a captain that we paid to fly up. We came back as far as Savannah. He was originally from Savannah. So we stayed in Savannah a few days; matter of fact, we had something wrong on the boat, we had to get it fixed. Savannah's a nice city and we enjoyed going around, nice restaurants and so forth.

"The guy on the yacht that I trusted the most was Louis Mikowski, who was the chef, really good chef, Polish, of course. We said, 'Louie, we don't feel like going the rest of the way back on the boat, we're going to fly out of here.' So they brought the boat the rest of the way back. I had a terrible time with crews. Then I hired captains just as needed, on a contract basis, because to have them on your payroll, they stand around and look pretty, and they don't do a damn thing.

"I hired an old-time captain, quite good, to take us over to Cat Cay, we were going to have a board meeting over there. So I asked any of the board members if they wanted to go along, and, if so, to come to the house at such-and-such a time. I think Ray Quadt was the only taker. When we were not much more than to Cape Florida, where the lighthouse is, the captain said, 'This boat doesn't seem to be picking up the knots it should be.' I said, 'Well, why would that be?' He said, 'I think you've probably got a lot of barnacles on your propeller.' I said, 'Hell, I just got them all taken off three months ago.' Can you imagine, in three months' time, behind the house there, barnacles form very quickly. The propellers, instead of cutting through the water, they were *balls*, they were just round balls!

"Cat Cay is about fifty miles, so if we were cruising at our normal speed, we'd have been there in three, three and a half hours at the outside. It took us about nine or ten hours! The worst of that was, you have the drift of the Gulf Stream going north, and you figure that all in. When we finally got to the islands, we were almost to Bimini. And that's a pretty good run from Bimini down south to Cat Cay. By now it's pitch black, nighttime, and it's tricky to get in there. You go straight toward a rock, then you make a ninety-degree turn, then you make another ninety-degree turn, before you're in the water toward the docks. In the dark, that was tough. Of course, we had the searchlights, but it's not like daylight.

"When we got in, all the directors had eaten, and we went to a late supper. Next morning, we had the mate go down underwater to clean off the propellers, they were just like balls. We were going to proceed to Nassau. Prior to leaving for Cat Cay, our chef Louie said, 'I don't really want to go on this cruise,' because he was on the first one up to Charleston, and he didn't like it, he was in the galley all the time, fixing three meals a day, and cleaning up and all. I said, 'Hell, if you're not going on the trip, I'll have to let you go, because I'm not going to pay your salary while you're sitting here and we're gone.' So we hired a new chef, and a steward who came along with the chef. The new chef and steward were worthless, and we sent them back to Miami. Now we have nobody but a captain and a mate.

"We called back to Miami to see if we could find a steward. We called these uniform places, and they quite often have guys that they kind of line up. What that means, if you hire them, then they buy their uniform there. Well, we got a guy to come over who was a jewel. His name was Blaine. Blaine had worked on boats for many, many years, and when he got there, he looked the part of a butler. Mrs. W. took to him right away. And we said, 'We have no cook, we can't find a cook.' He said, 'Well, I cook,' and he did and he was good. So he filled two jobs."

LATE THAT SUMMER, because of his excellent work as area manager, Rick was promoted to district manager of Columbia, SC, where he remained until 1979. His responsibilities included Physical Security administration, Operations, and Sales for all TWC offices within the district, including field training of supervisors.

"That gave me five additional offices, all of which were at a loss," he remembers. "We picked up Greenville, South Carolina; Ashville, North Carolina; Charlotte, North Carolina; Raleigh, North Carolina; and New Berne, North Carolina, which was over on the coast. I thought: Okay, I've got to do this systematically. I took a couple of my staff, went up to Ashville first. In one hour's time, I could tell it was *never* going to make a profit. Closed the office, basically on the spot. Transferred the stuff out, reduced the inventory, shipped it to other offices that were in the system, put the office under Raleigh, because we still had business there that we had to maintain. I put a supervisor in charge, gave him a small increase. It was a wham-bang-thank-you-ma'am type of a deal, but we had to cut the losses quickly. Then moved to Raleigh. Raleigh was an enigma to me. We got it profitable, but it would be in and out of the profit area. But we eliminated the major bleeding.

"There was Greensboro, also, I forgot about that. Then went to

Greensboro. I was having some problems with the manager, who had had some good experience in the company, he was very knowledgeable, but had just gotten lazy. My tactic with him was: I'm going to make him my district manager of Physical Security. Because he knew guards real well. And, since he was lazy, I wouldn't give him a *chance* to be lazy. He had to travel to these other offices. And it worked out well, he started moving to the other offices, and would report what was happening. Ultimately, it didn't work out, and we had to separate. He was considerably older than I was, and I think he thought he was just taking orders from a young kid, and couldn't handle it. It hurt him, I think, in that regard.

"Anyway, we basically followed this pattern. Not in one fellswoop. I did Ashville and then came back, and then, a few weeks later, we'd go to Charlotte, and we worked it that way. Ended up closing Ashville and closing New Berne. Then we opened an office in Charleston, and I think that was really kind of a personal wish, and we never could get it going. So we ended up closing it later. But we got all the others into a profit and felt very good about it."

CLEARLY, 1977 was an outstanding year for TWC, and a number of management objectives were achieved. Total domestic sales were $117.884 million, but, with the addition of foreign sales, the total reached $134.016 million. Net income increased to $2.707 million, a 20 percent increase over the previous year, to become the highest increase in earnings in the history of the company. The largest contract ever negotiated in TWC's history, to that point, was signed with the Alyeska Pipeline Service Company to provide security services for the 800-mile trans-Alaska pipeline. The $12 million contract covered a seventeen-month period.

22

Jan began her career with TWC full-time on Monday, January 2, 1978. After twelve years of marriage, she was separated from John Thorsen in March 1977, and divorced in December 1977. At that point, it was financially necessary for her to work. Although she had a teaching degree, she did not want to teach. "I didn't want to be in a school around children all day," she recalls. "It's okay if you're married, but I kind of wanted to get out and meet people. I wanted to become part of what was going on with the corporation. It took me a long time to adjust to the chips you're given, instead of what you planned. That was a big lesson. I think I sat down with both Mother and Dad and asked what would be available, or where they saw me. Because I had to work.

"I didn't get a wonderful settlement. They split property fifty-fifty, but he had a lot of property I wasn't aware of, that my name wasn't on. I got two years rehabilitative alimony, they call it, to kind of get yourself back on your feet. I didn't know anybody who had gone through a divorce, at the time, but now it seems there are support groups and things, and I later found out that a lot of friends that hadn't gone to college, or wanted to go on, got rehabilitative alimony until that was completed. I wish I had asked for enough alimony to go back to school and get the law degree that I'd been wanting then. I always had wanted one. I didn't want to work and be a mother. I just couldn't see how you could do it. I didn't want somebody else raising the kids. The luxury of deciding whether you're going to work or not was taken from me because of the split. I mean, you have to go to work."

When Jan was separated in March 1977, she did not tell her parents for at least two months: "I don't know, I guess I was embarrassed, and I was afraid they were going to say, 'I told you so,' and I just didn't tell them. At that point, my uncle [Harry], Dad's brother, and his kids would always come down for spring break. To Fort Lauderdale. It was about a week or two weeks after this had happened, and I took the kids and went up there for a couple of days. So, actually, they knew before Mother and Dad. That was March, and I didn't go to work with the company until January.

"Leading up to all this, I had to find care for the kids. Because you're there [at the office] till six at night—five-thirty, six—and I had to find somebody who could pick them up at school. I was trying to maintain their status quo as much as possible. You know, Scouts, and dancing class, and all the different things. This was March of '77, they were nine and ten. Tanya was ten in April. Even though I knew the finances weren't going to be there, I just didn't think it was right to have them give up everything because of something that John and I were going through. John's big thing was, 'Sell the house,' you know, and use the money from the house, but that would've meant taking them away from some sort of stability, and it was too premature, I felt.

"So, I went through a non-English-speaking woman who gave them rice and beans every night. It was hysterical! That didn't work. Then I finally found a gem named Ina Moryouseff. She's still in Miami. She had come from New York, no children, divorced, and all she wanted was a home for her—she had this huge dog named Lips. Because that's all you could see, his lips, because of all the hair. It wasn't a St. Bernard, but it was like a St. Bernard. English sheepdog, I guess. And we had a fenced-in yard, because we had a dog, a little dog, at the time, a Lhasa apso. I just loved the woman, she was a real overweight Jewish lady, my age, and she had enrolled in school to be in child development. That was my main concern when I'd interview anybody. I didn't care what they did to the house, to my mother's chagrin, I just wanted them to play with the kids, and to teach them, and be with them, and *care* about them.

"I had a cleaning lady twice a week, I guess, at that time, and I pushed her back to maybe once a month or twice a month, whatever, and Ina used to laugh, she'd say, 'I gotta be the only maid in Miami who has a maid!' But she was great with them. She had this little Volkswagon Beetle. I'd come home, and they'd be in the middle of cutting out paper things or drawing, and she was fabulous with them, I just loved her to death. So I put her in a—I had a little office room, an extra bedroom, and she slept there. I don't know whether she made dinner for the kids, maybe she would start it, I don't remember about dinner. But Thursday she had off, because the girls had Scouts, and that was at school, so by the time they finished, I could pick them up.

"When I got into the company, I first went into International. Of course, we were at 3280 Ponce, and International was across the street *and* at 3280, downstairs, on the north side of the building. I reported to Bruce Berckmans [vice president], a big, tall guy, handsome, used to be with the CIA. I think, initially, I was supposed to learn where we were and what we were doing in International. I don't know *what* they were going to do with me. I think, long range, it would've been sales. I know Ed Kuncar was busy with his Libyan students over at the University of Miami, and Fernando Carrizosa had just received his MBA in 1976. Part of the time I'd be down there, and part upstairs. Never did any traveling with International.

"It's hard for me to separate a personality with business. It's a knack, and I just don't have it. I look at somebody as all in one, and business is part of it, you know? If I've got a problem with somebody about something else, I'll tell him, even though it doesn't have anything to do with business. Or try to smooth it over. And that probably wasn't the best situation. I don't know if it ever got me into that much trouble. But I think people would come to me with grievances, and I took it to heart and tried to do something about it. Maybe it didn't have anything to do with the P and L, and that's what I was supposed to be thinking about.

"I remember one time I had a lunch with Mr. Goldsmith, who was president of our Alaskan operations at the time. He was in town, and the gentleman I was reporting to, Mr. Berckmans, thought it would be good for me to go to lunch with him and Bill Bitter, who was vice president of Labor Relations, a real smooth guy, gray hair, he wore it long, wore the best of clothes, he had an upstairs office, and he would go back and forth between New York and Washington. So it was Mr. Bitter, Mr. Goldsmith, and myself. And, you know, I was used to looking at my watch, because you get an hour for lunch, that was it. This lunch went on for an hour and fifteen minutes, an hour and a half, two hours. Well, I think Mr. Bitter had driven me to lunch, so I just couldn't excuse myself and leave. I guess I could have, but I didn't. And I caught all kinds of hell for that."

Fernando Carrizosa, president of Wackenhut International, Inc. (WII) since 1984, was manager of Latin American Services in 1978, and has pleasant memories of Jan at that time. "I was interested, because she could have been a great asset for me," he says. "In everything. She could have been my *partner* in corporate development. And that was my question to her: What is your five-year plan? I wanted to find out if she was serious about making a career in the company. And I wanted to see if she would be a partner. I would have somebody with the name Wackenhut who is smart, and willing to travel, and go for the gold."

Born in Bogota, Colombia, September 30, 1943, Carrizosa graduated from the Military Academy for Cadets, Colombia, in 1962, then served as a counterintelligence officer in the Colombian National Army, 1963–68. He joined the company's Colombian affiliate, Wackenhut de Colombia, in Bogota in 1968, simultaneously attended the Universidad Javeriana, 1969–72, where he earned his BA, majoring in industrial relations and business administration, and was assistant to the president of Wackenhut de Colombia when he transferred to TWC's headquarters in 1974. While serving as a special consultant to the Wackenhut Training Institute, he earned his MBA at Florida International University in 1976.

"The principal impression I received about Jan was good, generally speaking, but I was not by myself," Carrizosa explains. "There was also Bruce Berckmans, who she reported to, and who was thinking of her more realistically as a secretary or administrative assistant, rather than a partner, or someone who he could have trained to do better things. My impression was that she was serious, aggressive, and ambitious. Definitely. She obviously liked the business, and she was conscious of her career. I didn't have any problems with her skills and her willingness to do things. And I think that her little time in International was good for her. I don't know exactly what happened at that time, but, for me, in retrospect, Jan could have been something a lot different if she had remained with us."

"I remember another time," Jan recalls, "after I'd gotten out of International, I was put in—for a time, I was up at the front office helping John Ammarell as a secretary. And it was a nice working relationship with Dad's secretary at the time, an older lady who lived in the Gables. She was real sweet and kind.

"Then I went into Operations and reported to Jim Barkley. And, I remember, it was quite an adjustment to be at a desk all day. I felt like I was in a cage. I couldn't stand it. I was used to playing tennis, and being out, running around with the kids, and I just couldn't stand it. Bill Jackson was a runner, and I had taken up running. He ran on the golf course, Coral Gables Country Club. He told me about it, so I'd go over there, but with showering and changing and all that, I couldn't make it back in an hour. I'd be like an hour-fifteen, hour-twenty, but I didn't feel badly about that, because I dropped the kids off at school about a quarter to eight, so I'd get to the office at eight o'clock, instead of, technically, I was clocked in at eight-thirty, and I'd always stay till six or later. If I had to talk to the west coast, it would be later. So I figured I'd made it up, but we had a VP of Administration, Warren Altman, and a couple of times I'd come in fifteen minutes late—I don't know how he even knew when I left—but he'd be at the top of the stairs looking at his watch. Which was my signal to cut that out. I think, somewhere along the line, they said, 'Well, you know, we can't make exceptions, and it doesn't matter when you come in and what time you leave—an hour is an hour.'

"So then I started running at night. Late at night. Because I'd make sure I did homework with the kids, and get them to bed, and then I'd leave. I'd never do that today. I don't know how I did it. One night I had a bad accident. There was a school by our house, and the streetlights were down, and the fence was pulled away from the school, and I got caught up in the fence and came crashing down on my chin and was knocked out for a while. So that kind of put a damper on nighttime running. It was real hard for me to kind of juggle the whole bit. I really admire women today who do it.

"Then, with Operations, at the time, we had the company divided into four regions, and I was in the northeast. I had twenty-four offices, from Washington north. And, around that time, I guess I had met Roger [Ward]. I met him through an association with the company. Jim Barkley's assistant was Sandy Young. She worked administratively in the company, and was real good friends with Jim. Jim had been in the service, and Sandy was divorced from an Air Force pilot, and she didn't really sever her military connections. She was at the Homestead base all the time, a lot of her friends were down there. She said she was having a party and was inviting—she'd been trying to fix me up either with Roger or his roommate, Dave, she didn't know which one. She had mentioned him to me, and me to him, for several months, and both of us said we just weren't interested in a blind-date type of thing. And we finally met. He was a fighter pilot at Homestead, F-4s, just before the F16s came in. He was from Texas, he had been married, and they'd lived in Miami for about a year, I guess. Then he went to Korea, alone, and got divorced when he came back. I guess he had been in Miami maybe nine months or a year before we met. He had an apartment near Dadeland; didn't live on the base. His ex-wife and his son lived down by the base. He was thirty-one when we met in 1978.

"So, anyway, getting back to Wackenhut, I guess we were married by the time I was traveling to the northeast. Roger got out of the service the month after we were married. He left the service and worked for Wackenhut for a year up in Fort Lauderdale, then left the company and took a job in Washington—actually, it was in Arlington, Virginia—with a consulting firm that did a lot of military contracts. I didn't go with him because it was a consulting job and we didn't know how long it was going to last, and I didn't want to pull the kids out of school. Turned out, it lasted for two and a half *years!* And they didn't pay for trips home, so we'd see each other about once a month!

"Very stressful. We were living initially in the house that I had been in with John, and it just was real hard. I think it's an adjustment anyway, you know, I felt like I was in a tennis match at dinner, between the kids and Roger, and the whole thing was just—and I thought: Oh, maybe if we get out of this house, we can start fresh. And we bought an old home west of the [Dixie] Highway that was on an acre and a half, surrounded by some nice real estate. But this was old, and Roger's real handy, and his idea had been to rebuild this thing. But, shortly after we bought it, he went to Washington. Two and a half years.

"Before we bought the house and I was still with Wackenhut, I had a big blowup with Ina. That probably led me to getting married quicker than I would have. Although Roger doesn't know that. Ina would call me. I'd be in conferences at the office, and they'd say: 'There's an emergency call!' And I'd think: Oh, my God, it's the kids! And she'd be having trouble with Tresha, just back-talking, whatever. But it was like I'd have three children. And she'd demand my full attention whenever I'd walk in the door. I'd have to sit down and have this hour talk with her. I just thought there had to be a better way.

"Mainly, Tresha wasn't adjusting as well as I would've liked. She was trying to keep up with Tanya's crowd. A little hard to handle. I look back on it now, and it wasn't so bad, but Tresha was the wild one. Tanya did everything she was told, and Tresha would fight with me all the time. I just felt like I needed some help, so I asked Roger to come home. He probably would still be up there, but I cried 'Uncle.' Then he got a job with Key Power Technical Institute, and from there to Florida Power and Light, and they sent him to Juno Beach. So he was commuting from Juno Beach to Miami. The poor guy was never really home, and the whole reason he didn't become a commercial pilot is because he likes to be home and doesn't like *traveling!*"

TANYA LEIGH THORSEN, Jan's eldest, has vivid memories of those years. Born April 2, 1967, in Tallahassee, she graduated from Gulliver Preparatory School, Miami, in 1985, and earned her BA in sociology at Duke in 1989. For the past several years, she has been a coordinator of residential life at the University of Alabama, directly responsible for the safety and security of about 1,000 residents, and she supervises a staff of seventy. At the time of our interview, May 21, 1993, she was unmarried.

"I was just telling Mom a story the other day," she says softly, "one of the strongest memories that I have, when my parents were still married, so I was less than ten, I was probably six or seven. We lived in a house that had a pool. Pop [George] and Geech—I call my grandmother 'Geech'—that has a history too! She didn't want to be ever called 'Grandmother.' She didn't like that title! She thought GiGi was close enough to Grandmother, and she likes the extravagant, and it was French. It wasn't G.G., it was GiGi. Initially, when we were very little, it was 'Geegee,' we couldn't make the soft sound GiGi. Then it was shortened to Geech. When Rick's children were old enough to speak, and to call the grandparents anything, my grandmother said she wanted to be called Tye. T-y-e, after Tyecliffe: 'Call me Tye!' And Tresha and I couldn't shift over, we were like: *What?* It didn't go over with Rick's kids either. But she just didn't know what the kids should call her. Now they call her Geech too.

"The best memory I have, when we were still little, at that house with the pool, they'd come over, Pop and Geech would come over, Mom would have dinner parties or whatever, and have them over in the late afternoon when it was still sunny, and we were in the pool. Pop would always be in a velour tennis outfit, he played a lot of tennis, my grandparents played with my mom and dad quite often. When Tresha and I were little, we'd go over and watch them. But he just always relaxed in these velour tennis lounge outfits. And he'd wear those with sneakers. He was *big!* And he came over one day, and was sitting on our patio chair. Not in the sun, he was back away from the pool, and we'd come over, and we'd be all wet, and we'd drip on him. And he was real, you know: 'Don't *drip* on me!'

"But one day he was over and he had a cold. And he was all wrapped up in this velour thing, and I want to say it had a hood, because some of his things had a velour hood. But he sat there, and we came bouncing over—'Let's see Pop!' And we gave him a big bear hug, and he started to sneeze. And he said, 'If you stay with me, if you're going to sit on my lap, I'm going to sneeze so hard I'll blow the *roof* off this house!' And Tresha and I thought that was just the *neatest thing!* So we sat there on his lap, with our arms around him, waiting to watch the *roof* blow off!

"We would tease him about his nose, I've always joked with him. Honestly, that's the side of him that I see. The business side of him, I don't know. It was not my world. He was Pop, he was just my grandpa, who came to my tap and jazz recitals. And he was there when I was inducted into the National Junior Honor Society, and then the National Honor Society, he was just always there. Always there. And now, having lived away, I miss him.

"I envy Tresha. I have talked so highly of my sister to new people who have come into my life, when they get close to me. Because, honestly, being as close in age as we are, I see her, and look at my peers, and, without a doubt, she stands out as *the* most calm, at peace person I know. I don't know if that is entirely attributable to the relationship that she's found with God, but it is a large part of it. I don't doubt that.

"Christian Science doesn't have the kind of formal training that other religions do. Because they're only readers, who are lay people, members of the church who read to you. And yet, there is such an innocence and a sincerity with her, in a search, that I don't think she got into it with a professional motive. I think that's evolved. And, because of it, the people that I work with day to day, the college students who are preparing themselves for life outside of campus, and very career-oriented, because of the power of society that says you have to be, that demand is a material human argument. And Tresha doesn't see it. Not that she will deny its existence, but she's not *with* it day to day. Just because of the nature of the field that she works in.

"When we were children, she resented me, because I was older, I did everything Mom said to do, I was very obedient, and I got good grades in school. And all my teachers were then *her* teachers the next year, we were at the same school, and they expected the same of her that they had with me. There was a resentment. There was an undeniable love also. Without a doubt. And Tresha's my best friend now.

"But we went through high school differently. She was in a very fast crowd. Her sense of self was more affected, *externally*, by my parents' divorce, and her level of adjustment, than mine was. I stifled a lot. And because Tresha was so rebellious, searching for attention or whatever else it was, in Tresha's eyes, and indeed in many of our family members' eyes, Mom favored me. I was easier to raise, I didn't require as much disciplining, so I got the friendship of Mother. And the respect and the love and all that, shown that way.

"I don't like to consider myself a Christian Scientist, and *say*, 'I am a Christian Scientist,' when people ask me, 'What religion are you?' Because I don't practice it daily. I see doctors more so than my sister does. When people ask what religion I practice, my answer is, 'I was raised as a Christian Scientist.' Because I was. But, quite honestly, I don't think that my life would have come together the way it has, emotionally and professionally, without it.

"I've been dating a gentleman for the last four months who's from Huntsville, Alabama, and I've gone home with him quite frequently, and have gone to the Huntsville Christian Science Church there. He is not a Christian Scientist. He is a voracious reader, and saw the *Science and Health* book in my apartment, and asked me a lot of questions about it. He was raised as Church of Christ, and his ministers have talked to their congregation, saying that the Christian Science movement is a cultish movement, and they denigrate most everything that's not Church of Christ. He knew that he wasn't comfortable with that, but he's searching. And, because he loves to read, he started attending the services with me, realized the intellectual component necessary to even remotely begin to understand that faith, and has been turned on to it, probably because of that. The *Science and Health* that he's reading right now is because he loves to read, and he's reading it as a book.

"That's the way Mary Baker Eddy intended people to read it. She didn't found the church before she wrote the book. She wrote the book for people to read, and then she saw the demand, and created the movement. So that's the way he's been brought into it. He's still a student, he'll be graduating in August, and we met on campus at a leadership conference where I was presenting a program, and he was attending to get the leadership training.

"I don't take medicine. I don't take aspirin, I don't take Mydol when I have cramps, I'm not on the birth control pill. I mean, I just don't take things that are medicinal in nature. I don't take cold tablets. And with my benefits, as an employee of the University of Alabama, if something were to happen to me, I know that I would go to the hospital. I would go because I can, and I would go because

I'd feel safer, probably, that way. I don't think my faith is strong enough. If I was in a car accident and needed serious medical attention, I think that I would go.

"I think the best thing that Tresha did was go to Principia College [Elsah, Illinois]. She went to Prin very rebellious still, in her freshman year and into her sophomore year, did the things that the college students did there. I don't know how familiar you are with Principia, but all the faculty, all the administrators, all the students are Scientists. And yet, many are there because Mom and Dad want you there: 'And you're going to get into this, if we have anything to say about it, and we're paying your bills, and you're going to get into this.' And they rebel. They go to St. Louis and party, and pick up the fast life, because it's not there in Elsah, Illinois. She did that her entire freshman and sophomore years.

"For whatever reason, she decided that Principia was too sheltered and too quiet. She left and she went to Harvard to study for one semester. Honestly, I think I noticed more of a change in her then. When she returned, when she decided to leave Harvard—she could've stayed at Harvard—but when she decided to leave, go back to Prin, her heart was open, she was far more receptive to the principles and the way of life that she saw at Principia. She had decided that she was comfortable with that. And that's when I saw a change. Every time we would come home for the holidays, she was very calm.

"Harvard was so different for her. And, honestly, she confessed to me that the dating scene that she had while she was there scared her. It was different than what she had been exposed to at Prin. Because not everybody was from the same little mold. I know that she was very challenged academically. She always got great grades, always, and even with my high grades in high school, she was right there.

"Pop thought that I was selling myself short. He wanted me in the Ivy scene, he had wanted my mother to do the same thing, and she rebelled and went to a state school. He didn't recognize Duke as the intellectual institution that it is, just because he didn't know about it. But I love that man. He's my grandpa! He managed to come to every little thing that Tresha and I did when we were growing up. With a smile on his face. Big teddy bear, I remember him as a little girl, because he was so much heavier."

THE DATE is Thursday, August 26, 1993, the time is 7:55 A.M., the place is a two-story office building at 7800 Southwest 57th Avenue in South Miami. The sign on the wall outside Suite 219 has three lines of small, white, capital letters:

<blockquote>
CHRISTIAN SCIENCE
PRACTITIONER
TRESHA L. THORSEN, C.S.
</blockquote>

The door is open, the lighting is soft, the small windowless room is furnished to create an atmosphere of warmth and comfort, very much like a living room, bookcases, chairs, tables, cabinets, a large planter, two exquisite Monet prints, fitted carpeting, a desk in one corner, where Tresha (pronounced *Tree*-sha) is studying, as usual. She rises to greet us, relatively tall, slim, reddish-brown hair, smiling oval face that needs no makeup. Although we have met Tresha several times before, never in her office, her eyes continue to dominate her features, wide, blue, transparent even in soft lighting. Without any exaggeration, there is an "aura" about this individual that is impossible to miss and difficult to forget. It is an aura of *calm*. It defines her personality, and it is clearly more than the sum of its parts. The question is always on the tip of one's tongue: What is the *source* of such calm? Because there are obvious contradictions. On the surface, she is an extremely attractive, bright, eloquent, energetic but soft-spoken twenty-four-year-old lady. Beneath the surface, something complicated is going on, a chemistry that even she admits she doesn't fully understand, although it's been called to her attention for several years now.

Born in Miami, December 14, 1968, Tresha graduated from Gulliver Preparatory School in 1986, a year behind Tanya, attended Principia College, 1986–88, accepted a "visiting semester" at Harvard in 1989, and graduated from Principia in 1990. After nearly a year of working and traveling in Europe, she became a full-time Christian Science practitioner in 1991, at the age of twenty-two.

She speaks quietly, thoughtfully, about her earlier years: "I wouldn't say that I was rebellious. I think that I was exploring many different life-styles, because I wasn't finding satisfaction, I wasn't finding fulfillment, I wasn't finding completeness in the same old routines. I like to think back to the divorce, not because of trying to find a source for what happened in the rest of my experience, but it really was a *catalyst*, I think, for me, because I was eight, and, at that time, my world was shaped by what I valued as a standard. And, to me, that standard was love. The most eminent expression of that love was that of my parents, their love for me, their love for each other. That was my little unit.

"I don't remember my dad 'never being there.' We didn't have dinner together often, but when he was there he was very much a part of our lives. I'll probably always defend that, simply because he was just a great presence for me. I don't think I've ever defined a person's love for me by the *quantity* of time I've spent with them. That's probably helpful because, regardless of whether someone was there or not, does not at all define to me the *degree* of love that they had for me. It's something that you feel. I would never look back on my childhood and say to myself, 'My dad was never there.' Although, for others, looking at the situation, based on his hours at work, they might say that. But he was there for me. Because he was right in my heart always.

"I remember lots of weekends. I picture so many times just playing in the pool. Weekends were pool times, seeing him a lot. And, because of that, the divorce was a real shock. I didn't see that coming. Certainly, my parents argued, and that disturbed me, I remember, but not to any great extent. Why was it a shock? Because it was not in my definition of love. It was not in my definition of what was my security, of what was the fundamental element of my being. Which really was love. I depended on that.

"Now, at that point, when I was a child, to me, the source of that love was Mom and Dad. But what did the divorce do? Why was it the catalyst? Because it forced me to seek a greater source. If the love that *people* share between one another has that element to it, of the possibility of ending, changing, breaking, I can't depend on that. I don't want to think that that's all there is. As a child, I remember thinking about that a lot. I couldn't verbalize it the way that I'm doing now, but, as disappointed as I was with my parents, I thought: Well, wait a minute, you know, what's true about *divine* love? Because, growing up, I had learned that God was my real father and mother, and that a synonym for God was love. As it says in the Bible, 'God *is* Love.' Well, if *that's* true, is there something in that nature of love that I can *depend* on?

"Pop was definitely helpful to me at this time. I think my most powerful memories of him were during this time, because he was that source of constant companionship, in a way that perhaps neither of my parents could give to Tanya or to me, because of their own priorities and concerns at that time. Not because they weren't sensitive to it, but because their thoughts were wrapped up in themselves and their struggle that first year. And Pop was always real steadfast. I think my relationship with him pointed all the more to: Tresha, don't look to your parents solely and exclusively for the love that bases you, look to God for that.

"One of my greatest arguments with the entire family, with the exception of my grandfather, I often heard, 'Well, honey, it's okay, you *are* very young, and you won't understand this.' If I rebelled against anything, I rebelled against anyone ever telling me, 'You can't understand something.' Pop wasn't like that. Somehow, in his own way, his love saw the whole person. In other words, he didn't see a deprived or deficient child who lacked understanding, who lacked the ability to understand some real tough, perhaps grown-up issues. And I think what enabled him to do that was, he was seeing my true identity. What do I mean by that? Well, one of the basic premises of Christian Science is that God created man in his image and likeness.

"When you become so fully aware of that definition of man, of that concept of identity as the image and likeness of God, when it's something you really begin to understand, you *see* people that way. It's not as if you have to redefine it every time you're looking at anyone. And then what happens is that you begin to love them that way too. So, what happens is that the love you have for someone is so full, it's not capable of seeing weakness or seeing incapability.

"Pop always spoke to me as an adult. He would say, 'I know this is a tough time for you, but here are the facts.' Or he would just be a source of comfort. And, in that sense, perhaps he was the strongest *mother* I had during that time. His presence was just very dominant at that time, because his 'mothering' was also comforting my *mother*. And he was around a lot. Geegee was around too. I don't remember her presence so much, physically, I remember *feeling* her support. Now I call her Geech; when I was little, I called her Geegee. And now I call him Pop, when I used to call him Pop-Pop. Those were fun names, those were fun.

"I don't want to leave the impression that one gave more support than the other, because the relationship that I have with both my grandparents, Geegee and Pop, is one of the most important relationships in my family. My relationship with my grandmother is probably the strongest of anyone in the family with her. We just seem to know one another well enough to see through superficial elements of personality. We can relax with each other. I think she feels she can be herself with me more so than with anyone else in the family.

"I never accept limitations about a person, solely because I'm operating from a standpoint of loving what's true about them. I see everyone in their own, unique, individual expression, as an expression of God. So, whereas others might confront challenge, I see opportunity. Because I see the opportunity to redefine how I'm thinking about a person. Whether it's a human weakness, or a so-called personality difficulty. However the world would define it, I challenge myself to see beyond that. It's not that I ignore a weakness or a criticism, I just don't think that those have anything to do with our true being. And so, in order for me to be honestly developing a relationship with someone, I have to *un*see those weaknesses."

Although the subject of Christian Science has been mentioned previously in this study, going all the way back to George's childhood, it was not until we finished tape-recording this first, and quite lengthy, interview with Tresha that we began to realize the genuinely profound significance Christian Science has played in the man's life and career. The above excerpts were selected to reveal the emotional, psychological, and spiritual impact made on Tresha because of her parents' divorce.

The most intriguing question is, of course, exactly how much impact has the lifelong study of Christian Science made on the life of

George Wackenhut? The subject is of such an extremely sensitive and personal nature that George will not discuss it at any length with anyone outside his immediate family. Therefore, more substantive excerpts from Tresha's several interviews will appear in upcoming chapters, because it is of critical importance to understanding the man, his motivations, his tenacious work ethic, and, perhaps most importantly, how his spirituality has affected the lives of others.

JAN's initial attempt for a career at TWC lasted about eighteen months and, apparently, the children were the primary reason for her departure, especially Tresha. "I think under normal circumstances, if we'd had a regular family, I think I could've coped with it better and given Tresha what she needed," Jan reflects. "She always needed more attention, more time, even as a little baby. Always. And I just didn't have it to give her when I was working. It was just really hard. And she missed her father terribly. Really affected her deeply. I had her in counseling, and I just did everything I knew to do. In the summer of '78, I had met a practitioner, Joseph Heard. His brother, Alan, worked in International for a while. Joe told me of a Christian Science camp in Maine, Camp Newfound, for girls. You'd fly into Portland, and it was outside of that on Long Lake. I sent them and—oh, I felt like I was losing both arms that summer, I missed them so much. There was a four-week and a six-week term, and I sent them for the smaller length of time. It was a lot of money for me at the time, but we scraped it together. It was wonderful for them, they came back like different kids. Because they were around Christian Scientists, and it was just a real loving atmosphere.

"It turned out, they went every year from then until they were fifteen, and Tresha ended up counseling. Very, very nice part of their lives I think they'll cherish. I did get up there one summer to see it; drove them home. It was really incredible. I'll always be grateful to Joe for that. And I think the friends that they met, definitely with Tresha, led to her going to Principia, and then her career now.

"My dates are foggy, but after Ina left, I couldn't find anybody for the children, so I took a temporary leave of absence, that's what they call it, to try to give Tresha some attention. That was in mid-1979.

Then Roger and I married, and I got my real estate license. I worked it like a nine-to-five job, or more, because of the weekends. But it takes a couple of years to kind of get your contacts and get going. That's when I guess my selling ability started coming out.

"I didn't think it was going to be so difficult, because I knew an awful lot of people in Miami. When I first started, I went with South Dade Reality, because George Cademan, the president, was at our church. Their office was out in Perrine. I learned a lot from him, but the listings were down in Cutler Ridge. I switched to Casey Cousins because I had several girl friends who were doing very well. At the time, it was a lot of women who didn't really have to work; their husbands were extremely successful, so they'd pick up listings at cocktail parties and the ballet society and all that sort of stuff.

"So I thought: Boy, if I go in there and really need the money, and I'm willing to work, I should be able to do well. But none of my contacts paid off. My friends thought: Well, you're new, we'll go with somebody who's not new. Although, when you're new, you're really up on everything, because you've just been studying. Or, I'd have other people who didn't want me to know their financial situation, which is understandable. So I started from scratch.

"Every Sunday, I sat on open houses for people who had so many listings they couldn't be at all of them. That's how you do it in the beginning. You had to give so many hours a week—'floor time' it's called—answering the phone in the office, and if they called on an office listing, and you took the call, you could get that. So I did okay there.

"The turning point, there was a listing down in the Redlands, and somebody called on the phone to see it, and they met me in this limousine, accompanied by a van of thug-type men. They were Latin American. She would not drive with me. She said it was an all-cash deal. This had a landing strip with it! I mean, just perfect, right? It had been an avocado farm. The couple who were selling the house had a barn that they changed into a recreation area, a family-room area, but a big, big thing. It was a divorce situation. Well, the thugs got out and were *casing* the barn! I showed it to them one more time, and I remember calling my broker and telling her I felt very uncomfortable, that it was very obvious what the sale was about, and I didn't want to be involved. And she said, 'You're forgetting who your *fiduciary* is with.' They didn't care. It was just like the banks at the time.

"I was feeling very uncomfortable, and about that time, on a Sunday, I was sitting on an open house, and Gus Novotney [TWC's vice president of Sales] called me, and he said, 'We've got a sales opening, and you're the perfect one; would you consider coming back?' And it was just perfect, because I didn't like what was going on in real estate.

"Then that's when the traveling to the northeast happened. That's when I got into Field Support. I was in Operations before, but it was administratively, and this was as a Field Support person. This was in 1980. There weren't that many women involved in the company at the time; there were *none* who were traveling like that. I'd be out in Hartford, Connecticut, having to tell the manager that his services were no longer needed. Of course, I'd hear all the things about his family. I didn't mind the guys who were short-changing us, but the ones who were really trying were tough.

"I really had to play catch-up. Because you'd have a week out at an office, doing everything. Going out on new sales calls with the manager, meeting existing clients, checking all the P and Ls, and checking how they were doing their hiring, whether all the permits were in for the guns, all the legal business. It was a zoo. It was, for me. I would've liked to have known a little bit more about the office before I got there. Like, what's their main range of sales, and how long has the manager been there, and who's he got working for him? So the week I got back, I would be writing the report on the office I'd just been to see, and researching where I was going next. Then, when I was there, I'd bring a lot of the work back to the hotel, because I had not had enough experience.

"There was a big 'good-ole-boy' network. A lot of the men were ex-military. You know, what're they going to talk to *me* about? In a way, it was good, I think, because I brought part of Wackenhut to their area. I mean, there really was a George Wackenhut, and it was a family business. But a lot of managers—let's see, I was in my thirties at the time—a lot of the managers were at least ten, maybe fifteen, years older. So they would feel uncomfortable. Like, if it had been a man, they would've gone out to dinner with me at night. But as a woman, they'd either bring their wife along, and we would be talking wife things, and then I'd have to switch and talk business, or we just wouldn't do anything at night. I really didn't know how to handle that well. I felt better just not doing anything. But I didn't like to go out to dinner by myself. So I'd be in this hotel room alone, and thinking about the children, and it was just very lonely. Very lonely time. I think it could've been a lot more exciting had I been in a more stable position. Of course, now it would be *great*, because Roger's traveling and the kids aren't here! But, at the time, it was just really very stressful."

In November 1979, Bud Thompson was the first of the "original" senior officers to leave TWC. He had joined the company July 1, 1959, as director of Training and Inspection, and more than twenty years later, he left as executive vice president of Operations. During that period, the firm had grown from a small company to the third largest security and investigative organization in the nation with annual revenues of $148.217 million in 1979.

But, at age fifty-two, Thompson wasn't ready to retire by any means. In 1980, he and a partner bought Gables Air Conditioning, Inc., in Miami, a relatively large and successful firm, and he seemed happy when we talked with him in the spring of 1992. The walls of his office are covered with literally hundreds of TWC memorabilia. "I bought this company for my son, Ken, who's thirty-eight, he's married and has two children," he says. "I have a daughter, Geneva, who's twenty-one, and she's in the company here too. She's been studying at the University of Florida, in construction management. Now she's going to Florida International University, taking construction management. She runs my construction department.

He laughs softly when he talks about George; they have remained good friends. "After twenty years of watching George when he gets annoyed with something, his lips get very thin and he starts biting on a nonexistent skin there. He used to call me the Village Idiot. He was teasing me all the time, because George and I had a very good relationship. And, being with him so long, I used to come in on the board sometimes, and we were going to have a meeting or something, and I'd draw George's profile on the blackboard, and we used to laugh about the fact, and kid him about it, that if he ever loses his *teeth*, his nose and his chin will *touch!* Because he has this very protruding nose, and his chin sticks way out. And then, one of the jokes was, the distance between the nose and the chin was relative to how *mad* he was. Because, as he got madder, his chin and his nose would come together, because he was eating his *lips* off. He would do that. That was his sign of displeasure with whatever was happening. I drew that enough times, and he'd walk in the room, and he'd say, 'Thompson, God damn it, you did it again—I know you did that!' And I'd say, 'George, *I* didn't do that, I really didn't!' He could take a joke pretty good.

"In my latter time there, he and I were not on the best of terms, because I had said things that were going to happen, which he did not like. He didn't want it to happen and he didn't like that people knew that I had said things. Because I'd say in a meeting, if they asked me something, I've always been very frank. I always thought George liked that. He never wanted 'yes' people around him. He surrounded himself with people—I think I was aggressive, and probably a better businessman than a lot of those guys were. And Ammarell was a very reserved guy; he'd hold back the reins all the time. And he had an attorney in there, a very, very conservative attorney; if you asked him a question, he would give you the most conservative approach for the problem. George was smart enough to listen to all these people, he'd let them have their say, and then he'd make up his mind how he wanted to go. And many times, there would be one side or the other that would be rather upset with what he decided to do. But he was the boss.

"One of the things he used to do, which I admire greatly, and I copy it myself sometimes: You come in with something, he will push you against the wall, keep questioning and questioning, making you justify what you're saying. You just can't shoot something off, because he'll back you into the wall so you look like you don't know what you're talking about—unless you *know* what you're talking about.

"And I think another very good trait as a leader, he has an ability to do this: I would go in to him and say, 'George, this is what's happening here on the thing; this is what I think we should do.' He'd say, 'Well, I don't know that I'd agree with you, and what about . . .' He'd keep pushing you and pushing you. Until, after a while, you've given up everything you possibly can, so you say, 'Okay. You know how I stand. Tell me what you want to do, I'll do it.' And he'd go *along* with you then. You'd made your point, and you could stand behind it. You couldn't just go in there and bullshit him, because he doesn't go for that at all. That's a very brilliant thing I think that he has, it's one of his characteristics."

ELSEWHERE during that two-year period, on January 19, 1978, President Carter selected Federal Appeals Court Judge William H. Webster as FBI Director. On March 16, the U.S. Senate approved the Panama Canal neutrality treaty, and, on April 18, voted a treaty to turn the canal over to Panama by the year 2000. June 6, Californians in referendum approved Proposition 13 for nearly a 60 percent slash in property tax revenues. August 6, Pope Paul VI died at age eighty; the new Pope, John Paul I, sixty-five, died unexpectedly September 28, after thirty-four days in office; he was succeeded by Karol Cardinal Wojtyla of Poland as John Paul II on October 16. After a thirteen-day conference at Camp David led by President Carter, the "Framework for Peace" in the Middle East was signed on September 17 by Egypt's President Anwar el-Sadat and Israel Premier Menachem Begin.

On January 4, 1979, Ohio agreed to pay $675,000 to families of the dead and injured in the Kent State University shootings. January 16, the Shah left Iran after a year of turmoil, and revolutionary forces under Moslem leader Ayatollah Ruhollah Khomeini took over on February 1. Conservatives won the British election on March 28, and Margaret Thatcher became the new prime minister; on the same date, a nuclear power plant accident at Three Mile Island, Pennsylvania, released radioactivity that made worldwide headlines. June 14, President Carter and Secretary Brezhnev signed the SALT II agreement. August 27, Earl Mountbatten of Burma, seventy-nine, British World War II hero, and three others were killed by a blast on a fishing boat off the Irish coast; two IRA members were accused on August 30. Iranian militants seized the U.S. Embassy in Teheran and held hostages on November 4. December 27, the Soviet invasion of Afghanistan stirred world protests.

23

THE DECADE OF THE 1980s was, by all accounts, the most exciting and challenging period for TWC in terms of worldwide expansion, unprecedented revenues and profits, changing technology, major new government accounts (including the largest in the company's history), the move into an ultramodern headquarters building, and the inevitable restructuring of top management. The decade would also have its downside, with the departure of several key senior officers who were instrumental in helping George to build the company, and, finally, with a personal tragedy in the Wackenhut family, the death of George's brother Harry.

The year 1980 was memorable for a variety of reasons, one of which was the long-awaited and eagerly anticipated opening of a new division in February, Clarence M. Kelley & Associates, headquarters in Kansas City, Missouri, and specializing in investigations of arson fraud, and a wide range of white-collar crimes against business.

Clarence M. Kelley, the first man selected to succeed J. Edgar Hoover as director of the FBI (1973–1978), and a close personal friend of George's, was subsequently elected to the TWC board of directors.

Born in Kansas City, October 24, 1911, Kelley graduated from the University of Kansas in 1936, earned a law degree from the University of Missouri at Kansas City in 1940, and was admitted to the Missouri Bar in 1940. He began his career with the FBI on October 7, 1940, served in offices from coast to coast, retired on October 24,

1961, then became police chief of Kansas City for the next twelve years.

Kelley was nominated by President Nixon to be director of the FBI on June 7, 1973, and the Senate unanimously confirmed the nomination on June 27, 1973. He retired from the position on February 15, 1978.

The announcement of his association with TWC gained extensive national media attention, and was first published in the February 5, 1980, issue of *The Kansas City Star*, under the by-line of Bill Norton:

C. M. Kelley Joins Florida Security Firm

Clarence M. Kelley, former FBI director and former Kansas City police chief, has joined the Wackenhut Corp., a Florida-based private security firm, to head a division being established that will focus on arson fraud and other white-collar crime.

The announcement was made in Coral Gables, Fla., by George Wackenhut, president of the security firm, the third largest such firm in the world.

For Kelley, the job will absorb about half his time as he sandwiches speaking engagements and other security-related work, including liaison for security at the upcoming GOP national convention in Detroit.

Kelley, contacted at home today, said he and Wilburn K. De Bruler, former assistant FBI director in charge of planning, will form the new branch of Wackenhut in Kansas City. "We're going to have as our core the investigation of arson," Kelly said, "but it will encompass all the various kinds of investigation. Our purpose is first to establish an office in Kansas City and, with that having been successful, then throughout the country.

The security firm, for which Kelley is seeking to hire ex-FBI agents, will supplement rather than supplant publicly financed law enforcement agencies. Primarily, Kelly said, his investigators will not be looking at arson as a criminal act but as the insurance fraud related to it.

"When someone burns a building or a house or something like that, it's a fraud against an insurance company," Kelley said. His theory strikes at the profit motive of arson.

"If you can take away the prize they get, the money, then you've made a strike." Kelley is hopeful that cutting the profit motive will create "an additional barrier to the spread of this thing."

He was quoted in Miami as saying, "Arson has become quite a problem throughout the country. It's one which I think needs a double thrust—from the public and private sectors.... Millions are lost through arson and there's a lot of suffering as a result of it."

Fire officials say the intentional torching of vacant houses and failing businesses is becoming an epidemic that costs insurance companies hundreds of millions of dollars every year and sometimes costs lives.

Kelley and De Bruler had attempted to establish a similar type operation with a management group in Washington, but disagreements over project funding led to a split.

"Mr. Kelley approached me last summer and it took us this long to get all the details worked out," Wackenhut said. "We are tickled to death to have him."

Wackenhut Corp., among other things, provides private security for corporations and some government installations, investigates insurance claims and installs and maintains electronic anti-theft systems.

Kelley said his association with Wackenhut is not connected to his work for the GOP in Detroit. A formal announcement on Kelley's selection, while reported in the press as final, is not expected to be announced formally until mid-February.

Kelley was police chief here from 1961 until July 1973 when he returned to the FBI as director. He had served as a special agent for 21 years before his first retirement.

Kelley's salary with Wackenhut was not revealed, but the firm did say that he would stand for election as a company director during the April 28 annual meeting. He will be director of the Clarence M. Kelly & Associates division of Wackenhut.

There was no mention of Kelley's joining TWC in *The Miami Herald*, but, less than a week later, the paper was back at its campaign of poking fun at Tyecliffe, including a photo of the home and its finished landscaping in the February 10, 1980, issue. This time, the staff writer, Martin Merzer, also had some fun with the Wackenhut genealogy and family crest (the crest is also pictured). But, apparently, George had long since learned to take it all good-naturedly.

A Tip of the Hat From Wackenhut

Much already has been written about Tyde Cliffe [sic], George Wackenhut's 18,000-square-foot medieval castle smack in the middle of Coral Gables.

Featuring four buildings, a pool, tennis courts and a man-made cliff, the estate sparked years of complaints from neighbors outraged over the flamboyant architecture.

But not very much is known about the crest that Wackenhut wears on his blazers and on a very-solid-gold ring.

And even the story of the crest's origins illustrates the contrasts surrounding the man. He loves to show off the crest; and he doesn't mind puncturing the illusion.

It seems it all started a few years ago when he and his wife, Ruth, were in West Germany and decided to hire a genealogist to trace the Wackenhut heritage.

But wait, let George tell the rest:

"This guy got it back to the 13th century and he wanted to know if I wanted a family tree. And I wrote back 'no' but could he determine our family crest.

"The next thing I know, he writes back and tries to tell me as politely as possible, in his broken English, that sheepherders didn't have a family crest.

"Then, we find out that Wachenhut—spelled with an 'h' instead of a 'k'—means the top-watchman. And I'm thinking that would be really great [considering his line of work] but we spell it wrong.

"It turns out that spelled with the 'k,' Wackenhut means hat-tipper. So that's it: I come from a long line of hat-tippers."

But Wackenhut didn't let that stop him—he commissioned the genealogist to create a family crest. It shows a knight in armor, holding up his sword in salute. The knight is surrounded by eagles, symbolizing courage.

"It's all really something that the guy concocted," Wackenhut says.

But he loves it anyway.

At the quarterly meeting of the board on July 28, 1980, three new directors were elected: Charles J. Simons, T.F. Walkowicz, and Frederick M. Glass. Simons was a veteran of forty years' service with Eastern Airlines, rising from accountant to chief financial officer and highest-ranking corporate officer after the president. Although he retired from Eastern earlier in the year, he decided to continue as vice chairman of the Miami-based airline until May 1981. Simons also served as a director of various other companies and was on the executive council of the Harvard Business School Association. In 1994, Simons retired from the TWC board.

At the time of the election, T.F. Walkowicz was president of the National Aviation & Technology Corporation of New York, a mutual fund with investments in airlines, aerospace, and high-technology companies, and with assets of $90 million. He was a member of the National Research Council, and a director or trustee of a number of high-technology and scientific-industrial companies.

Frederick M. Glass, a financial management consultant based in New York, was also a director of numerous companies, served as chairman of the audit committee of three publicly listed companies and five mutual funds with assets of over $150 million. Glass had held a wide range of top corporate posts in the airline, car-leasing, banking, and insurance industries, and was a former chief attorney for the Civil Aeronautics Board. In 1992, Glass retired from the TWC board and became a senior consultant to the chairman.

Before the end of the year, TWC, through two of its subsidiaries, had renewed two major contracts. Wackenhut Services, Inc. (WSI), won a three-year renewal of its contract with the Department of Energy for security services at the Nevada Test Site. The contract was awarded in competitive bidding with ten other security firms, and represented an estimated $20 million in revenue. American Guard and Alert, Inc., concluded negotiations extending its present contract for the trans-Alaska pipeline for two more years along the 800-mile pipeline. The contract with the Alyeska Pipeline Service Company, agent for eight pipeline companies, represented more than $10 million in revenue.

December 30, 1980, was a milestone in the history of TWC. On that morning, the twenty-six-year-old corporation was listed on the New York Stock Exchange, as reported on the front page of a "Ticker Tape Extra" in the January 1981 issue of *Pipeline:*

Wackenhut Now on N.Y. Stock Exchange
TWC Joins Nation's Most Important Corporations on Big Board

The Wackenhut Corporation is now on the New York Stock Exchange. It is the only security and investigative organization listed on the prestigious "Big Board."

When TWC shares began trading on the Exchange last Dec. 30, the firm joined a select group of the nation's largest, most important corporations.

Following tradition, TWC President George R. Wackenhut purchased the first 100 shares of the company's stock to open trading on the Exchange that day.

The corporation listed 3,010,943 shares of common stock which were previously traded on the American Stock Exchange. The assigned ticker symbol for more than 3,700 tickers across the nation remains "WAK."

David L. Calvin, executive vice president of the Exchange, welcomed Mr. Wackenhut and a group of senior corporate officers and directors on the NYSE floor, which now has 22 trading posts.

"The listing of The Wackenhut Corporation on the New York Stock Exchange is of great personal satisfaction to me and is a significant milestone in the steady growth of the company," Mr. Wackenhut said while visiting Post No, 2, site of trading of all Wackenhut shares.

"We welcome this opportunity to be better known to the investing public," he added.

"It will afford our existing and potential shareholders a broader market for their shares, add prestige to our operations and enhance opportunities for additional national and international recognition," Mr. Wackenhut said.

The Wackenhut Corporation was founded in 1954. It first went public in the spring of 1966 and was traded over the counter until the company was listed on the American Stock Exchange on Oct. 9, 1967.

La Branche & Company Handle TWC Stock

You won't find his name on the Wackenhut payroll or see him at TWC headquarters. But James G. Burke has been hard at work for The Wackenhut Corporation since last December 30.

On that date, Mr. Burke began specializing in TWC stock on the trading floor.

Mr. Burke, 48, a veteran at the NYSE, is with La Branche & Company, which was designated by the NYSE's Allocation Committee to handle Wackenhut stock. La Branche has been trading on the NYSE for more than half a century.

Another of the registered specialists handling TWC stock at La Branch is George M. L. La Branche IV, grandson of the founder of the firm.

La Branche & Company represents some of the most prestigious firms listed on the NYSE. Among them are AT&T, Atlantic Richfield, Cannon Mills, E. F. Hutton and McDonnell-Douglas.

The NYSE operates in such a way as to enable the forces of supply and demand to determine prices. However, when there is a temporary disparity between these forces, specialists such as Mr. Burke and Mr. La Branche act as buffers.

They buy or sell for their own accounts, thus making it possible for stock to move from one price to another on reasonable volume and without unreasonable price fluctuations.

By year's end, TWC's financial condition had never been stronger, despite a series of dramatic challenges, not the least of which were unprecedented inflation and interest rates, and an uncertain business and economic climate. Fiscal 1980 was the fourth consecutive twelve-month period of record-breaking revenues, with sales of $177.457 million, compared to $148.217 million in 1979—a gain of 19.7 percent. This did not include $21.051 million in sales of unconsolidated foreign affiliates, which rose 30 percent over the previous year.

In February 1981, two major contracts totaling more than $21 million were awarded to Wackenhut International, Inc. (WII), one in Saudi Arabia, the other in Argentina. The $14 million contract with Saudi Arabia called for WII to provide training and supervisory guidance to fire- and crash-rescue personnel at fifteen civilian airports over a two-year period.

WII joined with an Argentine partner, Autotrol, S.A., to win a contract for more than $7 million from the Argentine Atomic Energy Commission. It covered the design, engineering, and installation of an electronic security system at a new nuclear power generating plant near Cordoba, Argentina's third largest city. Autotrol, S.A., is an engineering firm headquartered in Buenos Aires. The contract was managed for WII by Wackenhut Systems Corporation, another wholly owned TWC subsidiary that handled design, engineering, and development of total security systems.

The Wackenhut-Autotrol proposal was selected by the Argentine Atomic Energy Commission from among six submitted by international consortiums in a worldwide tender. Although TWC had provided security services for a number of nuclear plants in Holland, Italy, and Belgium, the Argentine contract marked the company's entry into the Latin American nuclear power market.

WII was involved in two other fire-related contracts with Saudi Arabia. One was a $1 million pact under which a firefighting force was set up at Jeddah International Airport; the other was a $1.7 million contract to provide fire service communications systems at thirteen Saudi Airports.

Fernando Carrizosa, president of WII, smiles as he recalls his first meetings at headquarters with George, and, after nearly twenty years in the United States, his speech still retains strong remnants of a Colombian accent. "When I first came to headquarters [in 1974] and met Mr. Wackenhut, my first impression was a mixture of reverence and intimidation," he says. "The image that Mr. Wackenhut provided, at that time, was of a very strong paragon of honesty and professionalism. He was a champion of those things. Absolutely straightforward and a very strong figure. When I was in the presence of George, in the beginning, I sat on the edge of the chair, and I was overly conscious about what *I* said, and afraid that I was not understanding everything that *he* said. I was also afraid that my answers would not be as detailed, as meticulous, to satisfy his need to know. I also talk about 'reverence' because, as time passed, he changed into a father figure.

"Many of the old timers say that he has mellowed, that he is more open, and that we can reach him easier. It is true that everyone in International who comes in to headquarters likes to see him, likes to talk to him, and regards him with the most respect and reverence. Not for what he has *done*, but for what he *is* to them.

"With the exception of the chairman, most people at headquarters were completely oblivious to what was going on in International. Mr. Wackenhut always had the time and interest in what was happening to International. There has been a gradual change. As a matter of fact, during the 1980s, we started growing to such an extent that we could no longer be ignored.

"From 1979 to 1980, I was director of Latin American Services at headquarters. We started a big expansion into other markets, like Central America, where we started looking at Guatemala, Costa Rica, Mexico, and the association of some of our other operations. We started planning the development of armored car companies in Colombia and in Ecuador. We also started looking into Honduras. In some of these countries, we began running into legal difficulties, jealousies from the military institutions that were concerned about our presence. A few of the others wanted a piece of the action. I remember that in Costa Rica, a relative of the president wanted to help us set up operations, but wanted 'liberated' [free] shares. In Honduras, a member of the military also wanted a few shares.

"Therefore, some of these preliminary efforts were not very exciting. However, following the best tradition of Wackenhut—persistence can conquer—we finally were able to find a good partner in Guatemala. We started Wackenhut de Guatemala in 1978, with Roberto Alejos, who was introduced to the company by our former director of Public Relations, Mr. Hal Hendrix. It was a fifty-fifty operation in which I spent a lot of time and effort. Unfortunately for the taste of Mr. Hendrix, it looked like my efforts were not as effective, and I had a few problems getting involved with Mr. Alejos and Mr. Hendrix and their executives.

"After a couple of serious negotiations, we took the financial responsibility, as well as the management of the company, and we fixed it our way. Today, it is a beautiful operation, it is flourishing, and we brought local management up to Wackenhut standards. Now it is one of our model operations that provides assistance and support to the neighboring countries. Over 700 men are involved in the Guatemala operations and it is recording $2.5 million in revenues annually, which is very significant in that country.

"During that same period of time, Mr. Wackenhut, with the help of our director, Seth McKee, was introduced to the Nikon Building Services Group, which resulted in the operation of Wackenhut Keibi in Japan.

"In 1980, we consummated our agreement to enter into Mexico as a minority stockholder by the hand of an insurance group belonging to the Cichihuahua Group. This company was one of the horizontal integration divestitures, and the group wanted to enlarge the core business and to provide a better service. The managerial concept was sound, but in practice it was not operational, due to the habits and the culture of the salesmen.

"In Mexico, at that time, it was forbidden to use foreign names, and the Mexicans were adamant in not using the Wackenhut name or logo, because ours was going to be the first security company in the country of Mexico. And it truly was. However, the Mexican constitution does not provide for armed private security at all. There are historical reasons for it. So our company could not use weapons in a country that requires pistols. And we had to start—and still do today—to fight all concepts of security, and introduce security without weapons.

"Our first manager was a very nice Mexican professional in the area of human resources by the name of Ruben Contreras, who used to work with the Televisa Group as a vice president. Televisa is a very big Mexican television network. Ruben was a very active person, and he tried to get the corporation as a majority stockholder, which was very difficult, and after two years of efforts in developing our majority partner, we decided not to continue, and we looked for other partners.

"Henry B. Ford, our partner in Panama, introduced us to the Boroto Group. I spoke with various executives and we agreed to buy shares in the insurance group. This was the start of our Mexican group, Servicios Professionales de Proteccion y Seguridad, which today has four companies—in security, alarms, cleaning, and real estate.

"We started going to Chile and Peru, and that was the time of planting the seeds of these very small operations. We kept a very low profile but, little by little, in the Annual Report, the names of the companies were starting to appear and multiply.

"The 1981 contract for firefighting at Jeddah International Airport was brought by Les Lobaugh, and Bruce Berkmans was involved with a consultant by the name of Ray Klaus. It was in the aftermath of an accident, a tragedy in which several people burned in a plane. So the Saudi officials in civil aviation decided to install modern crash, fire, and rescue capabilities, and at that time we went over and offered our services to furnish British firefighters in all the airports of Saudi Arabia.

"Prior to that, in 1976, the brand-new Jeddah International Airport was a conceptual design project that Les Lobaugh got through Skidmore Owens and Merrill, SOM, one of the largest architectural firms in the United States. They needed security design and engineering. Les Lobaugh, under Mr. Kirk, with the help of a group of consultants, provided the complete conceptual design, which is probably the largest security design made by a private security company *ever*. We are very proud of what we did on that. Keep in mind, this is still, I believe, the largest airport in the world, and has a fifty-mile perimeter. Ed Kuncar was our resident manager in Jeddah for three years."

At about the same time that Carrizosa was director of Latin American Services at headquarters, 1979–80, Rick Wackenhut was returned to headquarters and appointed director of the Physical Security Division, responsible for domestic guard operations, support services, and physical security administration. He had served as district manager of North and South Carolina since June 1977.

"When I came back to headquarters and took over Physical Security in 1979, I reported to Gus Novotney," Rick says. "When I first got there, I had only three or four people reporting to me. I went to Gus at that time and, subsequently, to my father, and said, 'I'm sorry, this isn't going to do it, you can't control the country the way it needs to be controlled with only three or four people here. I need to build an organization, and I realize what that's going to do to overhead, but I've got to do it.' Gus said, 'What're you talking about?' I said, 'I need people assigned regionally.'

"I brought in two or three guys from the Carolinas—they used to call them the Carolina Mafia—that were area managers I hired that were successful, and brought them in on my staff. Then I selected other successful area managers and brought them in. Now it's a training ground for area offices, but at the time it required bringing in good, competent area managers as a staff for me. Because we had a lot of losing offices. So I used them in the same capacity and in the same style in which I acted when I was a district manager going to the offices that were losing money. And the way I cleaned them up, I used these guys to go out and clean up offices around the country. So that was the concept. And it worked. We got most offices into at least a service profit.

"When we moved to Miami, we moved into a house, 9000 Southwest 97th Terrace, behind Baptist Hospital, in that area. An old '50s-style home with terrazzo floors, but it had something like twenty-seven fruit trees in the backyard, it used to be a grove. That was great. We squeezed oranges all day long and just had a great time. It was a fun house, and that's where we really started raising Jennifer, now called Jennie, and had our second daughter, Lisa. We went from that home to 6342 Southwest 109th Street, off 67th Avenue, and lived there for a number of years.

"In 1981, as vice president of Operations, I still reported to Gus. I believe at that point in time I picked up Investigations. Rather than just having Physical Security, we evolved from that concept to a true regional concept. Ken Leazette and Bob Palioca reported to me at that time. They had reported to Gus, and then I think it shifted and they reported to me, and Gus took on some additional sales responsibilities. Anyway, the regional guys then reported to me for a period of time, and it became pretty clear that they were kind of—I'll say a different generation, but I don't mean that in the *age* generation, although that was there also. It was a different mind set of how business needed to be done. They were more at the end of their careers, I was more at the beginning of mine, and the job wasn't getting done. A fair amount of that also translated to Gus, which was very awkward, because my wife and I liked him and his wife very much. And yet, it was clear that some changes needed to be made. So that was a tough time."

At the quarterly meeting of the TWC board of directors in June 1981, Robert E. Chasen was elected a member of the board, as well as executive vice president of the Systems and Services Group. Born in Newark, New Jersey, July 3, 1916, he earned a BSC degree at Benjamin Franklin University in 1943, then served as a special agent in the FBI, 1943–52. He joined the International Telephone and Telegraph Corporation in 1952, where he was elected president and chairman of the board of the Federal Electric Corporation, a major

ITT subsidiary, and later served as ITT group vice president of the Government and Commercial Services Group. In 1977, after twenty-five years with ITT, he retired to accept the post of United States Commissioner of Customs, which he held until late 1980. In 1993, Chasen was still a member of the board of TWC, in addition to serving as a senior consultant to the chairman, and he is president of Robert E. Chasen and Associates, Inc., a management consulting firm.

In the summer of 1981, TWC was awarded a long-term contract to provide security services to the New Jersey Sports and Exposition Authority's huge complex of facilities known as the Meadowlands. The value of the contract was estimated to be in excess of $4 million. More than 400 uniformed TWC security personnel were assigned to protect the Meadowlands complex, which includes Giants Stadium, the newly opened Brendan Byrne Arena, and the Meadowlands Racetrack.

The stadium is the home of the New York Giants NFL football team and the New York Cosmos soccer team. In addition to football and soccer, the 76,000-seat stadium also is used for concerts, expositions, and other outdoor events. With 21,000 seats, the Brendan Byrne Arena provides a wide variety of indoor events ranging from basketball and soccer to concerts and circuses. The New Jersey Nets were scheduled to be the Arena's professional basketball tenant, and the Cosmos soccer team would also use the Arena's facilities. The Meadowlands Racetrack plays host to horse racing fans 282 days or nights a year, with programs of thoroughbred and standardbred racing. Average daily attendance is more than 17,000. The track is also the site of The Hambletonian, the premier trotting race in the world.

During the same time frame that Fernando Carrizosa and Rick Wackenhut were assuming high-visibility positions at headquarters (Fernando became vice president of Latin American Operations in 1980; Rick became vice president of Operations in 1981), another individual started to emerge from the ranks by the name of Alan Bernstein, who would, after several false starts, eventually become president of the Domestic Operations Group and one of two executive vice presidents of TWC.

Born Alan Barry Bernstein, April 22, 1947, in Brooklyn, New

York, he graduated from Brooklyn Tech in 1964, and from the University of Rochester in 1969 with a BSEE degree (bachelor of science with a major in electrical engineering), and later went on to earn his MBA at Cornell in 1982. He married the former Katherine Anne Lippert on May 3, 1969. "Immediately after that," he says, "I went to work for Eastman Kodak for about nine to twelve months, worked in their engineering department. After that, I moved to Florida, went to work for a company called Florida Security Systems. Worked there for about three years, then went in with a guy called George Fenton, the Fenton Company, he was really a factory rep for electronic security devices.

"At the time, we had sold some products to Wackenhut, through the Fenton Company. We were selling some electronic components for the Wackenhut 4000 Access Control System. I met a gentleman by the name of Harold Berlin, who was an employee of Wackenhut, and, through him, I met a couple of other people. They needed a test engineer. And, at the time, I was not really satisfied with traveling around the state, and basically didn't like what I was doing, so I got a job with Wackenhut Electronics here in Miami in 1974.

"The first time I met George Wackenhut was probably a couple of weeks after I had actually been employed. Interesting circumstances. During the time I was a test engineer, I did a lot of work with the alarm central station that was here. I grew up in the alarm business, because my father owned alarm companies, my grandfather owned alarm companies, and, to this day, my brothers still own alarm companies. We were doing some testing on standardization of products. I had put a paper together, basically saying that the company was buying the panels, and all of the equipment needed to install alarms, from twenty or thirty different companies. And the reason why we had so much inventory, and so much money tied up in inventory, is because we weren't standardizing.

"So, apparently, that memo got to George, or to somebody near his level, and Bud Thompson brought me over to talk about it, and he introduced me to George Wackenhut. And at that time, they transferred me from WEI, which was electronics, into WESC, I think that was the original name of the company. I went over and worked as a test engineer, and helped standardize products for Wackenhut in the Alarm Division.

"Within a very short period of time, the general manager of that department got into a battle with Bud Thompson. Bud was on the phone with him, on the speaker, and I just happened to be in the general manager's office, and Bud basically *fired* him on the phone! At the time he fired him over the phone, and the guy was packing up, Bud said, over the speaker, 'Who's in the room?' And, you know, I told him I was in the room. He didn't know me, except for that one meeting we had on the memo, months before. Bud said something to the effect, 'Well, I'd like you to come over to headquarters.' I went over to headquarters, and he said, 'Do you think you could run the alarm group over there?' And I said, 'Yeah, my father owns alarm companies, I ran some of my father's companies.' So he said, 'Well, you're the new general manager!' Without exaggeration, that's how it happened! I mean, I was in the right place at the right time, and Bud made me general manager.

"Then he introduced me to Murray Levine, because, at that time, the alarm group reported to the local area manager. Now, I had met Murray once before, because when I went to apply for my original job, Murray had actually done my polygraph. Murray was doing polygraphs and doing area manager work.

"And then I went to work as the general manager of the alarm central station in Miami. That would have been early '75, I would say. Stayed with that job for about a year and a half. We turned it around, we made some profits, we were doing well, when a man by the name of Bob Edwards, who was the vice president of the Alarm Division—we owned the alarm company in Los Angeles, Puerto Rico, Miami, and Baltimore—he said, 'Look, we have a serious problem in Los Angeles. You did a good job here, would you consider going to Wackenhut, Los Angeles, and take over the alarm operations there?' I said, 'Yes,' and approximately mid-1975, I went out and took over the alarm operation, and worked there for about a year and a half.

"After that, I left the company. We came into some money, and my wife and I had basically made a decision between us that it would be a lot of fun to go ahead and do what we always talked about when we were in college, which would be—we didn't have any children yet—to just kind of relax and live on a farm in Oregon! My brother-in-law, who is in Oregon, and my wife's sister, we all bought this farm in Oregon. And, as I jokingly said nine months later, 'A boy from *Brooklyn* doesn't belong on a *farm* in *Oregon!*' So, Kath and I decided we're going to move back to Miami.

"I had no job, we had nothing, and we just came back to live in our house—we kept our home here in Miami all that time. During my time with the company, I had developed a relationship with the Wackenhut family, Rick and George, and when they knew I was back in town, they said, 'Why don't you come over? We don't have a job as a general manager, but why don't you come back as *something?*' This would've been late '77, in that time frame.

"I worked as a *salesman!* And, I must say, it was probably the best couple of years of my life, working as an alarm salesman. Not only was I free to do a lot of things I wanted to do, but it was good money for the late '70s, and I was having a good time. Not working very hard in the sense that I put in a lot of hours, but I liked selling. So, to me, it wasn't working very hard.

"Then, around 1979-1980, the position of general manager of the alarm central station again opened up, and George called me and said, 'Why don't you consider taking the job?' The reason why I questioned it was because it was really a pay cut. I wasn't going to get commissions, I was going to be tied down to a desk, the responsibility was going to be much different. But I said I'd do it.

"I did that until 1981, when, once again, I had an opportunity to go into business with my family. My father had sold his companies to the Honeywell Corporation, all his alarm companies, and my brother decided that he was going to buy a piece of the business that Honeywell was not that interested in. So, my brother and I bought it from my father. The name of the company was Security Systems, Inc. It was a division of Rochester Central Alarms, which was the main company that my father owned. Very quickly I realized that it was not something that I wanted to do. Quite frankly, I forgot what it was like to work in a family business.

"Long story short, we had been up near Ithaca, New York, and I had about six months left of my graduate degree, so I went over to Cornell and finished up my MBA degree in 1982. And, again, because of my wife's position, there was no great hurry. But all during that time, not only did I communicate with Rick and George, but also with a guy named Bob Chasen. Bob and I had become very friendly before I had left, primarily because of some of the work I was doing for Bob. So I talked almost every other week with Bob and Rick.

"I was down here on some personal business when I saw Rick and Molly, and Rick said, 'Why don't you come back?' And I said I would come back. At that time, I made a personal commitment to Rick and to George that if I came back this time I would not leave again. That would have been in early '82."

In June of 1982, the second of the "old-time" senior officers, Bob Kirk, decided to retire. Coincidentally, Kirk had also left TWC twice before. He started in October 1961 as contracts manager, resigned less than a year later, then returned in late 1962. After becoming a key player in landing both the Kennedy Space Center contract in 1964 and the Nevada Test Site contract the same year, he resigned for the second time on June 30, 1970, at the age of fifty-one. In his letter of resignation to George, dated May 12, 1970, he stated his reasons in part:

> This action is being taken after many days and hours of consideration on my part. It is no longer physically possible to maintain the momentum necessary to accomplish all the requirements of the assigned responsibilities. Further, I sincerely believe that new blood and new ideas will carry the Company forward at a rate which may even surpass that of my past eight and one-half year tenure . . .

At the time, Kirk was senior vice president of WSI. He returned again in 1971, and was credited by George in assuming the major responsibility for obtaining the huge contracts for both the construction phase of the trans-Alaska pipeline in 1974, and for the operational phase of the pipeline in 1977. When he retired for good on June 1, 1982, at the age of sixty-three, he was president of Wackenhut International, Inc., and he was given a huge wall plaque inscribed with the signatures of his International executives from all over the world.

Kirk now lives in the beautiful resort town of Homosassa, Florida, just north of Tampa, and since retirement he has been a special consultant to the chairman. When we talked with him in November of 1992, he was in excellent health, along with his wife Christa, and playing golf almost every day. His face lit up when we started talking about Murray Levine, one of the most colorful characters in the history of the company.

"I *hired* Murray Levine," he recalls. "I think it was October or November of 1964. The reason I remember that, I was sitting in George's office when he was going to interview Murray, and Murray has always been rather direct. But after he came out of it, Murray said, 'Gee, I'm going to be happy here.' I said, 'Murray, there's one thing I'm going to tell you. I want you to go back to my office with me and, right off the bat, we don't do any so-called low-pricing.' I said, 'I feel strongly that if we try to undercut our competition, we'll fall flat on our face. Every job, we're going to go higher. No matter what the argument, we're going to go higher.'

"Before coming with us, I think Murray had been with Globe in Jacksonville. He was always anxious to stick his nose into something, to see what the score was, and I think he just wanted to see if he could possibly get in here. I believe I was the first one to interview him. I liked the guy, and I liked the approach he had, and I liked his apparent tenacity toward getting business. Outwardly, Murray is a clown, and he's always been that way. People always liked him and, as they got to know him better, they liked him even better, because Murray always said what he felt. I never heard of Murray trying to stab anybody in the back. He's very outgoing. And he could handle George, too—I tell you, at times, it's amazing the stuff he got by with. To this day, I believe Murray Levine accomplished more for TWC than any other person except George Wackenhut."

Murray Levine, who celebrated his thirtieth anniversary with TWC on February 4, 1994, is vice president of the South Florida Region and of Custom Protection Services. In the early 1980s, he started working at headquarters, then moved to the area office in Boca Raton, Florida, in January 1991, where he also makes his home with his wife Barbara (McDonald), who is the TWC development representative in the Boca Raton office. His son, Drew, is the TWC area manager in Fort Lauderdale.

Born in Philadelphia, October 28, 1930, Levine graduated from

Simon Gratz High School in 1948, and never attended college. "My first real job, I was a manager for Globe Security in Philadelphia," he says. "I opened up their office in Jacksonville, Florida, in 1959. I was first exposed to Wackenhut when I called on the Martin Company in Orlando, Florida, where I observed probably the finest-looking security force that was in the business. I became disenchanted with Globe for many reasons, they're not important, and sought to join Wackenhut.

"Interestingly enough, I contacted a client of mine, Lou Libby, who knew George Wackenhut, and they had done some work together. He was a former agent, and he was head of security for the Winn Dixie Stores. I told him I had an interest in joining Wackenhut. He made a call. Hence, I appeared at their headquarters at 3280 Ponce de Leon Boulevard in Coral Gables.

"I was first exposed to the 'legend' at that time. I interviewed with him, and also with Bob Kirk and John Ammarell. But the interview with George Wackenhut was interesting, because he scared the pants off me. At that time, he looked like a young Don Shula, with a jutting jaw and a crew cut. He was in marvelous physical condition, and his eyes—he would look *through* you when he talked to you. I was in front of a living legend and I admit that I was quite nervous. The calming factor was Bob Kirk. They asked all the questions that one asks. We came to a meeting of the minds, and I joined the company February 4, 1964. I was thirty-three years old.

"I joined Wackenhut to manage the Jacksonville office. Unfortunately, I had a one-year noncompetitive agreement to ride out, so when I went to Jacksonville, Globe enforced the agreement, so I had to make up time before I could go back. As a result, I came back to Miami and did some sales in the Miami area, then went up to Baltimore-Washington to open up the Baltimore-Washington office.

"At the end of that time, I went to Jacksonville and opened up the Wackenhut office there. I set out to do what I was employed to do, and that was to establish Jacksonville and put it on the map. Indeed, within two years, it was a going concern. Then John Ammarell had a discussion with me about coming to headquarters to help them expand, and to hire and train new managers around the country, and teach them the Wackenhut ways, and get various offices going.

Which I did. The offices were in Chicago, St. Louis, Honolulu. To hire, train, and get an office going required about a month, maybe two months in some cases.

"Following that, I wasn't too pleased with the road travel, and I suggested to John Ammarell that if they ever separated the Miami operations from corporate headquarters, I wanted to be considered for the Miami office. There was no Miami office, everything operated from the corporate building.

"So, I had to go to Hawaii for some company business, and, when I got back, the corporation was awarded the Governor's War on Crime. Hence, they needed space at headquarters, so they said, 'You're the area manager in Miami.' This was in 1967. I had to quickly go out and, within forty-eight hours, find office space, transfer everything, and start the Miami office. That first office was in a 30,000-square-foot empty space on Federal Highway, where we rented 2,000 of the 30,000 square feet. Following that, it was on Bird Road, then we moved to the Doral area, and eventually to the Government Center, where it is now. Actually, I took both the Miami and Fort Lauderdale offices. Opened the Fort Lauderdale office from scratch. The gross revenue of the two offices in '67 was about $500,000.

"During that period, *my* highlights were being accepted by this corporation. Because what I found was that the upper echelon and area managers had considerably better backgrounds than I did. And they were considerably better educated. Retired generals, colonels, special agents of the FBI. And it was difficult for me to think that I could be a fit. What I found over the ensuing years, I could run rings around them. Which pleased me no end.

"In the '70s, we improved pay scales and benefits of guards, took them out of the minimum-wage category, and acquired contracts that this company was desperate to get, like Pan American World Airways, and other major contracts that helped in the building of the office. As I said, when we took it over, the two counties were about half a million a year. Last year, the two counties represented about $29 million. Obviously, in this business, you win and lose contracts, and not all losses are our fault. Some of them went out of business, like CenTrust and National Airlines. I can't remember ever losing a major contract because of service. Lost them for various reasons, low bids, out of business, or going in-house, like *The Miami Herald.*

"Somewhere in that period, I took over the Palm Beach operations. Highlights: I sold their first nuclear contracts, that was Florida Power and Light, Turkey Point, and St. Lucie, which, in effect, launched us into the nuclear business.

"I came back into headquarters in the early '80s as director of the Southeast Region. In the regional program, my region consisted of everything from the Carolinas to the Keys. I became a vice president in the mid-1980s, and I was at headquarters until January of 1991. First it was the region, then South Florida, then South Florida and the Custom Protection Division.

"Custom Protection was my baby, but it was really what I felt George Wackenhut represented. After leaving Globe and coming here, because I wanted to be with someone who was professional, I found that Wackenhut did quality work in the government jobs, but we weren't much different than our competitors in the private-sector jobs. We were different only with respect to the quality of management that we had. The quality of management is not enough when it comes to delivering a good product. A good product is predicated on background training, pay levels, and all the incentives you need to retain people and have them perform well. The good product was as vacant with us as it was with Globe or anybody else.

"I found that our competitors were without honor, and that this company did have that touch of class. Even though we were in a body-slinging business, we always retained that touch of class. Which I liked.

"What George Wackenhut and I have is an absolute love affair, where I am as comfortable talking to him as I would be in talking with members of my own family. Although, professionally, I hold him in awe, I know a human side of him. He projected in the '60s, especially with that jutting jaw and the crew cut, the epitome of a right-wing Nazi. Miami, in those days, was a big Jewish community, especially on the Beach. And one time, Dick Gerstein, who was the state's attorney, said to me, 'How can you work for him? The man is a right-wing *Nazi!*' And, knowing him as I did, George was anything *but.* Although he's America-first, and extremely on the right, so am I! I'm to the right of *him!* I've seen him in situations, as tough as he is, where he had to make some very tough decisions, especially where it came to people, and he was very humanistic. It's a side of him that not too many see.

"But one of the cutest things I ever saw with him, when we were on Ponce de Leon Boulevard, I found out who the *real* boss was. And it was *Mrs.* Wackenhut. Because one day, I was sitting in his office, and she happened to be, in those days, movie-star quality. Absolutely beautiful woman. We were talking about some business matter, and she came in and berated him about something, going a mile a minute, and his lips started to disappear. She turned on her heel and was about to leave, and his eyes dropped, watching her *can* go out the door. Then he had a big smile on his face. And, as tough as the two strong personalities are, it's the love affair of all time."

HISTORICALLY, the first two years of the decade of the 1980s were highlighted by the U.S.-Iran hostage conflict. On January 29, 1980, six U.S. Embassy aides escaped from Iran with Canadian help. February 2, the FBI's undercover operation "Abscam" (for Arab scam) implicated public officials. April 7, the U.S. broke diplomatic relations with Iran. April 25, eight U.S. servicemen were killed and five injured when a helicopter and cargo plane collided in an abortive desert raid to rescue American hostages in Teheran. July 27, the Shah of Iran died at age sixty. September 17, Anastasio Somoza Debayle, the ousted Nicaragua ruler, and two of his aides were assassinated in Asuncion, Paraguay. September 19, following an invasion, Iraq troops held ninety square miles of Iran. November 4, Ronald Reagan was elected president in a Republican sweep. December 4, two U.S. nuns and a lay worker were shot dead in El Salvador. December 4, John Lennon of the Beatles was shot dead in New York.

On January 18, 1981, an agreement between the U.S. and Iran freed fifty-two hostages held in Teheran since November 4, 1979. January 20, Ronald Reagan took the oath as the fortieth president. March 30, President Reagan was wounded by a gunman, along with his press secretary and two law-enforcement officers. May 14, Pope

John Paul II was wounded by a gunman in Rome. July 7, President Reagan nominated Judge Sandra Day O'Connor, fifty-one, as the first woman on the Supreme Court. July 18, 110 died and 188 were injured when an aerial walkway collapsed in the lobby of the Hyatt Regency Hotel in Kansas City. August 3, U.S. air traffic controllers staged a nationwide strike. August 11, President Reagan dismissed the strikers.

24

BUDD KNEIP, who joined TWC in mid-September of 1982 as director of Power Generating Services, was another young executive who would quickly be promoted to the ranks of top management within a relatively short period of time. When he was interviewed in October 1993, he had been senior vice president, Corporate Planning and Development, since 1988. Born Robert Charles Kneip III in Chicago, March 8, 1948, he was raised in a number of Midwestern cities, because his father was an executive with Kaiser Aluminum and was required to relocate each time he was promoted. However, Budd (his nickname since childhood) spent all of his high school years in a suburb of Minneapolis, graduating from Hopkins High School in 1966. When he graduated with honors from the University of Iowa in 1970, with a BA in history, he received offers of financial aid from four very fine southern graduate schools, Virginia, North Carolina, Duke, and Tulane, as well as from Iowa, to continue his studies in history.

Kneip selected Tulane because he was offered one of the very lucrative NDEA Title IV fellowships (National Defense Education Act, an act passed during the Eisenhower Administration), funded by the federal government. It paid all tuition, fees, books, plus a stipend of $300 a month for the first year, escalating to $340 the second year, and $400 monthly for the final year. As it turned out, it was an excellent choice, because the faculty at Tulane included one of the premier scholars in colonial American history, the area of his primary concentration.

In the summer of 1972, the history department at Tulane, along with at least fifty other graduate schools, received a solicitation from the Atomic Energy Commission to nominate three graduate students for an internship with the AEC.

"The AEC had a full-time history staff," Kneip explains. "They had, I believe, four full-time paid historians doing nothing but writing the history of the Atomic Energy Commission. Richard Hewlett, who was the AEC historian, had written several prize-winning books, including *Nuclear Navy* [1974], which was, I believe, nominated for the Pulitzer Prize, so they took that program very seriously. Curiously, they vested in the historian's office the responsibility for developing their internship program. They had four slots, and they would take the brightest humanities students they could find, put them in those slots, and they reported to the secretary of the Commission, and worked directly with the five presidentially appointed commissioners. Their role was to give educated laymen's opinions on scientific policy. It was a fascinating program. Very well conceived. And, since it was run by the historian, he tended to solicit from the history departments of the various graduate schools.

"So, that summer, he solicited something like fifty graduate schools, asking for three nominees each, and there was only *one slot* open! My ex-wife was from Washington, DC, and we always had a pleasant time visiting family there, and I was just about to start the third year of the fellowship, so I was already thinking: What am I going to do when the money runs out? The chairman of the history department gave me an application for the internship and I filled it out. I sent it in and didn't hear anything for a number of months and—lo and behold—they called and asked me to come up and interview. In November of '73, just one month before that third year ran out, I got an offer to go to Washington and join the Atomic Energy Commission. Which I did. I had been awarded my MA in May of 1972. During the remainder of the term and through early 1973, I was preparing for my doctoral exams, which I passed in the summer of 1973.

"I started out as a policy analyst in the secretary's office, and the next year I was promoted to lead policy analyst. I reviewed all the policy that was done out of one section of the secretary's office.

"I believe it was 1974 when the Energy Reorganization Act was passed. That act dissolved the Atomic Energy Commission and broke it into two organizations. One was the Energy Research and Development Administration, known as ERDA, and the other was the Nuclear Regulatory Commission, the NRC. ERDA had a very short two-year life; it became the Department of Energy. The NRC continued along. The theory was—I think it was flawed—but the theory was that you could not vest in one agency the ability to research and test product, on the one hand, while at the same time license its use.

"Be that as it may, I opted to move to the regulatory side, and stayed with the NRC in the office of the secretary through 1976. I ended up being an assistant to the secretary of the NRC, which sounds grandiose, but, in fact, there were a couple of assistants, so it wasn't that big a deal. But it was one of those nice things to say over a manhattan at lunch! In Washington, the name of the game is what title you could drop! I stayed there as we got the agency off the ground, and it was a long time before we had our full slate of presidential appointees. It was a five-man commission, and there were a lot of political battles about who was going to get placed on it.

"After we got those things established, I was asked to go over to the contract section to help structure their procurement regulations. I was with Procurement Policy and Planning, I believe it was called, for the remaining years of my government career. I left in 1978, because I was running out of tenure to complete my Ph.D. When I left Tulane in 1973, I had already received my master's in 1972, and I had passed my doctoral exams in 1973. You only have seven years after you are admitted to candidacy to complete your Ph.D., and I was beginning to run out of those years. I really wanted that degree finished, since I had gone 75 percent of the way. I still had to complete the dissertation. Now, while I was in Washington, I did take advantage of being in the secretary's office: I had special Library of Congress privileges, I was allowed to check books out of the Library, and I also had a study in the rotunda of the Library itself. It was very, very nice, because I had one of the sets of Madison's notes on the Constitution right over my right shoulder while I was writing!

"I did take advantage of that time to do a lot of research. But it's very difficult to do the concerted kind of writing, and to find that time, after work and on weekends. I'd get up early in the morning and I'd drive down—or later take the subway—to the Library of Congress, and I'd work there all day Saturdays. It was a difficult process, and when it came down to actually structuring the dissertation, I couldn't do it and work full time.

"So we packed up everything and went back down to Tulane. I finished it up there and was awarded my Ph.D. in 1980. When you get down to the end of the Ph.D. process, when all of your readers have read the document, and have substantially approved it, and there aren't any big research gaps, then it's a matter of refining the language in a couple of places. Maybe you have go back and fill in a hole here and there. You have a lot of administrative work. Back in the days before word processors, you had to use special dissertation paper that was bracketed in the corners, all of the typing had to fall within those brackets, and you were not allowed any erasures, whiteouts, or strikeovers. All footnotes had to be done inside those brackets, which meant you had to find incredibly skilled typists to do that, and it was a very expensive and time-consuming process. Back then, I paid a dollar a page, and I had a four-volume dissertation. I think I paid about $1,500—which I didn't *have!* But it was just a process you had to go through.

"When you begin to wind that down, you do have some time. You have to be resident at the school, because it's just impossible to organize all of that from afar. At the same time, it just wasn't in my nature to sit around. I could've had some graduate assistant teaching jobs in the meantime, but I had a wife and we had a child, and so it was one of those circumstances where the resources had to be a little bit more substantial. Plus, my wife at that time, who is now my ex-wife, was very materially driven, and was somewhat unhappy at the penurious circumstances of being a graduate student, and really longed for the days when we both had careers. For example, we were featured on the cover of *Money Magazine* in May of 1976 as typical of Washington's up-and-coming couples, we had a nice house in Alexandria, Virginia, and now here we were back in New Orleans as graduate students again, and she just couldn't quite make the passage back!

"I had no trouble with it, but it's one of those things, one of those little bumps in the road that end up driving you in various directions. So, having had the time, I knew there was a big DOE project in New Orleans. I want to say it started around the late '70s, maybe '77 or '78, and that was the Strategic Petroleum Reserve. SPRO, as we used to call it—now it's just the SPR—was a joint venture out of California between the Ralph G. Parsons Company, and Gilbane, both big construction companies, who took on the task of building the Strategic Petroleum Reserve.

"It was a fascinating project. Of all the sites, and I believe there are eight of them now, all but one of them was 'solution mined,' as opposed to 'conventionally drilled.' The purpose of the SPRO—this was after the oil embargo of '73-'74—was to bury reserves of raw petroleum, and have the capacity to pump it out and ship it to the major pipeline systems of the country in short order. The best place to store oil is in salt, because the liquid doesn't migrate through the salt. And the southern Louisiana Gulf Coast, and over a little bit into Texas, has some of the world's richest and deepest salt reserves. Most of those cavities were solution mined.

"Fundamentally, you drill a hole, and you put two pipes in there. You run a hose down one of them, a hose with a computer-controlled nozzle, and you had, in a sense, a sonic diagram of what the reserve formation looked like. Then you pump water in at high pressure, and aim the hose, and it literally carved out domes to the exact dimensions you wanted. That left a brine in the bottom of this hole, and to get that out, you used the other pipe, and you pumped oil down into it. Oil is heavier than brine, so the oil would drop down to the bottom and would push the brine out of the top. A really basic, simple, and ingenious kind of process. It created a lot of problems, because the brine concentration was higher than the brine concentration in the Gulf, and it killed shrimp, oysters, and a whole host of other things.

"But they overcame those kinds of problems. Only one place, in New Iberia, at the Weeks Island facility, they had an old abandoned salt mine that Morton Salt had worked. That was the only one that was conventionally drilled that they would pump oil into. But the rest of these things, it was quite an interesting process, and the headquarters of that whole project was New Orleans.

"So I simply went down the road one day and knocked on their door, figuratively, walked into their offices, went to the head of the project, explained who I was and what my background was. And, of course, I'd come out of Washington as a contracting officer for the NRC, which was sort of a sister agency. It so happened, at that time they needed a subcontract administrator. We probably had over $100 million of subcontracts that we would let a year, and some of them were very strange. For example, workover rigs at about $1.5 million a pop. Just pick up the phone and call.

"But it was a very interesting project. Within a couple of months, I moved up to become head of the entire procurement function. I ran the prime contract with the Department of Energy, which was in the hundreds of millions of dollars. All the subcontracts, which were also hundreds of millions of dollars, and all the small purchasing, which ran millions of dollars—everything from pencils and paper clips to facilitators to make sure when they said they were going to deliver pipes, pipes were delivered. The relationships between the prime contractor, a company called Dravo, out of Pittsburgh—they established a special firm down there called DUCI, Dravo Utility Contractors, Inc.—the relationships between DUCI, who I worked for, and the DOE were very, very strained, and this was sort of the last year of their contract. It was general knowledge that they weren't going to maintain the contract.

"I knew that going in, but, again, it was something to do, and it still allowed me time to go back and finish up the Ph.D. They were very considerate over there, and if I needed that half-day or a day to go do a little research, or to polish up part of the dissertation and just work the mechanics, I had plenty of time to do it."

Kneip's dissertation, titled *William Hooper, 1742–1790: Misunderstood Patriot,* was submitted to the graduate school of Tulane's department of history on June 27, 1980, together with a required three-page abstract. The first paragraph of the abstract gives intriguing insights into his subject, a little-known but brilliant political theorist, who was a signer of the Declaration of Independence:

> America's revolutionary past cannot be fully understood without a closer examination of the individuals who directed events at the colonial and state levels. In North Carolina, William Hooper assumed the posi-

tion of spokesman for his colony's and state's interests during that crucial period just preceding and following independence. He championed autonomy in local matters in colonial Assemblies, organized North Carolina's first provincial congress and led that delegation in the Continental Congress from 1774 through 1777. During the course of that service, Hooper's colleagues recognized his talents and awarded them by inviting him to participate in those momentous decisions which altered the political history of America and the Western world.

During his tenure as manager of procurement for Dravo, the prime contractor for SPRO, 1980-81, Kneip had his initial meeting with George Wackenhut, and it was on a quasi-adversarial basis. "One of the subcontracts that had been signed for security at the project, before I got to the SPRO, was with The Wackenhut Corporation," Kneip recalls with a smile. "At the time, I don't think all the sites were done when it was signed. I think there were perhaps five sites completed. The DOE had wanted security, there was a very aggressive security manager at DOE, whose name crosses Wackenhut history at three or four different points down the road. His name is George Miserendino. George was there, and George has an awful lot of strong points; one of them, however, is not his flexibility.

"He liked Wackenhut because of the work it had done at the Nevada Test Site. I mean, Wackenhut was then—and still is—known as the premier provider of security at these complex government projects.

"So Miserendino insisted that Dravo write a contract with Wackenhut, which isn't always good, because the contractor likes to feel they have some control over a project in a contract. But Dravo didn't really resist, because Wackenhut stood out on its merits anyway. But the flaw was that they wrote a fixed-price contract. What that means is that you contract to provide, say, five guards at—pick a figure—four dollars an hour. And they'll each work forty hours, and that's the end of it. You agree to a figure in advance. It will cost you x-millions of dollars for a year.

"Well, that doesn't work out on a dynamic and vital project that is in the process of being built. Every time a new well-head would open, you need to put more people there. You couldn't do it on a fixed-price contract without negotiating an amendment. Otherwise, you don't protect yourself. When you come to submit the bill, and you've exceeded that fixed-price allotment, you don't get paid.

"So it got to be a bit of a contest. George Miserendino wanted things done, and he wanted them done *now*. Bob Frye, who was president of WSI at the time, and a very fine, ethical gentleman who had years and years of experience in this arena, and who also has one of the most temperate dispositions of anybody I've ever met, kept sort of gently reminding Miserendino that Wackenhut couldn't do these things without amendments. And the amendments would get way behind, so it might be weeks before an amendment could get done. In the meantime, Wackenhut is experiencing costs and, in theory, they have overrun their contract, because they don't have an executed amendment, and they don't really have the authority to *bill* for it.

"By the time I got in there, these guys were having regular meetings. Bob Frye would fly into town and he'd sort of rub his head and try to convince Miserendino, or get him to understand, what the problem was. And it really just got down to a nasty, contentious battle between Miserendino and The Wackenhut Corporation.

"The contract was set to expire anyway, so I started the solicitation process which would lead to either a renewal of the Wackenhut contract or the selection of a new contractor. The whole process required many, many months, because it was *the* largest service contract at the SPRO. There were bigger contracts for things like workover rigs, and well-heads, and stuff like that, but as far as a service contract goes, this was in the millions. We did change it from a fixed-price to a cost-plus, so this was a big, big contract. Collectively, we wrote a very good set of specifications.

"All the major security providers in the U.S., plus some of the smaller firms, attended the pre-bid conference, and submitted bids. We finally narrowed it down, and we found that Pinkerton, Wells Fargo, and Wackenhut were the three that made what we called the 'best and final' range. I don't remember what the numbers were, I think when we started out we had about fifty different firms. A massive number of people showed up. Our first pre-bid conference, we had to go to an auditorium. At the time—I mean, you had the

Nevada Test Site over there—but this was new blood in the system, this was a brand-new contract, it brought everybody out of the woodwork. In terms of aggregate dollars, it was still smaller than NTS, but it was so exciting, because you were always adding new sites, it went over seven different locations in two states. You had licensing problems, you had coordination between the parishes in Louisiana and the counties in Texas, the feds, the state, local sheriffs—I mean, it was a very, very complex contract.

"So we had three firms left, one of which was Wackenhut. Well, it turns out, Wackenhut had made some mistakes on the solicitation. The pricing was all wrong. In some cases, pages were duplicated, pages didn't fit, so we weren't sure what the pricing was. Technically, they were certainly as good as anybody else, but the experience—because they'd been there—hurt them. And that was an honest appraisal by my technical board; I was not a voting member. So, in a very close contest, Wells Fargo actually prevailed on the contract.

"But during the orals—and this was when I first met George Wackenhut—during the orals, George Wackenhut attended with the management team. And it was a very tense meeting, because Wackenhut knew that they were the incumbent, but there were tensions with George Miserendino and the Department of Energy. The proposal, as I said, had some flaws in it. The technical group had a lot of questions about it. And then we had all the pricing screwups, and it made it very, very difficult to get through it. It was probably, I recall, maybe a two- or three-hour oral discussion. Then we broke and we came back for some critique.

"I had to be fairly pointed and say some fairly harsh things about Wackenhut. But I tried to couch it in professional terms and in positive terms. And, as it turns out, I must have, because a couple of years later, through a real quirk of fate, the way I got hired was kind of an interesting story—George Wackenhut *remembered* that. He remembered how I'd handled it. There are so many people in this world who would have been petty about it, and said, 'Yeah, I remember that son of a bitch, he's the one who took the contract away.' Instead, what George remembered, and he told me a couple of years later when he hired me, was that I had done a very difficult task professionally and diplomatically. And that's what appealed to him.

"When we get to the story of my joining Wackenhut, one of the things that made such an impression on me was that kind of attitude. You know, that chapter was closed with George. And I've noticed that about George over the years, when something is done, it's done. You try to learn whatever lessons you can from the event, you try to build off it and be better, but I've *never* seen George complain or worry or whine about an opportunity when it's *gone*.

"Wells Fargo won the contract. That was a significant issue for Wackenhut because, not only did they lose the contract, but it introduced a new player into government procurement. Up until that time, it was basically Wackenhut. And that also would come back to haunt them at Savannah River—in a small way, but, at the time, it caused some consternation.

"When the meeting was over, I went up to George and I said, 'Mr. Wackenhut, I'm pleased to meet you.' He was a legend already, and, of course, I wasn't an expert on security. I was an historian, an academician, but I didn't know much about security. But to everybody in the security business—and I noticed this even with the people who were on my technical board—George Wackenhut really inspired a certain amount of awe and respect, just by virtue of who he was. Of course, he was a very imposing figure, still had his mustache, very ramrod straight, stockier than he is today, and it was clear, watching the dynamics in the room, that everybody in that room was sensitive to George Wackenhut being present.

"I stayed with Dravo, they lost the contract, as expected, and the curious thing that happened, once Wells Fargo was awarded the security contract, they didn't know what to do with it. In retrospect, I guess if I had to look back and be critical, I would be critical of my board's evaluation of Wells Fargo's government experience, because they really didn't have much. In any event, Wells Fargo came to me when the Dravo contract was lost.

"One day, it was very strange, the president of Wells Fargo, Joe Gamble, flew into town. Well, I didn't need him for contract administration. Very nice man, former FBI agent, knew George Wackenhut. And it was in my office, which was very small, we sat down with the contract administrator, and we walked through some issues that we needed to deal with, and Joe Gamble just kind of sat in the back of the room. He was a big presence, in some respects, just like George was. Big, imposing guy, had these Leonid Brezhnev *eyebrows*. I mean, they just sort of started at the bridge of the nose and ended up somewhere around his hat size. They were incredible. Almost like *awnings!*

"When the meeting was over, the contract administrator got up, excused himself, and Joe Gamble asked me what my plans were going to be. I said, 'Well, Joe, I really don't have any.' And he came right out and said, 'We're having a little trouble administering this. You've got the background. If there isn't a conflict or an ethical issue here, would you consider joining Wells Fargo? And then, not only work this contract for us, but see if you can build government business?' I said I was flattered and would certainly consider that.

"They had a big regional meeting in Houston about a month later, and there had been some correspondence and phone calls, and they flew me over, and I spent three days with their senior staff, and just kind of listened. Then we came to an agreement. My job with Dravo was over; Wells Fargo had already won the contract; I was a nonvoting member of the board, so there was no way that I could've influenced that; and plus, there had been no conversation before that point.

"So I took that job and I stayed with them for just over one year, from April of 1981 to June of 1982. I was director of Government Affairs. And we were fairly successful, we won a couple of big utility contracts, a couple of small government jobs, and with the SPRO contract, which might have been about $10 million a year, we had about $50 million in business in that year. Unfortunately, Joe Gamble was bumped upstairs, he had some personality conflicts with Malcolm Baker, who owned Baker Industries, which in turn owned Wells Fargo. Joe was kind of my rabbi. There were a certain number of people, kind of a rump on the side of Wells Fargo management, who did not like government business because it was very low-margined, and a new president came in, a fellow by the name of Tom Ward, and we had a very amicable but definite separation about a year later.

"And they were very fair. I have no animosity with Wells Fargo. They gave me a nice severance package. But it was clear that government contracts were not part of their long-range plans. They did not want to build that up. They were after the guard business, they wanted the margins out of the guard business, and they were not concerned about the stability or the revenue cash flow that comes out of a government contract. Also requires different accounting practices, which they weren't interested in setting up. A lot of good reasons and I can understand it.

"Part of the package when I joined Wells Fargo, they asked me where I wanted to live. There was a guy who was a fairly talented writer who happened to run the Orlando branch, so I said, 'Fine, I'd like to move to Orlando.' So, for that fourteen months I was with Wells Fargo, I was in Orlando. Part of the severance with Wells Fargo is that they offered to move me anywhere in the world. If I wanted to go to London, they'd move me to London. I said, 'No, everything's back in New Orleans.' I was divorced by that time. I said, 'Why don't you move me back to New Orleans?'

"Now, one of the things I had to do during the fourteen months I was with Wells Fargo was re-bid the SPRO contract. Which we did, and we were successful. I did most of the writing at Wells Fargo's office in New Orleans, and it so happened that the office manager was a young lady named Cynthia Saladino, who turned out to later become my wife. That's how I met her. Cindy was just a workhorse, she was there twenty hours a day. She arranged all the service we needed, the typing, reproduction, the office space, the transportation. She had a very, very critical role in putting that thing together. And we were literally putting it together as we were delivering it. It was a massive effort. Two people with no resources. The company simply didn't know how to put one of these bids together. And, I mean, we were scrambling. Cindy and I were fairly close at that point, and I just decided that was my home, I knew everybody back in New Orleans, so let's move back there.

"I moved back in June of '82. And did a little consulting. Wells Fargo, in fact, used me as a consultant on three or four jobs, and I did some consulting with one of the aerospace companies in Louisiana. Had kind of a nice little deal going, not making much money, but sort of enjoying myself, working out of one room that I was leasing, and making ends meet.

"It just so happened—and you talk about the vagaries of business—the area manager for Wells Fargo in New Orleans was an old-time friend of Cindy's. He was a former assistant chief of police or something in the New Orleans police force. He had been a Wackenhut employee before. He spent one year with Wells Fargo, then Wackenhut recruited him back, so by the time I moved back to New Orleans—Frank Hayward was his name—he was the area manager for the Wackenhut New Orleans office.

"So Frank and his wife Evelyn, and Cindy and I, we got to be very close, and spent a lot of time together. In August of 1982, Frank had to travel to Coral Gables for a regular meeting of the Operations people. As he was walking down the hall in the old 3280 Ponce building, he had to pass Rick Wackenhut's office, so he stuck his head inside to say hello. Rick was on the phone, and he heard Rick say, 'You know, I wish we could find *someone* who could get a handle on these *nuclear* problems!' And he hung up the phone. The company had, I think, three, maybe four, nuclear projects, and the guy running it just wasn't getting the job done. So Frank says hi to Rick, and says, 'Incidentally, I got a friend of mine, he was with the DOE, and he was at the NRC. He's not working now and I think he might be interested in talking with you.'

"Well, at that moment, Bob Frye was walking into Rick's office. Rick asks Frank, 'Who is this guy?' Frank says, 'Budd Kneip.' And Frye says, 'Budd *Kneip?* Your *dad* knows him!' So Rick immediately picks up the phone, calls George, and says, 'You know someone named Budd Kneip?' George says, 'Yes, I remember him, he was the guy who handled the contract at SPRO.' Rick says, 'What do you think?' And that's when George says, 'He did a very professional, very effective job.' Rick says, 'I think he's free. He might be interested in the *nuclear* thing. I'm going to talk with him.' George says, 'By all means.'

"This was about late August of 1982. So I get a call from Bob Frye out of the clear blue. I'm sitting on the front porch having a beer, you know, typical Louisiana stuff, looking at the cypress swamp across the way, and I get this call from Bob Frye. He said, 'Mr. George Wackenhut would like to have you come and spend some time in Coral Gables.' I said, 'Bob, in all honesty, I've had all of the security business that I care to have,' He said, 'No, please come and visit.' I said, 'Well, I think not, Bob, I'm going to work for Pennsylvania Power & Light.' So then, George *Wackenhut* calls, and he tells me himself that he'd like me to come and see him! And George is a very forceful and powerful sort of a guy, very persuasive. I said, 'I don't want to come to Coral Gables under false pretenses. I'm not enamored of the security business, and I don't want you to spend your money on someone who is not likely to take the job.' He said, 'I understand that, I appreciate that, but come anyway.'

"So I hopped on a plane and spent a couple, three days in Coral Gables. And, you know, George doesn't take no for an answer. And we negotiated a package. It was kind of strange, because the incumbent in that job was still in the building. So I was kind of going up the back stairs while he's going down the front stairs. Because they just didn't want to hurt feelings or anything.

"Now I'm in the Miami airport, I've got a job offer in writing from Wackenhut. I call Cindy to tell her I have a job offer and I'm on the way home. We were planning to get married in the next couple of weeks, September 2. I called and I said, 'Hey, I've got a job offer here.' She said, 'Well, I hope you didn't take it, because Pennsylvania Power & Light called again and said not to take it until you talk to them.'

"Of the two jobs, the one I really wanted was the Pennsylvania Power & Light job. It was in the rolling hills of Pennsylvania, out in the country, land prices were cheap, nuclear power plants and utilities are lovely to work for. But the driving factor in the decision, ultimately, was that I had a three-year-old daughter [Stephanie] by my first marriage, and in order to get from Houston, where she lived, to this little town in Pennsylvania, was about four plane changes. And she couldn't do it. And I wanted to maintain a relationship. There were plenty of nonstops between Houston and Miami.

"Naturally, I was impressed with George Wackenhut. He made it very clear that this company was *not* like any other security company. I was very impressed with Rick. They were giving me lots of flexibility to run the job and form the department the way I wanted. But the driving force was that I just didn't want to sever relationships with my daughter. Because I had raised her, when I was in graduate school, while my ex-wife was working. So, when it came down to it, the money wasn't much different, the benefits were much better at the utility, but here I had a clear management opportunity to work with the owner and founder and chairman of the company. Cindy and I were both kind of southern in that respect anyway. I mean, I'd spent most of my adult life down in the south, and Cindy's family had been camped in New Orleans for many generations; nobody had ever left, except for vacations! So we just decided to come here.

"So, again, all these little vagaries. I ended up coming here about the second week of September of 1982, so I've just completed my eleventh year. It was very bizarre when I got here, too, because I worked for a guy who was a notoriously heavy drinker—we'll call him John Smith. He reported to Rick; Rick was head of Domestic Operations. The nuclear power plants, part of the problem with them was that—Wackenhut occasionally has this sort of organizational problem—they had five regional managers, and they were supposed to manage everything in their territory. Well, if a nuclear power plant fell in their territory, they felt it was theirs. The fact is, they couldn't manage it. And part of the reason for my predecessor's failure was that he didn't have the personality to politely tell them to get out of the way, without hurting their feelings, and yet still meet the clients' needs.

"So, here I fell into this, I worked for this guy who was a heavy drinker, and the only employee I had was a young lady who happened to be *sleeping* with this guy! So I would sit down with her, I would try to discuss some plans for the future, and she immediately, I guess, post-copulative whispering, would tell Smith what my plans were. And the next morning I'd walk in and Smith would call me and say, 'Well, I don't think those are good ideas.' Well, how in the hell did *you* know! And it really pissed me off.

"I was so aggravated with the situation, I'd gotten a follow-up letter from Pennsylvania Power & Light, and they called me at Wackenhut one day and said, 'Look, we'd like to have you reconsider.' And they said, 'We'll even reimburse Wackenhut for the moving expenses, and any of your down payment on your house and stuff, if you'll come up here,' I was ready to do it. I was honest with Rick, I said, 'I've had it with this. This is not a way to run a business.

I can't go out and work with my clients, because I've got a bunch of uninformed regional managers hanging over my shoulders. I can't sit down with my employee, because she's sleeping with my boss, and those two have got their own idea of what's going on, and I don't have a free hand to run anything. I've got an opportunity to go back to Pennsylvania Power & Light, and I believe I'm going to take it.'

"And I got in the car at that point, I drove all the way up to St. Lucie [a county north of Palm Beach], because I had a meeting with Florida Power & Light. Well, Rick said something to George—it's about a two and a half hour drive to St. Lucie—I get up there only to have George Wackenhut on the phone, saying, 'Come *back!*' So I immediately turned around, came back—so I spent five hours on the road to spend about fifteen minutes with the client—and George said, 'I understand you have problems.' And I explained it to him. He said, 'Well, we will *amend* those. Don't leave.' I said, 'Okay.'

"Then, it so happens that on Rick's birthday, which is November 11, he had a surprise birthday party at a local restaurant. Molly called me and invited Cindy and me to attend, but I couldn't, I was scheduled for a business trip to Iowa Electric, which was one of our clients. And it was at that birthday party that John Smith got loaded, fell down the stairs of the two-story restaurant where the party was, suffered a fatal head wound, and died three or four days later.

"There was a very strange, actually sort of macabre, but funny, story related to that. Before I left for Iowa City, Smith came over to me and said, 'You know, there's a little place in Iowa City'—and I went to school there, so I knew the town—he said, 'There's a little place in Iowa City that makes the best country hams.' He said, 'I'll give you the money, but would you buy one of those hams for me?' I said, 'Sure.'

"To get from Miami to Iowa City took about five different plane trips. So I get into Iowa City, I conduct my business, I'm there a couple of days, I don't get back until about midnight that Saturday night, the night of Rick's surprise birthday party, when Smith suffered his fatal fall. The morning before I left Iowa City, the area manager's shuffling me around, because I didn't rent a car, and I said, 'I've got to stop over at that place to buy a ham.' He says, 'Oh, another one of Smith's hams.' I said, 'Yeah.' He says, 'Yeah, the thing is, I always get stuck with the shipping bills.' Well, what Smith didn't tell me, the smallest ham they sold was about *fifty pounds!* So I go in, and I buy a bone-in-fifty-pound ham! Now, I got my bag, my briefcase, and a fifty-pound ham! I said to the lady, 'I've got a problem here, I didn't know the ham was that big, and I promised to take this back to Miami for a guy. Can you wrap it in such a way that I can carry it on the plane?'

"So they laughed like hell, wrapped this thing up within an inch of its life—probably added ten more pounds of wrapping to it—put it in something, jerry-rigged these two twine handles. So I had this thing that looked like a *tuba* wrapped in butcher paper, that I'm now carting off with my overnight bag and my briefcase!

"I drove from Iowa City to Cedar Rapids, flew from Cedar Rapids to St. Louis, then to Houston or Dallas, then into Miami. All the while carting this fifty-pound ham around. And it's starting to *smell!* It smells good, but it's starting to smell. And I was kind of monopolizing overhead space with this monster thing.

"So I get home about midnight, I get this thing back to the townhouse we owned, that Cindy and I had. Get in, have a drink, and my arms ache from lugging around this big damn stinking ham. Fortunately, it doesn't have to be refrigerated, because it's cured. So it's sitting there, and the thing covered the entire top of our washing machine. Cindy said something like, 'Well, I hope it's good.' And I said, 'Well, I bet it is, because, you know, Iowa hams, you can't beat 'em.'

"Next morning, I get up, Sunday morning, and I called Smith, I called his house. I called and I couldn't get anybody. And I called and called and called. I called the entire morning. So, finally, I called Rick. I said, 'You know, I've been trying to call John Smith all morning; I got a big ham I bought for him in Iowa City.' Dead silence on the phone. Finally, Rick clears his throat, he says, 'Budd, I'm afraid I have some bad news.' Then he goes on to explain to me that Smith took this two-story header and is now in the hospital in terminal condition.

"So I hang up, I tell Cindy what happened, we sit down and think about the guy. Finally, I look at Cindy, I say, 'What the hell are *we* going to do with his ham?' She didn't know, she comes from a good old New Orleans family, where you carve up a ham and go down and give it to the bereaved family. I said, 'Honey, I don't *know* the bereaved family, I don't know how close they were anyway, because he's been sleeping with the woman who works for me. I'm not going to just barge in and tell her I'm Budd Kneip, and here's your husband's ham!'

"So, what can I tell you? We couldn't waste good food. We ate the man's *ham!*"

HIGHLIGHTS of headline history during the year 1982 included the British victory over Argentina in the Falklands War, waged from April 2 to June 15. June 4, Israel invaded Lebanon in attacking the PLO. June 21, John W. Hinckley Jr. was found not guilty by reason of insanity in the shooting of President Reagan. June 25, Alexander M. Haig Jr. resigned as Secretary of State. June 30, the Equal Rights Amendment failed ratification. September 14, Princess Grace, at age fifty-two, died of injuries when her car plunged off a mountain road near Monaco; her daughter Stephanie, seventeen, suffered serious injuries in the accident. September 15, Phalangists killed hundreds of people in two Palestinian refugee camps in West Beirut. November 10, Soviet President Leonid I. Brezhnev died at age seventy-five; on November 15, Yuri V. Andropov, sixty-eight, was chosen as his successor. December 2, an artificial heart was implanted for the first time in Dr. Barney B. Clark, sixty-one, at the University of Utah Medical Center in Salt Lake City (Clark died March 23, 1983).

THE RESILIENCE and underlying strengths of TWC were demonstrated clearly in 1982. Throughout the year, the U.S. and most of the industrialized world experienced the most severe recession since the 1930s. Despite the tremendous challenges and uncertainties stemming from this global recession, TWC managed to sustain its steady growth pattern. In fact, the corporation set new records of financial achievement for the sixth consecutive year. Revenues in 1982 climbed to an all-time high of $228.351 million, an increase of 9.7 percent over 1981, while net income reached more than $5.7 million, for a gain of 19.7 percent over the previous year. Earnings per share also reached a new high level of $1.49, after restating for a 10 percent stock dividend declared in January of 1983, an upswing of 19.2 percent.

But if history is to attach labels on a year-by-year basis for TWC, 1983 could well be remembered as a benchmark year for a variety of reasons. The highlight of that year, beyond question, was an award by the Department of Energy of a three-year contract worth $81 million to provide security for the Savannah River Site, near Aiken, South Carolina. This contract was—and still is—the largest single government award to a private security company in history.

Winning the award was exciting, of course, but equally noteworthy was the fact that TWC captured the contract in competitive bidding against eighteen other security firms—a vivid demonstration of the corporation's international reputation for quality.

The following chapters give insights into why and how this single contract changed the entire philosophy, management, and operation of the company, and changed it dramatically. TWC would never be the same again, nor would its top management.

25

THE UNIQUE COMPLEX known today as the Savannah River Site (SRS) is one of the key installations in a program of nuclear production and research under the U.S. Department of Energy. Covering some 192,000 acres spread over parts of three South Carolina counties, the site's land area is about equal to that of the five boroughs of New York City. The primary mission of SRS is to produce plutonium, tritium, and other special nuclear materials for use in the nation's defense program. Weapons materials produced at Savannah River are sent to DOE facilities elsewhere in the country for fabrication into components.

While activities at SRS are still primarily defense oriented, some projects involve the peaceful uses of atomic energy. For example, plutonium-238 produced at Savannah River is used as a long-lasting fuel source for a nuclear-powered cardiac pacemaker. Plutonium-238 has also played a prominent role in the U.S. space program. Other isotopes produced at the site include californium-252, which has a variety of promising uses, including treatment of cancer.

The pressure of international tensions that developed as an aftermath of World War II prompted the Atomic Energy Commission early in 1950 to build the SRS to produce materials for both nuclear and thermonuclear weapons. On June 12, 1950, the Commission asked E.I. du Pont de Nemours and Company in Wilmington, Delaware, to undertake a new atomic project—the design, construction, and operation of what was to become the Savannah River Site.

Having designed, built, and operated the world's first plutonium production reactors at Hanford, Washington, in World War II, Du Pont had considerable experience in nuclear operations, and accepted the project on August 2, 1950.

The search for a site for the largest construction job ever undertaken by the Atomic Energy Commission began in June 1950. The Army's Corps of Engineers, which would acquire the land on behalf of the government when a site was chosen, assisted the AEC and Du Pont in locating a suitable plant site. One hundred and fourteen potential sites in eighteen states were examined before the South Carolina location was chosen.

On November 22, 1950, the AEC formally approved selection of 250,000 acres in Aiken, Allendale, and Barnwell counties. The historic Savannah River, which forms the area's southwestern boundary for twenty-seven miles, was one of the most important considerations in the final choice. The AEC formally named the facility "The Savannah River Plant."

The site lay in the inner margins of the coastal plains, pine covered, rolling, with sandy clay soil. It was a land rich in history and tradition. Here the first white men arrived five centuries ago. Close by was Silver Bluff, where DeSoto crossed the Savannah River in 1540 in quest for gold.

Ellenton, population 600—the largest town on the site—was destined to become the first incorporated community ever taken over by the government for an atomic facility. Here, too, were Dunbarton, a village of 231, and several smaller communities, including Hawthorne, Myers Mill, Robbins, and Leigh. In all, some 1,500 families—or about 6,000 people—were relocated in the interest of national welfare.

The SRS has been adjusted over the years and today comprises 192,323 acres, or 300 square miles. The U.S. government paid $18.-957 million for the site. From the perspective of more than forty years, it can be concluded that this site was ideally suited for nuclear operations.

Construction of temporary facilities began February 1, 1951. Operations commenced with the startup of a unit of the heavy water extraction plant on October 3, 1952, and criticality—the beginning of operations—in the first production reactor was achieved on December 28, 1953. Construction of the basic plant was completed in 1956 at a cost of more than $1.1 billion, including the land. Peak construction employment totaled 38,500 in 1952. After construction, a peak operating employment of 9,750 was attained in July 1956 at the height of plant startup.

The AEC contract originally signed by Du Pont in 1950 to design, construct, and operate the facility included all security services. It was a no-fee contract which provided that the AEC would reimburse Du Pont for all costs involved, and the funds were provided from appropriations approved by Congress. The agreement was renewed six times, with the latest renewal extending through September 1984.

However, independent assessments conducted as early as 1979 and 1980 by the DOE (formerly the AEC) and the General Accounting Office had clearly identified major deficiencies in the management structure underlying Du Pont's defective physical protection program. In January 1983, DOE exercises were conducted at Savannah River that resulted in the guard force refusing to take certain critical actions. It was also revealed that Du Pont had no plans or training to conduct other essential operations to protect the facility from theft of plutonium and sabotage of production reactors.

Therefore, because of mounting congressional pressure, particularly from Representative John D. Dingell, Democrat of Michigan, who was then chairman of the House Subcommittee on Oversight and Investigations of the Committee on Energy and Commerce, the DOE announced on April 11, 1983, its intention to select a new security services contractor at SRS. Nineteen firms responded to the DOE's Request for Proposal (RFP), including, of course, Wackenhut Services, Inc.

At that time, A. Robert Frye was president of WSI, and generally considered to be among the finest operational and marketing men in the security industry. Born July 29, 1926, in Dearborn, Michigan, he graduated from Dearborn High School in January of 1944, enlisted in the U.S. Army Air Corps, then transferred into the Infantry, graduated from OCS, and was a company commander with the Seventh Infantry Division in Korea when he received his honorable discharge in 1947. After three years at Hillsdale College, Hillsdale,

Michigan, he transferred to the University of Florida College of Law, and graduated in 1951.

Immediately after law school, Frye entered the FBI, serving as a special agent in Albuquerque, St. Louis, and New York, 1951 to 1958. When he resigned, he was a field supervisor in the Espionage Surveillance Section in New York.

"From 1958 to 1961, I was at Patrick Air Force Base," Frye explains. "I was a civilian employee of the Air Force, assigned to the Industrial Security Section. In '61, I joined Pan American World Airways At Cape Canaveral, and I was chief of security and law enforcement until 1965. I went over to Trans World Airlines, 1965 to 1968, when they had the contract at the Kennedy Space Center, and I was director of security. Of course, Wackenhut at that time was the subcontractor to TWA for security and fire services at KSC. So, in essence, I was the client, and that's how I became involved with Wackenhut.

"The first time I met George Wackenhut probably would have been about 1965, when the security and fire services personnel at KSC were being organized by unions. There was some concern by NASA as to whether we were going to have a strike by Wackenhut personnel, so three of us went down to Miami for a two day visit with GRW. The other two men were Bill West, the TWA corporate security director, and Dick Wilson, who was the TWA project manager at the Kennedy Space Center; he was my boss. We discussed the whole situation with George at considerable length. It was a no-holds-barred type of thing.

"I joined Wackenhut on July 1, 1968, and I came on board as director of Physical Security. I worked for Bob Kirk, who was vice president of Operations. Of course, I had known Bob back at the Cape, because he had been a previous chief of security police with Pan Am. We had known each other for about ten years. He was the guy who actually brought me on board."

Frye worked his way up through the ranks and was elected president of WSI in 1981. He remembers the SRS project with somewhat mixed emotions, because of a major fortuitous factor that could not have been predicted. "There was nothing magic about the Savannah River situation," he says with a smile. "The Department of Energy was, in essence, compelled by Representative John Dingell, who was chairman of the DOE Oversight Committee, to contract out for security services. What actually happened, Du Pont had received a number of unsatisfactory reviews, but the last one, in January 1983, was the straw that kind of broke the camel's back. And it was predicated upon the fact that Du Pont was just very proud of their *safety record!* They used to have big signs up there, you know, so many hundreds of workdays without an accident.

"During that last security review, I'm sure they had their people patrolling the plant in armored vehicles with heavy weapons, and DOE had this exercise planned, and Du Pont would not let any of their security people do things like jump over fences, because they might get *injured.* And Dingell went through the roof when that happened. So he said, 'Hey, we have to get a professional security firm in here *fast!*'" So, the Department of Energy at the Savannah River Plant prepared a Request for Proposal, and it had all of the major security firms involved in the initial RFP. It was about nineteen firms, it was everybody. Of course, this was a major effort. Even at that time, it was the largest potential security contract in the United States.

"Actually, what happened, that RFP came out April 11, 1983. It so happened that I had a heart bypass operation on April 10 of that year. And I was out of commission about forty-five days. Bob Chasen was the senior vice president of Wackenhut Systems at that time, which had responsibility for WSI and Wackenhut International. And, of course, Bob Kirk was still the president of Wackenhut International, and Bob had been involved in long-term government contracts, and he had been tracking that thing at Savannah River. We were always trying to get in there, but Du Pont would never subcontract.

"So, when the RFP came out, and with my unavailability to ramrod the proposal, they tapped Dick Wilson, who was the vice president of Business Development at that time. He was the guy who got stuck with that chore. Dick had been our senior vice president at the Kennedy Space Center from '78 to the first part of '83. Then, of course, we lost out on that thing, through no fault of our own. To give you an idea of how respected he was, before he left KSC, Dick was given the NASA Distinguished Public Service Medal, the highest honor that can be awarded to a civilian by NASA."

By another act of sheer coincidence, Dick Wilson joined TWC during the first week in April of 1983. But his background was positively ideal to be selected for such a critical assignment. Born Richard W. Wilson in Washington, DC, September 27, 1917, he graduated from South High School in Denver, Colorado, in 1935, and from the University of Denver in 1940 with a BS in physics. From 1942 to 1945, he served as a carrier-based fighter pilot in the U.S. Navy. Following discharge, he accepted a position with Trans World Airlines in February of 1946, not as a pilot but as an industrial engineer, based in Kansas City, and he was with TWA for the next thirty years. Through a series of organizational realignments, he became a regional director of foreign industrial relations for a period of ten years.

"Of course, at that point in time, TWA was a large international carrier with 'round-the-world routes," Wilson explains. "That was the primary reason I joined them, because of the opportunity to contribute to an international communications effort. Luckily, I was in fact able to serve with TWA for about fourteen years as regional vice president on international assignments in Europe, the Middle East, Africa, and the Far East. It was a very fulfilling opportunity. I took early retirement in 1975 and returned to Florida, where I had previously served with TWA at the Kennedy Space Center for a period of five years, 1963 to 1968. I was a vice president with TWA and project manager for the base support services at the Kennedy Space Center, which was one of the three or four major government contracts with NASA in introducing the Apollo Program. It was a nifty opportunity, a unique opportunity, as a matter of fact, because we had to implement an organization of 3,500 people. From zero up to 3,500 very rapidly, which doesn't happen very often.

"Then, in due time, a fellow by the name of Bob Frye contacted me," he says with a smile. "I went down to Miami and had a chat with Bob, and with George Wackenhut, and agreed to serve as the proposed project manager for Wackenhut Services at the Kennedy Space Center, if they were successful in getting the contract. And they were. So I had the opportunity to get back to an activity in the space program that was very important to me, and to serve for another five years. In early 1983, when TWA lost the prime contract, Wackenhut no longer had the protective services responsibility there, and I was asked to join with Bob Frye and George in Miami to assist in the pursuit of other U.S. government major business opportunities.

"I arrived there during the first week of April in 1983 and, lo and behold, my associate Bob Frye, whom I had known for a long, long time, and respected very highly, found himself in the hospital preparing for open-heart surgery. Concurrent with that came the opportunity that was most unusual, and that was the Savannah River Plant security job.

"I think it's important to stress that it was a *unique* business opportunity for The Wackenhut Corporation, and an opportunity for which Wackenhut had unique qualifications. It's really quite a dramatic story. Those of us who were very close to the situation—George Wackenhut himself, Bob Chasen, Bob Kirk, Bob Frye—all recognized that it was one of those business opportunities that come along only once every twenty years. Because it was, in fact, the largest private security force in the world. It was certainly potentially the largest U.S. government contract to a private security firm in history. And, I believe, it still *is* the largest.

"The Savannah River Plant was a facility that very few people *knew* about. Because it had been kept quiet for so long since its inception in 1950, that even those who worked there were not allowed to discuss it with outsiders. And there was a hell of a sizable work force that worked for Du Pont there. My Lord, as I recall, it was around 12,000 to 13,000 people. And, of course, Savannah River was a primary—perhaps *the* primary production facility for plutonium, and particularly tritium, that was used in nuclear weaponry. The facility was spread all over the place, over a piece of real estate of 300 square miles. Those 13,000 people had been educated to just keep quiet about what they were doing. And, apparently, they did a pretty good job of it.

"But, in any event, as time passed, more and more was known about what was going on in there. Contacts had been made with Du Pont to try to convince them that it would be in the best interests of

Du Pont and the U.S. government if they subcontracted security services to a professional security organization. But they didn't want that kind of help. As I recall, Du Pont had well over 500 people in security services at that time.

"It was a shock to Du Pont when they had one of their periodic physical security assessments, because this time the DOE used a military unit. They came in there to run a test, and the Du Pont security force just fell on its face. A big, fat problem, because a report was written, and it got enough circulation that it became a scandal to the jaybirds. Congress, the White House, the Secretary of Energy, all were under the gun, and that's when John Dingell got hold of it, the chairman of the House Subcommittee on Oversight and Investigations, who was raising so much hell on so many things critical to various branches of the U.S. government. And he lowered the boom on the Secretary of Energy.

"In turn, the Secretary of Energy turned to his staff and said, 'We've got to clean that act up and do it *rapidly* and *effectively* and get professionals in there!'

"Hence, when the RFP was rapidly drafted and contacts were made with potential support contractors who might be interested, it became quickly evident that the DOE wanted a first-class operation—super first class—and they wanted it quickly, so that a highly qualified outfit could get in there, and clean things up, and elevate the quality of security services to an extraordinarily high level.

"Now, you add all that up, and for a company like Wackenhut, which at that time, in 1983, had established a hell of a reputation for itself of being able to do a highly professional job in U.S. government facilities, we certainly had the experience, the reputation, the image, and, through George's direction, the integrity, we should be a front-runner in this competition, provided we were able to structure a proposal that, in writing, would reflect our understanding of the job, and our ability to do it, and to do it well.

"Unfortunately, the guy who normally would have handled such an opportunity and challenge was in the hospital. Bob Frye was—and is—in a class by himself. He had then—and still has—a reputation in the security business with one hell of a lot of people who come into contact with him as being perhaps the finest professional security operating and marketing man in the business. What he puts together, he puts together in a first-class manner, and with precision, and it generates a lot of business for the corporation.

"So, he was out of business there for a period of about six weeks. So Bob Kirk made the initial contact with me, I had just arrived on the scene, and he said, in effect, 'Here's an important opportunity and we want you to honcho it.' Kirk was very committed with all of the Wackenhut business activities for many years. He was a key wheel in the Nevada Test Site activities, and he knew John Goldsmith, who had been the WSI vice president at the Nevada Test Site, and was up in Alaska at that point, president of American Guard and Alert *and* Wackenhut of Alaska, and loomed as a logical guy to be the proposed project manager.

"There were five key people. You know, these proposals identify by name the key personnel in the proposed organization, and include their resumes. Goldsmith was the project manager, Pat Patterson was the proposed operational director, Jan Vandersluis came out of headquarters to head up administration, Lynn Williams was proposed as the assistant director of operations, and Bob Atkinson, director of support services. Both Williams and Atkinson came from NTS, and it was logical that we get some muscle out of NTS, because they were the ones who had the Department of Energy experience.

"As I recall, the proposal was a massive chunk of writing, five volumes, I think. It was a seven-day-a-week operation, and typically sixteen hours a day. So all you'd do is work and sleep and eat. It was a pressure-cooker, and that's the world that Bob Frye came out of and understands. And not many people really understand it.

"Kneip understands it. That was my first association with Budd Kneip, on the Savannah River proposal. I knew he was a bright guy, and I needed some expertise that he could supply. I asked for his assistance, and he and I worked shoulder-to-shoulder in the preparation of the proposal. Exactly what point in time he got into it, I don't remember."

Budd Kneip remembers all too well, and laughs out loud when he thinks about it. "I was in bed one Saturday morning, Cindy and I were planning to go down to the Keys. I had just completed a proposal for a brand-new nuclear power plant on the west coast of

Florida, Crystal River, which was the Florida Power Corporation. I had put that to bed and was very comfortable, I had mailed it in, I was tired, because it was a big proposal, and I thought I was going to catch a weekend of relaxation. I had known about Bob's heart bypass operation, but I had thought that things were taken care of. Apparently, Dick was having problems with generating the proposal, and he called George and said, 'I need help.' George said, 'Call Budd.'

"So I got this call at nine o'clock Saturday morning. Dick said, 'Can you come in?' I thought it was going to be for a *morning*. And it turned out to be *six weeks!* I came in that Saturday morning, and I'm sure everybody's recollection will be different in the telling, but Dick headed that proposal effort, I did a great deal of the writing on that thing, and put it into a cohesive whole. Saw the thing through to the end."

As Bob Frye recalls, when he returned to work about six weeks after his operation, the initial proposal was ready to be submitted to the DOE at Savannah River by mid-June. He had studied all of the material very carefully.

"About a day and a half before it had to be submitted," Frye says, "I got to talking with Dick, and I was looking at some of the questions that had risen during the pre-proposal conference, some of the answers that were given, and, looking at the structure of the organization that we proposed, I came to the conclusion that we were probably not submitting the deal that the DOE wanted to see. In other words, the big concern was, they had to make sure they satisfied Dingell, and his big concern about the protection of the nuclear assets. And I said, 'Dick, I think what we've got to do, I think we've got to have a specially dedicated Special Response Team.'

"The way that we had structured up until then was, we were going to have the people on patrol, and, if something happens, they drop their patrol duties, and go try to respond as a secondary type thing. But I said, 'No, I think the way this thing is going, I don't think *cost* is the paramount concern in this instance, I think the security protection is vital. As a result, you've got to have somebody on duty twenty-four hours a day, you've got to be able to respond immediately.'

"And what happened was, a day and a half before the thing was due, we added *seventy-nine people* for a Special Response Team! Dick and I made that damn decision, and one of the things we had to do, Ron Valentini was the guy who was doing the cost at that time, and Ron had *conniptions,* because he had to stay up all night and recalculate the added cost! Now, the idea of adding a significant amount of people, you're talking a couple of million bucks, and that's just never done. I mean, if anything, you *cut* costs.

"But, because of the fact that I was convinced that we really had to have it, and I convinced Dick, too, and he went along with it, we priced it out, and the next day he called Bob Chasen and said, 'Here's what we're going to do.' And Bob swallowed his teeth and said, 'Well, if you guys are convinced, we've got to do this thing.' And I know GRW had *apoplexy!* He really did! But the initial proposal went in that way."

Budd Kneip remembers a humorous anecdote that occurred just before the actual submission, and it certainly gives insights into George's reputation as a meticulous perfectionist. "At the last minute, we were producing the cover for the final document," Kneip recalls with a laugh. "It had met all of the criteria we'd designed for it, it had passed muster, George was intimately involved in every facet of this, from pricing to interviewing candidates for project management positions.

"Curt Bachmann, who was our head of sales at the time, was going to deliver this proposal, hand-deliver the volumes to the Department of Energy outside of Augusta, at Savannah River. He was scheduled to leave on a five o'clock flight that afternoon. There were probably six or seven flights a day from Miami to Atlanta, and then every other hour you could get a little connecting flight from Atlanta to Augusta. Then you rented a car and drove out to Aiken and went to the site. Curt was ready to go at five.

"I went in to George with a cover for the document. George approved it. We started to bind the thing, showed George the 'final' of one of the five volumes. Now he didn't like the cover. Back in those days, our typical cover for a proposal was a very heavy, blue, almost a construction-type of cover, and it felt like it had fibers in it. I think they were pressed, rather than actually part of the material. But it was very heavy. And it had a border of gold embossed around it.

"Then, if you wanted to produce something really special, we had a hot-press gold-stamping machine. This thing would heat up to about 500 degrees, you'd set the logo in it, you'd roll a piece of gold foil in, insert each individual cover, and you would *press* on this damn handle with all your might. You had to do it for each individual cover. And I think we had to deliver three sets of five volumes each. Fifteen covers.

"So George wanted that. He wanted the Wackenhut logo in gold. Everybody's temper was—we were on edge at that stage of the process. So I really lit into George. And, typical George, he was so focused on the project that—hey, say what you want, we're going ahead with it! I was way out of line, but George has an ability to transcend that kind of pettiness. And he knew I'd been busting my fanny on this thing. And he knew that all of our tempers were frayed on this thing. So he just ignored it.

"Now it's after five o'clock, Curt has long since cancelled his reservation on that flight; he's made a reservation on the seven o'clock flight. I took a bunch of covers down to the Training Department where the hot-press machine was located, I looked around, everybody had left the building, and I didn't know how to *work* the hot-press machine! Finally, I found some young kid who used to work in the Training Department; his name was Chuck. I said, 'Chuck, do you know how to work that damn hot-press machine?' He says, 'Yeah, I've seen it used a couple of times, let's plug it in and try it.'

"Okay, he plugs it in, and this thing heats up red-hot, it has to emboss gold foil. So, sure enough, we get the logo in there right, we try one. And now, mind you, about one out of every three didn't print the logo clearly. So, if you wanted fifteen, you really ran twenty to twenty-five of them, and then you picked the best fifteen. So Chuck gets this thing all cranked up, we try a test copy, and it works! I take it straight to George to make sure it's exactly what he wants. So George thinks it looks fine.

"Now we set up this assembly line. I would feed in on one end and I would press down on the handle; Chuck would roll the gold foil and pull the finished product out. And you had to do that carefully or else the gold would peel off and you'd lose part of the logo. So Curt's looking at a seven o'clock flight now, I'm feeding these things in, and I'm not paying a whole lot of attention, because I'm trying to keep the assembly line going. Unbeknownst to me, Chuck is just pulling one of these things out of the machine, his hand is still in the general area, and I press down—and, of course, you wanted to lay into it a little bit to make sure it took—well, I caught the corner of the fleshy part of Chuck's *hand!* He was in such shock, he couldn't even *scream!*

"For a couple of seconds, I didn't know anything was amiss, I continued to lay into the handle. And, of course, I swear you could smell burning flesh, because it's a 500-degree press! Finally, Chuck squeaks out this howling sort of sound, I lift the handle fast, and I can see the corner of his hand is embossed with the Wackenhut *logo!*

"We got through the process without any further mishaps, but then we had to bind all fifteen volumes with the new covers, and Curt missed his seven o'clock flight. As I recall, he got out on an eleven o'clock flight that night, got to Atlanta, then had to wait until early the next morning to catch a commuter flight to Augusta. He spent the whole night in the Atlanta airport, got the first flight out at like five o'clock in the morning. He got the thing delivered, and the rest is history. Chuck eventually went off to Savannah River as a trainer, still with a Wackenhut logo on his hand!"

On Friday, July 22, 1983, the board of directors were gathering for a week-long meeting at the famed Pebble Beach Resort and Country Club in Monterey, California. "We were out there, and George rented the Fairway House that's situated right on the first tee," Kneip remembers. "Everyone else stayed in rooms at the resort, but George and Rick and I stayed at Fairway House. We had the place to ourselves, which was really a big, beautiful old house. On Friday evening, we got a completely unexpected call from the Savannah River DOE requesting our 'best and final' proposal by Monday, August 1, including a restructured wage and benefits package.

"I had to hop a plane at four o'clock Saturday morning and fly all day to get back. We had a very short time-fuse on this thing. By this time, Dick Wilson had gone back up to central Florida, where he lived, and there was no one else around. What had happened, the Savannah River DOE had come back and said, 'Everything is beautiful, but you guys underestimated the wage and benefits package!'

"See, this was not only the biggest thing Wackenhut had done, but it was the first of its kind, really, in the industry. Yes, Nevada Test Site was big, but a much more clearly defined mission. But this was the first time that DOE had, in a sense, decided to go out and take an entire sector of its business, including the management prerogatives that go along with the function, and turn that over to somebody. So they weren't even sure how to structure the solicitation. And the industry wasn't really certain how to respond to it.

"So we had to do a complete restructuring. And, of course, that rolled throughout the entire proposal. We weren't just answering fourteen or fifteen questions, we were restructuring the entire proposal. But until George could get back from the board meeting on Sunday afternoon, I was sort of his surrogate there. Until we could get Dick Wilson back, and Bob Chasen, who was at the board meeting, I was kind of standing in for those guys. And they expected, when they got back that Sunday afternoon—they came right in from the airport—they expected to have this thing formulated, and we could agree upon the plan that afternoon and go forward.

"Well, we managed to get over that hurdle, we went back to the sixteen-hour days routine for eight straight days, but we got the revised wage and benefits package inserted into the restructured proposal and submitted the 'best and final' by Monday, August 1."

According to Bob Frye, within the next week he received notice that WSI was selected as one of the three finalists. He didn't know then who the other finalists were; the government procurement regulations were such that the DOE didn't reveal which firms were considered to be within the competitive range. "Before the final selection was made," Frye says, "we had a personal visit from the DOE-SRP general manager, Dick Denise, and the guy who was his contracts manager, Bob McFeeley. I think they visited all three firms that were finalists. Well, when they came down to Coral Gables, we gave them a dog-and-pony show that knocked their socks off! GRW orchestrated the whole thing. We rehearsed for *days!* It was held in the conference room. He must have run forty people in front of the DOE representatives. George's game plan was that teams of managers would come in, sit in assigned seats across the conference table, tell Denise and McFeeley who they were, what their jobs were, how they related to Savannah River, what we were going to do, and it went off like clockwork. One team would exit, the next team would enter, everybody had their best suits on, and it was quite a production. It was outstanding. And Denise admitted afterward, 'You know, you guys really impressed us.' They went away, and the net result was, of course, we were subsequently awarded the contract."

The first press release issued by the Department of Energy in Washington, DC, was dated August 11, 1983. It was one of several to be issued over the following six months in which the actual statistics of the award would be significantly changed.

DEPARTMENT OF ENERGY SELECTS SECURITY SUPPORT SERVICES CONTRACTOR

AIKEN, SC—The Department of Energy (DOE) has selected Wackenhut Services, Inc., of Coral Gables, Florida, to provide security support services at its Savannah River Plant (SRP) near Aiken, South Carolina. It is anticipated that a contract with Wackenhut Services, Inc., will be awarded by August 26, 1983. The contract value is approximately $41,000,000 for a 30-month period.

Wackenhut will employ approximately 460 uniformed security inspectors to provide a full range of security protection and law enforcement services at SRP. There will be an additional 50 contract personnel in management and support positions.

DOE announced its intention to select a security services contractor at SRP on April 11, 1983. Nineteen firms responded to the Request for Proposal issued on that date.

In announcing the selection, Richard P. Denise, Acting Manager of DOE's Savannah River Operations Office, stated, "DOE looks forward to working closely with Wackenhut. Their experience and expertise will help assure the highest standard of security at SRP. A six-month transition is planned for Wackenhut to assume security functions from the current patrol force."

Dick Wilson reflects on how critical Bob Frye's last-minute decision was: "In due time, as we learned more about the story of the competition, and the DOE thinking and attitudes, it was that decision that probably won it for us, aside from what we considered to be a quality proposal with some proposed key personnel who should have been able to do an outstanding job.

"In retrospect, we realized how important that discussion was that night. And I credit Bob Frye with putting his finger right on it. I don't know how much you know about open-heart surgery, but Bob had a triple bypass. My recollection is that it was triple. At least triple. He's the most dedicated guy I think I've ever known in my life when it comes to loyalty, and being unselfish, and going the extra mile. With open-heart surgery, you're supposed to take things real easy for a while. And he was back, thinking and working, really much too soon. But his effort to get back into the thick of things, after that kind of a medical experience, certainly was a major contributing factor to the ultimate success of the corporation in obtaining that plum. And it was a real plum. The biggest plum in the history of the company. And we knew it. We knew what we were after.

"The other thing I want to highlight, which I think fits what you're looking for, is that The Wackenhut Corporation, from birth to this day, is in the image of George Wackenhut. And because it is, and because of his integrity, his professional and personal integrity and reputation, the DOE looked with favor to our company, with our track record and our experience. And, ultimately, when they visited headquarters, to meet face-to-face with the executives who ran the show, don't underestimate the importance of that presentation and the discussions that took place. Because George is at his best in that type of situation. Dick Denise and Bob McFeeley got the chance to meet George Wackenhut again, and had the opportunity to have a dialogue with him again. A different man under similar circumstances could fall flat on his face and lose the contract. But he very well may have won it at that meeting."

The next press release from the Department of Energy was issued August 23, 1983, the day that WSI officially began its four-month transition period, to be followed by a six-month negotiation period prior to signing the definitive contract. An excerpt:

WACKENHUT SERVICES, INC., BEGINS SECURITY SERVICES
Transition at Department of Energy's
Savannah River Plant

AIKEN, SC—The Department of Energy (DOE) and Wackenhut Services, Inc. (WSI), of Coral Gables, Florida, today entered into a letter contract permitting WSI to begin immediately the transition process to assume full responsibility for security services at DOE's Savannah River Plant (SRP). The letter contract, with an estimated value of $1.9 million for an approximate four-month transition period, was signed by Richard P. Denise, Acting Manager of DOE's Savannah River Operations Office, and George R. Wackenhut, President and Chairman of the Board of Directors, The Wackenhut Corporation.

DOE announced on August 11, 1983, the selection of WSI to provide a full range of security protection and law enforcement services at SRP. During a six-month transition period, a definitive contract, for approximately $40 million for a two-year period, will be negotiated between DOE and WSI. . . .

That autumn, a serious scandal about the Department of Energy was brewing, initiated by Representative John Dingell, first reported by *The Wall Street Journal* on October 31, 1983, under the headline, "Major Security Flaws Found at U.S. Sites That Produce Parts for Nuclear Weapons," then sensationalized by syndicated columnist Jack Anderson, who did his own investigation by hiring a helicopter to fly at low altitudes over the Savannah River Plant. His story broke in newspapers on November 26, 1983. A few excerpts:

Five Linked to Nuke Goofs Awarded Medals, Bonuses

Five senior Energy Department officials have been identified by congressional investigators as responsible for a serious lack of security at government plants. Their fate: they have been given achievement medals and generous bonuses.

Rep. John Dingell, D.-Mich., chairman of the investigating committee, wrote recently to Energy Secretary Donald Hodel to complain: "This is a curious reward and punishment system."

The House investigation was inspired by my own report on the inadequacy of security measures at sensitive research facilities that produce defense-related nuclear material. To see how vulnerable the plants were to terrorist attack, I hired a helicopter to fly one of my associates back and forth at low altitudes over the Savannah River nuclear plant in South Carolina. The overflight was never challenged.

Dingell's year-long, secret investigation concluded that DOE officials deliberately misled both Congress and the White House regarding security at the nuclear facilities. Yet five key officials singled out by Dingell's investigators for blame received over $115,000 in bonuses and merit awards.

How was this possible? Simple enough: internal DOE documents show it was a case of bureaucratic incest in which the officials gave each other the high achievement ratings that won them the awards. My associates Indy Badhwar and Tony Capaccio have seen House documents that identify the five DOE officials, the actions they took that drew congressional criticism—and the rewards they received. Dingell's letter identifies them as: . . .

Robert Morgan, manager of the Savannah River operation: he took part in suppressing the critical security assessment and was accused of misleading Congress about safety at the facility. Last January, a new assessment of Savannah River found safeguards to be in a "shambles." Since 1981, Morgan has received more than $26,000 in awards, and this year he was given a gold medal.

The House investigation found some shocking security lapses: sensors and alarms that didn't work; guards who couldn't shoot; and guards who, in one exercise, "fired on one another rather than the (mock) attacking force." . . .

Elsewhere, major news events of the year 1983: January 25, Pope John Paul II signed the new Roman Catholic code incorporating changes brought about by the Second Vatican Council. April 4, the second space shuttle, *Challenger*, made its successful maiden voyage, which included the first U.S. space walk in nine years. June 15, the U.S. Supreme Court declared that many local abortion restrictions were unconstitutional. June 18, Sally K. Ride, thirty-two, became the first U.S. woman astronaut in space as a crew member aboard the space shuttle *Challenger*. August 15, the U.S. admitted shielding former Nazi Gestapo chief Klaus Barbie, sixty-nine, the "Butcher of Lyons," wanted in France for war crimes. August 21, Benigno S.

Aquino, Jr., fifty, a political rival of Philippines President Marcos, was slain in Manila. August 30, a South Korean Boeing 747 jetliner bound for Seoul apparently strayed into Soviet airspace and was shot down by a Soviet SU-15 fighter after it had tracked the airliner for two hours; all 269 people aboard were killed, including sixty-one Americans. October 23, a terrorist explosion killed 237 U.S. Marines in Beirut. October 25, the U.S. and its Caribbean allies invaded Grenada.

BACK AT TWC, 1983 marked the seventh consecutive year of record-breaking financial achievements in revenues, income, and earnings per share. Although revenues from the huge award by the Department of Energy for security at the Savannah River Plant had not yet made a significant impact by year's end, according to the 1983 Annual Report, revenues reached $238.936 million, an increase of 4.6 percent over 1982. Net income was $6.412 million, a gain of 11.4 percent. Earnings per share totaled $1.66, up from $1.49 the previous year.

WSI, in addition to inaugurating services at Savannah River in 1983, also won a $46 million, three-year extension of the contract for total security at the DOE's 1,350-square-mile Nevada Test Site, a contract it had held since 1964. TWC had exactly 100 offices in the U.S., and in twenty-seven other countries.

One of the company's most valued board members, James J. Rowley, resigned late in 1983 for personal reasons, after serving since 1974. In April of that year, George was delighted to announce that Frank C. Carlucci was elected to the board; Carlucci, who was then president of Sears World Trade, Inc., a Sears Roebuck subsidiary, had formerly served as deputy secretary of Defense, and deputy director of the CIA, among other prominent government positions. On April 24, John Ammarell retired as executive vice president, after nearly twenty-five years with TWC; however, he remained chairman of the executive committee of the board. On April 29, Jan Wackenhut Ward took her second leave of absence from the company, after almost two years of constant travel, primarily to devote more time and attention to her daughters, Tanya, who had just turned sixteen, and Tresha, who was then fifteen. In December, Rick Wackenhut was named senior vice president, Operations, in charge of all physical security and investigative services for all TWC companies.

MAJOR WSI personnel changes at Savannah River were published on the front page of Volume 1, Number 1, of WSI's *Savannah River Plant Pipeline* in February 1984:

WSI NAMES JOHN C. EVANS TO DIRECT SRP SECURITY

John C. Evans has been named Senior Vice President and General Manager for Wackenhut Services, Incorporated (WSI), at the Department of Energy's Savannah River Plant.

Mr. Evans, a former Colonel in the U.S. Army, moved to Savannah River Plant from Coral Gables, Florida, where he was Director, Executive Protection Division, at The Wackenhut Corporation, WSI's parent company.

He succeeds Jonathan P. Goldsmith, who has transferred to corporate headquarters in Coral Gables.

Shortly after taking charge at SRP, Mr. Evans announced the following top staff appointments:

* James M. Bowers, formerly Training Department Manager, moves up to Director of Operations and Training.

* Bob Atkinson, formerly Director, Support Services, is now Director of Safety and Inspections.

* Patrick Cannan, retiring Lieutenant Colonel and Public Affairs Officer for the U.S. Army at Fort Bragg, North Carolina, becomes the new Director, Corporate-Community Relations, effective next month.

During his 27-year military career, Mr. Evans held various assignments, including security and intelligence operations, combat infantry assignments in Vietnam, command posts through brigade level, and duties with the organization of the Joint Chiefs of Staff.

He is a graduate of the National War College and holds a Master's degree in International Affairs from George Washington University in Washington, D.C.

Mr. Evans is recognized by the American Society for Industrial Security as a Certified Protection Professional (CPP).

The final, negotiated contract was signed on March 27, 1984. It was for a period of three years, with a total estimated value of $81 million, almost double the original estimate for a two-year contract. The official DOE press release was dated March 28, 1984:

Wackenhut and Department of Energy Sign Contract for Security Support Services at Savannah River Plant

AIKEN, SC—The Department of Energy's (DOE) Savannah River Operations Office (SR) and Wackenhut Services, Inc. (WSI), of Coral Gables, Florida, have entered into a contract for WSI to provide security support services for the Department's Savannah River Plant (SRP), located near Aiken, South Carolina.

The contract, signed March 27, provides for Wackenhut security services from August 23, 1983, through September 30, 1986, and involves an estimated $81 million.

The three-year contract was signed by Dr. Goetz K. Oertel, Acting Manager, SR, on behalf of the DOE, and by George R. Wackenhut, Chairman of the Board and President of The Wackenhut Corporation.

Wackenhut is providing a full range of security protection and law enforcement services for the plant. During a six-month transition period which began in August 1983, Wackenhut assumed security responsibility for separate facilities, with complete security control of the plant assumed on February 13, 1984.

WSI currently employs more than 500 uniformed security personnel at the SRP, with an additional 75 personnel in management and support positions.

On September 29, 1988, WSI won a five-year renewal contract at Savannah River in a highly competitive environment. September 30, 1993, WSI won another five-year renewal contract, again competitive, with an estimated total value of $320 million. Now called the Savannah River Site, instead of "Plant," WSI employs about 1,100 uniformed security personnel.

Today, a forty-member staff of instructors conducts ongoing basic and specialized training programs that also include physical conditioning, first aid, and field exercises. State-of-the-art equipment provides computerized decision training. In addition to two helicopters and three patrol boats, the WSI mission requires 123 vehicles, 1,900 weapons, and 685 communication radios.

And, yes, SRS continues Bob Frye's original idea of a Special Response Team. SRT members epitomize the skills and professionalism inherent in the WSI protective force. Comparable today to any major city police SWAT team, the SRT is available on the site twenty-four hours a day for emergency situations or disruptive actions.

And to think George almost had *apoplexy!*

26

THE WACKENHUT BUILDING, a rectangular four-story structure enclosing an atrium with trees, flowers, and fountains, was ready for occupancy in March 1984. Situated at 1500 San Remo Avenue in Coral Gables, opposite spacious Riveria Park, the $18 million building has 160,000 square feet of office space, and a garage with more than 500 parking spaces, including ample space for visitors.

To construct the building, TWC entered into a limited partnership with the firm of Terremark, Inc., a developer in Miami, and the BEC Corporation, a British investor. Designed by the Miami firm Architectura Totalis, the general contractor was the BEC Corporation, and interior design work (other than the floors occupied by TWC) was accomplished by Wolfberg, Alvarez, Taracido and Associates of Miami.

The ground floor, which includes second-level mezzanine space, and half of the second floor, was initially rented out. TWC originally occupied half of the second floor and all of the third and penthouse levels.

Ruth Wackenhut, who designed the interiors of the first two headquarters buildings, had total responsibility for interior design of the TWC floors. This included selection of all furnishings, carpeting, paintings, sculptures, plants, and the most imaginative "penthouse" suites for senior officers ever seen by visiting interior designers.

Bill Scherle, who was manager of TWC's General Services at the time, helped plan and supervise virtually every aspect of the move, which was accomplished over a ten-month period, weekends only, on a departmental priority basis. Born William R. Scherle in Rochester, New York, August 9, 1928, he graduated from Male High School in Louisville, Kentucky, spent two years at the University of Kentucky, where he majored in journalism and psychology, and was working as a designer for a steel company in Louisville when he was drafted into the Army during the Korean War. Subsequently, he decided to become a career officer, serving more than twenty years before he retired as a lieutenant colonel. He joined Wackenhut at headquarters in 1973, and retired on Valentine's Day in 1992.

"We owned three buildings on Ponce at the time of the move," Scherle says, "and when the time came to relocate to this new facility, starting in March 1984, it was a tremendous logistical problem, because we were moving from those three buildings, plus the building we leased for the Legal Department, plus an entire floor of a building that we leased for International.

"The new building was not under construction yet in 1981, when we first started to consider moving, but it was in the planning stages, and I had seen a model of it. I was always scouting around, looking for other locations. I had seen the model of the building, mentioned it, described it, described its intended location, but nobody seemed to be interested. One that we seriously considered was the Barnett Bank Building on Douglas, and another one was the Federal Reserve Building at the north end of the Gables. Mr. Wackenhut never wanted to move out of the Gables. Almost every time we went to look at a building, Mrs. Wackenhut went with us, because she was very much involved right from the beginning.

"One day, I walked into Mr. Wackenhut's office, and there sitting on the table in the middle of his office was the model of the building I had already seen. It was called The Atrium in the Gables back then. I believe that was in early 1982, and that became the target from then on. It still wasn't under construction. The lot had not been developed at all when the decision was made to go into the joint venture, the limited partnership, to build it.

"Total construction time was about a year and a half. They ran into tremendous problems when they started digging at the west end of the building, because they had to go so deep to develop the basement parking area. They ran into water, and it kept flooding and flooding, and they finally had to build a containment area, and pump water until they could gradually fill in with cement and fill, and eventually reinforce it, and start laying the basement for the parking area. There would be five levels of parking on top of that.

"Every week we had a meeting with the Terremark representatives and the BEC Construction people, they had a temporary office across the street from the construction site in one of the small office buildings to the south of us. That was a weekly get-together where we would look at progress. We had all the subcontractors come in and we would talk about how we were going to lay out the building once we got the shell up, how we were going to arrange things. Mrs. Wackenhut attended all of those meetings, and Mike Simpson was very heavy into the planning, as well as Cal Harris.

"Wolfberg, Alvarez, Taracido and Associates continued on with architectural service, but sort of dropped out of the interior design aspect of things. At that point, Mrs. Wackenhut wanted to bring in Sal Bosco to help her with the interior design. Sal was a friend of the family, he helped with the interior design of the yacht. Sal's statement is usually very bold, and I think that's shown heavily in the penthouse design, the massive column work, the bold doors, that heavy symbol on the doors, which, incidentally, is an African *fertility* symbol! Few people know that. Sal came up with that, and he and Mrs. Wackenhut worked very closely together. He did his own set of architectural design plans for the penthouse, which were very complex. Very detailed, because of the tremendous amount of woodwork, the work around the ceilings that you see in all the penthouse offices."

The three elevators in the building, including a glass elevator in front, are each equipped with an electronic keypad for preventing unauthorized access to the penthouse, and the four-digit combination is changed periodically. Each of the penthouse offices, with the exception of George's, has an entire wall of picture windows that overlook rectangular, walled-in garden areas with trees, plants, flowers, and statues, giving the pleasant illusion of tropical patios. "I believe the garden areas were in the original plan," Scherle recalls, "although Mrs. Wackenhut probably selected the plants, trees, and statues. Sal's work was totally interior, along with Mrs. Wackenhut. Everything within the shell; I don't believe they had anything to do with the shell of the building.

"You also have to look at the woodwork, the desks and the furniture, and you notice that it has trimmed corners, it's not rectangular like the rest of the furniture in the building, so that just gave it another bold statement and another unique appearance. That penthouse furniture was manufactured in Canada, and it's all custom-made. The man's name was Lon Sniftter. He did a lot of work for some of the major penthouse complexes here along the coast in Florida, for banks and hotels and offices. All of the furniture is mahogany. The finish is Victorian Mahogany, that's the name of it. And it blended in with the mahogany corridors, the covering that's on the columns and the walls.

"The outfit that did the woodwork in the penthouse, their effort was very protracted, because of the detail. A lot of the trim was cut right here on the premises. Their work put us behind schedule, for occupancy of the penthouse, by about three months. It seems to me that we were targeted to finish the penthouse in November of 1984, but we didn't get it finished until January of 1985. In the meantime, we had to vacate the old headquarters buildings, we had most of the people over here, so we took Mr. Wackenhut and wedged him into a corner on the third floor, in a conference room that he could occupy as a temporary office. And we put as many senior officers as we could around him, the ten or twelve vice presidents who would eventually be the occupants of the penthouse.

"The Billing Department was the first to move in, and I believe it was in March. Payroll was next, because we were still tied to that fragile payroll schedule. So everything had to be timed so that we would have no breakdown in activity. Obviously, most of the moves were made on the weekends. We did what the moving industry calls a 'load-and-go' type of move. We had large vans, but you never tried to fill the van all the way. You didn't bother stacking anything. Once you had the floor filled, you moved the van and got it out of the way and started loading another one. So, on a weekend, we could probably move about twenty van loads.

"When the vans arrived at the new building, another difficult logistical problem for the moving company was that they were not permitted to use the glass elevator in front. So everything had to be loaded on the two back elevators, then pushed on dollies, some of it all the way to the front of the building, which was about 350 feet. To protect the carpeting, they had to lay huge beaverboard mats the whole length of the hallways.

"The other major problem, and probably the most difficult one, was moving the computer operations. We had to get the deck prepared on this end, all the cabling and wiring. With IBM's assistance, their technicians, and our electricians, and the people we were working with from BEC Construction, we set up a temporary section in this new computer room to accommodate enough equipment to keep us operational until we could move the second phase of the computer room over here. So, basically, we had to be operational at both ends for a while. I think it was about a week, a week overlap, when we were operational with mainframe equipment and supporting equipment at both ends, both headquarters buildings.

"We had to get additional air conditioning into the computer room, because that's all self-contained air conditioning. And the air conditioning systems, because of their size, had to be hoisted by *crane* from the atrium area to the third-floor balcony by the elevators. It was the only way to get them into the building. We had to remove the balcony railings, remove the glass-paneled walls and doors from each side of the balcony, then lift the air conditioning units by crane up and over the balcony wall, then drag them on dollies through the halls. Then we had to put everything back together again before the office opened Monday morning. We had to do that three different times with the air conditioning systems that were brought in, so those were very delicate weekend operations.

"Then we had a problem getting the computer room system totally operational. The Halon system in there is supported by tanks of a chemical that's automatically dumped if there's a fire. What it does, it sucks all of the oxygen out of the air and smothers the fire. It sucks the oxygen out so fast that when the alarm goes off, you've got exactly thirty seconds to get out of the room before the system dumps the chemical. Well, we were installing telephones, and one of the technicians was trying to run some wire to the back panel for the telephone system there. He found a conduit and ran a 'snake' tube down the conduit, and he hit a circuit that triggered the *Halon* system! It was the wrong *conduit!* The alarm went off, everybody went nuts, they were scurrying out of that room like rats before the system *dumped!*

"We had constant problems during various phases of construction and interior design of the building. For example, in a building of this size, you have to have your alarm system continually activated. And when construction was going on, this caused a lot of problems, because dust and dirt would activate the *smoke* detectors. We were just halfway moved in here and the smoke alarm system—very loud—was going off every other day! Scared the *hell* out of everybody! Then we had an actual disaster on the south side of the third floor. They had just laid most of the brand-new carpet when something accidentally triggered the *sprinkler system!* And before they could shut that off, a very large section of the carpeting was absolutely drenched, ruined, and had to be pulled up and replaced.

"I guess one of the last and most difficult projects was installing the big, graceful, spiral staircase that leads from the third floor reception area to the penthouse. It's so wide and heavy that it had to be prefabbed at the shops of the people who did the woodwork in the penthouse. They constructed it in sections and then it was assembled and hoisted into place. When an executive in the penthouse is expecting a visitor, his secretary is called, she comes down the spiral staircase, and escorts the visitor up this beautifully carpeted staircase to the penthouse.

"I believe the big vertical sign 'Wackenhut' went up on the front of the building sometime during the spring of 1985. We had a difficult time getting the approval required from the City of Coral Gables. A representative from BEC Construction and I went to a night session of the Coral Gables City Council and presented our statements and designs and exact dimensions, and it took several months after that presentation before they came around to approving the sign. It seems to me that it was around March or April of '85 before the sign actually went up."

George's office itself occupies the entire east end of the rectangular building, close to the glass elevator, and was completely designed and furnished by Ruth. The heavy wooden double doors from the balcony open to a waiting room occupied by his executive secretary, Esther Nicholas, and a second set of double doors—always open—lead to his main office, paneled in a dark, rich rosewood, accented with gray-blue stone. Facing his extra-long mahogany desk are twin chairs in the shape of elephants, handmade in Thailand, complete with real tusks. Although there are no windows, an extended glass ceiling panel near the rear wall was designed by Ruth to introduce daylight; she created the same effect for the board of directors room at the west end of the penthouse. For private conferences, there is a smaller office with a door to the left of George's main office, far more informal, with a wooden round-table and chairs, and rough, blue-gray stone walls. George calls this his "inner sanctum," and the walls and glass cabinets are filled with his personal memorabilia. In a small room near his bathroom is an old-style barber's chair, where he has frequent haircuts. The "inner sanctum" has the feel of a small living room in a hunting lodge, relaxed and completely private, and many of his most important meetings and decisions still take place in this informal atmosphere, as they have from the time it was completed.

As TWC was getting settled in its new headquarters building, Wackenhut Services, Inc., was working on another major proposal, headed by Bob Frye, who was then vice president of Proposal Development, to establish and operate a Central Training Academy (CTA) for the Department of Energy, located in an isolated part of Kirtland Air Force Base in Albuquerque, New Mexico. This time, WSI was selected over ninety-two other companies who responded to the Request for Proposal—including ten finalists—in highly competitive bidding for the three-year, $5 million contract. This marked the first time that a U.S. government training academy had been contracted to private industry.

An estimated 800 DOE-related personnel from throughout the country were scheduled to be trained each year at the new facility, including security managers, training officers, tactical response personnel, field trainers, firearms instructors, and hostage negotiators.

The DOE appointed Roy Crouch to be director of the Academy. WSI's newly elected president, Paul V. Roundy, selected William A. Meincke to be vice president and general manager at Albuquerque.

During twenty-six years with the FBI, Meincke served in supervisory and command positions in several FBI offices and at FBI headquarters. He was assistant director in charge of all FBI training from 1976 to 1977.

Thomas G. Hays, a captain with twenty-six years in the Los Angeles Police Department, was appointed deputy general manager of operations. Before leaving LAPD, Hays served as director of training.

WSI has held the contract since its inception in 1984 and presently employs a full-time staff and faculty of seventy-three, supplemented by an adjunct faculty. The current contract was awarded on a competitive basis and totals $10 million for the next two years, with options to extend to five years.

Many excellent magazine and newspaper articles have been written about the Central Training Academy over the years, but among the best in actually describing what WSI's instructors do on a daily basis was published in the April 1991 issue of *Soldier of Fortune* magazine, written by Peter G. Kokalis. A few excerpts:

Nuclear Snake Eaters
Inside the DOE's Secret Training Academy

It is arguably the finest training facility of its type in the world, staffed by the most highly regarded full-time and adjunct instructors in professional circles, and provides training to some of the most elite SWAT units in this country. It is not open to the public.

Few, outside the very fast lane in which Special Response Teams (SRT) move, even know of its existence. "It" is the U.S. Department of Energy's Central Training Academy (CTA), located in an isolated and desolate area deep within the confines of Kirtland Air Force Base in Albuquerque, New Mexico.

The DOE maintains and provides security for all U.S. nuclear weapons and components in inventory as well as other unspecified national security assets. The CTA's mission is to train the mostly contract personnel who provide security at the 47 DOE sites throughout the country to effectively and efficiently protect vital national security interests. Other municipal, state and federal law enforcement agencies and certain U.S. military units are accommodated at the CTA on a space-available basis. More than 3,000 individuals graduate from the CTA's numerous training cycles each year.

Established in 1984, the CAT provides instruction in the following fields: Special Response Team—Weapons and Tactics, Crisis Negotiations and Management, Dignitary Protection, Sniper Observation Team Training, Tactical Leadership, Fire Team Tactics, Explosives Identification, Armorer and Rangemaster Certification, Officer Survival, and Safeguards and Technical Training such as Material Control and Accountability.

Special Response Team training is offered at three levels. SRT 1 covers basic teamwork and covert tactics. SRT 2 includes teamwork, planning and dynamic factors. At this time, the most advanced SWAT course offered is the two-week SRT 3. SOF [*Soldier of Fortune*] recently attended three days of the second week of SRT 3 to observe the training firsthand. There were 24 students in this class, all volunteers, and all DOE security inspectors with the exception of several police officers from New Mexico law enforcement agencies. . . .

Together with the dynamic entry exercises held in the fun house and the final exam that all must pass on Friday of the second week, the SWAT obstacle course is a centerpiece of the dynamic tactics training. The obstacle course is run with all tactical gear, including ballistic vest, both MP5 and handgun, and the basic ammo load. . . .

CTA training is as realistic as possible. The training situations I observed closely simulated the stress encountered in firefights with opponents that shoot back—to kill. CTA's fun house—with no ceilings and an overhead catwalk for instructors to observe and critique the dynamic entry exercises—approximates the physical and mental environment that SRTs can expect when forced to clear a building containing both hostages and terrorists. The complex and highly orchestrated tactics employed in dynamic entries involve intricate choreography and for obvious reasons cannot be revealed. All we can say is that the geeks who think a properly trained SRT will enter a building like Don Johnson and Phillip Michael Thomas in a *Miami Vice* episode have an abrupt and fatal surprise in store for themselves.

While at this time there is no SRT 4 level course, CTA does offer a one-week Tactical Crisis Resolution course that covers full team movement, day and night vehicle assaults, and culminates in a full-blown operation that includes an open air-initiated assault with participation of the Crisis Negotiations class.

The DOE's Central Training Academy is the American response to terrorism. Those fortunate enough to graduate from SRT 3 are the beneficiaries of the most advanced antiterrorist training currently available—anywhere. Purposely low profile and underheralded, CTA-trained SRTs can match acts with any of the world's more highly publicized snake eaters.

But the year 1984 will be remembered for several other noteworthy happenings at TWC. First, on July 21, the company celebrated its thirtieth anniversary. Second, TWC experienced an unsuccessful attempt to change from a publicly owned corporation to a privately owned company. In the spring of 1984, George received an unsolicited proposal from a major New York investment banking firm offering to take TWC private through a leveraged buyout. The proposal called for paying the company's stockholders $24 a share. TWC engaged Dillon, Read & Company, Inc., to determine if the proposal was fair to shareholders. The finding was affirmative and the board of directors gave its approval to move ahead. In mid-December, TWC was advised by the New York investment banking firm that it was unable to obtain the necessary financing, and its proposal was withdrawn.

Revenues in 1984 reached $279.309 million, compared with $238.936 million in 1983. However, TWC reported its first loss—totaling $1.804 million—in 1984, or 47 cents per share, compared with income of $6.412 million, or $1.66 per share, in 1983.

On a more private note, at about the same time TWC was moving into its new headquarters building, Jan Wackenhut Ward, thirty-nine that year, started a new career with Mary Kay Cosmetics in Miami, knowing that she wouldn't have to travel constantly, as she had done with TWC, and hoping to devote more time to Tanya and Tresha, who were still in high school. "I liked a lot of it," Jan recalls, smiling. "I didn't go in to do facials, I went in to become a sales director, and the only way you could become a sales director was to recruit enough people that you had a unit, and you had to have thirty people that were in there for a good year. And they were in and out like gangbusters.

"I did what I had to do to get there. If they say on an average it takes ten interviews to get one recruit, well, maybe it would take me twenty. That was okay, I'd do the twenty. I schlepped up 800 apartments, and nobody would be there, and all the disappointments that you could have. But I kept going. I really did have blinders on with Mary Kay. And I had the luxury of not needing the income. I mean, it was nice, but I couldn't have done it if it were my sole support.

"When I became a sales director, it wasn't what I thought it was going to be. They had this whole rosy picture of everybody in it for the good of everybody else, and it was just like any other company. I don't know, I thought it was because it was all women—and I think many times women are their own worst enemies. They're out to get each other more than they would even a man. Particularly in business. I hope that turns around.

"I was killing myself. I was working seven days a week. For some reason, I wasn't able to recruit enough management material. If I could've had even two women that wanted to go into management, that would've relieved me of a lot of the recruiting. Because they have to have their own recruits. Everybody was just in it to make a few extra dollars each week. So I had sales meetings I held every Monday night, and for a while we were doing them in the office, in the training center, which was great, because I had all the audio-visual and everything. Then you'd have four people show—out of fifty! Very discouraging. Sales meetings, I had a monthly newsletter, I'd make myself have at least five interview appointments for recruits every day. Now, many times they cancelled, but I'd have at least five. I did my own skin-care classes to be selling product four times a week. Every Saturday and every Wednesday night, I had to train the new consultants that were coming in. And then I'd accompany some of them on their own—you know, get them started. Oh, it was a zoo. It was a zoo.

"Roger was real good in the beginning, Very, very supportive. But it took its toll. Took its toll. I just didn't want to give up. I'm not used to doing that. Although it sounds like I am, because I've been in and out of the company. But I didn't have anybody to blame but me this time. We won three cars, that was exciting, and I thought: Well, you might meet the person tomorrow that wants management. So you keep going and going. Finally, I had to say, 'Look, I've done everything, I went to every seminar that was available, got all kinds of awards, but that wasn't what I was after.'

"See, I wanted to be a national sales director. There are about fifty. And they make about—between $60,000 and $80,000 a month. A *month!* Good money for a woman. My national sales director, I was in club work with her years ago. She wasn't doing anything I couldn't do. But it just never came together. I finally had to stop and say: 'Wait.' You can't work this hard, and have all your goals seemingly in correct order—I mean, I wasn't wanting anything that wasn't honest or good, and I wasn't doing anything wrong to get it—and you're working this hard, it must be I'm supposed to be doing something else. I had to put it into a spiritual vein."

HISTORICALLY, 1984 had some significant highlights. January 10, the U.S. and the Vatican exchanged diplomats after a 116-year hiatus. February 7, President Reagan ordered U.S. Marines withdrawn from the Beirut international peacekeeping force. February 9, Yuri V. Andropov died at age sixty-nine, and Konstantin U. Chernenko, seventy-two, was named leader of the Soviet Union. February 18, Italy and the Vatican agreed to end Roman Catholicism as the state religion. March 30, President Reagan ended the U.S. role in Beirut by relieving the Sixth Fleet from the peacekeeping force. April 10, Congress rebuked President Reagan on the use of federal funds for mining Nicaraguan harbors. May 7, the Soviet Union withdrew from the summer Olympic games in the U.S., and other bloc nations followed. May 10, a federal judge found the U.S. negligent in 1950 atomic tests. May 11, Napoleon Duarte, a moderate, was elected president of El Salvador. July 16–19, the thirty-ninth Democratic National Convention, in San Francisco, nominated Walter F. Mondale and Geraldine A. Ferraro. August 20–25, the thirty-third Republican National Convention, in Dallas, nominated President Reagan and Vice President Bush. September 4, Brian Mulroney and the Conservative Party won the Canadian election in a landslide. October 12, British Prime Minister Margaret Thatcher was nearly killed by an IRA assassination attempt. October 31, Indian Prime Minister Indira Gandhi was assassinated by two Sikh bodyguards; more than 1,000 were killed in anti-Sikh riots; Gandhi's son Rajiv succeeded her. November 7, President Reagan was reelected in a landslide with 59 percent of the vote. December 3, toxic gas leaks from a Union Carbide plant in Bhopal, India, killed more than 2,000 and injured 150,000.

ALAN BERNSTEIN became vice president of Domestic Operations in 1985, replacing Don Bottom. Profits had dropped dramatically the previous year. "That job was really the start of me moving into the parent company," Bernstein explains. "I took over Don's position, less a couple of divisions. Just basically the Guard Division first. I operated the area offices through a five-person regional system. They had five regions at the time. One of the things I did immediately, I evaluated the five regions.

"I came back to George and said, 'George, quite frankly, you have five separate companies out there. Each regional vice president has his own little army, his own little fiefdom. If we're going to make the company move, and move in one direction, we need to do something.' So I suggested that we actually chop off all middle management. So we removed, and I eliminated, all middle management at headquarters. I fired or moved out to the field all of the regional people and vice presidents. We moved them back to operational positions in the field, or into other areas of the company. And that left everyone reporting to me. And, as I've often said, all of my professors for my master's degree must be rolling over in their graves, because that's just not normally done. But our industry seems to work better that way, when you have direct-line authority with a lot of people, and when you have a lot of good people in the field who in effect understand what their job is, and they take direction.

"Slowly, as I was successful in the Guard Division, Rick gave me Investigations, Nuclear, and other Domestic Operations services that I now control. That's really how my position has grown to the level it's in right now.

"I'll tell you some interesting stories. Knowing about George Wackenhut, George has always been a very impressive individual. Many years ago, when he wore the crew cut and he had big broad shoulders and a jaw that went on for a mile, he was very, very *intimidating* to me. George was always short on conversation, especially back then, and he would take command of a meeting, and I would never be *able* to speak to him—even when he was talking directly to me about a memo I had written! The memo was coherent and had a good plan, but for some reason I was unable to stand there in front of the man and basically feed back my ideas! I would just—*stutter!*

"It got so bad that Rick and I would talk about it, and he'd say to me, 'What the hell's *wrong* with you? You come in my office and you tell me everything that needs to be done, exactly how it should be done, how long it will take to accomplish, then you get in front of my dad and you become this babbling *idiot!*' And it was really true. It was some strange effect George had on me. I didn't realize that almost *everybody* went through the same thing at first. I think everybody thinks that it's just *them!* But it took years and years.

"They're very down-to-earth people, the Wackenhuts. And through some social things, my in-laws knew them, and Kathy, my wife, knows them. I would always call him 'Mr. Wackenhut' and Kathy would call him 'Russ.' As you know, Russ is his nickname to his close friends. I wouldn't dare call him *George,* let alone *Russ!*

"In the early 1970s, the first time I met Murray Levine was a great story, because George had pulled me into his office when I said I was talking with Bud Thompson about taking over the alarm operation. And he said, 'You've got to meet Murray Levine, because Murray is the guy you'll be reporting to.' It was a Wednesday afternoon, about two o'clock. So George had called for Murray and, of course, Murray was not in the office on Wednesday afternoon. About an hour later, after I had sat outside in George's anteroom like a little boy waiting to see the principal, this guy comes up the hallway, and I heard him screaming and yelling, this person, and I see him turn the corner, coming into George's office area, and he's wearing a *tennis* outfit, you know, white shorts, sneakers, and he has his racquet in his hand. And he says, 'What the heck does he want? I'm out there with the client playing tennis!' So George's secretary then, I think her name was Magruder, said George wanted to see us both, and she introduced us, and we went in. And, of course, Murray's comment was, 'Oh, another Jew in the company!'

"As we walked in, I went over and sat down on this little corner couch that he had, and I thought Murray was going to sit on this big yellow chair that was in front of George's desk. Well, Murray walks behind the desk, sits on George's lap, and *kisses his ring!* And here I am, I think I was like twenty-five, twenty-six, and I was just overwhelmed by George *alone*, and here's this guy walking in, sitting on his lap, and kissing his *ring!* And I thought: Oh, my *God*, what have I got myself into?

"Around 1982, even though a lot of the older senior officers were still around, the Gus Novotneys, the John Ammarells, the Bob Kirks, Rick started to expand his control, and started to hire people who he was more comfortable with, but also, I think, were better educated and more business-minded, and, quite frankly, it started what I'll call the 'metamorphosis' of our company.

"Personally, and I've made this comment to George and Rick, I believe companies have a life cycle. People have life cycles also in business. There will come a day when Alan Bernstein is no longer right for this position. And I expect wholeheartedly that one day Rick will come into my office and say, 'Alan, we need to replace you,' or 'We need to move somebody else into your position who is better educated, has better ideas, has more enthusiasm and energy to get the job done.' We're in a very, very tough business. The life expectancy of people in our business, in the corporate world, is not very long. The fact is, I have been in this position longer than any other person. I've been fortunate because, until this year [1993], we've always had big profits. This year, that may not be the case.

"But the fact of the matter is that I recognize that. And I think that's the difference. Unlike John Ammarell, who started with George very young, and grew up with George, I will never be under the illusion that I'm here forever. I would like to be here for as long as I can be a major contributor. But I think the older guys just thought, for some reason, they grew up in an era where you worked for a company for a hundred years and then you retired. I'm not under that illusion and I don't think the people behind me are under that illusion either.

"In any event, during that time, the early '80s, Rick started to move a lot of people in, more aggressive people, with a different mind set. That doesn't necessarily mean that it was a better mind set. Doesn't necessarily mean that ours was better or theirs was worse. But we were *different*. We *are* better educated; we *are* more adapting to the life of the business today. Doing business in the '60s and '70s was much different than doing business in the '90s—and certainly by the year 2000. We're more internationally oriented, our clients are more national and international in scope.

"In fact, I have often said, if you look at the growth of The Wackenhut Corporation, it was tremendous. But if you look at the growth of the security industry during the same period of time, all we did was keep up with the rate of growth. I think that if we had had some really superstar management in the positions of John Ammarell, Gus Novotney, Bud Thompson, and a number of middle-management people—those vice presidents that I fired—we actually would be much larger than we are today. I really do believe that. Because the industry was growing at a little bit slower rate than we were growing. And if we had had aggressive sales marketing campaigns, if we had had aggressive area managers at that time, I think we would've been larger today than we are. I've said that many times to George and I've said that many times to Rick.

"I said the same thing to my father, who had been very successful on a much smaller scale, and he said, 'I'm successful; you're not yet.' George basically said the same thing! Many years ago, I asked him a question about advertising, and he said, 'No, we don't advertise.' I said, 'Well, *why* don't we advertise?' He said, 'I built this company from nothing to $250 million.' And my only rebuttal to that was, 'Well, maybe we'd be half a billion by now.' That was the only comeback you could have, because the man was successful, and is successful, and built the company brilliantly.

"I can tell you one story about George Wackenhut to give you an idea of how honorable an individual he is. We had a contract in Saudi Arabia for years, which really gave the company most of its profits for a long period of time—Jeddah International Airport, and

Only photo known to exist that includes George with other three original partners. Picture was taken at ex-FBI agents lunch in Miami, 1954. Partners names are italicized. Seated, left to right: James D. Hayes, Earl F. Warford, William M. Robinson, Bud Thompson, Don Lohmeyer; standing, left to right: *Ed DuBois, Jr.,* Paul Williams, *Bill Stanton, George Wackenhut, Ken Altschul.*

TWC's first headquarters building, 3280 Ponce de Leon Boulevard, Coral Gables. TWC moved in June 1, 1960, remained 24 years, then moved to The Wackenhut Building, Coral Gables, in 1984.

George's second motor yacht, a 50-foot Hatteras named *Security Risk,* was purchased in the summer of 1966.

Ruth and George at the christening party for *Security Risk.*

General Mark W. Clark became a good friend of George after joining TWC's board in 1967, when he retired as president of The Citadel (1954–66); he served on the board until 1975.

"Captain Eddie" Rickenbacker, America's greatest air ace during World War I, became a friend of George when he was president of Miami-headquartered Eastern Air Lines (1934–65), and served as a member of TWC's board, 1968–72. (Charlie Preston Studios)

Rick Wackenhut's graduation picture from The Citadel, as it appeared in the college yearbook, *The 1969 Sphinx*.

Rick and Molly (nee Ball) were married in the Summerall Chapel at The Citadel, March 13, 1971, while he was still serving in the Air Force's Office of Special Investigations, stationed in Washington.

OPPOSITE. One of the first aerial photos of the completed Tyecliffe, 1974, with *Top Secret* at dock. Estate required seven years to build.

LEFT. Tyecliffe's flagstone turret with stained-glass windows contains a circular staircase leading to the belvedere tower.

OPPOSITE BELOW. *Top Secret,* George's 104-foot ocean-cruising motor yacht. Her twin motor launches were named *Cloak* and *Dagger.*

Ruth created *Top Secret*'s interior décor in a mode of Viking antiquity, including hand-sculpted teak, oak, and ash for each area.

Jan and Roger Ward cut their wedding cake during outdoor reception at Tyecliffe, Coral Gables, on November 24, 1979.

Jan's proud parents dance in tent on lawn at Tyecliffe, with Jan and Roger in background.

Clarence M. Kelley, first man selected to succeed J. Edgar Hoover as director of the FBI (1973–78), joined TWC on February 5, 1980, and was subsequently elected to the board of directors.

December 30, 1980, TWC was listed on the New York Stock Exchange. Don Calvin, left, executive vice president of the NYSE, and George, flank James G. Burke of the firm of La Branche & Co.

In 1983, at the Savannah River Site, near Aiken, SC, the Department of Energy signed a contract with TWC that was—and still is—the largest single government award to a private security company in history. Signing for the DOE was Goetz Oertel.

Seven members of TWC's Special Response Team at the 192,000-acre Savannah River Site.

The Wackenhut Building in Coral Gables, Florida. Constructed in 1984, the $18 million TWC headquarters has 160,000 square feet of office space, and a garage with more than 500 parking spaces. Ruth had total responsibility for the interior design.

George was an advisor to U.S. Senator Paula Hawkins (Rep.-Florida) in 1984, during her meetings of the Senate Business Advisory Committee.

OPPOSITE. George's penthouse office occupies the entire east end of the rectangular building, paneled by Ruth in a dark, rich rosewood, accented with gray-blue stone. (Adjoining conference room, not shown, has décor of an English hunting lodge.)

The Wackenhuts' home on Cape Cod, 1986. Left to right: Wynne Leon, Rick, George, Ruth (kneeling), John Bolles, Budd Kneip, Marty Holleran, Bill Hill.

Rick with some classmates in Advanced Management Program at Harvard Business School, 1987. First row, Hew Stevenson; second row, Hack Kim, Tim Cole (who joined TWC in 1988); third row, Bill Ziegert, Paul Rizzo, Phil Block.

George chats with former classmates Tom and Jane Triol at the 50th reunion of the Class of 1942 at West Chester State Teachers College, West Chester, PA, October 10, 1987.

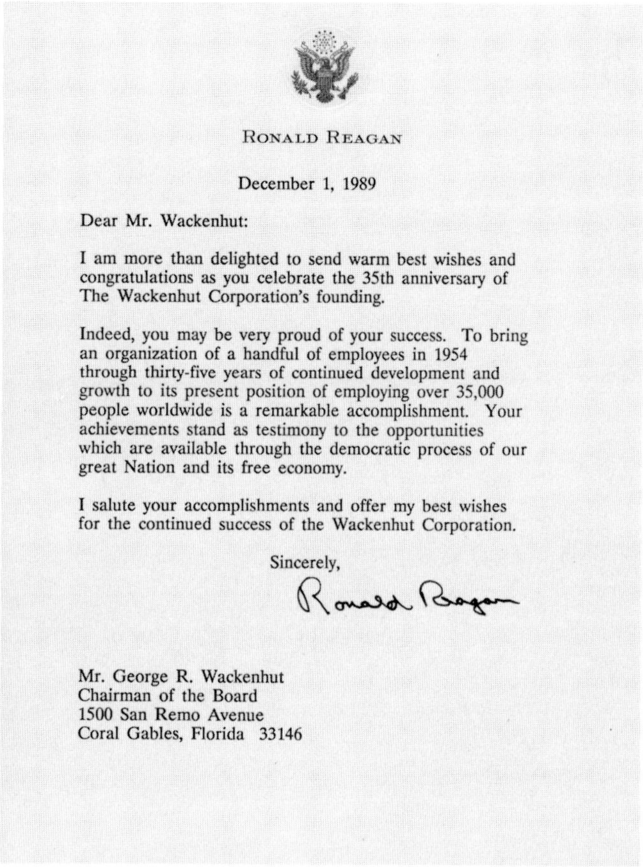

RONALD REAGAN

December 1, 1989

Dear Mr. Wackenhut:

I am more than delighted to send warm best wishes and congratulations as you celebrate the 35th anniversary of The Wackenhut Corporation's founding.

Indeed, you may be very proud of your success. To bring an organization of a handful of employees in 1954 through thirty-five years of continued development and growth to its present position of employing over 35,000 people worldwide is a remarkable accomplishment. Your achievements stand as testimony to the opportunities which are available through the democratic process of our great Nation and its free economy.

I salute your accomplishments and offer my best wishes for the continued success of the Wackenhut Corporation.

Sincerely,

Ronald Reagan

Mr. George R. Wackenhut
Chairman of the Board
1500 San Remo Avenue
Coral Gables, Florida 33146

In early December 1988, George received this letter from President Ronald Reagan shortly before he left office.

Thanksgiving Day, Cape Cod, 1993. Left to right: Greg Ward standing next to his father Roger, with Tanya, Jan, and George.

April 8, 1994. George and Ruth celebrated their 50th wedding anniversary in a house on the ocean at Vero Beach, FL, where they were joined by all members of the immediate family. Flanking George and Ruth in the front row are Lauren, left, 7 years old, and Ashley, 10 (Rick and Molly's youngest). Back row, left to right, Lisa, 12, and Jennifer, 17, with their parents Molly and Rick; Jan and Roger Ward, with Jan's daughters Tresha, 25, and Tanya, 27.

the hospitals we had over there. We were making, I want to say, $2 million in profits on a $12 million job. It was like a 15, 16 percent profit margin, *bottom line!* And we were going to *lose* it! This was 1984. A guy came to us and said, 'Look, if you give me two million, I'll give a million and a half to the sheik.' He said, 'I will make sure you retain that business.' And George said, 'We don't pay bribes to *anybody.*'

"Not only was he hurting his own company, but he was taking money out of his own pocket, because he still owns more than fifty percent of the company. So he was taking *personal* money out of his pocket by losing this job. But he had made a moral and ethical stand. And I was a party to that. To that conversation, when he said, 'We don't pay bribes to *anybody.*' Call it an agent's fee, a consultant's fee, whatever you want, that's a *bribe.* And he said, 'No.' You had to have great respect for the man, for his position, for his ethical and moral responses to business and to—just *people,* in general."

On July 1, 1985, in its first major venture into the social services field, WSI began operating its first Job Corps Center in Guthrie, Oklahoma, under contract with the U.S. Department of Labor. Job Corps Centers are federally funded residential vocational training schools for economically disadvantaged young men and women between the ages of sixteen and twenty-two.

WSI's two-year contract for operation of the Guthrie Center was then valued at $10.5 million and included three one-year options to extend services. The new division of WSI would eventually be called Wackenhut Education Services, Inc., and would develop into a significant profit center in the years to come.

"The year 1985 saw the company achieve two significant milestones," George says. "First, the passing of the $300 million mark in total revenues [$300.883 million], and the attainment of record earnings of $1.76 per share. This achievement represented an increase in revenues of 8 percent compared to 1984, and it took place while we improved the management structure in Domestic Operations, overcame the effect on international operations of the previous year's loss of a portion of our Saudi Arabian business, and continued to expand services to the government.

"Second, the creation of Wackenhut Education Services, Inc., was significant at that time, not so much for its impact on overall revenues, but for the fact that it represented a new corporate commitment toward diversification. In 1985, I suspected that the preoccupation of public officials with fiscal belt-tightening measures might lead to additional opportunities for us to expand our services to the government. I believed that the Gramm-Rudman Deficit Reduction Law and its follow-up proposals might lead to further explorations by government bodies at all levels to seek greater savings through privatization. Government budget cuts focused attention on the potentials for savings that exist when services traditionally performed by public employees and agencies are turned over to private concerns. Our government was getting into the business of getting out of business, and it made sound sense to me that we capitalize on the trends in this direction."

On August 26, TWC was selected by Pan American World Airways to provide full security services at its Worldport Terminal at John F. Kennedy International Airport in New York. Under the multimillion dollar, two-year contract—which became the company's largest airline contract—Wackenhut was also chosen to provide security for the airline's Pan Am Building headquarters in Manhattan, as well as the Pan Am computer center across the Hudson River in Rockleigh, New Jersey.

According to J.A. (Ed) LeBlanc, who was then director of Wackenhut Airline Services, the contract called for TWC to provide a variety of security services, including pre-departure screening of passengers, guarding all cargo and maintenance areas, assuming responsibility for all transit aliens or deportees going aboard Pan Am flights, and directing traffic control around the Worldport itself. Besides screening passengers boarding Pan Am flights, TWC inspectors also checked passengers of several Iron Curtain countries whose airlines operated out of the Worldport.

TWC operations at the Worldport were supervised by airport manager Jim Morris, who was assisted by administrative manager Tom Oates. When the contract went into effect, more than 300 Wackenhut employees were on duty at the Worldport, the Pan Am Building, and the Rockleigh computer center.

On October 26, Lieutenant General Joseph F. Carroll, USAF

(Ret.), stepped down from TWC's board of directors after fourteen years of distinguished service to the corporation. But the board unanimously voted to elect him to a new post, that of director emeritus, a lifelong title that would assure his continued association with TWC. A special tribute to General Carroll's exemplary service to the corporation was read by George, who then signed it along with the other board members: John S. Ammarell, Frank C. Carlucci, Robert E. Chasen, Frederick M. Glass, Willis M. Hawkins, Clarence M. Kelley, Dr. Robert Q. Marston, General Seth J. McKee, USAF (Ret.), Raymond A. Quadt, Vice Admiral William. F. Raborn, Jr., USN (Ret.), General Bernard A. Schriever, USAF (Ret.), Charles J. Simons, and Chesterfield Smith. General Carroll also received a framed photograph of himself with other directors, and a table clock carrying the inscription: "With deepest appreciation for your dedicated service and counsel, 1971–1985."

At the same meeting, Richard R. Wackenhut was elected to membership on the board. In so doing, the board recognized his thirteen years of experience in various assignments and in his recent contributions as senior vice president of Operations, a post he had held since 1983.

Later that year, Frank C. Carlucci departed the board to assume the position of director of the National Security Council in the Reagan Administration.

NOTEWORTHY historical events during 1985: January 20, Ronald Reagan, seventy-three, took the oath for his second term as the fortieth president. February 14, the Worldwide Conservative Rabbinical Assembly approved women in the clergy. February 18, General Westmoreland settled his libel action against CBS. February 20, Prime Minister Margaret Thatcher addressed the U.S. Congress, endorsing Reagan's policies. March 11, Soviet leader Chernenko died at age seventy-three and was replaced by Mikhail Gorbachev, fifty-four. March 15, Secretary of Labor Raymond J. Donovan, facing a fraud trial in New York, resigned; he was the first sitting Cabinet member to be indicted. April 13, tens of thousands marked the fortieth anniversary of the liberation of the Buchenwald death camp. April 18, Reagan became the target of wide attacks by Jewish leaders and others when he visited Bitburg Cemetery, West Germany, where SS troops were buried. June 14, two Shiite Moslem gunmen hijacked a TWA jetliner with 133 aboard, 104 of them Americans; on June 30, the 39 remaining hostages were freed in Beirut. August 9, Arthur James Walker, fifty, a retired Naval officer, was convicted by a federal judge of participating in a Soviet spy ring. October 7, PLO terrorists hijacked the *Achille Lauro*, an Italian cruise ship with eighty passengers, plus crew; American passenger Leon Klinghoffer was killed on October 8. November 14, a volcano eruption in Colombia left 25,000 dead and missing. November 19, Reagan and Gorbachev held a summit meeting and, on November 21, agreed to step up arms-control talks and renew cultural contacts. November 23, terrorists seized an Egyptian Boeing 737 jetliner after takeoff from Athens; on November 24, fifty-nine people were killed as Egyptian forces stormed the plane on Malta. December 12, the U.S. budget-balancing bill was enacted. Also on December 12, a plane crash in Newfoundland killed 248 U.S. soldiers en route home for the Christmas holidays. December 30, terrorists killed nineteen people at Rome and Vienna airports.

27

WHEN RICK WACKENHUT was elected president and chief operating officer of TWC at the board meeting of April 26, 1986, it signalled one of the predictable transitions that Alan Bernstein characterized as the management "metamorphosis" started in the early 1980s. George continued as chairman and chief executive officer, and his key role in the conduct of TWC's business was underscored by the fact that executives concerned with strategic and corporate planning, the corporate financial area, internal audit, and corporate relations still reported directly to him. But, at the same board meeting, Frederick F. (Buck) Thornburg, who was then forty-six (Rick was thirty-eight), was simultaneously elected to the board of directors and to the position of executive vice president of the corporation. Bernstein, also thirty-eight, was named senior vice president of Domestic Operations.

Thornburg had held various positions since joining Wackenhut in 1979 as associate general counsel. In 1981, he was named vice president of the Systems and Services Group, and the following year he was appointed corporate vice president for International Operations as well as president of Wackenhut International, Inc. He became senior vice president of Administration in 1983.

Prior to joining Wackenhut, he was a partner with the Indiana law firm of Thornburg, McGill, Deahl, Harman, Carey & Murray, and a law clerk to the chief judge of the U.S. Court of Appeals for the Seventh Circuit.

Thornburg received his BA in economics from DePauw University, and attended the University of Notre Dame Graduate School of Economics. As a Charles Halleck Scholar, he graduated magna cum laude with a JD degree from the Indiana University School of Law.

Alan Bernstein's thoughts on the transition: "I think the change came—the *real* change started—when Buck Thornburg jumped in as executive vice president, and took over John Ammarell's old position. To grow, any corporation has to have management that can drive it further than it is the day they take over. The management we had at that time had basically stopped, it had peaked out, it did not have the ability. George, I think, being the kind of person that he is, recognized that. Didn't *like* that, but recognized it. And I think Rick got a bad rap for being the one *pushing* it. It just so happens that Rick, at the same time, was growing and had ideas.

"So the need was to develop a second generation of management that could bring the company from, at that time it was about $300 million, to the billion-dollar stage. And that's why I say that one day somebody's going to walk in and say, 'Alan, you're at a billion dollars, you've just about capped your ability.' And there's going to be somebody that's going to be walking in behind me that's going to be able to bring us to $1.5 billion, or $2 billion, whatever that number might be."

Rick Wackenhut has vivid memories of his election to president and COO, and recalls approaching the position with a combination of pride, humility, and a certain amount of self-doubt. "We all have our insecurities, and I felt: Am I ready for this yet?" he says. "There wasn't really going to be that drastic a change, but it was difficult, psychologically and emotionally, to think: All these years, my father's been president of this company, and now I've got the title. So there was a considerable amount of that. I felt very proud, because my father has operated with one very prominent consistency: He may feel something personally, but he'll turn to the board, from a business standpoint, and say, 'Here's the issue, this is what I'm proposing; you decide.' He stays out of it. And he stayed out of this one entirely, and it was the board that truly elected me. I don't know, I don't think I'll ever get over the feeling of being my father's son. You know, the negative aspects of it. Always following that home run hitter to bat. Those types of things. Which is tough. No matter how confident you are in yourself, there's always somebody out there who's saying, 'Oh, you know, it wasn't him that did it, it was because of who he is.'

"Unquestionably, a lot of things have come my way because of who I am. But I don't think I'd be here if I hadn't done the job. In a mom-and-pop company, yes, but you can't in this company. Anyway, that was one thing, and then one that's a little more comical: To me, it was such a major thing that I was elected president, but the announcement in the newspaper the following day was a *one-liner!* Pat Cannon [director of Corporate Relations] had not blown it up, he just sent in a basic press release. It was handled with a one-liner, along with so-and-so just became manager of Southeast Bank. And I looked at it, and I just went, 'Jesus Christ!' In retrospect, it gave me a healthy sense of perspective, and I needed that."

The elections of Rick, Buck Thornburg, and Alan Bernstein, although major, represented only part of the transition that took place at that April board meeting. Three other relatively young men were also elevated to the status of vice president, and they would all prove to have significant impacts on the company: William E. (Bill) Jackson was elected vice president of the Western Region; Kenneth C. (Ken) Ketterer was voted vice president of Human Resources; and James P. (Jim) Rowan was elected vice president of Administration. In addition, George Zeiss, who joined TWC in 1978, after serving thirty-five years in the FBI, was voted vice president of Client Relations.

Another aspect of that particular board meeting that could be interpreted to fall into the definition of Bernstein's 'metamorphosis' was the departure of three long-time members of the board: Clarence M. Kelley, Vice Admiral William F. Raborn, Jr., USN (Ret.), and Chesterfield Smith. Kelley, former Director of the FBI, joined the board in 1980. Admiral Raborn's service—fifteen years—was the longest, dating back to 1971. Smith had been on the board since 1977, and would later return.

April also marked the retirement of Warren Altmann, after twenty-seven years at TWC. Altmann, who had been director of Operations Administration, joined the company in 1968 when the

Reliable Reporting Company of Long Island, New York, merged with Wackenhut.

At the annual shareholders meeting, April 25, George announced the creation of TWC's Anti-Terrorism and Crisis Management Division, and appointed Conrad V. Hassel, an internationally known expert on terrorism, as director of the new division.

Hassel had served as a special agent of the FBI for twenty-three years. When he retired in 1984, he was chief of the FBI's Special Operations and Research Unit, a group that studies potential "crisis problems" such as terrorist attacks or hostage incidents that might involve the FBI. He obtained an MS degree in criminology from California State University and was awarded his JD from Duquesne University in Pittsburgh. The author of numerous articles on terrorism, Hassel had been guest lecturer on that subject at England's Scotland Yard and at the Royal Canadian Mounted Police headquarters in Canada. Since his retirement, he had served as security consultant to various foreign governments.

In George's address to the shareholders, he said, "The move reflects the increasing concern of the worldwide business community to make adjustments to meet the spread of international terrorism. The Wackenhut Corporation has felt the effect of the current situation with increased inquiries and concerns with respect to security on both the domestic and international fronts. Corporations may be forced to deal with bomb threats, kidnappings, extortions, product tampering, and an entire gamut of disruptive actions which may take place with no advance warnings. It is our intention to be prepared on short notice—or no notice—to move a support team, tailored to the particular situation, and with the correct mix of experts, to wherever it is necessary."

Earlier in the year, Domestic Operations introduced its first annual "Area Manager of the Year" awards banquet in Miami on March 1, a competition that would become extremely popular over the years. George F. Stewart, who had been area manager in Indianapolis for the previous seven years, was named Area Manager of the Year for 1985. Stewart and his wife received a seven-day, all-expense paid trip to Hawaii, plus $500 in spending money.

Alan Bernstein's idea was to select ten top managers from area offices throughout the country each year, all chosen on the basis of three major criteria: (1) increases in sales for the area offices; (2) management performance in accordance with established corporate policies; and (3) overall profitability of operations.

The top ten managers and their wives were flown to Miami on an all-expense-paid trip for the awards banquet, held that year at the Kings Bay Resort Yacht and Country Club. The ten finalists were, alphabetically: Kenneth M. Crawford, Sarasota, Florida; James C. Fleming, Jackson, Mississippi; James D. Gorham, Memphis, Tennessee; Kenneth B. Lezatte, vice president, New York District; Elmer Nelson, Ashland, Kentucky; Edward J. Sanbourn, Washington, DC; Selvin M. Smith, Richmond, Virginia; George F. Stewart, Indianapolis, Indiana; Donald C. Taylor, Casper, Wyoming; and James O. Widel, Sr., Norfolk, Virginia.

The managers and their wives were met at Miami International Airport by headquarters executives as they arrived on Friday, February 28. Friday evening, they were guests at a cocktail party hosted by George and Ruth. Saturday morning, they were given a tour of the new headquarters building, and Saturday afternoon they were free to enjoy golf and tennis at their resort hotel. At the Saturday evening banquet, none of them knew who would emerge as the top award winner. The suspense continued right up to the moment that George Stewart's name was read.

In addition to the Hawaii trip, he received a plaque as Manager of the Year, and he and his wife each received specially designed watches. The nine runners-up also received plaques attesting to their achievements, and specially designed watches were given to each of them and their wives.

At the close of the banquet, a special cash drawing was held for the top ten managers. Ruth Wackenhut picked three sealed envelopes, each with a name, from a fishbowl. As she did so, a dramatic drum roll was played by a member of the band. Donald C. Taylor of Casper won first prize, $10,000. Elmer Nelson of Ashland won the second-prize bonanza of $3,000, and Edward J. Sanbourn of Washington, DC, hit the third-prize jackpot of $2,000.

During July's quarterly board meeting, Washington consultant Nancy Clark Reynolds became the first woman elected to the TWC board of directors. At the time, Reynolds was president of the prestigious Washington, DC, public affairs consulting firm of Wexler, Reynolds, Harrison & Schule, Inc. A native of Boise, Idaho, and daughter of a U.S. Senator, she had an exceptionally varied career in television, state government, public relations, corporate business, and government relations.

She was the first woman co-anchor at San Francisco television station KPIX-TV when Governor Ronald Reagan of California appointed her as his assistant press secretary in 1968. Two years later, she was named special assistant to Governor Reagan. In 1976, she moved to Washington as associate director, national affairs, for the Boise Cascade Corporation. The following year, she became the first woman vice president and corporate officer of the Bendix Corporation.

The mother of four children, Reynolds had held various presidential appointments, including service on the President's Advisory Committee on Trade Negotiations; as U.S. Representative for the United Nations Commission on the Status of Women; and as Co-Chair, U.S. Delegation to the U.N. Decade for Women World Conference in Nairobi.

She was a member, board of governors, of the Ronald Reagan Presidential Foundation, and served as the director of congressional relations for the 1985 Presidential Inaugural Committee.

In August of 1986, WSI was awarded a multimillion-dollar three-year contract to provide security services at eight Strategic Petroleum Reserve sites operated by the Department of Energy in Louisiana and Texas. WSI won the award from Boeing Petroleum Services, Inc., prime contractor on the SPR project for the DOE. Ironically, it was a contract that WSI had decided *not* to bid on, and the circumstances were complex and intriguing. "Boeing ran a very careful and very clean procurement process," Budd Kneip recalls. "They started soliciting in the spring of '86. Boeing was such a large government contractor in its own right, they really understood government contracting rules, and they created a process that was meant to not only develop the best subcontractor for the job, but also to assure that there would be no protests or other administrative problems that would hinder the award or otherwise delay its implementation.

"So they went through very carefully designed steps in inviting bidders into the bidding process. Every single security and services company in the United States bid on this contract. It was as broad a competition as any contract WSI had sought up to that time. The initial list of attendees had to be in the neighborhood of fifty companies.

"It was a very complex site and had a very complex operating history. At one point, every single site had a *different* security contractor. This goes back to the years when I was first employed at the SPRO, which was the late '70s and very early '80s. The Strategic Petroleum Reserve was viewed as an opportunity to advance small business and minority contracting objectives. So each site was competed individually, and small businesses and minority businesses were selected to provide security at each site. There was no coordination. It was not the most practical way to run a security program for a complex project such as this. But that approach was still fresh in the minds of an awful lot of people.

"This was in the early springtime and, as I recall, Boeing announced its intentions throughout the DOE community, in *The Commerce Business Daily*, that they would be soliciting, sometime in the future, for a security subcontractor at the Strategic Petroleum Reserve.

"You have to remember WSI's circumstances at that point. We had acquired the Savannah River Site in August of 1983, we had had some initial operating problems throughout '84, it was a very big task, it consumed an awful lot of time, and WSI's overhead structure was not as sophisticated as it is today. It was very lean. So Savannah River continued to consume a great deal of the time and attention of WSI management. In addition to that, the following year, 1984, we had been awarded the Central Training Academy, which was also a sophisticated and complex project. So, in the spring of '86, WSI, which was operating on a shoestring overhead budget, had kind of a 'full plate,' to put it in a colloquialism. An awful lot of time had been expended just managing these two unique projects. The Central Training Academy was totally out of the realm of anything that had been attempted anywhere before.

"When Boeing announced its intention to proceed with its solicitation for security services, WSI management had to look at it in terms of resources available, and had to evaluate the opportunity for success. Now, from DOE's perspective, WSI dominated the DOE market. It did then and it does now. So, WSI management sat down and evaluated our chances to win this award. They knew our management history, even though the WSI management team was relatively new. Bob Frye was still on the team, he knew the past experiences of Wackenhut at the Strategic Petroleum Reserve, and, of course, they had not been pleasant. Also, WSI management knew that we virtually controlled the DOE market, and one of the considerations had to be: Was the DOE going to consistently allow Wackenhut to win all the security contracts? Or would there be some pressure to spread the security responsibilities around?

"Well, that's a legitimate consideration. When I sat on the contracting side with the government, you had to look at that. You did not want to focus all your resources on one firm. This was the smallest of the major DOE projects, at the time, and it was a subcontract, not a prime contract. There were seven sites at that time [the eighth was still under construction], there probably had to be fifty people per site, so you're talking in the neighborhood of 350 to 400 people. And very complex, logistically. Another consideration was the incumbent, Wells Fargo. And, frankly, the industry scuttlebutt was that they were performing adequately.

"So when you took all the factors together, the time being expended on major DOE jobs, the potential to win yet another DOE facility, and then the incumbent's relatively strong performance, the decision was made early *not* to bid on that contract.

"When this first started to germinate, I was still working in Contracts, I was vice president of Contracts, and I was working very closely with WSI. I was still doing all the contract negotiations, all the G&A negotiations, all the fee negotiations, work terms and conditions in the contracts, so I was very well-versed with WSI and their facilities, and worked very closely with Paul Roundy, who was president of WSI at the time.

"I knew the SPRO very well, and I had a very proprietary feel for it. I had worked there as part of the prime contracting team. I had worked for Wells Fargo; in fact, had won the contract for Wells Fargo. It was only about three years removed from my employment there. I still knew an awful lot of the people around the site. I had a long talk with Paul, and I suggested that we really ought to take a run at it. And Paul's a very good marketer. His only problem was resource allocation; we just didn't have anybody. Paul had himself and Bob Frye as full-time employees. He had a part-time controller and a part-time secretary. That's all WSI *had!* So, when Paul looked at it, he just didn't have the resources to expend, given all the other factors.

"But I really wanted to take a crack at it. So I sat down with Paul, and Paul said, 'Look, if you can do it, fine.' I went up to the chairman and I said, 'I would like to take a shot at this proposal. All I need is somebody to help me with the costing, and I will do the whole thing. I will design it, I will write it, I will write all the "best and finals," I'll do it soup to nuts, I just need somebody to cost it, because it's very complex to cost.' Each site had to be costed differently, each site had different wage determinations, each *state* had different wage determinations, each state had different fringe benefits, different social welfare implications. So it was a very complex costing arrangement.

"George agreed to let me do it, and he let me borrow a gentleman by the name of Ron Valentini, who was a very skilled costing guy, probably the best I've ever run across, and also a very hard worker. His star was really rising at that point and everybody acknowledged his value to the corporation. I called Ron, he came up to the office, and he and I talked for a couple of hours about it, and he agreed, let's take a shot at it. We were both holding down other positions at the time, so a lot of this was going to be done in off-hours, around our main responsibilities. But we decided to tackle it, and Ron and I did it all by ourselves.

"When I looked at it, the approach to security at the Strategic Petroleum Reserve had been fairly conventional. The project itself was headquartered in New Orleans, and the sites were given a great deal of independent responsibility. So security had always tracked this process. The site security manager had the responsibility to run security on the site. I knew that if we were going to dislodge a strong incumbent, we had to do something very different. And here's where I had a leg up, because of my long experience on the site. One of the problems had always been, the further you got from New Orleans, the more disconnected you felt from the project. And some of those guys at the sites out in Freeport and Lake Charles sometimes didn't feel as though they were part of the corporation.

"So what I proposed, basically, was a headquarters operation in New Orleans, but also an east and west *regional* office. Each of the regional offices would run the daily responsibilities. They would run Human Resources, they'd run Training, they'd run Management, they'd run Outfitting and Purchasing, and then the headquarters operation could be relatively small and cost effective, and coordinate things, where cost efficiencies and administrative efficiencies made sense.

"So that's what we did. We constructed what I still think was a beautiful design project and one in which, in fact, if I were running the operation of the whole program, I would've implemented for the entire operations of the SPRO.

"The initial proposal was three volumes, very large volumes. One of those was a costing volume, the two others were six-inch technical binders. And I literally dedicated probably the next eight weeks to doing that, nights and weekends. I had good help in the Contracts group, so I was able to give them a lot of responsibility. Lina Trennert in Contracts is a very skilled lady. She had kind of grown up with me in the Contracts business, and she subsequently became director of Contracts. So she was able to relieve a lot of the burden, and I kind of closed the door, and that's what we did. And then Ron, again, was very helpful.

"As I recall, the approximate deadline of the initial proposal was sometime in early June. So somewhere around late May, early June, the proposal was due. What happened was that Boeing evaluated all of the proposals and came back with a set of questions to a smaller, sort of 'best and final' group. And those sets of questions were almost as profound as the initial solicitation itself. I ended up responding with another full volume of answers to the questions.

"Actually, at that time, we were not expecting to get very far. What we wanted to do, at a minimum, was show the DOE community that we had enough respect for their projects that we weren't taking them for granted, and we weren't picking and choosing just the projects we wanted to bid on. At a minimum, that's what we wanted to do. We felt we couldn't insult our major client by simply not bidding. So, although we wanted to win, of course, just submitting a credible proposal would have been satisfactory under the circumstances.

"Well, we were all kind of surprised when, lo and behold, we were picked in the final range and we were called to orals! I had found a management team, interviewed them all, and I had assistance from various departments: Human Resources assisted a great deal by identifying certain people and, of course, the WSI people assisted whenever and wherever they could. So we were able to get together a very credible management team, which was submitted with the initial proposal. We had used some devices that Bob Frye and Dick Wilson had developed for the Savannah River proposal, such as having every key manager sign a commitment statement. I think that was a great idea. Bob and Dick were the first ones to have really done that. The commitment stated that the key managers would serve at least one year, if we were selected.

"We had about two weeks to create an oral presentation. I went to George and Paul and told them that we had received notification, that we had to show up in about two weeks for some orals, and I would need both of them there. And again: 'Fine, do what you need to do.' So I went off by myself, again, with Ron's help, and we started to create an entire oral presentation.

"Ron and I took off for New Orleans about ten days before the orals. We sat in our hotel rooms and designed an entire oral presentation. For the first time in the corporation's history, to the best of my knowledge, we came up with a great number of audio-visual materials. We scouted up art shops in New Orleans and got all of our materials and created all of our graphics ourselves. I mean, sometimes, at three or four o'clock in the morning, we were sticking letters on boards, trying to create these graphics! We drew up entire maps of every site. It was really impressive, and a lot of fun, because Ron was a great guy to work with, and just didn't get flustered by deadlines. The guy was an incredible workhorse.

"We prepared all the presentations, wrote them out, the whole thing, used some of the resources of the New Orleans office, like typing and so on. It was almost a repeat of the process I had to go through with Wells Fargo, when I was the only guy preparing that proposal. We decided that I would act as the MC in the process, that I would walk-through the general plan, then turn it over to members of our management team to discuss specifics, and these guys would have a carefully prepared presentation. But we didn't want them to read it, we wanted them to *memorize* it!

"So, four days before the orals, I had the entire management team fly in, and we spent four full days *rehearsing* it! Four days, from eight o'clock in the morning to eight o'clock at night, just drilling that presentation. We wanted them to memorize their individual presentations, to understand the basics of the whole proposal, and it was like a schoolroom. Ron and I would pepper them with questions about what the proposal said, the whole thing. And, understand, I had a couple of guys there who were retired officers, and, at certain points, one or two of them began to chafe at the regimen that I was putting them through.

"George and Paul came in the day before the orals, and we drilled *them!* And, again, George is such an incredible guy, the focus to him was to win this contract, *period.* It didn't matter to him that a middle manager was drilling him on how to respond; George was simply part of the team. That's one of his incredible strengths. So we drilled George and we drilled Paul, and then we went through the whole presentation with them, all the management team having memorized their parts, and it went like clockwork.

"The night before the orals, we must've had a team of about ten, George took all of us down to the French Quarter to a really fine restaurant and treated us all to a terrific dinner. And, in his classic style, he said, 'I'm really proud of this group. Win, lose, or draw, it won't be because we didn't do a damn fine job. And I just want to thank you all.' I mean, that's the man's style. It's good and it's genuine. He means it. So we went out to dinner, we had a great dinner, and got a good night's sleep.

"The next morning, Boeing must've had forty people in the room. They had every single discipline represented, all levels of management, and we were talking to a big room. We brought our graphics in, our posterboards, our maps of the sites, and every member of our management team was confident. The orals took four hours, it took an entire morning. Boeing had given very strict instructions, they wanted an hour and a half presentation, then there would be a fifteen-minute break. Then they would come back with a host of oral questions; we were expected to take detailed notes. Then there would be another break. Finally, we were to come back and present the answers to the questions they had posed earlier—the fourth volume that I had shipped off—plus respond to the questions they had posed during the oral questioning period.

"By and large, people handled it in good form and in good humor, and we had a damn good presentation. We presented a very innovative program, based on the regional concept. It generated a lot of questions. It generated a lot of concerns.

"After the orals, we had lunch, then George, Paul, and the management team caught a flight back home. Ron and I had to spend an extra day there, just kind of cleaning up some loose ends, and submitting some additional information. So Ron and I saw everybody off on the plane, then left the next day, went back to Coral Gables.

"Less than a week later, Boeing asked us for a 'best and final' proposal. I think we had a two-week period to prepare a 'best and final.' In this case, we had to take the original proposal and, those areas that we changed were submitted on blue paper instead of white and had a black bar alongside the column where the change had been made. We had to submit the entire three volumes, and re-cost the thing because of the changes.

"So, I want to say that was sometime around early July. They really moved this process along. The deadlines were very short. We submitted the 'best and final' on time, then received notification that we were now officially in the competitive range, and that they would make their determination.

"We were notified in early August that we had won the three-year contract with Boeing, with an option to extend it two more years."

Rodger L. Hoff, a retired Army colonel, was appointed vice president and general manager for the SPR project by WSI, and he was headquartered in New Orleans, where Boeing also maintained its SPR project headquarters. Appointed as deputy general managers, Operations, were Gerald L. Kelly and Larry L. Jones. Kelly, formerly TWC area manager in Fort Lauderdale, was based in Beaumont, Texas, where he would oversee the SPR project's Western Region. Jones, a former division chief for Rockwell International at the DOE's Hanford Nuclear Reservation in Richland, Washington, was based at Baton Rouge, New Orleans, where he would supervise the SPR's Eastern Region. Dana Stevens, Jr., formerly manager of Accounts Payable at TWC headquarters in Coral Gables, was named director of Administration and Finance for the SPR project in New Orleans. Also assigned to the SPR project, as director of Training, was Victoria L. Wells; she had been the training program evaluator for WSI at the DOE's Central Training Academy in Albuquerque.

The value of WSI's three-year contract with Boeing was $25.3 million. However, revenues would reach $44.8 million if Boeing exercised its option to extend the contract an additional two years beyond 1989, which it eventually did, and WSI has held the contract ever since.

WSI began its start-up September 2, 1986, and completed takeover of operations at the eight sites on October 1. Of the eight sites, only one—the Big Hill site near Beaumont—was still under construction.

According to the Department of Energy in 1986, the Strategic Petroleum Reserve contained more than 500 million barrels of crude oil. This was more than four times the amount in storage when President Reagan took office in January 1981.

At the October meeting of the board of directors, two more relatively young men were elected corporate vice presidents: John W. Bolles and John M. Krysakowski, both of whom would assume significant responsibilities in the future, and both reporting directly to Alan Bernstein.

Bolles became vice president of the Nuclear Services Division, where he had previously held the position of director. A native of St. Paul, Minnesota, he was the administrator of Nuclear Security Services for Northern States Power Company before joining TWC in 1984. He earned a BS in business administration from the University of Minnesota, and his MBA from the College of St. Thomas in St. Paul.

Krysakowski was elevated to vice president of TWC's Central

Region, where he formerly held the title of director. He was president of Sanitas Security Services, Inc., in Bethany, Connecticut, before joining Wackenhut as head of Operations in New York City in 1982. He moved to headquarters in 1985 as director of Domestic Staff Operations, and was promoted to director in 1986 for what was then known as the Northern Region. His election to vice president coincided with his reassignment as head of TWC's expanded Central Region, an area comprising more than twenty-seven cities.

In November, the U.S. Immigration and Naturalization Service (INS) awarded a contract to WSI for the design, financing, construction, and operation of a 167-bed detention facility in Aurora, Colorado. The facility would be used for detention of aliens in the custody of the INS, the U.S. Bureau of Prisons, and the U.S. Marshals Service. The INS contract was originally for ten months, with options for four one-year extensions. Its total value, if all options were exercised, would be $8.8 million.

Although this was WSI's first contract in the field of comprehensive detention and correctional services, representing another step in Wackenhut's expansion into the privatization of public-sector services, within two years it would become Wackenhut Corrections Corporation, a wholly owned subsidiary of TWC, and, starting in the 1990s, it would blossom into one of the fastest-growing profit centers in the entire company.

In early December, the Nuclear Services Division won two major contracts with a combined value of $35 million for security services for Con Edison Company of New York, Inc., and Public Service Electric and Gas Company of New Jersey. At Con Edison's Indian Point II Nuclear Power Plant in Buchanan, New York, TWC would assume full protection responsibilities in February 1987. The contract for that site was valued at $15 million over a three-year period. At Public Service Electric and Gas Company's Salem and Hope Creek Generating Station in Hancock Bridge, New Jersey, TWC would take over security duties not later than May 1. The contract for those facilities was valued at about $20 million over the life of the contract.

HARRY WACKENHUT died on Monday, December 15, 1986, after suffering a massive heart attack on December 4. He was seventy-eight years old. In 1978, following his first heart attack, doctors had given him less than a year to live. Two years before his death, he had been suffering from glaucoma, arthritis, and loss of equilibrium. He died in Delnor Memorial Hospital in St. Charles, Illinois.

Pam Keller, his eldest, was forty-five at the time of his death, and recalls the circumstances. "He had a heart attack at age seventy. Eight years later, what finally happened that led to his massive stroke, he bit down on a grapefruit seed, and it broke the eyetooth off at the gum line. He called me at work, and I got permission to leave work and take him to a dentist, and Dr. Dickens said that he'd have to have oral surgery, because it was right at the gum line. There happened to be an oral surgeon right next door that they trusted. But he had to wait. He had to go to his cardiologist, be taken off the blood thinners, and make sure his blood was still coagulating at the right level before he had the oral surgery. The day of the surgery, my daughter Terri, God bless her, was able to take him for me. I happened to have a dentist appointment, that's why I couldn't take him. I was finished early, so I walked across and waited for him to come out. And when he came out, the dentist was saying he was such a great patient. And I remember kissing him on the cheek, and he said, 'No, that side's numb, we don't want to waste a kiss!'

"That night, he called about nine and he said that the novocaine wasn't wearing off. Those were the last words I ever heard him say. I remember saying, 'Well, don't be in such a hurry, Dad!' He had a massive stroke that night. For years, because I loved him so, I dreaded him leaving me. I pictured it happening just as it did, that one day I'd call from work, and he wouldn't answer. That day, I called an hour early. It was twelve that I used to call, and I called him at eleven. When he didn't answer, I called the neighbors, who kept an eye on him—he kept his door unlocked at all times—and they weren't *home*. So then I called the caretaker of the apartments, Frank. He ran over there, and he called me back, and he said, 'Pam, he's in a bad way. I called the paramedics.'

"It was one of the most traumatic times of my life. The paramedics had just gotten at his apartment, 1319 Prairie Street in St. Charles, and I recognized one of the police detectives that was there, Dan Klickhammer, and I said, you know, the little girl in me coming out, I said, 'My God, Dan, that's my *daddy!*' Terri was coming up the lawn the same time I was, I'd called her, so we got to the door, and they wouldn't let us go in there. They said we'd have to wait until he was at the hospital. In the meantime, I called everyone in the family to let them know.

"In the emergency room, the first time anybody saw him after the stroke, he was propped up a little bit. I was there, Scott, my daughter's fiancé, my brother, my daughter, my son, I think that's all. And I remember him looking at each of our faces with this *love* shining, and then looking at my son and raising his eyebrows, like, 'Oh, my goodness, even Rick!' I said to him, 'Dad, it must've seemed forever before we came.' And he raised his eyebrows in concurrence, because he could never talk after that.

"Then they brought him upstairs to intensive care. I remember going up there, and calling Joyce in New York, and I remember him being so uncomfortable in that tiny room, a unit right off the nursing station. We were out of the room when he had his second stroke. Before that, he was there, responding, you know, looking at us. After that, no. Oh, he knew we were there. He knew he was going to die. I remember talking to him when they tried to get him to swallow. I said, 'Dad, you've got to work on that swallowing. You've got to, because when they take you off the fluids, you've got to eat. That's why they're pushing you to swallow.' I could tell he understood me. At one time, Terry grabbed his hand, she said, 'Gramps, do you understand?' And he nodded his head.

"The day that he died, Terri was with him, she and Scott. I was at work. I know he decided to give up. They took him off the glucose, or whatever he was getting, and they gave him either water or Jell-O. And he couldn't swallow it. It just came back up. And he was so disappointed. Terri said, there's no words to say how disappointed he was. And, for the first time ever, he took her hand and he pushed her away. She said, 'You want us to go, don't you, Grandpa?' And he nodded.

"She got out, went to the elevator, which is right outside the nursing station, and glanced up at the clock. The time was exactly

11:07 A.M. That was when he died. He'd wanted her out of the room. He had made up his mind to let go. I know that. I believe that with all my heart.

"Dad was cremated. None of us saw him after he died. I've never been sorry about that. He had practiced Christian Science all his life. He got up in the mornings and did his lessons, he was constantly calling me to read excerpts from *Science and Health,* sending me articles from the various publications of Christian Science. I have to say, I think he hid behind it and denied a lot of things. At the same time, I think it's what kept him going. I remember one time in church. Wednesday night is testimonial night. I'm very happy that I did this. I went to a Wednesday night service with him, and, I don't know where I got the nerve, but I stood up and said—they usually say, 'I'm grateful for . . .'—and I said, 'I'm grateful for my father. He *lives* Christian Science. And, just like the sun, you can't help but benefit from the rays.' "

Joyce Wackenhut Hilbert, who was forty-one when her father had the stroke, and living in New York, flew to Chicago immediately with her husband Chuck. Over the years, she had always kept in close touch with her father, via telephone and letters. One letter from Harry, dated June 5, 1984 (four months before she was married), gives unusual insights into their relationship:

Dear Joy:
    I have been thinking about your problem and decided to jot down a few thoughts at random, and with no particular relationship to each other.
    You asked about Pam's drinking. This was going on some years ago when Pam was faced with a problem at home she simply couldn't handle. With one of John's kids and 2 of hers in the home and constant battles with John (and having no place to turn), she finally sought group help and that proved to be a turning point for her. I know that she has completely overcome the problem and now attends a weekly group called AL-anon. This group consists of people who have had to contend with others who drink (usually relatives) and are still fighting that battle. Thru group discussion they also discuss other alcohol-related problems. I believe this is a national organization and can be reached thru your telephone book. Pam thoroughly enjoys the meetings.
    After many years of suffering, I think I finally learned that I had to

stop looking for help from some person (or persons). When I was having marital trouble, I turned to everyone who would listen to me, but eventually I found that I had to look to God and to myself. This wasn't easy. But many times we are forced to work out our own problems. Believe you me, I was sorely faced with the test when I had to have your mother put in the hospital and when I had 4 kids and a full-time job—the youngest kid being Sal at age *one*. A similar time arose when Sal left for college at age 18 after being with me for 10 years. But in time everything worked out for the good, and for a long time I have been quite content to live by myself. Being content with yourself leads to other avenues of good.

I think you are going to have to find some group activity and, of course, keep very active in work. When I was at a very low ebb, I decided to join a local Toastmasters Club. This was tough for me because I had always been very timid when I had to talk before a group. I'll never forget my first meeting when I had to get up and give a short talk. Even now I have no idea what I said—I was shaking all over. But finally it got easier, and while I was never entirely at ease, I did reach the point of actually looking forward to those talks and the fellows I met in the club. At that time I also took on more Church work and read at Church for 3 years—every Sunday and Wednesday.

You will have to work hard on the "poor me" attitude. It accomplishes nothing but the development of further sadness. I had a friend years ago who was afraid of his own shadow. Then he started to talk sternly to himself and kept reminding himself that he was 10 feet tall and could handle anything. We played a lot of tennis together (and other games) and before each game he would say, "I feel sorry for you, because you are going to really get a beating today." He kept that up with every facet of his life and finally started to believe it. Thus, instead of most people turning away from his quest for sympathy, everyone truly liked him, because they knew what he was doing. I believe I, too, get much better results generally when I get "Harry" out of the way.

Honey, you are still young and have a lot of love left to give. I have seen that quality in you. So don't deprive others of that wonderful gift. And always know that I, and your sisters and brother,

Love you dearly,
Dad

Harry's constant concern and unconditional love obviously paid dividends. Joyce married Chuck Hilbert October 13, 1984, then earned her Ph.D. in philosophy at Hunter College in May of 1987, after working for it since 1977. "During the time that I was getting my degree, I was also working," she explains. "My dissertation was called *Social Deception in Everyday Life*. It was about the role that telling lies plays in close personal relationships.

"I feel close to my family, I'm especially close with Sally, and I think it actually started to become cemented that way when my dad had his first major heart attack [1978]. I flew out immediately, we all went in together, I was in the hospital, and I remember, all of a sudden, realizing: Where am I going to go if my father dies? Like, every year, I go home. Well, you know, if my father dies, where will home be? So I said, 'Sally, you're going to have to be my home.' And she has been. So I started going there every Christmas. And then, since I met Chuck, Chuck and I have gone there every Christmas.

"There was a period of time when I felt depressed all the time. That's not true for me any longer. I certainly feel a lot better about my life now than I did when I was in my twenties. I feel very grateful and thankful that my father loved us so much. That's probably an invaluable gift. Not all people get that gift. I love both my mother and father very, very, very much. So I didn't come away from all of the hard parts hating them, or anything like that, but rather quite the contrary. They must've connected in very meaningful ways to their children for us to have such strong feelings towards them. And, again, I'm glad that my father was always there for me."

Sally Bretl, who was thirty-two at the time of her father's death, reveals intriguing anecdotes about her family during times of crisis: "When Dad had his first heart attack, when I was twenty-five, I was now an adult, but I hadn't known Joyce too well, because she'd been living in New York for so long. She just flew in from out of nowhere, and she was just giving me her love. She would hold my hand, and she would tell me she would do anything for me.

"One night, Joyce and Pam and I slept in Dad's apartment, waiting for *the* call, which was so awful, and I must have been very fearful, because I really had no one else then. I wasn't that close to Joyce, because she lived so far away, and I wasn't engaged, I didn't really have anyone but Dad at the time. We had all been silent for maybe an hour, sort of lying down, trying to sleep on the living room rug, or whatever. I remember lying on the floor, trying to fall asleep, but feeling fearful, and almost feeling my body lift off the floor, you know, it was this weird, creepy feeling. It was really cool, because right when I started to do that, Joyce's hand reached over and just grabbed my hand. Right when that was happening! She was just so nurturing. And ever since then, we've been real close.

"Concerning my dad, if I think about a time that changed him, in terms of his spirit, that kind of thing, I think it was when he first got glaucoma. Because I was working at a camp at Lake Geneva here in Wisconsin, as a waterfront director. And there were cabins, and I had everybody come up and stay. Russ came up with Carol, Dad came up, and I think Joyce might even have been there. And he had just gotten word that he had glaucoma, which, for my dad, was his first real challenge as a Christian Scientist. I think that was where I saw him crumble more, fighting his faith and his fear, and turning toward medication for it, causing a real dichotomy within himself, concerning what he'd always taught us, and all his beliefs. He was so nervous and upset, he couldn't even spend the night, he drove all the way back home alone. Which was not the way I knew him. He just had to have eyedrops every day. It wasn't that bad. That wasn't the thing, I think it was more of the emotional stain. I think that was the thing that paved the way for him in terms of his own life changes, in terms of seeing that loss of control that people begin to see when they get older. I think that was when I noticed it most.

"The first heart attack, he went in to have an angiogram, and I went in and sat there, and he was conversant and so forth, and had me feeding him. And I remember leaving there and thinking: He could feed himself. Why was that happening? I just did it, you know, because, my gosh, this awful thing is happening to my dad. But he—it was just different."

Russ Wackenhut was forty-four when his dad passed away. After disappointing his father by not graduating from Drake University, he pulled himself together, joined Downers Grove National Bank in 1963, went to night school, and graduated from the Illinois Bankers School in 1971. In 1976, still attending classes at night, he graduated from Stonier Graduate School of Banking, a program sponsored by Rutgers University and the American Banking Association. In 1986, he had been an executive at Downers Grove National Bank for twenty-three years, and would become president in 1989.

"My sisters and I have stayed reasonably close," he says. "Really, my dad's passing brought us closer together. I mean, whole years would go by very easily where one of us didn't see the others. We certainly never got together as a group until my dad got sick. After he died in '86, we never *missed* getting together at Christmastime. The last several years, we've gone to Sal's place in Wisconsin. Before that, we pretty much went to our place in Downers, just because we were centrally located.

"We all felt extremely close to our dad, Pam so much so that we were all very much concerned about Pam when Dad died. He and she were part of each other's *daily* lives, whereas I would talk to my dad certainly on a weekly basis. There was a song that was very popular here about four years ago, called 'The Living Years,' where the gist of the song is that the singer *wished* that he had told his father these things while he was alive. The song gives me tremendous comfort, because I feel like I always told my dad. I think he knew how much I loved him, and I knew how much he loved me. Those are the kinds of things that people withhold. We didn't have that problem.

"I was certainly a wayward youth. I got through high school without ever having to study, and was on the honor roll most of the time. I never had to apply myself, and it came back to haunt me in college. I had to find myself. One job after another, and that sort of thing, and my dad had to forgive a lot, and he always did. He always did."

George wrote a eulogy for Harry's memorial service, held on Sunday, December 21, at Dunham Inn, St. Charles, Illinois, and attended by about fifty friends, including most members of the family. However, at the last moment, George was too emotionally upset to read it himself, and the same was true of all the family members who were present. Therefore, it was read by Sally's best friend, Laurel O'Connor:

> We are gathered together today in a memorial to my dear brother William Harry Wackenhut—the finest man, the most truly good and gentle man, I have ever known—the perfect reflection of love, the child of the living God.

Harry was named after our maternal grandfather, who beheld him as "the apple of his eye."

Our family moved from Philadelphia to Upper Darby on Harry's sixteenth birthday, December 11, 1924. He enrolled at Upper Darby High School and spent the balance of his junior year and all of his senior year there. During this time, he received "A" in every subject for all nine reporting periods. If ever there was a student who should have gone to college, it was he. He was not (in those days) eligible for a scholarship because of his shortened tenure at Upper Darby. Although our parents would have made any sacrifice to send him, Harry's deep-seated sense of responsibility said otherwise. Although economic times were good in 1926, our dad had just lost his job, so Harry felt compelled to go to work and contribute to the support of his parents and young brother. He got a job with Penn Mutual Life Insurance Company and stayed with them for over forty years.

Harry continued to contribute money to my parents for nearly fifteen years, until our mother refused to take any more after he married. Harry sent me spending money throughout my teenage years and helped defray some of my college expenses.

We shared a room together in our parents' home for many years until he was promoted by his company from its Philadelphia headquarters to Chicago as the assistant loan supervisor in Penn Mutual's Chicago office. It was my thirteenth birthday, September 3, 1932, and he walked with me on the boardwalk in Ocean City, New Jersey, before saying good-bye. How sad I was! Then how happy I was when he returned home for Christmas four months later. Unfortunately, I saw much less of him after that, but we exchanged letters religiously each and every week.

Harry was as much of a father to me as he was my big brother, perhaps because of our difference in age, or perhaps because of our dad's difficult time in business during the Great Depression. Harry and I never had so much as a cross word between us! When I was attending junior high school and was late getting home because of sports' practice, he would walk to the school to be sure I was all right. He worried about me every bit as much as any father would worry about his son!

Oh, what wonderful memories I have of him . . .

. . . As bat boy for his baseball team.

. . . Playing catch with him in our driveway.

. . . Meeting and sitting on the beach with him and his friends from Penn Mutual, and listening to their humor.

. . . Hearing one of them, as he approached Harry and his date on the boardwalk, say: "What's the matter, Harry, did you get stuck?" Obviously to his great embarrassment and to that of his date—but to his amusement, as well.

... Skimming a ball across the shallow ocean water on the beach at Ocean City.

... Our family's visit with him during the 1934 World's Fair in Chicago, at which time he was living in a rooming house on Chicago's South Side.

... Being best man at his wedding at a neighborhood church in Upper Darby in 1940.

... Meeting him and Fran in some railroad switching yard in Chicago on my return from overseas, en route to Philadelphia and Officer Candidate School in November, 1942.

... Returning by train to Chicago a week later to spend a week with them, their one-month-old son and their one-year-old daughter. Even though our mother and dad hadn't seen me for over a year, they insisted I go and visit Harry. They did not have to twist my arm.

... Harry and Fran's attendance at Ruth's and my military wedding at Aberdeen Proving Ground, Maryland, on April 8, 1944.

... The time we spent with Harry and his family in Downers Grove when we could not find a place to live in Indianapolis during my FBI days. Ruth and I moved in with two children and a dog. He kept my family until I found a house for them three weeks later.

... The time he and his family met me in Chattanooga, having visited Fran's parents, on my return from job hunting in Miami, and drove me to Indianapolis.

... His first visit with his family to our first home in Miami, when Sally, at age two, asked Jan what made the tail of her cat clock go back and forth; when Jan said she didn't know, Sally said, "Jan, you're stupid, aren't you? But I love you just the same."

... The times I was on business in Chicago and would have dinner with him, Fran, and the children at their home in Downers Grove, leaving at midnight to fly back to Miami.

... The couple of weeks Harry spent with Ruth and me after his divorce, during which time we were attempting to match him up with some good-looking divorcee from our country club.

... His attendance with Pam and John at Rick and Molly's wedding in Charleston, South Carolina, in March, 1971.

... My visit with him when we celebrated his seventieth birthday at

Pam and John's house in the country in 1978, where, after getting a cook's tour of John's new riding stables, in eighteen-degrees-below-zero weather, I got a real bad chill and didn't stop shaking for at least half an hour. Later that night, I drove with Harry back to his apartment. We had to remove many presents from the trunk of his car. He dropped his keys in the snow, and by the time we found them and emptied the trunk, I was shaking again!

... Meeting Harry, Russ, and Sally at the O'Hare Airport, where they had all made a special effort to meet me, as I was returning from Alaska. They listened to me elaborate on my first visit there and what it was like on the shores of the Artic Ocean in December with the temperature at seventy-five degrees below zero!

... Having the pleasure of his and Pam's visit to our home in Coral Gables on the occasion of my sixty-fifth birthday party.

... And, most of all, having been able to spend time with him this past October at our home on Cape Cod when he and Pam visited us there. Jan and her husband, Roger, were there as well. Ruth and I were able to show him some of the Cape, take him to a lovely place for dinner, and take him by boat to Martha's Vineyard. Ruth, Jan, Roger, and I are grateful for this experience.

If I were to continue, there would not be sufficient pages to record the happy things I remember.

When Russ called me shortly after noon on Monday, December 15, to advise me that Harry had passed on, I felt a sense of relief because neither he nor we wanted him shackled by mortal belief. After all, as in the words of the psalmist, wasn't he passing *through* the valley of the shadow of death? He hasn't died, he has passed *through* the valley and now, as always, he is perfect, complete, and every whit whole, therefore, harmonious and free.

The love and caring that Harry expressed throughout his lifetime could only have come from the fountain of all love. It has not returned unto Harry void because "Love is reflected in love." In the words of John, fourth chapter, we read, "God is love; and he that dwelleth in love dwelleth in God, and God in him." There, then, we have it—Harry dwelleth in God and is in the arms of Divine Love!

Should we not all then be happy, rather than sad? Harry has progressed to a higher state of being where freedom and heavenly happiness reign.

Oh ... he will be missed, but the loving memories of him remain with us all. Thanks, therefore, to our God and his God, the *one* God!

Major events in U.S. and world history during 1986 included: January 26, the *Voyager 2* spacecraft began to report the secrets of Uranus. January 28, the space shuttle *Challenger* exploded after its launch from Cape Canaveral, Florida, killing all seven aboard. February 7, Haiti President Jean-Claude Duvalier fled to France. February 26, President Marcos fled the Philippines after ruling for twenty years, as newly elected Corazon Aquino succeeded him. February 28, Prime Minister Olaf Palme of Sweden was shot dead. March 22, Union Carbide agreed to a settlement with the victims of the Bhopal gas leak in India. March 26, two scientific teams reported finding AIDS viruses. April 14, U.S. planes attacked Libyan "terrorist centers." April 17, three hostages were slain in Lebanon in reprisal for bombing of Libya. April 28, a major nuclear accident at the Soviet Union's Chernobyl power station alarmed the world. June 16, millions of blacks went on strike in South Africa on the anniversary of the 1976 Soweto uprising. July 26, Moslem captors released Reverend Lawrence Martin Jenco. August 14, the Senate Judiciary Committee approved William H. Rehnquist to be Chief Justice of the U.S. Supreme Court. August 15, the House voted an arms appropriations bill rejecting the Administration's "star wars" policy. September 29 and October 2, Congress overrode Reagan's veto of stiff sanctions against South Africa. October 17, Congress approved an immigration bill barring the hiring of illegal aliens, with an amnesty provision. October 21, Reagan signed an $11.7 billion budget reduction measure; on October 22, he approved a sweeping reduction of the U.S. tax code. November 4, the Democrats triumphed in the elections, gaining eight seats to win the Senate majority. November 6, a secret initiative to send arms to Iran was revealed. November 19, Reagan denied exchanging arms for hostages and halted arms sales. November 25, a diversion of funds from arms sales to Nicaraguan contras was revealed. December 19, The Soviet Union lifted its ban on rights activist Andrei D. Sakharov.

28

THE STRONG SPIRITUAL side of George's personality, reflected in the highly emotional eulogy that he had written but found impossible to read at his brother's memorial service, came as no surprise to the immediate family, particularly Tresha, who had just turned eighteen and was then in her freshman year at Principia College in Elsah, Illinois, the only college in the country for Christian Scientists, founded in 1898.

"My grandfather won't tell you this, but you should know more than you do about his spiritual life," Tresha says quietly. "One thing that I want to point out concerns the pastor of our Church. Many people often ask, 'Well, do you have a minister, or who's your pastor?' And it's important. The 'pastor' is two books: The Bible and *Science and Health.* And every week, there is a Bible lesson that's written in *The Christian Science Quarterly.* People who want to study Christian Science will study this lesson sermon. It's comprised of passages from both the Bible and *Science and Health*, and then this lesson is what forms the sermon on Sunday at the Church services. It's read by two people who have been elected by the membership as 'readers,' to serve three-year terms consecutively. There are twenty-six lessons, repeated twice throughout the year. That's an important element to know, because there's not a day that's gone by that my grandfather hasn't studied the lesson. Most serious students of Christian Science will study the lesson each day. That is the crucial element that has shaped the whole *focus* and *tone* of my grandfather's days. The lesson consists of six sections and there are usually four or five citations from each book. And that varies. He does that every day.

"You'll be discovering, the more you know about Christian Science, that it has everything to do with: 'What are you thinking?' Every moment. And: 'Are those thoughts divine or are they human?' And: 'How are you governing your thinking?' Well, the most important thing we can probably do every day, from the moment you're awake, is to set that *tone* for the day. And that's where studying the lesson plays an important—and invaluable—role in someone's life. You begin the day declaring: 'What's the authority here, what's governing today?' Declaring that 'This day is Mind's day—Mind's unfolding of itself—and I am the reflection of that intelligence at work.'

"If I asked my grandfather to define God, there's no question, he'd say, 'God is divine Love.' He'd also say, 'That Love is the source of our life, and that life is eternal.' That there is no afterlife, because there is no end to life itself. I know that is the ideal understanding that all of us are striving to live. Perhaps the ongoing, compelling force in the practice of Christian Science is the idea of working out one's salvation. Christ Jesus is an example, because he *showed* us how to do our own work. But his life example by no means relieves us of our own responsibilities. So I think my grandfather, knowing that, will always feel that it's our privilege to work out our own salvation, and that we do this perpetually, even after what is known as this human experience.

"When I'm meeting a new client and attempting to explain the basic tenets of Christian Science, I say, 'There are no *you will nots* in Christian Science.' There is no doctrine, there are no set of rules to heed. There is, however, a moral code that just naturally develops, based on the teachings that you're learning, and based on the integrity of effort to apply those teachings. Nowhere in Christian Science is it written, 'Thou shalt not use medicine.' And Christian Scientists will not say, 'I don't use medicine.' But their 'medicine' is not material. It's spiritual. 'Mind,' which is a synonym used for 'God,' is considered the only medicine.

"There is no rule in Christian Science against going to doctors.

The misconception has been perpetuated because it's based on hearsay. Perhaps the greatest element that the world has struggled with concerning what Christian Science proposes is the union of those two words, Christian and science. The world doesn't understand how you can try to draw together religion and science. And yet, Mrs. Eddy did so. Those two words, interpreted in Wycliffe's translation of the Bible, equal 'knowledge of salvation.' Science being knowledge, Christian being salvation. Basically, Christian Science is very much a study of what has been uncovered as the laws of God that Christ Jesus practiced. And how to apply those laws. And how to live the dominion rightfully ours.

"Basically, it's a declaration of independence. It's saying: Don't believe what the world is saying is true about your identity. *This* is true, and *this* is what you are capable of doing. One of the basic teachings of Jesus was, 'Repent ye: for the kingdom of heaven is at hand.' Well, 'repent' means, 'change the way you're thinking.' Change your perspective from believing that you're a mere mortal, full of imperfections, to realizing that you are, at this moment, the whole, pure, expression of God. And live out those infinite possibilities. What it does is free your thinking that you're bound by any limitations, regardless of whether it's emotional or physical.

"Three qualities stand out in my mind about my grandfather: Principle, integrity, and tenderness. A balance of those qualities. Maybe they overlap, but the point is, he is the only man I know who harmoniously blends both masculine and feminine qualities so beautifully. I think he can do that solely because of his understanding of what God is.

"Mrs. Eddy makes one statement in three words that I've lived with: 'Desire is prayer.' That 'desire' is molding and shaping the *choices* that you make. Because that desire is stemming from the true ideal of God that's voicing good to each one of us, that's propelling us forward. It's what Jesus lived. There is no judgment in Christian Science. One doesn't come into this with a blueprint of: Here's me—these are all my weaknesses, these are all my faults. Because, immediately, Christian Science embraces you with: 'No, this isn't who you are. You are *now* the image and likeness of God. Because of that, *this* is what's true about you.'

"And that is, that you *have* dominion now. And our lives are just opportunities to prove that. Because no matter what physical or emotional challenge arises, it's only that—an occasion to prove what's rightfully our dominion. That's why this is a science. That's why this is all about proving God's laws. But what enables us to do that is an understanding of those laws. And that's what the text of *Science and Health* is all about. To the degree that you're sincerely seeking, there *is* a practical way to live the spirituality that's rightfully yours. To me, spirituality is synonymous with truth, with true, honest living.

"I think what's true is that each of us lives what we believe and understand God to be, whether we're acknowledging that or not. I think the only thing that has to change, and will change, and it's inevitable that it will change, is an individual's understanding of God. How you *live* that understanding will naturally determine the life-style that you have. To start with the life-style and say, 'Change it,' is like starting with the *effect* and working back to the cause. If God is the source of our lives, then He is the only *cause* that determines all the decisions that we're making. How much are we tuning into that? How much are we heeding? How much are we listening to the ways it's propelling our footsteps forward? Those are the real questions. Those are the questions that my grandfather is constantly asking himself. That's what Christian Science is all about."

When we ask Tresha for her suggestions concerning a particularly appropriate epigraph to be used at the beginning of this biography, she doesn't hesitate an instant before reaching for a copy of the Bible, flips quickly to two books from the Old Testament and two from the New Testament, flags the four pages with small yellow stickers and writes the book, chapter, and verse on each sticker in her small handwriting.

She smiles as she hands us the Bible. "These are a few of my grandfather's favorites. Why not show him and let him choose one?"

CHRONOLOGICALLY, from the Old Testament, the first is from Proverbs, 3: 5, 6.

> Trust in the LORD with all thine heart; and lean not unto thine own understanding.
> In all thy ways acknowledge him, and he shall direct thy paths.

The second is from Isaiah, 54: 17.

> No weapon that is formed against thee shall prosper; and every tongue *that* shall rise against thee in judgment thou shalt condemn. This *is* the heritage of the servants of the LORD, and their righteousness *is* of me, saith the LORD.

From the New Testament, the first is from St. Matthew, 5: 5, 8, 9, 11, 12.

> Blessed *are* the meek: for they shall inherit the earth.
> Blessed *are* the pure in heart: for they shall see God.
> Blessed *are* the peacemakers: for they shall be called the children of God.
> Blessed are ye, when *men* shall revile you, and persecute *you,* and shall say all manner of evil against you falsely, for my sake.
> Rejoice, and be exceeding glad: for great *is* your reward in heaven: for so persecuted they the prophets which were before you.

The last is from St. John, 8: 32, with Tresha's note: "He *lives* by this one!"

> And ye shall know the truth, and the truth shall make you free.

The following day, when George reviews Tresha's four suggestions for what might be the most appropriate epigraph, he selects Proverbs, 3: 5, 6, and admits, just above a whisper: "I've given thought to those two verses before every major decision I've ever made for this company."

During the first few months of 1987, an event took place that clearly indicated the new direction and commitment of TWC toward the diversification of its services to business and government. On February 2, ground-breaking ceremonies took place for the construction of the detention facility in Aurora, Colorado, under a contract signed the previous November with the U.S. Immigration and Naturalization Service (INS). Within just ninety days, construction was completed, and the Wackenhut management staff admitted the first group of INS detainees. In the opinion of many government officials, it was difficult to conceive of a county, state, or federal agency acting in equal haste to meet a pressing community demand.

Michael E. Norris, formerly sheriff of Alexandria, Virginia, was appointed manager of WSI's Confinement Services, later to be called Wackenhut Corrections Corporation, a wholly owned subsidiary of TWC; he reported to George C. Zoley, who was then WSI's vice president for Government Services. In addition to overseeing the implementation of the new Aurora facility, Norris was given responsibility for the general marketing of Confinement Services, which included the design, construction, and operation of future correctional and detention facilities.

Earlier that year, WSI also executed a contract with the California Department of Corrections Parole Division for the management of a return-to-custody facility for technical parole violators, which was to be located in McFarland, and WSI was negotiating for a contract at a similar facility in Southern California, and with the Texas Department of Corrections for the operation of two minimum-security correctional facilities.

Clearly, George had recognized the opportunities available with privatization and was moving to diversify into the corrections field. The addition of these four sites would represent growth at a reasonable pace and in accordance with an established planning process. As a result, the company was starting to become a recognized industry leader in this emerging specialty in a relatively short time. Governments at all levels had begun to recognize the cost advantages inherent in the privatization of many of the basic services traditionally provided by local, state, and federal agencies.

On February 27, Alan Bernstein's Domestic Operations staged its second Annual Incentive Bonus Awards Banquet, this time at the Biltmore Hotel, a Coral Gables landmark. Selvin M. Smith, area manager in Richmond, Virginia, was named Area Manager of the Year 1986.

Again, the "Top Ten" managers and their spouses came to Coral Gables on an all-expense-paid trip for the banquet. In alphabetical order, the ten were: Frank J. Canzoneri, Buffalo; Kevin J. Enser, West Palm Beach; James D. Gorham, Memphis; Gerald L. Kelly, Beaumont; Fred W. Mays, Nashville; Arthur C. McPhail, Charlotte; Steven R. Norvell, Greensboro; Louis N. Schwartz, Atlantic City; Selvin M. Smith, Richmond; and James O. Widel, Sr., Norfolk.

Kelly was selected for his achievements as area manager in Fort Lauderdale. At the time of the banquet, he was deputy manager for WSI at Beaumont, Texas, in charge of Western Region security operations for the DOE's Strategic Petroleum Reserve.

As winner, Smith and his wife received an all-expense-paid trip to a major resort, with $500 additional spending money. His name was added to a new permanent plaque at headquarters which would list all yearly winners.

During March of 1987, George was honored by *Financial World* magazine as one of the nation's outstanding business executives. The occasion was *Financial World*'s thirteenth Annual CEO of the Year Awards Banquet held in Manhattan and attended by leaders of American industry. George was awarded a bronze plaque attesting to his selection as third-place winner in the magazine's "Services" category.

He was one of 2,400 CEOs of companies with annual revenues exceeding $100 million who were judged by an independent panel of analysts, economics experts, and other CEOs. Those 2,400 candidates were narrowed down to 183 finalists for gold, silver, and bronze awards. There was one gold winner (the CEO of Dun & Bradstreet) and ten silver winners. George emerged as one of the bronze selectees representing sixty-one categories. *Financial World* called the 183 finalists "the elite's elite" of U.S. business and industry.

IN THE EARLY AUTUMN of 1987, Rick Wackenhut was carefully screened and selected for admission to the Advanced Management Program of the Harvard Graduate School of Business Administration, an intensive thirteen-week course attended by 168 senior managers from a wide variety of industries throughout the world. Although extremely difficult, Rick remembers the experience as a critical ingredient in his development as president of TWC. In addition, it was during this course that he would meet Tim Cole, then an executive with the Martin Marietta Corporation, who would, within a year, become president of Wackenhut Services, Inc.

"I was reluctant to go for a number of reasons," Rick recalls. "Leaving my kids for thirteen weeks, and I think my youngest at that time was very small, and thirteen weeks to an infant is a long time. Fear of the unknown was part of it. Am I going to know as much as these people? Am I going to be embarrassed up there? Am I going to embarrass myself? What's going to happen? All of those thoughts and insecurities go through people's minds. But very shortly after getting up there and going through it—and there's no way you can get by without participating—it was just a tremendous experience. What it really was, more than anything, it made you realize that your level of competence, or your level of incompetence, was just as equal as every one of your peers. And that class was screened internationally. They ranged from the chief financial officer of the Brunswick Corporation to the head of all foreign investment for China. People from every continent, every country. And, more than anything else, was the networking that developed as a result of that.

"The dormitory was divided into two halves. Each half has eight floors. Each floor, on each side, is divided by two, and they were called 'can' groups. Each 'can' group housed eight men and/or women; they were coed. So, in effect, my 'can' group of eight people—and it was all men in my group—resided in separate rooms down a corridor, shared a common living room and conference table, and a little kitchen area. I got there fairly early on the day we were supposed to arrive, and in my room was a big red three-ring binder with lengthy biographies of all 168 students in my class. Each one of the eight rooms in my group had name tags on the doors. So I went down the hall, wrote down all the names of the people in my group, then went back to my room and studied the biographies of the other seven people in my group.

"The whole course was designed around the case-study type of curriculum. Very intensive reading, very intensive type of case studies, very complicated problems. It was quite an ordeal. You had to really work at it, and stay up for incredible hours, if you were going to actually do the cases yourself. A lot of people learned very quickly, in the thirteen-week program, to kind of split it up. If there were four cases to be done that night, each person in your particular group would do maybe only one of the four cases. Then you would convene at midnight or something and learn the results of each individual's efforts. Our group did not do that until probably the tenth or eleventh week. So we struggled through, doing all the cases ourselves, individually, for most of the time.

"Of course, I think the concerns or the fears of going to a class like that, being put into a melting pot with that many really top-level executives, makes you question your own abilities. And I think very shortly after the class started, everyone kind of felt a sense of relief that we were all either equally knowledgeable or equally lacking knowledge, that the mystique of people in these very high positions was not really that overwhelming.

"The long-term benefit of the program was not particularly in what was learned by doing the cases, although there was some academic improvement, obviously. The long-term benefit, I feel, is in the relationships that were developed with people who were ultimately going to be *the* top business people in the country—and in the world. For example, I'm planning a trip in two weeks to Australia, and I've sent off letters to five or six guys that I hope to see down there.

"The case-study method enabled you to broaden your horizons and recognize that there are a *lot* of different ways to solve problems, as opposed to how you may normally approach a problem. So, yes, that was a fundamental benefit of the class. The way that it was structured could not have been done better.

"Every morning at seven o'clock we were required to discuss the prior evening's cases in a one-hour discussion, prior to starting class. Each member of the 'can' group had to *chair* certain sessions in his own 'can.' Seven guests would come in, and the chairman's seven 'can' mates would go out to other sessions. When it became my turn, I would entertain guests that morning, and I would chair the discussions of the cases. That would last for a one-week period. In the second week, I was no longer chairman, and someone else in my 'can' group was chairman, and I went out to someone else's 'can' and sat. So it was like taking a deck of cards and shuffling them, to mix all these people.

"You had two different classrooms that were in session at the same time. You were divided initially into groups—A, B, C, and D. At first, A and B shared a classroom, and C and D shared a classroom. Then, A and C shared classrooms, and B and D shared classrooms. And you kept shuffling *that* way. In the evenings, they would encourage certain 'cans' to invite other 'cans' out to dinner. Or, for example, we had a Chinese gentleman in our group who invited all of us in his own 'can' out to a Chinese restaurant, and entertained us in his own style. I was invited, along with other people, by a Japanese gentleman—I don't know why he chose me—and about eight or ten of us went to this magnificent Japanese restaurant, and discussed business, and discussed what we did, and discussed those type of things. And he was entertaining people on a regular basis that way, building business contacts.

"So, it was this constant shuffling and mixing and moving around, and sharing of responsibility, and sharing of leadership, and then listening to someone else's leadership, that helped us all blend into a very cohesive group.

"The Advanced Management Program is the highest class that they give. The next level down is the PMD, I think it's Professional Management Development. If we were to take a high-middle-management person in our company, not in senior management, not in the very top level of management, he would go into PMD, as opposed to the Advanced Management Program. And the company must be $100 million in annual revenues, or above, or it was when I was there.

"We got very close to the faculty in a number of ways. The 'cans,' again, were encouraged to have off-site meetings, or after-classroom meetings, with the faculty, which included lunches. We often invited certain members of the faculty to our 'can' at lunchtime, where just the eight of us would share that professor for an hour or whatever the lunch period was. It was catered by the school. So, when we got to our rooms, the lunches were there, they were laid out and everything. We used the conference table that the eight of us shared, and we'd have one professor of our choosing for an entire hour, just the eight of us, to ask him all kinds of questions on his topics of expertise.

"There were a lot of functions in the evenings, when we would invite faculty members out to dinner, and they almost always accepted. I don't think they paid for a meal the whole time we were there, because you had all of these groups of eight people competing to take them out. They actually had ledger books, where they'd look up the dates, they'd say, 'Okay, I can only have lunch with you on that day,' or 'I can only have dinner with you on these particular nights.'

"Since it was as intense as it was, my routine was to do everything academic from the time we got up in the morning until the time classes were over. *Immediately* upon classes being over, a group of about six of us would race back to our rooms, change into workout clothes, into 'sweats,' meet downstairs, go to my car, and drive to an exercise facility, a racquet club that we joined within the first week of being there, and play racquetball for a good solid hour and a half to two hours. It got a lot of frustration out, it kept us in shape. This club was in Boston. We had to get on the expressway and drive to it. Great little racquetball club, they let us join just for the thirteen weeks of this program, and it was a tremendous release. We did that *religiously*, Monday through Friday, or every single day of the week, if possible, we'd do it. Then, as soon as we finished an hour and a half or two hours of steady exercise, we got back in the car, drove back to the campus. Dinners were optional, lunches were mandatory. So we'd either pick up some food on the way home or come back to the campus. What I'd usually do is go through the cafeteria, which was totally open, and I'd take handfuls of fruit and a couple of rolls, and go back to my room, and that would be my dinner.

"You had half-a-day classes on Saturday, so you were finished at noon on Saturday, and then Sunday night you had to start studying again, because you had homework over the weekend. In the summer of 1985, my parents had bought a house on Cape Cod, in Osterville, right on the water, so on certain weekends I invited some classmates to my parents' house. We had groups of between four to eight, so we usually would take two cars. We'd arrive Saturday afternoon, about three o'clock, and just relax for the weekend. It was a good time to unwind and relax. Generally, since my father was in Florida running the business at the time, my mother would join us and we would go out to dinner on Saturday night. Then, Sunday, we would just continue to relax, or drive around Cape Cod. One time, we went up to Provincetown.

"Tim Cole was in my class, but I didn't know him well. In fact, Henley Shelton, the guy I was very good friends with, said to me, 'You really ought to interview Tim Cole.' Tim was in Henley's 'can.' Somewhere around the eighth or ninth week, maybe even later, Henley said that Tim was not really dissatisfied with Martin Marietta, but he wasn't really satisfied either, with what he was doing, and would consider some kind of a change. So Henley set it up, and at lunchtime one day, Tim and I went off to the side and just had a general talk. At that time, I was looking for somebody to step into an important general management position. He sounded interested and it seemed to me that he had the credentials to do what we needed. So we talked and, upon graduation, I made sure he knew how to get in touch with Ken Ketterer, who was our head of Human Resources at the time, and made sure that the contact was made after I got back here. About a year later—it took about a year of negotiating and talking and waiting until the situation was right—a year later, he came with us."

Timothy P. Cole was born in Waterloo, Iowa, October 30, 1943. After graduating from West Waterloo High School in 1961, he enlisted in the U.S. Air Force, which subsequently sent him to the University of Oklahoma, where he majored in industrial management, minored in finance, received his BBA in 1972, and was elected to Beta Gamma Sigma, a national honor society for business schools. "I was active-duty Air Force while I was at the university," Cole explains. "The Air Force had sent me there, so I had a few side military duties, but going to school was my job. At Pepperdine University, I earned my MBA in 1975, majoring in management and administration. Once again, the Air Force had sent me to that school, so that was basically my full-time job.

"From 1972 to 1973, I was a price analyst, U.S. Air Force, Lockeed Missile and Space Company. That involved financial analysis on major proposals that Lockeed had submitted to the Air Force for products such as launch missile systems; satellite systems of a classified nature. We would evaluate their proposal from a financial and technical standpoint, establish a negotiation position, and then support the contracting officer as they negotiated the contract. That was at the Lockeed Missile and Space plant in Sunnyvale, California. From 1973 to 1976, I was a contract program manager. At that point, I became a warranted contracting officer, responsible for the day-to-day administration and management of the contracts that the Air Force had with Lockeed Missile Systems, mostly the Space Systems Division. Their products were mostly launch vehicles, second-stage rocket boosters, and then the satellites that went on top of the boosters.

"Then, from 1976 to 1982, I was deputy director of contracting at the U.S. Air Force Academy. I had responsibility for all of the purchasing and contract management of supplies, services, and construction. It was basically providing all the purchasing support for an 18,000-acre facility that had about 10,000 people on it, a small city.

"At the Martin Marietta Corporation, 1982-1987, I was director of subcontracts. That was in Orlando, Florida, and basically I was responsible for managing subcontracts with major suppliers of hardware and services to support large production programs. The largest was the Lantirn System, which was later used extensively in Desert Storm and other activities. It was a targeting and navigational system on the F-16 and F-15, and the total program was worth about $3.5 billion, of which $2.2 billion was under subcontracts with firms like Texas Instruments, Delco, Unisys, Grumman, and others. So that was my responsibility, to acquire the hardware to allow the integration and testing of the full system, and then delivery to the Air Force.

"From 1987 to 1988, I was program manager at Martin Marietta. In the aerospace world, that's really your entry into general management, and I think I was the second non-engineer in the history of the corporation to be a program director. They're an engineering company, so very seldom do they allow non-engineers to manage programs. The major program I managed was the Infrared Search and Track System, which went on the F-14, which allowed infrared detection of targets, as opposed to radar. It's a passive system, you use sensors that seek out heat, as opposed to radar. Radar, as soon as you flip it on, the world knows you're there, because you're emitting signals, so you then become a target yourself. This infrared system was passive, and it would allow you to track and engage targets at long distance, just based upon infrared or heat signatures. So that was very interesting.

"In the autumn of 1987, I was sent to the Advanced Management Program, Harvard Business School. I think it represented a significant investment on the part of the Martin Marietta Corporation. I was identified as a high-potential employee, so to prepare me for entry into the executive ranks, that was one of the mechanisms they used. They used the MIT-Sloane Program, and then they used the Advanced Management Program at Harvard. Since I had an MBA already, they decided to use the Harvard Advanced Management Program.

"That year, the basic cost to get in was about $30,000. And then, of course, you have the expenses associated with being there. Martin Marietta allowed me to travel home about every third weekend, so they had those costs associated with it. I would say Martin Marietta probably spent $60,000 on that program, because they insisted I had a computer in my room to facilitate communication with the office back in Orlando. We used electronic mail—real time. So there were a lot of hidden costs associated with that.

"Very diverse group of people, which really gets to the value of something like that, to sit and listen to these people, and the perspectives that the Dutch would have, versus the Japanese, and even the fellow from Mainland China, who was mostly in a receive mode the whole time. He'd tape all the classes, and then apparently he had some translators at night who would make sure he got the full drift of what was being said. It would be very difficult to come over here without a firm grasp of the English language, and come away with anything. So he had to work twice as hard as the rest of us.

"In the particular group I lived with, which was not Rick's—what they called 'can' groups—we had a Korean, a Chinese man from Singapore, a Canadian, a Texan, an Australian, we had quite a mix, and you really got to know these people very well. I've kept in touch with some of them, mostly by phone, I've visited a couple of them in various cities around the country. It's funny, I feel I could probably not speak with them for two years, but get in touch, and it would be like time had not passed. Because you really lived and played and worked very hard together for the almost three months that we were there. I guess it was Labor Day when we got there and we left a day or two before Thanksgiving, so it was a very intensive period of time.

"I met Rick through a third party, a fellow who was in my 'can' group, Henley Shelton, who became a very good friend of mine, and lived in the room right next door. And I think Henley, through racquetball, became friends with Rick. Henley and I talked a lot, and, of course, Martin Marietta being a major corporation, and me being a non-engineer, I knew that I was limited in what I could do in that company. Plus, I saw the handwriting on the wall about the aerospace business. They weren't going to continue to spend the kinds of money on weapons systems as during the Reagan years, in the '84-'85-'86 period. So I was on the lookout, and had almost left Martin Marietta a year or so before, to go with TRW, that had made a very lucrative offer, but it was right back into the same kind of business, and I wasn't interested in that. It would've been a general management position, but still in aerospace and defense. And I knew that could not continue forever.

"So, Henley knew of my desire to explore other opportunities, and I think he mentioned that to Rick, and then Rick and I had lunch one day. It was at the Harvard Faculty Club, and they had a spot for us to eat right upstairs. It was very nice. That was a first-class operation. I must say, the food was outstanding, the service was good, it had a great 'genteel' atmosphere to it. You just couldn't ask for more in a setting like that. Very conducive to forming relationships with people. Rick talked about a—I think a contract management position, and, of course, I had done that years ago, and I wasn't intersted in that. So I really didn't give it much thought, to be honest with you, and didn't know much about Wackenhut. This was fairly late, we were getting on towards the final couple of weeks of the program. We talked a little bit and just kind of left it—well, maybe he'd call, maybe I'd come down, but I don't think there was any real firm commitment on either part to explore anything.

"I went back to Martin Marietta and then we began to negotiate. Ken Ketterer was the man who contacted me when I came down the first time. I met with a variety of people. I think Paul Roundy was still the president of Wackenhut Services then. Buck Thornburg, I guess, was the executive vice president. I met Budd, met Alan, met Rick, and, obviously, the chairman. At that point, I think they wanted to offer me a job as a director of contract management, or some such thing, and I wasn't remotely interested in that.

"Several months passed, then I came down again. I think I came down about three times, as I recall. Then they offered me a job—this was when Buck was still here and Roundy had left—to maybe be senior vice president of WSI in some capacity, and I declined that as well. In August of 1988, I came down for kind of the final interview, where they basically offered the job of president of WSI, with the potential to become a senior officer, and the perks that go with that. Rick and I, and I think Alan Bernstein was along, we went over to the Beverly Hills Cafe to have lunch. I think we were still talking about the conditions under which I would come. And who, all of a sudden, comes into the restaurant, but the *chairman*. Takes the last chair at the table. I don't recall if he ordered or not, I don't think so. But it was clear he wanted the deal cut. He wanted this to happen. It made a very big difference to me. I'm not so sure that deal would've been made that day, had that not happened.

"I'll give you the most important insight into *why* it might not have happened. During the Harvard experience, our youngest daughter, Kelsey—it was just lucky I was home that weekend—she hadn't been feeling well. And my wife Betsy took her to the pediatrician, and they put her in the hospital. Her hemoglobin was way, way down. They weren't sure what was causing it, and one thing led to another. She was not producing red blood cells. So, they didn't know if it was leukemia or just some kind of infection. I stayed there a few days, while we sorted all that out. It turned out that she was finally in intensive care, they had to do bone marrow, they really thought it was something serious. She had what was known as transient aplastia anemia, in which your system stops making red blood cells. So she was at the point where they had to transfuse her with packed red cells. And she was about nine months old, and her system finally kicked in and started making them again. Had it not, she would have been transfused and treated with cortisone and a variety of things—all of her life.

"So at one point, earlier in our negotiations, an offer was made, and that was the reason I declined. Betsy just didn't feel comfortable at that point, leaving the doctors up there and coming down here. Because it was something that could have happened again, in which case it would've been a very serious condition. That was something that was in the back of our minds. When I came down here, I must say, I wasn't at all convinced that the conditions would come together that would cause us to leave Orlando. And a lot of it had to do with that singular issue, because she was being checked every couple of months to see if this was going to recur or not. Thank God it has not. Apparently, it's a condition that happens in infants, occasionally, around that six- to twelve-month period, and then they can either just never produce red blood cells again naturally, or the system just kicks in and starts again. In her case, it was a three-week period. It was really frightening. Because at nine months, obviously they can't talk to you, you can't get a feel for what really is happening.

"So it was a significant event for us, and it really caused us serious concern about changing jobs and moving, I must say, before the chairman kind of jumped in. I probably would not have come down here. But then that happened, and I came down in September, and then we finally got a house, and I think the family came down in early December. But, see, that was something that was so unlike the chairman. I mean, we were sitting there talking and, all of a sudden, it was like, I kind of felt that *he* felt: Hey, unless I jump in, this thing ain't going to happen. Because I think he probably sensed a reluctance, you know, because of the thing with our daughter. We wanted to move, but I'm not sure moving to Miami was ever part of our plans. It was a significant deal for us, and I think he sensed that reluctance or uncertainty, or some hurdles that needed to be overcome. And so he just seized the initiative and injected himself personally right into it. Without that, I'm not so sure it would've happened.

"I knew in that moment. It clicked with me. I mean, he was sitting to my right, he kind of leaned over, and I leaned over, and he said: 'Okay, what's it going to take?' And I said the number. And he said, 'Done.' I mean, then I knew this is the guy I want to work for. Somebody who's capable of cutting through all the bullshit, all the nonsense: Hey, what is it you want, and then I'll decide if that's acceptable to me, and, if it is, man, away you go! He cut through it all. That's how it happened."

THE YEARS 1987 and 1988 were packed with major news events in the U.S. and abroad: On January 20, 1987, William Buckley, one of the U.S. hostages held in Lebanon, was reported slain. March 4, President Reagan admitted making "mistakes" in the Iran-Contra affair. March 20, the FDA approved the drug AZT for treating victims of AIDS. April 27, the U.S. placed Austrian President Kurt Waldheim on the list of those banned from visiting the country. May 5, thousands of aliens began to seek legal status under the new amnesty law. May 16, the Soviet Union launched the world's most powerful rocket. May 17, Iraqi missiles killed thirty-seven Navy personnel in an attack on the U.S. frigate *Stark* in the Persian Gulf. May 18, British Prime Minister Thatcher was elected to a rare third term. June 25, Robert B. Anderson, seventy-seven, former U.S. Treasury Secretary, was sentenced for tax evasion. July 4, Klaus Barbie, seventy-three, former Gestapo wartime chief in Lyons, was sentenced to life by a French court for war crimes. July 7–10, Marine Lieutenant Colonel Oliver North, Jr., testified to a congressional inquiry that higher officials approved his secret Iran-Contra operations. July 15–22, Admiral John M. Poindexter, a former national security adviser, testified that he authorized use of Iran arms-sale profits to aid the Contras. July 23–24, Secretary of State George P. Shultz testified that he was deceived repeatedly on the Iran-Contra affair. July 31-August 3, Defense Secretary Caspar W. Weinberger testified to official deception and intrigue in the Iran-Contra operation. August 12, Reagan admitted the Iran-Contra policy went astray and accepted responsibility for it. October 1, a severe earthquake struck Los Angeles, leaving more than 100 injured and six dead. October 23, the Senate rejected Robert H. Bork's nomination to the U.S. Supreme Court.

January 2, 1988, the U.S. and Canada signed a fair trade agreement. February 11, Lyn Nofziger, a former Reagan adviser, was convicted of violating federal ethics laws. February 17, Marine Lieutenant Colonel William H. Higgins was abducted in Lebanon. March 11, Robert C. McFarlane, former national security adviser, pleaded guilty in the Iran-Contra case. April 4, Arizona Governor Evan Mecham was removed from office after his impeachment trial. June 20, the Supreme Court ruled against private-club membership restrictions. July 3, a U.S. Navy ship shot down an Iranian airliner in the Persian Gulf, mistaking it for a jet fighter; 290 were killed. July 17, the Democratic Convention nominated Governor Michael Dukakis of Massachusetts for president and Texas Senator Lloyd Bentsen for vice president. August 15, the Republicans nominated George Bush for president and Indiana Senator Dan Quayle for vice president. September 23, Michael K. Deaver, a Reagan friend, was sentenced for lying about lobbying. November 8, Bush was elected president and the Republicans swept forty states. December 1, the Soviet legislature approved political restructuring and a new national legislature. Also on December 1, Benazir Bhutto became the first Islamic woman prime minister, chosen to lead Pakistan's government. December 21, a Pan Am 747 (Flight 103), en route from London to New York, exploded in midair as the result of a terrorist bomb and crashed in Lockerbie, Scotland, killing all 259 aboard and eleven on the ground.

BACK AT TWC, revenues for 1987 were $381.972 million, a 16.2 percent increase over the previous year, while profits showed a dramatic upswing of 134 percent compared to 1986, reaching $5.660 million. This success was attributable not only to expansion of business in most aspects of the company's security, investigations, operations and maintenance activities, but also to an unusually strict austerity program and a number of management initiatives established early in the year to streamline operations. These included a realignment of the management structure to take full advantage of the field automation system that enabled TWC to manage its widespread activities with greater efficiency and less overhead. By year's end, the number of employees had increased to 28,000 worldwide.

During April of 1988, WSI was awarded a contract with the Texas Department of Corrections, valued at $10.5 million annually, for the operation and management of two 500-bed correctional facilities. The institutions, known as Pre-Release Centers (PRCs), would provide basic education, counseling, and training in pre-employment skills for inmates within two years of their release date.

WSI was also awarded a contract, valued at $2.3 million, for the operation of a 200-bed Return-to-Custody (RTC) correctional facility in McFarland, California. The facility would provide secure residential confinement with educational and counseling programs for technical violators under a five-year contract with the State of California Department of Corrections, Parole Division. This would be the first newly constructed RTC facility in California and it represented another step in TWC's expansion into the privatization of public-sector service.

As a result of these correctional activities, George announced the establishment of a new wholly owned subsidiary of TWC, named Wackenhut Corrections Corporation (WCC). It was also announced that George C. Zoley was named president of the new subsidiary. Zoley was previously vice president of Government Operations for WSI.

Earlier in the year, Domestic Operations held its third annual "Area Manager of the Year" awards banquet in honor of the top ten area managers, and Robert Fortney, area manager in Fort Lauderdale, was the winner for 1987. Fortney joined TWC in 1982 as a security supervisor in Fort Lauderdale. In 1984, he was appointed training coordinator at corporate headquarters, and became area manager in Fort Lauderdale in 1986. He earned a BA degree from Florida International University, and a master's degree in criminology from Nova University.

Retired General Paul X. Kelley, former commandant of the U.S. Marine Corps, was elected a member of TWC's board of directors at the April board meeting. General Kelley held the highest position in the U.S. Marine Corps prior to his retirement in June 1987, after thirty-plus years of active duty. At the time of his election, he was the senior vice president and director for corporate development of Star Mountain, Inc., a high-technology consulting firm in Alexandria, Virginia.

As a Marine officer, General Kelley commanded an infantry battalion in Vietnam in 1966, and during a later tour in Vietnam he commanded the First Marine Regiment, which was the final Marine ground-combat unit to leave Vietnam. He was the recipient of Distinguished Service Medals from the Departments of Defense, Navy, Army, and Air Force. During combat operations, he earned the Silver Star Medal, two awards of the Legion of Merit, and two awards of the Bronze Star Medal.

General Kelley was also a member of the board of directors for Allied Signal, Inc., PHH Group, Inc., Security First Trust of the Holden Group, the Freedoms Foundation at Valley Forge, and the Washington Center.

During August, the Department of Energy announced that WSI was selected for renewal of the contract to provide security services at the Savannah River Site for the following five years, at an estimated value of $300 million. At that time, the Savannah River installation included four active nuclear reactors and had taken on additional importance in its national defense role as the site of a naval fuels production facility and a nuclear waste processing plant. WSI employed more than 900 people at the facility.

That was the second major contract renewal for WSI during the previous nine months. The DOE's Nevada Test Site contract was renewed in July 1987 for five years at a total revenue of approximately $125 million. More than 600 personnel were employed by WSI at the Nevada Test Site.

Both renewed agreements were "Management and Operation" contracts, which operated under a different set of guidelines than service contracts in the respect that they may not have to be competed if the DOE is satisfied with WSI performances.

At the November board meeting, Chesterfield Smith, who previously served as a director of TWC, 1977–1986, was again elected to the board. A former president of the American Bar Association, Smith was a senior partner in the law firm of Holland & Knight, with Florida law offices in Bradenton, Fort Lauderdale, Lakeland, Miami, Orlando, Tallahassee, and Tampa, as well as Washington, DC. He was also a director of the Citrus & Chemical Bank of Bartow, and Batch-Air, Inc., of Miami.

Smith received his JD degree from the University of Florida in

1948. Since 1970, he had received honorary degrees from ten colleges and universities throughout the U.S. He was a member of Phi Beta Kappa, Order of Coif, Phi Kappa Phi, and Phi Delta Pi. From 1965 to 1967, he served as chairman of the commission that drafted Florida's present Constitution. During 1988, he served as chairman of the National Foundation for Advancement in the Arts, as vice chairman of the Florida Chamber of Commerce Foundation, and as president of the Florida Supreme Court Historical Society.

Finally, in November, George announced the formation of Wackenhut Nuclear Services Corporation (WNSC) as a wholly owned subsidiary of TWC, and he named John W. Bolles as president of the new subsidiary. WNSC staff members included Gary Sanders as director of Nuclear Operations, and Jeff Palmer as director of Radiological Services. Frank Finizia, Tom Shannon, and Bob Morton were named managers of Operations, while Debbie Jackson was manager of Proposal Development, and Bob Kindilien was director of Quality Assurance.

That month, WNSC project manager Joseph M. Johnson announced that all security systems at the South Texas Project (STP) electric generating station were ready to go into the lock-down phase in anticipation of full operations in early 1989. Through an innovative and creative management plan, the industrial security force at STP merged with the operational nuclear security force. This plan provided superior personnel to help maintain Wackenhut's standard of excellence in nuclear security services, sustaining a high degree of industrial and operational security without any loss of integrity.

The South Texas Project, once the largest construction projects in America, is located on a 12,200-acre site between Bay City and Palacios, near the Gulf Coast in Matagorda County. Upon completion, the plant would have the capacity to light more than 500,000 homes throughout South Texas and would help economic recovery, growth, and diversification.

At the close of fiscal 1988, TWC had completed its thirty-fourth year and continued its consistent record of yearly revenue increases. Revenues for the year crossed the $400 million threshold ($400.996 million), showing a 5 percent increase over the previous year. Profits did not exhibit a similar pattern, however, because of conscious decisions on the part of corporate management to invest in new lines of business, and to reward shareholders with an extraordinary dividend. The impact of these actions was to reduce earnings per share from $1.47 to $1.35, compared to the previous year.

Despite the fact that many American corporations seemed to be content to sacrifice long-term position for short-term profits, George had determined to resist those pressures and stayed his course during 1988. Consistent with a well-conceived Strategic Plan, the corporation continued to diversify into areas less vulnerable to the margin pressures typical of the traditional end of the security business, and position itself to take advantage of certain trends that George believed would begin to exert considerable market influence in the very near future. While not abandoning the core business that had provided the foundation of TWC's remarkable growth over the previous thirty-four years, he believed that the combination of these new ventures with the company's historical service and product lines would serve both the shareholders and the corporation better in the long run.

On a personal note, in May, George was honored by the University of Hawaii by receiving the 1988 Distinguished Alumnus Award. He had received exactly the same honor from West Chester University in 1979, despite the fact that he did not receive his degree there. He was cited by the University of Hawaii, where he received his BS degree June 15, 1943, for his "exemplary public service, and serving as a model for UH alumni."

29

MURRAY LEVINE smiles as he recalls the genesis of TWC's Custom Protection Division (CPD), which was his original idea, and the division quickly became the premier provider of security services to its specialized market niche. Today, it serves an increasing number of prestigious commercial clients who must have a high assurance of loss prevention as well as a high level of confidence in the effectiveness of their security programs in the protection of valuable assets. Beyond question, the CPD provides the highest practicable level of security service in the industry at this time, and the best qualified personnel to private-sector clients who will accept a higher billing rate for the assurance of quality personnel and services.

"Custom Protection evolved in late '88, early '89," Levine says. "We discovered that if there was a *good* security job, with good pay scales and benefits and advancement opportunities, it was in-house. Or it was our government jobs. Or they used on- and off-duty police. So while we were struggling, competing with Burns and Pinkerton and the rest of them, the locals, to get that piece of the pie, it was all predicated on price. Because we really couldn't say that we were much better, with the same labor pool.

"What we did in Custom Protection was every security company's dream. Our competitors all said, 'One day, we'll do this.' But, fortunately for us, they didn't have the balls to do it. See, if you're discussing a contract, or a job where you're guaranteeing a level of performance, and that buyer says, 'Well, okay, we'll give you a chance, but we can't pay those rates,' we wouldn't get up and say no. We finally said no. We made a conscious decision that we were going to hire people with law-enforcement backgrounds, degrees in criminal justice, military police backgrounds, and people who came out of elite units of the military. And we were going to put together a security force second to none. And, either they were going to pay the fee, or we weren't going to do the job.

"Currently, in South Florida—that's the three counties—Custom Protection has grown from two people, which was the first job, to more than 700, in five years. We've obtained contracts that we would never have obtained before. The first job, believe it or not, was in an Eckerd drugstore in late 1988, where we had commercial guards. The security director, Mr. Andy Mandetto, called me and said that he had a meeting with his principals, and they're going to go to twenty-four-hour stores. For that reason, they wanted armed policemen in there.

"My comment to him, and Andy is a retired New York City policeman, was that we can do the same job; however, we need the better pay scale, and we will hire people in this police category. I said this spontaneously. He said, 'I'd rather have Wackenhut than the police.' The reason that he and others would rather have us was that we have accountability. Whereas a policeman doesn't like to take orders from civilians. So, he said, 'I'll get back to you.' He went back to his manager and gave him my proposition, and they accepted it.

"We didn't have a special uniform. We scrambled, temporarily put them in blues, but hired and trained within those police parameters. Two guards. That account eventually became about eight people. Then, in accordance with the design of the whole program, we needed to separate them from what a commercial guard was. So I met with a uniform supply company—Levine Uniforms, to be specific—and looked at various combinations, and came up with the tan uniform.

"This is where the story gets cute. I had to pick up Mr. Wackenhut at the airport, he was coming in from some exotic meeting with a big client, at the private airport on Thirty-sixth Street. Driving him back to his office, I told him about the Custom Protection Division. He was listening with half an ear. I told him we went into a tan uniform, and all the reasons why, and he naturally asked the presidential question, which was, 'Did anybody approve it?' I dodged answering his question, because *nobody* had approved it!

"So he got back to his office, and, I guess, thought about it, and called me the next day, and promptly ripped me apart for entering into this division, and insisted on seeing the uniform. So we sent a guy over, dressed out in tans and the Highway Patrol-type hat. The uniform consisted of tan pants with a black stripe, black epaulets, black flaps on the shirt pockets. And the black gunbelt. And he said he didn't like the uniform! So, of course, I'm squirming at this time, because now, at this stage, I have about forty people in that uniform! That means eight sets per person, that's 320 sets of uniforms. Now, everybody in the United States likes it. Except George Wackenhut.

"Now we went through a couple of months of uniform display and selection. I was out visiting with a client, having lunch, and I got beeped. Called headquarters. It was Mr. Wackenhut. Needs to see me right away. I leave my client, pay for the lunch, and make a beeline to headquarters, rush to his waiting room. With a big smile on his face, he says, 'Come on in here, I'm going to show you the uniform that *we* want for Custom Protection!' Go into his office, and there sat a *gray* pair of trousers and a *gray* shirt that could be construed as a *bus-driver's* uniform! No trooper hat, he only liked the garrison hat. He *hated* the trooper hat! You see what I'm up against.

"Now, who helped him pick out this uniform? Mr. Sartorial Splendor, Budd Kneip. The two of these guys got together and conspired to put us in *bus-driver's* uniforms. A little-known fact is that George Wackenhut is *color-blind!* So I said to him, I said, 'How the hell can you pick a uniform when you don't even know what the *color* is?' Then he gave me the 'thin lip.' When he gets angry, his lips disappear. So, the only way I could get out of this gray uniform, I happened to remember that happens to be the *Pinkerton* uniform. So I delivered the argument that our elite division will be in the same uniform as the Pinkerton commercial guards. So we got rid of the *gray!*

"He still didn't like the uniform, and I took a chance. Mrs. Wackenhut was up at their house at Cape Cod. I said, 'I'll have Johnson from Lamar Uniform bring up twelve different variations, all colors, let Mrs. Wackenhut pick the Custom Protection uniform.' See, I know she's a decorator and she had impeccable taste. I *knew,* although she's going to look at a dozen uniforms, she's going to pick the same one *I* did!

"Lo and behold, they went up to the Cape with a model, the uniform company brought a model, and he went into all twelve different variations of uniform—green, blue, tan, gray, brown, everything. She picked the same uniform *I* did! She made two changes to the uniform that even improved it: She inserted the purple stripe for the black, and took off the black on the shirt-pocket flaps, which made the uniform even better looking. That happened five years ago, in 1988. That division has since grown, in South Florida, to more than 700 people.

"The Wackenhut commercial guard business has since declined in South Florida. There's a market for that, but leave it to our competitors. We go after the upper range. You can't be all things to all people. We still have some commercial guard business here, but our trend is toward Custom Protection. Our trend is toward that because: One, we have it; two, it's a winner; and three, after the competition gets it, *they* can't go back.

"Our competitors have tried to copy it only in the sense that they say, 'Me, too.' But they do the same thing that they did before. The competitors don't have an organized training program, they don't have training officers on the payroll, it's the same business as usual. I imagine one day somebody will catch on. But, after the past five years, we stand alone.

"It's a big investment. It's a lot of work. It's very costly. In the Custom Protection Division, between the time we interview and train and do the background, it can be as much as six weeks before the guy is on billable work. Which means, as you lose people for one reason or another, you're always behind the curve. Where, in the commercial guard business, it's a matter of a two-day training program, and they're not even drug-screened, and they're not psychologically tested, and the background investigation doesn't take you to their neighborhood, where you do a full field background investigation to the level of hiring a policeman. Our Custom Protection people have a two-week training schedule in the area offices.

"I got out of headquarters because one of my responsibilities was to move Custom Protection around the country. And I didn't have the cooperation of the area managers. There was resistance because there's a lot of work attached to it, it's a real yeoman effort to get it going. Either they didn't have the strength or the inclination or the desire to do anything other than what they were doing. We brought all the area managers down here for training. Training in how to do it, how to develop it, how to sell it, how to support it, and they went back, and it was business as usual. So I found I had the responsibility of developing this thing around the country, but I didn't have the authority. Because I would've fired half of them. I didn't want to be in that position.

"Miami was an established, going concern, and I wanted to get Palm Beach County and Broward County stepped up to the level that we had in Miami. I made that move about two years ago, and I have my son [Drew] running Fort Lauderdale. He's brought it from a $10,000-a-year profit office to last year's [1992] profit of $385,000. He's done that in a period of about two years. And we've turned Palm Beach County around, into a going concern, as well, with major accounts.

"In South Florida, we have thirty-two private community protection accounts right now. Barbara [his wife, a TWC development representative in Boca Raton] discovered that there was a niche in these communities for a lower-price guard, who is not a Custom Protection Officer [CPO], but had the personal qualities of the CPO, without the law-enforcement background. To operate gates, to have the personal bearing that was above and beyond the hamburger-flippers, had meaningful backgrounds in employment, and could've probably been a supervisor with a competitor, or even with us in the commercial guard business. And that rate structure fell between the CPO and the commercial guard. We call them Upscale Officers. It was a better payday, with incentives and raises. They wear the regular Wackenhut uniform, dressed up with patent-leather gear, and a Highway Patrol-type hat in blue. The CPO uniform today includes the Highway Patrol-type hat, the trousers and shirt are in tan, trimmed in black and purple on the trousers, and black epaulets on the shirt. They wear black Corafan gunbelts and holsters, and black patent-leather shoes."

It didn't take long for Levine's specially trained CPOs to pay tangible dividends and, in so doing, to achieve high visibility throughout the corporation, particularly in the Miami area office. The lead story on the front page of the May 1989 issue of *Pipeline* is a case in point, complete with photos of two CPS in their new tan uniforms:

Custom Protection Officers Receive Special Honors

Two Wackenhut Custom Protection Officers have been honored by respective clients for their efforts in thwarting robberies.

On January 21, 1989, a CPO employed by TWC prevented a robbery in progress at a Winn-Dixie Grocery Store by catching and handcuffing a man fleeing from the scene.

Lloyd Wilson, 37, an officer at Wackenhut's Miami area office, was reporting for duty at the store at the time and noticed a car parked with its engine running. Wilson entered the store and, as he did, a clerk alerted him, and Wilson noticed a man running out of the store.

Wilson ran after the suspect, who had gotten in his car and was about to drive off. The Custom Protection Officer reached through an open window (on the driver's side), and struggled for control of the steering wheel. Wilson then turned off the ignition. As he was about to get out of the car, the suspect turned on the ignition and ran over Wilson's feet in an attempt to make a second getaway.

At that point, Wilson and the suspect struggled more, and the store manager and another employee came to assist Wilson, who handcuffed the suspect until police arrived. Police later charged the suspect with grand theft and aggravated assault.

In an unrelated incident, another Custom Protection Officer from the Miami area office chased a purse-snatching thief for three miles before catching the suspect.

CPO Miguel Dominguez was on duty at the Three Sisters Store in North Miami when he witnessed a man snatching the purse of an elderly woman.

CPO Dominguez chased the suspect for 30 minutes before he finally caught him. Dominguez brought the suspect back to the store, where police were waiting to arrest him.

Members of Wackenhut's Custom Protection Division have experience in civilian or military law enforcement agencies or elite military units. Many have degrees in criminology or a related field, or are graduates of a law enforcement academy.

In the two large photos accompanying the story at the top of *Pipeline*'s front page, CPO Dominguez is congratulated by Eddie Rodriguez, TWC's manager of Physical Security for the Miami area office, and CPO Wilson is flanked by Rene Pedrayes, TWC's Miami area manager, and Bob Schweiger, director of security for Winn-Dixie Stores. From that issue on, Levine made certain that his unique CPOs received as much exposure as possible for the then-30,000-plus readers of *Pipeline* worldwide, and potential clients.

On January 23, 1989, Wackenhut Corrections Corporation began taking its first prisoners at the nation's largest private detention facility, when it started operating the 628-bed Central Texas Parole Violator Facility in San Antonio. WCC contracted for the renovation of the former Bexar County Jail, which would now be operated as a parole violator facility. The contract for the operation of the facility had a potential value of $15 million and was subject to state legislative appropriations.

In late February of that year, Ed Sanbourn, area manager of TWC's Washington, DC, office, was selected as Area Manager of the Year for 1988 at the annual banquet held in Miami. It was the fourth year that the corporation held its popular "Top Ten" competition for all area managers within Domestic Operations.

Sanbourn joined TWC in 1981 as a senior consultant, and later that year he became manager of Transportation Services. In July of 1982, he was named area manager for the Washington, DC, office. Prior to joining Wackenhut, Sanbourn was vice president for the Transportation Association of America.

Thomas J. DeGraw, area manager of the Los Angeles office, and Neil Jacobs, area manager of the Worchester, Massachusetts, office, were recognized for achieving the greatest percentage gain in sales, and outstanding budget performance, respectively. Additionally, Richard D. Ferner, area manager at Albuquerque, was singled out for having the greatest percentage gain in profits. Jimmy Gorham, area manager at Memphis, earned the use of a company car for one year in recognition for being selected as one of the "Top Ten" for four consecutive years.

TRESHA has vivid memories about her experience at Harvard in 1989, but she disagrees with her sister that the dating scene there scared her. On the contrary, she recalls that the different moral standards presented a challenge. "The real reason I left after two years and went to Harvard, I was rebellious against the hypocrisy that I felt was at Principia," Tresha says. "At that point, I was becoming much more of a student of Christian Science, I was digging into the Bible and *Science and Health* a lot more. Christian Science is very much a day-by-day, moment-by-moment, study and application. And, somehow, being at that school for the first two years, and for the first quarter of my junior year, made me value deeply what Christian Science really was all about, progressively. The summer prior to my junior year, I worked as a camp counselor that Tanya and I went to for Christian Scientists, Camp Newfound, in Maine. And always what stood out for me at Newfound, much more so than at Principia, was Christian Science *lived*. It was just an atmosphere that really showed how to live unconditional love. I was just immersed in it every time I was at camp.

"Principia is on a quarter system, trimester. So, going from that summer then, where I was a counselor, and just immersed in what I thought was an atmosphere that really attested to how to live Christian Science, back to the college, which did *not* feel like that at all, I think I was asking myself: Am I depending on a *place* for support? Am I *relying* on the fact that there are other people here who are calling themselves Christian Scientists? I think, at that point. Principia was just very comfortable and very, very familiar. You cannot fault the school. When I look back on it now, what I was resisting, I was resisting the pressure within my own thoughts of trying to resolve how to live, how to *practice* Christian Science within an atmosphere where I was not seeing *my* standard and *my* ideal of how I *thought* it should be lived. And I felt guilty, because I was criticizing and judging too many of my peers. Perhaps rightly so, but that guilt, plus wanting to be around a completely unfamiliar setting, where I could resolve these issues on my own, motivated my decision to leave.

"But also—and very much a part of this decision—wanting to challenge myself, wanting to know if Principia *was* a 'real' school, if it *was* intellectually challenging. I wanted to give myself that challenge because, as challenging as my courses had been thus far—and I had taken some tough classes—there was still that question: Are the Ivy League schools really better academically?

"At that point, I didn't know if I would transfer permanently, and what I did was, I had applied to Tufts and the University of Virginia and George Washington University, those three, and I had been accepted to permanently transfer. But if I had accepted any of those offers, there was no coming back. And, somehow, it was too much of a permanent decision for me.

"So Harvard offered a visiting semester, a visiting year, and I applied for it, and I was accepted. I don't think that meant anything to me, because, I mean, it's great for a school to be able to have a student come in for a year, so they get the tuition, but they don't have to give them a degree. So, being accepted to that didn't mean anything. Had I been accepted to Harvard in high school, that would've meant something. But I was accepted to study there for a year and I thought: Let's go, take a year there, just see it. Jump in and see if it's really what you want, then reevaluate what you want for the rest of your education.

"I think the underlying motive was that I was searching for my identity. I see that now, I didn't see that then. At that time, I thought the substance of a college experience is what shaped your identity. I don't think so now. In fact, I know differently.

"In any case, I went to Cambridge in January of 1989, and I didn't know a soul up there. I knew a few people who worked in the administration of The First Church of Christ, Scientist, the Mother Church, in Boston. But that was clear across the river from Cambridge; I didn't know anyone in Cambridge. I loved that. I mean it was just 'Let's jump in,' and something told me I could do it. I wasn't fearful at all. The only thing I was concerned about was making a mistake in my course selections. I had two weeks of time to do what they called 'shop courses,' and I probably sat in on about 100 classes.

None of the other kids did this, you know, their schedules were already set, but here's Tresha wanting to not let *anything* go wrong with this Harvard experience. Because, you know, my thought was: This *is* a once-in-a-lifetime opportunity, and I don't want to blow it.

"I finally settled on a Mid-East twentieth-century history course, a Rembrandt art-history course, a Victorian literature course, and a French course. All of the things that I was considering majoring in. How does Pop fit into this? He loved the fact that I was going to Harvard. Not because of the name of the school, but he loved the fact that I was challenging myself, and he supported me 100 percent. He thought it would be really good for me. I think he was trying to have me transfer there, so I could graduate.

"But I left Christian Science, in a way, I just put the Bible and *Science and Health* on a shelf, and I just didn't want anything to do with it. What I was rejecting was all the familiarity and hypocrisy that I had known at Principia. This was my new experience. But what happened was, I felt very lost. *Very* lost. I felt that I was wandering around in an unknown. And it had nothing to do with the place, because I was familiar with the place after a few months. It had nothing to do, really, with the fact that I didn't have a close unit of friends. Because I never really had that, I was always independent that way. I see now that I was lost spiritually. Because I had kind of just said, 'The heck with God for now, it's too difficult.'

"I was living in Cambridge. At first, I was living with a woman who was a Christian Scientist; somehow I was able to find out that she had a room for rent. It was a mile and a half walk from the university, but I loved it, I'd commute each day. Harvard wasn't at all a 'warm' place, by any means. What I always got a kick out of, I'd just naturally say hello to everyone, and always I'd get these double-takes, as if to say, 'Do I *know* you?' Anyway, I transferred from living with this woman, because it was just remote, it wasn't the whole campus experience. And I moved right into a dorm, into a single that was less than half the size of this room [her office]. It was called North House, and it was on the Radcliffe campus. It had been housing for women before Harvard went coed.

"I appreciated having that familiarity of friends around the hall. It was unique because at Principia I'd been in an all-girls house.

Harvard is coed by room; you have separate bathrooms, but across the hall and next to me and down the hall there were guys everywhere. And I just appreciated having those relationships. There weren't a lot of girls on my floor, not real close, but it was a real independent scene, even in the house.

"I never dated in college. I mean, there were friends I had, but I can't say I was dating. Frankly, I don't think I wanted to be bothered with all that because, while in my heart I wanted desperately to find that companionship, I was somehow intolerant of all the triviality of all that.

"What *was* a challenge at Harvard were the moral standards. Because it's a given at Principia, you just don't really have drinking and smoking going on in the houses—not out in the open—but at Harvard, you had it everywhere. At Harvard, I just put myself in those situations, voluntarily, and just held my own. I didn't drink while I was at Harvard, but I wanted to get to know people, and that seemed to be the only way. I sometimes amaze myself, looking back now: I love the sense of courage that I expressed during that whole experience. Because I'd find out about a party going on, and I didn't have a group of friends to call up and say, 'Do you want to go?' So I'd just pick myself up and go, and I'd walk into a room of 150 people, who I didn't know—I did this like five or six times—and I would just start introducing myself, or find some connection, and then eventually everybody realizes: Who's this new person?

"I think I shocked many people at Harvard, because they had never heard of Principia, and they had never heard of the visiting program that their school offered. And here I am, just doing this independently. But I think what resulted from that whole experience was, I learned how to be an independent thinker, at least intellectually. I realized that my professors were not authorities on *truth*, they were just individuals with interests that they had explored in depth, and were presenting what *they* had learned, *their* vision, *their* view. But that each one of us has that ability.

"I thrived on the whole city atmosphere, and the vastness of it, I loved that. I think I actually had more fun on the streets of Cambridge than within the Harvard gates. What made me feel lost was that I had just sort of neglected myself, my true self. What I mean by that is, I had put on 'hold' the study of Christian Science. That, added to the newness of the whole experience, is what made me feel lost. It wasn't so much the fact that people weren't warm and friendly, and it wasn't so much that I had new classes and new teachers, it was just that combination.

"One of the things about Christian Science is that when an individual is seeking healing, regardless if it's physical or emotional, they turn to prayer for that. And if that individual wants help, they turn to a practitioner. Well, I resisted turning to practitioners, because I always wanted to be able to prove what I was learning myself. I just wanted to be able to practice it on my own. Somehow, turning to a practitioner, to me, meant that I'd failed. And yet, after about four months of feeling lost, I finally resolved that I'd turn to a practitioner. Because I needed some help. I didn't care what my decision was going to be with my education, but I wanted to know how come I felt lost, why did I feel that I wasn't being honest with myself? Before I made that decision, I opened up the textbook, *Science and Health*, and I—I don't remember what I read, but in the words that I read, I felt like I'd come home.

"The practitioner that I eventually called was in Boston. It turned out to be the beginning of a wonderful relationship. The fact was, what I discovered at Harvard was that identity, completeness, fulfillment, all of those things, have little to do with what we do with our lives. But that security and fulfillment, our true identity, is discovered through our relationship with God. And once I had availed myself of that again, because I'd kind of turned my back on it, I was home. And it didn't matter that I was still having some challenges at the school, or feeling: What do I do with myself and my life and my education? The fact was, I knew where to turn to now, I knew where the source of love was.

"I give that background solely because perhaps I always knew that's where the source was. And that's certainly what Pop has *lived*, to me. In his own way, he's like a living testimony to that. God, whom he will define as 'Divine Principle,' that's the standard of our lives. That's what we have to turn to. That's what we have to base our thinking and acting on. And nothing else. I began to glimpse that at Harvard."

BACK AT HEADQUARTERS, TWC announced the formation of two new divisions in the autumn of 1989. On October 1, the corporation initiated a Special Investigations Division (SID), to be headed by Wayne B. Black, a former group supervisor of the Criminal Investigation Division of the State Attorney's Office. As director of the SID, Black's responsibilities would include direct investigative efforts that may involve any of the company's ninety offices in the U.S. or its representatives in more than forty countries throughout the world.

Black had fifteen years of experience as an investigator for both public and private sector organizations. Prior to joining Wackenhut, he was the lead investigator in the Tiffany Sessions kidnapping, and was credited with locating extensive funds that had been stolen by former financial consultant Henry Gherman, then serving a thirty-year sentence in federal prison. He was the recipient of awards and commendations from the U.S. Justice Department, the U.S. Attorney's Office in Miami, and the Drug Enforcement Administration.

On November 20, TWC formed a Maritime Security Division (MSD), headed by Kenneth Gale Hawkes, an internationally recognized maritime security consultant, admiralty attorney, and recent author of a comprehensive and authoritative book on maritime security. MSD's capabilities would include the expertise to conduct a variety of surveys, management appraisals, and risk analyses for individual ships, installations, fleets, or complex series of installations, irrespective of their locations throughout the world. Individually tailored implementation plans and procedures would supplement any initial survey activities.

As an example, the U.S. Customs' carrier initiative programs had recently mandated certain security procedures for maritime carriers, and strongly recommended additional measures to be taken to assure compliance. Most carriers did not have the expertise or assets to develop such procedures, and much of the documentation would require professional assistance to implement. The new division was prepared to render that assistance.

According to Hawkes, who was named vice president of Maritime Security, "There has been a need within the maritime industry for knowledgeable private investigations, crisis management team training and implementation, personnel selection and placement techniques, and security training within a maritime context. The Wackenhut Corporation has the assets to provide all of these services."

Hawkes served as an officer in the U.S. Marine Corps where, among other assignments, he was responsible for shipboard nuclear weapons security. Later, he attended the University of Miami Law School, where he earned a Juris Doctor degree. He was admitted to the Florida Bar in 1979. As a maritime trial attorney, he tried cases spanning the full range of admiralty matters, including personal injury, collision, cargo damage, environmental pollution, and negligent security. In 1989, Hawkes authored the book *Maritime Security*, published by Cornell Maritime Press, which was immediately recognized as the definitive text on the subject.

A past member of the board of directors for the Society of Accredited Marine Surveyors, Hawkes was currently a member of the board of directors for the International Maritime Technical Institute, and a proctor member of both the Maritime Law Association of the United States and the Southeastern Admiralty Law Institute.

Corporate operations under contract to the federal government, and particularly with the U.S. Department of Energy, received significant accolades during the year. The WSI security force at the Savannah River Site earned the highest possible rating after an inspection and evaluation conducted by a team from the DOE's national headquarters. Operations there and at the Nevada Test Site received excellent ratings in the most recent regularly scheduled six-month contract evaluations. Wackenhut security specialists performed unique protective services in weapons tests conducted at the Nevada Site during unusual conditions with observers from the Soviet Union present.

MAJOR EVENTS in world history during 1989 included: January 4, U.S. planes shot down two Libyan fighters over international waters in the Mediterranean. January 7, Emperor Hirohito of Japan died at age eighty-seven. January 20, George Bush was inaugurated as the forty-first president of the United States. February 14, Iran's Ayatollah Khomeini declared author Salman Rushdie's novel *The Satanic Verses* offensive and "sentenced" him and his publishers to death.

March 24, the ruptured tanker *Exxon Valdez* spilled 11 million gallons of crude oil into Alaska's Price William Sound. April 19, tens of thousands of Chinese took over Beijing's central square in a rally for democracy; in mid-May, more than one million Chinese in Beijing demonstrated for democracy, and chaos spread across the nation. May 25, Mikhail S. Gorbachev was named president of the Soviet Union. June 4, thousands were killed as Chinese leaders defended Beijing against the demonstrators. August 9, U.S. Army General Colin R. Powell was named the first black to become chairman of the Joint Chiefs of Staff. August 14, P.W. Botha resigned as president of South Africa. August 29, the *Voyager 2* spacecraft passed Neptune after making startling discoveries about the planet and its moons. September 18, Hurricane Hugo devastated a vast area from the Caribbean to South Carolina. November 7, L. Douglas Wilder, Democrat, was elected as the first black governor of Virginia. November 9, Deng Xiaoping resigned from China's leadership. November 11, after twenty-eight years, the Berlin Wall was opened to the West. November 30, the Czech Parliament ended the Communist Party's dominant role. December 15, a Romanian uprising overthrew the communist government; on December 25, President Ceausescu and his wife were executed. December 20, U.S. troops invaded Panama, seeking the capture of General Manuel Noriega; on December 24, Panama's resistance to the U.S. collapsed.

BACK IN CORAL GABLES, TWC's thirty-fifth anniversary year was also the thirty-fifth consecutive year in which the corporation experienced a growth in revenues, realizing $462.181 million, a 15 percent increase over the previous year. The year's net income of $5.874 million showed an increase of 13 percent.

George's relatively new (1987) direction and commitment of TWC toward the diversification of its services to business and government were clearly paying off.

30

WAYNE BLACK, who had joined TWC on October 1, 1989, as director of its newly created Special Investigations Division, would receive his first major assignment on March 1, 1990, a highly covert operation titled Case 427, that would quickly become the most notorious and publicized investigation in the history of the corporation, resulting in a congressional investigation, and more than three years of protracted litigation that would cost TWC's client, the Alyeska Pipeline Service Company, at least $10 million in legal fees before a settlement was reached on December 20, 1993.

Born in Dayton, Ohio, November 25, 1947, Black graduated from North Mot High School in 1966, served as a sheriff's deputy in Ohio, 1969–1974, before moving to Miami to join the Metro Dade Police Department in 1974, assigned to the Narcotics Unit, where he worked with a DEA task force investigating corruption and drug trafficking. From 1979 to 1982, he was a group supervisor in the office of then-Florida State Attorney General Janet Reno. In 1984, he began his own private investigative agency, Wayne Black & Associates, in Miami.

Since Case 427 was to become so enormously complicated, an overall view of the purpose and scope of the investigation can be found in a confidential memo from Black to J.P. Wellington, Alyeska's director of security, dated May 23, 1990, providing basic facts about the initial stages of the investigation:

On March 1, 1990, we initiated an investigation at your request to determine the scope of the problem involving theft of proprietary documents from the Alyeska Pipeline Service Company and identify those responsible. At that time, you suspected, but had no conclusive proof, that Alyeska employee Bob Scott had given proprietary information to Charles Hamel. In return, Hamel had given the information to The Wall Street Journal and other media.

RESULTS. We have been able to positively identify Bob Scott as one of Hamel's sources. There is the possibility that Scott may be violating federal law, that is, forwarding stolen material via the U.S. Mail from Alaska to Washington, D.C.

We have created the Ecolit Research Group which resulted in three Special Investigations Division investigators being in an undercover capacity with Charles Hamel. The results have been:

(a) The recovery of documents stolen from Alyeska.
(b) Admissions by Hamel regarding Scott and others, yet unidentified.
(c) The discovery that person(s) unknown inside the Alyeska legal department are supplying information and documents to Hamel or one of his other sources.
(d) Admissions by Hamel that he is doing what he is doing for personal gain only. Admission by Hamel that documents are stolen.
(e) We have been able to observe boxes of Alyeska documents in Hamel's possession in Washington alone.

INVESTIGATION IN PROGRESS. We continue to have weekly, almost daily, contact with Charles Hamel. Hamel plans to visit The Ecolit Group in Miami, followed by reciprocal visits to Washington and Alaska. Ongoing telephone toll analysis reveals sustained activity between Hamel and others involved. As new numbers develop, subscriber information will be obtained.

INVESTIGATION PLAN. Our general plan is to proceed on the present course, having continued contact with Hamel. As we gain his confidence, he continues to divulge information critical to Alyeska. Of great concern are Hamel's recent admissions regarding his "source" inside Alyeska's legal department. Our ongoing investigative plan involves the following:

(a) Continue undercover activity with Hamel.
(b) Identify sources of stolen documents in the legal department of Alyeska.
(c) Identify Hamel's other sources.
(d) Test for leaks in corporate headquarters.
(e) Test for recording devices during board meetings or meetings about Hamel.
(f) Continue telephone toll analysis, charting activity by event.

How can Alyeska best respond to the information gained from this investigation? Our investigative results could be and should be used to stimulate additional activity, both undercover and administrative. You now know that, with regard to Hamel, your legal department is not totally secure. Employee interviews and terminations could be initiated at the appropriate time. Additional document security measures should be taken immediately. Consideration of legal action, either civil, criminal or both, should be considered.

We are concerned about Hamel's allegation that he and George Miller (D-California) are friends and that he feeds Miller information about Alyeska from stolen documents. At the same time, Hamel admits that his only goal is to be reimbursed by Exxon or Alyeska for monies he feels owed.

CONCLUSION. We feel Hamel is truthful with our undercover investigators when he repeats his purpose for release of documents to the media, the Alaska Attorney General's Office, the Department of Justice, and even our research group. Hamel has never indicated that he is interested solely in providing information to a congressional committee to assist in any investigation. Likewise, we do not know if Congressman Miller or any member of his committee has requested Hamel or his sources to steal or otherwise obtain stolen documents from Alyeska. We are concerned that Hamel may be using his alleged relationship with Miller to extort or blackmail Alyeska or Exxon.

We have carefully reviewed the legal discussion found in Section 14 of this report dealing with the likelihood of unofficial involvement on the part of Congressman George Miller. While the cursory legal opinion was necessary, we feel no action needs to be taken at this time. Surely, future contact with Hamel will result in additional, more clarifying information about Congressman Miller. If and when Hamel even hints that he (Hamel) is assisting or acting as an agent of Miller, we will cease our undercover approach.

Exhibit List

1. Three pieces of paper given to investigator Ricki Jacobson by Charles Hamel on March 24, 1990.
2. Items taken from the trash of Bob Scott by investigator Rick Lund.
3. An envelope from Box 706, Zip 99686, addressed to Mrs. Gloria Ewell in Washington, D.C. This item was recovered by investigator Wayne Black after it was discarded by Charles Hamel.
4. Pertinent paperwork discarded by Charles Hamel and recovered on May 2, 1990, from the trash of Hamel in Alexandria, Virginia, by investigator Rick Lund.
5. A facsimile transmission dated and received on May 14, 1990, from Charles Hamel to Wayne Jenkins.
6. An Alyeska Pipeline Service Company work request dated April 15, 1990, and April 17, 1990. This exhibit is a stolen Alyeska document that was recovered from the home of Charles Hamel by investigators Black and Lund on May 16, 1990.
7. An Alyeska corporate operations administrative exchange report dated March 27, 1989. This document was recovered from the home of Charles Hamel by investigators Lund and Black on May 16, 1990.
8. Two Alyeska stolen messages recovered from the home of Charles Hamel on May 16, 1990, by investigators Lund and Black.
9. A legal memorandum from Carlos K. Goodman to Charles C. Ivie. This document was given to investigator Wayne Black by Charles Hamel on May 16, 1990.
10. A facsimile transmission dated May 17, 1990, from Charles Hamel to Wayne Jenkins.
11. A facsimile dated May 18, 1990, from Charles Hamel to Wayne Jenkins. This is a copy of The Wall Street Journal, Eastern Edition, dated May 18, 1990, regarding Alyeska.

In addition to Rick Lund, who was a contract employee specializing in sophisticated electronic surveillance techniques, Black had six full-time employees working on Case 427, all of whom were eventually subpoenaed to testify at the Congressional Oversight Hearings before the Committee on Interior and Insular Affairs, Washington,

DC, November 4–6, 1991, in the following order: Mercedes Iliana Cruz, Sherree Rich, Ricki Sue Jacobson, Rafael G. Castillo, Ana Maria Contreras, and Adriana Caputi.

When Ricki Sue Jacobson joined TWC in November 1989, she had no previous investigative experience; she had been a real estate agent since 1976, and was the mother of three children. For purposes of licensing, her position was listed as "private investigator intern." Black explained that her duties would basically involve property and asset searches, which would take advantage of her real estate background. In the initial weeks of her employment in the Special Investigations Division, she also worked on some surveillance assignments. Here is one excerpt from Jacobson's written opening statement before Congressman Miller's committee:

> In approximately February or March, 1990, Mr. Black asked if I would like to travel to Alaska on an assignment. Originally, I hesitated, because I do not like being away from my children for long periods of time. However, after being assured by Mr. Black that I would be gone only briefly, I agreed. I was not told the name of the client or the nature of the operation. I was given only the case number, which was 427.
>
> Mr. Black briefed me for my assignment during March of 1990 and I was due to leave around March 20, 1990. In my briefing, Mr. Black told me I would be attending an environmental conference in Anchorage, that I would be traveling under an assumed name, and that I was to have no public contact with Mr. Black or Mr. Rick Lund while in Anchorage. Mr. Lund was an investigator under contract with Wackenhut, who often worked with Mr. Black. My assumed name was "Ricki Eidelson." Eidelson is my maiden name and Mr. Black suggested I use it since it would be easy to remember. In the course of my briefing, I was also instructed by Mr. Black to become generally familiar with various ecological groups because I would be attending the conference pretending to be an ecological researcher for an environmental group in Miami. The environmental group I would be representing was called "Ecolit" and was a fictitious organization created by Wackenhut for the purpose of this assignment.
>
> After preparing in accordance with my instructions, I traveled to Anchorage on or about March 20, 1990. Prior to my departure, I was given false identification documents to support my assumed name.

These documents included a Florida driver's license issued in my fictitious name, business cards from Ecolit, and luggage tags. Mr. Black and Mr. Lund traveled on board the same plane, but we had no contact with each other, as per the instructions I had received. Mr. Black's assumed name was Wayne Jenkins, also supposedly with the Ecolit group. I believe Mr. Lund's assumed name was John Fox, though I am not certain. At this time, I still had no knowledge of the client's name, the nature of the operation or effort of which I was a part, or the name of any persons who might be the subject of any investigation to be conducted by Wackenhut.

After my arrival in Alaska, I traveled to my hotel, the Captain Cook, and registered. Mr. Black and Mr. Lund also traveled to the hotel, though separately from me. Shortly after we arrived at the hotel, Mr. Black and Mr. Lund met with me in my room and discussed various details of my assignment. The essence of their instructions was that I was simply to attend and take notes at the environmental conference scheduled to begin the next morning. However, in the course of this meeting, Mr. Lund also asked that I attempt to see the conference registration list and to let him know if the name "Charles Hamel" appeared on that list. That was the first time I ever heard the name Charles Hamel, and nothing further was said about him. When I inquired later about the list, I was told that a registration list was not available and I therefore reported to Mr. Black and Mr. Lund that I was unable to determine whether Mr. Hamel had registered at the conference.

On March 22, 1990, the third day of the conference, while I was seated with other conference attendees in the dining room of the hotel, Mr. Black approached me and whispered, "The guy we want you to eyeball is in the lobby." I believe these were Mr. Black's exact words. He then motioned for me to follow him. I was surprised, because I did not know anything was expected of me beyond my attendance at the environmental conference. However, I walked to the doorway of the dining room, and Mr. Black pointed out Mr. Hamel standing in the lobby area. Mr. Hamel was speaking with a man and a woman. I observed them for a few moments, but did not overhear their conversation. When they left the lobby, I returned to the dining room and later reported my observation to Mr. Black.

During the evening of March 22, 1990, the day the conference ended, I visited a local restaurant and bar with a fellow conference attendee. Upon my return to the hotel, I noticed Charles Hamel standing in the lobby area. Believing that Mr. Black and Mr. Lund would be interested in Mr. Hamel's whereabouts, I contacted one of them (I do not remember which) and advised him of Mr. Hamel's presence in the lobby. I was instructed to keep Mr. Hamel under observation and, if he left the lobby area, to follow him. After a short time, I followed Mr. Hamel into the hotel bar.

He was in the company of another gentleman and I learned later that his name was Rick Steiner. I sat a few stools away from Mr. Hamel and Mr. Steiner and, after a few moments, I used the phone in the bar and called Mr. Black or Mr. Lund (I do not remember which), and notified him of my whereabouts. A few moments later, Mr. Black and Mr. Lund entered the bar separately, as if they did not know one another, and took separate seats. After approximately twenty or thirty minutes, Mr. Hamel and Mr. Steiner left the bar. My observation terminated at that time. However, I believe either Mr. Black or Mr. Lund followed Mr. Hamel and Mr. Steiner out of the bar. During the time I was in the bar, I do not recall engaging in any direct conversation with Mr. Steiner or Mr. Hamel, and I do not believe that I did. However, I recall having brief eye contact with one or both of them in the course of various comments I was exchanging with the bartender.

Sometime after I returned to my room that evening, Mr. Black and Mr. Lund came to my room and we discussed the events of that evening and our travel arrangements home, now that the conference had ended.

I left Alaska on the morning of March 24, 1990. While waiting to board my flight in the Anchorage Airport, I noticed Mr. Hamel in the concourse area. I was very surprised that I happened to be booked on the same flight. After being seated in the coach section, Mr. Hamel noticed me and apparently recognized me. After exchanging a few words, he invited me to sit with him and I did. I was very nervous because my assignment was over and I did not know how to handle this particular situation. Since Mr. Hamel had just been the subject of our surveillance in the bar, and because I wanted to be very careful, I introduced myself using my assumed identity and purpose.

Mr. Hamel's destination was Seattle, the first stop on my flight to Miami. During the time we sat together, Mr. Hamel very candidly discussed many things of concern to him, including a lawsuit with Exxon, his own oil leases and problems he encountered with water being mixed with his oil. He also mentioned that he had various sources inside

Alyeska Corporation feeding him various types of sensitive information. He discussed secret meetings and even the suicide of one person involved. I did not understand much of what he was saying and felt very astonished and uncomfortable at the great degree of trust he was showing a complete stranger. In addition to these discussions, Mr. Hamel asked me a lot about myself and about Ecolit. In the course of that part of our discussion, he mentioned that he would be coming to Miami and that, when he did, he would visit Ecolit.

After I returned to Miami, I reported my experience with Mr. Hamel to Mr. Lund and then to Mr. Black, and subsequently dictated a memorandum to Mr. Black containing the same information. I maintained no activity logs during my stay in Alaska because I was told by Mr. Black that none of the usually required activity logs were to be maintained in connection with the Alaska trip.

Several days after my return to Miami, at the direction of Mr. Black, I contacted Charles Hamel one or two times at the number Mr. Hamel gave me on the airplane. The purpose of my phone call was to attempt to arrange an introduction between Mr. Hamel and Wayne Black (posing as Wayne Jenkins of the Ecolit Group). Mr. Black was present during my calls to Mr. Hamel and spoke with Mr. Hamel himself once the introduction had been made. Subsequently, it is my understanding that he made several additional phone calls to Mr. Hamel. I witnessed approximately two of the calls made by Mr. Black (Jenkins) to Mr. Hamel. I observed at least one of these telephone calls being recorded by Mr. Black. The device used was a wire with a suction cup attached to the receiver and the other end attached to a small tape recorder on Mr. Black's desk. I know other phone calls to Mr. Hamel were recorded because Mr. Black played for me the tape of at least one of the phone calls which he made to Mr. Hamel. . . .

Despite the above excerpt from Ricki (Eidelson) Jacobson's sworn statement before Congressman Miller's committee in November 1991, a badly distorted version of the events in the bar and on the plane, leaked by somebody to the press, resulted in the lead story on the front page of *The Anchorage Daily News,* Sunday morning, September 1, 1991, together with a photograph of Charles Hamel, and under the by-line of reporter Richard Mauer, whose story was quoted briefly in the Introduction to this book:

THE DETAILS OF DECEPTION
Dirty tricks used against Alyeska critic Hamel leave him bruised

The blonde was alone at the bar. Two men caught her eye. The woman knew just what she wanted. The men had no idea.

She stood up and breezed by their stools. She punched out a number on the bartender's phone. Her gaze bore into the men.

She hung up the phone and struck up a conversation. Her name was Ricki Edelson [sic]. She was tanned, 40ish, attractive and alone at Fletcher's, the bar at the Captain Cook, a long way from home. . . .

That same Sunday morning, more than 4,000 miles away, the lead story on the front page of *The Miami Herald* held the banner headline, "Spy web ensnared whistle-blower," and included a large four-color photograph of George Wackenhut. Careless investigative reporters meeting tight deadlines on a seemingly juicy story. But, in both stories, and in countless other newspaper stories nationwide, George Wackenhut's integrity had been questioned in public a full *two months* before the congressional hearings began.

During the sworn testimony of Sherree Rich, some of the so-called high-tech investigative techniques were revealed to the committee. Rich was hired by Wayne Black in August of 1990, after being interviewed at the Tampa office of TWC. Prior to that, she worked two and a half years for the Tallahassee Police Department, and three and a half months for the Hillsborough County Sheriff's Office on a special undercover operation. Following is an excerpt from her written opening statement:

> After completion of my background investigation, I was hired, and went to Miami for final processing and preparation for the operation. The final preparation for leaving to conduct the activity was to get a large amount of cash for use in setting up the undercover office.
>
> Mr. Wayne Black and I flew up to Washington on or about August 11, 1990. On the flight to Washington, DC, I was provided a number of articles to read about Exxon's activities in Alaska, environmental issues about oil spills, and the Alaska pipeline from Alaska newspapers. We were joined later by Rick Lund and Vern Johnson. We checked into the Crystal City Marriott Hotel, where I stayed for approximately four to five weeks. All of my hotel expenses were covered by Wackenhut.

During the first few days after arriving in Virginia, I was briefed on what my duties were to be in connection with the undercover operation. Initially, I was told very little about what the real purpose of the investigation was. I was directed to open and set up an office, posing as "The Ecolit Group," which I knew to be a false identity standing for "ecological litigation." This included opening a personal bank account in my name, with Ecolit on the check. I deposited several thousand dollars. It also included ordering cards with my name on the Ecolit card identifying myself as a "staff researcher." I also ordered cards for Wayne Black, identifying him as Dr. Wayne Jenkins. As part of my cover, I also joined the Library of Congress as a researcher. I ordered the Anchorage Daily News as part of the cover so that the office looked legitimate. I also purchased several books about environmental issues and several environmental posters, such as "Save the Whales" and "Save the Earth" as props.

The bogus office was located at 2341 Jefferson Davis Highway, Suite 525, in the Century Building, Arlington, Virginia. The office was in a suite of offices that shared common secretarial answering and reception services, and a common lobby. In order to appear legitimate, I also received daily telephone calls from Miami, posing as if it was the Miami Ecolit office, as well as faxes and occasional letters.

At about the same time, Mr. Richard Lund, posing as Mr. John Fox, rented a suite in the same location, called Overseas Trading Company. Although we were working together in this undercover operation, we pretended only to know Mr. Fox casually because he assisted in getting our computers. In fact, Mr. Rick Lund, and another gentleman named Vern Johnson, wired the offices with video and audio microphones and cameras for the purpose of recording all of the communications and transactions between Hamel and Black. This included putting in a video camera inside a portable stereo which was wired to Rick Lund's office where it was picked up on a receiver and recorder. The sound system was also wired through the ceiling panels to the office two or three offices down the hallway. I was present when all the wiring was done in these offices.

I was present during the time when Rick Lund and Vern Johnson wired Ecolit's office in Arlington, Virginia. We arrived at the QRC offices (where we rented the Ecolit office) at night. Rick and Vern ran wires from John Fox's office, International Overseas Trading, through the ceiling into the Ecolit office. Rick had attached the wires to a remote-controlled toy dune buggy. He used this vehicle to drive across the inside of the ceiling from his office across the intervening office to the Ecolit office, so he could get the wires to the Ecolit office. He ran the wire from the ceiling through a stanchion in the wall, cut a hole in the wall to bring the wire out, and ran the wire under the carpet. . . .

Tim Cole had been on the road constantly during the spring and summer of 1990. On July 1, he signed a two-year $13.2 million renewal contract with the U.S. Department of Labor for WSI to operate its Job Corps Center in Guthrie, Oklahoma. Under the terms of the contract, which was awarded after a competitive bidding process, WSI would provide academic and vocational training to 630 residents of the center. The contract was subject to three one-year extensions. Also in early July, Cole had negotiated and signed a two-year, $10 million renewal contract with the U.S. Department of Energy for WSI to continue operating its Central Training Academy near Albuquerque, New Mexico. Earlier in the year, WSI had signed a one-year, $5 million agreement with Olin Defense Systems Group, the prime contractor at the U.S. Army's Lake City Army Ammunition Plant in Independence, Missouri. That contract had four one-year options for renewal.

On Wednesday evening, July 25, 1990, Cole was at home when he received a call from John Tuck, who was undersecretary of the DOE at that time. "I remember it was funny, because it was one of the few days when I was home," Cole recalls. "It was about six o'clock in the evening and I was out washing my car. Betsy came to the door and said, 'There's a John Tuck on the phone for you from Washington.' And I thought: Oh, shit, we've either done something really *bad*, or this is obviously going to be a really interesting phone call. Because it was extremely unusual for someone like John Tuck to call me at home in the evening."

The call was about the security situation at a DOE nuclear weapons production facility named the Rocky Flats Plant, located approximately sixteen miles northwest of Denver, Colorado, and was then operated by EG&G Rocky Flats, a subsidiary of EG&G, Inc., headquartered in Wellesley, Massachusetts. The facility occupies 384 acres amid a 6,500-acre natural preserve (buffer zone). Rocky Flats was first operated by the Dow Chemical Company when it was constructed in 1952. Rockwell International operated the plant from 1975 to 1989. EG&G, Inc., had assumed operating responsibilities on January 1, 1990, and was providing its own security force. Actually, EG&G had taken over on a sole-source basis, because Rockwell had basically given up, and asked to be relieved of its responsibilities. However, the FBI conducted a night raid to test the new security system at Rocky Flats in July of 1990, leading to a very serious, classified incident, which was the reason for John Tuck's emergency call.

"I went in and took the call," Cole says, "and he talked about the extremely poor state of security at Rocky Flats. He stressed that this was really an extraordinary kind of thing, and that they had decided that the only way they were going to fix Rocky Flats was to bring in experts, the very best in the nation, to deal with it. Hence, as they examined the situation, they wanted to know what organization could come in and fix this. And he said, 'The Wackenhut name just jumped to the fore.' Consequently, he called me.

"He asked if we would consider assuming the security mission at Rocky Flats, under direct contract to DOE. Immediately, my comment was, 'Absolutely, yes, we would, and when would you like us to start?' And I believe his response was, 'Well, how quickly can you get there?' I said, 'I'll be there tomorrow, late tomorrow night, and I'll meet with Mr. Nelson the following day.' Which is exactly what happened. Bob Nelson was the senior DOE manager at Rocky Flats at the time. That conversation with John Tuck was probably a five-minute conversation, in which I expressed that we would put every possible corporate resource we had on the problem. Because, at that point, they had the major inspection and evaluation scheduled for October. And that was necessary before production could resume. Now, understand, that was at the point before the Cold War ended. DOE was still thinking of going back into production mode, so this was probably the singular most important event that could happen to allow them to get back into the resumption of production.

"After my talk with John Tuck, Bob Nelson called me maybe two minutes later, and we talked at length. He expressed his appreciation for us stepping up to this challenge, and said that if anybody could do it, it would be Wackenhut. He stressed that it was an extremely bad security situation, the culture was the root cause of the problem that had been formed over a number of years, that there was no documentation, no control of policies and procedures. The supervisor-to-security inspector ratio was twenty to one, and needed to be about seven or eight to one. They were short sixty-three men."

At noon on Thursday, July 26, 1990, the DOE issued the following press release:

Rocky Flats Announces Security Service Contractor

ROCKY FLATS—The U.S. Department of Energy (DOE) at Rocky Flats today announced the selection of Wackenhut Services Incorporated (WSI) as the security services contractor for the facility.

DOE Plant Manager Robert M. Nelson said he was pleased that the Secretary of Energy, James D. Watkins, had responded so quickly to the recommendations made by the Rocky Flats Office and its operating contractor, EG&G, to bring in a contractor with extensive security experience and immediate resources.

"We've spent the majority of the summer evaluating security and safeguards issues and procedures," Nelson said. "And as we recently reported, several serious deficiencies have been identified. These reviews and recent events have demonstrated an urgent need for this action.

"It is a real plus because it will provide the facility with standardized, well-tested procedures and modes of operation, and access to additional Q-cleared supervisors and inspectors," Nelson said. "In addition, the DOE office at Rocky Flats is being augmented with additional resources for safeguards and security oversight."

Phil Warner, EG&G Plant Manager, explained the transition would have no tangible impact on the guards currently employed by Rocky Flats. "The members of the force will remain with the new contractor, who will provide substantial expertise and additional resources," Warner said. "We will make this transition as smooth as possible for everyone involved. We will be talking with WSI this week and will make the transition in the near future."

Wackenhut Services Incorporated is based in Coral Gables, Florida. The firm currently provides security to numerous government and privately owned facilities, including DOE facilities at the Nevada Test Site, the Savannah River Plant, and the Central Training Academy in Albuquerque. WSI employs some 40,000 persons in 43 countries to include embassy, corporate and airport security.

"The telephone call was July 25, and I met with Bob Nelson at eight-thirty in the morning on July 27," Cole remembers. "We discussed what needed to be looked at, everything from the firing range, which was not safe, physical training was bad, there was a serious cultural problem. He wanted me to speak with the union president right away, and I'd already had that scheduled. We had to assume the collective bargaining agreement. A lot of the SIs had red badges, which meant that their 'Q' clearance had not yet been approved. There were about 100 people in that status.

"After the meeting with Bob Nelson, I met with Jim Vissar, the union president. He walked in with his number-two man, and I was there with John Evans, who was our senior vice president of Operations at that time. Mr. Vissar came in and sat down and pulled out a big jar of *Vaseline* and set it on the table. There was some comment, you know, he figured I was there to screw him, so he wanted to be ready for it! Which was not a very pleasant way to start it off. But the rumors were that we were going to *fire* everybody, we were going to bring in a whole new work force of 300 to 500 people. I mean, rumors were just running crazy: We were going to cut all the wages, cut all the benefits.

"But, of course, part of the agreement I had with Mr. Nelson was that we've got to leave everything basically status quo, in terms of pay and benefits. And, as these people transition from EG&G to us, their benefits have to remain absolutely the same, there can't be any reduction in either direct or indirect pay or benefits. He agreed to all that, so it was handled fine. But there were a multitude of things going on there that made it very difficult.

"Basically, we took the force two days later, Monday, July 30, 1990, at five-thirty in the morning, 'troop muster.' We had no offices. We had EG&G as a reluctant partner in this, they didn't willingly give this up. So we had that very tenuous relationship with EG&G. We had an organization within DOE that was in a state of complete flux. At that point, Bob Nelson was a temporary manager, and a lot of their organization was not yet complete. They went from being an area office to a field office. In DOE terms, that means different staffing and responsibilities. Before we came in, Rocky Flats reported to Albuquerque, and then Albuquerque reported to Washington. Now, Rocky Flats reported directly to Washington.

"Then, in early August, we had the Hiroshima-Nagasaki anniversaries. Rocky Flats is close to Boulder, and there's an anti-nuclear community of people there that always demonstrate. So, we were there, obviously picking up a new contract, hostile union, demonstrations coming up, a state of disarray within EG&G *and* DOE. So, in hindsight, I must admit I'm not sure I would've said, 'When would you like us to start?' It would have been a little more gradual transition.

"Over the course of the next nine months to a year, we brought in around 100 new people from sites around the country. And, of course, over the first year we were there, we brought the strength up to what it should have been. We had to keep the guard force that was already in place, because there was a union there, a local union of the UPGWA, United Plant Guard Workers. We had a relationship with that union from other sites around the country. I kept George and Rick informed, and I believe they briefed the board. But it was a very difficult transition, and continues almost to this day. I mean, Rocky Flats is such a peculiar and unique site.

"The estimated revenue for the two-year contract was $61.2 million, but that was underestimated. It was about $100 million. We had an interim sixty-day contract, and I think they added it as a modification to the Nevada Test Site contract. Then, Nelson and I signed a contract on October 1, 1990, and that was a two-year contract from that point. So we had about a two-month interim modification of the NTS contract that we used, then we had a two-year contract directly with Rocky Flats. Then it was re-competed in an early 1992 time frame, and ultimately we were selected for another three years, plus a two-year option.

"During the first two-month period, about half my time, or more, was spent at Rocky Flats. Over the first two years, I probably spent, I would say, a minimum of one week a month. Then, from January to April of '92, I ran the project, I became the existing general manager, and the DOE was being very, very, very critical, and we had another I&E that was scheduled in March, so I spent lots of time out there.

"Naturally, there weren't a lot of humorous anecdotes, because of what was at stake out there, in terms of trying to pass different kinds of inspections and evaluations in order to resume production. It was a very stressful period. I know DOE had several changes in personnel at the senior level; EG&G also had several. There were what I would call 'bodies all over the place.' I mean, people were being fired and retired and lots of stress. The Admiral had not visited Rocky Flats during the period that we had become involved. And I was told that he would not visit Rocky Flats until they had passed all of their inspections and evaluations, and resumption of production was cleared. And on that day, he would raise a flag on a ship's mast outside of the main portal that allows entrance into the production facility. And, sure enough, there's a ship's mast in front of the main portal. And there was never a flag raised on it.

"On a trip George Wackenhut made with me to Rocky Flats in mid- to late-1992, Admiral Watkins did visit, and there were several dignitaries there, and they had a ceremony in which the chairman made some comments. And they *raised the flag*, the American flag, and we had a Wackenhut flag, and a DOE flag, and it was quite an event. This was probably, I want to say July, in that time period of '92.

"We now have approximately 400 personnel in place at Rocky Flats. Our annual revenue today is about $40 million. It's kind of hard to put numbers on things, because of the way in which the complex is—not shrinking, but contracting—since the end of the Cold War. Because what they do, when you don't produce nuclear material, you just put it all in one place and store it, and that really alters your protection strategy, which alters numbers of people. But I think those numbers are close enough."

IN AUGUST 1990, the government of Venezuela presented a national award to George Wackenhut in recognition of the entrepreneurial spirit exemplified by TWC and its Venezuelan partner in the performance of private security and investigative services over the past twenty-five years. Venezuelan Minister of Labor Dr. German Lairet awarded George the Labor Order of Merit, First Class, at ceremonies in the capital city of Caracas.

In 1964, TWC formed a partnership with José Antonio Olavarria and Ricardo Zuloaga in Venezuela. That company, Venezolana de Seguridad y Vigilancia, C.A., was the initial international expansion for TWC. In 1990, Wackenhut International, Inc., had successful operations in more than forty other countries.

At the October 27, 1990, meeting of the board of directors, Sandra L. Nusbaum was elected vice president, Human Resources, the first female corporate vice president in the history of The Wackenhut Corporation. Nusbaum, who had been with TWC since 1981, was previously director, Compensation and Benefits, manager of EEO and Affirmative Action Programs, and a Personnel representative. A graduate of Florida International University, she was a member of the Personnel Association of Greater Miami, the American Compensation Association, and served on the board of directors for Family Counseling Services.

At the same board meeting, Michael A. DiGregorio was elected senior vice president, Finance, and chief financial officer of TWC, replacing G. Calvin Harris, the former CFO, who retired on August 31, 1990, after eleven years with TWC. DiGregorio had been vice president, Finance, since October 1989. Prior to that, he spent eleven years with the Gillette Company in a progression of financial positions, including a total of seven years of experience in Gillette's offices in Mexico, Spain, and England. Previously, he worked two years in the Audit Department of Touche, Ross and Company in Boston. A graduate of the University of Pennsylvania, where he earned a bachelor's degree in accounting, he also held a master's degree in financial management from the university's Wharton Graduate School.

When Wackenhut Corrections Corporation held dedication ceremonies November 29, to mark the opening of the newly constructed 610-bed medium-security Allen Correctional Center in Allen Parish, Louisiana, it achieved a significant milestone: The operation of eleven major correctional/detention facilities in seven states, all in less than four years. The Allen Center would be operated by WCC under contract to the Louisiana Department of Public Safety and Corrections. The facility would begin accepting prisoners on December 4, and was expected to be filled to near capacity before the end of that month, thus partially relieving overcrowded conditions in other state correctional facilities.

Louisiana Governor Buddy Roemer attended the ceremonies and congratulated both the Wackenhut staff and Louisiana officials for bringing the facility into operation. Other officials attending included Tim Cole, who had been promoted to senior vice president of TWC's newly created Government Services Group, WCC President George C. Zoley, Secretary of the Department of Public Safety and Corrections Bruce Lynn, State Senator John Saunders, State Representative James Davis Cain, and Allen County Sheriff John Claiborne Durio.

Situated on 857 acres, the center's design includes two dormitories with eight separate living areas, security walkways, a management building, an infirmary, a full-service laundry and kitchen, educational and library areas, staff training rooms, and central dining and recreational facilities. It was built by the State of Louisiana at a cost of $27 million.

WCC's warden for the new center was Larry Jeane, an experienced administrator previously employed by the Louisiana Department of Corrections. WCC would employ 210 people to operate the facility and its rehabilitative and support services; 73 percent of the employees were recruited from Allen Parish, and 25 percent lived in its neighboring counties.

Earlier in the year, WCC assumed management of the Monroe County jail facilities, under a contract to Monroe County, the southernmost county in Florida. WCC began operation February 13, 1990, and, according to George Zoley, "hired all former county jail employees, guaranteeing they would suffer no loss of wages or benefits." WCC was then performing the operation, management, and transport responsibilities for the 220-bed Key West jail, a substation in Marathon, and a forty-six-bed modular jail in Plantation. Another recent WCC contract was renewed by the City of Detroit, Michigan, to provide court security and detention services for the Michigan 36th District Court for another four years.

Before year's end, Murray Levine's Custom Protection Division negotiated a major contract and assumed security responsibilities for the Metro-Dade Agency's Metrorail, the relatively new twenty-one mile elevated rail line in South Florida that runs from the populous suburb of Kendall through downtown Miami all the way north to Hialeah. The contract for Metrorail included all stations along the route, plus additional stations on the 1.9-mile elevated downtown Metromover (peoplemover), and also a number of Metro-Dade courthouses.

To fulfill its new contract, CPD recruited, hired, and trained more than 130 Custom Protection Officers, whose primary responsibility would be to ensure the safety of Metrorail passengers. Following Levine's original requirements, the CPOs special qualifications included military or civilian law-enforcement training and background, academic and physical-fitness requirements, and completion of a special training program. Some of the officers were recruited from Wackenhut sites in other states, and all were licensed by the State of Florida. The Metro-Dade contract would be in effect for three years and would represent revenues in excess of $15 million. A minority-owned firm, Alanis Security, Inc., was a participant as a subcontractor to TWC, and would also provide security personnel with similar qualifications at designated Metrorail stations.

WORLDWIDE headline history for the year 1990 included General Manuel Noriega's surrender to U.S. troops in Panama on January 3. On January 22, the Yugoslav Communist Party ended its forty-five year monopoly of power. January 24, Richard V. Secord was convicted in the Iran-Contra affair. February 5, Nicaraguan opposition crushed the Sandinistas at the polls. February 11, the Soviet Communist Party relinquished its sole power. February 11, South Africa freed Nelson Mandela after more than twenty-seven years of imprisonment. April 25, Violeta Barrios de Chamorro was inaugurated as president of Nicaragua. June 26, President Bush broke his "no new taxes" pledge because of a budget agreement. July 2, Imelda Marcos was acquitted in New York of raiding the Philippine Treasury. July 6, the Western Alliance ended the Cold War and proposed joint action with the Soviet Union and Eastern Europe. July 20, a U.S. Appeals Court overturned Oliver North's Iran-Contra conviction. August 2, Iraqi troops invaded Kuwait and seized its petroleum reserves, starting the Persian Gulf War. August 31, East and West Germany were reunited. September 30, President Bush and congressional leaders agreed on a drastic budget-reduction plan. October 28, Congress passed a budget-reducing measure with new taxes and spending cuts. November 8, the Republicans were set back in midterm elections. November 17, Soviet President Gorbachev assumed emergency powers. November 21, leaders of thirty-four nations in Europe and North America proclaimed a united Europe. November 22, Margaret Thatcher resigned as British Prime Minister; on November 28, John Major succeeded her. December 9, Lech Walesa won Poland's runoff presidential election.

TWC's ANNUAL REPORT for the year 1990 contains a number of highlights that speak rather strongly for the excellent condition of the company at the close of the year: Record revenues of $521.191 million, up 12.8 percent from the previous year, accompanied by record earnings of $6.963 million, an increase of 18.5 percent compared to 1989, and an average shareholders' interest of 19.5 percent. This, of course, was the thirty-sixth straight year of increased revenues.

Although the covert investigation into the operations of Charles Hamel lasted less than seven months, it would have serious ramifications for more than three years. On September 25, 1990, J.P. Wellington, Alyeska's director of security, telephoned Wayne Black and told him that the owners had decided to terminate the investigation. Black immediately cancelled a meeting with Hamel scheduled for the next day. Black's instructions were to cease taping immediately and disengage from Hamel as credibly as possible without unnecessarily raising Hamel's suspicions.

Rick Lund immediately removed all electronic surveillance equipment. Sherree Rich stayed on in the Virginia Ecolit office for an additional month. Hamel called the office twice during the first two to three weeks. During the last (fourth) week, he called every day.

Hamel was quite upset. He stated that he had third parties interested in Ecolit and its inactivity had caused him embarrassment.

Black told Hamel that Ecolit had lost its funding and that he had obtained a new job in the insurance industry. The Ecolit office in Virginia was closed on November 1, 1990. Rent was paid for the Ecolit office in Miami through December 31, 1990, although no significant activities were being conducted from that office subsequent to September 25. However, Hamel remained in sporadic telephone contact with Black through December.

In a telephone conversation between Hamel and Black in late November, 1990, Hamel expressed his displeasure with Black's announcement that he was getting out of the environmental litigation business. Hamel said that he would try to get Congressman Miller to subpoena Black as a way of keeping him "in the business." Black told Hamel that he had nothing to tell Miller, because Ecolit had just started when its operations were shut down. Hamel agreed and did not pursue the idea of a subpoena from Miller.

Also in November, Alyeska employee Bob Scott was terminated for cause, unrelated to the Wackenhut investigation. Alyeska was advised that Scott had retained counsel in connection with his discharge. If Scott decided to sue Alyeska, it was entirely possible that the Wackenhut investigation would be required to be disclosed to Scott and his counsel through discovery. If that happened, Scott would obviously tell Hamel anything he learned about the Wackenhut investigation.

On December 21, 1990, Hamel telephoned the Ecolit Miami telephone number, which rang at Wackenhut headquarters. The call was answered by a Wackenhut employee. Hamel asked for Wayne Jenkins. When the Wackenhut operator was unable to reach Black, she called Adriana Caputi in Special Investigations, who returned Hamel's call. Hamel told her that he was anxious to speak with Wayne Jenkins.

The Ecolit telephone number was then disconnected.

31

THE PERSIAN GULF WAR was, of course, the major historical event of 1991, and exactly 201 TWC employees were called to active duty in the armed forces. When Iraq invaded Kuwait in 1990, after talks broke down over oil production and debt repayment, Iraqi President Saddam Hussein annexed Kuwait and declared it a nineteenth province of Iraq. President Bush believed that Iraq intended to invade Saudi Arabia and take control of the region's oil supplies. Therefore, he began organizing a multinational coalition to seek Kuwait's freedom and restoration of its legitimate government. The U.N. Security Council authorized economic sanctions against Iraq. On August 6, 1990, President Bush ordered U.S. troops to protect Saudi Arabia, at the Saudis' request, and "Operation Desert Shield" began. More than 230,000 American troops arrived in Saudi Arabia to take defensive action, but when Iraq continued a huge military buildup in Kuwait, Bush ordered an additional 200,000 troops deployed to prepare for a possible offensive action by the U.S.-led coalition forces. He subsequently obtained a U.N. Security Council resolution (November 8) setting a January 15, 1991, deadline for Iraq to withdraw unconditionally from Kuwait.

On January 16, 1991, Bush won congressional approval for his position with the most devastating air assault in history against military targets in Iraq and Kuwait. On February 22, Bush rejected a Soviet-Iraq peace plan for a gradual withdrawal that did not comply with all the U.N. resolutions, and gave Iraq an ultimatum to withdraw from Kuwait by noon of February 23. When this ultimatum was rejected, Bush ordered the ground war to begin on February 24.

During "Operation Desert Storm," in a brilliant and lightening-fast campaign, U.S. and coalition forces smashed through Iraq's defenses and defeated Saddam Hussein's troops in only four days of combat. When the Allies entered Kuwait City on February 26, the Iraqi Army set fire to over 500 of Kuwait's oil wells as a final act of destruction to Kuwait's infrastructure. On February 27, Bush ordered a unilateral cease-fire, 100 hours after the ground offensive started. On March 3, Allied and Iraq military leaders met on the battlefield to discuss terms for a formal cease-fire to end the Gulf War.

The first Allied prisoners of war were released on March 4. The official cease-fire was accepted and signed on April 6. More than 532,000 U.S. forces served in Operation Desert Storm. There were a total of 148 U.S. battle deaths during the Gulf War, 145 nonbattle deaths, and 467 wounded in action. No comprehensive casualty figures were released by Iraq.

In the April 1991 issue of *Pipeline*, published in a new tabloid-size format, and devoting a full page to the names and offices of all 201 TWC employees who were called to active duty in the armed forces, George wrote a column in the "Chairman's Corner" that provided a personalized perspective about the Persian Gulf War, when he quoted from a letter received from a young TWC employee who had been called to active duty.

Letter From a Soldier

Recently, our project manager at the Strategic Petroleum Reserve in New Orleans, Louisiana, received a letter from a protection officer who had been called to active service in the U.S. Army Infantry. His name is Spec. Michael Hebert and he was training at Fort Hood, Texas, scheduled to be sent to the Persian Gulf in March.

I want to share part of his letter with you, because I think this young man's comments are indicative of all the correspondence we have received, both in the field and at headquarters, from dedicated TWC employees who are currently serving in the armed forces of the United States.

Spec. Hebert writes:

"You have sent a letter showing your support for me and the rest of the employees who have been called up to serve our country. I would like to take this time to thank you for the training you have given me. It has played a big role in helping me to get ready for active duty. In particular, the training I received on the ranges helped me to obtain an Expert rating on the .45-caliber automatic for day, night, and NBC shooting. The training proved to be great.

"I sure hope that we do what we have to do over there and come back. I have never seen so many changes in people in my life. The rest of my unit has come together as one. I think we will get our mission done. Thank you for your support and caring. It has made me a little stronger."

The last paragraph of Spec. Hebert's letter made me smile: "Sir," he wrote, "Infantry soldiers never die, they just go to hell to regroup and come back to finish the mission."

As a former Army enlisted man and officer who served in World War II, I understand only too well how important mail is to anyone in the armed forces, particularly when you are far from home, family, and friends. Letters are extremely important to morale. I hope all of our employees, especially in offices that have men and women now serving their country, will make an effort to write individual letters of support.

By doing so, you will make an important contribution to our collective effort.

Earlier in the year, in ceremonies conducted at headquarters February 12, TWC's Nuclear Services Division was the recipient of Florida Power & Light Company's coveted Quality Supplier Award. In making the presentation, Bruce Guilbeault, FPL's director of Nuclear Materials Management, stated: "FPL is honored to recognize Wackenhut's Nuclear Services Division as a Quality Supplier for the year 1990. Your organization has distinguished itself through its commitment to the principles of continuous quality improvement and customer satisfaction. I might add that you are in fact one of the few companies among our 4,000 active suppliers to receive this award.

Wackenhut's commitment to quality places it at the forefront of a resurgence in American industry. Your achievement represents our common understanding that competitiveness is irrefutably linked with quality."

On February 18, George welcomed back a veteran of twenty-three years with the corporation, J.A. (Ed) Le Blanc, who was named president of Wackenhut Airline Services, Inc. For the past two years, Le Blanc had been president of Alert Management Systems, a subsidiary of the Pan Am Corporation, with responsibility for uniformed security service for Pan American World Airways and other airlines in Europe, the Near East, South and Central America, and the United States.

In his new position, Le Blanc would be responsible for developing TWC security services for the commercial aviation industry. He was associated with several airlines before joining TWC in 1966, serving as station manager for National Airlines in Philadelphia, and as district sales manager for Swissair in Cleveland. Starting with TWC as an investigator, Le Blanc later became manager of Internal Intelligence, area manager in San Francisco, and had several positions in Domestic Operations at headquarters. He became director of Airline Services in 1980.

In another major appointment during February, Arthur A. English, the former commissioner of the Alaska Department of Public Safety, joined TWC as vice president of Alaska Operations. English had a distinguished career in law enforcement and public service, including twenty-one years as an Alaska State Trooper. He was a 1977 graduate of the National Academy of the FBI in Quantico, Virginia. Prior to his cabinet-level appointment by the governor of Alaska in 1987, English was vice president of Purcell Security, Inc. He was born in Seldovia, Alaska, and was a veteran of the U.S. Air Force, where he served as an air policeman.

At Domestic Operations' sixth annual banquet held March 2 in Coconut Grove, Florida, for the Top Performance Club, Rene Pedrayes, area manager in Miami, was selected Area Manager of the Year for 1990. During that year, the total gross revenues generated by the Miami area office amounted to $17.471 million.

At the April board meeting, Alan Bernstein, who celebrated his fifteenth anniversary with TWC earlier in the year, was elected president of the Domestic Operations Group, and executive vice president of TWC. At the same meeting, Tim Cole was elected president of the Government Services Group, and executive vice president of TWC. Juan Miyar, who joined the company in 1973 as a staff accountant, was elected vice president, controller, and assistant treasurer of the corporation. The board also announced the election of Marc Shapiro as vice president of the newly created Marketing Department. Paul Brownell was elected vice president of the Tax Department. Edward Kuncar, who joined TWC in 1975, was elected vice president of WII's International Development.

July 1, TWC commenced a three-year, $8.1 million contract with R.J. Reynolds Tobacco Company to provide security and firewatch services to its headquarters and manufacturing facilities in Winston-Salem, North Carolina. Founded in 1875 by Richard Joshua Reynolds in the small town of Winston, the firm grew quickly and was incorporated in North Carolina in 1890. Quality products and successful advertising campaigns combined to make the company prosperous. During 1991, R.J. Reynolds employed more than 10,000 people in the state and utilized the most sophisticated automated manufacturing equipment available to process over 8,000 cigarettes per minute per machine for shipment worldwide.

Upon being awarded the contract, TWC immediately prepared a transition plan and organized a start-up team. Al Guastella, senior vice president, Domestic Operations Group, appointed Jim Shrum, manager of Operations, to head up the team. Shrum was assisted by two other managers of Operations, Cathy Ross and Mike Munk, and two quality assurance analysts from Computer Services, Danny Garcia and Ana Tirador.

Also in July, after nearly a year of research and negotiations, TWC announced the creation of Wackenhut Monitoring Systems, Inc. (WMSI), a wholly owned subsidiary that would specialize in providing electronic monitoring of probationers and parolees, and technological support to government and correctional areas.

In making the announcement, Rick Wackenhut named Tim Cole as president of WMSI and said that Cole would continue as president of WSI and Wackenhut Applied Technologies Center, Inc.

Named senior vice president of WSI was J. Allison DeFoor II, thirty-eight, a former sheriff of Monroe County, Florida, who was the Republican Party nominee for lieutenant governor of Florida as the running-mate of Governor Bob Martinez in his unsuccessful campaign for reelection in the 1990 gubernatorial race.

The genesis of the acquisition dated back to 1989, when Budd Kneip started research at the National Institute of Justice (NIJ), Southeast Missouri State University, and Kutztown University of Pennsylvania. Both universities maintained criminal justice departments that had a specific interest in electronic monitoring.

"Through initial discussions at NIJ and with individuals at those two universities," Kneip says, "we began to look at the marketplace—what was involved, what relationship it might have to what we're doing, and whether there was a heavy product end that we'd have to be sensitive to. We also had discussions with a couple of companies, one that manufactures the equipment, and one that manufactures and services the equipment."

As a result of that research, it was clear to senior management that the marketplace for electronic monitoring would be defined and informed by two constants: (1) as a consequence of the ever-increasing number of criminal prosecutions, jails and prisons would continue to be constructed, staffed, and maintained, thereby strengthening the market position established by Wackenhut Corrections Corporation; (2) there would be ever-increasing pressures on government agencies at local, state, and federal levels to relieve chronically overcrowded jails and prisons, and to explore alternative means of incarceration for offenders who obviously did not constitute a serious threat to society.

According to DeFoor, the NIJ began compiling figures on the utilization of electronic monitoring in 1986. "During those years," he says, "NIJ reported a sixteen-fold jump in the use of electronic monitoring. Experts generally attribute this growth to the expansion of programs targeted to offenders who would otherwise have been incarcerated."

Forced to make room for new prisoners, the parole boards, judges, and sheriffs had discovered that electronic monitoring made it possible to retain some control over offenders who must be released but who would not have been released except for severe institutional overcrowding.

"We did normal due-diligence," DeFoor says, "and found very high levels of customer satisfaction out in the field. We went to a representative sample of local and state administrations, places as diverse as Orange County, Florida, and Los Angeles, and in virtually all cases we found a very high degree of satisfaction with the whole philosophy of electronic monitoring."

How does the system work? Electronic surveillance systems that are used to monitor individuals at a specific location are generally divided into two categories: "active" and "passive."

Active systems are those in which a transmitter is attached to the participant's ankle or wrist with a tamper-resistant strap. The transmitter sends a signal every two minutes on a continuous basis. A Field Monitoring Device (FMD) is placed in the participant's residence and receives the signals from the transmitter. The FMD uses normal telephone lines to make reports to the central computer.

The FMD is capable of reporting each time a participant enters or leaves the residence or tampers with the equipment. The host computer can be programmed with an unlimited variety of schedules to accommodate the participants' work schedules. The active system produces an "alarm" with each exception to the predetermined curfew hours, or if the participant tampers with either the transmitter or the FMD. The alarm is transmitted immediately by telephone line to the central computer.

The central computer must be manned on a twenty-four hour basis. Instructions for the handling of alarms are dictated by the client agencies and are programmed into the central computer at the time a participant is added to the system. When an alarm is received by the central computer, the computer operator will follow the instructions concerning notification of designated authorities at the client agency. Notification can be immediate or as otherwise directed by the agency. Written reports are also available as may be required.

Passive systems are those in which a central computer places random telephone calls to the participant's home (or other specific place being monitored). The participant is required to use an electronic identifier, usually attached to his wrist, to identify himself. In other words, the equipment is passive and the participant is active, using the equipment for identification to answer a call from a central computer.

Passive systems are only able to verify that the participant is home at the time of the phone call, when in fact he may be gone in-between calls. In addition, random calls during night hours may be deemed to be an infringement on the rights of others living in the same location as the participant.

During 1991, electronic monitoring systems were being used in forty-seven states, at municipal and county jails, and in state corrections systems. The growth had been significant and steady since 1986. The preliminary estimate for monitored individuals in the U.S. during 1990 was 12,000. Estimates for the *potential* monitored population in the U.S. have ranged from 100,000 to more than one million.

In early August, Wackenhut Corrections Corporation expanded its services to an international scale when it won a contract to help design, build, and operate a prison in Australia to be called the Junee Correctional Centre, as part of a consortium known as Australasian Correctional Services. In addition to WCC, members of the group included ADT of Australia, and PTY Ltd., an Australian-based construction subsidiary of the Leighton Group.

The Junee complex would house up to 600 male prisoners and was being developed on 250 hectares of land outside the Junee township in southwestern New South Wales. Work on the site had already commenced when the contract was signed with the Government of New South Wales on August 7, and it was envisioned that the facility would be completed and operational by mid-1993. ADT and Wackenhut formed a joint venture known as Australasian Correctional Management PTY, Ltd., to manage the prison and explore other business opportunities. When completed, the Junee Correctional Centre would employ a staff of about 225 people.

CONGRESSMAN George Miller, a Democrat who had represented the seventh California district since 1975, was chairman of the Committee on Interior and Insular Affairs in 1991 when he wrote the following letter to George Wackenhut, via Telecopier and Federal Express, dated August 7, 1991:

Dear Mr. Wackenhut:

Pursuant to its authority under Rule X, clauses 1 (1) and 2 of the Rules of the House of Representatives, the Committee on Interior and Insular Affairs is investigating allegations that The Wackenhut Corporation and/or its contractors conducted undercover surveillance and investigation of Mr. Charles Hamel on behalf of Alyeska Pipeline Service Company and/or any of its member corporations (including Exxon Corporation and any of its subsidiaries or related entities) for the purpose of obtaining information on and/or interfering with Mr. Hamel's communications with the Committee.

In furtherance of this investigation, please provide the Committee on or before September 6, 1991, with all documents and records (including correspondence, memoranda, notes, reports, disks, audiotapes and transcripts of any audiotapes) in your possession or control relating to any investigation or surveillance of Mr. Charles Hamel, specifically including but not limited to: all such documents and records kept at 1500 San Remo Avenue in Coral Gables, Florida; all documents and records regarding Wackenhut Investigation No. 427; all daily activity logs, diaries, and telephone logs for persons involved in or aware of the undercover operation; all documents and records of payment made in furtherance of the undercover operation; all documents or records obtained in any manner from Mr. Hamel.

Please be advised that failure to preserve documents and records which are the subject of a Congressional investigation may be a criminal offense.

Should you have any questions regarding this matter, please contact Jeffrey Petrich or Linda Chase at (202) 225-2761.

On the same date, virtually identical letters from Miller were sent via Telecopier and Federal Express to: James B. Hermiller, president, Alyeska Pipeline Service Company; Pat Wellington, manager, Corporate Security, Alyeska Pipeline Service Company; L.R. Raymond, president, Exxon Corporation; W.D. Stevens, president, Exxon Company, U.S.A.; Alan Bernstein, president, Domestic Operations

Group, TWC; Wayne Black, who had been promoted to vice president, Special Investigations, TWC; Richard Lund, Special Investigations, TWC; and Gilfredo Mugarra, Special Investigations, TWC.

That's a total of ten men, none of whom wanted such potentially image-damaging information leaked to the press. However, just eight days later, when reporter David Bloom broke his exclusive story about the congressional investigation on the NBC affiliate WTVJ-TV in Miami, he held in his hand a copy of that letter, and even quoted from its opening paragraph. That exclusive triggered an almost immediate avalanche of national publicity.

By Monday, August 19, the publicity had become so widespread and exaggerated that Rick Wackenhut issued the following memo to all TWC managers, supervisors, and headquarters' department heads:

> There have been numerous reports on television and in the newspapers in the last few days regarding an investigation conducted by The Wackenhut Corporation.
>
> Unfortunately, the media has accepted statements from unreliable sources who are giving them inaccuracies and distortions regarding the investigative practices of the Corporation.
>
> As the Chairman of the Board stated to a television reporter during a videotape interview on the subject of the investigation, The Wackenhut Corporation "did nothing illicit, illegal, or even irregular. That, I can guarantee."
>
> The Special Investigations Division carried out a complex investigation to a satisfactory conclusion, and in a highly professional manner. However, Florida law and our typical client-investigator confidentiality agreements prevent us from releasing information regarding the specifics of the case.
>
> If we are able to provide specific responses to the allegations at a later date, we will do so, and keep our employees informed. In the meantime, we remain firm in the conclusion that all investigative techniques employed in this operation were legal, ethical, and in keeping with the high professional standards of our Corporation.

Congressman Miller's letter was answered on September 5, 1991, by James P. Rowan, TWC's vice president and general counsel, who stated in part:

Prior to your Committee's request, we had already turned over virtually all of the requested materials to Alyeska at their direction. In furtherance of your Committee's investigation, we have turned over copies of all such materials remaining in our possession to Alyeska, at their request, and we understand that Alyeska is in turn arranging to deliver all of these materials to your office in cooperation with the Committee's request, except for those Attorney/Client documents for which they may claim privilege. . . .

On September 6, David W. Marquez, Alyeska's general counsel, mailed Congressman Miller five document boxes containing sixty-one "file pockets" relating to the investigation. Some file pockets contained individual items, while others contained multiple items. In addition, Marquez attached to his letter a brief narrative describing the origin and course of the investigation. His narrative follows, in part:

Background

Alyeska had for some time prior to 1990 been concerned about leaks of confidential corporate documents and information. For example, Alyeska's Security Department had during 1987–88 attempted to identify the source of a hand-drawn diagram of Alyeska's ballast water treatment system that was furnished by an unknown person to Trustees for Alaska, Inc. During 1989, Alaska police authorities impounded a stolen vehicle that had been used in a burglary. The trunk of the vehicle contained a box of Alyeska documents that subsequent inquiry determined had been received by the Environmental Protection Agency ("EPA") from Charles F. Hamel ("Hamel"). Those documents were being returned to Hamel by the EPA when they (in a manner never determined) came to be in the trunk of the stolen vehicle. Finally, on January 30, 1990, during the course of an episode of the British television program, "The Scottish Eye," dealing with operations of British Petroleum Company, a highly confidential and privileged Alyeska attorney-client communication was shown on camera.

Shortly after the showing of the above-mentioned episode of the Scottish Eye, Alyeska President James B. Hermiller ("Hermiller") expressed his concern to Alyeska's Manager of Corporate Security, J. Patrick Wellington ("Wellington") about continuing leaks and asked Wellington for his suggestions.

The Investigation

Wellington proposed to Hermiller than an undercover investigation be conducted for the purpose of identifying leaks within Alyeska. Wellington advised against informing Alyeska in-house counsel of the investigation because at that time he was concerned that leaks might exist within Alyeska's legal department. Wellington also recommended against informing the owners of Alyeska of the investigation because any matter conveyed to the owners necessarily would become known to a large number of people in widely scattered locations. Hermiller accepted these recommendations from Wellington.

Upon Wellington's recommendation and with Hermiller's approval, Alyeska retained The Wackenhut Corporation ("Wackenhut") to conduct the investigation. Wayne B. Black ("Black"), Director of Wackenhut's Special Investigations Division, was in charge of the investigation for Wackenhut. Wellington instructed Black that the investigation was to be legal, with no "sex, booze or drugs," and was to focus on locating all leaks within Alyeska. Hamel was identified to Black as a recipient of leaked documents.

Wellington advised Black that Hamel was very talkative and that an undercover investigator might be able to win Hamel's confidence. Wellington suggested to Black that the Alaska Frontier Conference, to be held in Anchorage commencing on March 24, 1990, could provide an opportunity to meet Hamel, who might attend the conference.

Black created an unincorporated entity known as The Ecolit Group ("Ecolit"), which purported to be involved in environmental litigation. A small office was opened in Coral Gables, Florida, and business cards and brochures were printed.

On or about March 24, 1990, Wackenhut agents traveled to Anchorage. No contact was made with Hamel at the Alaska Frontier Conference but, by coincidence, Hamel and Wackenhut agent Ricki S. Jacobson ("Jacobson") were on the same return flight from Anchorage to Seattle. Hamel and Jacobson engaged in conversation for the length of the flight between Anchorage and Seattle. Hamel told Jacobson about his activities and was advised by Jacobson that she was employed by Ecolit, which was engaged in environmental research. Jacobson gave Ecolit's Coral Gables telephone number to Hamel.

Shortly after the Alaska Frontier Conference, Wackenhut agents went to Valdez, Alaska, to attempt to identify possible leaks within Alyeska. Ecolit advertisements were placed in local newspapers and Ecolit leaflets were placed on Alyeska employees' automobiles in an attempt to establish contact with Alyeska employees who might have been the source of leaked documents.

These efforts to locate leaks within Alyeska were not successful; however, Hamel became aware of the Ecolit activities and, on April 6, 1990, Hamel telephoned Ecolit's office in Coral Gables seeking to reach Jacobson. Black (posing as Wayne Jenkins, head of Ecolit) returned Hamel's telephone call and Black and Hamel agreed to meet the next time Black was in the Washington, D.C., area.

Investigation of Hamel's Sources Within Alyeska

The contact initiated by Hamel on April 6, 1990, together with Wackenhut's failure to contact any employees of Alyeska, caused Wackenhut to turn from a more general focus on locating leaks within Alyeska to a more specific focus on identifying Hamel's sources within Alyeska. Black first met with Hamel on May 9, 1990, at Hamel's home in Alexandria, Virginia. An additional meeting was held with Hamel on May 16 in Virginia. During this meeting Hamel stated that he had furnished information regarding Alyeska and Alyeska's owners to Congressman George Miller.

While in Hamel's home on May 16, Black and fellow investigator Rick Lund observed numerous Alyeska documents lying around the Hamel home and retrieved four documents from a group that Hamel described to them as "stolen from Alyeska."

A decision was made to audiotape or videotape all future conversations with Hamel in Virginia, where taping was determined to be lawful with one party's consent. It was felt that recording Hamel's remarks was necessary to preclude later misrepresentation of what had been said. Black was instructed by Wellington to press Hamel for the names of persons who were leaking Alyeska documents and information to Hamel and to stay completely away from and not pursue anything having to do with Congressman Miller, his Committee or his Staff.

Following Hamel's initial telephone call to Ecolit on April 6, 1990, Hamel's trash was searched on a number of occasions. Hamel's telephone toll records for some time periods were obtained and reviewed.

A conversation between Black and Hamel that took place in Black's hotel room at The Hyatt Regency Hotel in Crystal City, Virginia, on June 20, 1990, was videotaped.

The decision to open an Ecolit office in Virginia was made to facilitate taping Hamel under controlled circumstances and to attempt to identify Alyeska documents in Hamel's possession. Hamel was paid a total of $4,000 by Ecolit to cover his expenses and the expenses of his sources.

The Ecolit office in Virginia was established in mid-August, 1990. Several conversations with Hamel were audiotaped and videotaped between August 18 and August 30, 1990.

Involvement of Alyeska Owners

A decision to advise the TAPS Owners Committee of the Wackenhut investigation was made by Hermiller and others at Alyeska during mid-September. At a September 25, 1990, meeting, Alyeska's General Counsel presented to representatives of the three principal owners of Alyeska (BP, Exxon and ARCO) an overview of the investigation. After an exchange of views it was decided to shut down the investigation. . . .

In mid-September 1991, Richard Bonin, a producer with CBS-TV's *60 Minutes,* wrote George Wackenhut a letter from his Washington, DC, office, requesting the opportunity to interview him, and/or other TWC executives, concerning allegations that had been made about an investigation commissioned by the Alyeska Pipeline Service Company.

On September 30, 1991, George sent Bonin the following reply:

Thank you for offering to The Wackenhut Corporation the opportunity to be interviewed by 60 Minutes concerning allegations which have been made about this company and its client, Alyeska Pipeline Service Company.

As I believe you are aware, in March, 1990, Wackenhut was retained to conduct an investigation for Alyeska. A Florida statute and the agreement between Wackenhut and Alyeska provide that Wackenhut maintain the confidentiality of that investigation, and we will honor that statutory requirement and contractual commitment unless and until our client releases us from them. We are, therefore, not in a position to discuss the investigation.

We can state, however, that we specifically instructed our investigators that they were to conduct the entire investigation in strict accordance with the law. To that end, independent outside attorneys were retained, and those attorneys reviewed the conduct of the investigation as it progressed. For that reason, we believe that all of the investigative methods and techniques employed throughout the operation were entirely legal and proper.

We understand that your personnel expect to be here in Coral Gables during the week of September 29 in the hope of interviewing us. While they certainly may come to Coral Gables if they wish, we suggest that there is no need for them to do so since we feel bound to maintain our confidentiality agreement with Alyeska and therefore will not be able to answer any of their questions.

Once again, thank you for offering to us the opportunity of an interview with 60 Minutes.

Shortly before noon on Thursday, October 3, 1991, Steve Kroft, then forty-six, who had been a correspondent and co-editor for *60 Minutes* since 1989, was waiting across the street from The Wackenhut Building with a camera crew from CBS. Apparently, sources had told him that Wayne Black routinely walked to lunch with friends from the office between noon and 12:30. Black appeared about 12:15, and Steve Kroft called his name.

Precisely one month later, on Sunday evening, November 3, 1991, the night before the three-day congressional hearings were to begin, CBS aired a fourteen-minute segment about the Alyeska investigation on *60 Minutes,* with a Nielsen audience of 28.876 million households. Here is a verbatim transcription of that segment.

> *Steve Kroft, co-host:* When the seven major oil companies built the trans-Alaska pipeline fourteen years ago and began pumping oil from the North Slope to a tanker terminal in Valdez, they pledged to respect the environment and the safety of their workers. So when evidence began reaching Congress and the federal regulatory agencies that those promises weren't being kept, the oil companies decided to put an end to the problem by plugging the leaks—not the leaks in the pipeline, the leaks of damaging information reaching Washington.
>
> The Alyeska Company, the consortium of oil companies that owns and operates the pipeline, went out and hired one of the nation's largest private-eye firms to conduct an elaborate, expensive, and secret undercover investigation of one man, a former oil broker by the name of

Chuck Hamel. Why would the oil companies that own the Alaska pipeline go to so much trouble to silence Chuck Hamel? Well, if you visit the upstairs office of Hamel's Virginia home, you begin to get some idea. For the past decade, this has been the command center for his one-man war against Alyeska. What are all these documents?

Chuck Hamel: Well, this is—is Exxon shipping documents from some of their ships that polluted along the way, other oil companies who were doing some wrongdoings in Alaska.

Kroft: Where did you get this stuff? Where did this stuff come from?

Hamel: Well, it comes in the mail, a great deal, and in the fax machine. I get faxes. I don't know who's sending it to me.

Kroft: These documents and the information in them have cost Alyeska dearly. In 1987, it was Hamel who told the EPA about the release of cancer-causing compounds into the air at this terminal in Valdez. It cost Alyeska $30 million to correct the problem. And it was Hamel who told Congress that the pipeline was corroding. Last year, Alyeska agreed to fix it at a cost of up to $900 million.

Hamel: They're making a billion dollars a year on the Alyeska pipeline, profit, these companies. A billion dollars a year profit, and—and they've got—greed has gotten to them where that's not enough. They want a billion, plus, cheat a little on the environment and make an extra nickel.

Kroft: When Chuck Hamel first took on Alyeska and the oil companies a dozen years ago, he had the strongest of motivations: revenge. Hamel claimed they cheated him out of millions of dollars in an oil deal and then drove him out of the tanker business. When he began to fight back in court and in the press, Alyeska employees began slipping him information about safety and environmental violations.

Hamel: I was a funnel from their employees to the government. Their employees would never go straight to the government, they're all fearful of being discovered.

Kroft: Hamel not only protected their confidentiality, he got results. And, over time, he attracted a legion of Alyeska whistle-blowers.

Hamel: And they'd say, "Here's the problem: I have to do these things that are wrong, and my fellow employees, and we have no choice. We'd lose our jobs. We have families. We have children, like everybody else."

Kroft: At first, Alyeska tried to stop the leaks and identify the leakers by going to court to try and recover company documents that Hamel had turned over to the federal government. They lost. But Alyeska was so infuriated at Hamel's continued access to the company's inner workings, it went out and hired one of the nation's largest private detective concerns, Wackenhut, to try and shut down Chuck Hamel's pipeline any way it could. Wackenhut assembled an undercover team of former state and federal investigators. No expense and no dirty trick was to be spared. Tell me about that first encounter with the Wackenhut undercover team.

Hamel: That would have been in Anchorage, at the—Fletcher's Bar. It was late in the evening and this lovely young lady somehow was getting our attention.

Kroft: How was she getting your attention?

Hamel: Well, pretty blonde, tanned, and her clothing, if I recall—I think that her blouse was rather transparent. It just didn't fit the scene in—in—in Anchorage in March, eleven at night.

Kroft: A few days later, the same woman just happened to be leaving Anchorage on Hamel's flight.

Hamel: We sat down next to each other, and she told me she worked for an environmental group called Ecolit. Ecological Litigation.

Kroft: The woman told Hamel that Ecolit was anxious to help him by bringing lawsuits against Alyeska and the oil companies. In reality, the woman was a Wackenhut investigator, and Ecolit a Wackenhut invention set up for one purpose, to lure Chuck Hamel into revealing his sources. Former Wackenhut investigator Sherree Rich helped set up the phony environmental group. It offered Hamel office space, computer services, even cash.

Sherree Rich: He was having financial problems, and that's why they were such a good bait for him. Because they were this company that was on the same side as he was, with all this, you know, unlimited funds that could help him out.

Kroft: And you were at his service.

Rich: Right.

Kroft: Anything Chuck Hamel needed, you were supposed to give it to him.

Rich: Right.

Kroft: But first she had to make the company seem legitimate, so she rented office space near Hamel's home in Virginia.

Rich: I had brochures made up, and stationery, business cards. We had posters all around that were environmental posters. "Save the Whales," that kind of thing.

Kroft: She says the office was set up so they could secretly record every meeting with Chuck Hamel.

Rich: We had a desk over here with a stereo set up, and there was a pinhole camera in the stereo. And then we had microphones up in both of the vents here. So that anytime Hamel would come, he would be filmed.

Kroft: One man who frequently taped meetings with Hamel was Dr. Wayne Jenkins, the director of research for Ecolit. Since Ecolit was supposed to be suing the oil companies, Dr. Jenkins tried to get Hamel to reveal the names of potential witnesses. What's going on here?

Hamel: He's trying to get me to identify ship captains of ships that are dumping off the Florida coast, and I just wouldn't let him know who they were.

Kroft: And good thing for Hamel, because Dr. Wayne Jenkins is really Wayne Black, the man who ran the whole investigation for Wackenhut. Black also wanted to know who Hamel spoke to on the telephone, so he hired Ana Contreras and gave her a computer-generated list of Hamel's private telephone records.

Ana Contreras: All the numbers that he was calling, the times, the duration of the call, and see who Chuck Hamel was calling—if it was somebody within Alyeska who could be the person that was leaking documents to him.

Kroft: Where did they get this list of long-distance phone calls? Do you know?

Contreras: I asked them where they got it, and basically they told me that it was from a confidential source. That they paid $100 per toll, per—per set of records.

Kroft: Did it make you uneasy?

Contreras: Yes, it did.

Kroft: Why?

Contreras: Because I had been a customs agent prior to working at Wackenhut, and we used to subpoena those records with the government. We just couldn't obtain them from confidential sources.

Kroft: But Wackenhut and Alyeska didn't stop there. They even stole his garbage and found out things like when his mortgage was due, that his wife was on medication, even details of his private correspondence.

Hamel: They were looking to—to find anything compromising on me. They were looking to—to disgrace me, to discredit me.

Kroft: What they did find in his garbage was an envelope from this man, Robert Scott, whose name also appeared on Hamel's long-distance telephone records. Robert Scott was an Alyeska technician stationed at the Valdez tanker terminal. He now admits that he leaked confidential Alyeska documents to Hamel. Alyeska says you stole these documents.

Robert Scott: I'm not a thief.

Kroft: It's Alyeska's property. They say that you stole them and sent them to Chuck Hamel.

Scott: I am not a thief. If Alyeska wants to call it stealing, that's fine. But I called it doing my civic responsibility.

Kroft: What kinds of problems with Alyeska did you come across?

Scott: Air pollution, water pollution—I could sit here and tell you for an hour. I believe I could go nonstop for an hour.

Kroft: Did you ever raise these questions with Alyeska?

Scott: For a period of about eight or nine years, yes.

Kroft: What happened?

Scott: Nothing. Absolutely nothing. I might as well be talking to—to the wall.

Kroft: I want to show you a couple of documents. Take a look at this March 13, 1990, memo. That's a Wackenhut memo from the man who was running the investigation. It's a list of your long-distance phone calls that you made during a given period.

Scott: Well, I consider this private information.

Kroft: What's your reaction?

Scott: I'd spell this Gestapo.

Kroft: Here's another Wackenhut memo going through the contents of your garbage.

Scott: This is unbelievable.

Kroft: Did you have any idea this was going on?

Scott: Absolutely not! If I had, I would have been hid behind my garage door with my .25 automatic. I wouldn't have killed him, but I would have shot him in the legs.

Kroft: But Robert Scott and Chuck Hamel were apparently not the only targets of the Wackenhut investigation. Ana Contreras, the former Wackenhut investigator, recalls a conversation she had with Wayne Black.

Contreras: He came to my desk one day and he said, "Ana, this investigation is getting big. This investigation is so big it involves congressmen." Hamel was making contact with congressmen about the documents he was getting, and the congressmen were using the documents at hearings. And those hearings were hurting Alyeska and Exxon. And he said, "We're going to get them. We're going to really get them."

Kroft: The congressmen?

Contreras: Yes.

Kroft: Did he mention any congressmen in particular?

Contreras: He mentioned Congressman Miller.

Kroft: That's Congressman George Miller of California, chairman of the House committee that oversees operation of the Alaska pipeline system and a recipient of much of Hamel's information. Congressman Miller believes that Wackenhut was trying to compromise either him or his committee's investigations of Alyeska.

George Miller: They just decided that they were a little police department unto themselves, Wackenhut, Alyeska. They said, "We're like the government. We're worth billions. Look who we represent. Hey, it's just Chuck Hamel. It's just one guy. It's just one member of Congress. It's just one environmental movement." Come on.

Kroft: Congressman Miller says the pipeline company was out to silence its own employees, who are protected by federal whistle-blower laws, and not, as Alyeska claims, to retrieve stolen documents.

Miller: That's not what they were after. They were about stopping the investigations of my committee, and Chuck Hamel, who made a whole series of assertions to me, to the Senate committee, to the EPA, to other people, all of which turned out to be true. All of which would be very, very bad for Alyeska.

Kroft: After Congressman Miller announced that he would hold hearings into the Wackenhut investigation of Chuck Hamel, the president of Alyeska took out a newspaper ad apologizing for having ordered the investigation.

Miller: It's what criminals usually *do* do—is they apologize. They apologized after they were caught.

Kroft: You're calling them criminals?

Miller: I'm calling them criminals.

Kroft: Alyeska turned down our request for an interview, so did Wackenhut. But we did manage to catch up with Wackenhut's director of Special Investigations, Wayne Black, who the last time we saw him on videotape was using the name Dr. Wayne Jenkins. Dr. Jenkins, I presume.

Wayne Black: How are you?

Kroft: Or is it Wayne Black today?

Black: Wayne Black. How are you?

Kroft: Hi. Steve Kroft, with *60 Minutes.*

Black: Nice to meet you.

Kroft: Just want to ask you a couple of questions about the Alyeska investigation of Chuck Hamel. You proud of the investigation?

Black: I'm real happy with it. I think we did a—did a good job. Our people did a good job. We'd do it again if we—if we had the opportunity.

Kroft: You're proud of going through somebody's garbage? You're proud of surreptitiously recording conversations? You're proud of setting up phony companies and giving people a lot of bogus information?

Black: People don't bring stolen documents to us if we tell them that we're investigators. So it's—it's not like you can come right out and tell somebody who it is, and say, "Please, please bring me the evidence that—you committed a crime."

Kroft: Your client, Alyeska, knew what was going on?

Black: Yes.

Kroft: At every step of the way?

Black: That's correct.

Kroft: Why did Alyeska shut down this investigation?

Black: I wish I knew. But our role is finders of fact, and basically we're soldiers.

Kroft: Wackenhut apparently was proud of the investigation, too. It promoted Black to vice president. As for Robert Scott, Alyeska fired him for what it said was unrelated worker misconduct. Why do you think that Alyeska fired you?

Scott: For blowing the whistle, if you will.

Kroft: You're sure of that?

Scott: I am positive. I am positive, just as sure as the Lord makes little red apples.

Kroft: Are you sorry you did this?

Scott: Absolutely not. I would not change one thing, except that knowing what I do now, I might tell Chuck Hamel we better use some pay telephone and a different phone every time. And I won't put—I won't use—I won't put my return address on the letters, and don't put your garbage out. That'd be the only change I'd make.

Kroft: Did they get what they wanted? Did they get sources?

Hamel: They only got one that I know of.

Kroft: Robert Scott.

Hamel: That's correct, and they missed dozens.

Kroft: They still giving you information?

Hamel: I have new ones. I can't believe it myself.

Kroft: Starting tomorrow, Chuck Hamel, ex-Wackenhut investigator Sherree Rich, and her former boss, Wayne Black, will all appear at a congressional hearing to testify about everything they told us.

32

MONDAY, NOVEMBER 4, 1991, the House Committee on Interior and Insular Affairs met at 9:45 A.M. in Room 2226 of the Rayburn House Office Building with the Honorable George Miller (chairman of the committee) presiding. After a brief opening statement by the chairman and several members of the committee, Wayne Black was sworn in. He was represented by his own attorney, Jon Sale. Following is a verbatim transcription of the opening remarks, as published in the committee's official hearing record, titled *Alyeska Pipeline Service Company Covert Operation*, pages 4 and 5:

Mr. Sale. We have written a letter. We would like to invoke Rule 12(f)(2), and request all cameras and microphones be turned off. Mr. Black does not wish to be photographed or have his picture taken.

The Chairman. That is the right of Mr. Black under Rule 12 of the committee, since he is a subpoenaed witness. At this time, all photographing will cease, and the cameras will be turned off during the questioning of Mr. Black before the committee.

Mr. Sale. Mr. Chairman, we have one other procedural matter before you proceed. We would also like to invoke Rule 11 (k) (5) of the House Rules. Our position is that evidence or testimony at this hearing may tend to defame, degrade, or incriminate Mr. Black, and we are making this assertion in good faith. We are basing it on items such as the chairman's memorandum of September 24, which has been distributed to members, which accuse Mr. Black of violating federal and state criminal laws, and similar allegations have been repeated in *The Wall Street Journal* on Friday and *60 Minutes* last night. And we think that fundamental fairness requires that the committee take Mr. Black's testimony in executive session, and we request that this hearing be held in executive session, because of the reasons previously stated under that rule.

Mr. Lagomarsino. I understand your ruling was that cameras be turned off. I see one in the back with a red light on. And one in—

The Chairman. At the moment, we are engaged with Mr. Black's attorney. I think to facilitate turning off the cameras, the committee should recess for about three minutes so that we can allow that to be done by people in the outside and the people on the outside of the room.

Mr. Gejdenson. Mr. Chairman, I am not sure as to where the rules are, but the question I have is, should we finish with other legal motions or requests of Mr. Black's attorney, or do the cameras get shut off immediately?

The Chairman. I think out of fairness to Mr. Black, the cameras should be shut off immediately. It is his right as a subpoenaed witness before this committee. So I would ask that those who have the capability to turn off the cameras, turn them off now, and we will recess for three minutes so the people in the halls can make necessary arrangements.

[After recess.]

The Chairman. The committee will reconvene. Mr. Sale, as I understand it, your assertion is, again, what, that the testimony or the hearings would tend to defame your client. What is your reading of the rule again?

Mr. Sale. Mr. Chairman, it is our position that any testimony from Mr. Black, or in fact anything, any testimony in this entire hearing, in the words of the rule, may tend to defame, degrade, or incriminate Mr. Black, and that is why we invoke the House Rule, as well as Rule 11 (k) (5) of the House Rules and Rule 5 (b) of the rules of this committee, and our position is that the entire proceeding would have that effect upon Mr. Black. So our request is that the entire proceeding be executive session.

The Chairman. I think it is my understanding that the purpose of going into executive session with respect to Mr. Black is so that Mr. Black can take the Fifth Amendment. There is nothing in taking the Fifth Amendment that would tend to incriminate, defame, or otherwise prejudice Mr. Black. That is his right under the Constitution.

Mr. Sale. Mr. Chairman, I know that that is the law and that no adverse inference should be drawn against Mr. Black from doing that, and that is—and Mr. Black has nothing to hide, but I am afraid that when that is reported, it is not always reported that way, and that is why I think he has a right to do that in private. And I am not even sure that should be stated in public, but that is already done, with all due respect. . . .

Congressman Miller had already stated it in public, twice, the damage had been done, and that was all the mass media needed. Following procedural statements by several members of the committee, a vote was taken on a motion to convene in executive session, a roll call was taken, and the room was finally cleared of all cameras, microphones, reporters, and the public.

Next morning, November 5, long before George Wackenhut had his opportunity to testify before the committee at 9:45 A.M., newspapers across the country carried banner headlines with feature stories about the closed hearings and openly asserted that Black had in fact taken the Fifth Amendment. A typical story appeared that morning in *The Miami Herald*, written by reporter Heather Dewar, who filed the story from Washington.

Wackenhut Exec Testifies in Secret Oil Probe

WASHINGTON—Faced with a congressman's claim that "crimes were committed" during Coral Gables-based Wackenhut Corp.'s secret probe of an oil industry whistle-blower, a top Wackenhut executive insisted on testifying in secret before a congressional committee Monday.

One Wackenhut investigator refused to testify, asserting his Fifth Amendment right against self-incrimination, and the lawyer for a top Wackenhut executive confirmed that his client intended to do the same.

It was the first time in three years a witness has taken his Fifth Amendment before the House Committee on Interior and Insular Affairs, as well as the first time the committee has gone into secret session.

For months, Wackenhut vice president Wayne Black has promised congressional hearings would clear him of wrongdoing in a seven-month undercover investigation of Alexandria, Va., oil broker Charles Hamel, a thorn in the side of Exxon and seven other companies that control the flow of Alaskan oil.

Former Wackenhut employees have charged that Black and his team stole documents from Hamel, illegally taped telephone conversations with him, went through his garbage, and falsified driver licenses and other identification to set up an elaborate sting operation against him.

The ex-employees also have said that California Rep. George Miller, chairman of the committee that regulates the oil industry, was a target of the probe paid for by the Alyeska Pipeline Service Co., an oil industry consortium.

"I believe crimes were committed," Miller told a *60 Minutes* news crew.

And Monday, he opened two days [sic] of hearings into what he termed a "spy operation," saying, "It is important to find out why some of the largest and most powerful corporations in this country would resort to such elaborate 'sting' tactics to invade and destroy the privacy of Mr. Hamel, federal and state officials, environmentalists and ordinary citizens."

Face-to-face with Miller's committee Monday, Black, a veteran Miami investigator, passed up his opportunity to publicly vindicate himself. Instead, his attorney asserted Black's right, under House rules, to testify in secret and to impose the same veil of secrecy on other witnesses whose words "would tend to degrade, defame or incriminate Mr. Black.

By an 8–5 vote, the committee agreed to take secret testimony from five witnesses: Black, electronics wizard Rick Lund and their three principal accusers, ex-Wackenhut employees Ricki Jacobson, Sherree Rich and Mercedes Cruz.

Lund testified for 10 minutes and said afterward he had claimed his Fifth Amendment right to silence in response to all questions.

Black, who testified briefly, refused to say whether he took the Fifth Amendment. . . .

At 9:45 that morning, November 5, George Wackenhut was the committee's first witness, before a large audience of the press and public in Room 2226 of the Rayburn House Office Building. He was represented by Greg Baldwin, an attorney with the law firm of Holland & Knight. After being sworn in, George read his opening statement, published verbatim in the committee's hearing record, *Alyeska Pipeline Service Company Covert Operation*, page 10–13, prior to being interviewed by members of the committee.

Mr. Wackenhut. Good morning, Mr. Chairman, Congressman Young, and members of the committee. I am George Wackenhut, chairman of the board and chief executive officer of The Wackenhut Corporation. Mr. Chairman, last Wednesday, I delivered to you copies of three documents. I would like to have them formally entered into the record.

They are: The 1990 Annual Report of The Wackenhut Corporation, the resolution passed by the board of directors on Monday, October 28, 1991, and a statement of policy adapted several years ago setting forth ethical and moral standards for the conduct of business by the company. I would like also to preserve the right to supplement the record at a later date.

The Chairman. Without objection, the documents you referred to will be entered into the record. The hearing record will be held open for a specified period of time, but that has not yet been determined.

Mr. Wackenhut. Thank you. Mr. Chairman, I filed in advance a detailed statement which contains information I would very much like the committee to consider. While I will not repeat here what I said there, I specifically want today to emphasize three topics: First, your committee staff indicated to us that they believe that top management in Wackenhut did not approach this committee's investigation with the appropriate degree of seriousness.

Approximately eight weeks ago, in response to this committee's request for information and a consequent reporting by numerous newspapers on our alleged corporate activities, Wackenhut engaged outside counsel to conduct a full internal review and report on the 1990 investigatory events.

Our attorneys rapidly assembled a team of eight lawyers, with at least three lawyers working full-time, to conduct an investigation of the entire engagement. In less than two weeks after the pertinent material became available to them, our attorneys digested a massive amount of information in an effort promptly to respond to this committee's inquiries and ultimately to produce a preliminary report thereon to our management.

That effort, while ongoing, is now substantially complete.

Personally, Mr. Chairman, since receipt of your August 7 letter, all my concentration, as well as the valuable resources and efforts of my employees, has been focused on this hearing. I am consumed with the magnitude of this process and unquestionably it has had my full attention. I have very much taken your inquiry seriously.

The board of directors of The Wackenhut Corporation, the weekend before last, received a preliminary report by our outside counsel. Their reaction, too, was solemn and concerned. Indeed, the board of directors spent more time on this particular matter than they have on any other matter and any other business concern in the 37-year history of the company.

A brief review of what The Wackenhut Corporation has done between August 7 and the present puts its delay and silence into a perspective which I believe will demonstrate that Wackenhut has taken this committee and its investigation very seriously indeed. The prompt production of documents relevant to The Wackenhut Corporation's 1990 investigation conducted on behalf of Alyeska was not easy.

On April 16, 1991, almost four months prior to this committee's request, Alyeska requested us to deliver to the law firm of Paul, Hastings, Janofsky & Walker in Los Angeles the investigative file and materials that The Wackenhut Corporation produced or collected during the 1990 investigation.

We complied with Alyeska's request after they agreed to maintain these records for a period of 10 years and make them available to us for legitimate inquiries. That agreement with Alyeska delayed us in providing that privileged documentation sooner to this committee. Our own internal investigation of this matter has been delayed, too.

Alyeska authorized The Wackenhut Corporation on October 1, 1991, to release information fully to comply with this committee's request for documents. Alyeska then promptly delivered back to Wackenhut copies of some of the documents we had originally sent to the law firm in Los Angeles.

For the first time, The Wackenhut Corporation was in a position, practically speaking, to provide the requested materials to this committee, and three days later—specifically on October 4, 1991—we produced every document we could find in response to the congressional subpoena.

In addition to the management of Wackenhut requesting our outside legal counsel to review every facet of the investigation, the board of directors of Wackenhut also has itself established an independent board/committee which will—separate and apart from the management review I instituted—fully review to its own satisfaction all the claims and allegations raised relating to the Alyeska investigation.

This independent board/committee will then present a recommendation to the full board of directors specifically stating what, if any, remedial actions are necessary.

Second, the methods of undercover surveillance used by Wackenhut in the 1990 investigation are traditional and standard investigative techniques commonly used in private investigations. Information was obtained throughout the investigation using video and audio surveillance to tape meetings and telephone conversations in Virginia between Mr. Charles Hamel and our investigators.

Wackenhut knew that the only task was to identify the source of the Alyeska corporate documents in his possession in a manner that would permit the initiation of litigation against those persons responsible.

It was obvious that any illegal conduct by us would be counterproductive when the evidence and documents produced were ultimately to be turned over to a court.

Again, the purpose of this investigation, as far as Wackenhut was concerned, was only to identify the persons stealing documents and information from Alyeska so that an appropriate criminal and civil action could be brought against those persons. To that end, they carefully sought out and received legal counsel to preserve the integrity of the investigation.

Third, Mr. Chairman, contrary to reports, let me categorically state that Wackenhut did not conduct a covert investigation of you, your staff, any member of your committee, or any other member of Congress. I personally believe that any statement or inference to the contrary is absolutely false. I am convinced that it did not happen.

My outside lawyers advise me they would wholly agree. The only inquiry about any congressman conducted by Wackenhut in the Alyeska investigation was confined to a single trip to the public library.

Based upon the information given to me by our outside law firm, it is indisputable that on May 16, 1990, Mr. Hamel admitted to the investigators that he was receiving documents belonging to Alyeska. It was only from Charles Hamel that our investigators frequently heard the name George Miller.

Mr. Hamel said then that he and George Miller intended to set up the president of Alyeska, James Hermiller, at a hearing scheduled before this committee. Once Mr. Hamel first mentioned a member of Congress, Wayne Black immediately and properly sought legal advice from a prominent Miami attorney, William Richey.

Mr. Richey, as I understand it, will testify later today, but it is my further understanding that he unfailingly advised our investigators on the legality of each of their investigatory activities.

After I received the letter of August 7 from the committee, I got great satisfaction from a visit I had with Mr. Richey in which he told me that he knew of no illegality connected with the investigation and that I should be proud of the Wackenhut investigators, "who had conducted as fine an investigation as he had ever seen." Among Mr. Richey's firm advice to our investigators was not to in any way investigate a congressman.

I am sure he will reaffirm that advice. Suffice it to say, the only action taken by Wackenhut to investigate George Miller after receiving that instruction was for Mr. Richey to look up information in a library at his request. That was the beginning and that was the end of Wackenhut's investigation of any congressman.

When Wackenhut began the investigation, Alyeska told Wackenhut that corporate-sensitive documents were being taken from Alyeska and that the minutes of secret internal Alyeska meetings were being leaked to the press and others. Our assignment was to determine who appropriated the documents from within Alyeska's corporate offices.

It is not absolutely clear that the name of Charles Hamel surfaced at the very beginning of the investigation as a top operative in the receipt of the stolen documents.

Our recent review efforts have clearly affirmed to us that at no time during the course of our investigation was any member of Congress under surveillance, visually or telephonically, or was any member of Congress being investigated in any other way, shape or fashion.

At no time was the telephone of any member of Congress ever tapped. I am, and always have been, very disturbed about the concerns raised by this committee. However, I believe that many people have grossly exaggerated our conduct and the facts of the investigation.

Be assured Wackenhut will continue to scrutinize its investigators' conduct and methods of operations during the entire 1990 investigation until all legitimate future concerns are satisfactorily and permanently resolved.

The reputation developed by this company throughout the nation during the past 37 years demands no less. It is my purpose to do all that is needed to keep that reputation unblemished.

Gentlemen, thank you for this opportunity to address this committee. I now stand ready to take questions.

Although George had submitted, far in advance, a detailed ten-page double-spaced statement to the chairman and all forty-one members of the committee, describing The Wackenhut Corporation in general, its three distinct operating groups (Domestic Operations, Government Services, International Operations), and focused his attention on the Special Investigations Division, a unit of Domestic Operations, it was obvious from the beginning of the questioning period that few of the dozen or so members of the committee who were actually present in the room had read the statement, because, almost without exception, their questions about the company and its operations were naive beyond belief. This was particularly true of Congressman Miller, who dominated the questioning.

One example will suffice, which occurred about one hour into the hearing:

> *The Chairman.* Are you the largest security firm in this country?
> *Mr. Wackenhut.* No, sir.
> *The Chairman.* No. What are you?
> *Mr. Wackenhut.* Third.
> *The Chairman.* Third. But you are a national, international firm?
> *Mr. Wackenhut.* Yes, sir.
> *The Chairman.* Would you not guess, Mr. Wackenhut, whether or not there are legal requirements in the State of Florida?
> *Mr. Wackenhut.* There are legal requirements. Mr. Black is very familiar with them, as are our attorneys.
> *The Chairman.* Would you guess that there are federal regulations and laws with respect to extracting communications between two people?
> *Mr. Wackenhut.* There are, of course.
> *The Chairman.* And yet you do not engage in a policy of taking your people through the process of what would be expected. You expect all of your people to know the law. Essentially, that would be the case, because you do tell them they can only do that which is legal?
> *Mr. Wackenhut.* I am repeating myself, Mr. Miller. I have said three times now they contact an attorney when they have any questions.

As various members of the committee wandered in and out of the room, hurrying to and from other hearings, George answered questions of an incredibly repetitious nature for more than three hours (forty-six printed pages in the hearing record) before a recess was called at about one o'clock. As countless televised congressional hearings have proven over the years, with only a few notable exceptions, most committee members in this particular hearing did not do the minimum homework necessary to justify the time, energy, and expense of holding the hearing in the first place. The morning session was clearly an exercise in futility.

During the afternoon session, the committee reconvened for the purpose of taking testimony of three individuals, all sitting at the same table, flanked by their respective attorneys: William Richey, outside counsel of the Alyeska Pipeline Service Company, represented by Robert Jordan, an attorney practicing in Washington, DC; James Hermiller, president of the Alyeska Pipeline Service Company, represented by Gerald A. Feffer, an attorney practicing in Washington, DC; and J. Patrick Wellington, manager of Corporate Security for the Alyeska Pipeline Service Company, represented by Kenly Webster, an attorney practicing in Washington, DC.

Each of the three witnesses read a brief prepared statement, starting with William Richey, the outside counsel of Alyeska, who was a partner at the Miami, Florida, law firm of Richey, Munroe, Fine, Goodman and Armstrong. A graduate of Harvard Law School, he had practiced law for the past seventeen years. Before entering private practice, he was a prosecuting attorney with the Florida State Attorney's Office in Miami, where he served as the chief of the Organized Crime and Public Corruption Unit, and was later appointed chief assistant state attorney. Since leaving that position in 1981, his practice had focused primarily on commercial fraud litigation and white-collar criminal defense.

Two paragraphs of Richey's statement were particularly relevant:

> I would like to comment on some of the investigative techniques used in this case. I fully understood that Wackenhut was collecting abandoned trash, purchasing telephone toll records, and videotaping and recording its encounters with Mr. Hamel. Each of these practices can be undertaken legally, and I was confident that Mr. Black, who I knew had substantial experience in such matters, understood how to do so.
>
> These techniques may seem intrusive, but the fact is that they are common investigative practices in cases involving fraud and criminal wrongdoing, and in my opinion, were wholly appropriate to this case. You simply cannot rely on traditional investigative techniques or the

civil discovery process to obtain information from individuals who, like Mr. Hamel, are known to be trafficking in stolen goods or information.

Next to read his prepared statement was James Hermiller, president of Alyeska, who had at that time been in the oil business for some twenty-five years. In 1966, he joined Sohio as a chemist, then served with Sohio in a variety of positions until 1984, when he was appointed vice president and general manager of the Industrial Chemical Division for Sohio. In August 1986, he was appointed vice president of Refining for BP Oil. In May 1989, he became executive vice president and chief operating officer at Alyeska. He became president of Alyeska in October 1989, seven months after the *Exxon Valdez* spill.

Of course, the Valdez spill gave rise to an extraordinary amount of litigation. Alyeska and the other companies found themselves defending literally dozens of lawsuits. In the course of deciding how to deal with those lawsuits, Alyeska consulted with many attorneys, including the Los Angeles law firm of Gibson, Dunn & Crutcher. Those consultations with counsel were, of course, highly privileged and confidential.

Hermiller discovered documents from those consultations had been stolen in 1990:

> To my great distress, and to the distress of the owners of Alyeska, we learned at the beginning of 1990 that certain legal documents containing our confidential communications with our counsel in the Valdez litigation had been stolen or leaked. One such document was actually shown on a British television program called *The Scottish Eye*.
>
> The owners of Alyeska and I viewed the unauthorized dissemination of these highly confidential documents as intolerable. The theft or leaking of these documents, coupled with my preexisting concern over previous unauthorized dissemination of technical and legal documents, led me to conclude that steps should be taken to determine who was stealing or leaking the documents from within Alyeska. . . .
>
> In May 1990, the Miami law firm of Richey, Munroe, Fine & Goodman, P.A., was retained to furnish advice in connection with the investigation. The two members of that firm principally involved in advising Alyeska—Messrs. William Richey and Jonathan Goodman—both are

former prosecutors with a wealth of criminal law experience. It was my understanding that the Richey, Munroe firm remained involved in the investigation until its conclusion.

Also, in approximately July 1990, Mr. Wellington and I advised then-Alyeska general counsel Alfred T. Smith about the investigation. Mr. Smith, in turn, involved one of his top attorneys, Mr. Lon Trotter. Mr. Smith also retained the prominent law firm of Baker & Hostetler McCutchen Black, and Alaska attorney Edward Boiko. To my knowledge, none of these lawyers ever indicated any doubt about the legality of the activities undertaken by Wackenhut in the course of the investigation. . . .

Last to read his statement was J. Patrick Wellington, Alyeska's manager of Corporate Security, who had a thirty-five-year record of service in Alaska to law enforcement and other public positions, most prominently as commissioner of the Alaska Department of Public Safety, a cabinet-level position, and as director of the Alaska State Troopers. He had worked for every governor since Alaska became a state.

Although Wellington's statement was the shortest of the three, about two hours later, during the questioning session, he engaged in a heated debate with Chairman Miller about Miller's statements on *60 Minutes* the previous Sunday evening. The debate was initiated by Hermiller, and provided the only fireworks of the afternoon session:

> *Mr. Hermiller.* The objective was a single objective, and that was clear. To get our materials back to go ahead and sue Mr. Hamel.
> *The Chairman.* I understand that.
> *Mr. Hermiller.* I don't know if you do, Mr. Chairman, you have made statements during the last six weeks. I watched you on *60 Minutes*, Sunday night, condemn me and Alyeska as criminals.
> *The Chairman.* Uh-huh.
> *Mr. Hermiller.* That is, as far as I am concerned, unjust to do that before we even had a chance to come here today and have you listen to us. We were very scrupulous.
> *The Chairman.* As opposed to the characterizations of Mr. Hamel that he is an extortionist and so forth by the counsel sitting next to you, who said he only shook his hand yesterday. Yet you have, again, the Paul Hastings memo and others suggesting they don't see that at all.

Mr. Hermiller. Congressman, what you said Sunday night on *60 Minutes* went out to how many millions of people in the United States?

The Chairman. Oh, so it's just a question of how far you broadcast it.

Mr. Hermiller. No, it is not.

The Chairman. Let's lay down the gauntlet—

Mr. Hermiller. You have condemned us before we have gotten here. There is no reason for that. There is no *reason* for that. We have scrupulously throughout this thing avoided the kind of contacts that you are talking about here. . . .

Mr. Wellington. Mr. Chairman, why would you call us criminals then, if you haven't seen any evidence before we ever came here?

The Chairman. I think I have seen evidence that has only been counteracted by Mr. Richey's opinion of criminal activity undertaken with the surveillance of Mr. Hamel.

Mr. Wellington. By me?

The Chairman. We differ about that.

Mr. Wellington. By *me?*

The Chairman. You are an agent of the company. He is your agent.

Mr. Wellington. No, I'm asking you a question. By *me?* Have you seen anything that would lead you to believe Pat Wellington committed a criminal act?

The Chairman. By your agent.

Mr. Wellington. By *me?*

The Chairman. No. You have to take responsibility for your agent.

Mr. Wellington. You called me a criminal on TV.

The Chairman. No, I didn't.

Mr. Wellington. You said Alyeska are criminals.

The Chairman. And you are Mr. Wellington.

Mr. Wellington. Well, who do I work for?

The Chairman. Well, the fact is, you have to take responsibility for your agents.

Mr. Wellington. I think you prejudged us before we got here today. I think you owe an apology to me and my family for the comment you made without legal proof. Half of the things that were introduced today, if it were in a court of law, wouldn't stand up at all. And you've accused us of being criminals. . . .

After more than four hours of testimony, the committee finally adjourned at 6:35 P.M., and would reconvene in Room 1324 of the

Longworth House Office Building at 9:50 A.M. on Wednesday, November 6, where the committee would first hear from a panel of witnesses: Fred Garibaldi from British Petroleum America, former chairman of the owners committee of the Trans-Alaska Pipeline System; Darrell G. Warner, president of the Exxon Pipeline Company; and William C. Rusnack, president of the ARCO Transportation Company. The afternoon session would be exclusively devoted to the statement and testimony of Charles Hamel.

However, George Wackenhut would not be there. On the advice of his attorney, William Richey, he returned home on Wednesday morning, but not before reading many of the major newspaper accounts of the previous day's hearing. Most were accurate, balanced articles, reflecting the consensus opinion of the attorneys who testified, that there was no evidence of wrongdoing on the part of the Wackenhut investigators. Here is one excerpt from the November 6, 1991, issue of *The Wall Street Journal*, under the by-line of staff reporter Allanna Sullivan, who discussed a January 1991 report prepared by outside attorneys, hired by the owners of the oil companies, claiming that covert activities undertaken by Wackenhut left Alyeska vulnerable to federal prosecution:

> George Wackenhut, chairman and founder of the Coral Gables, Fla., security giant, said that a probe of Wackenhut by an outside law firm has concluded that there was no wrongdoing on the part of any Wackenhut operative. "And any inference to the contrary is absolutely false," Mr. Wackenhut said.
> An attorney for one of the Wackenhut operatives said the lawyers hired by the oil companies to prepare the report were off base. "There was no violation of criminal or state law," said Alan Weinstein. "Nobody in that law firm is an expert" on those issues.
> The report was not prepared by Alyeska, the consortium of major oil companies that produce and transport oil from the Alaskan North Slope, and which hired Wackenhut last year. It was, instead, the product of attorneys hired by Alyeska's owners to figure out whether the Wackenhut surveillance went too far. . . .

Only one newspaper of the dozens we researched that carried feature stories about Tuesday's hearings actually headlined and sensationalized the totally absurd allegation that Wackenhut planned to covertly investigate Congressman George Miller in an effort to trigger a criminal investigation of him. Naturally, it was the city's only major English-speaking newspaper, *The Miami Herald*, the staff writer was Wackenhut nemesis Heather Dewar, and her routinely biased story ran—where else?—on the front page of the November 6 issue:

Wackenhut Corp. Considered Probe Targeting Lawmaker

WASHINGTON—In their zeal to stop an oil industry whistle-blower, lawyers and sleuths for Coral Gables-based Wackenhut Corp. contemplated investigating a congressman on charges of receiving stolen documents, a congressional inquiry revealed Tuesday.

The idea was dropped or put on hold after attorneys advised the company that its plans to trigger a criminal investigation of Rep. George Miller, D.-Calif., could backfire and lead to obstruction of justice charges against Wackenhut.

Lawyers for the Alaska consortium that hired Wackenhut to stop information leaks concluded that the security firm might have gone too far in other aspects of the operation. The lawyers said in an internal memo that Wackenhut could be charged with wire fraud, mail fraud and interstate transportation of stolen documents.

Those revelations came in dramatic testimony Tuesday before the House Committee on Interior and Insular Affairs, chaired by Miller himself. The committee is probing Wackenhut's handling of an elaborate undercover sting operation aimed at Alexandria, Va., oil broker Charles Hamel, a thorn in the side of Exxon and six other big oil companies that control the flow of Alaskan oil.

In often heated testimony, Wackenhut founder George Wackenhut and Alyeska President James Hermiller defended the seven-month investigation, which they said never targeted Miller. "I wouldn't have touched that with a 10-foot pole," Hermiller said.

And Miami attorney William Richey, hired as a consultant in the case, called Hamel "an extortionist" who was trying to force Exxon to settle a long-running multimillion-dollar lawsuit. Hamel is scheduled to testify today as the last witness.

For a decade, Hamel has funneled information about oil company wrongdoing from workers in the Alaskan oil fields to the Environmental Protection Agency, the Justice Department and Miller's committee, which overseas the oil industry. The Alyeska Pipeline Service Co., an oil consortium, hired Wackenhut to stop him in 1990.

In conversations with Wackenhut operatives who were posing as environmentalists, Hamel continually bragged that he was close to Miller, said Richey and Wackenhut. The private eyes were told that if they ever met Miller, they were to reveal their true identities and "immediately discontinue all surveillance activities," Wackenhut said. . . .

The next morning, Thursday, November 7, Rick Wackenhut sent the following memo by E-Mail to all TWC area and branch offices, subsidiaries, facilities, and project managers, under the subject "Congressional Inquiry."

> During the last three months, there have been numerous reports in the national media regarding The Wackenhut Corporation and an investigation conducted by the Special Investigations Division (SID) on behalf of the Alyeska Pipeline Service Company. This media coverage included stories carried by major newspapers, wire services, network news programs, and a segment of last Sunday's *60 Minutes* on CBS.
>
> The Chairman of the Board, Mr. George R. Wackenhut, testified earlier this week before the U.S. House of Representatives' Committee on Interior and Insular Affairs, which held three days of hearings in order to bring out the facts regarding the conduct of the investigation.
>
> Although allegations had been made that some of the techniques used in the investigation were illegal, none of the charges were substantiated, and the Chairman was able to respond in a positive manner to the questions which were raised.
>
> Subsequent testimony by the legal representative of the Alyeska Company reinforced the Chairman's remarks and, in fact, praised the work of the Wackenhut investigators and their innovative application of fully legal investigative techniques.
>
> In keeping with the Corporation's 37-year history of maintaining an environment of integrity and professionalism in all of its activities and associations, the Corporation has cooperated completely with the public inquiry and feels very satisfied with its current resolution.

That same morning, George announced to the entire headquarters staff that there would be a special meeting held in the Wackenhut

Training Institute's large training room, called The Learning Center, which was then located on the second floor, at 11:30 sharp, and invited everyone in the building to attend. At about 11:25 that morning, George was in his office with Budd Kneip and Rick. "Props" had been obtained from the first-aid room on the third floor, and all three men were laughing as Rick applied bandages and cotton swabs to George's forehead and cheeks, then helped place his left arm into a sling. His tie was then loosened, his shirt collar opened, the three men left the office, and were joined by Fernando Carrizosa and George Zeiss, all laughing, as they took the glass elevator down to the second floor.

More than 300 headquarters personnel—many noticeably apprehensive—were standing in the The Learning Center when George made his entrance, limping slightly, leaning on Rick, and the applause and laughter were immediate and deafening. No one in that room needed to be told why he was wearing the sling and bandages or that he would be talking about the congressional hearings; all knew the names he would use, the dates, the events. But only a few senior officers knew why he was so obviously happy. He had received information the previous night that even the press hadn't learned. As he limped to the center of the room, still amid tumultuous laughter, the noise softened to almost total silence as be began to speak in his characteristically quiet way, without notes of any kind. Without his knowledge, we tape recorded his message. Following is a verbatim transcription:

"We were hired by a very good client, Alyeska, as of March of last year, in an attempt to determine who—one or more people—was leaking information about their company. You can appreciate the very, very company-confidential information from any organization—you want to stop it. In this case, it was even a client-attorney privilege that was taken, engineering drawings were opened up, all this was going to Charles Hamel. Hamel, in turn, was making all kinds of statements to the effect that would lead anybody doing the investigation to believe that Congressman Miller was part of it, and was actually conspiring with him to do these things. I never believed that, and I don't believe it now.

"But, for that reason, there was discussion by the investigators and the attorneys that we used here as to what we should do, because Hamel continued to talk about Congressman Miller and his closeness to him. And it was recommended at that time that all this be turned over to the FBI, where it could be brought to the attention of the attorney general, and let them decide what to do with it.

"About that time, the owners' committee—and the large oil companies that own Alyeska are called the owners, as a consortium—they decided, no, we'd better discontinue the investigation, because we're getting too much involved in things that we have no control over. Because we were taping, we were audio- and videotaping Hamel's conversations. And we were. And these accusations by him were being made. So the investigation was discontinued last fall.

"Since that time, some dissident ex-employees of this organization went up to Hamel and told him about the investigation. As a result, all this came out. We got a letter from the Congress stating that they wanted all the material that we had. In the meantime, it had all been handed over to Alyeska attorneys in California for safekeeping. That's what they wanted, that wasn't our idea, and we did it reluctantly. We didn't do it until they guaranteed they'd keep them for ten years, and then we could have them back any time we needed them.

"They then turned over everything. We got a further subpoena for anything else we found. We did find some other things. In the meantime, the investigative unit moved down to the ground floor, and that caused some confusion. But everything we had, everything we could find, everything we would continue to find, goes to the committee. There was nothing hidden.

"As a result, after I testified, and I answered the questions to the best of my ability—remember, I was not involved in it. They acted as if this company was a million-dollar company that was only involved in investigations, and in each case I should know what's going on. So I just pointed out to them that one-fifth of one percent of our entire operations involve corporate investigations, and that I didn't know everything that was going on.

"Before I testified, the attorney for Wayne Black requested under House Rule so-and-so that all the cameras be turned off. That was done; they had no choice. The second request was that the hearings about Mr. Black, the questioning of him, be held in closed session, because of the possible damage to his good reputation, under House Rule so-and-so. The chairman had no choice but to honor this request. Before that was all over, the minority chairman and the majority chairman, Miller, had gotten together and they decided that they would hold not only Wayne Black's testimony in private session, but also Rick Lund's testimony in private session, and the three ex-employees of this company in private session. So the whole day passed, Congressman Miller did not get his show on TV, they didn't have any press there to do anything about it, and the big break, of course, was that anything said that was bad was said in private.

"The following day, Tuesday morning, I was on first. After I had finished, there was a panel group consisting of Mr. Hermiller, who is president of Alyeska, Mr. Wellington, the head of security for Alyeska, who hired us, and Bill Richey, who is a very prominent criminal attorney here in Miami, who followed this investigation through its entirety. And, I'm telling you, he did a splendid job. He said all that Alyeska had asked for was to find out who was leaking the information, which they had a right to do, and all they wanted was to get this information. But they didn't want any more than that, and they wanted to call the investigation off. Alyeska wanted Hamel to be criminally charged and civilly charged, but the owners said no. So that was it. Then the committee started asking, 'Well, what about this law being broken?' And Bill Richey cited chapter and verse on every law that was said to be violated. If it was a Supreme Court decision, if it was part of a Supreme Court decision, and case laws all through the thing, he had answers for every single question they raised. No laws were broken.

"The attorneys advised me not to go back there again, so I was not there yesterday. However, it was reported by David Cornwell, our Washington representative, that yesterday morning they had—I don't know how many—three or four members of the oil industry testified. And when that was finished, then Mr. Hamel went in and testified in the afternoon. He gave his prepared statement. After that was finished, Congressman Miller and the members of the committee caucused in private, and I'm told that Mr. Miller said, 'I only have a couple of questions to ask Mr. Hamel and, remember now, if you question Hamel on all the things that we knew he had said and done, and all the lies he had told, it's going to be embarrassing to the chairman and to the committee.' So, one of the minority members, who had been asking questions on our behalf, said, 'Well, Mr. Chairman, if you ask him any questions at all, it would open up the flood gates, and I could be here for days, following up on that. I suggest that you decide that the people who have testified here before have committed no violations of any laws. If you agree to that, I'll agree not to ask any questions.' Mr. Miller said, 'I agree.' They went back into the committee room, no questions were asked of Mr. Hamel, and that was that.

"That's the latest information I have. But, hopefully, friends, the ordeal is over. Whether you'll ever see the good stuff in the press or not, we don't know. But that's not important. The important thing is what's here. Thank you."

IN THE SATURDAY, November 16, 1991, issue of *The Miami Herald*, staff writer Heather Dewar was at Wackenhut's throat again, this time about the resignation of Wayne Black:

Embattled Wackenhut Sleuth Quits

Veteran Miami private eye Wayne Black, who masterminded a covert Wackenhut investigation of an environmental whistle-blower, resigned Thursday amid new allegations of wrongdoing.

The resignation came hours after a Wackenhut Corp. employee and an ex-employee accused him of intimidating potential witnesses in a congressional probe of the undercover operation.

In letters sent to Chesterfield Smith, a member of the board of directors of the Coral Gables security company, Wackenhut private eye David Ramirez accused Black of planting false information designed to ferret out "traitors" in his office and of interrogating workers daily about the actions of employees involved in the congressional probe.

Neither Black nor company founder George Wackenhut could be reached for comment Friday. But a top Wackenhut executive and Black's lawyer said there was no connection between the letters and Black's resignation.

"Wayne has been planning to resign for a while," said his attorney, Jonathan Sale, who called the timing a "coincidence."

"We're very satisfied that Wayne didn't do anything wrong," Sale said.

But Smith, who got the letters, said there was a direct connection.

Smith said he showed the letters to company president [sic] George Wackenhut, who "reached the conclusion that it's not in the best interest of the Wackenhut Corp., its employees and its operations for Mr. Black to any longer be associated with them.

"Mr. Wackenhut was going to terminate Mr. Black, but Mr. Black said he understood the situation and tendered his resignation," Smith said. . . .

"Oh, the same old things," Robert Kneif [sic], Wackenhut senior vice president, said Friday when asked about Ramirez's and Freburg's charges. "We're comfortable with our position that most of these allegations are false."

Kneif [sic] said Black resigned because "for whatever reason, he felt more comfortable working for himself. He preferred not to work for a big corporation."

Smith said he hadn't had time to investigate the allegations. Nonetheless, he said, he agreed with the decision to terminate Black because of "all the turmoil and the agitation in the Special Investigations Division.

"The Wackenhut policy certainly was that there would be no investigation and no punitive action against any employee for any of their testimony," Smith said. "I invite any employee who feels they're being penalized because they were a witness or a potential witness to call it to my attention, and I'll see to it that the board of directors investigates it."

Smith said the company may eliminate the special investigations division, which was created by Black to run undercover or high-tech cases.

"This division, I am told, produced one-fifth of 1 percent of the company income, and it's caused us a great deal of concern and a great deal of trouble," he said. "I think serious concern is being given as to whether or not we want to stay in that kind of business."

Although the Persian Gulf War dominated the headlines during the early months of 1991, other world events of significance included the European end to sanctions on South Africa, April 15. April 18, a cholera epidemic spread through Ecuador and Colombia, after killing 1,100 in Peru and infecting more than 50,000. May 14, William H. Webster retired as director of the CIA; Robert H. Gates succeeded him. June 3, France agreed to sign the 1968 treaty banning the spread of atomic weapons. June 4, the communist government of Albania resigned. June 5, the South African Parliament repealed its apartheid laws. June 20, Berlin again became the capital of Germany. July 10, Boris N. Yeltsin was inaugurated as the first freely elected president of the Russian Republic. August 10, China accepted the nuclear nonproliferation treaty. August 18, a coup failed to unseat Gorbachev after Soviet hard-liners seized him; he credited Yeltsin for his rescue. August 24, Gorbachev sealed the Communist Party's doom when he resigned as secretary general. August 25, three Baltic republics won their independence. September 6, the new Soviet ruling council recognized the independence of Lithuania, Estonia, and Latvia. September 15, the charges against Oliver North were dropped. October 18, Israel and the Soviets resumed relations after twenty-four years. November 5, Robert Maxwell, sixty-eight, the British press magnate, was found dead in the Atlantic. November 18, Anglican envoy Terry Waite and U.S. professor Thomas M. Sutherland were freed by the Lebanese. December 4, Charles H. Keating, Jr., was convicted of fraud in the savings and loan crisis.

And finally, to the astonishment of the world, on December 25, the Soviet Union collapsed with remarkable speed after President Gorbachev's resignation. Constituent republics formed the Commonwealth of Independent States, which the U.S. and other nations quickly moved to recognize.

AT THE CLOSE OF 1991, and for the thirty-seventh consecutive year, TWC had once again succeeded in substantially increasing revenues over the previous year. All three major operating groups contributed to a 9.8 percent across-the-board increase during the year. The corporation had the enviable record of averaging double-digit increases in both revenues and profits for the past five years. Revenues increased to $572.527 million in 1991 versus $521.191 million in 1990. Profits jumped to $7.721 million as compared to $6.963 million for the previous year, an increase of 10.9 percent.

The congressional investigation was over, and George's integrity, questioned in public for the first time, had remained solidly intact. Unfortunately, Charles Hamel's powerful motives of revenge would return to haunt Alyeska and TWC for several years to come.

HURRICANE ANDREW hit South Florida in the early morning hours of Monday, August 24, 1992, and became the major news event of the year. Although it was headline news nationwide for weeks, the effect of its devastation on TWC and its clients was best described by the front-page story in *Pipeline*, written by Barbara McDonald:

Wackenhut Shines During Worst National Disaster in U.S. History

Colossal. Staggering. Incomprehensible. Those words can only begin to describe what the national media has labeled "the worst natural disaster in U.S. history," far exceeding the massive damage inflicted by the legendary San Francisco earthquake and fire of 1906.

Preparations for a worst-case scenario fell short only because the final script delivered by Hurricane Andrew made a mockery of those well-intentioned preparations. No amount of preparation by ordinary citizens or planning by the arsenals of disaster experts could have lessened the horrific devastation and catastrophic chaos caused by Hurricane Andrew. And the frustration of coping with individual disaster was compounded by the task of servicing clients who were also going through a living hell while in desperate need of security services.

This monumental task of servicing clients under unprecedented natural disaster conditions, when your logistical support system has been decimated, is beyond description. This report is only a feeble attempt to describe how this was accomplished by our Wackenhut personnel who diverted their energies from taking care of their personal devastations to that of taking care of our clients. What it took to cover our clients' posts can best be understood by starting at the beginning.

Before dawn on Monday morning, August 24, Hurricane Andrew came and conquered. The initial survey of the damage focused on Miami Beach and the north end of Dade and Broward counties. These areas were damaged to the extent of broken glass, downed trees, power lines, traffic lights, and minor structural damage. It was not until much later in the day, when media crews were able to creep into south Dade, that the devastation slowly began to take focus.

Devastation turned into decimation. Many of our employees at headquarters and security personnel from the Miami office live in the areas that bore the brunt of Andrew. Power was out in Broward County and all of Dade County, telephone and radio communications were almost nonexistent, and roads were impassable. Getting a readout on our coverage status was virtually impossible. One employee at the Dispatch Center had been in the dark for 24 hours trying to man the telephones for whatever calls could get through.

On Tuesday, August 25, the Boca Raton and Fort Lauderdale offices were inundated with desperate calls from non-clients who needed security protection from the looters. Many of these callers had security service with other companies who were unable to provide service to them. In fact, these security companies actually told their clients to call Wackenhut.

During this time, we were receiving requests for extra coverage from our clients. Of particular note is that 99 percent of our client demand was for Custom Protection Officers.

Obviously, the decision was made that the needs of our clients came first and that we would do everything possible to provide service for them. The employees of Boca Raton and Fort Lauderdale offices shifted into high gear to sustain client service for the Miami office. This required immediately shipping 23 Custom Protection Officers from Boca Raton and Fort Lauderdale to help cover posts in Miami.

Boca Raton clients, such as IBM, The Polo Club of Boca Raton, and Broken Sound, were eager to assist us in this effort by freeing up some of our Custom Protection Officers to protect clients in Miami. The CPOs were equipped with food, clothing, and sleeping bags. (In one instance, an elderly store clerk in Boca Raton insisted on contributing $20 to help buy sun block for our CPOs.)

At some of the posts, our CPOs stood 24-hour shifts because of the threat of armed looters. Also, the sound of gunfire by the looters made sleep impossible during rotated break periods. In extreme situations, these people were standing post amid the smell of rotting food and maggots. Other CPOs rested between shifts at corporate headquarters, which had been closed down for a week.

Our K-9 patrol (German shepherds) proved invaluable deterrents to would-be looters who approached our officers in armed groups. All it took was one warning that the K-9 would be unleashed to scare them away; and they ran, guns and all.

The rotation logistics became more difficult with each passing day. Fresh crews that were rotated had to be equipped with water and ice, which were rare commodities in Dade, Broward, and Palm Beach counties. Bottled water, ice, and other supplies had been shipped by stores in Palm Beach to Dade County, which is why a scarcity existed all over. Neighbors in Boca Raton bagged ice from their refrigerators to help us supply the need.

Traffic jams into Dade County were horrendous due to the thousands of relief caravans bringing in supplies. Telephone service remained a nightmare. Employees of the Boca Raton and Fort Lauderdale offices spent hours with nonstop redialing to the Miami office and Dispatch Center to coordinate logistics. (Many members of the skeletal command-post staff from the Miami office who were involved in these logistics, and security personnel standing post, had lost their homes.)

By the end of the week, our security needs were so great that we began shipping in approximately 100 officers from Georgia, Alabama, Louisiana, and Florida. Arrangements were made to house and bed them at headquarters. Because of our commitment to our client base, we were staffing our permanent accounts at normal rates and time-and-a-half for over 40 hours, as opposed to offers of $30–$40 per hour to non-clients. These higher rates were necessitated by officers' travel and living expenses, which non-clients were willing to pay.

This operation will result in a no-win, no-profit situation for TWC. The important aspect is that our permanent client base knows that we have done our best to service them under unprecedented conditions, with profit motive as the least of our concerns. When other security companies *could not deliver*, and pulled the rug, the South Florida Division of TWC energized itself in the name of service and commitment. Supervisors and management personnel tirelessly gave of themselves under 20-

hour work days. The super-human efforts of our employees redefined the true meaning of teamwork. They remain nameless; it's what they wanted.

It was a week of indescribable loss, pain, suffering, tragedy, and chaos, all of which has affected our Wackenhut employees in South Florida. The area looks like a war zone with more than 200,000 people left homeless, at least 70,000 homes destroyed, over $30 billion in damages, and military personnel and equipment everywhere. And the relief efforts have been further hampered by torrential rain, lack of water, ice, oppressive heat, mosquito infestation, sanitation health hazards, odors from rotting trash, and gridlock traffic. Despite all this, the beauty of human compassion surpassed the ugliness of Hurricane Andrew.

The conditions were heartbreaking, pure and simple. The mental strain for everyone was just overwhelming. There is nowhere to find relief when devastation is all around and people have only the strength to scramble for Band-Aid solutions until they can begin permanent rebuilding of their lives.

Part of that rebuilding is knowing that our company did not cave-in when others did. Even the payroll and other vital corporate functions were met through the efforts of an exhausted skeletal corporate staff, who also bagged ice between duties. Wackenhut delivered its finest performance during its darkest hour. It is to all the remarkable people who so selflessly gave of themselves to meet our clients' needs and TWC's internal operations that this article is dedicated.

As Barbara McDonald's article indicated, Hurricane Andrew inflicted its worst devastation throughout southeast Dade County—exactly where the majority of the Miami office and headquarters employees lived. Literally hundreds of their homes were destroyed or severely damaged, leaving them and their families suddenly homeless, without food, water, adequate clothing, medical attention, transportation, or money. The story of how TWC's personnel all pulled together to help each other is dramatic and unprecedented.

Soon after the hurricane, we conducted a Q & A interview with Al Guastella, TWC's senior vice president of Domestic Operations, who immediately assumed full responsibility for creating and implementing a Disaster Relief Plan. Guastella combined decisive leadership and tenacity with a quick and easy sense of humor and perspective that proved inspirational to everyone concerned.

Q: When did you realize how badly your employees were hit?

A: Monday morning, August 24, at nine o'clock, when I stepped outside and saw the damage to my house, and I realized the number of employees who lived in the area, and particularly south of us. That morning, I drove twenty-five blocks to Alan Bernstein's house to make sure he was alive. It took me an hour, it was an experience just trying to get there. His house was trashed, not a total loss, but significant damage, like mine. Then I called Jim Murray, who is our vice president of the New York-New Jersey District. Of course, it was business-as-usual for about eighty-five of our offices. So I had to put somebody in charge, not having our own communications here. I told Jim to take over, break down the country, talk to our key managers, and take care of business. The way we operate now, we give our area managers considerable authority, so it was just giving somebody the ultimate responsibility.

Q: On Tuesday, what were the basic conditions at headquarters?

A: There was no air conditioning, but we had electricity, so I set up shop just outside our ground-floor office in the atrium courtyard. I made a few phone calls. Bernie Reilly came in, I remember. Basically, my first concern was to account for my people.

Q: When did you set up the Command Center?

A: Wednesday. I took a long telephone cord outside, lots of water, set up shop out there, and talked to my managers. Obviously, I told Dispatch what we were doing, I talked to Jim Murray, I talked to Carl Page, Brian Reynolds. Marty Holleran worked the telephones admirably, trying to get in touch with people. We had a lot of telephone calls from the field, asking if everybody was all right, offering to come down and help.

Q: When you started learning how many employees' homes were destroyed or badly damaged, what actions did you take first?

A: The first person that called, on Tuesday, was Keith Lewis. Keith is a long-time employee, he had extensive damage. I got one of the road captains from the Miami office to take ice and water down to him. We had placed an announcement in the newspaper on Wednesday that generated some calls to our 800 number. The problem was, a lot of people were not getting newspaper delivery. So I asked Marty Holleran, on Thursday, if he could do something with the radio stations, which he did, and that generated quite a few more phone calls.

Q: Explain how you started to get supplies?

A: On Thursday, Ken Crawford, our manager in Sarasota, called and said, "What do you need?" I told him we needed ice, water, canned goods, cold sandwiches. He and his manager of Physical Security, Bill Rivenbark, drove down Thursday with the supplies. On Friday, George Kent, our manager in Fort Myers, drove down with similar-type supplies. Also on Friday afternoon, Bill Stodder came down from Lakeland with a lot of water, canned goods, two huge coolers that he put in the back seat of his car. Actually, he removed the back seat of his car to get the coolers in there, with a total of eighty bags of ice.

Q: Where did you get the big freezer?

A: Well, it was then that I realized that I needed somewhere to store and maintain this ice. So I called Bob Green, our manager in Tampa, and asked him to somehow get us a stand-up freezer that we could plug in here to preserve the ice. To give you an example, I was good for two or three bags of ice a day. By that time we had regular "customers" who knew we were here and alive and were depending on us. People from my department started filtering in and assisting. I couldn't have done any of this without their assistance. We established supply runs for people whose needs we had identified. On Saturday morning at 7:30, we met Bob Green and his area supervisor, Mike Watkins; they drove their trucks through the night with this big freezer and sixty bags of ice. Helping to unload it were Mr. Munk and Mr. Aldrich, Jim Sonntag, and many others. Bob also brought down about 100 sandwiches. For three days, we were actually feeding some of the out-of-town security officers, who were housed in headquarters, until restaurants in the area opened, and they could use their per diem.

Q: You hired a plane with a message trailer to get in touch with employees in the disaster areas who couldn't be reached otherwise?

A: That's right. When I realized that a lot of our people weren't getting the paper and couldn't listen to the radio, I used my American Express card and chartered a plane to fly around the disaster area with a sign behind it reading: "Wackenhut Employees Requiring Aid, Call 1-800-666-5350," our number here in Operations. So, it was a group effort. Marty Holleran helped me coordinate the radio ad and renting of the airplane.

Q: You also drove around to people's houses?

A: I tried to account for people myself. I went to Jim Rowan's house, Marc Shapiro's house, Al Arbuthnot's house, Keith Lewis's house. The work took different dimensions. I sent Jim Sonntag, Martin Aldrich, and Bob Shelly down to Keith's house with shovels, rakes, and a chain-saw, the whole thing, to do that kind of work. Jim Granan deserves so much credit, his house was trashed, way down in Homestead, but he was here at work, and we helped him out with whatever we could. Gil Mugarra in Investigations deserves a lot of credit, he came up with these family-kit packages, 100 of them, very popular items. Each box contains basic items such as soap, towels, water, canned goods, toilet paper, toothbrushes, toothpaste, soft drinks. There's another version that has female products, and another version strictly for babies. Bob Jankowski from Information Systems, who lives up in Broward, brought in ice on a daily basis, big chunks of ice that he made himself.

Q: Tell about those two truckloads of emergency supplies from Texas.

A: On Tuesday, I went around talking to department heads. And I found out through Bob Mianowski and Chuck Lister of the Corrections group that their people in Bridgeport, Texas, had put out an appeal for supplies. The people of the state of Texas responded to the tune of two eighteen-foot U-Haul trucks, filled top to bottom with boxes containing clothing and food. They loaded the vans, it took them about two and a half days to get here. They sustained a flat tire somewhere in Mississippi, which slowed them down, but they arrived here Sunday, September 6, about noon. We had people here every weekend, including Labor Day, because we feel that if we're here, and we've helped one individual, we've accomplished something significant. So, Sunday, we had a bunch of people here helping to unload the trucks. As the days went by, the main necessities went from water to ice, and then finally to clothing and money.

Q: You opened a special bank account for the Disaster Relief Plan?

A: On Tuesday, when I talked to Jim Murray, he said, "I'm going to take up a collection and I'm going to send you money—and I'm sending you cash—because I trust you, I rely on you. Use your discretion." He sent me $1,255 in cash. Other managers have contributed likewise. We've since opened a bank account, we're getting contributions by check. Now, basically, I've interviewed approximately 100 individuals in private, I've heard their stories, and I've helped them financially, using my judgment—taking into account whether they're single, married, married with children, the extent of the loss, where they're living, whether they have electricity or not. We've helped about 100 people in that fashion. We've even housed people here at headquarters, people who work in the Miami office. Most are security officers and a few clerical people who work at headquarters.

Q: You held a meeting of department heads on Tuesday, September 8, to explain how the Disaster Relief Plan was being implemented?

A: Yes. Now we're in the process of sorting out the clothing that came in from Texas, to make it available for people to look at and select. We've taken a suite of offices at headquarters that's vacant for the time being. I've had my "goons," as I call them, my managers of Operations—they're the young guys with the muscles—and I've had them move boxes from three "wholesale" areas and into the suite of offices. We've identified each large room as, for example, men's clothing, another room would be for ladies' clothing, another for children, and we're trying to break that down to boys and girls. We plan to offer this clothing to our employees, their families, their friends, their neighbors, even to strangers. Because that's the kind of company we are. When we were unloading Bob Green's freezer and ice on Saturday, August 29, an elderly couple drove by, and their eyes went wide when they saw all that ice. I walked up to them, I said, "Can I help you?" They said, "Can we buy some ice?" I gave them a couple of bags, I said, "We're with Wackenhut. Please take the ice and come back if you need anything else." So, we're here to help anybody that we can.

GEORGE J. SHANNON replaced Bill Scherle as manager of TWC's Building Services on March 30, 1992, just five months before Hurricane Andrew hit the headquarters building, and he would be working to repair the damages for the next two years. Born in Brooklyn, New York, June 23, 1927, Shannon went to St. Agnes High School in Rockville Center, Long Island, left after his junior year to join the U.S. Navy in 1944. When his Navy service was over, he entered South Side High School, also in Rockville Center, and graduated in 1947. After a large snowstorm that year, he hitchhiked to Florida and accepted a baseball scholarship at Stetson University in Deland, Florida, where he majored in business administration. After two years, he received an associate in arts degree in business from Stetson in 1949.

Shannon had been superintendent of buildings and grounds for the Catholic Archdiocese of New York for twenty-three years, with responsibility for 127 parishes containing over 400 buildings, before he retired in 1972 to become a building services consultant.

"When Hurricane Andrew hit on August 24, I arrived at headquarters the following afternoon about two o'clock," he says. "As I walked into the atrium, my first reaction was that of horror. It was just a total disaster. The whole skylight roof was on the floor of the atrium, trees were down, debris was just all over the place. I mean, it was just one hell of a mess. Al Guastella was there, and we were talking, and then Walter Mobley of General Services showed up.

"Walter and I just surveyed the whole place. I went immediately to the 'Chiller Room,' our air conditioning room on the mezzanine floor, just off the garage, to see what was going on. This is where our engines are, the centrifugal engines that supply all the air conditioning throughout the building. And nothing was running, of course, at that particular time, except our generator. The generator was running, and I was thankful for that. I made a few phone calls to Florida Power & Light to see what was happening. Within two hours, the electricity came on in the building.

"The cooling tower in the back of the building was hit, and we had a twelve-inch pipe up there that was just ripped off. I called a contractor to see if he could do anything about it right away. Well, they did come over the same day, and this was amazing. I knew them, and they were taking care of the building already, which is Parks & Thompson, Inc., and the president is Joe Gorski. They came over and we looked at the damage to the tower, because we couldn't run any air conditioning without that tower. We couldn't get any parts that day, naturally. But late Wednesday, we got the piece of pipe, Mr. Gorski had a piece in his stockyard. His man came over with it, Pat, and we managed to get Miami Plumbing opened, they had a couple of men come in. We needed a ninety-degree, twelve-inch elbow, and they had that in stock. We went up on the tower and sat there and put that thing together. And within three or four hours, I guess, we had the air conditioning running. This was still Wednesday.

"Of course, you still couldn't walk in the atrium. Of the 196 custom Plexiglass windows in the skylight, only ten remained intact. In the beginning, I estimated the cost of replacing those skylight windows at about $208,000. That was a quick estimate, because we didn't really know what that smoked Plexiglass cost. Actually, what it turned out to be, it was a total of $140,000 to buy and install it.

"On Thursday, I called Robert Fenton, who is a general contractor down here and had done work for us before. I knew from watching television that this whole area was a mess, and we couldn't get a GC, a general contractor. You need a GC to get the building permits in Coral Gables. Robert Fenton was nice enough to call me back and come over to the building on Thursday. We took a look at the outside damage, the 'what we could see' damage. So we decided to call the 'what we could see' damage Phase I. He was magnificent. We went right from there. I sat down with the insurance company, I negotiated for about $300,000. They wrote us a check immediately for $295,000.

"Phase I, we had to repair the soffits outside the building, the overhangs, that were hanging loose from the building. Now, immediately, we had to decide what we had to do to repair these things. We needed a plan, so we sat down and drew up a sketch to go to the Coral Gables Building and Zoning Department, because in Coral Gables you have to have a sketch and a plan for everything to get a damn permit. In the meantime, he was negotiating on the phone with a company in Fort Lauderdale who specialized in this kind of construction, scaffolding work, because we had to put scaffolds up on the sides of the building. So, we were only a week into this thing, we had the scaffolding up already.

"During the first three days, I had sixteen people in the building clearing up the mess down on the atrium floor. But we had a terrific amount of cooperation from the vendors that we dealt with. Therefore, we could move. Most of the Plexiglass panels from the skylight were down on the floor, and they just cut the trees and plants all up, so we had to pull up all the trees and plants, everything. Those panels measured four-by-six feet and weighed seventy-five pounds each.

"Phase I also included all the electrical work outside, all the closed-circuit television cameras at all the entrances that were all blown away and torn up. But, naturally, we concentrated on the atrium floor first, so we could move around. Phase I went on from late August of 1992 through January of 1993, and we spent the whole $295,000 on it.

"Phase II was all the damage that you *couldn't* see. Now, the wind hit us at about 145 miles an hour. First, we concentrated on our two tar-and-stone roofs that cover the penthouse and, actually, the offices right down to the first floor. What happened was that the roof attached to the parapet that goes around the outside of the roof, had separated. The wind had literally lifted the roof up like a rug, and put it down again. So, when you got down on your hands and knees, you could see how the wind had gotten under that and lifted it up. What it did was—the amazing thing—it laid it down like a blanket.

"The trees and plants and statues outside of the penthouse windows are in a recessed and sheltered space only about six feet wide, and they have an outside wall, so the wind really went over that area and didn't do much damage at all.

"So Phase II was really the roofs, and later the painting of the building. The original paint was a very light beige, almost an off-white type of color, and after all that wind and debris, it looked like it had been sandblasted, especially on the north side. We started painting the building in May of 1993. At first, we estimated that it would take just a few months, but we found out that it was an extremely difficult building to paint because it's so angular, particularly around the atrium. So the painting took from May of 1993 to

December of 1993, about five months. The color on the outside, along the street, and inside the atrium, is the same, what they call 'Winchester 73.' That's a gray shade, a very good paint. The bottoms of all the planters in the atrium are a little darker brownish-gray, and the tops of the planters are a brick-red color called Country Redwood.

"All of these colors were selected by Mrs. Wackenhut. She picked them out of the book that we gave her, and I think they look great. She has exquisite taste.

"So far, Phase II has cost approximately $300,000, and we still haven't finished all the incidentals [February 1994], but I estimate the total cost of Phases I and II will be around $700,000. I did all the negotiating with the insurance company, and the insurance basically covered everything. Any natural disaster that we have here is covered by our insurance.

"There was a fairly large fountain inside the atrium, behind the glass elevator, and that's gone now. After the hurricane, Alan Bernstein gave me a call one day and said to me, 'George, how much does it cost us to run that particular fountain?' I said, 'I don't know, but I'll certainly let you know in fifteen minutes.' So I checked with the kilowatts on the motors, and put it all together, and found out that it cost about $6,000 to $7,000 a year to run that one fountain! So I went up to see Alan and told him, and he said, 'Oh, my *God!*' So we went to see Mr. Rick Wackenhut and told him, and he said, 'George, can you fill that fountain in?' I said, 'Sure.' And then I said—I don't know why I said it—I said, 'But I think we'd better ask Mrs. Wackenhut first.' Which we did. I called Mrs. Wackenhut and told her, and she asked me a couple of questions, and she said, 'Cover it.' It was also her idea to cover the one in the front of the building, under the 'Wackenhut' name.

"The big fountain at the entrance to the building is still under repair. The top ledge, the sitting area, is now painted Country Redwood, but the inside, which used to be blue, is now painted black. That's what Mrs. Wackenhut wanted. Because the water will be white, of course, and when the water comes out of the black it will give you a brilliant crystal appearance that will look very nice, especially when it's all lighted. We had it running the other day.

"If I had to pick a date when all of the repairs from the hurricane will be completely finished, it would probably be May of this year. It will have taken from August of 1992 to May of 1994, and cost about $700,000."

When the hurricane hit, George and Ruth had been vacationing at their summer home in Cape Cod (Osterville, Massachusetts) for about a month. Rick and Molly and their children, and Jan and Roger and Tresha, decided almost at the last minute to move out of their homes and spend that night at Tyecliffe, because of the obvious safety it afforded, even though it was in such close proximity to Biscayne Bay.

Molly laughs as she remembers that night: "I guess we moved into that fabulous hotel about eight o'clock Sunday night. Because we really couldn't make a decision to stay there earlier. You know, it came so fast in the end. We were still boarding up and packing up. And Rick had planned that if it turned into a Category 4, he would pack the family into the car and head up north. But I knew we would be stuck on I-95. So I said, 'You're crazy, we can't do it, we're going to The Castle.' At which stage, he laughed at me and said: 'No one goes to the *water*, Molly!'

"Well, if you've seen that house, you know you're safe. Solid. We stayed upstairs in the movie theater. It was the biggest room, it was carpeted, my kids could put their sleeping bags down. We were the largest family. Rick slept and Jan slept, and I don't know how they could sleep through all that noise and confusion. Jan and Roger stayed in the French quarters, I guess it's called, where Nana used to sleep. Tresha bounced around; she stayed with my kids some of the time, with her mom some of the time. And then Rick went to sleep in one of the other bedrooms. There were two bedrooms up over the kitchen, and he was sleeping in one of those.

"My kids, three of them slept, one didn't—Lisa didn't. Thank God she didn't, because she's the one who felt the floor moving. See, underneath the movie theater is an open gallery. And the wind was somehow getting under there, and you could feel the floor moving. So, when she told me that, I said, 'Come on, we're moving!' So I took everybody out of there and moved them into the hallway. Just about that time, the wind got really bad, it ripped one of the shutters off the bedroom Rick was sleeping in. So I ran in there and said, 'Get out of bed!' And just as he got out of bed, one of the stained-glass windows broke. So we were really lucky.

"Next morning, the landscape was just awful. It was so beautiful to begin with, it was really hard to look at it. Gosh, I remember walking out and seeing fish in the driveway, all over. You could hardly tell where one area stopped and another began, because there was so much rubble everywhere. There was a big boat in the courtyard!

"The alarm was going all night. Not in the main building where we were, but we could hear it. It was the alarm in Mom and Dad's quarters and we couldn't turn it off. This was, of course, after the electricity went out, which was 3:30, I think. Then the generator came on. Anyway, so Roger and I decided that we were going to go and shut the alarm off. Tried to open the door, going over to their quarters. It was incredible, it was just wild. I mean, you can't imagine how much power there was to that wind. But he made it. I held the door while he went across to the other one, opened up their quarters, went down and tried to shut it off. I couldn't let the door slam because, at that stage, he could've been locked out! So, anyway, he got it off once, and then it went back on, and we just gave up.

"The funny part is, when we called Mom and told her we were going over to their house, she said, 'Don't take any pets with you!' Well, this is what we took with us: We took our two cats, our dog, and about thirty birds in cages! And Jan brought her two cats. Then, when we got there, Mom's two cats had been left outside, so we let them in. So we had six cats, one dog, and thirty birds! When Mom found out we had cats, she said, 'Whatever you do, don't let them in the French quarters bathroom!' That was exactly where the cats spent the night!

"I think we stayed three days and then decided we'd get back home and start digging out. The staff didn't stay there the night of the hurricane, but I remember they showed up the next day to see if everything was all right at the house. That's loyalty. They came to check and see how things were.

"When I saw our own house, I was grateful, I didn't expect to see it standing. It's all wood, so I never thought it would make it through. The reason I got to see it before anyone else is that Jenny and I decided, the next day, to take a walk, just down Casuarina to see things. When we got to the end of Casuarina, we just couldn't resist the urge. I said, 'Jenny, we've gotten this far.' And she goes, 'Mom, let's walk it.' So we walked home that day. I remember it taking forever, to climb over trees and go around wires and dig through. Because you couldn't find Old Cutler Road, where we live. It was completely covered with debris. I got lost, I know, four times, and I was on a straight road. When I finally came to our neighborhood and saw part of our wall, I knew where our house should be. I could see the roof, and I thought: Dear God, isn't that amazing? It was still standing. I mean, a lot of damage, but I expected it to be leveled."

PRIOR TO Hurricane Andrew, 1992 had an auspicious beginning for TWC. On January 1, Wackenhut Nuclear Services (WSN) commenced a new three-year, $7.5 million contract with Wisconsin Electric Power Company to provide nuclear security services at its Point Beach Nuclear Power Plant in Two Creeks, Wisconsin.

Shortly thereafter, Wackenhut Education Services, Inc. (WESI), a subsidiary of TWC, was awarded a $15.5 million contract by the U.S. Department of Labor to operate the 650-student McKinney Job Corps Center in McKinney, Texas. The two-year contract was subject to three one-year extensions.

TWC's Custom Protection Division (CPD) had initiated physical security and fare inspection service for the Tri-County Commuter Rail Authority, operated by the State of Florida, with fifteen stations extending through a sixty-seven-mile corridor between West Palm Beach and Miami. The CPD contract was anticipated to reach 1,000 hours weekly in early 1992. CPOs assigned to Tri-Rail were all armed and radio-equipped, and divided their time between the trains, station patrol, and vehicle patrol to maximize their visibility throughout the system.

Also early in the year, TWC's Domestic Operations Group had out-negotiated two rival, major security companies to purchase International Service Systems, a 15,000-hour-a-week, $7 million annual revenue security guard service with operations in seven cities. TWC had about two seconds to celebrate the successful acquisition before getting on with the task at hand: Hiring and outfitting 470 new employees, spending time with 140 new clients, expanding six area offices, and starting a seventh office from scratch.

On March 7, Carl E. Page, district manager for Ohio, and based in Columbus, was selected as Area Manager of the Year for 1991. During that year, the total gross revenues generated by the Columbus area office amounted to $5.583 million, an increase of $2.103 million over the previous year.

Promotions announced early in the year included that of Al Arbuthnot to vice president of Domestic Operations; James M. Sonntag to vice president, Operations; and Wynne Leon to vice president, National Accounts. Gary A. Sanders, who joined TWC in 1979, and had served most recently as vice president, Nuclear Operations, was promoted to president of the Nuclear Services Division. Daniel E. Mason, who joined TWC after ten years with the Coastal Corporation, and had recently been controller of Domestic Operations, was promoted to vice president and chief financial officer of the Domestic Operations Group.

At the April meeting of the board, Clark G. Redick, the former COO of UtiliCorp United, Inc., a multistate utility firm headquartered in Kansas City, was named senior vice president and general counsel of TWC. Redick was with AT&T from 1972 to 1988, having served as general attorney and assistant secretary, and was head of AT&T's law department in Kansas City with responsibility for a five-state area. He was promoted to vice president in 1986 and was the top AT&T executive in Kansas City before moving to UtiliCorp.

April and May were banner months for Wackenhut Corrections. In April, three contracts were executed that represented additional annual revenues of over $13 million. Opening ceremonies were held May 5 for the San Diego City Jail, under management by WCC. The 200-bed facility features three housing buildings and two additional units, one for administration and one for booking and health services. The facility was designed and built by Wackenhut at a cost of $5.5 million, and WCC signed a ten-year contract with the city, plus options for renewals.

New contracts for WCC also included a major agreement with the Immigrations and Naturalization Service (INS) for the expansion of the Aurora, Colorado, INS Detention facility to 300 beds. Construction of an additional 34,000 square feet of space, along with renovation of the existing building was already underway and scheduled to be completed in August of 1992. Wackenhut's 500-bed Kyle, Texas, Pre-Release Center, under a contract with the Texas Commission on Alcohol and Drug Abuse, would now provide the world's largest in-prison chemical dependency treatment program. This meant that inmates who have histories of chemical dependency would be housed at this facility and take part in the nine- to twelve-month intensive in-prison therapeutic program called "New Vision."

In Queensland, Australia, WCC was awarded a contract to manage and operate a 380-bed Remand and Reception Centre, located outside Brisbane, in a joint venture with Australasian Correctional Management PTY Limited.

On September 9, Tim Cole, president of WSI, announced that TWC was awarded a contract renewal for security and protective services at the Department of Energy's facility at Rocky Flats, Colorado, after a competitive bidding process. Cole said the contract was for three years, with two one-year renewal options, and that it would begin on February 1, 1993. Annual revenues were placed at approximately $50 million for the initial year, and WSI would be eligible for an award fee based on performance evaluation.

On October 1, WSI was selected by the Department of Energy's Nevada Field Office to continue providing protective services for the Nevada Test Site and related government facilities in the Las Vegas area through a five-year, $140 million contract that would continue through September 30, 1997.

October 19, Mirtha Latour, who started her career with TWC in 1962 as a typist in the Accounting Department, and who would go on to become director of Payroll and Billing, celebrated her thirtieth anniversary, to join the exclusive group of thirty-year employees in the thirty-eight-year history of the company, three of whom would attain the milestone in 1992, an historic first for TWC. Ansel T. Minick, manager of Operations in Jacksonville, reached his thirtieth on May 5, and Bernardo Galarza Cruz, a TWC security officer in San Juan, Puerto Rico, would celebrate his thirtieth on December 12.

HEADLINE HISTORY in the nation and the world during 1992: February 1, Bush and Yeltsin proclaimed a formal end to the Cold War. February 21, the U.S. lifted trade sanctions against China. February 27, the U.N. rebuked Iraq on the disposal of weapons of mass destruction. March 3, Bush apologized publicly for breaking his campaign promise and raising taxes. April 16, the FDA restricted the use of silicone in breast implants. March 18, South African whites voted for majority rule. April 1, seven industrial democracies agreed to aid Russia. April 9, General Noriega, the former Panama leader, was convicted in a U.S. court. April 14, the U.S. imposed sanctions against Libya. May 20, six industrial nations planned a nuclear cleanup for Eastern Europe. May 22, the U.S. ordered sanctions against Belgrade; the U.N. voted sanctions on May 30. June 16, Caspar W. Weinberger was indicted in the Iran-Contra affair. June 17, the last Western hostages were freed in Lebanon. June 29, the Supreme Court reaffirmed the right to abortion. July 1, a House panel exonerated Bush in the hostage-release inquiry. Also on July 1, the first food was airlifted to Sarajevo. July 10, General Noriega was sentenced to forty years on drug charges. July 11, the Democrats nominated Bill Clinton and Al Gore. July 13, the Israeli parliament approved Yitzhak Rabin's coalition government, dominated by the Labor Party. July 23, Israel halted new settlements in the occupied areas. August 20, the Republicans nominated Bush and Quayle. September 1, Bush pledged federal funds for Hurricane Andrew's devastation of South Florida. September 22, the U.N. expelled Serbian-dominated Yugoslavia. October 1, the Serbs resumed "ethnic cleansing" of the Muslims. October 9, the U.N. Council created a Bosnian "no fly" zone. November 3, Bill Clinton was elected president, Al Gore vice president, and the Democrats retained control of Congress. November 24, the last U.S. forces left the Philippines, ending nearly a century of American military presence. November 25, the Czechoslovak parliament approved a separation into two nations. December 3, the U.N. approved a U.S.-led force to guard food for Somalia. December 9, the Prince and Princess of Wales agreed to separate. December 14, the Russian parliament confirmed Chernomyrdin as premier in a deal with Yeltsin. December 17, Israel deported about 400 Palestinians. December 24, Bush pardoned six former Reagan Administration officials involved in the Iran-Contra affair. December 29, hard-liners ousted Premier Panic of Yugoslavia.

THE GENERAL ECONOMIC SITUATION in the U.S. gave the business community little to applaud in 1992, but TWC achieved some significant objectives, while managing a 10 percent increase in both revenues and income for the year. During 1992, revenues increased to $630.320 million, compared to $572.527 million in 1991, up 10.1 percent. Net income was $8.507 million, up from $7.721 million the previous year, a jump of 10.2 percent.

TWC's corporate goal of maintaining a sustained profitable growth pattern was achieved principally through the continued expansion of its international operations and the growth of its correctional business.

The corporation continued to benefit from the trend of municipalities seeking alternative and less expensive methods of providing for public safety. Private security officers would now supplement the services of law enforcement officers, without sacrificing the level of security and protection to the public.

34

Not so long ago, it would have been unthinkable. Starting January 1, 1993, it became a reality: Wackenhut International, Inc. (WII), had officially registered to open operations in Moscow, in a joint venture with the Commonwealth of Independent States (CIS), formerly the USSR. The joint venture, named "Wackenhut Russia," was under the supervision of Tony Sharpe, WII's senior vice president of Europe. Actual security operations started at the end of April.

Born Anthony H. Sharpe in Ilkley, England, April 22, 1944, Sharpe studied medical photography at the University of Leeds and was awarded the standard certificate by the City and Guilds London Institute in 1962. He then joined the academic staff at Leeds University Medical Centre for research in microphotography, pathology, biology, and teaching material. A co-author of several scientific papers, he filmed major surgical operations, and entered the Paris Film Festival with a movie on facial implants that was judged third in its class.

Sharpe immigrated to Toronto, Canada, in 1966, where he ran his own real estate business, owned a nightclub and some car lots, and operated a furniture-leasing program, all simultaneously. After several years, he decided that he should look for a more stable situation, and joined Anning Services, a firm specializing in investigations and top-level security.

"I started with them as a favor, actually, to set up their photographic department within the investigations group," Sharp recalls, smiling. "And I really just never left. I had various jobs with them in junior and senior management, and wound up as president when I was thirty-two years old. I started with them in March of 1968. The company was amalgamated with two other security companies to form Wackenhut of Canada in January of 1970."

Before the end of that year, Sharpe was promoted to manager of investigations in London, Ontario, and, in 1972, he was named area manager in Kitchener. He was appointed regional manager in 1974, then vice president of Operations in July of 1975. Eventually, he was appointed president, Wackenhut Canada, Ltd., in a letter of authorization from Bud Thompson, dated December 16, 1976.

After ten years of continued profit and growth in Canada, Sharpe was transferred to his native land in the United Kingdom as managing director and CEO of Wackenhut U.K., Ltd., in 1986, then became WII's vice president of Europe and Canada in 1992. During his tenure in England, he opened new offices, offered new services, and developed one of the most diverse and largest aviation divisions in the U.K., with more than fifty clients.

"I was there for five and a half years," Sharpe says, "and during that time we were starting to look at Europe and had a handle on a couple of things we wanted to do. I think the corporation had gone through a couple of people trying to develop the European operations, and it didn't work out for various reasons. I had a fairly good knowledge of the area, having traveled through Europe for years when I lived there as a young man. So I suppose it made sense, using a British passport, with EC availability.

"So we started to look at it and put some thoughts together. And, eventually, I was transferred here [headquarters] to do that. The first one was Russia, although we had started looking at Czechoslovakia—as it was then, earlier—but we actually opened in Russia. We filed for registration on January 1, 1993, got licensed in April, started operations toward the end of April, and our first real billing was in May. We had a general manager, a field support manager, and myself.

"A lot of Western businessmen have been hit by crime in Russia and it's ever increasing. We want to be able to help these companies to have honest security and provide the protection that they require when running a business. We started in Moscow with Peter Gurinchuk as general manager, and he's still with us. Gurinchuk is a former Petrovka-38 colonel. He was in the public relations department and has many contacts in the media, which has helped us, and I believe he has the right kind of personality for our business and for business ethics in general. During the initial year, television, radio, and print coverage was fostered, and local contacts assured a significant impact. We're also assured that business flow should be steady with the initial concentration on physical security. Following this period, we plan to focus attention on the need for electronic surveillance, residential alarms, and related security equipment."

According to Sharpe, Moscow today, with a population in excess of nine million, and an average of three million visitors at any given time, is not unlike the U.S. Wild West, with significant business ventures springing up on a daily basis. Laws for structure and taxation on business ventures have been changing, sometimes weekly, but the end result is a copy of Western-style structure moving closer to our common business practices.

During 1994, WII was offering security service for physical assets, buildings, hotels, warehouses, retail stores, and factories. Bodyguards are provided for business visitors, both foreign and national. The same guards also act as drivers, escorting executives for the duration of their visit. They are armed and equipped with the latest electronic communication devices. In addition, WII provides cash-in-transit protection for hard-currency retail stores, and, utilizing the same vehicles, protects the transportation of valuables for dealers and import-export companies. WII also offers full business services, including secure accommodations, translation office services, background checks, appointment escorts, and legal services.

Oleg Krasovskey, a Russian attorney with twenty partners, is one of WII's partners, and an integral part of the business structure. He is well-connected and a well-known Afghan war hero with many supporters for a foreign venture in security.

"We expanded into St. Petersburg in the early part of 1994," Sharpe continues. "It's a different style of city and it has a lot more organized crime. In June 1993, we opened with the Czech Republic, which, at that time, was all of Czechoslovakia, in the city of Prague. We took over a company with about 120 guards. They were in need of some organization and needed discipline in European and American standards. We also opened a small operation in France, with a single client, and, unfortunately, we had a near-death situation with the gentleman who was assisting us to build that business, so it's kind of taken a back seat at the moment. But we have one client in Paris. We are also in Greece, and have been there for some time. At the end of 1994, we hope to open in Mainland China.

"By the end of 1994, I expect to be in some more countries. It will depend upon how the opportunities go, but we have an opportunity in Poland, and we will be in Slovakia in a couple of months time. We have an opportunity in Bulgaria that we'll probably take, and we're looking at a joint venture in Italy right now. We have a possibility in Estonia, and we probably will look at some other Eastern European countries. Hungary is another possibility.

"I think Wackenhut International could grow a lot quicker if certain parameters were opened up to us, and I think the corporation is starting to look at that. That's obviously a biased opinion to some degree, but it's clear that you can make quicker and bigger returns in these areas where there's less competition. The currency may be a little bit suspect, but certainly it's not in the established European countries now, and I think you can include countries like Hungary and Poland and the Czech Republic, because there's no real problem with money any more, it seems to have stabilized, and we've got proper channels to get the money out.

"Russia is a little more difficult at the moment, with a fluctuating exchange rate, but certainly the returns are very good, and we expect them to continue to be so. But we expect competition there, obviously, this year. We knew we'd have about a year grace period, and in that period of time we've established ourselves with probably close to sixty guards now. We're looking at expansion in St. Petersburg and Krasnodar in order to keep building. I think we'll probably be bigger in St. Petersburg, in short order, than we are in Moscow.

"Crime in Moscow and St. Petersburg is very high and you've got to look over your shoulder all the time. Because so many people are out of work, they're desperate, they're hungry. Times are very difficult there, and the crime factor has just escalated beyond anybody's initial thoughts, and seems to have taken a stronghold. So I would recommend a driver and a bodyguard. The bodyguard can usually speak enough English to get by, and it needn't be a limousine. We're using cars with a little bit lower profile, so that we're not quite so obvious."

Effective in early January 1993, James L. Long, formerly senior vice president and general manager of Wackenhut Services, Inc. (WSI), at the Savannah River Site, was promoted to the position of president of WSI, and would move to headquarters. Long previously served as general manager of Protection Technology, Idaho, at the Department of Energy's (DOE) National Engineering Laboratory, and as director of the Security Force Department at the DOE's Pantex nuclear weapons manufacturing facility. He commanded Military Police units and attained the rank of lieutenant colonel while serving twenty-one years in the U.S. Army, including combat service in Vietnam and Grenada. He earned his BS degree, cum laude, from the University of Tampa, and his MA in business management from Central Michigan University.

Tim Cole, who was then executive vice president of TWC, as well as president of the Government Services Group, relinquished his additional position as president of WSI to devote more time to his responsibilities for the parent corporation. Lawrence Brede, Jr., who had been manager of Security at the DOE's Pantex plant, near Amarillo, Texas, was named general manager at the Savannah River Site.

Also in January, WSI's protective force for the DOE's Nevada Test Site was involved in a highly publicized antinuclear demonstration consisting of staged protests conducted by a number of groups, including the Western Shoshone Nation, the Veterans for Peace, the March Across America for Mother Earth, the 100th Monkey, and the Veterans Peace Convoy. The first day of the week-long protest was conducted at the DOE's Las Vegas facility by a group of approximately 150–200 demonstrators, who then engaged in a sixty-five-mile walk to the Nevada Test Site, demonstrating to traffic along the way. When the marchers arrived at the Site, they were joined by other protest groups.

Of the estimated 2,000 activists present, 699 were arrested by WSI and other law enforcement agencies. The majority of those arrested were cited for trespass and released. However, several were cited by the Nevada Highway Patrol on more serious charges and were transported to the Las Vegas Metropolitan Police Department Detention Center.

Protesters were more violent than during previous demonstrations. Several foreign nationals were included among those arrested. Efforts of the demonstrators to confront authorities and instigate incidents had continued to escalate over the years. As always, WSI-Nevada Operations personnel, as well as the Las Vegas Metropolitan Police, the Nye County Sheriff's Office, and the Nevada Highway Patrol, exercised constraint and control while confronting and arresting the protesters.

Also early that year, Gary A. Sanders, the newly promoted president of TWC's Nuclear Services Division (NSD), announced a new five-year contract with Vermont Yankee Nuclear Power Corporation, his first major contract since his appointment as president the previous April by Alan Bernstein, TWC's president of the Domestic Operations Group.

Under terms of the contact, NSD would provide nuclear security services at the Vermont Yankee Nuclear Power Plant in Vernon, Vermont. The ultramodern complex of buildings that make up the Vermont Yankee nuclear facility is located on the west bank of the Connecticut River just above a hydroelectric power station constructed in 1909. Vermont Yankee began operation in November 1972. Since then, the plant's 540,000 kilowatt unit had produced enough electricity to serve more than 500,000 homes and the industrial needs of several communities.

Prior to the award of the contract, senior officers of Vermont Yankee Nuclear Power Corporation met with Alan Bernstein, Bob Kindilien, NSD's director of Nuclear Quality Assurance, Jan Vandersluis, manager of Nuclear Operations, and Gary Sanders, as part of the evaluation process.

In his new position, Sanders would have overall responsibility for the operation of security contracts at TWC's nuclear accounts throughout the United States. All TWC nuclear project managers would report directly to him for operational guidance and support, and he would maintain complete profit and loss responsibility for these accounts. He would also be instrumental in formulating nuclear policies and procedures at NSD sites. During transitions, he would oversee start-up operations and participate in labor relations negotiations. An active client relations program had been consistently maintained by Sanders since his promotion.

Sanders, who joined TWC in 1981, had held several key positions with the corporation prior to his appointment, including area supervisor in Atlanta, GA; area manager in Lexington, KY; field support for the Western Region; and manager of Power Generating Services at headquarters. In 1987, he was promoted to vice president of Nuclear Operations.

Born in London, England, June 21, 1952, where his father was stationed as a U.S. Air Force pilot, Sanders came to the states when he was about four years old. His father retired in the early 1970s as a colonel, after extensive travel, including service at the Pentagon. "We finally moved to Columbus, Ohio, where I went to both junior and senior high," Sanders says. "I graduated from Walnut Ridge High School in 1970. Shortly after graduation, I wasn't sure what I wanted to do, except that I knew I wanted to fly. My goal in life was to be a military pilot.

"When my father graduated from the Air War College in Alabama, he was stationed at the Pentagon. That would be in 1971. They bought a house in Virginia, and I went to night school at the University of Maryland, and that's when I learned to fly. I got my private flying license at that time. After that, I went to Ohio State University, got my credits transferred, and graduated with a BS in social welfare in 1975. Then I received an MS in criminology from Florida State University in 1977."

Prior to joining TWC, Sanders was a crime prevention specialist with the City of St. Petersburg Police Department, 1977–1979, conducting research in burglary and robbery investigative techniques. His responsibilities included contacting businesses and residences within specific locations and providing crime-prevention techniques. From 1976–1977, he served with the Police Executive Research Forum, conducting research on burglary and robbery investigations in St. Petersburg, FL.

"My father knew Jim Poisant, who was at that time head of the Wackenhut Training Institute, and he suggested that I call him," Sanders continues. "I did, and Dr. Poisant told me that there was a Career Development Program starting at Wackenhut, and I sounded like an ideal candidate for that. There were many delays after that, and I finally asked him, 'What if I just came to Miami and was available for an interview?' He said, 'I think that's a great idea, why don't you just do that?' He gave me a time, and I drove here, and stayed at what used to be called the Holiday Inn, just up the Dixie Highway, across from the University of Miami.

"I'll never forget, I was scheduled to come in the next morning at the 3280 Ponce building, the old headquarters, and I'd forgotten to bring a *tie!* And here I am, it's late at night, I have no idea how to get one, and I've got an eight o'clock meeting the next morning! I'm desperate, I'm going crazy, and I find a maid who's walking around, she doesn't speak much English, so I use sign-language, and I say, 'I need tie, *necktie,* I forgot my tie!' She says, 'You wait, I find.' She comes back about ten minutes later, she knocks on my door, she's got about *fifteen* ties! Says, 'Which you like?' Apparently, these are ties that people had forgotten over the years, left in their rooms, and she'd collected them. So I picked one out, gave her five dollars, and went to bed happy that I had a tie to wear to my meeting!

"There was a senior staff meeting every morning. And Poisant had me come to the switchboard to let him know that I was there. And I was called up to this senior staff meeting! I had no idea this was going to happen. I remember George Wackenhut was there, Richard Wackenhut, John Ammarell, Gus Novotney. I was called into that room, sat at the table in front of all these people, totally unprepared for this sort of a meeting. Richard Wackenhut turned to me and said, 'Gary, why should we hire you? Can you tell me why The Wackenhut Corporation should be interested in hiring you?' I remember answering that question, but the incredible pressure of this setting—not even sure, really, if I had a formal interview scheduled! And I was *hired* right there in that room, on the spot! But I was told that they really weren't sure when this new program was going to kick off.

"The thing that impressed me most, even to this day, was the professional attitude and demeanor that they had. Always very businesslike, but still very personal at the same time. They always had their coats on, they were always dressed very well, and the way they carried themselves. Especially George Wackenhut. Because I'd read about the corporation, I'd gotten an Annual Report and done a little homework. I was almost in awe that I'd met this man who had created this corporation. And, to this day, I still feel that. It's the man's presence. I still feel that way today when I talk with him. But, at the same time, they both appear to be very kind, and easy to talk to, and I think they try to put you at ease.

"I was hired first as an area supervisor in Atlanta for a six-month period. One of my first assignments was to go to the Arrow Shirt Company and stand post, in uniform, and armed. So I started pretty much at the bottom, which was the idea of the program, to expose you to the business, what it's like to be a security officer, and then work your way up with a planned progression, as part of the career development. I thought it was a great idea. I'd never worn a uniform, I'd never carried a weapon. I was there for six months, then on to Lexington, Kentucky, as area manager. I was brought into headquarters in February of 1983 by Bill Jackson, who was then director of Physical Security for the corporation. Started at 3280 Ponce as a manager of Field Support, Western Region. Living in Miami, responsible for the Western Region, traveling out west, often weeks at a time. Next, I was manager of Power Generating Services. When that became the Nuclear Services Division in December of 1984, with John Bolles as president, I was director of Nuclear Operations. I became vice president of Nuclear Operations in 1987.

"John Bolles left the company April 1, 1992, and shortly after that I was appointed president. Any time a position like that opens up, or somebody leaves, for whatever reason, I'm sure George, Rick, and Alan say: 'Who is the best person to fill that slot? Is it somebody we have, like Gary Sanders, or should we bring in maybe somebody from our government sites, or from some other utility? What would be best for the company?' So I never assumed that it was automatic that I would get that position.

"I was running the division on a temporary basis after John left. What I think really weighed in my favor was that I had, over the years in Nuclear, gotten really close to our clients, had a very positive relationship with our clients. Being vice president of Operations for six years, I was directly involved in everything that was going on.

"I think it was five to seven days after John left that it was announced. I was told by Alan, and then quickly talked to Richard Wackenhut and George Wackenhut. And they just expressed their confidence in my abilities and the potential we had in the business. And that they were very comfortable in that decision. The first thing I felt was relief that I got the opportunity, because I was very confident that I could do the job. The apprehension came shortly after that, when the realization came that I'd always worked in a job where there was always somebody over me in my division. It suddenly dawned on me that, as Harry Truman said, 'The buck stops here,' that I was now in that position, that there were no more levels above me in this division. But, at the same time, I guess I realized also that the way you deal with that is that you perform, you do the job, and our job is obviously involved in selling the business, growing, and maintaining positive client relations.

"So, for the first immediate period of time, I was nonstop travel, reassuring clients, which was our first goal. Our nuclear clients are normally very large sites, some in excess—one contract in excess of $8 million in revenue a year—and we have very personal relationships with them. So I wanted to reassure them that, if anything, business was going to improve, that was my goal, that there were not going to be any dramatic changes. I mean, they just needed to be comforted by that. I was able to do that, and Alan helped me a great deal. Alan Bernstein traveled with me to many of the locations, made phone calls to others when it wasn't possible to travel, and so that helped a lot, too. Just reassuring. And we got real positive feedback from the clients.

"That was the first step. We had to do that. And my belief has always been, in this business, my philosophy, client relations are the key. In Domestic Operations, which I was in previously, previous to December '84, you have a lot of contracts. You know, an area office may have fifty or so contracts, some very small. We now have thirteen contracts, and they're very large. I know these clients personally. They know me personally. Normally, there's one client security manager representing the utility, and that's the individual that's key, really, to both our project management having a positive relationship, and corporate having a positive relationship.

"Some of that stems back to my previous positions, where I transitioned some job sites, I started them up myself, I was there during the transition. So, you develop a very close relationship that carries over the years. And I've always been involved heavily in the operations of the day-to-day business. Maybe more than I really should, right now, but I like to *know* what's going on, I like to be *involved* in decisions, when it comes to issues of maybe labor or personnel, where it involves legal matters. Directly involved. And I am to this day. And I think they appreciate that.

"Frank Finch wrote the Vermont Yankee proposal. We were aware of them going out to bid, and the proposal was submitted probably in the June time frame of 1992. That's how long that process takes. And then follow-up meetings. For Vermont Yankee, particularly, the contractor prior to Wackenhut hadn't been changed in years. I think maybe twelve years. It wasn't a major company, which maybe made it a little more difficult for us. I believe it was Green Mountain Security, which is literally a ma and pa company. But, politically, they were tied in. I think her husband is the chief of police in the local town. So, there were real political ties, but the utility wasn't really satisfied with the service they were getting, because they're a small operation. They wanted to go with a company like Wackenhut that was recognized, that had expertise in all areas, a broad spectrum of security. They felt they could benefit from that. And the National Regulatory Commission, which regulates the industry, was also pressing them, I think, to make that change. And we have a very positive relationship with the NRC.

"So that was a long process that led right up to Thanksgiving. They still had not made a change. I recall traveling up there two days before Thanksgiving. They had a meeting the day before Thanksgiving with Alan Bernstein, and Jan Vandersluis, I believe, also went from my staff, and Bob Kindilien, our director of Quality Assurance. And we did a presentation right before Thanksgiving. It was *then* we were told that we were selected. Very tough decision to make that change, but, they felt, a very positive one. That was an extremely competitive proposal situation.

"I think one of the primary reasons Vermont Yankee selected our corporation was—in addition to what we have corporately available and our expertise in all areas—the Quality Improvement Program we have. The way we do business makes us different. In Nuclear, we're pretty advanced in that quality aspect, where there are formulated procedures on how you deal with business, how you deal with problems running up through the quality processes, how you deal with terms and conditions of a proposal, meeting those terms and conditions, and just how you really manage the business. So that set us apart and they liked that.

"In our transition, they were particularly concerned that we didn't upset the security officers, who were long-term employees, some of them going back to day one, literally, and I think that goes back to the early 1970s. There are approximately sixty employees at that site. They were concerned about their well-being, that they weren't inconvenienced, that they weren't upset, that the morale remained high. Those are areas that we take a lot of pride in during a transition. We do that by going out to them, on shift, and saying, 'Your salary is not going to change, your benefits are not going to change,' and so on. When the application process needs to be done, the paperwork part of it, we don't make them come to us, off-duty or whatever, we try to arrange to have that done right on the job site, so we don't inconvenience them. Tom Shannon, who headed up that transition, was there Christmas Day. We bought turkeys and had turkey dinners for the people who were working. They had never seen anything quite like this. That starts you off on the right foot, I think, and then it's continued from there. So it's been a very positive experience for them.

"Since that time, we have added Kewaunee, which is in Wisconsin, southeast of Green Bay, on Lake Michigan. That was a Burns site. Burns had been there a number of years—I believe seven. Again, there was a concern with the transition, but it went well. I visited the site recently, and I'll usually go up to an employee and say, 'How do you like the change? How do you like what you've seen so far?' And they're just all smiles, and happy to have our company there. So that's always nice to hear. You know, your fear is that they're thinking: Well, we're just going to change patches, change from Burns to Wackenhut—who cares? You don't want to let that happen. You want them to *know* that something's different. And I think the *way* we're different relates to the resources that we have, the Quality Improvement Program. For example, Mike Goodboe, vice president of the Wackenhut Training Institute, went up to Vermont and conducted the training at the site himself, so they could see that we're a corporation that truly has the substance that we talked about, and that we are going to benefit the security officer because of these programs that we have. That starts you off on a positive note, and I think their performance is going to improve as a result.

"I report directly to Alan Bernstein and he leaves me pretty much alone. I take that as a real positive. Because Alan is not the type to always do that. If there's an area that he thinks needs attention, he's the type of executive who will devote whatever time it takes to straighten out or improve performance in an area, and he has not done that here. I view that as his confidence in our ability as a unit to take care of business. And we do, frankly. I mean, I've had two different clients come in recently to our headquarters, talk to George Wackenhut, Rick, Alan, and me. I didn't know what they were going to talk about, but it was very positive. What they said was, essentially: 'You have the right programs, you have the right approach to business, and we want you to know, Mr. Wackenhut, that your competitors are using *you* in Nuclear as their *model!*'

"Laissez faire is generally not the management philosophy at Wackenhut. As a matter of fact, there are areas that I'm amazed that George Wackenhut is involved in. And they may be *seemingly* insignificant issues. I remember two that come to mind. One is business cards. There must have been a time when George Wackenhut saw a bill for the cost of how many business cards we were buying company-wide. He absolutely put a stop to that, unless *he* approved it. The other time was Federal Express. Apparently, at some time, an awful lot of people were sending things by Federal Express, and I'm sure it was being abused. As soon as Rick Wackenhut saw how expensive that was, he put a stop to that, unless *he* approved it.

"I was called up to George Wackenhut's office one time when I was in Nuclear, and he had a bill from the National Rifle Association, and he said, 'What are we paying this for?' I had approved it, that's why he called me in. I said, 'It was required for one of our project managers at one of our sites. It's a contractual requirement to have NRA qualified instructors. To do that, we have to have members.' He said, 'Is it billable?' I said, 'Yes, it is.' He said, 'How do you know that?' I said, 'Well, it's in our contract, you know, when we costed the contract, that was considered.' He said, 'Okay.' So, sometimes, while it may appear, in my case, that there's a laissez faire type attitude toward me conducting business, it's simply because they're comfortable with the way I'm conducting business. But by no means are they hands-off management.

"To this day, George Wackenhut goes to incredible detail that often shocks me. Just before a recent board meeting, George Wackenhut walked up to me and said, 'I understand that Houston Lighting & Power is coming out for bid soon; I believe June, is that right, Gary?' I said, 'Yes, sir, the contract runs through June 30 of this year.' He said, 'Well, give it your best.' I walked away, kind of shaking my head, and Alan happened to be standing nearby, and he said, 'What's the matter?' I related the conversation to him, then I said, 'How does he *know* that?' Alan said, 'That's George Wackenhut.' So things like that happen regularly with him. The level of detail. To this day, his total involvement in the business just fascinates me.

"The first few times I met him, the setting was probably some of the training settings for our Career Development Program, where we'd be called in for training, and George Wackenhut would speak. He was much more—I think 'aggressive' is the word, and forceful in his comments and presentations. Still pleasant, but quite different than now, where he's more—I guess 'introspective' would be the word.

"Shortly after coming into Nuclear, which is the '84 time frame, so that's ten years ago, I was called up to his office, because John Bolles was out of town, who was my boss at that time. It was about the Crystal River account that we had. We had a unique situation there, where we had a collective bargaining agreement with the union, and the wages of the employees would go up, *but*, because of the way the contract was bid, our bill rate would not go up to recover the increase in wages for maybe three months down the road. So, for that period of time, we would *lose* money. And, again, reviewing information, as he's always done, George Wackenhut saw that and demanded an answer: 'Why is this happening? Why are we losing money at this job?' And I was the one called up to answer that. I'd been in Nuclear probably two months, and certainly not involved in the bidding process of that contract, because we were coming to the *end* of that contract. I had no idea how it was priced, why it was priced that way, how that happened, how the labor contract was negotiated that way.

"He was very forceful in his questioning, and I was in the 'elephant' chair, the famous 'elephant' chair that I was told never to sit in again, and I know why now. Sitting right in front of his desk, trying to answer questions, you know: 'How can this happen? How can you do business this way?' And I said, 'Well, sir, I wasn't even involved in the bidding.' He said: 'I . . . don't . . . want . . . that . . . excuse. *You* tell me how this happened.' So I told him how that *could* happen, and I said, 'I *assure* you, we will not let that happen again.' And that seemed to satisfy him. That was the message he wanted to send. But I learned from that moment that the alibi that I wasn't even involved didn't cut it with him. And I said to myself and to others: 'I will never do *that* again.' "

EARLY IN 1993, it was announced that General Thomas P. Stafford, USAF (Retired), a member of TWC's board of directors since 1991, was awarded the Congressional Space Medal of Honor at the direction of President Bush in the final week of his Administration. General Stafford, a pioneer NASA astronaut who commanded the first flight of the lunar module to the moon, also commanded the crew that joined with a Soviet spacecraft in 1975 to improve relations between the two nations. He flew both the Gemini VI and IX missions in 1965 and 1966, during which he developed rendezvous principles and techniques that remain in use today.

General Stafford, who retired from the Air Force as a lieutenant general in 1979, was quoted in *Pipeline* as saying: "This is the greatest day of my life. I'm very proud to have contributed to our nation's future in space, and I am deeply grateful for the opportunity to have participated in the beginning of America's venture into the new and endless frontier."

On February 27, Elmer R. Nelson, TWC's area manager at Ashland, Kentucky, who won the lion's share of awards at the previous year's banquet for the Top Performance Club, but missed out on the big one, was selected Area Manager of the Year for 1992. This marked the eighth year that TWC had held the competition for area managers within Domestic Operations.

That year, for the first time, Domestic Operations introduced Gold Club and Silver Club selections for the top-selling business development representatives. Gold Club members, who attended the Top Performance Club banquet, were Michael G. Bannon of Somerset, New Jersey, Melissa K. Matthews of Huntsville, Alabama, and Barbara McDonald of Boca Raton, Florida. Named to the Silver Club were William Cox of Greensboro, North Carolina, and Robert DeBarr of Los Angeles.

At the conclusion of the banquet, George Wackenhut announced that Melissa Matthews was selected as the Top Business Development Representative for 1992.

IN APRIL, James L. Maynard was promoted to executive vice president of Wackenhut Education Services, Inc. He was formerly senior vice president. WESI, headquartered in Richardson, Texas, at that time operated Job Corps Centers for the U.S. Department of Labor in McKinney, Texas, and Guthrie, Oklahoma. It had become a premier provider of educational programs for disadvantaged youth since entering the field in the mid-1980s.

At the July meeting of the board, Richard C. DeCook was elected senior vice president and chief financial officer of The Wackenhut Corporation. Prior to joining TWC, he had been vice president of Financial Planning and Control for the Trinova Corporation, a worldwide company headquartered in Toledo, Ohio, with $1.7 billion in annual revenues. DeCook spent more than fourteen years with Trinova and advanced through a series of financial management positions with the parent company and its subsidiaries. He holds a BBA degree from the University of Michigan, and is a CPA. Before joining Trinova, he held executive positions with the accounting firm of Ernst & Young.

During August, TWC noted with regret that Renard Ricker, a former executive who filled several key positions in the corporation during the 1960s and 1970s, had passed away. Ricker joined the corporation in 1967, after a distinguished military career, and was initially the branch manager for security operations in Fort Lauderdale, Florida. In 1968, he went to Honolulu to manage TWC operations in the State of Hawaii. From 1972 until his retirement a few years later, he was director of European Operations, and the first person to serve in that position for the corporation.

Prior to joining TWC, he was a U.S. Army officer in the Military Police Corps, and his years of service (1943–46 and 1951–66) spanned World War II, the Korean conflict, and combat service in Vietnam.

Ricker, aged eighty-one and in excellent health, died in an automobile accident. A resident of Kansas, he was visiting his sister in Morristown, New Jersey, at the time of the accident, and had just participated in a high school reunion in his native city of Philadelphia.

He was a brother-in-law to Ruth Wackenhut, and was married to Ruth's sister Evelyn, who passed away in 1968. Ricker was survived by his wife Micki; his daughter Barbara (Dusty); his son-in-law Hugo Knoblauch; six grandchildren; twelve great-grandchildren, and his sister Kitty Coughlin.

In September, George Wackenhut was appointed to the national board of the National Soccer Hall of Fame, located in Oneonta, New York. National Soccer Hall of Fame board president John Biggs announced the appointment of George and five other prominent businessmen with present and past connections with the sport. Biggs stated: "The demonstration of support at this level is a monumental step forward towards our goal of building perhaps the most significant sports museum complex in the world, the National Soccer Hall of Fame and Wright National Soccer Campus."

The Hall of Fame was founded in 1979, and in 1993 consisted of the National Soccer Hall of Fame interim museum in downtown Oneonta and the sixty-one-acre Wright National Soccer Campus a few miles away at the edge of the city. The campus would eventually be the home of the new museum, have eight soccer fields, a small stadium, and an indoor facility.

THE 1994 INFORMATION PLEASE ALMANAC revealed some intriguing statistics about life in the United States during the year 1993: Total estimated population was 258.3 million. The median age was 32.9 years. Total households numbered 91.947 million. Non-family households totalled 64.517 million. The number of owner households was 59.846 million. The estimated number of homeless individuals on any given night ranged from 500,000 to 600,000; homeless families, 125,000–150,000. Unmarried households, 2.586 million. Single-parent households (female), 6.599 million; (male) 1.153 million. Families maintained by women only, 11.692 million. Widows numbered 11.477 million; widowers, 2.333 million.

In the field of religion, Protestants totalled 61 percent (Baptist, 21 percent; Lutheran, 8 percent; Presbyterian, 4 percent; Episcopalian, 3 percent; other Protestant, 13 percent); Roman Catholic, 25 percent; Jewish, 2 percent; other, 5 percent; none, 7 percent.

Vital statistics included: Births, 4.084 million; births to unmarried women, 1.165 million; deaths, 2.177 million. Leading cause of death was heart disease, about 930,000 Americans. Marriages were estimated at 2.363 million; married couples, 52.457 million. Interracial marriages, 994,000. Divorces were estimated at 1.215 million. Legal abortions totalled 1.590 million. Life expectancy at birth for males was seventy-two years; for females, seventy-nine years. Persons without health insurance amounted to 35 million (13 percent of the population). Total AIDS cases reported as of June 1993: 315,390; of these, 194,334 deaths were reported.

Civilian labor force highlights: Total labor force as of June 1993 was 127.5 million. The nation's largest employer was the U.S. government with about 3 million federal employees. Women in the labor force, aged sixteen and over, amounted to 57.798 million, or 45.5

percent of the labor force. The unemployment rate in June 1993 was 7.0 percent.

Income and credit: per capita personal income amounted to $19,-841. The median family income was $35,776. The median single-home price was $103,700. Persons below the poverty level totalled 35.7 million, or 14.2 percent of the population.

Conveniences: Estimated households with at least one television set was 93.1 million; with two or more sets, 59.584 million. The yearly average household TV viewing per day was seven hours and forty minutes. Households with VCRs was estimated at about 58 million. Computers used in the home were estimated to be between 30 million and 35 million.

THE 1993 ANNUAL REPORT OF TWC included a "Letter to the Shareholders," signed by both George and Richard Wackenhut, and dated March 15, 1994, that reflected significant insights into the state of the corporation as it approached its fortieth anniversary in 1994:

> Reflecting on 1993 brings mixed emotions. On the one hand, we are pleased to report an increase in revenues for the 39th consecutive year, and look forward to being able to make the same announcement twelve months from now, as The Wackenhut Corporation celebrates its 40th anniversary.
>
> On the other hand, Corporate earnings for the year tempered our satisfaction in achieving another year of record revenues. Continuing margin pressures, driven by intense competition in our core business and the slow recovery worldwide, contributed to lower than expected operating income. These factors, coupled with the decisions to retire a portion of the long-term debt early, write-down certain intangible assets and increase reserves of our casualty reinsurance subsidiary, resulted in a drop in earnings for 1993. The favorable cumulative effect of accounting changes for income taxes during 1992 makes the drop in 1993 earnings appear even more dramatic. Nonetheless, we are comfortable with management's responses to these circumstances, and are optimistic that earnings will recover during the current year.
>
> In part, our optimism is a by-product of sustained positive trends in

margins through the last quarter of 1993, and some notable marketplace successes. During the close of 1993, the State of Florida selected the Corporation to provide security services at rest stops along the State's Interstate Highway system. The Custom Protection Officer program had been designed for just such purposes a few years back, and the presence of these specially selected, high-caliber Wackenhut personnel had an immediate and marked impact on security at rest stop facilities, a problem which had created grave concerns for the State. We are proud of our contributions in this regard.

During the first eight weeks of 1994, The Wackenhut Corporation was the beneficiary of four significant contract awards. The government of the United Kingdom selected Wackenhut Corrections Corporation to build and operate a 771-inmate prison, the largest prison to be turned over to the private sector in that country; the U.S. Department of Labor awarded Wackenhut Education Services an additional Job Corps Center, the third in its system; the Commonwealth of Puerto Rico contracted with our international subsidiary in that country to supervise and operate the toll booths on its highways beginning March 1; and the State of Florida selected Wackenhut Corrections for the design, construction, and subsequent operation of a 750-inmate prison. All of the foregoing confirm the wisdom of our decisions to diversify our services and focus on privatizing heretofore public sector functions.

We are bidding farewell to four members of our Board of Directors who have been with the Corporation for a combined 97 years. John Ammarell joined the Board in 1959, and Raymond Quadt two years later, in 1961. These two gentlemen have been involved in many of the formative decisions which made the Corporation what it is today. Chesterfield Smith first became a member of the Board in 1977, and Charles J. Simons was elected to membership in 1980. They have been trusted advisors during their terms of service, and all four will be sorely missed.

We must also note with sadness the deaths of two others who served on the Corporation's Board. General Roscoe Robinson, Jr., whose tenure was far too short, died last July, and Frederick Glass, a retired member, passed away in June.

Our gratitude is extended to the current members of the Board and our highly capable senior management team for their contributions to our many successes, as well as to our shareholders and customers for the confidence they have demonstrated in our services. We pledge to continue to strive to meet, and exceed, all their expectations.

Actual revenues for 1993 increased to $664.160 million, compared to $630.320 million in 1992. Net income in 1993 reached only $2.165 million, as opposed to $8.507 million during the previous year.

3 5

COMPLICATED PEOPLE resort to complicated camouflage, and in researching the life and work of George Wackenhut, we have attempted to catch glimpses of the face behind the mask as it changed over more than seven decades. If there is a common denominator in definitive modern biographies, it is the stylistic technique to render, rather than state, by viewing the subject through the eyes of as many individuals as practicable, and to make the basic chronological structure analogous to a musical composition in the sense of inculcating major and minor recurring themes. This final chapter will make a concentrated effort to render highly personal evaluations of George by individuals who have worked closely with him over the years, many of whom we have not heard before, and conclude with the clearest expression of the dominant theme. This is also the chapter in which we will attempt to render realistic and defensible conclusions about George's life and career, his relative strengths and weaknesses, his major achievements and disappointments.

Listen to Alan Bernstein: "Here's an analogy about George that I have in my mind. I believe that he has these two lists left on his desk. And, at seventy-four, he'll think about these lists for however much longer he has to live. On the left-hand side, there's a list that's about sixty pages thick, legal-size pages, and every line is filled up with his accomplishments. And you can go down the success factors of George Wackenhut, and this is a very long list, and it's a very thick book.

"But on the right-hand side of his desk, there's a notepad with, I think, six or seven items, maybe seven to ten items, of things that George feels he *didn't* accomplish. And, what I've noticed over the last couple of years with George, he is *driving* to accomplish these things. Examples of these things: The worldwide investigative company. To be in the electronics business, to take his company and move into that, he always had that vision of being in the electronics business. So the secondary acquisition of the Stellar ETP, the secondary acquisition of the NUSAC, that other company we bought, were decisions that I think George Wackenhut would not normally make. But they were on this *list*. He wanted them to be successful. For some reason, he doesn't feel he was ever successful in that segment of his business, which is totally wrong, but this list on the left-hand side of his desk, it's so big and so powerful that he's not *looking* at it any more. He's not looking at this list of what he's done that's great, he's looking at these four or five items on his notepad, and saying, 'I've got to do something about these, I've got to accomplish these tasks.'

"And, to me, he's focusing on the wrong side of the desk. I've said that to him a couple of times, I've said, 'George, the notepad over here is *nothing*. Look at the list over *here*, because these are big, thick accomplishments.' I mean, how many people from his background, middle-class Philadelphia family, grew up with nothing, starts a company with *nothing*, and builds a company worth more than half a billion dollars in thirty-nine years? Amazing. Amazing that he could do that."

Jim Hastings, who was TWC's general counsel, 1970–1987, agrees with Bernstein about George's obsession with electronics and his drive to make that business a success. "One thing that impressed me over the years I worked for George as general counsel," Hastings recalls, "was his tenacity in seeking to achieve his goals for the corporation. In the early-'70s and mid-'70s, we had a subsidiary known as WPSI—Wackenhut Protective Services, Inc. The main business of this subsidiary was home and business alarm systems. Another product of WPSI that was very important to George was the 'Bloodhound,' an electronic device installed in cars that would indicate to a surveillance team where a car was and in what direction it was moving. They had many problems with the Bloodhound which greatly exasperated George over several years.

"Finally, George set aside one full day a week to meet with employees of the subsidiary and its president in an attempt to work out solutions to the problems. Also, many hours during the week, he would neglect TWC's problems in order to make a success of WPSI. All to no avail.

"Eventually, the alarm business was sold, and WPSI was no longer an operational company. He had hoped to 'spin-off' this subsidiary so it could stand on its own feet. It never came to fruition, but it wasn't because George didn't try."

Willis Hawkins, who spent more than forty years with Lockeed, and played a major role in the design and development of aircraft, missile systems, and space vehicles, served on TWC's board from 1974 to 1991, and has fascinating insights into George's interest in electronics. "As I look back on my history as a board member for George," Hawkins says, "I realize that I was one of a very few board members who had not come from a politically charged, nationally prominent career. I'm not sure how this happened, but it was probably 'Red' Raborn who suggested me because of my early technical endeavors with him when we invented the 'Polaris' missile.

"However it happened, I found myself to be a slightly divergent member of the board, anxious to see George expand his company into more technically based fields where he had a product rather than a service to offer. From listening to George, I was certain that this was his dream, too. After a while, however, it was apparent that this would mean delegating a part of his company to someone with a different kind of expertise, and this conflicted with George's constant drive to be a 'hands-on' leader, including all new endeavors.

"Thus, any new technical initiative had to produce immediately. In electronics—or any product—studies for the government, even services for government agencies, constant supporting research and development effort is required and complex, expensive proposals are necessary—all of which was met with a certain amount of impatience from George. With George at the helm, the team had to get with it and produce. Fortunately, this instinct, though tough on new 'start-up' business efforts, produced a tight ship.

"George's hands-on operation was humorously demonstrated when the board had one of its meetings in the Dominican Republic. One of his offshore activities had developed a surplus of funds which could not be transported to the United States. George's solution: Spend it there! It was a wonderful experience, enhanced by George doing most of the monetary exchange for all of the board members personally—with great gusto—en route on the airplane. He drove a fun-filled but hard bargain.

"My years with George were years of constant new experiences requiring challenging different judgments, but the constant consistency was George. He wanted to do the best possible job, no matter what it was. He has kept his hand firmly on the tiller and, even with myriad diversions, the company has prospered. I'll bet he's still dreaming of some new tasks to tackle—but they'd better show signs of success soon or they'll be gone!"

Gary Sanders has a particularly intriguing insight: "Currently, he seems more reflective. For example, the loss of FPL. We had FPL a long time, Turkey Point, since 1972. We felt maybe unfairly treated in the bid process, and we were deciding what to do about that in a senior meeting. And George said, 'Let's think about this. I'm going to be gone someday. You are going to be here. Do we really want to *challenge* them? Do we really want to *attack* them? Or do we want to let this happen, lick our wounds, and then have a better prospect of doing business with them in the future?' Now, from what I understand about George, that is a dramatic change. Because I think George is the type to charge ahead and get answers, and it was George Wackenhut who was trying to urge some caution.

"By the way, we did kind of charge ahead and wrote a rather strong letter, for George's signature, that to this day is hurting us. The letter went to the CEO of the utility and others, and there were a lot of claims in that letter of maybe unfair treatment of our company—just what George cautioned us about—that left a lot of wounds throughout the utility. Those people are still there. I've done my best to overcome those wounds, I've overcome a lot of them, but most recently we were supposed to bid for that FPL contract in April 1994, and it was just extended fourteen months. Those are things that happen as the result of a letter like that. It didn't get us anything, other than some bad blood. But it was George Wackenhut that was urging the caution, which I guess surprised me a little, because the George Wackenhut that I had *seen* was not one to hold back and say, 'Let's just let it go.' But that's exactly what he was doing."

The "reflective" dimension that Sanders alluded to has, in fact, been present during most of George's adult life, particularly in his spirituality, which he will not discuss. However, that dimension assumes consistently definitive overtones in his private correspondence with longtime friends.

One example is a man named Ray Farley, who was in George's graduating class of 1937 at Upper Darby Senior High School, and grew up about three blocks from where Ruth lived in Drexel Hill. He was the youngest of ten children, and his father was a blacksmith. When we talked with him at his condo in Hollywood, Florida, on January 14, 1993, he appeared much younger than his seventy-five years, but he had recently been stricken with the so-called Lou Gehrig's disease, which made speaking very difficult. Mary, his wife of thirty-eight years, helped to interpret his words. After more than thirty years of government service, including high-level positions with the Department of the Treasury, Internal Revenue Service, he retired in 1977.

"I kept in touch with George, of course, and he wanted me to come down to Florida and work for him when I retired," Farley says. "But when I retired and we moved down here in 1977, I found that I had too much to do raising my family of two sons. I've kept in touch with him two or three times every year and he always answers my letters quickly. I mean, he's very busy, but he's never too busy to keep in touch with his old friends.

"I'm the last of my family to remain living. We had two sons and lost both. One of them, Raymond, Jr., was married with three children, and lived in Indiana. He worked for the Worthington Steel Company. We were very, very close to him. On May 3, 1990, he was killed in an accident on the job. Mary and I were absolutely devastated. We went to the funeral in Indiana, and no one from my side of the family attended, because I don't have anybody in my family left. It was awful. Nobody seemed to understand. I wrote to tell George about it, and he responded immediately. His letter moved us deeply, and I've kept it, of course. It lifted our spirits during the worst time in our lives. I'll never forget his kindness and understanding during that time of need."

George's letter, dated June 13, 1990, reads, in part:

> There is little that anyone can say at a time like this. However, perhaps you might find some consolation in a passage from the Bible, Second Corinthians, Chapter 5: "We are confident, I say, and willing rather to be absent from the body, and to be present with the Lord." And in answer to your request that I keep Raymond in my prayers, I believe that it is you and Mary that I need to keep in my prayers—Raymond is already present with the Lord.

In reading George's personal correspondence over the years and talking with a wide variety of his oldest friends, we find that most of these relationships are not only lasting and fiercely loyal, but overwhelmingly based on humorous memories of the past.

Bud Hunter, for example, has known George and Ruth for almost sixty years and remains among their closest friends. Bud's sister Lillian graduated in George's class at Upper Darby Senior High School, and Bud graduated six years later. At Columbia University, he played football for the famed Lou Little and—to the best of his knowledge—he still holds the school record of most yards gained per carry in a single game—16.4 yards per carry.

"The first time I ever noticed Ruth, I was about twelve, and I guess she was about fourteen," Hunter remembers with a smile. "It was Easter and Ruth came out in this blue Easter outfit. In those days, you know, you had to have an Easter outfit or you didn't go out. She went around with a couple of girls who were next-door neighbors of mine. She lived two streets over, at 937 Cornell Avenue, and she came over in her little Easter outfit to 828 Childs Avenue. And she was *spectacular!* She was over there with the Caruthers girls, and somehow I found a way to spend the whole day in close proximity!

"Years later, every year, I always send her flowers at Easter, with a little poem referring back to those days when I first saw her in her blue Easter outfit. Still do! George gets the biggest kick out of it. I never dated her, of course, I was two years *younger!* That just wasn't done. I would love to have dated her, she was quite spectacular, quite beautiful, and still is. She's always been one of the loves of my life.

"She has a marvelous sense of humor and she's bright as can be. Great wife for George. You know, she brings him out. George told me that Ruth had wanted to recapture the nostalgia of Ocean City, where we all used to go in the summer on vacation. Now, you have to understand, when we got to Ocean City, we would rent a room with a bathroom down the hallway. And we would put three or four or five people in that room. But we were right near the beach. Within a block, a block and a half from the beach.

"Well, Ruth wanted to recall that nostalgia. So she goes up to Ocean City to buy a place. And, of course, Ocean City has changed considerably. Tremendous changes, and there was no nostalgia there. So she went up to see Cape Cod, and that brought back memories. This was about 1986. Here's George telling me: 'Hey, she went to Cape Cod, brought back memories, we bought a *cottage!*' I said, 'Well, tell me a little about the cottage, George.' He said, 'Well, it's got 7,500 square feet in it!' I said, 'George, that sure would bring back the *memories*—of four or five of us crowding into a room of possibly 144 square feet, with a bathroom down the hall! I can see how that will bring back all those *nostalgic* memories of our visits to Ocean City!' He said, 'She's up there furnishing it now.' I said, 'Well, George, you know, you're down here, she's up there, she's going to spend a quarter of a million dollars furnishing that house!' It wasn't three weeks later, George called me, he said, 'Bud, she's already *passed* that number you quoted!'"

Chesterfield Smith, a senior partner in the huge law firm of Holland & Knight, who first became a member of TWC's board of directors in 1977, and finally retired in January of 1994, reveals a few good-natured "chinks" in George's armor. "Certainly, George Wackenhut has always been his own person, and his past indicates that he will be so in the future," Smith asserts. "Significantly, he is a plain-spoken man, always telling it exactly as it is. His style is specific, direct, and unequivocal. He is a friend who you know will be a friend forever.

"But this great person I have described is not without chinks in his magnificent armor. He works too hard and he should play more. He doesn't have a sufficient interest in recreation—golf, fishing, tennis—just in work and more work. Other people think of a weekend as relaxation and pleasure with one's spouse and friends; he thinks of the weekend as a period when he can, without interruption, consider overhead reductions so that the margin of profit of The Wackenhut Corporation can be raised to a better level.

"He is so conservative in government that he makes partisan political judgments which edge over into his other areas of interest and activity. He is as interested in national defense as Senator Sam Nunn or General Schwarzkopf, and usually better informed, but he will advance argumentative positions on government, national security, politics, or taxes without knowing for sure that the facts really are as he perceives them to be. He always asserts his positions, whether they be informed or uninformed ones, freely and vigorously. At dinner parties, he can get quite agitated when too many other participants disagree with him.

"Just recently, President Clinton was in Miami to make an address. George Wackenhut invited me by telephone to attend as his guest. When I declined because of a conflict, he stated that he did not know who else to invite since, 'You are the only Democratic friend I have.' Sad, but true, and sometimes he gets irked enough to at least temporarily remove me from the friendship list. But I always get back on the list.

"Certainly I can say that almost always George is my friend in all possible ways except those involving political philosophy. He always has expressed the belief that all of his corporate directors, except me, were conservative Republicans. I am glad to now advise him that at least a few others have been, and are, Democrat and liberal—although most often in the closet.

"Over the seventeen years that I have served as a director of his company, I have seen him do a magnificent job of presiding over an ever-changing and diverse group of experienced and uniquely qualified members of the board of directors—men, women, financial wizards, military men, corporate executives, doctors, lawyers, newspaper publishers, airline executives, university presidents, and former high officials in government. He stood vigorously and vocally for his beliefs, but he could, and always did, listen to others. When his views turned out to be minority views, he accepted the majority position with utmost grace.

"He personally grows very fond of the individuals on the board. When they leave for retirement or for other causes, he is prone to be very emotional about the departure. Fortunately, he gets over it soon, so that in six months to a year, he seems to many to like the new directors just as well, or even better, than the departed old friends.

"George has come as close as a man can come to being exactly what he appears to be. There are no secrets. He is what he is. Indeed, George Wackenhut is The Wackenhut Corporation. As over time George has grown, so over time the corporation has grown; and, as over time George has changed, the corporation has changed. I am proud to be his 'liberal friend'—who has never been in the closet."

Although Ruth agrees with Chesterfield Smith about George's continuing to work too hard, she has grown philosophical about it over the years. "He's basically a very happy man in what he's doing, because his work is his first wife," Ruth observes. "I'm his second wife. Wait a minute, I'm moving into third, I think TV is moving into second. He has a tremendous sense of humor, and he expresses it more so when he's around people. Don't forget, a man's home is his castle, and he can act whatever way he wants around home. So, there are times when he wants to be completely left alone. He doesn't want to discuss anything, he doesn't want to talk, and I leave him alone.

"Russ is always thinking. And if he has a deep problem to solve, you see it in his face. I mean, I know right away. When he feels more relaxed, or if he just doesn't want to think, it shows in his face. It shows in his face when he's not feeling well. It shows in his face if he's in pain. And it shows in his face when he's feeling devilish.

"Concerning Tyecliffe, he said to me, 'I want you to have complete protection and privacy as you wish it, and no one can get in unless you want them to.' That's what he said. So, I feel very secure. I love my privacy. I feel like I'm on my own little island. Now, I'm a night person, and I love to swim at night. And I love to walk around at night. But he doesn't want me out without him. And, you know, he's tired. Even when he was younger, I'd say, 'Come on, let's go swimming!' He'd say, 'No, I don't want to go in the pool.' We've lived here for twenty years, and he's never been in the pool. Can you *imagine* that? He's never been in the *pool!*

"I don't really call it a 'pool,' I call it a little pond, or a little creek area. I don't feel it's in the shape of a swimming pool. I love the cascade, and I love the shallowness, and then I love the bridge. And the kids just adore it. I do like the evening because of the stillness and the moonlight. I just love it, and it's very relaxing. But he's a wreck if I go and swim at night. A wolf's going to get me! A muskrat's going to get me! A possum's going to get me! A raccoon's going to get me! Something's going to *get* me! And he *worries!* He says, 'Suppose you *drown!* Suppose you get a *cramp!*' I said, 'I have a great idea: You sit on the bridge and *watch* me!' "

Gus Novotney, who spent nineteen years with TWC in positions ranging from area manager to senior vice president, retired in 1984. "Prior to my retirement," Novotney recalls, "I asked George when he planned on 'throwing in the towel.' He said, 'Gus, what would I do if I retired? This is my play thing that I thoroughly enjoy.'

"One of his many attributes that created loyalty and 100 percent effort by the employees is that he never failed to give a pat on the back and credit where credit is due. For example, I remember working on a request for a proposal for a multimillion-dollar contract for the Meadowlands in New Jersey which was quite involved and very time consuming. During the course of preparation, George received a telephone call from a member of our board of directors telling him that we should discontinue our efforts on pursuing this contract, because he had inside information that the Meadowlands contract would be awarded to a competitor.

"George informed me of his conversation with the board member, which was obviously disheartening to both of us, and said to take it off the front burner. 'However,' he said, 'if you want to continue your efforts until they make their decision, be my guest.' After our proposal had been submitted, we were given an opportunity to make a presentation. We felt at the time that this was essentially a courtesy to Wackenhut as one of the qualified bidders. In any event, we made the presentation, which was spearheaded by George.

A short time later, Wackenhut was awarded the contract! George called me into his office and said, 'Gus, I take my hat off to you. You refused to give up when the odds were against us, and even when *I* suggested that you put it on the back burner. You did a *hell* of a job. Congratulations!' That meant a great deal to me.

"On the negative side, because of his aggressive nature in accomplishing his goals, George had little concern for organizational structure and lines of reporting, which made it frustrating at times to work around. However, he always managed to restore peace and order.

"On the lighter side, one year I was reviewing annual pay increases with George, and it so happened that I recommended Rick Wackenhut for a slightly higher raise than the norm. George said: 'Gus, why are you *doing* this? I don't want any special treatment for Rick because he's my *son!* If anything, he has to work *harder* for his increases than anyone else!'"

The "negative side" that Novotney found frustrating at times, the so-called open-door policy in George's availability to employees, is considered a positive aspect by Bob Chasen, who spent twenty-five years at ITT, then was appointed United States Commissioner of Customs, 1977–80, and served on TWC's board of directors, 1981–92. "George's most outstanding attribute, in my opinion, was his ability to *listen*," Chasen recalls. "He was the best listener I ever met. He always would hear you out if you came in to talk to him about something. And this encouraged people to say what they had to say, because he made it comfortable for them to provide him with information which he knew might turn out to be of substantial value.

"He not only would listen, but he would do something with the information he obtained. I was in a large corporation other than Wackenhut for twenty-five years, and there were many executives who made decisions, but the superior executives were the great listeners."

Of course, the open-door policy could be carried to extremes. "During my first year as a member of the board," Chasen says, "George appointed me chairman of the cost-reduction committee. This was 1981. We were sitting in the conference room of the old headquarters building, all the senior officers of the corporation, talking about how we could reduce costs. Suddenly, the door opened and a stranger poked his head in and said, 'Who's the chairman of this cost-reduction committee?' I raised my hand. He said, 'Let me tell you something. If you want to reduce costs, you start with *that* guy!' And he pointed his finger right at Wackenhut himself. And then he left.

"I knew it was some kind of gag, but I didn't know what kind of person would do something like that. Well, it turned out to be the one and only Murray Levine, and that was his way of expressing himself, which, I later found out, was to say just what he thinks, whenever he feels like saying it!"

Bob Kirk recalls an anecdote when the open-door policy didn't apply, because George was out of town and he had to make a critically important decision almost immediately. He was president of Wackenhut International at the time. "Late one evening in the latter part of October, 1978, while I was still at the office," Kirk says, "I received a call from a top official of E-Systems in Dallas, Texas. E-Systems was a contract communications company that specialized in electronic surveillance. The man's name was Bobby Wolfe. He had one question that needed an immediate answer: Could I meet with him and top United States State Department officials the next day in Washington, DC? And, of course, the answer was yes.

"At the meeting, attended by five State Department officials and the E-Systems official, Bobby Wolfe, I was asked if Wackenhut could provide a large security force in the Sinai to protect E-Systems employees engaged in operating three electronic surveillance facilities located at high strategic points in the Sinai, to replace a United Nations force of 120 men?

"I replied that it could be done, but it would take direct assistance from the State Department to accomplish the task. Two direct actions were immediately necessary. First, passports would have to be processed and delivered to the TWC office in Miami in three days, complete with visas for both Egypt and Israel; normally, it would take ten to fifteen days. Second, Wackenhut would be given a waiver to use a foreign air carrier; this action was mandatory, due to the fact that independent contractors being employed by the United States had to use American air carriers if the area was serviced by an American airline, but such was not the case in this area.

"This was all agreed to, and late in the afternoon papers were signed and the operation began. The same day. I brought in a well-qualified security force chief down from Anchorage, Alaska, who had served with Wackenhut on the pipeline, to take over the acquisition and processing of personnel for the entire task.

"One of the requirements that was extremely difficult was that all of these people had to be well-trained and qualified in several types of weapons. However, all of the personnel were acquired and processed, all of the passport applications were approved, the visas issued, and all of the necessary logistics were planned. It was necessary that all of the individuals have five separate immunization shots prior to leaving the United States.

"Since it was necessary to spend many hours flying to Tel Aviv, and then proceed to the bases by ground transportation, we had seven days from the date of the contract to be on the sites. In less than ten days, Wackenhut had replaced the 120-plus United Nations troops with twenty-nine TWC personnel. To this day, I don't believe George even gave me permission to sign the *contract!* The project was handled successfully for more than one year."

Following our initial interview with Tresha in Chapter 22, we posed hypothetical questions concerning how much impact the study of Christian Science made on the life of George Wackenhut, and, perhaps more importantly, how his spirituality had affected the lives of others. Jan's second husband, Roger Ward, now president of Ward Consulting Group, Inc., in Miami, offers very tangible insights into both questions.

"I first met Russ face to face at Ocean Reef Yacht Club in 1978," Ward recalls. "Jan and I had just started dating, and we were driving down so I could meet Russ and Ruth for the first time, and to attend a party aboard their boat, *Top Secret.* Jan forgot to tell me it was a 104-foot motor yacht. Through Jan and others, I already had an esteemed image of her dad. He was a self-made person who, over the past twenty years, had built his company from scratch into a major corporation. Planning to leave the Air Force at the end of the next year, with the dream to start my own business someday, I could not wait to meet Russ. Seeing *Top Secret* made me even more eager to discover how he made all this happen.

"Our first meeting provided me with a lot of insight about the man. Later, I would find that insight was only the tip of the iceberg. Russ was the perfect role model I had envisioned—a powerful-looking man, stately, impeccably dressed, comfortable in his element, a gentleman with a beautiful wife. At the party, you could see the admiration of the guests toward him, each competing to speak with him or to be noticed in his presence. He would have been the center of attention, except that he gave that honor to his charming wife Ruth.

"Jan and I had a great time, even though I slept in the crew's quarters and her in one of the staterooms. Over the course of the weekend, I found out I was not the only one who had a lot of questions to ask. Anyone could see that I was dating the delight in Russ's life, and he had a full line of questioning for me. However, both Russ and Ruth made me feel welcomed and comfortable at this first encounter.

"Then, on the tennis court, I gained my first insight into how Russ started and built his corporation. He was as strong and as quick as a pro—and he played to win. Losing was not something he understood. I was thoroughly humbled that day on the court.

"Jan and I were married in 1979. Asking Russ's permission was the worst board-room presentation I ever made. But, in the end, he was willing to do anything that made his daughter happy. Over the years, I have learned a great deal about Russ. I know now that success had little to do with him being driven to win or wanting all the power and wealth that surrounded him. He loved the sport of *business.* I could see he played this game of business harder and with even greater determination than our tennis game at Ocean Reef. My feeling is that he used the business as a means of keeping score. He did well in business not only out of his perseverance to win, but because of his spiritual qualities.

"He is not only a remarkable businessman, but a devoted husband, father, and grandfather. His domineering style at the office is complemented by a tenderness that is boundless. He is almost childlike whenever we are all together on holidays or when we get together at the Cape. His eyes will fill at church when a particular message touches him or while reading a special card from one of the family, particularly from the grandchildren. You sense he is never far away when needed. He confided in me that the only regret he ever had about starting his business is that it stole precious time away from Jan and Rick and their kids.

"During a period when I was struggling to get my own business off the ground, Russ gave me a copy of an article from *The Christian Science Sentinel*, by Carl J. Welz, titled 'Demonstrating Demand.' He said he used it during the years of building his business. It was dated December 9, 1961, and this was 1983, and he still used it as a guide. I read it and put it away like most articles I get. I wanted to learn from him how you really *made it* in business, not from something someone wrote in a church journal.

"But for some reason I kept it and continued to reread it from time to time. The more we talked over the years, the more I understood what he had discovered in this article. The article talked about the qualities a person must have to be in demand and receive economic value from others. It spoke about skill, promptness, ingenuity, honesty, helpfulness, thoroughness, adaptability, efficiency, as all desirable qualities. George had all of these qualities, but I think his perception was that these were just the minimum prerequisites to even play the game. The article went on to describe other qualities, less tangible to human consciousness, which spelled out the difference between real success and mediocrity. These were spiritual qualities, what his Christian Science religion called attributes of Divine Principle.

"You won't find these attributes at any business school—spiritual wisdom, unselfed love, conscious immortality, and perceptive justice were just a few that were described. Reading the definitions helped a little in understanding their meaning. However, seeing Russ put them into practice made it clear to me that he had modeled his life after the attributes of a leader, and the teachings he learned about through his Christian Science religion. I have seen him demonstrate these qualities.

"The article concludes by saying, 'One who appears to be doing all this and still does not succeed may need humility.' I have never seen Russ seek or want recognition for the work he has done. He seems to know that the demand for one's services is demonstrated from one's self. These qualities may sound corny, but I can assure you that no one thinks George Wackenhut is corny. He exhibits all these attributes. Now dog-eared, I carry this article with me everywhere I go. It is in the back of my calendar appointment book, and I refer to it frequently, knowing I have a better understanding of the true qualities of leadership through examples set by George Wackenhut."

Nancy Clark Reynolds, who is presently a senior consultant for The Wexler Group, Inc., a governmental relations and public affairs consulting firm in Washington, DC, had the distinction of becoming the first woman elected to TWC's board of directors in 1986, and has vivid memories of how that happened. "One day in 1985," Reynolds says, "I was talking with former Secretary of Defense Frank Carlucci, who was an old friend of mine from Sears World Trade, where he had been chairman and CEO. He had been a board member at Wackenhut, and he asked me if I would consider serving on the Wackenhut board, if they were interested, because they had no women on the board.

"I was intrigued, and he gave me an Annual Report, and then I was even more interested by the idea. Frank told me about George and his remarkable background. So, after several telephone calls, George asked me to come down and talk about it.

"George and Ruth took me to dinner in Coral Gables, and it was like meeting part of my family. They reminisced about their early life, and how they started out, and talked with great pride about their children and grandchildren, and I kept thinking, you know, this is what America is all about. And then George said, 'I can't tell you how much I admire your former boss, Ronald Reagan.' Because I had worked for Reagan for ten years.

"We got on the subject of politics, and this country, and I thought: Here's a true *patriot*. This man has a clear idea of who he is, what he stands for, and what he wants to accomplish. I was impressed by his unswerving loyalty. George warned me, in a friendly, funny way, that I was going to be the only woman on the board, and I had to expect a lot of kidding, and some resistance from a couple of board members who opposed the idea of a woman on the board. Now I'm chairman of the EEOC committee, which was formed when I went on the board, and I must say, George has been particularly supportive of me, and so has Ruth.

"One thing I've observed, sometimes George is very quiet in a meeting, but you can just see that computer going in his brain. He'll come out with questions and then make decisions in an understated way. So I think the title of this book, *The Quiet American*, is a great description of George. I just think George is a remarkable gentleman. He has a great equanimity about him. I think that's important, because everybody looks immediately to the chairman to see how *he's* going to react, or what *he's* going to say. And when a mistake has been made or something hasn't worked out, he very calmly moves on to the next subject. But he's very firm in what he thinks. I've been on a special committee of the board regarding what happened with the Alyeska investigation, and George's reaction to all our questions has always been calm, logical, and truthful."

Former Secretary of Defense Frank Carlucci, who had been a TWC board member, 1983–86, just before he was appointed to his Defense post in the Reagan Administration, 1987–89 (he had been deputy director of the CIA under President Carter, 1978–81), is presently chairman and CEO of The Carlyle Group, in Washington, DC. One event stands out in his mind during a TWC board meeting that he believes is characteristic of George's integrity. "At one board meeting," Carlucci recalls, "discussion centered around a harassment lawsuit obviously instigated by a law firm with 'graymail' in mind. Shortly after making an outrageous demand, the plaintiff offered to settle for $25,000. If we failed to settle, they threatened to demand documents by the truckload and to depose all the directors.

"The directors felt that, personal inconvenience aside, the discovery process would be disruptive to the company. Hence, the outside directors were unanimous in urging George to settle. When the vote came, all voted to settle, save George. He voted against, stating that he recognized the problems, but he had to stand on principle. The lawsuit had absolutely no merit. While he would abide by the board's decision, he could not go on record as agreeing to settlement at *any* price. A man of principle indeed."

General Seth J. McKee, who retired from the U.S. Air Force as a four-star general in 1973 after thirty-eight years of military service, joined TWC's board in 1974, and observed George in action until his retirement in 1992. "If George has a shortcoming," McKee says, "it would have to be his loyalty to, and his support of, subordinates who fail to measure up to expectations. On infrequent occasions, he was prone to defer severing activities or individuals in order to give them 'one more chance,' although I am quite sure that his astute business acumen advised him otherwise. On the other hand, he was never slow to make the hard decisions when failure to do so would have had significant impact on the welfare of the company."

Another former TWC board member (1974–1991), and also retired from the U.S. Air Force, General Bernard A. Schriever, recalls George's loyalty to his employees. "In late 1973," Schriever says, "I received a call from George inviting me to become a director on the Wackenhut board. I was surprised, since I didn't know George, nor really anything about the company. But I did know three or four of the sitting directors, and they were the type of people I like to work with. I told him I would come to Miami and visit with him, which I did. Our meeting went well.

"I was convinced George was the type of person I would want on *my* team. So, why not on *his?* I accepted his invitation and I was never disappointed. George is a born leader. He instills loyalty because everyone knows that, in his case, loyalty is a two-way street. He's also one of those rare individuals gifted with both long-range vision and understanding day-to-day management capabilities. In addition, he's a fierce competitor and a staunch believer that right is right and should in all cases prevail.

"Frivolous lawsuits, which are quite frequent these days, enraged George. Lively board discussions would invariably follow with legal cost becoming a major focal point. As I recall, after the dust settled, and various options had been considered, a satisfactory solution was always found. I also recall that in no case did we ever bend the truth."

Richard H.W. Maloy, who has his own law firm in Miami, has known George for forty years. "I met George shortly after he had started a private investigative firm with three other former FBI agents, across the street from my law office," Maloy says. "He located a 'deadbeat' who was trying to avoid paying a judgment my law firm had secured for a client, and that was the beginning of what is today a forty-year friendship.

"In those years, George was the most powerful man I had ever seen. He looked as if he could pull a redwood out of the ground by its roots. I met Ruth some years later. She was so beautiful she 'should have been in pictures.' To say that they were an attractive couple is a gross understatement.

"In 1962, George hired me as the first general counsel of his corporation. He never tired of telling people of how being 'in-house' counsel was a vast improvement over my former status of being an 'out-house' counsel. As a matter of fact, he never tired of poking good-natured fun at me, but I knew the high regard he had for me, or I never would have remained his lawyer, and I expected the ribbing. If he ever stopped, that would have been a sign that our friendship was at an end. Thankfully, he never stopped.

"George worked longer hours than any man I ever knew. He was thorough and meticulous. We traveled together a lot in the years I worked for the company. After a full day, upon our return to the hotel, about midnight, he would always invite me to have a 'nightcap' with him. Initially, I was grateful for the first chance of the day to relax, but it wasn't long before I realized that this was just George's way of setting up one more conference. He inevitably pulled a yellow pad out of his briefcase, handed it to me, and asked me to recap the day's events so that we could determine whether we had made any mistakes that needed correcting in the morning.

"One gets to know a person quite well when they travel together frequently. During those trips, I learned of the deep love he had for Ruth, Jan and Rick, of his strong faith in God, and the sensitivities which he masked with an austere exterior. On one occasion, after I had left the company, he must have detected that I was in a depressed mood, for the next day he called me and took an hour of valuable time getting me out of my rut. We philosophized, talked about God, and traded jokes. It worked. I used to tell him he got his fabulous sense of humor from his Irish grandmother! [Actually, she was English.]

"I left TWC because, with a young family, I could not take all the traveling that the job entailed. When George was unable to dissuade me, he gave me his blessing, and ordered my successor, Vic Keay, to give me as much outside work as they could spare. Over the years, I earned substantial fees and handled some very interesting legal work as a result.

"Suffice it to say that for forty years George has been my friend, my former employer, my former client; but when I think of him, and I do that often, I think of him as my brother."

George smiles when he recalls the very early years in the Ainsley Building when, after landing the National Airlines account in 1955, he had to "pass the hat" around the office almost every Friday in order to meet the weekly payroll for his twenty guards. Lewis B. Whitworth, who is now a retired circuit judge, remembers that the monetary situation hadn't changed much in 1956, when the fledgling company was beginning to win other guard contracts.

"In 1956," Whitworth says, "George employed me to operate the background investigation organization named Fidelifax in Miami. During the period I was with George, we were able to enlarge and improve our branch of the business that was being set up by former FBI agents nationwide. But I quickly learned that George's real interest was in the security business.

"Even though we had only a handful of guard employees, I remember George saying, 'I'm going to build one of the largest security companies in the world.' Then Friday would come and the time to pay the guards had arrived. The search for enough cash to survive another week would begin.

"First, a review of the 'receivables' file. Then, if no help there, we would perhaps visit an attorney for one of the companies utilizing the guards. And then, if that failed, on at least one occasion, a trip to the bank to borrow enough money to keep going for another week.

"After a few Fridays like that, I said, 'I don't know how you stand this pressure, George, I could never do it.' For almost thirty-eight years, I have remembered George Wackenhut's answer: *'That's the difference between you and me!'* I think that was the moment when I accepted the fact that Wackenhut would become one of the largest companies of its type in the world. George possesses qualities of resolution and firmness of will that are simply unequaled in other people.

"I remain an admirer of George. It was a privilege to work with him. And, by the way, the *difference* between us has now amounted to more than half a billion dollars!"

Raymond A. Quadt is presently chairman of Mariah International, an Arizona mining company, and vice chairman of Sunstate Bancshares, Inc., an Arizona bank holding company. He joined TWC's board in 1961, retired in January 1994, and looks back over his thirty-three years of association with George by relating one specific anecdote that remains frozen in his memory. "I am reminded of an evening in the late '60s or early '70s," Quadt says, "when George invited a group of directors, including Captain Eddie Rickenbacker, to a catered private gathering at the Kennedy Space Center.

"The waitresses serving us were pretty, young, and vivacious. While their service to all of us was complete and excellent, it wasn't long before we realized they had all surrounded Captain Eddie, who charmed them with his good humor and anecdotes. He held their undivided attention for much of the remainder of the evening. We were all understandably jealous of the overwhelming attention Captain Eddie enjoyed from the ladies, and George was heard to admiringly murmur words to the effect that, 'I wonder if any of us will ever achieve the charisma, personal magnetism, and celebrity status of a Captain Eddie?'

"In his own way, however, I believe George has accomplished just that, in his astute guidance of TWC to its present spectacular heights. Those of us who were closely associated with George over the years while he structured the TWC success can only commend, with the greatest sincerity, the wisdom, energy, drive, and versatility with which he achieved his goal."

Maria Hester, who was George's administrative assistant from 1983 until she retired on February 18, 1994, after thirty-one years at TWC, shared some interesting insights with us just before she left. "I started working for TWC in the summer of 1962," Hester says with a smile. "As far as I know, I was the first Cuban hired at headquarters. I worked for three months and resigned to go to San Francisco to get married. After one year, we decided to move back to Miami. San Francisco is not the place for someone from the tropics. I missed the palm trees, blue skies, sunshine, moonlight, and beautiful ocean around this city.

"Before I left San Francisco, I wrote to Mirtha Latour so she would let William Bitter know I was moving back to Miami and would be very interested in coming to work for Wackenhut again. When I arrived, I called him. He said, 'We don't have an opening now, but you are hired. We'll find something for you.'

"Those were very different days. Headquarters consisted of the second floor at 3280 Ponce, and that included what we call today the Miami area office, and the uniform, equipment, and supply room. It was a time when all the females in the office took turns in keeping a huge coffee maker full of coffee at all times, and everyone had to pay, I think it was five cents a cup. I remember some girls being sent home, on their own time, to change into more businesslike attire, when the office manager thought what they were wearing was not appropriate.

"Believe it or not, the payroll checks were handwritten. If we needed several copies of a document, we had to cut a stencil and run the number of copies on a machine full of ink that was very hard to wash off your hands. Birthdays were celebrated in the conference room and everyone in the office was invited. As we grew, they decided to change the cake celebration for a day off, because it was really getting difficult to assemble everyone in one room at the same time. We all knew each other back then and felt like we were out to conquer the world.

"And the world started to be conquered little by little. Every contract won was like a victory for each one of us. Then things started to change. The tenants who occupied one-half of the first floor were asked to move out, and the other half of that floor, which consisted of a covered parking garage, was built into more office space. Then came the purchase of the parking lot next to the building, another building half a block away, another building across the street, and another parking lot next to it. In the end, we were also renting space in two other buildings.

"At the same time, downtown Coral Gables was growing very

fast. In the summer of 1962, there were two restaurants, and they weren't even in the Gables. One was The Hasta on Thirty-seventh Avenue, where Tony Roma's is now, and The Pub on Coral Way. Then arrived that wonderful culinary delight called French cuisine. The first French restaurant to open in Coral Gables was Chez Vendôme, and that is why I chose it for my retirement luncheon—sentimental reasons. After that opened, we had them by the dozens, and every occasion that called for a celebration was very properly celebrated in one of those restaurants.

"While all this construction was happening, something else was happening too. Mr. Wackenhut started to have Tyecliffe built in 1968. I think that added a lot of pleasure to his already very hectic schedule, but, like everything else, it came to an end, and finally the Wackenhuts moved in about 1974. I remember that in the beginning Mr. Wackenhut started to hold weekly staff meetings at Tyecliffe, and all of the men would return to the office complaining because they said there wasn't one comfortable chair in the whole place!

"Then we moved into this very beautiful headquarters building in 1984, which we are all very proud of, so elegantly decorated by Mrs. Wackenhut, and with plenty of room for everyone to work comfortably. But something strange happened. We kind of lost touch with each other. I don't think a day goes by now that I don't see a new face, and I don't have the slightest idea of who that person is or where that person works. I guess, in a certain way, I left my heart at 3280 Ponce.

"Since I first met Mr. Wackenhut, I had a lot of respect and admiration for this formidable man. He instilled guidance and security, which was a very comfortable feeling. Some people used to be somewhat intimidated by his demeanor, but I never felt that way about him. His name was synonymous with integrity and honesty, and every time someone asked me where I worked, I always felt great pride in saying, 'I work for The Wackenhut Corporation,' and, if they did not recognize the name, I felt kind of offended.

"One thing that really impressed me about Mr. Wackenhut was his anticommunist stand. He and Mr. Ralph Kiel in Public Relations wrote a publication called *The Wackenhut Security Review*, that came out sometimes monthly and sometimes quarterly, starting in

1961, which disclosed everything that was corrupt about communism. I was also impressed to see someone with such strong ideals and doing something about them. It was extremely interesting material to read.

"Just before we moved into this new building—eleven years ago, to be exact—I was transferred to be Mr. Wackenhut's administrative assistant. I will always treasure this association, and I am very glad that it happened when all the success had already been accomplished, because then I was able to know his 'gentle' side, not just the aggressive businessman that I had known him to be during my first nineteen years with the company. I have felt very much at ease working for him. He is extremely organized and methodical, has a great sense of humor, and his points of view about life, family, country, and politics could not be more compatible to mine. I have always enjoyed listening to what he has to say.

"I always thought that I would retire at the same time he did, but all this changed when, about a year ago, I asked him what his retirement plans were, and he said, 'Feet first.' I couldn't wait that long."

Budd Kneip touches on a subject that has not been adequately explored in this study, but it is an extremely important intangible: The unique "culture" of a family business. "With the size and scope of The Wackenhut Corporation, it's easy to forget that this is basically a family business," Kneip observes. "It bears the indelible stamp of its founder, and the culture that has emerged as a result is as important a contributor to its success as any other single factor. In fact, one of the subtleties of planning at Wackenhut is to accommodate the culture to the demands of a substantial business venture.

"When one joins the company, he or she must understand and accept that fact. And some people can't. There is not the structure or compartmentalization that typifies so many corporations of a similar or larger size. While that can easily be mistaken for an undisciplined management style, it has actually helped to protect the company from the calcification that so frequently happens when entrepreneurial organizations evolve into a different form.

"But what that offers to the individual who is willing to work within our unique environment is a rare opportunity in this era of 'downsizing' and 'reengineering.' George creates a lot of room for people to grow. All one has to do is demonstrate talent, and that person will be afforded the potential to capitalize on it. I liken it to the draft strategy of the old Dallas Cowboys, who used to go for the best talent available, then find a spot for them. With my academic background [a Ph.D. in history], I would have been typecast in a much different capacity, if I had been hired by a big company at all. But George gave me the chance to grow and develop. Although I could never adequately repay him for the faith he's had in me, I believe the company has benefited from my being here. And you can rest assured that I would never do anything to intentionally abuse that trust.

"I'm not alone in feeling that way. Until recently, we didn't have the compensation packages that companies our size typically offer. Yet people stayed, and, if you survey the employee base, you will find that there is this intangible sense of belonging that is difficult to replicate elsewhere. Again, it's not for everyone, but it's important to those who have succeeded here.

"There are numerous references to family throughout this biography, and the role it has played. Without overstating the case, this company is a very real extension of that concept to George. Family means something to him; it has obligations and responsibilities on both sides. It can have aggravations as well. But, if honored, it can transport the employment relationship into a different dimension. George is paternalistic about 'his' people without being patronizing. You are invited into this corporation as much as you are hired.

"The Wackenhut culture is one of the strengths of this corporation. It provides flexibility, encourages innovation, and enhances responsiveness. If guarded and nurtured in the coming years, it will be the greatest legacy George leaves to the company."

Three major milestones would occur in 1994, and when we tape-recorded an interview with Rick on April 15, 1994, he had just returned from the celebration of one of them, and spoke so eloquently about the other two, still to come, we decided to let him have the last say about his father in this biography. "On April 8, 1994, my parents celebrated their fiftieth wedding anniversary by renting a house up in Vero Beach that was really outstanding," Rick says smiling. "It was a five-bedroom home, right on the ocean, with a boardwalk going out to the beach. You basically just opened up the doors, and there you were, right on the beach.

"For this occasion, they actually rented the house for two weeks. Most of our family went up for the better part of a week. Those who came were, of course, my mother and my father, who were there; the next to arrive were Molly, myself, and our four children; very shortly after that, the next day, Tanya and Tresha arrived; then Jan arrived; and Roger came in a little bit later during the week.

"It was really a fun week. It was probably one of the best family gatherings that I have experienced, and, in fact, Molly commented that it was *the* best Wackenhut family gathering that she has attended. It was very relaxed, there was a lot of laughter, there was a lot of communal feasting around the table. It was a very large family atmosphere. I taped the entire weekend on videotape.

"My sister and I were absolutely at our wits end on what to get them for a gift. About a week prior to going up there, in somewhat of a panic state, trying to figure out what to get them, I was leafing through a magazine that came to me in the mail, and on the inside front cover of the magazine was an advertisement for a game. It was called 'The Collectors Edition Monopoly Game.' Each of the houses and hotels were made out of pewter; the houses were silver-plated and the hotels were gold-plated. The board itself was made out of mahogany, with green felt, and all hand-painted, and just a very top-level game. That did it for me. I called my sister and I said, 'I think I have their gift.' I believe they're going to just have it permanently set up somewhere on some game table in their house, because it truly is a piece of art.

"Anyway, while we were up there for the week, Molly and I and the kids did a lot of fishing on the beach, brought it into the house and cooked it, and that was a lot of fun. We drove around Vero Beach, my parents were looking for another home, possibly up in that area, so they did a considerable amount of house-hunting while they were up there. We visited the Mel Fisher museum of sunken treasure. In that visitation, my father and I both bought some coin necklaces for our wives. They're actually 'pieces of eight,' the eight-real piece, and each one of them has an emerald in the setting, surrounded by gold to make the pendant to hang on a necklace. They're really nice pieces, dating to about 1568. My father and I both enjoy this very much—the *reality* of the history. It's one thing to hear the story, and to read about it, but to actually hold the coin that was under the ocean for about 425 years, and then to see it around your wife's neck, is a wonderful thing. That anniversary was the first this year of the three major milestones of 1994.

"The second milestone, that will be coming up shortly, is the fortieth anniversary of the founding of the corporation, July 21, 1994. And to reflect on how far this company has come in those forty years is mind-boggling. I'm forty-six now and I'll be forty-seven in November, but I remember having my seventh birthday November 11, 1954, and sitting on the floor of our little rented apartment on San Remo Avenue, just across the street from what is now our headquarters, and opening my presents, one of which was a silver dollar, because I was collecting coins back then. To think of that space in time, which does not seem long ago to me, and to see how far this company has come in that period of time, is just almost beyond comprehension. The task has been a tough one, but not without a tremendous number of rewards.

"The third milestone in 1994 will be my father's seventy-fifth birthday on September 3, and it affects me very emotionally. He has maintained a lot of the acuteness of his senses, and his mind, in the business arena, is as sharp as I think it ever was. When you live with someone for almost forty-seven years, as I have, you never think of that relationship terminating. But obviously it will, one day. And I only wish there was a way of turning back the clock, or stopping the clock at this point in time, because, like anyone who feels very close to their parents, you never want to see that relationship end.

"I'll be very deeply affected when he is no longer here. But I will be forever grateful for what he taught me in integrity, what he taught me in work ethic, what he has taught me about life, and certainly about this business. He's a tough taskmaster and a tough teacher. But I would not be as well groomed, as I feel I am, had he not taken that particular approach. Yes, I will be deeply hurt, not just for the passing of a loved one, but for the loss of the real leader of this corporation.

"I would've liked to have seen my father have more hobbies. He has no hobbies whatsoever, except the business. A simple matter of taking out a fishing boat for an afternoon, and dropping a line, even if you aren't the one fishing. To enjoy some of the recreational pleasures that life has to offer. I actually feel sorry for him in the sense that he was never able—for whatever reason—to divest himself from business endeavors, and just go enjoy a hot dog at a ball park. Or to engage in coin or stamp collecting. Or to have a favorite spot in the yard where he raised rare plants, or something along those lines. You know, pick any relaxation that most people have. Even traveling. Horses. Just any type of secondary vocational endeavor.

"You have to be able to relate to things that you may be missing before you can determine whether you miss them or not. I don't think he has the capability of even relating to what he's missing. He has never allowed himself to get involved in any type of side activity, shy of sports, when he was much, much younger, and he was participating in sports, and he participated in them to the fullest extent that he could. As he got older, he tried to continue some of that, through playing tennis, and trying to keep himself physically fit. And there's a comparison there, because he's commented on a number of occasions, 'It's a bitch to get older,' and so forth, meaning that he really misses some of the sports activities he used to engage in. But, take anything else as a hobby or a sideline, it's nonexistent, so he has no comparison.

"So I would have to say, yes, I think he *is* happy, in the fact that he's still active in the business, and he's still involved in it. I think his happiness is waning a little bit, because he feels he's not as quick or as sharp as he used to be. At seventy-four, who is? So he gets irritated at himself when he thinks that he's not remembering something, or when he thinks he's not responding as quickly as he feels he should. But even with that, he's quicker than most guys half his age. So that's something else to be said to the fact that he'll never retire.

"This is a personal observation of mine, but I think fairly accurate: When he is away from the office, especially during the summers when he goes up to Cape Cod, I've had a number of occasions where I would visit him during the vacation time. It is amazing to me how much *older* he appears, and how much older he acts, when he's away from the office. When he comes back to the office, from minute one, when he walks into this building, he looks *ten years younger*, he's more alert, he's more vibrant, and he has much more *energy* than when he's on vacation."

That final paragraph speaks volumes about the man, his work, and his motivations today. And, of course, only Rick could possibly have that critically significant insight.

Appendix

Wackenhut - Stammtafel

Aberlin I/1
* um 1475/80 † nach 1531
Hofbauer, Richter
⚭ ....

Jakob II/1
* um 1510/15 † vor 1574
Hofbauer, Richter
⚭ .... Waldburga

Egenhauser-Stamm

Jackob III/1
* um 1540/45 † 1625
Hofbauer
⚭ um 1565/70, Maria........

Hans III/2
* um 1545/50 † vor 1607
Bauer
⚭ um 1570........(Weißhaar?)

Hans IV/1
* um 1566/70 † 1613
Bauer
⚭ um 1590 Barbara.......
(⚭ 1618 Jodokus Kircher)

Jakob IV/2
* 1570/72 † 1635
Taglöhner
⚭ I. vor 1595 Maria........
⚭ II. 1619 Margaretha vid. Ott

Michael (IV/3) E1
* um 1572 † 1625
Taglöhner
⚭ 1598 Maria Braun

Hanss E2
* 1607 † 1661
Bürger
⚭ 1632 Anna Waltz

Michael
* 1643 † 1650

Johannes (Hanss) E3
* 1648 † 1722
Burger, Richter
⚭ 1676 Anna Schaiblin
⚭ 1689 Margarete Steiner
⚭ 1699 Barbara Braun

Johannes
* 1681

Michel
* 1985

Georg (Jerg) E4
* 1678 † 1746
Bauer, Richter
⚭ um 1705 Maria......

Jakob
* 1687

Lukas
* 1699
† 1699

Hans Jakob
* 1693

Hans E5
* 1705 † 1771
Bürger, Flößer
⚭ I. 1734 Anna Braun
⚭ II. 1749 Anna Volz

Georg E6
* 1715 † 1766
⚭ 1747

Johann Georg E7
* 1738 † 1813
Schneider
⚭ 1768 Magdalena Großhans

Michael
* 1748

Michael E8
* 1769 † 1832
Schneider
⚭ 1794 Magdalena Haintel

Johann Georg E9
* 1770
Tuchmacher i. Altensteig
⚭ 1796 Sophia Frey

Johann Georg E10
* 1796 † 1834
Schneidermeister
⚭ 1824 Elisabetha Rath

Michael E11
* 1798 † 1877
Weber
⚭ 1825 Maria Oertle

Johann Martin E12
* 1806 † 1863
Schneider
⚭ 1835 Lucia Hammer

Johann Georg E17
* 1840 † 1893
Weber
⚭ 1869 Christina Mohrhardt

Johann Martin E18
* 1844
ausgewandert n. Amerika

Johann Adam E21
* 1873 † 1940
Weber, Händler
⚭ 1899 Katharina Ottmer

Johann Georg E22
* 1876 † 1945 i. Spielberg
Bauder in Spielberg
⚭ 1901 Barbara Bühler

Adam E30
* 1902 † 1971
Muller

Friedrich E31
(Fritz)
* 1905

Johannes E32
* 1906 † 1973
Schneidermeister

Karl E33
* 1909

Wilhelm E34
* 1910

Ernst Martin E35
* 1913

Gottlieb E36
* 1916 † 1942

Zwerenberger-Stamm

WACKENHUT

Endris III/3
* um 1548/52 † 1625
Zimmermann, Richter
⚭ I. 1572/75 Katharina
⚭ II. 1614 Magdalena vid. Brözing

Auberlin (III/4) Z2
* um 1555/60 † 1632
Hofbauer in Zwerenberg
⚭ I. 1586 Maria vid. Ganßhorn
II. 1591 Maria Roller

Hans Z3
* 1594 † 1635
Bauer
⚭ 1623 Lucia Morath

Georg Z4
* 1604 † 1635
Bauer
⚭ 1627 Barbara Schill

Aberlin Z5
* 1606 † i. Ettmannsweiler
⚭ 1632 Waldpurga Burkhardt

Michael
* 1611

Jakob
* 1614

Aberlin Z6
* 1627 † 1699
Bauer, Schultheis
⚭ I. 1651 Maria Schwefflin
⚭ II. 1673 Christina Schülin

Georg
* 1629 † 1680

Georg Z8
* 1659 † 1727
Bürger, Richter
⚭ 1695 Magdalena Schaible

Christian Z9
* 1664 † 1735
Schmied
⚭ vor 1701 Anna Maria

Johann Martin Z10
* 1666 † i. Berneck
⚭ 1708 Maria Wurster

Jakob Z11
* um 1671
Bauer
⚭ 1704 Maria

Abraham Z12
* 1675
Bürger
⚭ 1699 Sibylla Wagner

Conrad Z13
* 1679 † 1754
Bäcker
⚭ 1698 Barbara

Michel Z14
* 1683
Bürger
⚭ 1710 Anna Maria Rapp

Matthias Z15
* 1691 † 1724
Schneider
⚭ 1717 Anna Lodholz

Hans Jerg Z17
* 1696 † 1735
Bauer
⚭ 1724 Barbara Dürr

Christian Z18
* 1712 † 1795
Schuhmacher
⚭ 1736 Anna Catharina Maier

Johann Georg Z27
* 1725 † 1782
Richter, Hofbauer
⚭ 1748 Barbara Seeger
⚭ Maria Schleh

Johannes Z32
* 1751 † 1801
Hofbauer, Richter
⚭ 1776 Barbara Seeger

Heinrich Z33
* 1762 † 1831
Bürger
⚭ 1789 Eva Seeger

Johannes
* 1801 † 1863
Bürger
⚭ 1828 Justine Herter

Heinrich Z
* 1809 † 1890
Bürger
⚭ 1838 Anna Bock
⚭ 1840 Elisabeth Faßnacht

Johannes
* 1857 † 1911
1881 n. Amerika ausgewandert
⚭ Christine..........geb. 1854

William Henry
* März 1888 † 1961
Pennsylvania

Frederik
* Mai 1890
Pennsylvania

Frank
* April 1895
Pennsylvania

John
* Oktober 1896
Pennsylvania

William Henry (Harry)
* 12-11-1908 † 12-15-1986
⚭ Frances Boyd † 12-10-1983
Chicago, Illinois

George Russell
* 9-3-1919
⚭ Ruth Bell
Coral Gables, Florida

Pamela
* 11-9-1941
⚭ Paul Rittgarn
Elgin, Illinois

Russell
* 10-10-1942
⚭ Carolyn Rimnac
Lisle, Illinois

Joyce
* 5-31-1945
⚭ Charles Hilbert
New York, NY

Sally
* 7-12-1954
⚭ James Bretl
Mukwonago, WI

Janis Lynn
* 2-16-1945
⚭ John Thorsen
Miami, Florida

Richard Russell
* 11-11-1947
⚭ Mariane Ball
Miami, Florida

Teri
* 4-11-61

Rick
* 6-14-62

David
* 8-2-67

Robert
* 1-6-70

Thomas
* 6-30-92

Matthew
* 12-17-82

Ben
* 10-31-85

Nick
* 7-3-89

Tanya
* 4-2-1967

Tresha
* 12-14-1968

Jennifer
* 5-10-1977

Lisa
* 10-2-1981

Ashley
* 9-17-1983

Lauren
* 10-31-1986

THE WACKENHUT CORPORATION
1994 CORPORATE STRUCTURE

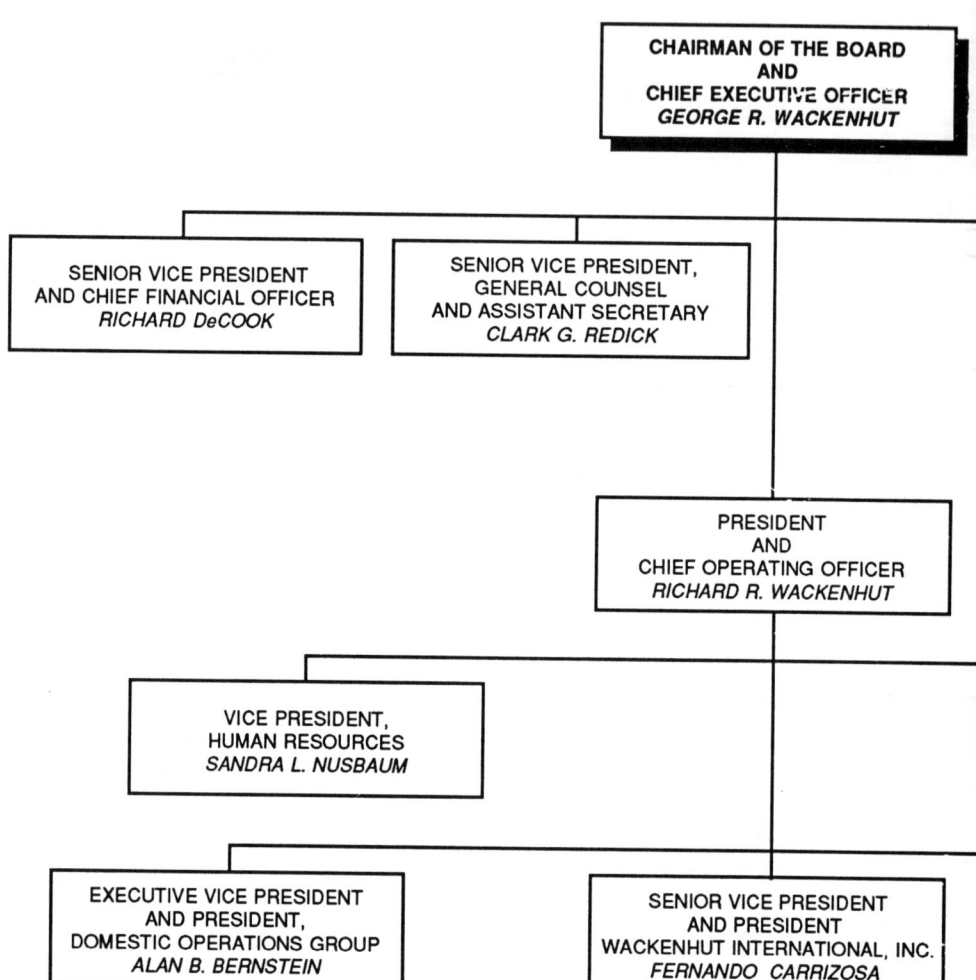

SENIOR VICE PRESIDENT,
CORPORATE PLANNING
AND DEVELOPMENT
ROBERT C. KNEIP

VICE PRESIDENT,
CLIENT RELATIONS
GEORGE A. ZEISS

EXECUTIVE VICE PRESIDENT
AND PRESIDENT,
GOVERNMENT SERVICES GROUP
TIMOTHY P. COLE

Designed by Suzanne McLean

Bibliography

Alyeska Pipeline Service Company Covert Operation. Oversight Hearings, Committee on Interior and Insular Affairs, House of Representatives. Parts I–IV, November 4–6, 1991. Washington, DC: U.S. Government Printing Office, 1991.
Ammarell, John S. *History of Wackenhut.* Unpublished manuscript, 124 pages, 1991.
Baseball Encyclopedia, The. New York: Macmillan Publishing Co., Inc., 1974.
Bernstein, Carl, and Woodward, Bob. *All the President's Men.* New York: Doubleday & Co., 1974.
Bible, The Holy. King James Version. Boston: The Christian Science Publishing Society.
Bond, Colonel O.J. *The Story of The Citadel.* Richmond, VA: Garrett & Massie, Inc., 1936.
Chicago Manual of Style, The. Fourteenth Edition. Chicago: The University of Chicago Press, 1993.
Clark, Mark W. *Calculated Risk.* New York: Harper & Brothers, Publishers, 1950.
Commandoes, The, Company H, Class 57. Ordnance Officer Candidate School. Philadelphia, PA: The Majestic Press, 1943.
Eddy, Mary Baker. *Church Manual of The First Church of Christ, Scientist, in Boston, Massachusetts.* Boston: The First Church of Christ, Scientist, 1895.
———. *Prose Works Other Than Science and Health.* Boston: The First Church of Christ, Scientist, 1925.
———. *Science and Health with Key to the Scriptures.* Boston: The First Church of Christ, Scientist, 1875.
Golan, Jay. *Frommer's Comprehensive Travel Guide to Philadelphia, '91–'92.* New York: Prentice Hall Press, 1991.
Hullabaloo, The 1947. Baltimore, MD: The Johns Hopkins University Press, 1947.
Information Please Almanac, The 1994. Forty-seventh Edition. Boston and New York: Houghton Mifflin Company, 1994.
Kneip, Robert C. *Hooper, William, 1742–1790: Misunderstood Patriot.* Unpublished Ph.D. dissertation. New Orleans, LA: Tulane University, 1980.
Lawson, Edward. *The Haverford School: A Century of Service, 1884–1984.* Haverford PA: The Haverford School, 1984.
Literary Market Place 1993. New Providence, NJ: R.R. Bowker, 1993.

Lovegrove, Richard, and Orwig, Tim. *The FBI.* New York: Exeter Books, 1989.
Ordnance School, The. Aberdeen Proving Ground, Maryland: 1943.
Random House Encyclopedia, The. New York: Random House, 1990.
Powell, Lyman P. *Mary Baker Eddy: A Life Size Portrait.* Boston: The Christian Science Publishing Society, 1930.
Random House Dictionary of the English Language. New York: Random House, 1987.
Rickenbacker, Captain Edward V. *Seven Came Through.* New York: Doubleday, Doran & Co., Inc., 1943.
———. *Rickenbacker.* Englewood Cliffs, NJ: Prentice-Hall, Inc., 1967.
Rickenbacker, William F., ed., with notes and introduction. *From Father to Son: The letters of Captain Eddie Rickenhacker to his son William, from boyhood to manhood.* New York: Walker and Company, 1970.
Savannah River Plant, The. Savannah River Operations Office, U.S. Department of Energy. Aiken, SC: 1980.
Shaffer, G. Wilson. *Recreation and Athletics at Johns Hopkins: A One-Hundred-Year History.* Baltimore, MD: The Johns Hopkins University Press, 1977.
Shirer, William L. *The Rise and Fall of the Third Reich: A History of Nazi Germany.* New York: Simon and Schuster, 1960.
Sphinx, The, Volume 69. Charleston, SC: The Citadel, the Military College of South Carolina, 1969.
Sturzebecker, Russell L. *Centennial History of West Chester State College.* West Chester, PA: Tinicum Press, 1971.
Theohairs, Athan G., and Cox, John Stuart. *The Boss: J. Edgar Hoover and the Great American Inquisition.* Philadelphia, PA: Temple University Press, 1988.
Wallechinsky, David, and Wallace, Irving. *The People's Almanac.* New York: Doubleday & Co., 1975.
Who's Who in America, 47th Edition, 1992–1993. Wilmette, IL: Marquis Who's Who, Macmillan Directory Division, 1992.
Wolff, Leon. *Lockout.* New York, Harper & Row, 1965.

Periodicals

Amlong, Bill. "Private Eye Lowers His Tower." *The Miami Herald,* November 22, 1968.
Anderson, Jack. "Five Linked to Nuke Goofs Awarded Medals, Bonuses." Syndicated newspaper column, November 26, 1983.
Bohne, Grace Wing. " 'Social Security' Was the Byword." *The Miami Herald,* July 31, 1973.
Boston Evening Globe. "Rickenbacker Found Alive." November 14, 1942.
Dewar, Heather. "Wackenhut exec testifies in secret on oil probe." *The Miami Herald,* November 5, 1991.
———. "Wackenhut Corp. considered probe targeting lawmaker." *The Miami Herald,* November 6, 1991.
———. "Embattled Wackenhut sleuth quits." *The Miami Herald,* November 16, 1991.
Fiaka, John J. "Major Security Flaws Found at U.S. Sites That Produce Parts for Nuclear Weapons." *The Wall Street Journal,* October 31, 1983.
Friedrich, Otto. "Day of Infamy." *Time,* December 2, 1991.
Frady, Marshall. "It is a *Joyous* Thing to be a Kirk Republican!" *The Saturday Evening Post,* July 29, 1967.

Glass, Ian, and McHale, Joan. "Roger Jolly And So Was the Crew . . . At Wacken's Hut." *The Miami News,* January 28, 1969.
Harper's Weekly. "The First of the War." January 19, 1861.
Kokalis, Peter G. "Nuclear Snake Eaters." *Soldier of Fortune,* April 1991.
Los Angeles Times. "Rickenbacker's Plane Missing." October 24, 1942.
Mauer, Richard. "The details of deception." *Anchorage Daily News,* September 1, 1991.
McDonald, Barbara. "Wackenhut Shines During Worst National Disaster in U.S. History." *Pipeline,* October 1992.
Mercury, The. "The War Begun." January 10, 1861.
Merzer, Martin. "A Tip of the Hat From Wackenhut." *The Miami Herald,* February 10, 1980.
Miami Herald. "Spy web ensnared whistle-blower." September 1, 1991.
———. "Wackenhut Shares Offered." April 27, 1966.
———. "Adding Up a Year of Struggle: Andrew By the Numbers." August 24, 1993.
Miami Review. "Notice Under Fictitious Name Law." July 23, 1954.
Miller, Susan. "Neighbors Whittle His Tower Power." *The Miami Herald,* May 29, 1968.
Norton, Bill. "C.M. Kelley Joins Florida Security Firm." *Kansas City Star,* February 5, 1980.
Oswald, Jack. "Speeding Charge." *The Miami News,* June 5, 1967.
Petit, Mike. "Wackenhut's Home His Castle." *The Miami Herald,* May 8, 1968.
Pipeline, The. "Message from our President." January 1, 1962.
———. "Wackenhut Now on N.Y. Stock Exchange." January 1981.
———. "Custom Protection Officers Receive Special Honors." May 1989.
———. "Letter from a Soldier." April 1991.
Rigsbee, Fred. "A 'Woodcarver's Paradise' Docks Here." *Charleston Evening Post,* April 1, 1977.
Savannah River Plant Pipeline. "WSI Names John C. Evans to Direct SRP Security." Aiken, SC: February 1984.
Sellers, Elaine. "Clark's 10 Years at Citadel Marked By Great Progress." *The News and Courier,* March 16, 1964.
Sherril, Robert. "A Political Happening Named Claude Kirk." *The New York Times Magazine,* November 26, 1967.
Sullivan, Allanna. "House Panel Demands All Data, Files of Firms' Surveillance of Witness." *The Wall Street Journal,* August 19, 1991.
———. "Alyeska Firms Were Told Surveillance of Critic Left Them Open to Prosecution." *The Wall Street Journal,* November 6, 1991.
Tucker, William. "Bay Corpse Still Mystery." *The Miami News,* June 5, 1967.
———. "Now, About That Tower On Wacken's Hut." *The Miami News,* August 26, 1968.
U.S. Department of Energy. "Department of Energy Selects Security Support Services Contractor." Press release, August 11, 1983.
———. "Wackenhut Services, Inc., Begins Security Services Transition at Department of Energy's Savannah River Plant." Press release, August 23, 1983.
———. "Wackenhut and Department of Energy Sign Contract for Security Support Services at Savannah River Plant." Press release, March 27, 1984.
U.S. News & World Report. "When a State Opens Its Own War on Crime," May 22, 1967.
Warren, Spencer. "Why America Slept." *National Review,* December 16, 1991.
Welz, Carl J. "Demonstrating Demand." *Christian Science Sentinel,* December 9, 1961.

About the Author

JOHN MINAHAN is the author of eighteen books, including the Doubleday Award winning novel *A Sudden Silence*, the million-copy best seller *Jeremy*, produced as a major motion picture by United Artists in 1973, and *The Great Diamond Robbery*, produced as a two-hour television film on CBS in 1988. An alumnus of Cornell, Harvard, and Columbia, he is a former staff writer for *Time* magazine, and was a writing instructor on the Faculty of Arts and Sciences at Harvard, 1987-89. Minahan and his wife Verity live in Miami.